FOUR YEARS ON THE WESTERN FRONT

FOUR YEARS ON THE
WESTERN FRONT

By a Rifleman

BEING THE EXPERIENCES OF A
RANKER IN THE LONDON RIFLE
BRIGADE, 4TH, 3RD AND 56TH DIVISIONS

First published 1922 by Odhams Press Ltd.

ISBN 0 948 13046 6

Dedicated

TO

MY MOTHER AND FATHER

INTRODUCTION

THE following account of adventures with the London Rifle Brigade is based upon letters sent home by the writer during the War. In some cases they are quoted verbatim, with merely the addition of names of places originally banned by the censorship, but the majority of letters have been woven into a narrative in order to overcome the piecemeal effect of hundreds of disjointed paragraphs selected at random. The account has been amplified by information gleaned afterwards, but events are portrayed as far as possible in the light in which they appeared at the time of their occurrence, rather than re-written and altered because after-events proved certain hopes or fears to be groundless.

It is difficult for a ranker to see very far beyond his own nose, and it is obvious that this narrative cannot be so descriptive of the events of the Battalion as that written by, say, the Colonel. It is not supposed to be a history of the L.R.B. But to prevent the account becoming too trivial an endeavour has been made to record not only what lay in the immediate vicinity of the writer's notice, but certain general experiences of the Battalion and, to a smaller extent, of the Division.

No apology is made for loose construction of sentences and various literary defects. Even where letters have not been quoted verbatim, much of their original language has been deliberately retained in the context and the numerous faults will no doubt be overlooked by charitable persons, in view of the conditions under which the letters were compiled.

FOREWORD

Of histories of the War there is no end, nor will there be for many years, yet I venture to think that this book—though not termed a history—will fill a corner of its own. Many in high places have published their views and intentions ; not so many, if any, who started the War on the lowest rung of the military ladder and served over three years in a regimental transport have given their hopes and fears to the world.

The author of the book was a civilian on August 4th, 1914 ; he longed again to become one on November 11th, 1918, and gained this end on January 16th, 1919. Landing in France on January 25th, 1915, he served in the ranks of the L.R.B. through the second battle of Ypres, joining the transport section when the Battalion was on L. of C. in the summer of that year.

Distinctions have often been drawn in my hearing between service in the trenches and in the transport. My reply was always that I would sooner sit in a trench than drive twice a night through Ypres. To my mind greater courage was often required for the latter. Alone one can master one's natural fears, but a transport driver has to do this and at the same time control possibly a couple of dumb animals, who cannot be expected to know what depends on their behaviour.

Aubrey Smith before the War was unknown to me. He will forgive me when I write that he was just one of countless thousands of young men who worked in an office in London. He felt the call when War broke out, and joined the London Rifle Brigade apparently because others in his office had done so already. That he never regretted the step is clear from his book. I can answer for it that the regiment, too, so far from having any complaint, had cause for congratulation.

Transport sections are either good or hopeless. That ours was uniformly good and always a happy party was in no small measure due to its component parts of which Aubrey Smith was one. We read of the others in the pages which follow. Esprit de corps of the most intense description often took the place of Army discipline, and it was an honour to be a rifleman in the L.R.B.

Largely taken from letters home, the following narrative lacks correctness in one particular at any rate. No mention is made of the fact that the author was awarded the Military Medal in August, 1917, and a bar to the Medal in November, 1918. Probably only the fact that he is now in China and that this foreword has to go to press next week, admits his readers to what he obviously meant to hide.

ARTHUR S. BATES, Lieut.-Colonel,
Commanding L.R.B.

BEMBRIDGE,
August 21st, 1922.

CONTENTS

FOUR YEARS ON THE
WESTERN FRONT

CHAPTER I.

TRAINING DAYS.

(*August, 1914—January, 1915.*)

Enlistment—Training in luxury—Billets at Haywards Heath—Warned for draft—
Trouble with Military Police—Parading for Overseas.

My summer holiday lasted from August 1st to August 15th, and on my return the office was scarcely recognisable owing to the rush there had been to join the Army. Tyler and Farquharson had got into the Artists; Kidd had found a Scottish regiment; while Whittle, Heath-field and Merrilees had joined Wood, who was already a member of the London Rifle Brigade.

Thomson and I feared that with this drastic reduction of the staff we should not be allowed to leave, but the firm lost no time in assuring us that we were not indispensable and we therefore went round to the Headquarters of the L.R.B. and craved permission to enlist, in a manner that would have won the hearts of recruiting sergeants in later days. The L.R.B., however, did not seem any more anxious for our services than the office was : they were over-strength and had closed their roll. Nevertheless, as a special favour, they allowed us to put our names down on the waiting-list for the 2nd Battalion, having ascertained that we had been to public schools and that we would sign on for foreign service. Gernat, another of the office staff, put his name down also.

On 1st September, the drill-hall was opened to us and, like so many people who have been waiting for hours to see a prize-fight, we swarmed in and scrambled over one another in our anxiety to pass the doctor and swear allegiance. We speedily made urgent requests to join Wood and Company in the 1st Battalion at Crowborough, but our efforts were unavailing and only a few ex-territorials managed to work

the transfer we so much desired. So Thomson, Gernat and I accepted
our fate, which—as events proved—gave us a far more gentle introduction to the rigours of Army discipline and discomforts than we
would have experienced in Crowborough Camp.

For weeks we simply played at soldiers.

Our officers came along in driblets, and, though most of them had
had territorial or similar experience, they managed to get us into hopeless tangles in our drill and constantly consulted the N.C.O.s as to the
best means of extracting us. Our N.C.O.s consisted partly of those
recruits who had a smattering of drill and partly of people who possessed
an aptitude for bawling loudly. Of the individuals, be they officers,
N.C.O.s or privates, I remember very little. A large number of them
were destined to remain in training for a year or so, finally coming to
France as a complete unit in the 58th Division. Others found themselves drafted to the 1st Battalion in France within a few months,
among whom were included Thomson, Gernat and myself.

We had no rifles and our uniforms were incomplete, but I fancy that
the Army had issued out toothbrushes and pocket-knives : they were
also profuse with their pay, and we got allowances for living at home,
for travelling and other things, which were on quite a generous scale—
for the Army—and they enabled us to have good lunches, at any rate !

We left home by the " directors' train," put in two hours' drill at
Charterhouse or Embankment Gardens, had a short march in the
afternoon and returned by the four o'clock train to bathe our feet in
" Tiz." Whatever else we accomplished at this time, we certainly
improved our voices and on our return from route marches the sedate
City offices could recognise our approach by the charming strains of
" Who's your lady friend ? " echoing down Queen Victoria Street.

We were a very jolly party in those days and we felt we were having
a glorified holiday. For one thing, we thought the War would soon
be over and that there was only a remote possibility of our being
required. As the messenger said to me when I called at the office one
day in October : " There are twenty millions fighting together, and,
if everyone only fired ten rounds a day, it makes two hundred million
cartridges fired daily. Now, sir, how can they keep that up till
Christmas ? "

And then came the announcement that the 1st Battalion had been
ordered off to France, and this at the end of October ; but it was well
understood that they were only going out as a stop-gap until Kitchener's
Army could relieve them and it was said that they were merely going
to be put on the lines of communication.

Shortly after their departure, the Army found us billets at Haywards
Heath, but, though they found us uniforms and obsolete rifles as well,
equipment was entirely lacking. So came the first farewell to home,
and one misty morning we departed for our training area, amidst the
cheers of the onlookers at London Bridge.

We were billeted in twos and threes on the hospitable inhabitants,
who waited at their doors to see who their " guests " were to be.
Some fellows found pretty girls waiting on the doorstep to welcome
them and their probably less fortunate companions heaved a sigh as
they moved on to see what their fate might be. Some found kindly
aged people, in whose homes they were assured of a good welcome :
one or two struck people who looked as though they might be " kill-
joys " and the troops watched these receptions with broad grins on
their faces ; but the best fun of all was afforded by the look of blank

dismay on the face of our most famous authority on alcohol when he found himself billeted on a clergyman !

Thomson, Gernat and I found comfortable quarters and we lived as we might have done at home, having meals with our " landlords," sleeping in proper beds and rising just in time for breakfast in the mornings.

Our parade each day was at 9 o'clock and at 1.30 our training was over. We really had a most slack time and, instead of becoming hardened for the fray, we were like turkeys fattening up for Christmas. The only hardship we ever endured was headquarters guard, which we only suffered once and then we were excused duty all the next day. Even on field-days we took mackintosh-sheets with us so that we should not get damp when flinging ourselves on the ground !

In December they started to " ear-mark " twenty-five men from each company as a probable draft for the 1st Battalion and it was, for the most part, selected with a view to keeping up the standard of the 1st L.R.B. and consisted of picked men, chosen for stature and general smartness. How we three came to be included, I do not know, but we assumed it to be on account of the insistence· of our request to join our comrades, which had now thoroughly got on the Captain's nerves. The " first draft " became an object of much attention and it was soon decided that we should do a little shooting.

The prospective draft, some two hundred strong, shortly proceeded to Jarvis Brook, near Crowborough, for practice at the targets. We spent a week there, mostly indoors—on account of the weather. It took us half the mornings to prepare the targets and, by the time a few of us had fired, it was time to fall in and march home again. The consequence was that we only fired about twenty rounds each during that week and did not shoot again until we were in the firing-line. As far as I remember, most of my shots did not appear on the target at all, and there seemed to be many other fellows of equal brilliance. Officers and everybody considered this a huge joke and there did not seem to be any attempt to give a little extra practice to the poorer marksmen.

Everyone's attention seemed to be much more concerned with the damsels of the village, and I believe the experience of Thomson—who spoke to a girl in the dark and walked to her gate with her, there contriving to light a match and gaze upon her face, resulting in an " Oh, Lord ! " and a hasty retreat—was not uncommon. At my billet there was a little girl of thirteen with spectacles, whose great enjoyment was to attend the local cinema and, to please her mother, I agreed to escort her there one night, trusting that my friends would not see me. But Fate was unkind and, passing beneath an arc-lamp in the village, a party of my company, whom I desired least to see me, burst into roars of merriment and they would not let me hear the last of it for many a day.

During our stay there, a rumour came round one day to the effect that the 1st Battalion had lost half their numbers and required a draft—an announcement which created quite a sensation. Apart from the fact that this might herald our immediate departure, most of us had friends in the 1st Battalion and we were anxious for news of them.

Could it be true ? We had heard that they had been holding a quiet part of the line, but had they actually put them into the fighting ? Could it be that this affair that we were treating so lightly, with our jokes about shooting and the village damsels, was something much more serious ? Few of us had given much thought to that terrible struggle that had been going on for the past three months on the other side of the Channel ; few of us realised that, while we were spending afternoons in idleness and evenings in cinemas, it was touch-and-go in Flanders as to whether the Germans would break clean through our single line of troops and reach Calais. Of course, none of us could be expected to depict accurately that mire of mud and water in which at that moment our own friends, Wood, Whittle and Merrilees, and thousands like them, were eking out an existence. Perhaps, had we been able to look across the water and gaze upon the trenches, we should not have been keen to go across and share their misery ; but the words " trenches " and " shells " had no meaning for us—we had neither seen the one nor heard the other—and we therefore yearned to be in company with our friends and share their experiences. We really came to fear the War would be over before we had had an opportunity of seeing any operations and taking part in its wind-up.

Although the rumour turned out to be much exaggerated, the 1st Battalion was in fact losing a number of men from frost-bite, chills and general sickness, in addition to a few casualties, and they required a big draft as soon as possible. Twenty ex-soldiers were immediately despatched in a small draft, while preparations were made to fit out the balance with equipment.

After Christmas leave our " training " was intensified, but it could not be claimed at the end that we were really versed in the art of war. We had only dug one trench and that took us three days to complete, working in relays and with the assistance of picks and shovels : precious little practice for men who were to hack desperately with entrenching tools and bare hands to get cover from fire ! We had let off twenty rounds of ammunition from obsolete rifles and some of us had not even hit the targets. We had marched a few miles at a time without equip- ment, with the aid of a band, refreshed by frequent halts and fortified by an abundance of good food. These feats, together with a real proficiency in presenting arms and saluting, comprised the sum total of our military achievements when we set sail for France. What we really needed was practice in carrying weights over slippery ground, filling sandbags, laying wire and throwing bombs, and instruction in the gentle art of cooking !

One incident occurred before we left Haywards Heath which seemed for the moment to jeopardise my chances of going with the draft and it arose from the fact that I was afflicted with a most unfortunate laugh, which had become so noticeable that, whenever I gave vent to it upon a route-march, the troops echoed it from the head of the column to the rear. Now it was my misfortune to attend the cinema a few evenings after an uproarious exhibition on the part of the soldiers in the audience, which had provoked the proprietor into complaining to the military police. This resulted in a strong force of regimental policemen picketing the hall every night in search of offenders and it so happened that on this particular occasion the pictures were extremely funny and, sitting in the front row of the balcony, I laughed loud and long at the incidents on the film. This outburst was in every instance mimicked by the remainder of the audience, as on the route-marches, and the consequence was that the hall echoed from end to end with the din.

Though I was unaware of it at the time, every policeman had his eye upon me and was perfectly convinced that he had hit on the ring-leader of the hooligans : at the close of the performance, therefore, I felt a tap on the arm and, in spite of the indignant protests of my land-lord who was with me, one of the regimental police took my name and number, looking in my hat to confirm my statement.   I was apparently accused of disorderly conduct and no arguments had any impression on the unpopular little bounder who thought he had secured his first conviction.   The only thing for me to do was to appeal to my Company Commander, whom I found recovering from his evening repast.   I admitted that my smile was not as musical as it might be, but assured him that there had been no intention to misbehave, and good old Captain Johnson tried to hide his smiles, for he had had previous samples of my mirth.   Wherefore, when the official complaint came in next day via Brigade, he made a truthful explanation on my behalf and the little policeman was baulked of his prey.   I recognised him two years later on the Somme as a subaltern and I remember he got most annoyed because my horse insisted on breathing down his neck.

The preparations for the departure of our draft were pushed on with all possible speed.   We were medically examined and inoculated against typhoid.   All manner of equipment was issued out in driblets, from packs and mess-tins to entrenching tools (which we had not handled before).   Our uniforms, though clean, had to be handed in and brand new ones were issued, presumably because we were shortly going to plunge into Flanders mud !   Our badges were blackened, lest the Hun should find good targets.   All these things took many days to complete and our impatience to be off increased with every delay.   A special Church service was held in our honour and the rector made a very touching reference to the fact that some of us would probably not return—alas ! this was only too true.   I only hope that many of those who eventually drifted to other battalions through transfers and commissions came safely through the War, but to my knowledge only four of those two hundred men were destined to go right through with the 1st L.R.B.

Final leave was granted to us, and this proved to be a more heart-rending affair on this occasion than on subsequent leaves.   That last evening at home, the lump in the throat, my mother's brave attempt to appear as usual, the impulse I felt to throw my arms round her which must be checked lest her assumed cheerfulness break down in that moment, the emotion in my father's voice : all these excruciating feelings seemed to overwhelm me and make me dread the final parting.   They were bad enough in later days, even when we were more accustomed to grief and our finer feelings were rendered more callous by the tragic events around us ; but on that first occasion, leaving home for the unknown, it told upon one's parents and almost made one question whether one had done the right thing in being so anxious to leave home training for service in France.   My own people came down to Haywards Heath for the week-end after the final leave.   They talked about cheerful things, but the hours were tinged with sadness. . . .

At last January 20th arrived, and the Overseas draft paraded early in the morning.   Owing to a re-arrangement, Thomson was put back until the next draft, but the detachment from Q Company was otherwise unchanged and included Sergt. Fulkes, Lance-Corporal Pace, Gernat and Vallentine, whose names will reappear in the narrative.   Vallentine, known later as " Kimbo," was destined to share many experiences with me.

The townsfolk had gathered round the green in hundreds to give us a great " send off " and, after a speech from the C.O., and a few words of advice from the Sergeant-Major *re* the utility of gallipots, we marched off to the station. The whole route was lined by the remainder of the battalion waving their hats on their rifles and behind them on the pavement were civilians, all shouting at the top of their voices. It was a very happy idea and it put us in excellent spirits. In the early days one did get a right royal send-off ; later the enthusiasm waned.

The station was still more crowded and we had to fight our way through to the platform. Moreover, as many of the regiment and populace as could crowd into the station followed in our wake and swarmed over the platforms and railway lines, handshaking and cheering, the din was appalling. Finally, about 10 a.m., our train pulled out *en route* for Southampton and, as we got a last glimpse of the crowd waving us farewell, we carried away a very pleasant reminiscence of the kindly townsfolk and happy " training " days of good old Haywards Heath.

At length we had started on our journey for the unknown.

CHAPTER II.

En Route for the Front.

(*January*, 1915.)

An assortment of drafts—Cooking under difficulties—Farewell to Southampton—
Our Channel escort—Arrival at Havre and Rouen—Learning the truth about
the War.

SOUTHAMPTON is a dirty, dingy, depressing town, with such an
atmosphere of gloom that it is calculated to damp the ardour of the
keenest soldier. And, much to our dismay, instead of going straight
on board the transport, we were marched off in the direction of the
town, where we promptly struck the most unsalubrious quarter : our
route lay past public-houses and squalid little shops and our destination
turned out to be a school which had been commandeered by the military.

As we trooped into the building, a regular babel of heathen tongues
could be heard, and, so far as we could see, the great hall was overflowing with soldiers from various battalions, squatting about in
ungainly attitudes, their kits beside them on the floor. Others were
parading in small parties and there seemed to be half-a-dozen roll-calls
proceeding at once. It did not appear possible to find floor-space to
accommodate us, but we were eventually pushed into two class-rooms
jutting out of the main hall, wherein we each sought out a couple of
square feet of floor and dumped our rifles and equipment.

Considering it was bitterly cold and there was neither hot food nor
anyone to cook for us, you can imagine our feelings as we surveyed
the surroundings. This was the first semblance of a hardship we had
experienced, which is my sole excuse for mentioning it. For two hours
we awaited orders and then it was announced that we should sleep
where we were squatting and that we could wander round the town
if we cared : tea would be ready about six o'clock.

Our fellow-sufferers consisted of drafts from practically every
Territorial unit that was by then in France : Artists' Rifles, Queen's
Westminsters, Rangers, H.A.C., Highland Light Infantry, Royal Scots,
Cheshires, Yeomanry—all contributed their quota and the variety
of dialects was most disconcerting. The first thing that struck me about
some of these drafts was their delightful freedom from discipline. Many
seemed to be under the charge of officers whose duty was to see them
safely on board the steamer and then return to their training camp,

and certain battalions with less esprit de corps than the London units cared not a fig for any orders or regulations. We could hear N.C.O.s frantically shouting to the Welsh to fall in, the only effect being a muttered comment from the motionless figures on the ground. Just before lights out, we were treated to a regular entertainment when the Cheshires' sergeant attempted to hold a roll-call. Every name as it was called was answered by at least half-a-dozen voices in unison shouting " Here, sergeant," and presently other units joined in until a chorus arose every time the N.C.O. opened his mouth. The latter finally gave it up in disgust amidst much cheering and laughter.

We had made " pillows " of our packs and blankets of our overcoats and, as it was the first time I had slept on the floor, I found it extremely difficult to get to sleep. The pack was too big and too hard for comfort and my face was level with another man's feet. . . . We were just dozing off towards midnight when a runner arrived, turned on the light and informed Sergt. Fulkes that two men would be required to get up at 4.30, light fires and cook the L.R.B.'s breakfast. Since none of us had acquired the art of cooking to a marked degree, this announcement set up a titter, above which my unfortunate laugh was very noticeable. My name was, therefore, the first that occurred to Fulkes, and I found myself detailed to perform this distasteful job in company with another, as inefficient as myself. Of course, the draft knew at once that they wouldn't get any breakfast, but, instead of grumbling, they laughed the more.

Wretchedly cold, I turned out in the dark to find the playground white with snow, which was still drifting down. Already the H.L.I. had a magnificent blaze between two iron bars, supported by bricks : the foundations for the fires ran in long lines from one end of the playground to the other. Several other units had fires well under way and we selected an unused portion of the fire-trench next to the H.L.I. Nobody seemed to be in charge and it was some time before we were able to find any fuel ; then, armed with paper, wood, coal, dixies and bacon, we took up our position and endeavoured to strike matches in an exceptionally heavy snowstorm : within five minutes all the paper was burnt and there was nothing to show for it. So my companion set off in search of further supplies while I, in my ignorance of Army ways, left my post in order to find the water-pump. Alas ! little did I know of the subtle art of " winning," otherwise known as " scrounging," that strange moral code by which the theft of anything from a hut down to fuel is considered a smart piece of work, provided you are not foolish enough to get caught. The motto of that code is : " Damn *you*—*I'm* all right," which delightful sentiment was freely expressed when you had comfortable quarters or ample rations, or a leave warrant, or a clean shirt, and somebody else had none. The Army breeds in every soldier two diverse traits of character : extreme devotion and self-sacrifice, and a desire to attend to one's own wants without consideration for the interests of others. I was too raw to have acquired the " scrounging " habit and was not even put wise to it. Therefore, the Highlanders deserve nothing but congratulations having caught me " on the hop " and pounced upon our coal and wood in my absence ; the bacon might have disappeared too, but they had sufficient for their requirements.

On my return, the light from the neighbouring fire doubtless reflected misery upon my face. There was no doubt where our fuel had gone to : the H.L.I. dixies were nearly boiling, being licked by flames which illuminated the whole playground. I shall never forget the sight of those cheerful souls, squatting down in the snow and singing Lauder's songs, while I wrestled with a flickering fire until 7.30, my eyes streaming with water from the thick smoke and my face and hands grimed with coal. Presently the L.R.B.s arrived in driblets and enquired after their tepid dixies and, with their assistance, we endeavoured to make up for lost time. But most of them breakfasted that morning on bread and jam, followed by a second meal at 9 o'clock, consisting of a mug of tea and a rasher of smoky bacon. That was the first and last occasion on which I was appointed as official cook.

Before dinner there was an inspection of all the units in the playground and the Cheshires caused much amusement by singing on parade and arriving in twos and threes several minutes after the official hour for the parade. After the meal, some of us sauntered into the town ; the snow and slush, the muggy atmosphere and dingy shops, all conspired to make us " fed up " with the place and we grew more and more impatient to get over on the other side and see what the firing-line was really like. We heard a little about it from a despatch-rider whom we met in a tea-shop and who professed to have just returned from France. He told us of limbers he had seen calmly proceeding along roads when shells had burst and left no traces whatever of the vehicles ; and we were treated to graphic descriptions of men standing in trenches with water above their waists, tales specially designed to make our flesh creep. But no description could convey what the conditions really were, and, beyond instilling vague fears into our hearts, he told nothing which destroyed our confidence that we held all the trumps on the Western Front.

At night we went to a music-hall, where the greater part of the audience consisted of soldiers and sailors with lady companions : the various recruiting and patriotic songs made a great hit. Elgar's work, " Land of Hope and Glory," was rather new to me then and its strains conjured up pictures of the fireside at home, where they were even now looking for postcards from me. Outside, the streets were full of soldiers, the majority being in excellent spirits, doubtless produced by convivial scenes at the public-houses which one could smell everywhere, and this visual proof that Kitchener's Army was in being was greatly reassuring. After a few months they would be able to relieve us at the Front. Rumour said that several new divisions had been formed and that considerably over a million men had already joined up—what an unpleasant surprise for the Germans, who had scoffed at our contemptible little Army !

Certain units sailed for France some hours before our turn came. Apparently, there were submarines in the Channel and the voyage had to be made at night : moreover, our actual destination was a carefully guarded secret and even the Captain of the transport steamed off under sealed orders.

After dinner on January 24th we were gazing upon the Southampton landing-stage from the deck of an old Argentine cattle-boat, wondering when we should see that shore again. As a matter of fact, it was four years almost to the day—January 17th, 1919—before I set foot on that pier again and then it was with heart so full that it is impossible to describe adequately the feelings that overwhelmed me, for ten hours after that I was a civilian once more.

As we started our cruise down Southampton Water, about four o'clock, we were all standing on deck waving our hands to well-wishers

on shore and in neighbouring boats. We passed down that Water a
in a dream. How could it be possible that here everything was goin
on as usual—the repairing of ships, the cranes working, the South
Western trains probably carrying passengers back to beloved Waterloo—
when just over on the other side there were fighting, shelling, killing
mutilation and all the other horrors of war? A ferry passed u
conveying workmen to their homes; intent on their own cares, the
gave but a fleeting glance at the cargo of home-sick ones just departing
The last glance we got of England's shore was after dusk and we wer
approaching Portsmouth. A thousand pairs of eyes gazed upon i
until twilight fell and scarcely a word was spoken. . . .

Now there were only searchlights and signals to be seen. The forme
played upon us and our engines slowed down and finally stoppe
The flashing lamps from the ships around us gave the impression tha
a myriad vessels and forts were concerned with our arrival. For hou
we lay there with the water lapping against our side, reflecting on th
extraordinary might of our Navy, by virtue of which our shores wer
kept clear of the invader and we soldiers could be transported to figl
upon soil other than our own. After all, it was a consoling though
that we were going to conquer the Germans on foreign soil—even if
belonged to the unfortunate French, it was better than making a me
of the Eastern Counties! There was something about Portsmou
Harbour that inspired confidence: the Navy seemed so very wi
awake.

Presently, lights drew near to us and we could make out the for
of our escort on either side: then our engines moved again and o
two destroyers dashed about on each flank, sometimes plunging forwa
and crossing our path, at others nestling close to our stern, the ve
embodiment of activity and the guarantee of our safe passage acro
the Channel. At ease as to our protection, we went down into t
depths of the ship to lie down in cold and smelly old cattle sta
digesting our first meal of bully-beef and biscuits. In the blackn
of the night we were heading straight for the War zone—Englan
peaceful and placid, lay behind us.

Although we did not know for which port we were bound, we we
not surprised next morning to find ourselves outside Havre, where t
1st Battalion had disembarked. One or two French destroyers circ
round us, waving greetings, and we all sang the "Marseillaise." Th
one of the officers on board the French boats announced through
megaphone that the British Fleet had sunk the *Blucher*, one
Germany's best warships. Loud cheers! We were assuredly winni
the War!

Enthusiasm was increased now that we were in sight of "La Be
France" and we got a bit tired of waiting when morning turned
afternoon and there was still no sign of our landing. We were looki
forward to that magnificent reception which we had heard was accor
to British troops on their arrival in France and we were all ready
march through the streets in grand style as the deliverers of th
country.

It turned out, however, that our real destination was Rouen, so
miles up the river, and that we were waiting for the tide, in orde
complete our journey. The British destroyers had returned as
obtrusively as they had first come and, when we went forward ag
it was a solitary voyage. Leaving the sea behind, we entered the R
Seine. Eagerly we scanned the banks, gazing for the first time—

many of the men—upon this foreign land where all the happenings of
the past few months had actually occurred. I do not know what we
really expected to see, whether we expected hospitals or ruins or mar-
shalled armies to line the river, but we certainly could not detect
anything unusual about the villages which we passed. For the most
part, there was bleak, empty country upon either side of us. In some
places civilians came down to the water's edge and shouted " Vive les
Anglais," to which we responded heartily : and I suppose it was really
an inspiriting sight to these folk to see a ship, crammed with reinforcements, gliding up-river towards the War.

We gathered in groups and sang songs, each battalion endeavouring
to give a more effective programme than the others. One of the
L.R.B.s went forward and listened to the Westminsters singing glees
and, upon returning, made frantic efforts to stimulate the vocal production of our party. Generally speaking, the atmosphere was one
of levity, but in the midst of it a fellow called Marshall told me perfectly
calmly that he knew instinctively that he had seen England for the last
time, which put a damper on me for at least five minutes ! As darkness
gathered, the little illuminated cottages beside the river looked most
picturesque : old men and women, attracted by our singing, continued
to come to the banks, holding up lanterns and raising feeble cheers.

Presently it got decidedly chilly and, as the smell of the cattle stalls
was too repugnant, I squatted down near a hatchway, and, in spite of
people frequently stumbling over me, this proved to be my bed for the
night. We reached Rouen at 11 p.m., but there was nothing to be
done until the morning ; however, as soon as it was possible to take our
bearings at daybreak, we were all " up and about," gazing out at
the river-scenes, which reminded me very much of the Clyde. Huge
arc-lamps still spread their rays uselessly around.

We found we were moored alongside a wharf where food, forage and
stores of all kinds were piled into huge dumps. Vessels in the vicinity
were being unloaded by British soldiers and activity was in evidence
as far as the eye could see. Close at hand were grouped a collection
of girls bearing baskets of fruit and chocolate, endeavouring to throw
refreshments on board, in return for the English pence that were hurled
down from the deck.

" Bonjour, monsieur. Comment allez-vous ? " enquired one bright-
eyed damsel, with a shawl over her head.

" Oh, swish ! " exclaimed an individual, who was evidently listening
to a French girl for the first time. His comrades grinned approval.

" Say, how many oranges for a penny ? " he continued.

" Two for seexpence," replied Mademoiselle.

" Phew ! Chuck us 'arf a one then."

Her reply was as unexpected as it was amusing.

" *You* damn fool," warbled Mademoiselle, flushing, and she moved
away.

Several French workmen hung around, pointing out this, that or the
other about the appearance of the troops, and farther in the background
were a French soldier or two and a gendarme. Unfortunately, the
water supply was very limited and we could scarcely get enough to
shave in ; our wash was, therefore, a " lick and a promise," which
rather hurt our self-respect, as we were about to meet the criticism
of these gallant Allies.

After breakfast we got the order to put on our coats and packs,
and one by one we tramped down the gangway and " fell in " on the

wharf in our best parade manner. This operation attracted more onlookers, including regular British troops who assembled to find out what stuff the latest Territorial drafts were made of ; and, by the time we set off down the street, there were numbers of people standing in groups to watch the procession.

It struck me as a trifle odd that there was very little enthusiasm or cheering : evidently the people of Rouen had grown accustomed to the sight of British troops and the old scenes of welcome were not to be repeated.   Possibly it was because it was felt that they needed stirring up, that our officers came along and told us to sing.   So we struck up : "Here we are, here we are, here we are again."   It was a failure. Old soldiers from the Mons Retreat stood by, minus their hatbands and shoulder titles, which had been given to civilians as souvenirs, and, as we rolled out our chorus, they smiled—cynical, knowing smiles—and there was a twinkle in their eyes.

"You won't be singing soon, mate," said one grinning onlooker as we passed.

We tried again with "Gilbert, the Filbert," and at least half-a-dozen Regulars remarked, "You wait till you get oop there, choom."   This took the ginger out of our efforts and we relapsed into silence.   One of the other drafts shouted, "Are we downhearted ?" followed by the usual resounding "No !" which echoed down the narrow street. This provoked a group of cavalrymen to derisive laughter.   "But you . . . soon will be," shouted one of their number.

We couldn't understand it at all.   We were giving the Germans a thorough hiding.   Why, here in Rouen, we had seen such hundreds of British soldiers that the sight galvanised us into blind optimism. Why should these Regulars be so confoundedly cynical ?

On we marched, up a long, long hill, and after a ten minutes' halt to recover from what was really a supreme effort on our part, in full kit, we continued our march past countless camps and marquee hospitals until we reached No. 2 Territorial Base Depot.

Our welcome to this uninviting, bleak camp took the form of a long exhortation from the Commandant about breaking bounds, naked lights and so on, with dire threats of punishment.   We were also informed that a few days ago Private —— had been shot because he was absent when his draft paraded for the front.   After ten minutes' muffled cursing on the part of the weary troops, we were taken to our portion of the camp, where a dozen men were ushered into each tent.

I took an early opportunity of visiting the Regulars' camp next to ours and of getting into conversation with one or two infantrymen in the Y.M.C.A. hut.   I was anxious to obtain first-hand information as to the conditions at the front and the prospect of a speedy termination of the War, and some of their statements were a revelation to me.

I had imagined from the newspapers that the retreat from Mons had been a great strategical move, in which we had inflicted such loss on the advancing masses that we had seriously weakened the enemy's man-power ; this had been followed by the brilliant advance, for the purpose of making which Joffre had retired so far.   This again had been followed by a most successful action on the Aisne, of which I knew little, and then our British Divisions and Cavalry had shifted up into Flanders, continuously outflanking the Germans ; here they had dug in and were opposing an impenetrable front to the enemy, completely barring the way to Calais.   We only needed another strategic move when the weather improved and the Huns would be pouring back to their own frontiers. This, in short, was the situation as it had been presented by the Press and as it was believed by the majority of the British public.

The shreds of information that I was able to piece together, now, revealed a rather more depressing state of affairs. It would be wrong to imply that there was any lack of confidence among these hardened old warriors in their individual superiority over the Germans, in the justice of our cause or in the ultimate success that would be theirs. But they all believed that it would be necessary to have Kitchener's first million, and even double that number, on the Western Front before a final decision could be made.

Their losses had been terrible. The retreat from Mons had reduced their numbers considerably and they had been opposed by forces infinitely superior in numbers and particularly in artillery. Their physical exhaustion remained their chief impression. Worn out with fighting then and on the Aisne, they had been transferred to the north, where the line had swayed to and fro in the desperate effort of the Germans to smash their way through to the coast. A most momentous struggle had taken place all around Ypres and especially by the Menin Road. Here, in the last days of October, our thin little line had been subjected to heavy assaults by masses of the enemy, with orders to break through at all costs. The German artillery fire was overwhelming and considered to be six times as heavy as ours. Our infantry had thrown back one attack after another, without a spell of rest, as there was nobody to relieve them. They had had no reserves and, when at times the front trenches had been lost, it had looked as if the Germans would sweep right through our line. On such occasions, the situation was only restored by the advent of a dismounted squadron of cavalry or by a detachment of " odds and ends " being flung into the breach. The London Scottish and the Northumberland Hussars, both Territorial units, were used in the emergency. On October 31st the most critical moment arrived and never had things looked so black. On November 11th, the Prussian Guards had made a supreme effort which had been broken at a heavy cost to both sides.

The result was that some units were decimated, others had lost from one-half to three-quarters of their men. Divisions had dwindled to Brigades, Brigades to Battalions, the 7th Division had been practically annihilated.

Owing to the weariness of both sides and the advent of atrocious winter weather, the fierce struggle had eventually died down, leaving the Germans in possession of all the high ground from Ypres, on the left of the British line, to La Bassee, on the right, including Hill 60, Messines and the Aubers Ridge. Parallel to them, in a disadvantageous position, ran the British water-logged trenches, where the enemy's observation made all daylight movement impossible.

At this stage several Territorial regiments had been sent up into the line to reinforce the Regulars, who were so depleted in numbers that in some places there was only one man to two or three yards of trench. From the drafts we saw at the Base, these included, in addition to the L.R.B. and those units already mentioned, the Liverpool Scottish, 1st Herts, 4th Suffolk, Kensingtons, 2nd Monmouths, 7th Argyll and Sutherlands, the Northampton, Essex and N. Somerset Yeomanry and the Oxford Hussars. During the months of December and January, two more divisions—the 27th and 28th—arrived on the scene, consisting of Regulars withdrawn from garrison duty abroad. In this way the line was being strengthened and rest was afforded to the remainder of the original divisions.

The faces of those with whom I conversed showed traces of the nerve-racking experiences which they had undergone, but they were very stout-hearted fellows.

" How long do you think the War will last ? " I asked one of them.

" Oh, only another few months," was the reply.

" You reckon we can beat the Germans by then ? "

" Oh, yes, when the Territorials and Kitchener's Army come out we shall let 'em have it, you see. We shall do for Jerry all right this spring."

Another said : " We'll have to get two million men out here, but I reckon it will finish this year."

And in spite of the odds being so much against us, it was impossible not to be optimistic after listening to their views. Something instinctively told them, as it told me, that all would be right in the end, and our only misjudgment was that the end would come soon. Nevertheless, I thought I knew now why they had smiled.

CHAPTER III.

FIRST IMPRESSIONS OF THE FIRING-LINE.

(*February-March*, 1915.)

We join the 1st Battalion—Taking up rations, etc.—Billets in Ploegsteert—Front-line breastworks—Rest in Armentières—Digging fatigue—In the trenches—Continuing the round.

WE spent five days in the Base Depot, where there was no work to do and nothing of interest occurred, unless it be that the water was frozen for the greater part of the time, so that our washing suffered in consequence.

On the evening of January 31st we marched down to the station in company with other drafts and entered comfortable compartments in a train that was to conduct us up the line, and next morning our own particular draft descended on to the metals at Steenwerck, where sundry guides and a transport waggon awaited us. We had seen various transports in fields and British soldiers at the stations and, now that an occasional boom could be distinctly heard, it was evident that we were up in the War zone at last.

We marched to the village of Romerin, where the L.R.B. Transport Section was stationed, and some Regulars of the 11th Brigade, to which the L.R.B. were attached, turned out of their billets as we passed and surveyed us with interest. They looked a sturdy lot of men, with bronzed faces and very cheerful expressions. "Are you for the L.R.B. ?" they asked. "They're a fine lot o' lads. Good luck!" They even raised cheers.

After dinner at Romerin we continued our journey along a very muddy and uneven road until we came to the village of Ploegsteert, commonly called "Plug Street." Considering that this place was only just a mile from the front-line trenches, it seemed extraordinary that it should be so intact ; there were some rather shelled buildings in one spot and a battered church, but labourers were doing their usual work and it might have been far from the War. So occasional was the firing from the guns that sometimes quietness reigned for a quarter of an hour at a time. Now and again an aeroplane, with several puffs of smoke around it, could be seen in the clear sky. It was war under the best conditions, in this village, at any rate.

One company of L.R.B.s was billeted here and seemed glad to see

us : many of the draft had friends with the 1st Battalion. It was
a matter of luck whether we should be split up into various companies in such a way that our friends would be with us, but Gernat
and I were fortunate in that respect and found ourselves drafted to
" D " Company. With us came " Kimbo," E. Hudson, Cox, Marshall
and other men from " Q " Company, but some of the latter became
separated here. The four companies of the 1st Battalion apparently
took it in turns to do three days in the trenches, three days in rest at
Armentières, three days in "support" farms just behind the line and
three days in billets at Plug Street. Wood and the others were at
that moment at Armentières, which meant that I should not see the
trenches for some days : we were to join them on the morrow.

We slept that night in a biewery, somewhat cold but comfortable,
and could hear a little " popping " of rifle-fire which ceased an hour
or so after we were " in bed." Next day we did very little in the
morning and afterwards marched to Armentières, where we at last
found the men we wanted in a large hall, with straw to lie on and
parcels strewn around. Wood and Whittle looked extremely fit, but
Merrilees was not up to the mark ; as for Heathfield, he had got facial
paralysis from exposure and returned to England. Needless to say,
this was a very happy meeting, and when we succeeded in getting in
the same section of the same platoon as Wood and Company, our
joy was great. The only other members of that section were the
corporal, named Miles, and a fellow called Bourke.

Naturally, we went out that evening to celebrate our arrival and
had a good meal at a restaurant, where I listened to many amusing
anecdotes from Wood and Merrilees. Two days before, a shell had
burst just over their trench and they had made a dive for the dug-
outs. Merrilees was asleep and he felt Wood grab his feet and dart in.
Whittle, with his usual appetite, made a dive for shelter with a rasher
of bacon in his hand and was unable to get in, so he dashed for another
dug-out which he reached, with the bacon, long after the effects of
the shell had passed.

Everybody seemed cheerful and few that I saw showed signs of any
breakdown, but I understood a good number were away sick in
hospital. The regular arrival of the post and plenty of food parcels
cheered everybody up and I found a large mail waiting for me.

Next afternoon, the Company moved up into support, each platoon
occupying one farm in the rear of the trenches, but the members of
the draft from England were put in a barn near Ploegsteert, whence
they were to do fatigues and gradually become accustomed to the
firing-line.

The ensuing experiences can best be told by extracts from the letters
written on the spot.

4/2/1915. " . . . Last night we came to a barn, about
three-quarters of a mile from the trenches, and I found myself
billeted in a loft. After dark, our section had to take up rations
to a support-farm nearer the trenches. It was very dark and it
is marvellous that anyone can remember the route. Leaving a
lane, we turned into a field (needless to say that all the way we
trod in very thick mud) and sloshed along beside a wide ditch
of water, which was the only thing I could see, except the outline
of the man in front. Can't you picture it ? Field after field
separated by ditches : occasionally we cross a small stream
boarded by a couple of planks and the party slows up to allow all

to cross over : then on again. We turn to the left and tread through some water but a flare goes up on the horizon and we are able to pick our way for a few seconds. A muddy field, all glistening with water and the outlines of short stumpy trees are visible against the sky. We spot a narrow brick-path, which we follow, and presently have to jump a stream. One man stumbles and the party has to wait for him : another, overburdened with a rather heavy sack, calls out ' losing touch,' and the pace is shortened. My package is a sack and a huge piece of bacon tied on top, which nestles confidingly against my neck and hair and makes me feel I am not alone ! Soon we tread a very muddy turnip-field and have to duck a piece of wire overhead, which the first man discovered at the price of his hat. It is very interesting and weird and the flares serve to make it still more unusual. These flares go up frequently, sometimes three at a time. A few bullets whistle over our heads but, strangely enough, we don't seem to notice them. At last we approach our destination — a dark farm. We tread a cinder-path leading up to it and enter to see a platoon of men comfortably settled down there on straw, with a nice blazing fire. After depositing our loads we turn back, and, by this time, having grown more accustomed to the light are able to see something of our path. I find that what I had taken to be a ditch of water, which I carefully avoided, is really a wet path and that a muddy bridge I had so gingerly trodden is several feet wide !

" We arrived back and went to bed on straw, only to be awakened and told to put all equipment on and go to sleep in that attire. There have been a few shells flying overhead to-day and falling on some position far in our rear and the noise does not seem at all alarming. It is a swishing sort of sound, ending in a huge explosion. Some of our guns are quite near us, replying to the German fire."

5/2/1915. " . . . I had to go up to our trenches last night with a party who were carrying provisions, sandbags, etc. We halted at a little inn to get some of the things and it was really funny to see the proprietor carrying on his business within a few hundred yards of the trenches, selling coffee and beer to the troops, with an incessant ' Pop-pop ' of rifle-fire going on outside." (Months afterwards we heard he had been shot as a spy, having had a secret telephone connected with the German lines.) " At this estaminet, known as the ' Demi Lune,' the party of us waited for some time for further stores to be brought up by a transport wagon. My bundle was a packet of a hundred sandbags, which was as much as I could manage, as they were loose and kept slipping. We advanced in single file up the lane, where the mud was not too terrible if you kept right in the middle. Presently my load began to drop in portions and I had to keep picking the muddy sandbags up and shouldering them again, so that I got left behind. My discomfiture was increased by the amount of rifle-fire that was going on, and the bullets kept hitting trees and walls by the wayside with as loud a crack as the shooting of them makes. The flares seemed very close now, and I had not the least idea where to go. Fortunately another of our men came along and helped me put my bundle together : he knew the way and told me the places where it was necessary to duck down.

c

He said it was an unpleasant road for casualties from stray bullets, and I was very glad to be able to dump my load for a moment behind a barricade.

" Have you ever wondered what happens when a lane goes over across the British and German trenches ? I always thought that the trench was cut right through the lane, but it is not necessarily so, and I must say that when I saw this barricade I was amazed. Erected right across the road is an immense wall of sandbags as high as a man, and it is continued for some yards on either side of the road. In the case of this barricade, a lane happened to turn to the left at that spot and so the wall of sandbags continued beside the lane. Just here the German trenches were eighty yards away. Behind the sandbags were regulars (Essex) and there were little low huts of sandbags where those not on guard could sit and lie down. Presently the barricade came to an end, which left me with a most uncomfortable feeling as, across the open to the right, were, of course, the German trenches. Soon we passed another barricade and went on beyond it. A flare went up and we flopped flat, unobserved, the trenches being now a little farther away. The next place we came to was our Headquarters trench beside the road, where we dumped our loads. A short walk over the field to the right would have brought us to the L.R.B.'s front-line trench. . . .

" We are doing drill in the daytime here and shall not see Wood and the others until to-morrow. It is very nice listening to the British guns which are very active round here. Now I understand all that is implied when the bulletins say that ' Artillery duels have taken place.' German aeroplanes come along occasionally and get fired at. You may see several puffs of smoke in the air but, in order to detect the aeroplane, you have to look about a mile away and half a mile higher. The guns on both sides don't seem to get the range in the air very easily. If the airman succeeds in locating the position of the guns we get shells whizzing over us intended for our batteries. Yesterday these shells fell in Ploegsteert and in the fields around, but the British did not reply much. To-day our artillery has been very busy, without any reply so far from the enemy. The firing-line is so different from my conception of it. The entire countryside is quite flat, consisting of green or ploughed fields, with groups of trees in the distance and lines of willows between the fields. Here and there are farmhouses, thatched cottages and small houses, and with the sun shining the panorama is a very placid and peaceful one. Except for the noise of firing and the ' Pip-pip ' of the rifles, we might be in Kent ! "

8/2/1915. " . . . This is the third day of our stay in billets (in Ploegsteert). Sergt. (now Corpl.) Fulkes, Cox, Sweeting, Gernat and I are in a house in the village and have the front room to ourselves for sleeping and eating and the people are very obliging. Fulkes and I speak French sufficiently to ask for all our wants. We have not been posted to our sections again yet, so Corpl. Miles and the others are in a billet farther down the street. What an absolute treat to sit down at a table again for a meal ! We have our food cooked by the ' landlady,' who also makes tea and provides milk and won't hear of us using our enamelled plates and mugs or even our own knives and forks !

No, she provides crockery and cutlery and washes up afterwards and we feel quite at home. When back in civilised surroundings it is very funny how a hair on our plates worries us, whereas we swallowed all manner of things in the barn. We are most particular now about clean knives, and the butter we bought, which was so perfect in the barn, is recognised as white lard when surrounded by ' tea-things.' The Army food is good and rations are plentiful : we can also buy almost anything in the village, but the ' boutons noirs ' have a reputation for possessing money and the shopkeepers charge them much more than they do the regulars.

" We marched (to Nieppe) to the baths yesterday, which we were very glad to have. They consist of huge tubs of hot water to hold about twelve men, and you have to drop down some distance from the top of the tubs to the water. We got a complete set of clean underclothing, which did not necessarily fit us, and I changed mine with a big fat man who was in rather a fix. While we were in the baths our uniforms were ' baked ' in a kind of oven to disinfect them. On returning here, I went round with Wood to a deserted village school and played the piano for about half an hour ; it *was* such a pleasure to touch one again.

" Last night Wood's landlady had made a fine boiled roly-poly jam pudding and I asked the good wench at our billet to make one. Being of the peasant class, she had never made such a thing before and all signs and explanations were useless, as our French was not advanced enough to describe the recipe. Fulkes and I pointed to bread and pretended to roll out dough and spread jam and threw the imaginary pudding at the oven, but the woman only laughed. . . .

" I have only been on guard once. On that occasion one nervous sentry thought he saw something move, which was really a harmless dust-heap, and called us all out (the guard, I mean). It was rather exciting and we didn't grumble. The only person who grumbled was a man who had had some rum before retiring to bed and, on the command "Guard, turn out!" thought he was part of the guard and turned out with them! When we had gone some distance, he realised that it was a day or two before that he had been on guard."

12/2/1915. " . . . This is my third day in the front-line breastworks, having left billets on the evening of the 9th, and we shall be relieved to-night. We came up by the lane past the ' Demi Lune ' which I described before, and, having got to the front-line trenches, filed along to the left until we got to some breastworks. The trench is so full of water here that these breastworks have been built on the ground. Ours is a long low bivvy not very much above ground-level, made of sandbags, planks and earth, and well covered. It is divided into three compartments, each holding three men, or a portion of them— for our feet stick out in the open and the space is very limited. We are in a big field and our trenches are on one side : to the right they are manned by our company for some few hundred yards and then the (Essex) regiment continues the line onwards in the direction of (Armentières). To our left is another breast-work, manned by our platoon, and beyond them there is a considerable space before the (East Lancs) trench begins at the outskirts of (Le Gheer). Three hundred yards away is the German trench, which we observe through a periscope. The field itself is a mass of wet brown mud, without anything growing, but with thousands of cans and empty tins thrown about near the trenches

" All we do is to cook meals, read, write and keep guard. We start off with a sip of rum to warm us and then cook bacon as best we may on an improvised brazier deposited on a duck-board path behind our breastwork. Everything is done under difficulties, as we have to keep very low to avoid being seen, and from morn to night we are unable to straighten ourselves. The Germans appear to have superiority of fire, as regards musketry, in this part of the line. They have snipers posted and plenty of loop-holes and keep up a constant fire all day long. ' Ping ! Ping !' we hear continually as they hit one object or another in the vicinity. It seems to be the aim of one sniper to reduce a certain house to ruins, as he keeps chipping off pieces of brick. As for us, we keep silent. As far as I can see, the whole British line keeps silent and treats them with contempt. As a matter of fact, it would be difficult to reply if we wanted to, as we haven't any loopholes and it would be madness to stand up and fire over the top. But the sniping doesn't do any good, except in so far as it forces us to lie low. At night time, unfortunately, he may work mischief, as the man on sentry-duty has to stand up for two hours and peer into the darkness. This brings me to the sorrowful bit of news that Merrilees was hit on the first morning in the next breast-work to us, just before dawn. The wound is not serious, but he was grazed on the chest by a rifle-bullet ; they managed to get the stretcher up and to take him away just before it was light enough for the Germans to see, otherwise he would have had to stay there till dusk. He went away making his usual witty remarks and we were very sorry to lose him. I don't suppose we shall see him out here again. The average casualty-list for the company in the front-line is only one man per three days. Lieut. Forbes was unfortunately killed by a sniper yesterday."

15/2/1915. " . . . On being relieved on the night of the 12th, we made our way gaily down the Demi Lune Road where a wagon was waiting to take our packs. Then we tramped along to the billets in (Armentières)—where we met Wood first of all—and had a very good night's sleep. Next day we cleaned ourselves up and Wood and I went out in the town, where we found a pastry-cook who not only stocks ' gateaux ' but also keeps a piano. The result is a permanent invitation to his house and we went again next day. That night we were awakened at midnight and had to put our kit together ready to move : we also had to have a meal and drink tea, though nobody wanted any. Fortunately the whole thing was a false alarm. . . . "

" This seems like a big military town in England and the appearance of a French soldier is, of course, a rarity. The thing that strikes you most is the enormous number of motor lorries driven by the A.S.C. There is a long straight road (from Nieppe) by these billets and sometimes the convoys extend as far as the eye can see and continue to pass for a few minutes. Then you will see a company or two of very spick and span troops, who are obviously new arrivals, and there will be an almost unending line of horses being taken out for exercise in the other direction.

In the streets you will see Hay's Wharf wagons, County Council
conveyances, etc., and everything seems to be connected with
the Army. ' To the Follies,' ' A cock fight will be held in this
estaminet,' etc., meet the eye, and menus are exhibited in more
or less faulty English in some of the estaminets. . . .''

21/2/1915. " . . . We are billeted in (Ploegsteert) again
now and go in the trenches to-night. I must tell you about a
digging fatigue we had on 16th when we were in the support farm
again. Now that the mud is removed from my coat and trousers
I can relate it without bad language. We arrived in the field
of mud in which the front-line trench is situated about 8.30 p.m.,
having carried planks of wood up there from the estaminet. The
night was dark, but we had to stoop all the time, as we were working
in the rear of the trench, filling sandbags, and if a flare went up
we had to crouch right down in the mud. Sandbags have to be
filled with mud and water and in the dark the operation is a very
awkward one, for half of each spadeful misses the bag and pours
down the putties and boots of the person holding it. The mud
you stand in comes nearly to the top of the boots and is much
deeper in places. We all wore our mackintosh capes, which are
very spacious and reach almost to our feet, and, as we perpetually
stooped, we kept tripping up and treading on the capes, which
were soon as muddy inside as out. When I had dug a small hole
it enabled me to sit in the mud and put my feet and legs in the
hole.

" After a number of bags were filled we had to carry them a
distance of 150 yards to an emplacement on the right, stooping
and wading through the slosh ; we trod on turnips and slid off
them, our feet turning right over in the mud, sometimes tripping
up. This is all very well until a flare goes up. Then you instantly
flop down flat in the slosh and crouch for about twenty seconds.
On you go again, stooping and treading on the mac, falling over
turnips : another flare, another flop : then you feel yourself
slipping and find yourself in a shell hole, knee deep in mud and
water, sprawling about against the slimy sides. Several swear-
words follow, and you try to get out, but become tied up in the
cape. I fell in such a hole twice and to put my hand anywhere
on boots, puttees or trousers was to get it as slimy and dripping
as when I sprawled in the mud. We left off the task at 11.30
and went to bed about half-past-midnight, very glad to rest our
backs after the stooping. One man wearing waders or gum-boots
had been digging for half an hour and found he had absolutely
stuck in the mud and couldn't get out. The only way out was to
withdraw his feet, stand on a bank in his socks and tug at the
boots with his hands. But even this was too much for him, and
another man had to come up, and, with gloves on, they tore away
the mud from the boots and eventually freed them. But this
time, the man who had come to the rescue found he had stuck
and he also had to get out of his boots and dig them out. *Some*
mud ! . . .

" The new draft from the 2nd Battalion had arrived, and Thomson
will probably get on our section. It is nice to see him again,
also Aimes, Hudson, Dennis, Stapleton and others, who are all
in " D " Company. . . ."

23/2/1915. " . . . We came in the trenches the night before

last and leave to-morrow: Wood, Bourke, Gernat and I have one bivvy and we have not had at all a bad time. This section of trench is six or seven feet deep and the duckboard path is three feet wide. There are raised platforms to fire from, but in the daytime the sentries use periscopes and only look over the parapet themselves after dusk.

"The German snipers, who are in special pits right out in front of their own trenches, try to hit these periscopes as soon as they appear. They are excellent shots and no sooner has the sight made its appearance than the bullets start ripping up the sandbags sending showers of mud over the occupants of the trench. To-day we rigged up a dummy one and they at once started to waste their ammunition on it, while we used the proper one in a different part of the trench. The reason that we were particularly anxious to use one at that moment was that a real live German had actually been seen: true, he was but a mere dot in the distance, walking along behind their reserve trenches, probably emboldened by the fact that we scarcely ever fire, but he was the first that had been seen for a very long time and hence the excitement. Peeps through periscopes: peeps through our one loop-hole: great preparations for taking a shot through the latter! These having been completed, puzzle—find the German! He reappeared later, and we all took it in turns to look at him, and then one of our men potted at him. Whether he hit him or not is unknown, but it greatly disturbed the German snipers. The idea of a British soldier shooting a rifle in the daytime! Pop! Pop! Pop! Their bullets struck the place where our shooter had appeared, one after another, all in the same spot, sending plenty of earth over us. Whatever their average shooting is like, their snipers at any rate are very good shots. They are gradually shooting down the barbed wire outside our trench, but we send out a party at night to repair the damage.

"Yesterday it was very misty and we could not see far in front of the trench. This afforded an opportunity to the E. Lancs on our flank to go out on little expeditions in search of German helmets, etc. There are dozens of German bodies in front of our trenches, where they have lain for three or four months, and we can see them distinctly in the daytime and occasionally smell them at night. The Lancs soon appeared in our trenches with German rifles, bayonets, pouches, buttons, etc., which fetched various prices up to fr. 4. Thus encouraged, they set out again and brought back plenty more. I shouldn't have liked the job!

"Just as we were going to cook some dinner on the brazier yesterday, the Germans started shelling an already wrecked house some 100 yards to our left, and plugged in the shells sometimes twelve to the minute. Of course, we had to seek the protection of the 'bivvies' and lie down there, and I fell asleep for forty minutes. When I woke up, the British were sending shells over behind the Germans most vigorously. This is the regular after-dinner programme and nobody takes any notice of it.

"At the present moment, some wag in the German trench along the line on the left is signalling with a plank the shots which the Lancs have just fired, just as if he were recording bulls at a rifle range. . . .

"There seems to be no remedy for cold feet and a number of

our men have gone away with frost-bite. When you wake up you usually find them like two lumps of ice, even though each foot be in a sandbag and covered with a mackintosh sheet."

2/3/1915. ". . . We still continue our twelve-day round. This is my third day in this farm, and we go to billets in Ploegsteert to-night. The farm is 600 yards from the trenches and I have had an opportunity of using a carefully concealed observation-post, from which I have seen all the neighbourhood and right across the German trenches. It is a lovely day and you cannot realise that this is the firing-line. Even the trenches are most difficult to distinguish and only the battered houses show anything is unusual. I was on guard last night from 9 till 11 and 3 till 5, and continue to-day for two hours in six. The place where I did the guard was depressing, as just in front of me was a solitary little grave where a cavalry major was killed on October 21st last year.

" Whenever you are near the firing-line you can see them shelling the Convent (at Le Gheer) just behind the Lancs' trenches, and half of it still stands. When they have nothing better to do, they shell that house. Yet the Lancs continue to garrison it. They just turn out, stand behind the wall and put on a pipe, waiting while they shell the other side of the building, and when it is all over they go inside again. Those Lancs are a cool lot of chaps. The other morning I saw one walking along the little lane behind our trench, smoking a pipe and carrying a walking-stick. He walked two or three hundred yards and back again and did not get hit. Another day two came over to our trench about something, in broad daylight, and on the way back the Germans started potting at them and they had quite an argument in the middle of the field as to whether they should walk or run. One wanted to run and the other didn't, and the argument was still continuing when they reached shelter. . . ."

5/3/1915. ". . . Two days ago I had an irksome occupation, as it was perpetual digging for 4½ hours in drizzling rain, with nothing to relieve the monotony. The soil was very sticky on account of the rain and you can imagine what it would be like to dig soil in your garden and put the spadefuls on a barricade some feet high, with all your movements hampered by a huge mackintosh cape and rain nearly all the while ! The spades were pointed, and I, being rather an ' unhandy ' man, chased clods of earth all over the place without succeeding in picking them up. When I did get half a spadeful, I gave it a violent jerk, but the mud stuck hard to the spade and wouldn't shift. Extracting my feet with some difficulty, with half of Belgium on each foot, I made another effort to throw the earth on the heap, resulting in the spade nearly smacking Thomson in the face and a little piece of mud hitting Wood on the nose. The remainder stuck to the spade. And still it rained . . . . Then I plunged the spade in the earth, leant too far forward and fell over it ! Great fun, but still we made an appreciable difference in four hours !

" This afternoon I was playing the piano in the deserted hall when a regular came in and told me I had better leave soon as the Germans might be replying to some guns close by. The shells came over soon after I had left, but there were only four of them and they all landed in a field. Accordingly I returned to the piano again, but this time my play was cut short by the appearance of three Somersets, all rather merry with beer, I fancy. They asked me to play the melody again, asked each other to listen to Paderewski, remarked on what a fine audience I had and waxed enthusiastic over my footlights. After one or two incoherent questions, which I found it difficult to answer, they proceeded to waltz together and asked me to strike up the music. This was scarcely encouragement to continue good music, which might have called forth eggs at my head, so I found it was getting near time for tea—and went ! "

9/3/1915. " . . . I got back (to Armentières) quite safely from the trenches yesterday night, after a very cold day and occasional falls of snow. During our stay there, I have not fired a single shot, but have continued my night-watchman's training and am getting used to seeing things in the dark. The posts of our barbed wire entanglements no longer appear to be advancing Germans : the only things that seem to advance are empty-tins, but they never attack us. . . .

" If you stand up long enough looking over the parapet, it is very easy to imagine anything moves : this is *not* the effect of rum, as this is only taken when you come *off* sentry-duty, to warm you sufficiently to forget about icy feet and doze off to sleep. When we left the trench after dark there was scarcely a shot to be heard from when we first emerged to when we got out of ear-shot. I expect the Germans were keeping warm round their fires."

CHAPTER IV.

PLOEGSTEERT WOOD.

(March-April, 1915.)

The 11th Brigade—Neuve Chapelle—Trenches in Ploegsteert Wood—The wood itself—The enfilade trench—Battalion at rest.

WHEN our 1st Battalion reached the firing-line in November they were attached to the 11th Infantry Brigade of the 4th Division, the latter holding the line from just south of Messines to north of Armentières. The particular portion covered by the 11th Brigade was in front and to the right of Ploegsteert Wood, though the Germans were not finally driven out of the fringe of the wood until December 19th. For instruction purposes the L.R.B.s were attached to the R.B.s and Somersets and sent into the trenches with them, thus affording these regulars some measure of relief in their vigil : and no body of men ever had larger hearts and more reassuring words than these troops. They confessed afterwards that, on hearing that Territorials were to join them, they never thought they could " stick it," and were astonished to find the L.R.B.s put up with the discomforts so cheerily. These regulars insisted upon cooking all the meals, relieved our fellows of all possible fatigues and generally set out to be as obliging as they could. We knew them and they knew us by name : we shared out our parcels and newspapers and generally rubbed along exceedingly pleasantly.

After a few weeks, the L.R.B. were given a trench of their own to hold, thereby enabling the other regiments to shorten their front and get more rest. This trench was situated on the right of the Brigade, beyond the Hants and E. Lancs and had until then been practically undefended, owing to the extremely attenuated line we were holding. It was the trench in which I found the regiment when I arrived in France, and it was said to be unrecognisable then compared with the quagmire which they had taken over at first.

What struck me very forcibly from the start was the truth of the statements of the old soldiers at the Base that the enemy were being held by bluff, and that our line was but a fringe between the Germans and the sea. In our own section, for example, one company held two or three hundred yards of front with from 150 to 160 men. Behind this were two or three fortified farms held by another company ; a mile back was another company billeted in Ploegsteert, while the remaining company was three miles away in Armentières, behind the 6th Division front. To the rear there was no infantry at all. The rest of the 4th Division front was similarly held. In fact, the entire British front, from Ypres to La Bassée, held now by 12 divisions, I think, was so weak in numbers that a big enemy concentration at any point would have caused extreme embarrassment to the staff. True, such concentrations had been withstood a month or so before, but the situation had been extremely critical. More troops were, however, arriving and, with the advent of the 46th and 48th Midland Territorial Divisions at the end of February, one of which marched into Armentières in column of route under the noses of the enemy, it was possible to thicken our front slightly.

Sir John French took advantage of this to order an offensive, and on March 10th at 7.30, when we were in Armentières, the guns of the 2nd, 8th and Indian Divisions south of us opened a bombardment of the enemy's positions. After half an hour the attack started and the battle raged for three days. We all thought it would mean the complete rupture of the German line and hopes ran high. As a matter of fact, of course, we captured the ruins of Neuve Chapelle and some four fields, at the cost of thousands of casualties. Barbed wire and machine guns were not to be destroyed by a half hour bombardment, consisting principally of shrapnel. It was our first lesson and should have been enough.

Shortly afterwards the 46th Division took over a portion of the front and we gave up our trench for the Ploegsteert Wood position, while the 11th Brigade extended to the north. A few weeks later the 1st Canadian Contingent prolonged the English front around Ypres and took over a few miles from the French up to Langemarck. We entered the new trenches on 22nd March, having continued our old routine up to that date and the best description of our conditions there will be conveyed by further letters written in the trench.

23/3/15. "Yesterday afternoon we came up to our new trenches, which we were able to enter in daylight. They are about fifteen yards from the edge of (Ploegsteert) Wood, where I have so often tramped down 'Piccadilly' and the 'Strand' when on fatigue from the village, but our route this time lay in the direction of 'Tower Bridge.' We have a good position here, and the regulars, whom we have relieved, have worked hard during the last month or so. This is not really a trench but a huge wall of sandbags and we tread on ground level. The trenches which used to be here have long since become filled with water and it has been found necessary to build above the level of the ground. Behind the wall of sandbags is the passage-way, which is all that existed in the olden days when the battalion first came out here and shared these 'trenches' with the regulars : but now there is a long bivvy in the rear, built of logs, with sufficient space for 18 men to sleep on thick boards under a splinter-proof roof : this is very different from the crowded bivvies in the other trenches, where we could not stretch our legs out.

"Along the top of the wall of sandbags dead branches have been placed, through which we keep our look-out, with the advantage of the wood as a background. How the Germans must envy us our position ! It belonged to them some weeks ago, before they were driven out of it completely by the British ; their old trench is a few yards away, between ourselves and the edge of the wood, and, in addition to this, there is a stream between the trenches and more than one series of barbed-wire entanglements, which makes it difficult for them to attack this position. They are now in the field which skirts the wood and have dug their trench about two hundred yards away; they are now on the skyline, whereas we are less visible, although we do not put our heads up more than we can help. There is very little firing indeed and during the night scarcely a shot came in our direction; they are supposed to be Saxons opposite us and they are apparently not going to exert themselves unless we provoke them. As it is more comfortable to walk about the wood without many bullets coming through, we shall keep quiet. It is very nice to be able to leave the 'trench' and take a stroll in the wood to stretch one's legs. I am going out shortly with Bourke, as two men are allowed to be absent at once, for an hour.

" It is beautiful here this morning, the sun is shining brightly and the birds are singing in the tall trees which tower upwards as far as we can see. Sometimes quite thirty seconds pass without the sound of a shot anywhere, during which time it seems as if I were in Pembury Woods on a lovely summer morning. We have not had enough hot weather to bring out the smells badly, though they are commencing and in some places are already objectionable. There has been so much fighting in this wood that there are hundreds of dead buried in it and some streams are somewhat polluted with them. The worst smell comes from between the lines, where there are many bodies lying around.

" Between the trenches there are one or two ruins of houses, now not any higher than a man, with about three small walls remaining, riddled with bullets, and pictures of desolation. If ever I am sent out on listening patrol, I may make a closer acquaintance with them. Of course, I have not had any time to find out much about the immediate neighbourhood, but I have already noticed that our line is by no means one continual wall, but a series of barricades, some nearer the edge of the wood than others and connected with each other by corduroy paths. . . ."

24/3/1915. " . . . When I went for my walk in the wood yesterday I found corduroy paths in all directions and countless shelters, huts and sign-posts had been made, which point to four months of hard work. I went down a path, past the officers' bivvies, which were marked 'Hope Cottage' and 'Shrove Villa,' past a barricade with the sign-post ' Ye Olde Jug and Giblets,' and then after a short walk came to ' Primrose Hill,' where a roof of a hut was covered with budding primroses. Then came ' Baynes' Bivvy,' ' The Tabernacle ' and ' The Tourists' Peep.' Shortly afterwards I reached the ' Tower Bridge ' and made my way to ' Piccadilly Circus.' Five ' roads ' meet here and a huge motor sign-post has been erected, with a big red triangle denoting ' Danger.' The notice ' Drive slowly : School at bottom ' is rather superfluous. I don't know whether it was Regent Street I followed next, but I soon passed ' Somerset House ' and the ' Palais de Justice,' and then went for some distance without a turning. All the way we encountered men carrying planks, barbed-wire, etc., and as I did not go into that part of the wood where we have hitherto done all our fatigues, I realised more what an enormous amount of work is done here." (In spite of all defence preparations, extending over three years, the wood was captured by the Germans on April 11th, 1918.)

" The wood consists of many tall trees and dead undergrowth, but in many places one can see for quite a distance, partly owing to the number of trees that have been cut down or smashed by shells. Numerous small streams run under the paths, some of them crossed by well-constructed bridges : the water varies in colour from yellow to green and sometimes opens out into a big morass, with signs of deep footprints in it. Turning off at Spy Corner, we presently reached our trench again, the whole stroll taking an hour, without our seeing a quarter of the wood.

" In the early days many civilian snipers were caught in here and shot, and although the Belgians are not allowed in the wood, one or two suspicious persons have been seen. There are a number of spies about.

" We are here for nine days, doing guards for two hours in six. During my sentry-go last night the Germans could be distinctly heard shouting and talking. They had probably just heard of the sinking of our warships in the Dardanelles, as they seemed very merry. Soon afterwards we heard a drunken German shouting a song at the top of his voice, but they quietened down by midnight and for the period from 4 to 6 a.m. very few shots came over. In the night we only get an occasional star-shell over at this point, just to show they are awake. . . ."

One day was much like another in the Wood and there was little time for sleep, with one thing and another. Sandbag-filling parties, water-carrying parties, wood-carrying parties, meals to cook, rifle-cleaning and the incessant sentry-duty occupied our time, by day and by night. Heightening the barricade, listening-patrol and building block-houses made an occasional change of work.

At the end of the month I went to the sick-billet in Ploegsteert with septic fingers, caused by getting dirt in cuts, and I was unable to move my trigger-finger, thus being useless in the front-line. On April 6th, however, I had joined the company again, this time in what was called the " Enfilade " trench, so named because it ran out towards the German line at right-angles to the Wood and enabled us to attack the flank of any German advance. The German trenches bent back slightly at this point but, nevertheless, the " Enfilade " trench stretched out towards them until it got within 85 yards of a ruined estaminet in their hands ; thence our front-line turned to the left again and kept closer to the enemy.

This trench was a maze of communication trenches, dug-outs and small sections of front-line, which were a seething mass of mud. The parapet overlooked an artificial hedge, through which one gazed at a veritable sea of slush as far as the German line. Behind the " trench " was a low mud wall, and in rear of that an old three foot trench used for drainage ; owing to the excessive rain and failure of our " pumping station," the water in this had risen to the level of our trench and dug-outs and had submerged the bridges. The entrance to my particular bivvy was through a narrow passage of slimy mud, and the floors, walls and ceiling of this residence consisted of the same substance. There were traces of sandbags in the roof, which was so low that we could not sit upright ; these got rid of all the water they didn't want in wet weather by dropping it on to the inmates below. Four of us had to sleep in it and the men farthest from the entrance had to scramble over the others to get out of the door, and groans and swears were heard as you put your knees or hands on their ribs, or a muddy foot in their faces.

When one came off guard my bivvy would probably not have to provide a sentry for the next two hours, so that there would be four of us sleeping there at once. One night I crawled in and struck a match, four matches in fact, and eventually lit a candle. Then I had a look round and saw that the two men between whom I had to sleep were spread out without leaving me an inch of room. I crawled over the first one—incidentally waking him—and called out to the second to move. Only a grunt resulted. I raised my voice and asked him to move again. He shifted about six inches after a struggle and then said he couldn't get any farther, so I woke the 4th man and told him to make himself smaller. His equipment got caught and when he had done his best midst much cursing, there was about room enough for a rifle. By this time, smothered gasps of agony arose from No. 2, whose shins I was kneeling upon, and No. 4 had dozed off again. I perceived my blanket was over the legs of the latter gentleman, while the groundsheet had disappeared, and eventually No. 2 admitted that it was near his head. Then the candle fell over and, amid much cursing on the part of everybody, I set it up again. On recovering my belongings, I eventually wedged myself between the two sufferers and, by so doing, forced No. 2 out, but he settled himself down again by pushing No. 1 farther into the wet bog at the entrance. . . .

At 1 o'clock No. 4 had to mount guard and *I* was one of the trodden ana oppressed. He got his equipment entangled with mine and cursed like a trooper. Then at 3 a.m. my turn came again. In the daytime there was not much opportunity to rest as we were always being called on to do digging, bailing and other odd jobs, chiefly caused by the flooding of trenches and the collapsing of earth. As can be imagined, we did not carry away with us very beautiful impressions of that trench.

For me, this was almost the last front-line experience at Ploegsteert, as April 12th found me in hospital with poisoned hands, a complaint by no means uncommon owing to the foul soil that begrimed one's flesh for days on end. When one's hands became cut and sore, the dirt frequently caused septic poisoning to set up. The hospital was the 11th Brigade Field Ambulance at Steenwerck, and while there I had many chats with the Somersets and others ; twice the patients were conducted to an R.A.M.C. concert party. Most of the day we sat out in the open enjoying a rest, and I quite enjoyed the freedom from sentry duty and sandbags.

On April 18th, to my surprise Wood and Thomson called to see me and brought the news that the battalion was resting in barns near the village and that all the 11th Brigade was being withdrawn for rest and training. They were keeping a place for me in their billet and urged me to leave as soon as possible, which I was unable to do for another two days.

I found the regiment in the midst of preparations for sports tournaments, races, company concerts and other enjoyments : " D " Company very soon had their musical evening in a hall in the village and, although the piano was atrocious, the concert went off very well. Everyone was in excellent spirits and looked forward to weeks of recreation and rest.

True, the news that the Queen Victoria Rifles, our "sister" battalion, had suffered heavily at Hill 60 caused a momentary flutter. It was commonly supposed at that time that the Territorials, who had come out to fill the gap until the arrival of Kitchener's Army and had been through the winter campaign, would shortly be relieved or at any rate not utilised for the "Great 1915 Offensive." That the Q.V.R.s had taken part in a British attack on Hill 60, near Ypres, came as a great surprise. Perhaps we might be called upon to take Warneton and we conjured up visions of wading across the No Man's Land at Ploegsteert. There was no doubt that the news was true, for we saw some of their men in ambulances on the way to Bailleul.

But ours was a quiet part of the line: they could attack up north as much as they liked so long as it did not affect our rest at Steenwerck. So we dismissed it from our minds and proceeded with our sports preparations in high spirits. The dark dismal winter season was over; now we had the joyous spring, the drying ground, the advent of Kitchener's two millions and the approaching collapse of the Hun !

CHAPTER V.

The Second Battle of Ypres : Opening Stages.

(*April 22nd–29th, 1915.*)

The opening bombardment—Preparing to move—En route for Ypres—Bivouacs at Poperinghe—Scenes at Vlamertinghe—The march to the Salient—Digging in at Fortuin—Filling the gap near Zevenkote—Three days' bombardment.

Scarcely had we finished our tea on April 22nd when a furious bombardment started up in the Ypres direction, by far the most violent that we had yet heard. In reality it was the opening of the famous German gas-attack on the French, and heralded the Second Battle of Ypres. We did not realise that the stroke came from the Germans and that most of the cannonade represented the reports of their guns and the explosions of their shells ; we believed that a greater British attack than that at Neuve Chapelle had started.

All that evening it continued without intermission and as it grew dark one man after another laid aside his books or his letters and joined the little knots of spectators, watching the flashes in the northern sky and debating upon what our objective could be in the great attack. However, as it was not on our portion of the front, it did not interest us sufficiently to interrupt our sleep, and it was only when the guard woke us at dawn that we learnt that the cannonade had lasted all night and had afforded a sight so well worth watching that each sentry's two-hour guard had passed by with incredible rapidity.

Indeed, the noise seemed to have grown in volume. The air was quivering with vibration and the bombardment seemed more like a perpetual rumble than a collection of separate reports. After breakfast we had a route-march to Bailleul and did a little open-order work ; upon returning to Steenwerck we were informed that we were " standing to " and must not leave our billets without permission. This announcement caused a certain amount of excitement as it now began to dawn upon us that, as we were in reserve, we might be despatched to any part of the line. Later in the day our doubts were finally settled, for a message came round that we were to entrain first thing in the morning : extra ammunition was to be issued out, much to our consternation ! We were also advised to discard all surplus kit, to clean our ammunition and rifles, and to write letters home. These interesting occupations took us the entire evening to carry out, to the accompani-

ment of an increased pandemonium up at Ypres that struck a chill
to our hearts. Attack or defence—and we knew not yet which it
might be—nobody could honestly say he was eager to plunge into the
fray, considering things from a personal point of view. There was
an eagerness to prove the worth of the battalion, since the Queen
Victorias had sprung into fame, but if this could be proven at a
minimum of personal discomfort—well, so much the better.

Next day (April 24th) found us on the road, transport and all, and,
now that we were definitely moving, our spirits revived and we sang
" Timiloo " and " Ragtime Navvy " on the way to Steenwerck Station,
where a collection of cattle-trucks awaited us. The transport continued by road and was to meet us near Poperinghe, so the entraining
did not take very long ; but it was some time before we steamed out
of the station, crowding round the open doors and taking a last glimpse
at the rear of the Ploegsteert section of the line, which we were leaving
behind us for ever.

When we reached Hazebrouck, where we switched off on to the
Poperinghe line, there was a considerable delay while other trains
passed by us. To our great delight we found a trainload of the 1st
R.B.s alongside us, so that the 11th Brigade was evidently on the
move and we were not an isolated unit being withdrawn from the
4th Division, as we had feared. " Cheerio, L.R.B.s," was their
greeting : "we're in for it this time all right." And somehow one
felt that it didn't matter if we were, so long as we had these cheerful
Regulars with us. Over beyond the station was a main road, and
as we sat munching our biscuits we watched an endless stream of
motor ambulances coming down from the direction of Ypres, while
a few were speeding the other way. Never had we seen so many of
these vehicles, and the fact that the convoy appeared to be an endless
one reflected very heavy casualties up in that inferno : had we
reasoned it out we must have concluded this from the volume of the
gunfire, but the visible proof brought the fact home to us. Another
disquieting sight was a train full of refugees, poor, miserable beings,
who had taken with them a few belongings and were crowded into
cattle-trucks, men, women and children together, with no homes
to go to and their own dwellings probably pounded to dust.

Soon after the R.B.'s train had started off ours followed, and we
proceeded at a snail's pace as far as Caestre, where more refugees
passed us and the din of battle grew louder. As yet we had no news
of what was happening and we asked one of the R.T.O.'s orderlies.
He mentioned something about the use of gas and a German advance
of five miles and Turcos running like blazes. We received this news
in a dull-witted sort of way and did not appreciate its significance
at all. As a matter of fact, someone told us at the next station that
the Canadians had made a fine advance, recaptured the lost ground
and forged right ahead. Between the two reports, we were still
undecided as to whether we were making a big offensive, since we
could not reconcile ourselves to the attack being made by the
Germans.

Late in the afternoon we stepped out on to the platform at Poperinghe
and threaded our way in single file over the prostrate bodies of wounded
French and Algerian soldiers, who were probably waiting for a train
to take them away. They were the ghastliest sight we had yet seen,
some being blind, others limbless and most of them looking pathetic
in the extreme. Outside in the street was a company of French

Territorials who watched our parade with great interest. Having formed up, we marched along a road to the south and were ushered into a very large field, where the other regiments of the 11th Brigade had already bivouacked round the hedges (excepting the East Lancs, who had been temporarily left at Ploegsteert). Here we chose a suitable spot and, casting off our cumbersome kit, squatted round in groups and debated on coming events or remained silent, according to individual temperament. There was a farm in the centre of the

SECOND BATTLE OF YPRES

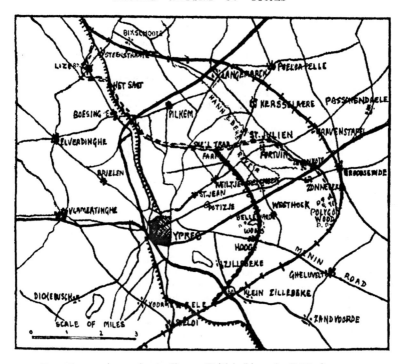

➖❙➖❙➖	Approximate Franco-British Line, April 22nd.
⩵⩵⩵⩵⩵	Approximate position after first and second gas attacks, April 26th.
⚬⚬⚬⚬⚬⚬	Approximate New British Line, May 3rd.

field, where we tried to get some coffee, but we found it crowded with Somersets and others and it was hopeless attempting to get served. Word came round that we were the last line of reserves and that we probably should not be wanted—an instance of the sops that are served up to the gullible ranker.

At dusk the arrival of the transport with cookers aroused our enthusiasm and thoughts of a mug of hot tea overshadowed all else. After satisfying our thirsts we started to erect bivvies with our ground-sheets, as the Regulars were doing, but Colonel Bates succeeded in finding a few barns as billets for the L.R.B. (God bless him !) and we were soon trooping off on to the road again, leaving our unfortunate

D

comrades to pass the night in the open field amidst drenching rain, which was still falling in the morning.

" D " Company were packed into a loft of straw, but, although feeling tired, it would be wrong to say we slept soundly that night : the gun-fire was so close now that, in addition to the incessant roar, we could make out the individual reports of the larger guns, of which we unfortunately possessed so few. We woke up many times and I, for one, dreamt about the bombardment so that, sleeping or waking, the noise of the guns dominated my mind. We were called at 4 a.m. and had to have breakfast and be clear of the farm in an hour. The remainder of the 11th Brigade were already marching off and we followed in their wake. Owing to the absence of the East Lancs, our brigade had been reduced to four battalions, so that instead of being " attached " we now ranked on a par with the Regular units and were going to do exactly the same as they. This was a feather in our caps and we felt quite pleased about it.

Away to the left, parallel to us, ran the main Poperinghe-Ypres road, outlined by an avenue of tall trees : a clump of them in the distance, with some buildings, represented Vlamertinghe. On this road we could distinguish through the drizzling rain the same string of ambulances hurrying to and fro and parties of troops arriving in motor-buses. Nearer to us were contingents of Belgian soldiers digging trenches, looking cold and miserable. Occasionally we could see the flash of a gun in the distance. To either side of us, as we wended our way along a muddy track, lay fields and hedges, dotted with isolated Flemish farmhouses, a most bleak and depressing piece of country. At one of the farms the Essex Yeomanry lined up to watch us pass : we also saw cavalrymen about, always a reassuring sight.

When we got to the outskirts of this village, we were halted by a brewery on the main road and then crowded into the second floor. How many other units were squashed into the building I do not know, but we were certainly so uncomfortable inside that many of us descended to the street again and stood for an hour or so watching passers-by. The majority of these consisted of slightly wounded men, since there was such a run on the ambulances that only the bad cases could be put on board. Even others, more seriously wounded, decided to " foot it " and chance being picked up, rather than hang about indefinitely for a seat in an ambulance. A large number of these men were Canadians, but dozens of British regiments were represented, to say nothing of artillerymen. From one and another we asked for news of the fighting and some of the slighter cases drew up for conversation. They all told conflicting stories and none knew really what had happened except on their own particular bit of the front. But we gleaned sufficient to learn that the Germans had let loose clouds of poison gas, which had asphyxiated the French corps on the northern part of the salient and driven them back five miles to the Yser Canal. This had left the Canadians' flank open and the situation had been and still was most critical. Several told us that the Canadian Division had been practically annihilated, which was, of course, true. All spoke of the terrific preponderance of the German artillery which had obliterated their trenches, and many, with reddened eyes and wheezing breath, had experienced something of this vile gas, though those who had had its full force were either dying at the dressing-stations or else were already covering that plain where this outrage had been perpetrated. It appeared that the Canadians had momen-

tarily saved the situation by a spirited counter-attack, while some of
the original line was still holding firm, but the pandemonium still going
on up in the salient and the thousands of wounded who were continually
arriving showed how serious the position was and how black was
the future for the newly-arrived battalions in reserve.

Sickened by the sight of these broken and maimed men and the
perpetual flow of motor ambulances, I re-entered the building and
penned a note to my people which I enclosed in a hurriedly-scrawled
letter to my cousin, with instructions to hand it to them if the worst
should happen to me : this was no sooner completed and a very feeble
attempt at skilly mechanically consumed than we were ordered to
evacuate the brewery and congregate in the open field at the back,
where the transport was drawn up, and the bombers were told to fall
in and march down to a grenade store. This party included myself
and several others who had never thrown even a dummy bomb with
sufficient accuracy to justify our being trusted with real ones, and
we pitied the battalion that had to rely upon our efforts with live
grenades. Our route lay through the village, which was a scene of
bustle and activity and crowded with transport. We passed a field
ambulance where there were about a score of men crowding round
each Red Cross car, dozens of stretchers lying out on the pavement
and numberless cases out in the grounds. The majority of the latter
were gas cases and nothing could be done to save them : black in the
face, blinded and gasping, they were undergoing a slow, agonising
death. It made us boil with rage to think that such a devilish device
had been introduced into warfare and we were determined to show
short shrift to any German we saw.

The village was full of troops, and frightened old women stood at
their doorways watching the coming and going of soldiers and the
passing of innumerable transport wagons. Interspersed with the
khaki figures were decrepit old Belgians pushing along on wheelbarrows
all that they had saved from the wreckage of their homes in Ypres or
to the east of it. Some led horses, others pushed perambulators, still
others carried their belongings tied up in a sheet ; while many carried
birds in cages and weird trophies. With their womenfolk and children
they trudged wearily over the cobble-stones and answered all questions
with much waving of hands and arms and the two words " Beaucoup
bombard ! " Many of the women and girls were in tears, and the
inhabitants of Vlamertinghe who watched them with so much pity
were destined to be in a similar plight shortly, for next day the village
was heavily shelled.

We eventually reached the grenade-store—a Canadian one—and
having loaded ourselves up with the missiles, returned to the battalion
who were sitting about where we had left them, smoking cigarettes
in moody silence or addressing spasmodic remarks to their neighbours.
Rations for the next day were soon served out and I suddenly realised
my water-bottle was empty ; so I crossed over to a neighbouring cottage
and induced them to boil me some water. The inmates were not
accommodating, however, and it seemed curious that they should be
so ungrateful to the British who stood between them and the German
Army.

Presently the Colonel sent for all the officers and N.C.O.s and held
a council of war. How eagerly we awaited their return in order to
hear our fate ! It was Cpl. Miles from whom we learnt that an attack
was at the moment proceeding at the north-east corner of the salient

and the Staff didn't know quite what was happening. We had to make for an unknown spot near St. Julien and dig in there. No one knew whether Canadians or Germans would be in front of us, nor whether, if we were not careful, we should find ourselves surrounded. Nobody really knew anything. The principal thing was to advance to the head of the salient and " dig like blazes."

With these cheerful orders ringing in our ears, we marched off in fours at dusk, heavily laden with packs and bombs and wearing our overcoats, our transport—also fully loaded—following us in the rear. In the middle of the village we halted to allow what seemed an endless line of troops to pass ahead of us. They were our friends of the 11th Brigade, all as jolly and as merry as could be. We fell out for a moment amidst the Canadian onlookers who stood, two or three deep, on either side of us. Some of them had been relieved that day and remnants would probably come down that night.

After a considerable delay and a halt between the road and the railway line just beyond the village, we started on what will always be, for me, the most memorable march of the war. We split up into platoons with connecting files to keep touch in the front and rear, proceeding at such a pace that it amounted to a " double " and the connecting files absorbed half our platoon. I was suffering from very sore feet and was hobbling along with a limp which did not improve my temper or my language.

Straight ahead of us lay Ypres, marked by a huge conflagration caused by inflammatory shells, and tall pillars of flames towered into the sky. The Germans had been shelling it for days with 17-inch guns, and every few minutes one of these deafening crashes resounded in the town : consequently it was with a feeling of relief that we presently beheld a sentry with a lamp, in the middle of the road, switching us off to a track leading half-left across a field. This enabled us to avoid passing through the centre of the town. The pace became trying on this rough ground and the messages, " What's the hurry ? " and " Go slow in front " were constantly passed on, but no reply came back nor did the speed diminish. A convoy of gun-limbers dashed past us in the opposite direction, careering across the open ground and urged on by the drivers. We could now see the gaunt, ruined tower of the Cloth Hall distinctly outlined against the glow on the right, and also the pall of smoke that hung over the surroundings. Gradually it loomed nearer and we found ourselves in the northern outskirts of the city, where, making a detour round some dead horses, we descended a hill and came to the Yser Canal at the bottom. Crossing this, we turned to the right on the farther bank and immediately after-wards took the St. Jean Road eastwards. This particular corner, our transport told us afterwards, was the most unpleasant spot of all on their nightly journey with rations and they always took it at a canter. As it was, we saw traces of the buildings having been very much knocked about and portions of limbers beside the road.

Just past this point we had our first halt, and scrambled up onto the bank, where some of us foolishly began to encroach on our water-ration ; Woodward, next to me, had not filled his bottle at all and so took a drink from mine. How I longed for that precious liquid next day ! Salvoes of four shells at a time whizzed over very near the road and burst on the right. In other directions also there was a good deal of commotion, caused, unfortunately, by the enemy's shells and not by our own guns. By this time we began to feel decidedly wobbly inside!

After ten minutes, we staggered to our feet and resumed the march with strict orders that there was to be no smoking : it was soon evident that we were not the only people on the road and it became more difficult to keep together. There was, in fact, a great deal of traffic and noise : wagons, troops and teams tearing past us, orders being shouted out, and a general feeling of excitement, which was increased by the shells which whizzed overhead and sometimes burst quite close to us. There were at least three lines of vehicles in places and advancing convoys got jammed with retiring ones ; amidst these, motor ambulances throbbed and wormed their way forward. The pedestrians added considerably to the congestion and we were nearly ridden down several times, but we all kept moving somehow. Naturally we were continually met with the eternal " Who are yer ? " and we ourselves asked the same question many times. One officer rode by, from the direction of the line, and followed this query by remarking : " Courage, lads ! You're going to a hot place." " Nice cheerful old bird, I must say," said Wood, who was chirpy at all times.

The first village we came to was St. Jean, about a mile and a half from Ypres, and I have dim recollections of a battered church on the left and some cottages on the right : some of the latter were emergency dressing-stations and lights peeped through cracks in the darkened windows. Some shells had just been over and caught some vehicles on the road and the thought struck me how I should hate to be perched on a horse with shells about. It was here that we first detected gas in the air. Our eyes started to run copiously so that we could hardly see and many of us sneezed. The air was laden with a sickly and not unpleasant smell, evidently caused by " tear-shells " : beyond the village this wore off, but there still lingered a certain heaviness about the atmosphere which told that the air in the salient was not as pure as it should be. Perhaps it was this that gave us a great thirst, causing our mouths to become very dry. Yet we dared not drink the entire contents of our water-bottles as we felt inclined to do.

In St. Jean we halted in order to draw a pick and a shovel between three men from a store, which was also a dressing station. I take it that the other units ahead of us had also done this, since we were delayed before we reached it. We got a glimpse here of some Canadians who had just been relieved : they passed by in ones and twos and it was the most unceremonial retirement from the trenches we had seen. Without valises, and shedding as much as they dared, they came along almost at the double, tired through they were—anxious to get out of shell-range as soon as possible : they had a repartee for every remark and, to set our minds at rest, said it was " not so dusty up there."

The guns continued to pay a good deal of attention to this road and some shells burst in the middle of it, laying out the best part of a platoon of the R.B.s : when we moved on again it was not very pleasant passing the spot where it had happened. Some of our transport were hit in the village too. They seem to have brought every vehicle up to this point, presumably under the impression that they might be wanted, and at any rate they had no settled horse-lines to go to : but this shelling decided them that it was only necessary for the machine-gun limbers and the medical cart to proceed and the rest sensibly made their way back to calmer regions.

The amount of transport grew less from this time onward, but evidences that we were on a Road of Death appeared more frequently, we saw groups of dead men, dead horses, wagons blown to bits, houses burning and smouldering, and we smelt the stench of the carcases, the fumes of shells and traces of gas. We passed on and through the village of Weiltje as in a dream. . . .

The flares were more noticeable now and they appeared so far behind us that the terrible nature of the salient was at once evident. We could see the rockets used by the French far behind us to our left and due north the British and German ones continued in a line that drew nearer to us : over on the right also we could make out star-shells miles back by Ypres, and yet they extended to a point that must have been over by Zonnebeke. Due east, however, all was in darkness and that was where the line was in such confusion at the moment. All along the Gravenstafel Ridge there was a great shroud of darkness : as a matter of fact, at 2 p.m. there had been a severe attack with gas against the 8th Durhams at that point and at 7 p.m. they had fallen back with heavy losses.

To the left we heard occasional machine-gun fire and the crump of shells. Twice we heard terrific bursts of rapid fire which may have meant partial attacks; these occurred on either side of us and were accompanied by dozens of flares.

In course of time we passed through the hamlet of Fortuin, consisting for the most part of smouldering ruins, and some little distance on the other side received the order to halt. On the side of the road was a barn, silhouetted against the sky, and, on the other, a hedge beneath which we lay down. Across the lane itself a smashed tree prevented our limbers coming any farther and, near by, a tall, well-built German lay dead : I went over and peered at him in awe and was particularly impressed by his heavy top boots. It was the first time I had seen a German at close quarters.

After about an hour's wait, during which the C.O. had been out reconnoitring, we advanced and filed into an open field on the right where we lined up along a hedge facing eastward. " A " Company went first and ours was the last on the scene, so that our left flank rested on the road. Having extended to about a yard between each man we got orders to dig in behind the hedge in which gaps were to be made to give us a field of fire. We were to be as quiet as possible, as it was not known who was in front. The Sergeant-Major told us to " dig like the devil." It was then after midnight and we must be under cover before dawn.

At the very outset of the operations we heard the report of a gun, a sudden swish and a crash on the other side of the hedge, followed by the whining approach of a portion of the shell. In that brief second we wondered whom it was making for, and then there was a howl, followed by shouts. A light was cautiously switched on and we found it was Burles, who had a beautiful little wound in the leg. The lucky man was despatched down the road again and his spell of the Second Battle of Ypres was done : the unwounded ones had to remain on and await their turn.

His shouts had caused uneasiness, as we had been told to keep quiet and when I discovered a dead man, whom I had to move, lying on the particular stretch of ground where I was about to dig, it was more unnerving still. Many shells fell in the vicinity and the desire to obtain some shelter lent us strength in our wrestle with the clods of earth. The greater part of the digging had to be done with entrenching tools, since the spades had to be shared, and, on our knees, we hacked away at the ground and flung it up in front of us by the hedge, working frantically against time, and wet-through with perspiration. We left our packs and overcoats on the ground behind us, but in spite of that it was very warm work. We kept having to leave off our work to bob down for shells coming over, but our section managed to get down some distance by three o'clock, alternately using picks, spades entrenching tools and bare hands.

Meanwhile the limbers had been unloaded and one machine gun had been posted at the end of the hedge so as to command the road, a fact which pleased our platoon, as we were next door to it. Although we did not know it at the time, the R.B.s and Somersets were digging in somewhere half-right and the Hants were far away beyond them on the Langemarck-Zonnebeke road. Between them was a weak place, filled, after a fashion, by the 8th Durhams, part of the Northumbrian Division of Territorials, who had only arrived in France from England a few days before and had been rushed straightway into the battle-line. To our left was St. Julien, and the tactical situation was so extraordinary that to meet an attack from that village we should have had to face completely round, looking north. None of this was, of course, appreciated at the time and all we thought of was getting our heads below ground.

By the time the first dim light of dawn appeared we had succeeded in getting down a fair depth and were still engaged in scooping out the earth, chiefly with our hands. We had been unable to join up with our immediate neighbours on either side, but about five of us got down into our particular section. Before doing so I crept over to see whose body I had moved a few hours before. It turned out to be one of the London Rangers, and one of our sergeants, who had been out reconnoitring, said that the place was strewn with them in front.

We were now able to look about us and peered anxiously through the hedge : our rifles lay on the parapet, peeping through clearings we had made. Before us was a field covered largely by a yellow sort of mustard-plant and eighty yards ahead was a platoon of R.B.s who, unknown to us, had dug in across our line of fire and promptly had to move elsewhere. The country appeared to be flat in front : there was a bit of a wood, and the road had a hedge on the left. One solitary building about 150 yards away lay straight ahead. To our left there was a little way-side crucifix on the far side of the road by a gap in the hedge : to the right our new trench seemed to stretch as far as the eye could see. Behind us was a hedge and one or two of our guns were concealed near by.

At dawn there was an increase in the volume of the German artillery fire, and away on the right the Durhams were attacked and two companies, according to records, enveloped. On our immediate front there was no sign of the enemy and, having toiled away for an hour or so after daybreak, widening and deepening our trench, we ravenously devoured some sandy bacon and bread and washed it down with a drop of our fast-diminishing water-supply.

Soon after breakfast an objectionable German aeroplane spotted our position and, although they were shelling all the other trenches,

roads, farms and gun positions the whole time, they found a few to
spare for us, and ten minutes later there was a blinding flash, an
explosion, a cloud of smoke and then a shower of earth fell about us.
This was followed by another. They had burst on the top of the next
section of trench, where they had not dug as deeply as we had. There
was a cry of " Stretcher-bearers wanted," a cry that we were destined
to pass up the trench many times in the next few days. Three had
been killed and three wounded : two were killed simply by concussion.
Poor old Tucker, Pepper and Woodward ! It seemed too awful to
realise. But this was just the commencement of our casualties and
they started to mount up in all companies from this time onwards.
Our wobbly feelings increased : so did our thirsts. By dinner-time
the last drop had gone from my bottle. I felt sticky and filthy, my
hands were caked and grimy and my fingers were septic again. A lot
of earth had gone down my neck, but there was nothing to be done
but grin and bear it.

In the early afternoon machine-guns grew busy on our left. The
French by the Canal, the Lahore Division by Pilkem and a Northumbrian Brigade close at hand by St. Julien were making an attack.
The British batteries were putting up a brave little fight, but they
were insignificant in numbers and their supply of shells was restricted.
Our wounded going down saw the Northumbrian Brigade coming
up to Fortuin for the attack and say that they were absolutely shelled
to pieces before getting there. The attack was a failure. The
Northumberlands got as far as the outskirts of St. Julien, but were
compelled to fall back, and by 6 p.m. had reached their original
trenches again. The Indians had been met at the enemy's line with
clouds of poison-gas and had fared no better.

At dusk we furnished a burying-party for those who had been
killed during the day and marked their graves in the field behind
us. Simultaneously we got orders to prepare to move and the more
optimistic thought a relief was at hand. But they were doomed
to disappointment, for when we set off we followed the trench to
the right and moved off across field after field and into shell-hole
after shell-hole, making in the direction of Zonnebeke ! The whole
neighbourhood was most desolate and barren and we had no idea
of our bearings at that time. In fact we could not see any trenches
that gave us any clue : there were no equipment, no bodies, no
trace of battle. It seemed as if we were at the very head of the horseshoe, when we turned up in the direction of Zevenkote and passed
by a small copse where two of our field guns were sheltered, seemingly
far from anywhere. They were facing in absolutely opposite directions ! How could this be and what did it all mean ? Surely we
had plenty of guns, plenty of troops ? Why should we be seemingly
in a tight corner after four days of battle ? All these questions
occurred to us and remained unanswered, for the situation was
inexplicable. We had all been far too optimistic as to the speedy
termination of the War and had not yet appreciated the strength
of the forces against us.

Near this copse we lay down for hours in a cold wind, while others
searched for the new position where we were to dig in once more.
We were to fill a gap on the left of the Hants and they seemed to be
an interminable time finding them. Around us now were some gigantic
shell-holes, bigger than any we had seen before, and most of them
were half-full of water. In desperation, having been parched since

midday, I crawled to one of them and, making a cup of my hands, took several sips which tasted so metallic that for the next half-hour I expected to be poisoned. While lying out on this barren piece of field several of us managed to doze off for a short while, being the first doze of any kind for over 40 hours. Before midnight we got the order to move on again and presently joined the Langemarck-Zonnebeke road by an inn, where a small lane branched off to the left. On the road was the L.R.B. Transport convoy with a lot of pack-ponies, which had just been prevented by the Hants from wandering into the German lines. The trench held by that regiment lined the road as far north as this point and our allotted position was a line bending back from the road, parallel to the little lane I mentioned. It ran across a field and the battalion extended, as on the previous evening, with " D " Company on the left. The R.B.s joined us on the other side and made no secret of their joy that it was we who flanked them : we appreciated their encouragement at all times and it was particularly welcome now.

No. 16 Platoon found itself "squeezed out " in these operations and dug a small trench some ten yards behind the main one, the lane running between the two. A poor soldier and various packs on the ground led us to suppose it was the scene of the previous day's

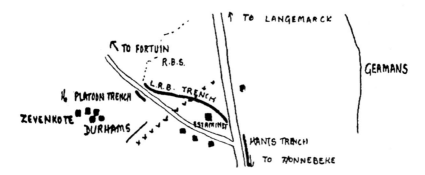

fighting. What struck us as most odd were the barbed-wire entanglements which crossed the lane, and therefore our new trench at right angles ! Moreover, near by were some Durham troops, also in a trench at right angles to our own, facing our right flank.

The shells they were sending over were 5.9 howitzers and they were peppering the ground where they thought we were likely to be making a new line. I had scarcely removed the turf from my allotted place, when I was told off to fill water-bottles in the little inn by the fork-roads. Unfortunately the entire regiment was endeavouring to supply its needs from the one pump in the scullery here, and, since the sink had got stopped up, the pump was not in proper working order, the room was under water and all operations had to be conducted without a light, it can be imagined that considerable confusion reigned. I lost two bottles in the scramble, but filled the others somewhere about 1.30 a.m. By the time I returned, my companions had dug down over a foot, and considering I had to be completely under cover by the morning, I set to work like a demon. The ground was very hard on top and all of us experienced more difficulty than on the previous night. As the trench became deeper, we lay flat and scooped out the soil, but, though we had something to show for it by daybreak, it was not so deep as our original handiwork.

The Germans were not to be seen. About three-quarters of a mile in front of us was the Gravenstafel Ridge from which the Durhams had recently been driven. A few hundred yards behind us were a few buildings representing Zevenkote : we were on a small eminence which fell away to the right enabling us to see the road to Zonnebeke and the village itself in the distance.

When the enemy observed our new position they got the range to a " T " and we discovered, to our cost, that they could bring fire to bear on us from three sides. In the exposed position we were particularly vulnerable from the right, where they simply enfiladed us. We could hear the howitzers fire, the swish and moan of the shells through the air gradually approaching us and, finally, the crash just behind our trench, which shook the earth and sent showers of dirt down upon us. Often during the next two days I timed the sound of the gun to the explosion and it was six seconds. The last two were nerve-racking : we ducked for dear life, cringing at the bottom of the trench where we squatted or knelt. Sometimes as many as twelve and often as many as eight of these high-explosives would fall around our own section of trench in one minute. After five minutes the batteries would turn their attention to the next section and then the next and you would try to get a doze or eat some rations. You might get ten minutes or so's respite and then you would be shaken by another close burst.

Early in the day we started the cry for " Stretcher-bearers " after each shell that alighted in the trench or on the parapet, and these fellows had to get outside and run for the place where they were wanted, because the trench was so narrow that it was an impossibility to pass anyone. In the next dug-out a shell landed on the roof and buried Sergeant-Major Thomas : elsewhere a lot of fellows were unfortunately buried alive, as we were unable to dig them out in time. This happened right down the line and it is really a marvel that anyone survived. Our section was most fortunate so far.

It was most depressing not having more artillery support ourselves. We knew nothing of the loss of fifty guns by the French and of the British losses. Behind our trench we had one little battery that sent over about ten shrapnel shells per gun each day on to the ridge opposite and, even though we got hundreds in return, they cheered us up immensely.

In the afternoon the French resumed their attack farther away on the left and our bombardment diminished somewhat. We squatted for hour after hour, but could get little or no sleep, and when night came we had to set off for Zonnebeke to meet the ration convoy, while those that remained improved the trench. Our transport had most extraordinary luck and got our rations up every night while other regiments frequently had their limbers blown up. Every road radiating out from Ypres was kept under most harassing and continual fire and it was a most difficult matter to bring supplies to the infantry and the guns. Yet our convoys always found us and, in spite of some casualties, kept us well fed, while the cooks at Elverdinghe prepared cut-up cold meat every day, which was sent up in boxes, and thereby earned our everlasting gratitude. .

News that Italy had declared war and that the British were " through " the Dardanelles was circulated amongst us, ostensibly coming officially from Corps H.Q. Both reports were sheer fabrications and caused us to place little faith in subsequent Corps announcements, which were frequently made with the object of cheering us and had a doubly depressing effect when their misstatements were apparent.

There is no need to recount in detail all the horrors and discomforts of the three days spent in that enfiladed trench. Shelled intermittently and unable to strike back, we lay at the mercy of the German guns on the Gravenstafel Ridge. Of the enemy we saw nothing. One night two platoons of the R.B.s went out on patrol on the far side of the Zonnebeke Road and never returned at all. On the second day, some of the enemy shells contained gas and at one time many of No. 15 Platoon were lying out in the lane near our trench recovering from the effects.

At last, on the night of the 29th, after some 170 casualties, including Capt. Otter, Captain Johnson, Lieut. Flindt and many other officers, we were ordered to quit this trench after dusk and move to the St. Julien front, where we should indeed see something of the enemy.

Just before we left, Wood was filling water-bottles at the broken pump in the estaminet down the road when four shells fired from howitzers plomped suddenly in the building and its garden. Out he came at once and it stands to his everlasting credit that he brought all the water bottles in his arms—even though they were empty!

CHAPTER VI.

THE SECOND BATTLE OF YPRES: GAS ATTACK AT ST. JULIEN.

(*April 30th–May 3rd*, 1915.)

On the St. Julien front—The Bombardment of May 2nd—Release of the gas—
"Enemy advancing"—Casualties—Attack repulsed—Reinforcements—No
stretchers—A horrible trench—Withdrawal of May 3rd.

WHEN we quitted our Gravenstafel trenches on April 29th we had
to take our ammunition with us : the bombs which had been brought
up from Vlamertinghe had been buried in the trenches by bursting
shells and consequently, on this occasion, I assisted in carrying a heavy
S.A.A. box, in addition to overcoat, pack and full equipment. After
a tiring journey over many fields and through hedges, it was a relief
to find ourselves eventually at the rear of our new trench and to
be able to dump our loads. It was our fifth night without any sleep
and the idea of coming to a trench that was already dug for us, instead
of having to make our own cover, cheered us up somewhat, although
it was depressing enough to get no relief from this infernal salient.

We found, however, that the trench was about two to three yards
wide, which was simply courting casualties, for, if there was one
thing we had learnt in the past few days, it was the need of having
one's trench as narrow and deep as possible to minimise losses. What
we saw before us was an old second-line trench of the French, which
was apparently as crude and impossible as when it had first been
made. The battalion holding it had done nothing to improve it
and naturally complained of heavy casualties. They were one of
the Northumbrian Division battalions who had been rushed up from
the Base into this inferno and seemed dazed and in a semi-stupefied
state. Apparently they had no orders as to where they should go
and we crouched for a long time on the parados of the trench waiting
for them to move off. I believe that in the end they were told that
the only thing to be done was to occupy the trench we had just left
This they did eventually and they had a terrible experience for the
next few days.

Having occupied our death-trap, we found there were about two
hours to go before daybreak and, though very tired, we decided to dig
a narrow trench in front for the sake of our lives. Accordingly,
No. 16 Platoon started on the work, though other portions of the

battalion acted for themselves in this matter, some finding the trench system satisfactory and others, I fancy, not troubling about it. It was, of course, impossible to finish it by daybreak and so we spent that day in the wide trench, resuming the work at night and connecting our new system with the trench one in two places.

When daylight came we took stock of our new surroundings. In the first place, we now faced north, being on the upper side of the salient and protecting the Fortuin Road which lay behind us. We were almost at the extreme north-easterly point, but another regiment prolonged our line to the right, a battalion of Yorks Territorials, yet another of those sacrificed units of the Northumbrian Division. Their trench was behind a hedge, where they were less likely to be attacked, but at the point of their junction with our 16 Platoon the hedge turned off at right angles to our line and ran out towards the Germans as far as we could see.

The L.R.B. trench then continued in a westerly direction, with its left flank (" A " Company) close to the Fortuin Road at a point near to the spot where we had dug in upon the first night.

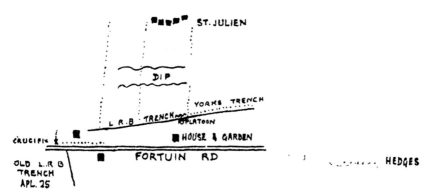

Before us, about eight hundred yards away, were the outskirts of St. Julien, that village that had been so valiantly held by the Canadians and subsequently won and lost again. Our trench ran across an open field and there was little but grass between us and the village. About three hundred yards away there was a dip and we could see a good deal of that yellow mustard-flower growing there. Behind us there was a small house, in the garden of which was stationed one solitary field gun, the only artillery backing for the whole of this portion of the line.

It is easy to understand that we should ask ourselves, " What is our artillery doing? Where is Kitchener's Army? Where are our aeroplanes? Whenever shall we be relieved ? " For days the Germans had been doing just what they liked : they shelled us unmercifully and we had to submit, our reply being pitiful ; their aeroplanes flew low down above our trenches, observing what they pleased, while our anti-aircraft guns were not to be seen or heard ; they would not come out for a hand-to-hand fight unless the wind be in their favour and they could first place us hors-de-combat with poison-gas. A more unequal struggle could not be imagined : on their side was a preponderance of all weapons and devilish devices and on ours there were merely infantry battalions who did their best to interpose themselves between the Germans and Ypres and continually filled up the ranks of the other infantry as they were blown to pieces.

We were not shelled so badly in our new position as we had been in the enfiladed trench, although the enemy could shell us here from the right and rear: and we were able to look over the parapet and range on various objects. We found that the nearest house of St. Julien was about 820 yards away, and we tested this by firing at a corner of a ruined wall and observing the brick-dust flying up, by means of field glasses. This range was to prove a useful one : the German trench ran round the outskirts of the village.

Thirst, dirt and vermin were three of our greatest troubles : we never took our clothes and boots off, we never washed, and we were perpetually grovelling in mud—my trousers had two gashes, eight inches by six, through kneeling for day after day. As for water, the pump in the cottage behind us only gave up a teaspoonful after much effort and we eventually started to dig in the trench, where we had the good fortune to strike water and the hole gradually filled with water again. so that we had a miniature spring, which our section used with great glee.

Our narrow trench in front was completed finally by the morning of May 2nd. Corpl. Miles was on the extreme left, then came myself, Thomson, Wood, Whittle, Pace, Bourke and Fulke's section. Gernat had departed with sore feet. Aimes, Marshall, Hudson and many other Haywards Heath " Q " Company friends had taken themselves off with wounds. Sergt. Wimble was in charge of our platoon. Cartwright was, I believe, the only officer left in " D " Company. Our platoon, however, had been very lucky and Corpl. Miles' section particularly so, as we had not suffered a casualty. From our left it was some little distance to the next platoon, there being an unused portion of the old French trench in between.

In front of us, at a distance of some twenty yards, our wiring party had put up a single strand of wire, a travesty of an obstacle to the Germans, should they attack us. But our patrols had been out over half a mile from our line and seen nothing of the Germans, a lot of empty French dug-outs being the only feature of interest.

Behind us, so far as we could make out, there was no reserve line of trenches, and if our line were pierced all other regiments holding the head of the horseshoe would be taken in rear. Further towards Ypres there were more troops in trenches and more guns, but there was no concentration at the point of the salient, as the staff intended to occupy a shorter line as soon as practicable. In the great game of tactics that was being played by the heads, the 4th, 50th and 28th Divisions were counted as good as sacrificed in order to safeguard the forming of our new front nearer Ypres.

A great boon came to us that morning in the issue of some very primitive respirators that had been hastily despatched from home. They consisted of a pad of gauze with elastic attached, to fit round the mouth and nostrils in case of a gas attack. They had been treated chemically, but we had to pour water on them if it was necessary to resort to them. They were issued as a palliative and could not be expected to be efficacious in the event of a prolonged dose of fumes. Needless to say, we took special care of these and they gave us confidence.

Our rations and letters from home had been brought up by the faithful transport as far as Fortuin, where we met them at night, and the drivers said that the hell extended all the way back as far as Vlamertinghe and that most of the other regiments' convoys had been blown up in the course of the week : ours was the only unit to receive its rations intact every night, we were told.

In the afternoon of Sunday, May 2nd, the artillery fire, which had been increasing in volume, swelled up into a regular barrage. No. 15 Platoon had several direct hits in the trench and I don't know what happened to the other platoons beyond them. Soon after 5 o'clock, having no officer or senior N.C.O. left unhit, and no stretcher-bearers, they sent along to Corpl. Miles to come and bandage, among others, Webb—who had a leg blown off. Some minutes later poor Miles returned, very pale and blood-stained. He squatted down in his corner of the trench.

" God ! Isn't this awful ? " he said, and he was very nearly in tears.

The intensity of the fire had increased still more.

" I should think this is going to be an attack," I said to him, and he nodded assent. If only it would mean a cessation of the shelling it would be a relief. Nobody in particular was acting as sentry, and I got up and looked towards St. Julien. There, rising in whitish green clouds by the outskirts of the village, pumped from their diabolical cylinders, rose the gas that we had heard so much about.

" Look over there," I shouted to Miles. " Do you reckon that's gas ? "

" I should think it was," he replied, after getting up and gazing at it. " Squat down and get your respirator ready. Pour some water on it from your bottle. Pass the word up, ' Respirators ready.' "

The message went round the traverse and we made our preparations, which included opening our ammunition pouches.

Then Thomson shouted a message which had come from the right. " Enemy advancing," and we leapt up to the parapet. Almost simultaneously we got the gas. First of all I got a whiff of it and clapped on my respirator, but instead of damping it the water had saturated the gauze and, to my horror, I fancied I couldn't breathe through it. Everyone's eyes were running and we were seized with coughing. In desperation, I foolishly tore the respirator away for a moment, as I felt unable to breathe, and promptly choked the more. At last, just when—in my panic—I thought I was " done for," I discovered that by breathing through the gauze and exhaling through the nostrils it was possible to get some air inside, and, as the gas seemed to be passing off, it was possible to carry on after about three minutes which seemed three years. As a matter of fact, we did not get the full force of the gas.

We could see little figures darting about among the ruins and running down the hedge towards us. A number of them seemed to be making westward to attack elsewhere and every moment or so we saw them run from one building to another. We opened fire at long range ; I opened rapid, others choosing their own targets. The enemy shrapnel and H.E. barrage was terrible, the former bursting ten yards in front of our trench and making it almost impossible to put our heads up. All along our trench, one man in every three had a head or arm wound within the space of a few minutes. We could not hope to experience our section's usual immunity under such conditions.

Corporal Miles was the first to get hit and then Wood got a bit of shrapnel in the arm. While Thomson was attending to him, I got Miles' field-dressing out of his tunic and bound up a hole in his wrist that was spurting out blood.

" My pull-through is in that overcoat there," said he. " Tie it tightly round my arm just above it. . . . There, I shall be all right now. Range 300 yards. See that yellow stuff; they're deploying there. Open rapid."

Wood had meantime made his way to the wide trench at the back where poor old Pace was being bound up by amateurs. He had had his leg blown off and his arm was nearly severed. Just beyond Whittle two men were killed outright, one was hit in the leg and two others were wounded in the head, one of whom made an awful noise moaning for the next hour until he unfortunately succumbed to his wound.

We had to duck down repeatedly and, in the meantime, some of the enemy approached and opened out under cover of the dip ahead of us, and actually got a machine-gun trained on to our parapet! To make matters worse, a German aeroplane approached and calmly sailed along our trench to register the shrapnel barrage for their guns.

Our field-gun at the back was doing splendidly and every shell it sent over cheered our hearts. At first it knocked pieces off the houses in St. Julien and then shortened its range and sent bursts of shrapnel at 300-400 yards where the German infantry was deploying. The gunners were evidently using a reserve supply of ammunition, but it was hopelessly inadequate for the occasion.

The din was indescribable. In addition to the crashing shrapnel barrage above our heads and the barking of our 18-pounder, there was a rattle of musketry to our right and left. It was, in fact, the third gas attack, and extended all along the northern part of the salient as far as the French. The French 75's in the distance and our own firing nearer Ypres added to the general uproar, but we were only dimly aware of it in those moments.

Looking back over our left shoulders we could see one or two figures making a rush for our trench in an effort to reinforce us : those that reached it dropped down near 14 Platoon and none got so far as our company's right flank. The Yorks on our right, behind their hedge, kept passing down the message, " Keep a sharp look ' oot ' on the left," and, so far as we could make out, were under the barrage without actually being attacked. If the Germans got through on our front or on our left, the fate of the Yorks, the 11th Brigade and any others in the salient was sealed.

Suddenly the barrage stopped and we manned the parapets with merely the German machine-gun fire to contend with, the occasional " Swish ! Swish ! Shish ! " of the bullets as it swung round in our direction caused a momentary disappearance of our heads. We emptied our magazines as far as we could into the mass of shaking yellow plant where the Germans—astounded at the failure of the gas and at the concentration of our fire—seemed loth to spring from cover and advance. All along the trench, rifles and machine-guns blazed away in the fading light and our field-gun doubled its efforts. No German came within two hundred yards of our portion of the trench : it was impossible to make headway. Other companies on the left said that the enemy advanced against them in close formation, but the L.R.B. trench held firm.

Farther away, to the west of Fortuin, other units were less fortunate, having suffered much more severely from gas-fumes. Indeed, one battalion was almost entirely asphyxiated and lost their trench, while our line was captured in one or two other places, whence the enemy were ejected later in the evening. The Argyll and Sutherland Highlanders on our left actually advanced through the gas and attacked the oncoming infantry. The French by the Canal more than held their own.

When it was quite dark, Corpl. Miles, who had behaved splendidly, said " Good-bye," and made his way off on foot, as did all the others able to walk. Much to my consternation, however, I found that Wood, while lying in that rear trench, had been hit in three more places—the abdomen, knee and wrist : he was in a bad condition and must have a stretcher. Thomson was with him then and would try to get a stretcher along. Whittle, somewhat the worse for gas, Bourke and myself, joined later by Corpl. Hall, were now the sole occupants of No. 14 Section's trench, and I was the left-hand man. Beyond me there was a big space held by no one. We seemed abandoned to our fate. Sergt. Wimble went off to take command of a company or something, and a mere handful of 16 Platoon remained

We could hear a lot of shouting and talking in German out in front of us, followed by the noise of picks and shovels. They were throwing up a trench under our very noses and shouting at one another as though we did not exist ! We received the order to economise with our ammunition and therefore did not fire without instructions. We merely oiled the bolts of our rifles, laid them on the parapet and waited. . . . The shelling had ceased and except for distant shells there was little to be heard but the digging in front and the moaning near at hand.

About half an hour passed like this and then some Northumbrian Territorials arrived to thicken the line and about three found their way into our bit of trench. How welcome they were ! I had just had visions of Germans rushing up and pouncing on me from the left. Their arrival was none too soon, for shortly afterwards there was a burst of rapid firing towards Fortuin which swelled and grew nearer and spread like some infection until our company found itself, within some five seconds, engaged in giving the Germans the most rapid rifle fire it was in our power to produce. A flare went up from our line and opposite us we could see dark shadowy forms by our strand of barbed-wire. What we saw and what other companies witnessed there seems a lot of disagreement about. Others say the Germans advanced to attack them : I can only say that I saw at least three forms quite distinctly which flopped down when our flare went up. The noise of musketry on this occasion was louder than before, as there was scarcely any shelling and, moreover, our trench was more fully manned. We kept it up for three minutes or so, and, whatever may have been the intention of the Germans, they were certainly severely punished, for they could not have dug themselves very much cover : in the morning there were several of their dead lying out in front.

As soon as I could I went to see Wood and found him fully conscious, but extremely badly wounded : it was impossible to move him without a stretcher, it seemed, and Thomson said they were going to try and send some along, but at present they had only two for the whole battalion and there were many, many cases to carry to the dressing-station. I did what I could to comfort him and also spoke to poor old Pace, who lay perfectly calm and collected at the bottom of the trench next to Wood. Limbless and suffering terribly from loss of blood, he nevertheless smoked a cigarette and waited patiently for a stretcher that we dare not tell him was most unlikely to arrive.

In our portion of the trench a Northumberland sergeant, untrained in warfare, was the senior N.C.O.

" Have you got any bombs ? " I asked him.

" Aye. ———— brought soom along."

" Is he here ? "

" Aye, but he ain't a bomber. Now, let's see, who can throw a bomb ? ————, are you a bomber ? "

" Noo."

" Waal, never mind. Catch 'old of these 'ere. All you've got to do is to take the pin oot and buzz it. . . "

Later on, while the digging in front of us was still in progress, one man in three was detailed to dig a pit for himself a yard or so behind the rear trench, to reduce the probable number of casualties through crowding together, and it fell to my lot to leave the front trench and seize a pick and shovel.

Thus on this eighth successive night there was to be no sleep, and for the fourth night there was a new piece of digging to be done. It savoured very much of digging one's own grave, and the only consolation it afforded was that, unless a direct hit came upon the little pit, there was not much danger of being wounded : in the event of a German attack these isolated holes would, of course, be vacated and their occupants take their places in the firing trench. There was no time to be lost, and I therefore set to work in earnest. I was down about a foot in depth when a steady tramping close at hand signalled troops on the move, and, looking along the trench, I found a long file of infantry trooping by.

" Who are you ? "

" We're the East Lancs. Are you the L.R.B.s ? "

" Yes."

" Cheer up, boys. We're coming in your trench ! "

Joy of joys ! Our old Ploegsteert pals, the battalion that had been left behind when we moved, had just arrived on the scene. All of them regulars and reservists, what had we to fear side by side with them ? They jumped down into the trench and stood shoulder to shoulder with the remnants of our men and the Northumbrian reinforcements. The whole outlook had changed now. These men had not had eight days' nerve-racking experiences to damp their spirits, and they were full of fun.

There was no ration party that night, as we had orders not to leave the trench, since no man could be spared : our transport brought them up to the usual place, however, and dumped them. Although " D " Company therefore had no food at all, it transpired afterwards that the East Lancs volunteered to get the L.R.B. rations and sent off a party, who returned towards morning reporting failure to find them.

" We were determined to get *some* grub for you fellows," they said, so they purloined somebody else's ! This was not sufficient to supply all our men, however, and I think " A " and " B " Companies received most of it.

Long before my pit had reached an appreciable depth, Wood called for me, and I made my way along to him. The failure of the stretchers to arrive, the seriousness of his wound and the pain were most distressing, and both he and Pace implored me to get them stretchers.

" I can't last through another day of it," murmured Wood. " Get me away to-night, for God's sake ! "

" Bring a stretcher. Oh, bring a stretcher . . . " moaned Pace.

" They'll be along soon," I said reassuringly, knowing it to be a lie. Whatever could I do ? It seemed most probable that they would have to be there for another twenty-four hours. The Germans might get into the trench ; or the wounds might prove fatal. I decided to find an officer and urge him to do his best for them ; so I set off down the wide trench in the direction of Fortuin. Just round the corner I enquired for an officer, and was told there might be one farther along. The trench I passed along then was a nightmare. Wounded lay on either side waiting for stretchers : some of them did not move at all. Dead bodies in various attitudes had been removed from the front trenches and deposited here. On and on I stumbled, little heeding the entreaties of these poor helpless creatures—for what could I do ?— until at last I came upon 13 Platoon where Lieut. Cartwright still remained on. Whether he was wounded and went down later I do not know, but he was not with us the next night. I explained the situation to him, describing the urgency of it, but he could only tell me there were scores of others waiting also and only two stretchers for the whole battalion and no hope could be held out at all. He gave me some morphia to administer, and then, raving and cursing at the Staff, the inadequate arrangements and our lack of everything from stretchers to ammunition, I made my way back and did my best to comfort them. They were despondent when I arrived without the stretchers.

" I'm going to die, Aubrey. . . . If I don't get away to-night, I shall die," groaned Wood. Can you picture my feelings ? Powerless to render practical assistance, I eventually gave place to another fellow who came to stay with them, and resumed my " grave-digging," which was completed by daybreak.

At any other time, the position in which I found myself would have afforded a ludicrous comment on modern warfare, but there was no call for humour in those surroundings. Squatting down in a hole, some four feet deep by three and a half long, wearing an overcoat and caked in mud from head to foot, I faced another day of unknown horrors. Perhaps the Germans would shell us heavily again and I should be com- pletely buried without anybody in the trench being any wiser ; perhaps I should be wounded and no one would be able to render me any assist- ance ; at any rate, I had the whole day before me to reflect on these and other things. No rations having arrived, I opened my haversack and pulled out a tin of bully beef, two biscuits and some tea-leaves, on which I proceeded to make a breakfast. I pulled out of my pocket my last letters from home and friends and re-read them ; the former were full of courage and hope, some of the latter told of theatres, bathing-parties, dances, petty quarrels, and a hundred and one trivial things which seemed to occupy everyone's attention at home. " When are you going to finish this war ? " they would end up. It was the only reference, perhaps, to our hardships. Until everybody in England realised that we were at present hopelessly outmatched, that our production of shells must be increased a thousandfold, that we must have millions more men under arms, we should not be putting our backs into winning the war, and thousands of lives would be sacrificed. . . .

Presently I began to get thirsty and, as it seemed possible to crawl from my hole to the trench without being seen, I seized my water- bottle and set forth. A horrible sight met my eyes, for two dead bodies had been placed over the back of the trench and faced me, a couple of yards away, directly I gazed out of my shelter ; they were men I had been speaking to but yesterday. When I got to our trench I asked Corpl. Fulkes for news, and he said the Germans had dug themselves in about fifty yards away and cautioned me not to show a finger above the parapet.

" They've sniped poor old Henderson this morning. Killed him outright. He's in the back trench there. We simply daren't look up. They've got loopholes in their parapet and their snipers are very busy. Water ? Our hole has dried up, but there's a small spring about thirty yards along there in the Yorks trenches. . . . Poor old Pace ! I'm afraid he's done for. There's one advantage to the Germans being so close—they've stopped their shelling."

I next went along to Wood and stayed with him some time. The trench was a litter of old equipment, rifles, overcoats and mess-tins, many of them blood-stained and several trodden into the ground. Beyond was a litter of corpses. What a spot for dangerously wounded men, who ought to have been in a comfortable bed in hospital ! Pace and Wood now seemed quite resigned to waiting until nightfall, when Wood declared that he would walk down somehow if he could not be carried.

The sun was shining and it was quite a hot, sultry day. The two stretcher-cases had got their water-bottles full, but the " spring " had no more water in it, and so I set off towards the Yorks trench. In the remaining ten yards of the back trench between my pit and the hedge which marked the end of the Yorks position, a more blood-curdling sight than any of the others made me pause in terror. Here were some ten or twelve men lying in all attitudes of death, the corpses of both 16 Platoon and of the next regiment, men who had died outright and men bandaged up about the head who had died of their wounds. The second man had been placed there that morning ; it was that cheery little Lance-Corpl. Henderson, sniped in the head but an hour or so before. Amidst them was a figure, bandaged over the eyes, badly wounded on top of the head, and he was struggling to get to his feet. He was a little fellow whom I knew in Haywards Heath. I went up to him and held him. By this time he was in a sitting position. I asked how he was feeling.

Apparently he had been blinded and he was also suffering somewhat from gas and the ugly wound on his crown ; but he had all his wits about him and spoke quite calmly and collectedly.

" Cheer up, old chap ! You just lie here. You're all right. Don't try to get about. Just stay quietly where you are. I'll bring you some water in a minute."

He murmured " All right," and sank down on that shambles, fortunately unable to see about him. Then, stepping over the bodies, I came to the traverse and went round it. On the other side were some eight or nine wounded Yorks, lying on the ground on each side of the trench. They begged me to get them water. Beyond them were the remnants of this stunned and stupefied battalion, most of them sound asleep. Here and there a sentry was on his feet, leaning against the parapet—dozing sentinels who scarcely turned to watch me pass. The men were, after all, quite new to warfare of any description, having been in England a fortnight before. No wonder they were dazed and surly.

The hole containing water was a little way along their trench, and I filled the bottle and took it to the wounded Yorkshires. Poor fellows .

They were parched with thirst and yet not one of their own men was attending to them. The water was far from pure, but they much appreciated it and I refilled the bottle and made my way back to the blinded fellow in our own trench.

I felt quite sick with these sights, and when I found this man groping about amongst the dead and feeling their outlines it was almost more than I could stand. If he realised what surroundings he was placed in, it would make him feel a hundred times worse. I led him farther away, gave him the water, and said he must stay there and not wander round.

"But I want to get out. . . . I can't see. . . . I'm all alone. . . . Where are the others ? "

"They're just here. You'll get out all right to-night, old man. Stay quiet."

Then I asked Fulkes if a man could look after him from time to time, and presently made my way back to the hole at the rear of the trench and sank down to doze and forget the sights I had seen and the growing hunger within me.

*   *   *   *   *

The roads and fields had been swept by fire all day, but our trench had been immune from all but rifle-fire. That night, however, there was a severe attack behind us, the 1st R.B.s being badly mauled, and the Germans got into some parts of their trench. Both they and the Somersets were much cut up, but they showed a good front to the enemy.

As a matter of fact, a retirement from this salient had been ordered two days ago, and some stages of it had been carried out already. It was all the more remarkable that these two German attacks did not upset all our plans. For the task was not an easy one to perform. All round the top of the " horseshoe " our troops were to withdraw silently that night, commencing at ten p.m. In some places the front line was only a few yards from the enemy, so it can be imagined what caution was necessary. If he became aware of our intentions before the withdrawal were completed, the result would be disastrous. The contemplated retirement covered the whole front from Hill 60, which had been retaken by the Germans on 1st, to the Shell-trap Farm near Weiltje. Zonnebeke, Frezenberg, Fortuin, Zevenkote, Polygon Wood were all to be abandoned to the enemy, and I hope he enjoyed the smell. All the wounded were to be evacuated and all equipment taken away or destroyed.

The retirement in certain places commenced at dusk, but we were not to leave our trench until the other troops to the north went— viz., 12.45 o'clock. The R.A.M.C. were soon on the scene with stretchers, and Pace, suffering intensely, was placed upon one ; but he was, unhappily, not destined to live. Wood refused to wait a moment longer than necessary and disbelieved our promises that stretchers were coming. Two East Lancs, exceedingly happy and well fortified with rum, offered to lead him down, and it seemed best that he should hobble along lest through accident he should have to be left behind. The two Lancs were a bit too merry for my liking, and when they started to lead him east instead of west, I began to doubt their efficiency as guides. But Wood knew the way and guided them aright, and I saw him depart supported on either side, happy in the knowledge that he would soon receive proper attention. The blinded casualty was also removed, but he died in hospital.

We next proceeded to collect all the rifles, boxes of ammunition, etc., and bury them near the road, the spots being duly noted by our Colonel, ready for the return " push." Next came the dead bodies, which we determined to bury decently instead of abandoning them to the Germans. All this was done without arousing the enemy's suspicions, while in the " No Man's Land " between the two lines, our patrols were active to keep him preoccupied. One of our men out on patrol, on seeing a German, shouted " Hands up." The German dropped his rifle, and our youth escorted his prisoner in proudly, the latter being over six feet high. One of our listening patrols, consisting of three men, was captured in a scrap, and we heard afterwards they were alive.

Two of the East Lancs, who had discovered a bottle of rum earlier in the day and were now completely helpless, would have to be left in the trench ; it was impossible to move them. There were many stretchers on this night, but they could not be used for drunken men. The evacuation of the wounded from the salient was very efficiently carried out. Many cellars in Zonnebeke were filled with them, but dozens of ambulances drove up to convey them away, and in all 780 were taken from the front, apart from the walking cases.

When the hour came, we filed noiselessly out of the trench and moved off behind it towards Fortuin. Some of the East Lancs were left as a bluff, to fire their rifles occasionally and give the Germans the impression that the trench was held : these men were to follow at midnight. A flare or two went up, and we flopped down, afraid that we should be discovered and that an attack or shelling might begin. We seemed to make too much noise ; but the enemy gave no sign, and with great relief we filed on to the road, where, with as fleet a step as possible, we wended our way along past the field on the left where we had dug in upon the first night, past the graves of Pepper, Tucker and Woodward, past the spot where we had halted by the dead German on that memorable march up there. On and on we went, leaving behind us those hideous trenches, those thousands of bodies and those shell-swept roads and fields. At Weiltje we passed ambulances, but a short while before we reached it we saw our new front line on either side of the road, manned by new troops, while barricades of barbed wire were ready to be stretched across the road when the last man had gone past. The enemy were not to realise our trick until the next day, and our trenches were shelled by them long after our departure. The regulars who had been left behind withdrew in safety and without the loss of a man—even the two Lancs who were the worse for rum " came to " the next morning and, finding their friends gone, managed to make their way down to their battalion again.

To the right and to the left the star-shells rose, marking the terrible salient as they had done nine days before, and for miles we plodded on without appearing to get far from the line. Through St. Jean we passed on, throwing nearly everything we possessed into the hedges and ditches, for we had hardly strength to carry ourselves along, let alone equipment and other encumbrances. Machine-gun ammunition, bandoliers of cartridges, entrenching-tools and other articles were cast aside, and the road was lined with the equipment of all those units that had passed before us. By daylight we were over the Canal, and feeling at last we were in comparative safety, lay down for a rest. But after a short halt we resumed our tramp, endeavouring to keep our " fours " as well as we could, and it was here that I first saw the kindly face of Lieut. Wallis, ultimately Lieut.-Col. Wallis, of our battalion, who had evidently been attached to " D " Company, in the absence of all our officers. Whereas most of us looked haggard, unkempt and far from merry, his face was wreathed with encouraging smiles as he walked first with one, then with another, not saying very much but heartening everyone up with his presence.

At last we entered a field where our cookers were drawn up, and a very sympathetic party of cooks, transport-drivers and Q.M.S.s stood there ready to wait on us " hand and foot." Here was civilisation—of a sort—after nine days and nights in hell !

CHAPTER VII.

The Second Battle of Ypres: Final Phase.

(*May 4th-20th*, 1915.)

Rest in Elverdinghe Woods—Vlamertinghe Chateau—In the trenches again—German attack of May 13th—Retirement of the cavalry—Reinforcing the front-line—After the attack—Pillage and plunder—Withdrawn from the line.

Our roll-call, immediately after breakfast, was rather a heartrending affair, everybody being anxious for news of friends in other companies. From an original strength of, I suppose, seven hundred, our fighting strength now totalled about three hundred. The majority of the officers, senior N.C.O.s and stretcher bearers were casualties; the signallers and bombers and machine-gunners were denuded and it was difficult to find more than a nucleus of any speciality section.

Considerably refreshed by the hot soup and tea, we shortly moved to the wooded grounds of a big chateau, which harboured many troops. Here I took my boots off for the first time since April 24th and, since my feet had been sore then, it can be imagined that they had not healed in the meantime; moreover, the septic fingers had naturally not improved. There was a stream close at hand and never has a swim seemed so delightful: I think everybody had a bathe and a wash and shave and then went to sleep, happy to be free at last from shells and the menace of gas.

That evening we marched with the 11th Brigade to Elverdinghe Woods and built ourselves " bivvies " under the trees in most pleasant surroundings. The weather was mild and we had an issue of blankets, so it was possible to look forward to a complete night's rest. We were further elated to receive a ten-days' accumulation of parcels and with our battalion that meant two wagon loads. The Brigade Post Office always said that our mail was more than double that of the other four battalions put together. Now we had all the parcels for those who had become casualties and, since our own were more than we really needed, it can be imagined that the surplus was considerable.

The next day these were opened by order and the contents were put in heaps according to their nature. There were hundreds of packets of chocolate and sweets of all kinds, biscuits, cakes, apples and oranges; scores of tins of fruit, pills of every description, mufflers, underclothing (which we badly needed and helped ourselves to), cigarettes and all kinds of personal gifts. It was as if the contents of some huge grocer's and confectioner's shop had been dumped down in Elverdinghe Woods. We had such a surfeit of our own parcels that there were few things we desired : we read many pathetic little messages on slips of paper enclosed with the parcels, messages addressed in many cases to men we had seen pass away. Then the happy inspiration came to us to give these goodies to our Regular pals of the 11th Brigade, particularly the Somersets and R.B.s with whom we had had most to do. So they were told to send over men with blankets and they opened their eyes wide when they beheld the eatables. They had not many parcels and this made a red-letter day for them. Intensely delighted, they bore away load after load and gradually cleared the supply. We were sure the senders of those parcels would not have wished for any better disposal of their contents.

Every morning now we got up and drew our breakfast when we woke up, at any time from 7 till 8 o'clock, and we slept by day and by night. Occasionally aeroplanes came over and three sharp whistles warned us to keep under the trees or put out all candles. Sometimes we wandered to the edge of the wood and watched the movement of troops. There were many French soldiers in the vicinity and our Transport told us that a lot of reinforcements, particularly French artillery, had come up within the last few days. The Colonial troops were weird : they marched along with all the paraphernalia of a clothes-store and cook-house upon their backs, including extra boots, frying-pans and saucepans, and we heard that they had recently conducted a bayonet attack near the canal without casting off any of this impedimenta.

On the 7th the Regular regiments of the Brigade moved off again towards the firing-line : they had been made up to strength again with new drafts from home. We were instructed not to move with them, no draft had arrived for us and, so far as we knew, none was on the way. Our numbers had been further reduced owing to sick men being sent to hospital. One had to be very ill to get there, however, and many were merely given pills to cure their various ailments.

On the 8th there was a very heavy German attack on the new line, and had we been with the rest of our Brigade we should have been in the thick of it once more. Our Brigade was covering the village of Weiltje and held the trenches between there and Shell-Trap Farm and, owing to the terrific nature of the bombardment, the Germans broke through on the right and captured the village. In the rear we could only hear the heavy guns, which gave the impression that the Germans must be having a very uncomfortable time " up there." Their aeroplanes were very active and continually came over in our neighbourhood. In the afternoon at 3.30 there was a counter-attack, in which Weiltje was retaken, and from that hour until well into the night the Brigade and particularly the E. Lancs were engaged in desperate fighting. The Germans had made a great effort and had at one time badly dented the line, but once again they had been foiled in their attempt to capture Ypres.

The attack had an effect upon our rest, however, and that same day we had to leave our bivouac and move to some more woods, leaving them in turn upon the morning of the 9th. From them we marched for miles behind the French portion of the line until we came down to Vlamertinghe Chateau. The move was an ominous one as it brought us nearer the firing-line and, since they had called for volunteers for stretcher-bearing, signalling and other specialities, it appeared as if we should be used again. Whittle and I joined the Morse Code class but it led to nothing, as will be seen later.

This chateau was occupied, I think, by a corps headquarters and we heard that, as its owner was a German, it was considered immune from shells and bombs. But some shells fell near the heavy batteries in the vicinity, which were firing as much ammunition from their scanty supply as they could afford. The grounds in which we encamped now were well wooded and we had to keep well under cover of the trees, from which we could see something of the village of Vlamertinghe. How different it had been exactly two weeks before! Then it had been crowded with troops and transport; now, all the soldiers and vehicles that had to pass used a track that avoided the main street, which was frequently shelled: this track passed close to our bivouac. There was a good deal of traffic on it and most of it went by at a trot; it was not a very healthy locality.

Our section felt the loss of Miles and Wood very much. Lance-Corporal Hall had charge of it now, and the remnants of it drew closer together in bonds of sympathy. There was one new lieutenant in our company and Lieut. Wallis was temporarily in command of it, otherwise we were without officers and Sergt. Mamby became Acting Sergt.-Major.

After tea we had orders to leave our packs with a few men and take picks and shovels with us on a digging fatigue nearer the line. When we set off it was still light and only one company left at a time. Although this would seem to minimise the risk of observation, especially at such a distance from the Germans, we had scarcely walked half a mile before shrapnel was sent over to the road exactly where we were passing. There were one or two cottages near at hand and, in view of the fact that several civilians had been arrested as spies during the past two weeks, we felt convinced that our position must have been signalled to the enemy. We took cover quickly in a ditch and had to wait there nearly ten minutes before proceeding. Thereafter we made our way across fields, unmolested, the countryside was bleak and war-marked, with relics of old trenches and broken-down cottages to be seen now and again, and occasionally a dead horse in a ditch would cause many handkerchiefs to be extracted. We crossed the depressing disused Ypres–Staden railway line and a bridge over the Yser canal and continued on a sandy road until we came to a farm-house a little north of St. Jean, the ruins of the house still smouldering, having probably been set alight by a shell.

It was quite night-time now, but there was a bright moon which enabled us to see a fair distance. Ypres was lit up by burning buildings and the Germans still seemed to be giving special attention to the town, in which gigantic shells burst with much noise from time to time. The flares continually rose from the line on our left and sometimes gave the impression of a Brock's benefit. Our task was to dig a reserve trench from a point on the Pilken Road to a point not far from Weiltje, facing north, and since the sooner we completed it the sooner we should be back in our bivvies again, the work was over soon after midnight. Our labours were undisturbed by shelling, as the efforts of the Germans at dawn the next morning were directed against the Menin Road portion of the salient. Shell-Trap Farm, to the north of Weiltje,

was a great bone of contention, however, and changed hands two or
three times during the next few days, but all was quiet in that direction
·on this occasion.

The 10th of May passed quietly beneath the shade of the Chateau
Woods, and the only sight of interest on the following day was the
arrival of dismounted cavalry, who marched past in an unending
stream in the direction of Ypres. Although about to relieve a weary
infantry division, they wore bandoliers and spurs—a quaint equipment
for the trenches !

We followed them in the evening to dug-outs near the Yser canal,
where we promptly furnished a digging fatigue to carry on the work of
preparing a vast underground palace for a divisional headquarters, a
monument to our labours and the industry of others which doubtless
served a useful purpose right up to the end of the war. In our spare
moments, next day, we had a bathe in the Yser canal, but it was understood that if an aeroplane came over we were to get out or get under !
There were many engineers' bridges across this sluggish stretch of

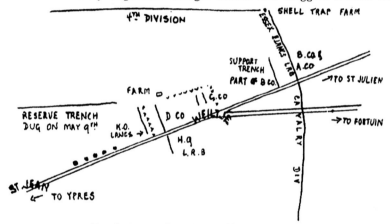

Rough sketch of position on May 13th, 1915.

water, all of which were registered by the German artillery. It was not
a very simple matter to get a direct hit on them, however, as the banks
of the canal were fairly high and most of their shells buried themselves
in the banks or plunged with a terrific splash into the water. Nevertheless, the crossing of the bridges was usually effected " at the double,"
and very few took the trouble to use them as a diving-board.

We got news here that the British had started an offensive at
Festubert and that the Germans had sunk the *Lusitania* with hundreds
of women and children on board. Commenting upon the latter in a
note written at the time, I wrote : " What a lot of things there are to
inflame the anger of the British soldier. . . . As for gas, I see the
Times thinks the question of whether we should use gas or not should
be left to the opinion of the soldiers at the front. There are no two
·opinions about it here." Even at that date the British people had not
persuaded themselves that an unscrupulous foe must be met by his own
methods.

When evening came we definitely moved for the trenches again.
There was a slight reorganisation of the firing-line that night and many
units were relieved. From the right of the French the 4th Division

carried the line through the Shell-Trap Farm to the Weiltje-St. Julien road at a point five hundred yards east of Weiltje. The L.R.B. were to put " A " and " B " Companies in the trenches, starting on the left of this road, and I suppose their front was about two hundred yards or more. On their left were the East Lancs, and on the right of the road the Cavalry Division started, though some of our men were given a position on this side of the road also. The cavalry held the centre of the salient and carried the line round to the Bellewarde Lake by the Menin road. Our " C " Company moved into a system of trenches forming a kind of redoubt in a field to the left of Weiltje, and " D " Company and Headquarters lined up and dug a trench on either side of the Weiltje road, some two hundred yards west of the village.

In the digging we had a casualty or so from shells, but generally it was a quiet night—the lull before the storm. Little did we realise that on the morrow the Germans were to make their most colossal attempt to break our line, an attempt that was very nearly successful. The shortening of our line had enabled the British to hold it with fewer men and therefore increase their reserves ; our artillery, also, was not so negligible as it had been at the top of the salient. But the same remarks applied to the Germans. If their gun-power had been so formidable when spread out round the huge semi-circle about Ypres a fortnight ago, how much more terrible would it be when all those guns were drawn closer together and probably reinforced by others, trained on to a far shorter length of front ! They had the range to a nicety. They had already pounded the trenches and the barbed wire to smithereens on the 8th, and there was little protection afforded by our front line.

We had dug down sufficiently deep to be able to sit down and rest after our efforts, and by dawn the majority of us were taking things easy before proceeding to erect ground-sheet shelters and improve the bottom of the trench. The dawn had broken squally, raining and cold, and there was every prospect of our trench becoming a mass of slime before an hour or two had passed.

Suddenly every German gun seemed to open fire at once. We looked up and saw the whole of the panorama a mass of puffs of smoke. Everything from shrapnel and small explosive to tremendous " coal-boxes," which sent volumes of black smoke and clods of earth thirty feet and more into the air, plastered the countryside in front of us and to right and left. The worst punishment was inflicted upon the front-line trenches, which were wreathed with smoke. " Coal boxes " alighted in them continually, and sometimes three or four great geysers of smoke and earth rose simultaneously upon that short stretch of ground held by the East Lancs and our "A" and " B " Companies. But the Germans had other targets besides the front trenches, and they sprinkled every field behind them with such a liberal supply of high explosives that it became a problem as to how to send reserves forward. The village of Weiltje, now a mass of ruins, was a particular object of bombardment, and frequent shrapnel clouds over the road itself made it impossible to use it for any purpose. Every clump of trees, farm and field-gun position seemed to have a gun trained on to it and an aeroplane observer who watched the whole salient later in the day described the plain as being wreathed in fire and smoke so that it seemed impossible for anyone to exist on it.

Five minutes' bombardment of this nature would have pulverising effects, but there was no sign of abatement after an hour had gone by.

The front line by this time must have been smashed out of all recognition, and we saw many wounded coming down, very glad to have been hit. They hurried on to the dressing-station in St. Jean as fast as their legs could carry them. None but wounded left the trenches, however, and we admired the men in the front line for " sticking it " so well. Knowing many of the other company men, as we did, we were very anxious for our friends eight hundred yards ahead of us. As our trench was a new one it had not been registered by the Germans, and the only shells that fell near us were promiscuous ones, forming part of their back-area barrage.

Suddenly we were alarmed to see the cavalry falling back upon the right. According to records, in a short space eight hundred shells fell on a line of little more than a mile and their trenches were choked with dead. The 8rd Dragoon Guards were buried alive. Some of the cavalry came back through the village of Weiltje, their hats gone and in some instances their rifles smashed or missing. It was certainly most disconcerting, and we expected to see Germans appearing at any moment on the right, but the infantry attack had not yet commenced. Some of the cavalry came into our trench, and presently they all went forward again. It was impossible to see what was going on, other than on our immediate front, so that we could not determine the extent of the withdrawal upon the right.

About 7.0 a.m. the Germans captured Shell-Trap Farm on the left, and reinforcements of the 2nd Essex, who had held the Ploegsteert Barricade on the right of our old trench, came over our trench, advancing in open order ; their packs had been left behind and they carried their rifles with bayonets fixed as though they meant business. Their advance was a grand sight to watch, for they went forward in a long line stretching across two fields, as steadily as though they had been on Salisbury Plain. One or two shells fell amongst them and parts of their line were for the moment obliterated by wreaths of smoke, but they never wavered and, if any men fell, they closed the ranks again as they went forward. Right up the slope they went—for the front line was on an eminence that could almost be called a ridge—and then they disappeared from view. Wounded coming down later were in good spirits and said the farm was retaken. Soon the King's Own Royal Lancs from our Division (12th Brigade) arrived and occupied a hitherto deserted trench along the hedge just behind us, and it became evident that the front-line of L.R.B.s would need reinforcements. We got the order to dump our packs by the hedge and leave our ground-sheets where they were and to be ready to move forward. We surveyed the ground over which we should have to pass and watched the wounded coming down. It was raining hard and the ground was turning to mud with that rapidity for which Flanders soon earned a reputation among the troops. The din of all the shells,. which had now lasted without break for four hours, was growing in density, and our own guns were very busy in the rear. The large shells sent by our bigger pieces could be heard whining high up in the air as they passed above us, neither the report of the gun nor the sound of their burst reaching us ; but the batteries of field artillery barked just behind us and we could hear the swish of the shells and see the puffs of shrapnel. Our guns were still firing that high proportion of shrapnel which was proving so useless for smashing down trenches and barbed-wire.

Our Company went forward in parties of four, and Lieut. Wallis started first. Our first objective was a trench just this side of the brow of the hill, where some of "B" Company were stationed, out of sight of the front line and about a hundred yards from it, and we were to make as much use of shell-holes as possible in getting there. When it came to my turn, I went with Lance-Corpl. Hall, Thomson and Bourke, and we started off along a hedge which ran towards the line, slipping along in the mud and going at the double. As I mentioned before, "C" Company were stationed in trenches to the left of Weiltje, and when we got level with them we found the preceding four in a shell-hole, so took cover ourselves until they moved on. Presently the leading four got to the trench and the following group took their place. All the parties then sprang up in turn and occupied the shell-hole just vacated. The reason for this was that the support trench was not very big and it was already full of troops of our own and other units : these kept on supplying reinforcements for the front-line, who made their way across to it in ones and twos, and, as soon as these had left, there was room for the next four men who were promptly signalled to in an adjacent shell-hole. We must have been some eighty yards from the support trench when there was a lull in the call for men and we had to wait a considerable time. The ground here was studded with small shell-holes and we chose one each and flung ourselves flat in the mud for safety. There was no question of avoiding wet and mud—we had neither mackintoshes nor overcoats— and we simply had to make friends with the mud and wallow in it. We promptly got covered in it from head to foot but we did our best to keep our rifles in working order : my bolt had an old sock tied round it for protection.

With shells falling in front, behind and to either side, I lay as flat and as far into the mud as was possible, praying that a second shell would not fall precisely where its predecessor had cut out this hole for me, every minute seeming like an hour ; the rain fell pitilessly and drenched us through and we remained on and on until past ten o'clock. Then the move forward commenced again and, within half-an-hour, I found myself in the support trench, where the first person I saw was our dear Company Officer, Lieut. Wallis.

"I say, this is hell, isn't it ?" he said serenely. "I'm not enjoying myself at all."

His very candour and the twinkle in his eye brought smiles to our begrimed faces. He stood there, arrayed in his Burberry, looking over the parapet. But there was nothing to see. From the trench the ground sloped upwards for twelve yards or more before the ground again became level and the first sign of the enemy we should get— if he broke through—would be his foremost ranks appearing just over our heads. We speculated upon what a surprise it would be for them to be greeted by the muzzles of our rifles. What was happening just over the brow of the hill ? We could not see the "coal-boxes'" smoke rise from where we were, but we could hear them and those that fell nearer to us sent down odd fragments of earth from time to time. Although I did not know it, more than one infantry attack had already been attempted and our fellows, rising from the mass of wounded about them, stood to the parapets and poured rapid fire into the Germans. The latter seemed undecided and occasionally could be seen running to and fro in front of their trenches, nonplussed by our resistance. Again and again during the day they attempted to attack but did not reach the L.R.B.'s trench. They got through on the left of us and were thrown back again and fierce hand-to-hand fighting occurred round the Shell-Trap Farm.

The situation on the right was very serious, as the Cavalry some distance away had fallen back hundreds of yards, making an ugly gap through which the Germans were able to work their way in behind the left Cavalry Brigade, of whom there were not many left. Sergeant Belcher, with eight L.R.B.s and two Hussars whom he had picked up, was holding a long stretch of trench on the other side of the road. All day they hung on there, opening fire whenever the enemy attempted to advance, and bluffing them into the belief that the trench was strongly manned. By this plucky stand it was held that he had saved the whole right flank of the 4th Division and he was subsequently awarded the V.C. for his action, while two of those who were with him, I believe, ultimately received Military Medals. The stand of the whole of that front-line was, of course, a splendid example of tenacity and pluck and my heart went out to those " A " and " B " Company men who were holding on so well. " B " Company were now all in the front-line.

For dinner we munched meat and muddy bread, then, finding that our turn for reinforcing would not come yet, Bourke, Thomson and I turned into a small bivvy where our heads were dry but our legs stuck out in the rain. It was not possible to sleep, for one or the other of us kept getting cramp and we were wedged so tightly that one could not move his position without the consent of the other two. At half-past-two there was a magnificent charge of dismounted cavalry away on the right, which it was not our good fortune to see. The 10th Hussars, the Blues and the Essex Yeomanry advanced and after a struggle retook the lost ground. But owing to the severity of the gun-fire, exactly ranged, they had to fall back and by the evening there was a serious dent in our line a mile to the right.

Several fellows of ours went up to reinforce during the afternoon, but dusk came before it had fallen to the lot of our platoon to advance. The shelling of the front-line had died down now and the peppering of the fields had also been relinquished. The Germans had had their opportunity—for they could easily have broken through with any zeal—and they had let it slip through their fingers. As soon as it was dark, the bulk of " D " Company that were left, which did not amount to many, went forward over the brow of the hill, slipping over the muddy ground and falling into yawning shell-holes. We then realised the fate that had overtaken many of the men who had crept forward to reach the front-line during the day. They had had to traverse a hundred yards of level ground—level but for the shell-holes—swept by the enemy's bullets, and a number of them had been hit. We saw them lying in the holes whither they had crawled, and many of them, unaided and stranded, had perished in their miserable cavities. The wounded both from the shell-holes and the trench were taken away with all possible speed, but the carrying of a stretcher across a slippery field studded with pitfalls is not an easy job and it became exceedingly difficult in the pouring rain on a pitch-black night.

I was detailed to do a four-hours' continuous sentry-duty in the front-line trench and I slipped down into it wondering whatever it would look like. It had been a very wide—an absurdly wide—trench, but it had had its parapet blown down in so many places and so many direct hits in others that it now bore little resemblance to a trench at all. Lieut. Trevelyan was the only officer left alive in it and there appeared to be about one man in ten yards of trench, to my left. There were many men lying on the ground, but unfortunately they were dead or stretcher-cases awaiting removal. To my right there was a space of some eighty or a hundred yards to the road which I could see when a flare went up. This was completely destroyed and there was not a single person in it. It was as uninhabitable as it is possible to imagine, since no part of it had apparently escaped a direct hit : it was here that our machine-gun section was destroyed.

I had a most lonesome feeling. Supposing the Germans advanced now, they could walk right over that space, down the hill and through Weiltje. With sufficient numbers they could break right through the British line. How could I deal with a few hundred men rushing up from the darkness ? The sentry ten yards to my left came along for a few words' conversation.

" Been here all day ? " I asked him.

" Yes. . . . I was with ' B ' Company in that trench behind there. When ' A ' copped it badly we came up to reinforce quite early in the morning."

" Have they attacked you ? "

" Rather ! They got in by the Lancs. I wonder how long we've got to stop in this cheerful spot ? "

" Well, I'm on sentry-duty for four hours. I expect it will last all night."

" Heavens ! When are we going to be relieved from this infernal salient ? What's the good of an offensive at Festubert ? Why can't they bring the troops up to relieve us ? "

" You'd better go back past that traverse—there's a big gap on the other side of you."

" Not nearly so big as the one on your right ! Well, so long ! "

Trevelyan came along presently and told us we were to be relieved at nine o'clock, but it was about midnight when the advance guard of our relief slushed along through the mud and asked who we were. Then an officer jumped down into the trench and Trevelyan, who, by the way, had done wonders that day, came out of the darkness and spoke to him.

" We're coming to relieve you," said the other. " What's the trench like ? "

" Pretty bloody," remarked Trevelyan quietly.

" So I see." There was no other comment from the officers.

There was plenty of grousing from the ranks of our relief, however. On learning that our battalion were being relieved after only a day in the trenches, they started spluttering with wrath.

" And we only taken out the day afore yes'day ! One day's blinkin' rest and up we come again. We was seven days in the trenches afore we was relieved. . . . Bloomin' Territorials ! "

At one o'clock we returned to our original trench from which we had set out that morning, to find our packs rifled and nearly all our mackintoshes and ground-sheets taken, including my own. By this time there was a pool of water in the bottom of the trench, but we sank down into it for a time until we found it would be impossible to get any sleep under such conditions. We then went off in search of bits of wood to put in the bottom of our " home," and spent about an hour in this manner. Towards morning we filled our water-bottles from our water-cart, which had been left in a yard down the road and sorted out rations at the back of the trench. Then, chilled and wet through, we lay down in all the slush and tried to snatch forty winks.

Dawn broke without any recurrence of the previous day's outburst, the Germans had given up the fight. From that moment they proceeded to withdraw many of their heavy guns to meet the Anglo-French offensive in Artois. This offensive met with better success on the French front north of Arras than with the British at Festubert. Here our attack was a most costly failure, as the majority of our men were hung up on the barbed-wire and the survivors returned to their starting-point. Kidd, from our office, was killed in this assault. The 14th of May, therefore, gave an opportunity to both sides to nurse their wounds. It also enabled them to brood over their unhappy plight, as, devoid of the excitement of battle, we now began to appreciate our miserable physical conditions.

We awoke, chilled to the bone, wet through, and smothered in mud, determined to " win " ground-sheets and mackintoshes without delay. It was not more difficult to detect them than it had been to locate our fuel at Southampton, since the King's Own in the trench behind us were all wearing macs, with plenty of them to spare, which were being used for their bivvies. I seized one which was as muddy inside as out and many others did the same, leaving the King's Own swearing volubly. The next move was to pillage the neighbouring ruined houses in search of bits of wood, doors, etc., with which to improve our surroundings. There were plenty of such houses between Weiltje and St. Jean and those that had not got smelling horses rotting in their dining-rooms made suitable fields of conquest. Most of them were minus roofs and walls and all the contents of the rooms were laid bare to the world. It seemed sacrilege to touch them and yet . . . half the contents were already destroyed by shell-fire and the remainder would doubtless be blown to smithereens within a week. Why not provide for our present comfort while the woodwork still remained intact ? I passed a regular procession coming up the road, carrying doors, planks, chairs and other articles, and soon entered a ruin on the right where some dozen men were trooping round from room to room. How forlorn and sad the place looked ! The rafters, plaster, bannisters, furniture and stoves smashed to bits. In the sink was the crockery, just as the people had left it when they had to flee ; broken lamps stood on the tables, old newspapers and books lay about : pictures hung at absurd angles on the walls, with the glass smashed. We hardly paused then to think of the wretchedness and unhappy lot of the owner who had long since left his dwelling to the tender mercies of the troops : perhaps he was one of those whom we had seen pushing a perambulator along the Vlamertinghe road. If he could see us smashing the legs off his table to obtain supports for a roof which we had just procured by wrenching a door off its hinges !

Thomson appears wearing a bowler hat : another man has unearthed a bottle of red wine ; still another has discovered eighty francs in a drawer. Lieut. Wallis arrives and smiles with glee. " Make yourselves as comfortable as you can, boys," says he. " There are plenty more houses down the road and they won't be there next week."

The men cart their plunder to the trench and return for more. Gradually materials accumulate in readiness for a supreme bivvy-building competition and this is soon put into operation. For my part, finding the door too wide, I put two planks in the mud at the bottom of the trench and the door over the top as a roof : then I clamber down between the muddy sides and sit down with my back against a traverse.

For one who has not been to the War, it is difficult to imagine what it is like to sit for hour after hour in a narrow trench, looking at bare earth on either side and another man sitting in front of you. A mass of wet slimy mud from head to foot, you cannot move without bringing fresh layers of it on to your sodden uniform and more sploshes of it down your back. Occasionally, in order to stimulate some circulation in your numbed feet you lift them up out of the mud and bang them down again ; then, to avoid cramp, you turn over with great effort on to your side and lie on your waterbottle, this action bringing your knees against one muddy side of the trench and your feet against the other.

All these conditions pertained to our life in that Weiltje trench and the only relief to the monotony came in the form of a sick-parade, at which we were frankly advised to go sick in order to get a walk into St. Jean and a cup of Bovril at the dressing-station.

At one period of the day, when it had come on to pour with rain again, Wallis walked down the trench and, reaching our little group, remarked :

" I'm feeling jolly miserable." His face did not reflect it.

" Do you know the attendant at the Holborn ? " he asked. " Well, I'd just like to be him now, showing gentlemen in one side and ladies in the other. What a soft job he has, eh ? I don't like this game at all."

With the arrival of the sun in the afternoon and the partial drying of the trench, everyone's spirits improved. Rain and sun influence soldiers' happiness more than shells and casualties. Our losses the day before had totalled 91, bringing our Company strength down badly ; but it was not this fact so much as the mud that caused such cursing on the 14th. When I discovered two sandbags to put inside my trouser legs to keep the wet material away from me, my delight knew no bounds. I had lost my gloves, but, sitting in the trench and using a fountain pen and a muddy piece of paper, I had already written home for a new pair. For tea, Bourke and Whittle heated a mug full of cocoa over two candles and shared the drink with Thomson and me. Three sips of this worked wonders. We only needed news that we were going to be relieved to complete our joy.

That evening we moved off to the trench we had dug a few nights before when we had set out from Vlamertinghe upon a working-party and, thanks to our labours on that occasion, there was not much to be done to the trench to make it habitable. Whittle and I dug a little deeper and, having brought wood with us, made a serviceable bivvy in a very short time : when this was accomplished sufficiently to keep out the rain, we promptly lay down and slept soundly until morning.

Although we did not know it, our continuous spell in the firing-line was now drawing to a close. While we were still cursing the Dardanelles campaign for using up forces which should have been on the Western Front, while we were yet bemoaning the fact that it was five weeks since we had had a hot bath or a change of underclothing (some of us had secured the latter) and a week since we had shaved, the wires were buzzing with the news that we could not yet be made up to strength again. The 2nd Battalion was now being trained as an individual unit and the 3rd Battalion, which was started about the end of 1914, was not in a position to supply sufficient drafts. A small draft en route for France was stopped and ordered back again. We should have to be withdrawn and reconstituted, with a new machine-gun section and fresh signallers and first-aid men, before being sent into the firing-line again.

We went to one more trench upon the evening of the 15th, when we were to be " schoolmasters " to a Territorial Battalion unversed in warfare, and tell them all there was to be known about trench work. We recognised this as a sop to us for moving nearer the line again, but when it was announced that we were to do nothing in the way of digging or sentry-duty and that we could take plenty of sleep, things did not seem so bad. We found corrugated iron for bivvies and made ourselves comfortable, except for the difficulty of keeping warm, but, needless to say, when all the men in the other unit were out digging, there was still plenty for us to do. However, once the work was finished we slept well on into the morning.

On the 16th we returned to the Canal and occupied bivvies built into the banks. Close at hand was the remainder of the 11th Brigade who were delighted with the fact that we could not be made up to strength (rumours of which were now very strong) and ungrudgingly wished us a long rest and a despatch to England, though they themselves, poor fellows, were likely to return again and again to the firing-line, continually being made up to strength. Few things touched us more during the War than the way in which the genuine friendship of these Regulars, who said all sorts of nice things about us in a perfectly sincere way, was proven by their desire to see us " well out of it." The Staff officers also came along with rumours of our being made an officers' training corps, of going home to England, or being put on lines of communication. My Company officer, Captain Otter, returned to us and one or two other recently-arrived officers made their appearance. So did some parcels ! With water drawn straight from the foul Yser canal and boiled over " Tommy's Cookers " we made ourselves cocoa, cafe-au-lait and other delicacies so precious to the interior of a soldier.

Three days were spent in this position, our definite orders to move arriving on the 18th and our departure taking place on the following day. As we lined up on the Canal bank, our joy at being relieved was intermingled with regrets that we were leaving that good old 11th Brigade. The Staff wished us a cordial farewell, saying that they hoped we should return to them one day, while the four Regular battalions—or such remaining in them as remembered us at Ploegsteert —lined up and cheered as we set off across the Canal, watching until we were out of sight.

Before mentioning them for the last time, it is worth recording that four days later there was another big attack on the 4th Division from the Shell-Trap Farm southwards. The 11th Brigade being in reserve did not suffer so badly as the 10th and 12th. On this occasion a great cloud of gas, three miles in length and forty feet in depth, swept down on our lines, accompanied by a bombardment with gas-shells. Four and a half hours afterwards the emission continued, but the Essex, reinforced by the E. Lancs and Rifle Brigade, held on all day and even made attempts to counter-attack. Ground had to be given on the right, however, and that night the front was withdrawn finally to a line running through Weiltje, the Germans occupying that ghastly trench which had been held on 13th by " A " Company. This was the end of the German attempts on Ypres in the spring of 1915.   The R.B.s and Somersets also did particularly well in a charge north of Ypres on July 6th, when they captured and permanently held a portion of the German line.

And there with regret we must leave that gallant Brigade for good.

On the morning of May 20th, after an address by General Snow in the grounds of Vlamertinghe Chateau, we boarded London motor omnibuses which were drawn up in readiness on the Vlamertinghe Road.   No curious populace turned out to see us depart, nor did crowds of Canadians gather in the village as they had done on that night of April 25th, watching the endless line of troops and transport on the move.   The place was now deserted, as we had judged when we had seen it from the Chateau grounds some days before.

It was a beautiful spring morning and as we passed under the trees overhanging that fateful Poperinghe Road, leaving the war behind us, it seemed impossible that such a blighted stricken piece of country could lie so near at hand.   What regiment in the British Army has not marched up that Poperinghe Road a corporate body of men and returned weeks, maybe days, later as though it had passed through a furnace ?   How many that went up never returned at all ?   In the Second Battle of Ypres alone the figures were so serious in proportion to the number of troops engaged that some of the casualty lists were suppressed for over a year.   During the war, 250,000 British officers and men were killed and wounded in that salient alone.   Can it be wondered at that the Poperinghe Road spelt tragedy from beginning to end ?

As we passed Poperinghe we saw the first civilians : although big shells had fallen in that town, it was not badly knocked about and gave us the first glimpse of civilisation.   Thence we passed through Steenvoorde and Hazebrouck, waving our hands to all and sundry in our joy at having lived to see such towns again, while the townsfolk gazed in amazement at the ragged, slovenly, tatterdemalion, muddy crew that shouted and sang songs as they passed down their main streets.

On and on we went, the freshness of the breeze and the brightness of the landscape cheering us up to such an extent that our spirits rose higher and higher, and every mile that was placed between ourselves and Ypres added further to our hilarity.

Our destination was the village of Tatinghem, close to St. Omer, where we met the transport who had trekked thirty-six miles in eighteen hours, truly a creditable performance for men who were not much less worn out than were we ourselves.   With them, also, the thought that they were putting distance between themselves and the Weiltje Road spurred them onwards.

Thus ends a very incomplete record of what was a complete and definite phase of our adventures in France.   The Battalion as reconstituted, was an entirely different one, and I am thankful to say that it never went through such a trying or protracted period in the trenches in any subsequent battle.

CHAPTER VIII.

On Lines of Communications.

(*June–August*, 1915.)

The question of commissions—Railway work—In hospital—Three days' leave—
Guarding prisoners—Police duty—A French billet—A Flemish railhead—
Trip to the Mont des Cats—Work and play at Caestre.

A QUESTION that occupied nearly everyone's attention and the greater part of our letters home, during the weeks succeeding the Second Battle of Ypres, was the desirability of taking commissions. It had been a most difficult matter for the L.R.B. to get commission papers through, as the C.O. would not sign the recommendations for outside regiments ; there were then about 95 per cent. of the battalion eligible for the commissioned rank, so that, if this restriction were withdrawn, he would find the whole of his men whittling away until there was no unit left. Whittle, Bourke, Thomson and many others had long been using influence at home to get colonels in newly-forming units to apply to Col. Bates for them to return to England and become one of their officers. Such applications were always acceded to by our Colonel, and since Whittle's papers had already come through and been signed while we were on the Canal bank, together with other men's applications, the majority of us proceeded to write to all friends and relatives who might know colonels, asking them to leave no stone unturned to secure our return to England to serve as officers with new units. The great attraction was not the star on our shoulders but the prospect of an unlimited period of training in England, and the thought that Whittle, Bourke and others, who had already done some judicious " wire-pulling " at home, would soon be recalled, while the remainder would still be doing fatigues in France, was the primary cause of the general demand for commission papers that now ensued. Some were immediately successful, while others waited months for their papers to come through ; still others, including myself, did not possess the influence in the required quarter.

There was much discussion on the merits of the question. We had " done our bit " as privates and N.C.O.s. There was a great shortage of officers in the scores of new battalions just forming. The C.O.s, when they heard of an L.R.B. man who had been through the Ypres affair, were only too glad to apply for him. Why not take

advantage of this opportunity of getting back home for a while ?   The
3rd battalion of the Territorial units would be the best battalions to
try for, but Thomson, Bourke and many were getting commissions
in Kitchener's Army.   For the moment, beyond the pulling of strings,
little was done, so the craze did not affect our numbers, which were,
moreover, considerably increased by the return of men from the base,
of slightly wounded and sick cases discharged from hospital, and by
the arrival of a draft of fifty.

For some days we remained at Tatinghem, taking things very easily ;
we were within a mile or so of St. Omer, where attractive shops of all
kinds, baths and very nice-looking French girls were among the many
delights of civilisation.   The Artists, who had been retained at G.H.Q.
as an officers' training corps, paraded the streets of St. Omer looking
spick and span in their untarnished uniforms ;   beside them, our
fellows—still attired in the torn, dirty and soiled garments of the
trenches—looked too slovenly for the Military Police, who asked if
we could not dress ourselves more decently.   The remarks came very
ill from men who had not seen the firing-line and they received suitable
retorts from those they accosted.   There was a piano shop in St. Omer,
much to my delight, and a fellow named Collins, who was an excellent
violinist, frequently shared an hour's music with me there.   St. Omer
was, by the way, the home of G.H.Q. and there was a large number
of Staff officers in the town.

At the end of the month we heard we were to be put on lines of
communications, together with the remnants of the Rangers and
Kensingtons, the whole forming one composite battalion which was
to relieve the 5th Welsh.   The latter regiment was split up into numerous
little parties of men, with their headquarters at St. Omer, the majority
of whom were engaged at various railheads in guarding stores, stations
and bridges, unloading trains and lorries, conveying prisoners to the
Base and cleaning up goods-yards.   On lines of communications one
might be anything from a policeman to a dustman or a railway-porter,
but no job could be as bad as sitting in an enfiladed trench, waiting
for the Ministry of Munitions to construct armament factories !

On May 31st a number of us were despatched to Berguette, two
stations from St. Omer in the direction of Bethune, where our task
was to shunt about trucks and unload them, also to guard a large
Engineers' dump.   When there was no work to do, the fatigue party
had to wait about from 8 a.m. until 5 p.m. in case anything arrived.
There were guards to do at night and the crazy old R.E. officer responsible for the dump came round on tiptoe on the first two evenings
to surprise the sentry at 1 a.m. at the imminent risk of being shot
dead.   Our billet was an empty house close to the station.

Berguette was only a tiny village, where the inhabitants were most
hospitable :   they were delighted to find many of the L.R.B.s could
speak French, for the Welsh had not been proficient in that respect,
though they had won the villagers' hearts.   The surroundings were
peaceful and the guns sounded as a mere rumble in the distance.
What a delightful change !   We could stop here for the duration
of the War !

It was my ill-fortune, however, to be still suffering from septic fingers
which the month without treatment had rendered worse ;   of course
there was no doctor at Berguette, and this meant my having to walk
back to Aire, a good-sized town some distance away, which was the
headquarters of one of the Indian Divisions.   The hospital here had

different wards for British and Indians, but all the attendants and orderlies were Indians. As I thought, once I got to hospital they made me bring my kit along there and stay; this was a bad beginning to my friendship with the damsels of Berguette, who were doubtless falling on the necks of Scholefield, Hettler, Clarke and the rest of them.

The hospital had an air of novelty about it, for it was new to me to see all these Indians about, dressed in khaki shirts in lieu of tunics, presumably because the ordinary uniform was too uncomfortable for them. In my ward was an Irishman who talked a little Hindustani and frequently had wordy arguments with the Indian orderly who was responsible for the tidiness of his bed. As fast as the Indian put it straight, amid much cursing on the part of the Irishman, it got upset again, which caused the orderly when he next walked that way to wave his arms and rush up to re-arrange it, protesting the while in Hindustani and broken English that it *must* be kept tidy. More fun could be got out of the inmates of hospital wards, though they were usually unaware of it, than from any other source. This Irishman had acquired a smattering of French which he was airing to me with much pride and an atrocious accent. The phrases were of one kind only : " Vous etes tres gentille mamsell ! " " Vouli-vu promenade avec moi," and " Embrassez-moi veet," were the most polished ones.

My stay at this hospital was short-lived, as I was transferred to a stationary one at St. Omer, almost within a stone's throw of the camp where the L.R.B. who remained in this town were stationed. There were nurses in some of the wards here and I looked forward eagerly to hearing a tender female voice talk in English once more, after five months without even the sight of an English girl. On the first morning my desire was realised : one of the nurses came up and gave me a good bullying for using the wrong washing-tub. After this my desire to listen to them somewhat diminished.

The principal amusement in this ward was the regular performance of an exceedingly fat and very tall " Jock " who repeatedly fell off his bed. Whether his size was too big for the article of furniture, I don't know, but several times he fell "plomp" on to the floor, whereat he would sit up, rub his eyes, put his bed straight, place a pipe in his mouth and lie down again. We soon got to know what the thump meant and took little notice of it.

Our duties were not arduous, though I made one attempt to scrub the floor. This was my one and only effort in that direction, however, as it took me half an hour to clean a few square feet, over which I used two buckets of water and got up wet to the skin ! Most of my time was spent in reading, writing and talking to an L.R.B. guard who were in a tent by the gate.

On June 8th these men heard that everyone was to get three days' leave, starting immediately ; the original 1st Battalion men were going first, but it would not be long before it came to my turn. Nothing else counted after that ; my thoughts were confined to planning what would be the best means of spending three days in England. There must be a concert, and there were some thirty or forty people, living anywhere from London to Brighton, whom I wanted to see ; then there were the office friends, and, above all, I *must* interview some colonel of a regiment at home and, having satisfied him, return to France secure in the knowledge that he would be writing out to apply for me. At the first rumour of leave being granted, all those who had been " swinging the lead " at base depots and hospitals for months—

some since Christmas—with various complaints such as frost-bite, rheumatism, etc., suddenly found themselves cured and hastened back to join us. Some had already done so on hearing that we were out for a long rest, but nearly a hundred men turned up to claim their leave ! Many of their old complaints returned when we formed up again later. The thought of leave seemed to make all the difference to my desire to quit hospital, too, and every day that passed without my being discharged increased my impatience.

On June 11th I succeeded in rejoining the L.R.B.s in their camp, where Bourke and Whittle were waiting for their turn to come. They had been relieved from their stations down the line by men whose leave would be due later on, which somewhat perturbed me, since I might be despatched on the same errand. But the only errand on which I was sent was " post duty," which involved travelling to Bethune *via* Hazebrouck and dropping bags of mail addressed to the L.R.B.s at the various stations, finally returning to St. Omer *via* Lillers and Berguette. It was a most interesting journey, as it enabled me to see the various places and get an idea of the work done at them. Our men seemed to be coalheavers at one place, railway clerks at another and traffic superintendents at a third : everywhere they were in the best of spirits, well-billeted, well-fed and pleased with life. The journey enabled me to spend an hour or so at Bethune, some five miles from La Bassee, a fine town, full of Jocks from the 9th Division, recently out from home.

My turn for leave came on June 16th, when we set off by train from St. Omer, slept on the boat at Boulogne and left next morning at 10.30. By tea-time I was in my home again. It seemed incredible that such a short distance separated peaceful Kent from the scene of war on the other side of the Channel. It seemed as if we reached Boulogne directly we had left St. Omer ; then the sea voyage was much shorter than that from Southampton, and no sooner were we in those English railway carriages again than we had whirled up to London. How unchanged everything looked ! Business was going on as usual ; about one young man in four was in khaki, everyone spoke as though we had won the War. However, it was reassuring to know that munitions were being turned out in much larger quantities and that we were now specialising in heavy guns in which Germany had stolen such a march on us. Recruiting was going on everywhere, but many considered themselves indispensable who would have been doing better service in France. Every schoolboy seemed to be getting a commission and I heard from several sources that there should be no difficulty over anyone who had seen service, belonging to the L.R.B., becoming an officer forthwith.

The three days went by like lightning and there seemed to be only one morning to spare for the purpose of interviewing a colonel. The 3rd or 4th reserve battalions of the 1st, 2nd and 3rd London Regiments offered the best chances, so it was to their headquarters that I proceeded. Alas ! two of them expected their C.O. at any time, but he was not there and my only hope was the 1st London, whose Adjutant was very busy. The taxi machine ticked on and on, while I waited the sweet will of some " jumped-up little bounder " whom I consigned, in my wrath, to eternal shell-fire. For over one hour I waited and it was nearly twelve o'clock. There was only one more hour in which to see the folk at the office, as this was a Saturday and I should be leaving for France again on the following afternoon. Everyone in the neighbourhood of that orderly-room had cause to know I was there : I tried every means to interview that Adjutant, but the red-tape that was still so rampant at home rendered them ineffective. At last the quest had to be given up in despair and, in disgust, I decided to let the matter slide : to make matters worse, when I got to the office nearly everybody had gone home, including those I most desired to see. From those two points of view, then, my three days' battle leave had not been a success. Others made better use of their holidays, because their interviews had already been arranged with colonels whom they or some friend of theirs knew. They invariably passed satisfactorily and went home within the next month or so.

On my return to St. Omer they sent me down to Berguette again, where I met Thomson, who was going to see Colonel Bates on the 25th in reference to a commission in the 21st Middlesex, whose Colonel had applied for Bourke. Whittle soon departed to take his commission in the 2nd Londons. Many friends drifted away from this time onwards and there was so little prospect of " D " Company being even a ghost of its former self that I took up the question again, writing direct to one or two C.O.s and receiving replies to the effect that they would very much like to see me if I could arrange to get leave for the purpose. The only place for their letters was my breast-pocket, as it was impossible to get special leave for any purpose whatever. One must wait until another leave came round.

In the meantime we were all very happy at Berguette. On this occasion Thomson and I had the pleasant duty of guarding a reserve ammunition train by night and sleeping or taking walks by day. Near the station was a stream, upon the bank of which we chose a secluded spot and stripped for a swim in the afternoons. It was such a lonely place that we never used bathing-costumes until one day a detachment of French females came along the tow-path and offended our delicacy by waiting for us to come out of the water. After that we wrote home for bathing costumes or else desisted from swimming in daylight.

The Army does not believe in letting one remain long in one place : whether they thought there would be too many marriages with French girls if the soldiers saw too much of them, it is impossible to say. At any rate, they soon decided to take me away again and the end of the month saw me back at St. Omer, with Scholefield and Gernat. Our principal occupations here were attending signalling classes, guarding a few promiscuous prisoners and heaving road-making material from one barge to another. What did the nature of the work matter when we had tents to sleep in, plenty of food, innumerable shops and no shells ? Up in the Ypres direction frequent rumbles told us that others were having an unpleasant time, which made us all the more satisfied with our lot. They were now training fresh signallers, and volunteers for machine-guns were being instructed at the Army School at Wisques, signs that our respite would not last for ever.

Italy was now in the war and, in spite of the gigantic Russian reverse, we somehow hoped that peace would suddenly be announced or that an unlooked-for turn of the tide would speedily appear. With a view to testing the views of the Germans on this subject, we conversed with one or two of the prisoners whom we guarded in a barracks where they were allowed to take exercise and sit about in the sun once a day. They consisted of some half-a-dozen Saxons, two of whom had voluntarily entered our lines and given themselves up, and one Prussian. They were small men, rather pale, with close-cropped hair and a typically

Teutonic face, but without the arrogant air that many prisoners had. The exception was the Prussian, who refused to walk with the others, because he presumably thought himself superior. We had one or two conversations with one fellow, who was a dentist, and another who spoke excellent English. Neither of them thought the war would last the summer, or that either side would gain a supreme victory. When confronted with having descended to using poison gas, they declared that they had not been in the "gas" region, but they were under the impression that it was only used in shells and that, in any case, the French had used it first. They were somewhat amused when we told them they would soon be in England, as they imagined their submarines were making the seas impassable. Our food much impressed them, one declaring that it was better than the average workman's pre-war food in Germany. The Saxons fed at one end of their room and the Prussian at the other !

On July 8th I gave a dinner-party to Collins, Gernat, Scholefield and another in a famed restaurant where the thirst of these colleagues outstripped the extent of my purse : accordingly I had to borrow ten francs from Gernat under the table in order to meet the bill. At this shop there were three very refined and attractive French girls whose aid I invoked when I lost a piece of sticking-plaster which had covered my hand. After a frantic search, imagine the discomfiture of everyone when I discovered that I had sat down upon it !

Permission was granted about this time for men, who could not be applied for from England, to join the Artists' Officers' Training Corps and take a commission in a " line " regiment up at the front. This scheme involved five days' leave only, which defeated the whole object of those who were trying to join reserve battalions, namely, the obtaining of a long spell at home. Leave was going round again and men preferred to wait until all other sources failed before joining the school, from which they would probably be posted to any regiment that required officers, regardless of their particular wishes. Only a few, who " didn't care what happened to them," availed themselves of the class in question among the Artists, in which, by the way, was another of our office staff, Cooksey.

The next place I visited was a small village near Hazebrouck, known to the troops as " Tee-en " but spelt " Thiennes." We were sent here to supplement the local L.R.B. detachment, and my principal job was policeman's work.

17/7/15. " To-day my arduous duties (at Thiennes) commenced. Rising with the lark at 7.15, I washed and then finished off eggs and bacon, marmalade and tea by five minutes to eight. Then I donned my belt and bayonet—it is considered sufficient to show you're a policeman in the Army if you wear these two articles—and sauntered down to the station on my own to take up my post.

" What a matter of luck it is on lines of communications ! You may be at some docks and work like a navvy all day, or you may get to some quiet little country place like this, where everyone is more or less his own master. The station is the most forsaken one I've ever seen. Two aged porters trim hedges, and collect tickets if anyone happens to alight from the two passenger trains per day. An officer superintends the gigantic station arrangements in his office, while his orderly sits on a seat, twirls his thumbs and waits all day for something to turn up. The only other official of note is myself—how some people have greatness thrust upon them ! I am a policeman, a kind of special constable, and my belt and bayonet are supposed to work wonders ! No one is very sure about what my duties are, but they all agree that it would be as well to hang around to see that the motor-lorries don't knock down the gate-posts at the entrance to the yard and that nobody makes off with a railway truck when I'm not looking. Theoretically, I walk up and down the yard on the alert from 8 a.m. till 5 p.m. Practically, I come in the station to avoid the rain, sit down on a seat and write a letter.

" There are fields and woods all around and the railway track itself is overgrown with grass and weeds, as is usual on French lines. Some enterprising officer farther up the line has put a party of men on to weeding the railway track, much to the amusement of the French people, who have never seen such a thing done before ; but I'm pleased to say that we haven't such zealous superiors here and, so long as the policeman doesn't agitate for more work, they will be quite content to let the weeds remain where they are.

" Just as I had written the above, a corporal came up to inform me that some forty lorries had already arrived and asked me whether I intended to regulate the traffic or not. I said that, as the rain had stopped, perhaps it would be as well to see if there had been any collisions, so I hastened out to the yard ; I felt I'd be such a lot of use if anything happened to one of the lorries. However, the gate-posts were in good condition, though six lorries had already entered the yard without consulting me and there were thirty-four more to come. Soon an officer came up and told me to let in twelve at a time and see there were no collisions, conferring all sorts of powers on me until I thought I was as important as the Munitions Act. So I proceeded to the front lorries to instruct six more to enter the yard, but, finding the drivers had departed elsewhere for breakfast and the lorries were immovable, I discreetly returned to my post.

" After standing at the gate on duty for over an hour without any movement on the part of the convoy, lorries started to arrive from the back of the queue first, passing the others on the road. One after another they came and there were very soon twelve in the yard. If I stopped the thirteenth and the others behind it, it would block the road and the gateway, thus preventing lorries from getting out, so I was in a dilemma. I seemed to be overwhelmed with automobiles on all sides, some were even preparing to leave the yard and there threatened to be as complex a congestion at this gateway as opposite the Bank of England, with only one poor special constable to deal with it. Like the hero in some novel, I rushed down past the oncoming hordes, inquiring for the individual who had ordered this sudden onslaught, as it was impossible to turn them back once they had started. At last I found the individual in a public house and I told him politely but firmly how matters stood, but even my belt and bayonet did not signify much to him : he was an A.S.C. sergeant !

" By the time I arrived back at the gate I found the lorries at the front of the queue were now going into the yard right merrily, one after the other, without any hindrance, so I stopped the procession and learnt from one burly driver that another sergeant had beckoned him in. After telling him to halt until I found this sergeant, I entered the yard, where I saw so many wagons that it seemed as if the officer who had given me my instructions would have a fit if he saw them too. The N.C.O. was not to be seen and before I got back to the gate four more lorries had entered. Instinctively I hummed to myself : ' A policeman's life is not a happy one, happy one,' but there was little to worry me after that. Motors came and went away again like clockwork, under the command and direction of some Boer War regular sergeant, who whistled for four more when he thought he'd have them— and there were no collisions and no broken gateposts. The yard was full, but when the officer himself came on the scene he did not have a fit : he thought how well everything was going. So I just sat down on a box and opened your parcel, which had reached me even in this outlandish place, having some dates for lunch and lapsing into silence. It seemed like having lunch in the Old Kent Road with all the motors about and their natural smell, instead of being at a little French wayside station close to the Forest of Nieppe.

" The orderly from the station came up and told me he had had nothing to do all the morning, whereat I confessed that the A.S.C. were getting along very nicely without my assistance and that even the belt and bayonet were not of much use to me in exercising the powers granted to the gate-keeper. In fact we agreed that we were not the slightest bit of use to anybody and resolved to bring a book with us to read after dinner, which we did.

" Most of the lorries had then left the yard and there were few people about, so I began to feel like a policeman again, patrolling the empty train with much dignity—when it didn't rain. It rained nearly all the afternoon. My duties ceased at 5 p.m., when I left the station and came back to the farm to finish this letter. I am now free until to-morrow night, when I shall do a night guard over the place, look at the numerous passing trains and ' watch the wheels go round.' What a life ! "

After a few days spent at this kind of work, the railhead was moved elsewhere and our party was withdrawn to St. Omer, but we had not been there three days before Thiennes required a fatigue party for some other purpose and another detachment was drafted off there, in which I happened to find myself. On this occasion I was the R.T.O.'s clerk, whose duties were to sit in an estaminet or telephone from the station to neighbouring places, each call taking several minutes. The second visit to Thiennes was not of interest except for the extraordinary billet that Gernat and I and another fellow had. We were allowed to choose our own billets, but there were not many available and the three of us selected an estaminet. It had its drawbacks, but one could so well observe a side of life there that was quite new, that it was worth remaining there.

27/7/15. " . . . Gernat succeeded in finding various spiders, ants, moths and other creatures in the bed the first night, by the aid of an electric torch, but, after using all sorts of powders, finally settled down comfortably. Last night, when I slept in it, it looked tolerably clean. Ma and Pa sleep over part of the room, one son over another, Juliette next door, and two other youngsters in the wine-cellar reached through a trap-door from our room.

The landlord, a bearded drayman, who is out most of the day except for an occasional return with a barrel of beer, has a nasty habit of expectorating on the floor, eating garlic and hiccoughing over the assembly. His wife is an old hag with a sallow complexion, some four feet high, wearing an absurd pair of old glasses that continually fall off. His voice—a terrible, screaming croak— got on our nerves within half an hour of our arrival. Equally trying is the voice of Juliette, a wench of some three and twenty summers, portly, ungainly and not by any means handsome— the sort of sight in curling pins that puts you off your breakfast when you see it preparing your meal first thing in the morning. The eldest boy squints and he will always place himself in front of your nose, wherever you happen to be. His great delight is to pinch people.

" One or two visitors come in to watch the English soldiers have their meals in the living-room, the only room apart from the bar, and the entire family likewise gathers round and stares. They think we eat enough for one meal to last a French family a week.

" An exciting thing happened yesterday morning : I mention it to show how such people enjoy themselves. When the landlord appeared, to leave a barrel of beer and, incidentally, to have a glass of the liquid at the counter, another drayman entered with him. The latter gentleman's chief amusement seemed to be to take a mouthful of beer and eject it like a spray all over Juliette, causing a great hubbub. Juliette screamed, we laughed and Madame yelled. Monsieur the landlord said nothing but promptly finished off the drayman's beer, retaining a mouthful which he ejected over the drayman. This struck us as such an extra- ordinary way of taking revenge that we had to leave off writing and watch it. We saw the drayman squirting beer in all directions, while the landlord followed him round, taking mouthfuls of beer as fast as he could and squirting it over him. Then came Madame with a flying leap, kicking the drayman on the shin, whereupon another shower of beer shot forth. However, after all the excite- ment, both landlord and drayman departed, leaving pools upon the floor. This is war in a little French village. You never see our gallant Allies downhearted ! "

Even sojourns in estaminets come to an end, and on the 28th we returned once more to St. Omer in order to relieve some of the Ken- singtons at Caestre on the 29th. About this time the British took over a stretch of the firing-line south of Arras, and the Kensingtons, as well as many of our own men, were despatched to the Doullens neighbourhood for detraining and other purposes. Those who were sent on this work were extremely fortunate, for, in the districts around Amiens and Doullens, British soldiers were a novelty and very well received by the populace. Caestre, to which my party was sent, was a wretched Flemish village, only two stations away from that dreaded place, Poperinghe. On our way up to Ypres it had been our first stopping place after Hazebrouck. This was the first time I had been nearer to the Ypres portion of the line than Hazebrouck since we had been on lines of communications, and the roads, buildings and surrounding country reminded me very much of the landscape nearer the line. The station was the railhead for one of the divisions up in the salient, their rations arriving here by train to be transferred to motor lorries, which in turn took them nearer the line to the A.S.C. of the various brigades in the neighbourhood of Poperinghe. Our duty was to furnish guards and clean up the yard, not a particularly intelligent job, but then the Army does not look for intelligence in the ranks and cannot discriminate between various units. They put navvies on to telephone work and clerks on to picking up sardine tins on railway lines !

We were nominally in charge of an officer here, but he rarely interfered with us, since he spent most of his time in his " mess " in the village ; his military bearing and fondness for red-tape were all right for the Army in England, but were ill-suited and unwelcome to the L.R.B. detachment, who were somewhat rebellious at having to sweep up yards at one moment and turn out spick and span on sentry duty the next. The senior N.C.O. was Sergt. Belcher, V.C., a very genial, unassuming fellow, who lived with the men. Among the other men I met here were Trendell—destined to become a great friend—Harbord and Chrisp. It must have been Fate that put Chrisp and myself in this party, for our meeting altered the whole course of my life in the Army. He was a driver on the L.R.B. Transport Section and had been with them since mobilisation, but when the Composite Battalion was formed the regimental transport was disbanded, with the result that Chrisp and some fifty to sixty other men had returned to their companies. He was a very witty individual, to whom I quickly took a great fancy.

We were camped in tents in a field close to the station, and on guard the very first night I realised that, however distasteful our job, it was far better than the trenches : for before daybreak a dull boom broke the stillness of the night, followed by a very distant rumble signifying rapid artillery fire. The boom was a mine sprung by the Germans, who were now making another attempt to get Ypres, via Hooge, on the Menin Road. On this occasion they called into being another vile ally, viz., liquid fire, which was sprayed in huge jets from their line into the trenches of the 14th Division, who had to give ground. Next day we saw one or two hospital trains pass through and some days later we had the task of sorting out the welter of burnt and charred rifles, equipment and clothing, which had been salved.

On the 9th of August the British made their counter-stroke at 3.15 a.m. and it was with an eerie feeling that one stood on guard and watched the innumerable flashes in the sky that told of so much metal hurling through the air on to the enemy's lines. This attack took place on both sides of the Menin Road and succeeded in recovering the lost ground : the wounded who passed down in hospital trains on this occasion were in excellent spirits and appeared to have inflicted considerable punishment on the Germans.

A few days later I took a bicycle one evening and set off in the direction of the Mont des Cats, a tall hill noticeable for miles around, on the top of which stood a monastery. From the top of this, on a fine day, you were reputed to be able to see miles beyond the firing-line, northwards as far as the sea, southwards to La Bassee and behind you to Cassel and even St. Omer. In the daytime I never had the time to spare, but after tea there was nothing to prevent a little joy-ride ; in about half an hour I had reached the hill, while a fifteen-minutes' climb brought me to the top. Several sightseers were there as well as myself, and I think I am right in saying that it was from this eminence that many of our war correspondents gained their fantastic ideas and their censored information about the firing-line. Through a pair of field-glasses, kindly lent me by a R.A.M.C. man, I was able to follow the whole of the firing-line from the neighbourhood of Dixmude, past Boesinghe and Ypres to Wytschaete, where the view was blocked by Mount Kemmel; to the right lay Armentières and the approximate position of Ploegsteert could be gleaned. Below us to the right was Bailleul, while to the left was Godearsvelde, next station to Poperinghe. Yes, that must be Poperinghe and somewhere among those trees there was Vlamertinghe, that village of awful memories. I could see the ruins of Ypres quite distinctly among the trees and beyond—dim ridges that seemed to dominate the city. In that indistinct background all the details that were lacking could be filled in from memory, the Gravenstafel Ridge, Zonnebeke, St. Julien: they were all there, in a nutshell as it were, yet it was impossible to make out where the British and Germans faced one another. Occasionally a white puff of smoke, unaccompanied by any noise, arrested the attention; next it was the twinkle of a gun-flash in the trees around Ypres. These were the only signs of war. Just below us two armies were locked in conflict—and behind us . . . a few low ranges of hills beyond which, though we could not see it, we knew was the sea. We were fighting with our backs to the sea, holding on to the narrowest strip of land, for every inch of which there would have to be a fierce struggle, since every inch meant so much. Fascinated to the utmost, it was difficult to take my eyes off the panorama and it was only when the light really faded that I started back for the camp, my thoughts full of those stirring events of April and May that now seemed to have faded into the past.

Our duties would have been more arduous had we not carried on a campaign of passive-resistance against a bullying, self-assertive R.A.M.C. lance-corporal who was put in charge of the sanitary conditions of the station and its surroundings. This person's idea of our working day, when on sanitary fatigue, was that his slaves should work from 7 a.m. until 8.30, walking along the railway-line with a sack, with the object of picking up all the paper, orange-peel, matches, buttons, tins, straw and cigarette ends. His next scheme was for the washing-place to be cleaned up, this being situated in a quagmire by the side of a green slimy pond in a distant field : he never propounded any sound scheme for the sanitising of this spot and, beyond the hiding of cast-off garments in bushes and the dressing of the empty petrol (washing) tins " by the right," he got nothing accomplished. Another job that he organised was the emptying of rubbish-boxes, followed by the lighting of an incinerator. In the afternoons the yard had to be swept beautifully clean after the lorries had left, all the hay, straw and other untidy eyesores being swept up and put out of sight. Since he proposed that this work should be started long before the unloading had finished, with the result that no sooner had a place been cleaned than it was smothered again, he promptly came into conflict with the members of our party. His unpopularity so increased that he found himself ostracised from society, so much so that one day, when he sulkily looked in our tent—with the obvious intention of remarking that some job had not been properly finished— Lindsay looked round the group of men and calmly asked :

" Did anyone call the Corporal ? . . . No ? Nobody wants to see you. Good day."

At which the Lance-Corporal disappeared.

What used to annoy this self-important individual particularly was the invariable request for fuel when he ordered one or other of us to light the station copper for boiling the drinking-water for the R.T.O. and our detachment. There was apparently none issued for this purpose and the Kensingtons had evidently searched high and low for wood and coal. The only means of obtaining any, unless you happened to be on intimate terms with the local French coal-merchant, was to beg it off an engine-driver. Begging, we told the Corporal, was a thing we could never descend to : stealing was out of the question. Therefore, if he wanted his fire lighted, he must find the fuel. The plan was successful : he usually spent an hour a day hunting for wood and coal, the only real work we ever saw him do !

Our spare-time was enlivened by the antics of Chrisp and another man named Cox, who developed the wager fever and either made bets or tossed for money from morning till night. Had they confined their gambling to card-playing they would not have aroused unusual interest on the part of the others, but simple gambling and wagers soon became stale and they were not content unless some sensational bet was being made. Chrisp bet Cox five francs that he couldn't hit a target with a revolver at ten yards and Cox took it on. So the whole camp adjourned to a neighbouring field to watch the shot. Cox got the shot almost in the bull and therefore won the bet. Thereupon Chrisp challenged Cox to a cricket-match, betting him three francs that he would be able to bowl him out in twelve bowls ; the bet was accepted by Cox, whereat the whole camp adjourned to the cricket-field, where stumps, bat and ball were found and the exciting " match " took place. This time Chrisp won, but Cox promptly bet him three francs that Chrisp could not bowl *him* in twelve turns, and another game took place amidst general excitement. The match over, Cox having won, all the stumps, etc., were put away again and we returned to camp, Chrisp being the loser on the day ; however, a wager on a walking match round the field next morning brought them even again and they stood precisely as though they had not put themselves to all that trouble ! This sort of thing took place every day and helped to make the wheels of time go round.

Thus the month of August rolled by ; endless lorry convoys passed daily, occasionally troop trains filled with drafts stopped on their way up to Poperinghe, at other times hospital trains brought down the men whose places the drafts had gone to fill. Our chief enemies were wasps and the Sanitary Corporal : our best friends were letters and parcels from home, which arrived regularly, and two very attractive girls in the village. The average Flemish female is an unattractive sight, attired in unbecoming clothes and sabots, jabbering hard in a tongue akin to German and frequently showing unmistakable dislike of the British soldier. My friend Zoé was a blonde of seventeen, with a pretty face and an attractive manner, and I was much flattered when, having to go into Hazebrouck one day at the same time as I was taking the post there, she condescended to travel in my carriage. At Hazebrouck I waited for her to return and watched her thread her way through the many British soldiers on the platform who gazed admiringly upon her. Then, choosing the most conspicuous spot, I advanced, relieving her of her parcel, opened a carriage door and ushered her in, stepping in after her. This left the entire station gasping, for it was most unusual for a French (or Belgian) girl to openly accompany a British soldier anywhere in France : the priests in many places forbade it and it always led to gossip. The carriage-full of Tommies into which we stepped were equally envious and I felt as proud as could be. At Caestre, I carried her parcel home and went round next day for a cup of coffee. Alas ! a day or so later she saw me picking up orange peel on the railway line, dressed in fatigue uniform ; useless to pretend I was searching for a lost franc—she had discovered I was a rag-and-bone man ! She didn't seem pained or even surprised—she just looked through me and passed on. That was the end of my dream of Zoé and, incidentally, the end of my profession as a sanitary man. In sheer desperation I told Belcher I must have a change of work and I was about to help the cook prepare meals when the order came for me to go back to St. Omer and my last hope of recovering my self-respect in Caestre vanished for ever.

CHAPTER IX.

Re-Forming the Transport Section.

(*September–October*, 1915.)

Volunteers for the first-line transport—Detraining Kitchener's Army—First adventures with horses—Prisoner escort—The Battle of Loos—Driving lessons—With the L.R.B. Transport.

" WELL, Smithy, why don't you join the transport section ? " asked Chrisp one day while we were together at Caestre.

" I don't know anything about horses and, for another thing, I haven't thought about it," I answered.

It appeared that the regimental transport section, which was at present non-existent, might be re-formed shortly and owing to some twenty or more transport men having taken commissions they would soon be calling for volunteers to undergo a course of riding and driving, in order to make the numbers up to strength. Chrisp anticipated being made a lance-corporal shortly and seemed very pleased about it.

The attraction of being one of the transport men appeared to be that, however unpleasant the conditions of driving, however dangerous the road and to whatever time you stayed up in delivering the rations and ammunition, there was always cover of some sort to come back to when the job was finished, where an hour or so's sleep might be snatched in peace. This advantage was a very considerable one and, after recalling how I had loathed the roads at the Second Battle of Ypres and how I had pitied the men stuck up on horseback in the traffic blocks when I could rush for the ditch if necessary, I none the less came to the conclusion that it would be a good plan to try to join it. Trendell was of this opinion and he and I had become fast friends now. Harbord also announced his idea of volunteering. It was Chrisp who finally decided for us.

" I'm going to write to Sergt. Gordon (the transport sergeant)," said he, " and tell him that he simply *must* have you on the section on account of your laugh : it will send the fellows into hysteria. Not only that, but we're keen on parodies and haven't an accompanist for our concerts."

So, when the official list came round calling for volunteers and some of us put our names down, Trendell, Harbord and myself, having been specially mentioned privately by Chrisp, found ourselves selected to proceed to St. Omer to interview the transport officer, Capt. Russell. This was at the end of August, but it was another fortnight before the nineteen men were definitely chosen for the riding-course and, in the meantime, we were liable for the usual work that cropped up in the St. Omer headquarters camp.

We found here that during August many had left to take up their commissions : leave for the battalion had been stopped for four weeks now, so that those who, like myself, were waiting for their next leave in order to interview colonels saw the prospect of getting commissions soon growing more remote. When Thomson had applied for two days' leave in order to interview a C.O. who wanted to see him, he was told that " leave wasn't granted for that sort of thing ! " Now, however, an application had arrived for him, this being worked by " Lieut." Bourke of the 21st Middlesex, and after three evenings spent in celebrating his luck, he departed for England on the 7th of September. Poor Tommy ! it was the last we saw of him, as he was killed the following year but one. Wood, we heard, was getting on famously now. He had lain at death's door for a month at Le Treport, but had finally got on the road to recovery and was now enjoying himself at Reigate. Greensmith, another of the office staff, having now reached the eligible age, took a commission in the R.N.A.S. Whittle, after training in England, had gone to Malta, en route for the Dardanelles. Merrilees, I believe, was still in England, but expecting to sail for Egypt. Tyler, yet another of our office staff, was recovering from a shattered shoulder, received at Ypres. Everything seemed in a state of uncertainty and flux.

A new draft arrived from the 3rd Battalion, who were at once put on to doing guards and special training : our machine-gun section's preparations were well advanced : the transport was about to draw new horses and vehicles, and everything pointed to our being made up to strength as a fighting unit once more.

We learnt that Kitchener's Army, which had been coming out gradually for some time, enabling us to take over more line south of La Bassee and again south of Arras, was arriving steadily now, and for two days we saw an endless stream of infantry and artillery fresh out from home marching from the coast, through the outskirts of St. Omer and onwards to the front. If they were not going to relieve the Territorials, as we had once fondly hoped, they were at any rate going to adjust the balance on the Western Front and prevent our fighting against such odds a second time. Moreover, we heard that big guns were now beginning to appear and that we were accumulating ammunition for an offensive.

On the 10th we made a closer acquaintance of Kitchener's Army, for the L.R.B. were called upon to supply a detraining party for some of the 21st Division, which was about to arrive at Audruicq, a station between Boulogne and St. Omer, and, as there were not enough men at our camp to spare for the purpose without utilising the transport party, we were called upon to depart for Audruicq while we were still in doubt as to which of us would be retained for the course.

Audruicq was not far from St. Omer and possessed a siding suitable for the detraining of troops ; close to the station was the empty garage of a private house, which we made our billet, and the folk in the residence were most hospitable, being Belgian refugees of the best class who were temporarily living there. The town was an important depot of the reconstituted Belgian Army, who wore khaki uniforms with big

peaked caps and leather gaiters, a great improvement on their original
costume ; both Belgian soldiers and French inhabitants were most
obliging and before a day had passed we began to wish we had spent
the month of August here, instead of at Caestre. Being so near the
coast as this, we had to put up with taunts from troops in leave trains
passing by, who leant out of the windows and remarked, " You're
too far forward, mate." It was probably too early in the War to
justify the retort " We were in the trenches before you thought of
joining up," for no doubt practically all troops going on leave had
been out for at least six months.

For two days the detraining went on, trains arriving every four hours
with great regularity. We got warning of their approach so that,
while they steamed slowly through the station, we hopped on to the
trucks and started our work, knocking away the pieces of wood which
prevented the limbers, field-kitchens, guns, etc., from slipping about,
and unwinding the thick rope that passed round the spokes of their
wheels from one length of the train to the other. The trains stopped
just beyond the station, preparatory to shunting the vehicle part
into one line of the siding and the cattle-trucks containing the men
into another. Our task occupied the whole of this time, even working
as smartly as we could, as there were not enough of us for the job.
Then, having got to the siding, we rushed ramps up to the trucks and
either unloaded the vehicles or led terrified mules and horses down
the gangways. These brutes travelled eight in a truck, four on each
side, and they had become very restive and frightened. It was sometimes a difficult matter to induce them to walk down the ramp, especially
at night.

When the artillery arrived, a hundred people seemed to be giving
orders at once. The senior officers rushed up and down and bawled,
the subalterns all wanted to show how important they were, sergeant-
majors and sergeants gave fierce orders and swore volubly at the
drivers—in fact, all was bustle and confusion. They wished to detrain
in a totally different manner to that in which we had been instructed,
with the result that, while we were waiting with a ramp at one truck,
they would be cursing us for not being somewhere else. Many of
the drivers took possession of the ramps and carried on the work as
if we hadn't been there, so we promptly struck : we were not doing
it for pleasure and they appeared to know better than we did what
they wanted. At night, artillery officers once or twice flashed torches
in our faces as we came up to lead horses from the trucks and shouted,
" Who the blazes are these men ? " On one occasion we thought the
best thing to do would be to go back to our billet and sleep, which we
did : nobody missed us.

This was the first French place the 21st Division had seen. These
troops had arrived from England in most cases about twelve hours
before and had straightway been put into trains. One can imagine
the interest they evinced in their surroundings and the innumerable
questions they asked us as they stood about in the yard waiting to
march away. Not only was it the first time they had seen French
civilians, but regulations in regard to estaminets were new to them.
On the arrival of one train I saw two men dash off furtively to an
estaminet for some liquid refreshment, whence they returned most
disgusted to find that no British soldiers were served before 1 p.m.

It was amusing to see these North-countrymen of Kitchener's Army
going up to a stout old French civilian and saying :

" Well, 'oo's goin' ter win ? "

The old gentleman smiled benignly and ejaculated with some difficulty :

" I—not—understand."

" 'Oo's winnin' ? I says," shouted the exasperated questioner, at which the Frenchman merely smiled again.

" Oh, love-a-duck," was the comment, " can't the Froggies understand blinking English ? "

The impression created by these fresh troops was very good. Both the French and Belgians—not to mention ourselves—thought they were a tough lot of men and the sight of them was most cheering.

We only remained at Audruicq until the 14th, but on the morning of the last day I made a discovery which stood me in good stead on many subsequent occasions when temporarily penniless. I found that you touch a kind spot in a Frenchwoman's heart when you are nice to her children, and when rations are short and you have spent your last sou, it is politic to look round for some child to lavish your attentions upon ! Feeling peckish upon the day in question and having not a copper upon me, I spied through the window of a confectioner's shop a portly woman and a little daughter of about five, and straightaway entered with much bravado in the hope of getting something for nothing.

" Bonjour, madame," I said, with a profuse smile.

" Bonjour, monsieur," said the great big fat woman, standing with hands on hips, reminding me of a rather kindly Madame Defarge.

" Je n'ai pas de l'argent. J'ai fini mon dernier sou. Je n'achete rien. . . . Mais je vous ai vu et je pense que vous avez le visage le plus joli dans tout ce village——" (Collapse of Ma into fits of laughter.) " Oui, vous avez les yeux bleus et les dents blancs—" (arrival of a second daughter, aged thirteen) " —et j'aime beaucoup les yeux bleus. Je pars demain et je veux dire ' Adieu ' avant que je pars pour la guerre." (Much laughter from all.)

The little girl takes hold of my hand and wants to come to the station with me and I start talking to her. Mama's heart melts. The only souvenir I have to give away is a black button which I present to the daughter. At this Madame sends the girl for a pear and presents it to me. I protest volubly, but very soon eat it. After further conversation I am presented with a cake, which goes the same way ! On turning to go, there is much blubbering on the part of the little kid, but she is consoled when I give her a photo of a dog and goat show, just received from home, whereat Madame is so touched that she begs me to go in and say " Good-bye " to her husband. In the back room I find Pa with two girls and a boy engaged in making chocolate fondants. After one or two pointed remarks, I am asked to try a taste and they are remarkably good. When I eventually leave, everyone is in a good temper, scarcely realising that I have not spent a single sou, but that I am richer by a pear, a cake and a few fondants. So I determined never to despair if at any time I was " broke."

The evening of the 14th found us back at St. Omer, where we thought we were at last to be interviewed by the transport officer, preparatory to our riding course, but the new troops arriving from home were intent upon giving us no rest, so that the same detraining party was despatched the very next morning to Wizernes in order to meet the trains containing, I think, the 4th Canadian Division. When we arrived we found that we had been rationed with such a rotten piece of meat that our amateur cook declared that nothing would be ready for us until 5 o'clock. Even then it was practically uneatable and, since he had only one dixie, he could not make us tea. There had been an issue of pay on the previous evening and we bought ourselves a meal in the town.

It was fun detraining the Canadians, who had far less of the " Brasso" and dazzling appearance than Kitchener's men. They did not mind how they got the vehicles off the train or who gave orders, nor did they attempt to dress their mules by the right when they had got them in the yard. The men showed rather an inclination to explore the village and it was some time before they could be collected together to march off. We did not have much opportunity of studying their peculiarities, however, as the would-be-transport men were relieved the next day by some new draft fellows and we departed to St. Omer once again.

Captain Russell, the transport officer, was waiting to inspect us. He had weeded us out of a list of some eighty names and there were still a few to be rejected. He gave preference to those who had been all through the Second Battle of Ypres. Unfortunately West and Cooper, two " D " Company men, were rejected as being too heavy, but " Kimbo " Vallentine, my friend of recruits' days, was chosen, while the three names mentioned by Chrisp were put on the permanent list. So I found myself, on the 16th of September, definitely enrolled on the L.R.B. transport section, thus being thrown with a set of fellows who were to face everything that turned up for the next three and a half years, although, from one cause and another, several changes were to take place before the final phase of the War. There were a few men in the draft just out from home who had been through a transport course in England, who were admitted to the section, reducing to about thirteen the number of company-men selected, but one or two of the old transport hands welcomed the chance of going through a riding course and made our numbers up to twenty.

The training was to be a thorough one, under the direction of the warrant officer in charge of the A.S.C. at General Headquarters, a unit that probably had a higher standard of discipline and general turn-out than any other A.S.C. in France. Fortunately their camp was only a few hundred yards from ours, so that we could sleep in our own lines and go over for our lessons in between meals. We were to assist the A.S.C. drivers and learn all we could in the early morning, this being followed by riding lessons and lectures on wagons and harness.

18/9/15. " Our transport training began yesterday, when we got up at 5 a.m. and worked hard all day until nearly six o'clock at night. It is estimated that, if we go through this course for a month, those of us who are not shaken to atoms or laid out by horses will be quite efficient to take charge of some of the battalion's transport : the work will be fairly strenuous during this training.

" Of course, my knowledge of horses is extremely vague and, when I was introduced to my steed, I think I could have told you which was her head and which was her tail, and that is about all. I found subsequently that she also possessed hoofs which she introduced to me in a very forcible manner !

" I christened her ' Martha ' and, in my opinion, Martha was once a ' star ' turn at Sanger's Circus or Buffalo Bill's 'Wild West.'

As soon as I took her to have a drink, leading her by a rope, she broke into a canter, but I hung on grimly until she politely trod on one of my feet ; at this I swore hard and called Martha names until someone came to the rescue. My toes felt as if they had been crushed by a steam-roller. Before I took her to be watered, she had to be groomed : this consisted of brushing her hard for about three-quarters of an hour, although she was nice and clean within ten minutes. This operation takes place three times a day, and, if I were only half as clean as Martha, I should be happy. Martha's ticklish round the neck and tried to eat me every time the brush went near it. For breakfast she had hay and corn, also a piece of my coat, while her master ate bacon and horsehair, principally horsehair.

" Learning to mount and to put on a saddle came next, this being followed by a class of instruction in harness, which thoroughly bewildered us. There are dozens and dozens of different straps and buckles and links with unheard-of names which convey nothing to you, and all I can remember about the lesson is that there was a huge sergeant-major with a very red face glaring over me and shouting, ' What is the name of this ? ' and holding in his hand a silly bit of strap with a buckle on the end. I couldn't for the life of me distinguish it from an ordinary strap and nearly told him so, but it turned out to be the ' traces pieces leather with quick release,' so I thanked him kindly and said I'd make a note of it.

" After this we took the horses off to drink again, passing the L.R.B. camp en route, where the onlookers had many sarcastic remarks to make about their new transport. They roared with laughter just because I tried to push Martha a few feet to the right and all my efforts failed to move her an inch. Then she had some more grooming and another feed of hay and oats : you might include some sugar in the next parcel to relieve her monotonous diet.

" Directly after dinner the excitement began. By way of digesting our food, we saddled up and paraded immediately after our meal, ready for our riding-lesson. Then, having found a quiet spot, we got the order to stand by our horses, whereupon Martha started talking to the horse next door and the officer blamed ME ; and when I had to throw the reins over her head she lifted it so high that they stuck on her ear and remained there until I mounted. Of course, I tugged at them when I tried to clamber on her back, causing her to move forward, so that by the time I had dropped into the saddle she was half-way across the field, but by vigorous pulling at the reins I brought her back into position again somehow.

" Unfortunately our officer had a weak voice, so that I only heard what I had got to do to *start* the horse, while all the other remarks were lost in the wind. Well, we started off but there was soon quite a gap in front of me, although we only walked at first. I was at a loss as to what to do. I said ' Trot ' and ' Gee-up,' but I couldn't get her to hurry until the horse in front started getting skittish, and then Martha commenced quite a little circus jaunt. I have a faint recollection of being bumped up and down violently, clutching the saddle and finally seizing the reins and tugging hard. The officer had no sympathy to spare and actually

swore, not at Martha, but at me. I didn't discover the action
for making a horse trot until afterwards : you have to dig it with
your heels. Unfortunately I gave her a nice prod with them at
the critical moment when our officer had us at attention and was
addressing us. It started Martha off on a trot all on her own
and I had a most uncomfortable time getting her back to her
place ; even when she got there she insisted on standing with
her back to the officer and she simply wouldn't turn round, even
when I called her ' Martha.'

" Our exercises were naturally a bit mixed up, as it was the
first occasion, and the officer looked in vain for the leading horse
after we had been round a few times ; in fact he stopped us at
last and said that, if we went round once more, he didn't think
he'd be able to find his way out, so that ended the proceedings."

On the following day we rode a good deal without stirrups and
after that we got on to jumping, but in the evenings we felt somewhat
sore. We were now put into a special line of tents in the L.R.B. camp,
and rationed separately, so we were beginning to be recognised as
transport men at last, although we might not appear to be so when
carrying out such ridiculous antics in a neighbouring field. In a few
days we were issued with riding breeches which completed the illusion.
The remainder of the battalion were carrying on as usual, but they
were on the verge of being relieved in all their wayside stations and
formed into a fighting unit once again. Rumours to that effect were
very strong and now that still further drafts had arrived it was clear
that our return to the firing-line would not be long delayed.

Before this relief was effected, however, one great event happened
on the British front which should be mentioned at this point, and that
was the autumn " push " for which everyone had been waiting, in
other words, the Battle of Loos. For months we had been storing
ammunition for this great " push," having learnt our lesson from Neuve
Chapelle and Festubert, but our resources were not yet great enough
to give us that overwhelming superiority which we needed. We
had sufficient for an overwhelming bombardment on the morning
of September 25th and again on September 26th, but after that our
reserve stock was very seriously depleted. There was not sufficient
to carry on with equal intensity for an indefinite period and we had
to look carefully at our available supplies. The early morning bombardment sounded so clearly at St. Omer that we left off our work to
listen and our enthusiasm knew no bounds. Here at last was the
great offensive ! Kitchener's Army was at them ! We had been
keeping this up our sleeves all the time and now the German line would
be broken ! We almost danced for joy. Later we heard that the
village of Loos had been captured and the German line pierced on a
front of several miles in conjunction with the French on towards
Arras. We did not know that even now we had not nearly enough
big guns or high explosives nor had we accurately estimated the strength
of the German defences and his total available reserves.

On the 26th every available man had to leave the L.R.B. camp in
order to convey German prisoners to the base and they had to call
upon the twenty who were undergoing intensified riding course, as a
last resort, to the annoyance of the A.S.C. officer responsible for our
training. We were taken away from it, with apologies from Colonel
Bates, and assurances that we would be returned at the earliest possible
moment. Accordingly that evening found us at Chocques where

some thousand German prisoners were formed up in the station-yard. It was dark when we got there and we could only see their outlines by the light of the station lamps. This was the first time we had seen such numbers and the sight was, of course, a very inspiriting one. Acting on the principle that the riding-school detachment was not to be utilised if possible, and finding that there were more than enough guards for the prisoners on hand, the officer in charge arranged that we and several others should pass the night at Chocques and see whether there were any fresh batches next day. We were at the moment intensely disappointed over this, but heard afterwards that the Germans had such a deplorable odour about them that our guards, travelling in the same cattle-trucks with them, were only too glad to reach the base and hand over their charges. Those prisoners with whom our men got into conversation were perfectly confident that Germany would win the War : they were buoyed up by the gigantic successes against the Russians and the knowledge that, so soon as their Eastern Front had been disposed of, the Germans would transfer all their forces to the West. Their failure to reach Paris was a disappointment to them, but they thought it was only a matter of time.

After passing the night in a small camp beside the station we proceeded early next morning to Bethune, the big town behind La Bassee almost on the border of the great conflict that was going on amidst the slag-heaps and pit-shafts of Hulluch and Loos. We lay half the morning on the platform and then entered our billet—an old barn—within a stone's throw of the station. We could not leave the premises for long, in case anything turned up for us to do. However, we wandered out by turns and went to inspect the captured German guns which were drawn up in the market-place. The town was full of soldiers, principally divisions of Kitchener's Army, and we saw several wounded, some of whom hobbled down the road to the station. The sight of them brought tears to the eyes of many French girls and women, standing at the doors of their houses as they passed, and one girl brought out cups of hot coffee as fast as her sister could make them. We learnt from one and another that the battle was not such a success as we had hoped for : in fact it was a disappointment. We had gained one village and a piece of the surrounding country, but were finding it difficult to retain what we had captured and, indeed, had had to face incessant counter-attacks by strong forces. The attack was notable as being the first occasion on which the British had used gas in retaliation for the German use of it at the Ypres battle, and in those parts of the line where it was used our men went over the top wearing respirators. The effects, both of the gas and the preliminary bombardment, appeared to have been unequal and we received most glowing accounts from one wounded man while another was pessimistic. The original attack had been made with six divisions, and a couple of them were met by unbroken obstacles not far from their starting-point, the same trouble of Festubert repeated. The troops on the right had done much better, but had eventually been brought to a standstill, all units suffering very severely. At this juncture the 21st and 24th Divisions had been brought up, the former being that one we had recently detrained at Audruicq, and since all the wounded were cursing these poor troops unmercifully it is only fair to appreciate how these tired men arrived in the firing-line after forced marches, never having been under fire before. Without being told that they were being sent straight into battle they were rushed up with no meal to warm them, cold, hungry and fagged out, sent forward to the captured German trenches on the 25th in the middle of the night and plunged into the continued attack on unknown territory in the morning. The attack was made with the flank in the air, against unbroken wire and subject to a severe enfilade fire. They marched straight into a heavy German counter-attack and retired in some disorder. Poor wretches ! they should never have been put into the offensive, particularly when they were so inexperienced and knew nothing of France, let alone Hulluch and Loos and the general contour of the battlefield, which should have been known to all the storming troops. Needless to say, our losses had been very heavy and, in some units, absolutely appalling. On the evening of the 26th, when we had arrived at Chocques, the British line was already somewhat contracted, but on the morning of the 27th, when we were waiting in vain for prisoners at Bethune, the situation was still more critical. Early that day we were pushed off Fosse 8, the key to the whole of the captured position.

It is really beyond the province of these records to dwell further upon the fortunes of this glorious but unsatisfactory " push," since we had no part in it. Yet it was the biggest battle in which the British Army had yet been engaged and the fact should be noted before dismissing it in a page or so. Desultory fighting took place for weeks afterwards, but whatever deeds of heroism were accomplished, it could not be denied that our effort had merely resulted in the capture of one village and a few slag-heaps, and the entire army felt a keen disappointment at its outcome.

Having waited for a day or so for further prisoners who did not arrive, we were ordered back to St. Omer to continue our interrupted riding course, in which we made rapid progress, so that we were shortly put on to driving, although the long-rein " coach-and-four " type of driving such as the A.S.C. adopt was not to be our system on the regimental transport, where the " ride and drive " system was, of course, universal (that is, sitting on one horse and keeping the other animal " up to the scratch "). Nevertheless, it was most useful to learn the long-rein driving and it stood us in good stead on certain subsequent occasions.

10/10/15. " . . . We are having enjoyable times now and the more accustomed we become to the horses, the easier it is for us to avoid getting kicked or turned into a tasty hors d'œuvre for the horses' dinner. Though they never get a taste of us, however, they still show a strong inclination to gobble up our tunics if we have left them lying on the rope and they gnaw the rope itself into shreds. Martha is one of the worst offenders because she is very ticklish and gives vent to her feelings when she is being groomed, by gnawing her head-rope viciously : she also makes wanton attacks upon the unoffending horse next door. She can be quite docile when she likes and occasionally I have fondly imagined that she likes me because she has rubbed her face confidingly up and down my leg, but afterwards, when I've seen her doing exactly the same thing to a wooden post, it has dawned on me that she probably had a slight irritation and no affection at all. I always slap her to show my affection, but this is a very silly way of doing it, for the other day, when I gave her a terrific slap as a punishment for attacking her next door neighbour, she evidently took it as a sign of high approval and encouragement and straightway renewed her efforts, leaving me to nurse a tingling and very painful hand !

" Our riding and jumping lessons are most exciting and I will say that Martha turns up trumps when there is any jumping to be done. Nearly all the horses refuse the obstacles, some of them after much persuasion gingerly walk over them, but, fortunately for me, my mount heads straight for them. The first time I alighted on her neck, but since then I have managed it better, even without stirrups.

" Yesterday I went out driving a wagon, the official driver sitting beside me ready to catch the reins if they fell or seize them if I was heading for a ditch. I had not realised before how difficult it is to turn a corner and started to manipulate the first one when we had almost got past it, nearly colliding with a post. Presently we got on to cobble-stones and I longed to catch hold of the rail for safety, for it was a horrible wobbly little seat and I wondered what would happen if we came to a bump in the road. The next corner I took a trifle too soon and we took a slice off the pavement. The tracks which the wheels of the wagon made were very comical at first—they zigzagged across the road like a " wiggle-woggle " and the man beside me began to look a bit sea-sick, but presently I mastered the art of keeping them straight.

" There is only another fortnight's training now and we shall then join the battalion who are all together again, doing drill, cleaning rifles and polishing equipment all day long—doing everything, in fact, to make themselves as smart as when they left home. And when they're spick and span, with polished hat-badges and everything bright, they will be just in a fit state for some old officer to come along and say : ' They'll do fine for a winter in the trenches,' and off we shall have to go. I know them so well by now ! Polishing of equipment is so often the preliminary to departing to a place where it will show up when it isn't wanted to ! However, we have no right to make comments at present for we do not know really what will happen to us and this cleaning mania may, after all, be merely an effort to stimulate the brass polishing industry. The Army loves everything to look shiny and at (Caestre) I should not have been at all surprised to receive instructions to polish the railway lines with Brasso. . . ."

The battalion's training was taking place some five miles away, at a charming little place called Blendecques, where the various out-buildings in the grounds of a magnificent chateau afford billets for most of the unit. The transport section had the use of the palatial stables and lived in an empty house. Some thirty of the old section, with several new draft men, were already there when we joined them towards the end of the month ; some of the original 1914 horses, which had been sent away on the disbandment of the transport, had been recovered, but the bulk of the animals, together with vehicles, had yet to be drawn from a remount depot. The old A.S.C. warrant officer came over from St. Omer and gave us a lesson or two in the " ride and drive " system, without vehicles behind us, and on the strength of this tuition some of us were selected amongst the drivers who had to fetch the new animals and limbers from the depot. Much to the delight of everybody, the remounts proved to be horses, not mules, and they seemed to be a good looking contingent.

Now came the critical moment for the decision as to what work the new arrivals were to be given on the newly formed section and it would perhaps be as well, since this book will deal with first line transport work, to mention the different branches of that work.   Our section consisted of :—

    11 limber drivers, each with two horses (2 tools, 4 machine gun, 5 ammunition).

    2 water cart drivers, each with two horses.

    4 field kitchen drivers, each with two horses.

    1 mess cart driver, with one horse.

    1 medical cart driver, with one horse.

    11 grooms, each with one officer's charger (liable for brakesmen's, spare men's and other jobs).

about 10 pack-pony men, each with a pony.

    1 T.O.'s batman.

    2 cooks.

    2 wheelers.

    2 shoeing smiths.

    1 forage man and a few spare men.

    4 N.C.O.s (Sergt. Gordon, Corporal Simmonds, Lance-Corporals Chr:sp and Main).

It was originally rumoured that most of the newly-trained men were to be made drivers, but this caused such righteous indignation among the old hands who had been on this work since mobilisation that it was sensibly decided to appoint only about half a dozen of us to that post.   It was considered to be the post of honour and those who were given grooms' and other jobs felt disappointed at the time, Vallentine particularly.   There were many of the original men, however, who frankly averred that they would not have a driver's job for anything, as there was too much work attached to it.   Of the absolutely new arrivals, Trendell, Harbord, Cooper (a different Cooper to that in " D " Company), Barnett and myself were given pairs of horses, while Leach and Cornford from the 3rd Battalion also became drivers. Though the matter was thus compromised, as it were, it was clear that we were not looked upon with favour by the old transport men and our advent would probably have been equally unwelcome had we all been given pack-ponies and spare men's jobs.   There was no friction, merely a keeping-apart of the new and the old, as is inevitable in such cases, but no distinction was noticeable after a few months.

The transport section, as reconstituted, was comprised of a very decent set of fellows, practically all of whom were in offices in civilian life.   Solicitors', merchants', bank, Stock Exchange and other clerks formed the bulk of it, there being only one or two there who really had anything to do with horses before the War.   Being of the same social status as the transport officer and the N.C.O.s, who had in their turn been rankers on the same section, we did not suffer from that complete crushing of independence and iron discipline so much in vogue.   We were treated as gentlemen and could talk on friendly and equal terms with either Captain Russell or the N.C.O.s when not on parade.   Moreover, the bulk of the fellows could be relied upon to do their allotted work without continual supervision and criticism, so rampant in artillery horse-lines.   Rifles were inspected about once in two months and the only semblance of drill was the falling-in after " stables," when " dismiss " was accomplished with a smart click, a right-turn and a very smart salute.   Loathing army red-tape and drill as I did, I seemed to have fallen upon a sort of Paradise.   Trendell

" messed " with me and we met several men with whom we were able to come to closer friendship later. Two of these were friends of Trendell's, Hobson and Figg, and the latter, though not yet in the same mess, was destined to prove a real friend of mine, second to none. Conibeer, another future friend and companion in many pleasures and hardships, was little known to me then. The various individuals will be introduced into this narrative, as it proceeds, according to the circumstances in which they imprinted themselves on my memory and, since many of them will doubtless read this record, I hope that any remarks will be taken in good part.

CHAPTER X.

FRENCH FLANDERS.

(*November*, 1915.)

Last days at Blendecques—An unfortunate trek—Billets in Flanders—Short rations—My horses prove to be a dud pair—A typical picket—The year's events—More drivers' troubles—And some compensation.

ON my appointment to the position of driver, I was given charge of a pair of horses who had already been " christened " and entered into the sergeant's note-book as " Jack " and " Tar." The person responsible for this appellation was, I believe, an ex-company cook named Baker, and, knowing him as I do, it is wonderful to think the names were not more idiotic than that. They were described as a water-cart pair and I had visions of long spells of rest when the battalion was billeted where they would not need water-carts. This illusion was, however, quickly dispelled for it appeared that, although I should drive one of the two water-carts whenever there was a trek from one place to another, I should take my turn with all the other pairs to do whatever jobs were required when once we had settled in one spot.

We carried out much the same programme for " stables " as we had with the A.S.C., though ours was not so strict and laborious. The harness had to be kept clean and in a soft condition and the bits and stirrup-irons were supposed to be free from rust. Our duties lasted from 6.30 a.m. until 5 p.m. with intervals for meals, and about once a week it fell to everyone's lot to do a night picket with five other men, working in three shifts of four hours each, with two men on at each shift. I had one picket before leaving Blendecques when, having the good fortune to win the toss, I chose the first shift, which passed quite quickly. We were supposed to look round the horses continually, but a fellow known as Gunboat Smith (not the boxer !) was my companion and he initiated me into the mysteries of keeping picket according to his standard, which was none too conscientious. We sat down and wrote letters most of the time, enlivened by some hot cocoa made on the embers of the cook's fire, about eight o'clock. The sergeant came round after we had been on duty for some two hours and said two horses were loose in one of the stables. Fortunately, at that moment Gunboat had just set out on his first inspection of the horses that evening and he assured Sergt. Gordon that, having returned from that stable but ten minutes before, the horses in question must both have broken loose within the last second or so, so to speak. To this Gordon objected that they had finished up most of the feed of hay which had been deposited at the back of that stable for distribution amongst its eight horses by the second picket and must have been eating stolidly for an hour or more ! Gunboat's reply was inaudible.

We had a section concert before leaving Blendecques, the success of which was considered by a certain number of individuals to be much enhanced by the liberal supply of liquid refreshment provided in the form of a beer-barrel and many bottles of white wine, purchased for the occasion. The N.C.O.s and one or two others thought the supply had been rather too liberal and the candid remarks passed about certain individuals rather too forceful—consequently there was an address by Captain Russell the next day. Many were then suffering from splitting headaches, however, and it was almost superfluous to refer to the misconduct of the previous evening. The concert and its attendant celebrations were really symbolical of our farewell to lines of communications and the inauguration of the re-born section which, although much changed, was just recognisable at the end of the War, whereas, long before that time, the remainder of the battalion had lost every link with the 1st L.R.B. as we knew it in 1914-15.

Early in November we got orders to join the 3rd Division, which happened at that moment to be resting in the neighbourhood of Cassel and Steenvoorde (a few miles west of Poperinghe), and there was a two days' trek before us in order to reach their area. This applied to the transport section, but the companies were to travel in motor-buses, as they had done when coming down from Ypres. The change in our fortunes was not a popular one. Had we been returning to the 4th Division or to " Plug Street," or going to that ideal portion of the line south of Arras which the British had recently taken over from the French, where we heard that guns were not fired from one week to another, we should not have minded so much. But it was too bad of the authorities, we grumbled, to send us back to that infernal Flanders and to Ypres, of all places—for that was what it meant.

The move was a collection of misfortunes from beginning to end, starting when one limber broke down in the main street of Blendecques. Our route lay through Aire and Ebblinghem, and a short distance from the latter village we came to the first estaminet we had seen for some time with a Flemish name on it, instead of a French one. We were not in Belgium, but in that north-east corner of France, known as French Flanders. It came on to rain at the same moment and, in view of the evil reputation which the Flanders weather had gained by this time, it was a coincidence which could not fail to evoke derisive remarks from the troops. The rain continued steadily from now onwards, and by the time we reached our first night's halting-place—Hondeghem (close to Caestre)—it had developed into a deluge. Just as it was dark we drew up in a big field, erected horse-lines between two or three limbers, and gave the animals their well-earned feed. We were longing for our own deferred dinner, but it took the cooks nearly two hours to prepare it, as there was no shelter for them.

The picket had an unenviable vigil in the open field that night, as Flanders rain had set in with a vengeance, but, whereas they gave vent to their feelings throughout the night by their customary explosive language, the horses stored up their resentment until we started off in the morning. One or two drivers had some difficulty in starting and, just as my turn came to move off with the convoy, Tar, soaked through, cold and bad-tempered, simply refused to move. Neither coaxing nor whipping did any good and he finally sat down in the mud, so that eventually we had to bring to the rescue an extra pair of horses, who pulled the cart on to the road. They left us here to return to another jibbing pair and it was only with much persuasion that Jack and Tar could be induced to take the hill. The rain was coming down in sheets and my pair edged away from it to the side of the road, making it most difficult to drive them straight and to prevent my leg being broken against the limber-pole.

When we reached the top of the hill we waited for the remainder of the convoy which presently arrived with Gordon. He promptly led us straight on, in blissful ignorance of the fact that the first half of the convoy, under Captain Russell, had turned to the right. We discovered our mistake after about half an hour and then decided that we must right-about-turn. The road was narrow and the ditches beside it were deep. Tar jibbed once again, refused to turn round, reared up when flicked by Watkins' whip, and then backed the cart slowly but surely into the ditch. The language that floated around baffles description. Remarks were made about transport novices. Watkins—one of the other drivers—looked livid. Some dozen men, drivers and spares lent their weight to a drag rope while a stouter pair of horses was brought from one of the cookers, the united efforts resulting in the cart being at length pulled on to the road, turned in the right direction and handed over again to the faint-hearted water-cart pair and their unreliable driver.

Much to my joy, the next pair that tried to turn also gave vent to their feelings and ditched a field-kitchen on which one of the companies' dinners was cooking. Imagine the faces of the cooks when they saw their fire extinguished and the boiling water being tilted into the ditch ! The delay wasted about an hour and we eventually retraced our steps, feeling very sore with everyone and everything : the new-comers to the section were recalling the sunny reflections upon the nature of transport work which they had made under the ideal conditions at Blendecques.

Our destination was the typical Flemish village of Ryveldt, about two miles from Cassel and nine miles west of Poperinghe, thus putting the firing-line about sixteen miles away. The battalion were to be billeted in various big farms which were dotted round the neighbouring country, the one with the muddiest field being allotted to the transport section. The vanguard of our men had done most of the hard work in erecting the lines and were waiting for details of the first experience with the new drivers, the old hands naturally chuckling with glee at our shortcomings.

When we had disposed of our horses, we turned to see what billet had been provided for us and were directed to the farmhouse at the entrance to the field, one of those three-sided Flemish farmsteads, with an evil-smelling midden and refuse-heap in the centre. We were inclined to put on our gas-masks when making a detour of this foul heap and when we had to pass through a narrow passage with pig-sties on either side our inclinations almost amounted to resolutions. Up a rickety ladder we climbed, emerging in a low-roofed loft filled with straw, situated over the pig-sties. This was our billet. There was loud abuse of our dear Lance-Corporal Hurford, who acted as transport Q.M.S., for not having secured a better residence, but he merely grinned and informed us that the N.C.O.s' billet was a glorified dog-kennel. It was truly a pungent abode. The reek of the midden outside rivalled the stench from the pigs below and the noise made by the latter served to increase our disgust. Had the billet not had such a crazy means of exit it would have been more tolerable, but the yard and passage-way were extremely muddy and the step-ladder was not exactly an efficacious boot-scraper ; consequently, everybody who entered the loft with muddy boots attracted the straw to his feet and wandered about with great lumps of straw sticking out on either side of his boots. After a few days the loft was scattered with lumps of straw plastered with mud which had been conveyed there by this means.

At dusk we repaired to this dubious bedroom. Lighting candles and sticking them on our mess-tins, we determined to make ourselves as comfortable as possible and commenced to divest ourselves of some of our soaking wet clothes. Already several men had hung wet mackintoshes and overcoats on various nails and pieces of wire, so that before long my candle had been extinguished and my " bed " was well on the way to becoming a bath. I felt too exhausted to argue much ; besides, my own mackintosh was making a pool on Trendell's bed, while my overcoat was moistening a parcel of Leach's. The cooks were preparing a dixie of tea, which was the only thing we were living for at that moment, though an aching void within told us that food would also be very welcome. We had, however, already eaten our rations for that day and looked hungrily for the arrival of Hurford with the next day's supply, upon which we should have to draw in our extremity.

Presently our acting Q.M.S. arrived with a sack, which was hauled up into the loft with some difficulty, and proceeded to issue out the rations according to " messes." The average number in a " mess " was four, but some parties drew for two, some for three, others for five ; here and there one single man clamoured for his just proportion and, in desperation, Hurford brigaded two or three irreconcilables together and treated them as a mess, regardless of their feelings. The difficulty of splitting up cheese, tins of margarine, jam, etc., among such varying quantities can be imagined. This system of rationing on the transport lasted throughout the War and nearly drove poor Hurford off his head at times, especially when someone would suddenly change his mess and upset all his calculations. For convenience, Trendell and I rationed with Leach and Cornford, thus forming a temporary mess of four drivers.

With a sinking at heart we learnt that rations were very short, in fact, one loaf between five instead of one between three, as it should have been—with other issues cut down proportionately. There was no explanation of the shortage. One loaf between five meant two slices each for the whole of the next day and we always felt we could eat that amount for breakfast alone. Reluctantly we put the precious food aside for the morning—out of sight so that our mouths shouldn't water nor the mackintoshes drip upon it—relying upon a cup of tea and the next day's cheese issue to satisfy our hunger. It was a curious thing that when food was in abundance, as on lines of communication, we did not possess enormous appetites ; but when we had to allowance our half-slices of bread, estimating that we couldn't eat more now because we should want a little for the next meal, as we did—not only at Ryveldt but on many subsequent occasions—we seemed suddenly to have a craving for twice as much as we normally ate. Moreover,

H

appetites increased in cold weather and the food issue for the next few weeks particularly was very short indeed.

Next morning, having been called at 6.30 by the picket, the earliest risers went down to the kitchen of the farmhouse and endeavoured to purchase " tasses " of coffee before " stables." The family were not particularly amiable. Indeed, when one looked at the state in which the British troops had made their field, they could hardly be expected to fling themselves at our feet with gratitude. But they got paid well for it, for I saw their billeting book, which represented a considerable indebtedness mounting up for the British Government. Not satisfied with this, they profiteered in chicory and called it coffee, supplying it in very small cups, minus sugar and milk, for the modest sum of 10 centimes, representing some thousand per cent. profit. The buxom daughter and the lout of a son were rather repulsive creatures and we had no love for either of them ; they fitted in well with the general atmosphere of Flanders.

There was a water-trough in the yard, which could be filled from a slimy pond close by, a job for which Gerrish, Long and other pack-pony men were delegated. Near by, the cooks, Spinks and Waters, were doing their best to prepare breakfast under an outhouse with no wall upon the side facing the midden, which lay a couple of yards from the frizzling bacon. With a mug of tea in one hand and a plate of bacon in the other, it may be imagined how difficult it was to mount the ladder into the loft : yet there was nowhere below where we could have our meal, while in the open it was raining. The chief drawback to the step-ladder was that the man mounting it just before you would knock lumps of mud down into your teacup ; even if you waited until he was out of sight it was unsafe, for bits of straw came fluttering down into your plate of skilly as he scrambled away from the top of the trap-door. After a few meals had been spoilt in this way, some of the men betook themselves with their food to a cowshed and sat on milking stools and wheelbarrows.

Ablution and shaving were miserable tasks. The only place where one could perform the former was out in the rain, while shaving had to be conducted in the narrow alley-way between the pig-sties, looking-glasses being propped up on the ledge separating us from the swine. If shaving-brush or soap fell off the uneven bricks they went down into the mixture of mud and straw at our feet. A chilly draught blew along the passage, rendering shaves a painful operation, while every time anyone descended the ladder the toilet preparations had to be suspended to enable him to pass out into the yard.

Every day certain drivers had to go out on duty. The whole object of the section was to deliver food, water, fuel, post, ammunition and tools, machine-guns and ordnance to the battalion, no matter where they were, nor how long it took to reach them. That fact may be taken for granted throughout the whole of this narrative. Some driver was always out on duty, even if he were not actually concerned with " delivering the goods " ; he would be drawing clean clothing from the baths, fuel from the dump, water at the nearest refilling point, ordnance at the A.O.C. stores. There is no need to go into detail over this daily routine : over the difficulties of harnessing up horses with our racks a long way away : over the frequent complaints that the horses or harness were too dirty : over the hurried breakfasts and shaving operations when out on an early morning job.

My troubles with my pair of horses soon began to develop in earnest.

One day, when hooking into the water-cart, I foolishly left Tar on one side of the pole while I led Jack round to the other. In a minute he was kicking his heels in the air and away like the wind, dashing through the yard past the sergeants' billet and out into the road. Some were amused—others merely cynical. It was all right—it was only Aubrey Smith's horse !

Two or three mornings later I had a recurrence of the jibbing trouble. The water-cart, having sunk a little in the mud, required a horse with a little heart in him to start it. Tar waited for Jack to pull and, finding he could not move it, declined to make any effort. He finally sat down on his tail in the mud, nearly breaking both my leg and the pole. Macloughlin, our best driver, Bill White, a horse expert, and others of equal brilliance took my place and used the whip unmercifully, but fared no better than I. Finally, they changed the horses over and put the saddle on Tar. The sergeant mounted this time, wearing a sharp pair of spurs, and spent ten minutes in futile efforts to move him. This being of no avail, another pair was put on to the work. I was glad they had all failed, as it took some of the odium from me. This performance took place two or three times and it was disquieting to think I should have to rely on such a pair of horses " up the line."

A night or so after we arrived I had my first picket at Ryveldt. The six men who happened to be on divided themselves into couples, according to the particular companion they most desired or least detested for the night's vigil, and then tossed up for shifts. I won the second toss and chose the last shift, from 2.30 to 6.30 a.m., which should have given me an uninterrupted sleep of six hours, but the thought of turning out and sitting about in that dark cold field for four hours haunted my dreams and caused me to wake up half a dozen times imagining the picket was calling me. At length, about half-past one I could sleep no longer ; something told me the dreaded hour was approaching and several times I thought I heard the approach of the next picket. He came up at last, flashing his lamp into my face. Pulling an overcoat on and seizing a muffler, I groped my way out into the yard, followed by Trendell. It was a pitch dark night and we felt our way with some difficulty over the field to the horse-lines, yawning the while ; then we trudged round the horses with the off-going picket, checking their numbers by the light of the lamp. About a dozen of them were pegged out by themselves, owing to being kickers or precious beasts too good to be kicked, or mange-suspects or else rope-chewers, so it took about ten minutes to complete the round. Rain was falling and I asked the others if they had any shelter. They pointed to the heap of forage, covered by a piece of tarpaulin, informed us that—owing to a cracked glass in the lamp—the candles had been gutting, handed over a short piece that had got to last us until day-break, and then took themselves off to their " bed " in the loft.

Picket in an open field was very different from picket in the stables at Blendecques where, with a roof over one's head and something to sit on and little probability of disturbance among the horses, one could sit down and write letters or make cocoa by the light of a good lamp. Hardly had the sounds of the departing shift's footfalls in the mud died away, than there was an outbreak of kicking farther down the lines. If in the morning it was found that bad kicking had been going on, the picket were held to blame and charges of having been asleep were imputed, so that at the sound of the outburst we groped our way among the various pack-saddles and piles of this, that and

the other strewn about the ground and endeavoured to locate the
disturbance. However, by this time all was quiet ; the miscreants
stood looking perfectly innocent. It reminded me of a class-room at
school where an uproar would cease upon the sudden approach of the
headmaster. We could only shout a few bullying remarks to make
them cower, after which outburst we returned to the forage.

About half-way through the picket, when going round counting
the horses for the third time, I found there was one missing : by now
I was using a candle which I had found in my overcoat pocket. Trendell
came round again with me, but we disagreed as to the total, so had to
tramp round once more. Yes, there was surely one less than when
we had taken over : the next thing to do was to find the missing horse.
We were in a large field which was not so muddy at this stage that
all traces of grass had disappeared and, indeed, there was a considerable
stretch of meadow on one side. We made for this and did not have to
wait long before we heard a masticating sound and saw a form loom
up out of the blackness. It was the pony " Zonnebeke," trailing
round with him, on the end of a rope, his picketing-peg, which the
softness of the earth had enabled him to pull up with ease. As we
approached he quickened his step and broke into a trot when we closed
in upon either side. Stalking horses in a muddy field on a pitch black
night would have been a tedious job if the hunt had been a short one,
but since the greater part of our picket was monopolised in this manner,
it was enough to try the patience of Job. No wonder the language on
the transport was more flowery than in the companies ! We stumbled
and the lamp went out : we ran into pegged-out horses unawares and
nearly got kicked into the middle of next week : we chased " Zonne "
round and round, not giving him any rest lest he eat too much wet
grass and die of colic ; and, finally, when we had tied the runaway to
a limber, we returned to the forage to find one horse with his head
buried in a sack of oats and another loose one rapidly devouring the
next day's hay issue.

It seemed as if daylight would never come, and it was, as a matter of
fact, still almost dark when we called the men in the loft at 6.30 that
morning. reminding them again twenty minutes later that " stables "
were at seven. It was rather good to be up and watch all the others
stirring in their sleep dreading the thought of getting up ! As for the
two men who had turned in for the first time at 2.30, we really pitied
them. They were like two logs of wood and had to be dragged out of
bed when the whistle went.

In the evenings there was nowhere of interest to go and nothing to
do. The village was a poky little place with a few estaminets and one
mingy shop where you could get scarcely anything to eat. Supper
was an impossibility : there was nothing to eat for it and food was
unprocurable at any price. Two men who wrote home stating that
rations were short had their letters confiscated by Captain Russell ;
even when writing for parcels our requests had to be put in a most
diplomatic way.

Nothing changed one's spirits from buoyancy to utter despondency
or vice versa quicker than a shortage or surfeit of rations. Given a
shortage and inability to buy food, one's outlook on the War changed
immediately. Add to this grievance an existence in perpetual rain
and mud and a billet such as ours was and it can be imagined that it
would require a very real success to make us joyful. As a matter
of fact, the war news was at this time none too inspiring and it was

with pangs of disappointment that we looked back on the year's work and then contemplated a second winter in this benighted land.

What had we to show for our efforts up to the present ? While the German efforts at Ypres had failed, our own attempts to break the German line had been no more successful. Neuve Chapelle, Festubert and Loos had all been disappointments. Foch had twice attempted to capture the Vimy Ridge and had failed. The French offensive in Champagne had fizzled out. On this Western Front, the armies faced one another in practically the same trenches they had first occupied a year before.

Very different was the state of affairs on the Russian Front. There the Germans had been sweeping all before them ever since April, capturing hundreds of guns and hundreds of thousands of prisoners. Poland was in their hands, Galicia re-occupied. The tragic Dardanelles expedition, which—though keeping the Turks occupied—had drawn from the Western Front forces and munitions badly needed there, was a pronounced failure. Kitchener had gone to investigate in Gallipoli and we expected at any time to hear that we had withdrawn from the peninsula : this was not actually effected until January 8th. Then we were witnessing the crushing of Serbia. Bulgaria had joined our enemies on October 4th. Greece had proved unreliable and seemed partly hostile. We had landed forces at Salonika, which meant another " side-show " for us, with its incessant demand for reinforcements, artillery and ammunition. As a matter of fact, our division very nearly got orders to proceed to Salonika, while others actually left France for that theatre of war.

On the other hand, we felt that we should see the pendulum swing the other way on our front in 1916, for we had actually witnessed the arrival of these new British divisions we had heard so much about and they were still, no doubt, detraining. What we had not seen was heavy artillery, but we knew that this too must come to hand next year, in view of Mr. Lloyd George's efforts at home. The naval blockade had been tightened and Germany was assuredly beginning to feel the pinch.

Figg, Trendell and I frequently discussed these things as we sat on picket or went for a walk along the dark Winnezeele Road before returning to the first floor of the pig-sty to sleep. We were on high ground and could see the flares rise, fifteen to eighteen miles away, marking the firing-line which we should see once again in a week or so. The 3rd Division had held the south-eastern corner of the Ypres salient, near St. Eloi, when in the line, and we understood they were returning to the same place when their short rest was over. What would the transport work be like up there ? What would 1916 bring forth ? Should we have open fighting, in which we should encounter ambushes or have to leave our horses and engage in a bayonet charge ? It was impossible to conceive what the next year had in store for us : we could only work our way steadily through our second winter in France and trust to luck.

When our transport field became really too impossible, owing to the churning of mud by the horses, we shifted our lines to a meadow on the other side of the road, where conditions were more tolerable. I fixed up a pole between two trees as a harness rack and brought my pair to the spot whenever I wished to harness them, since there was grass at hand and they made no attempt to quit the spot. However, one day a certain Watkins, who had recently received a bottle of pickles as a reward for clean harness, had his leather-work spread out upon the ground after an hour or so's hard work at washing and greasing it : when my back was turned and Watkins was temporarily absent, Jack got down and rolled, first in the mud and then on top of all Watkins' clean harness. A veil may be drawn over what the driver said when he surveyed the damage, but I gathered that his opinion of the new drivers upon the transport section was not a high one and that, if he had his way, certain changes would be made. I was beginning to wish they might, myself. Why should I, who had rapidly acquired the reputation of having the dirtiest harness upon the section, also be burdened with a pair of horses that Macloughlin " wouldn't touch with the end of a barge-pole " ?

They surpassed themselves on the occasion of a great march-past which was to be undertaken by the whole of the 8th Brigade, before the Divisional General. We had to look as " posh " as possible and spent days in making the vehicles and everything else look smart. At the critical moment when the transport section was leaving the lines in order to take its place behind the companies in the great column of route, Tar had conscientious objections to the whole affair and refused to move. Curses and taunts from everybody. The sergeant arrives with a whip. Corporal Chrisp arrives with a whip. Several spare-men come up. Captain Russell, horribly annoyed, canters up with a suitable epithet at the tip of his tongue : on arrival, he lets it forth. Tar collapses and sits on my clean harness in the mud. Much confusion. The cookers draw out and leave me, looking with disgust upon the snorting beast and the ruined breeching. When the last vehicle has disappeared Simmonds rides back.

" You'd better unhook and bring them along as a spare pair," says he.

So Jack and Tar are led off in shame by a driver in disgrace, leaving a beautifully cleaned and painted water-cart to mind the field until our return.

Few other incidents occurred during our week or so's stay in this village. One night C Company burnt their billet down and the blazing barn must have been visible from far beyond the German lines. This occurrence thoroughly alarmed the proprietress of our farmhouse and she started to make herself objectionable. Some of us had moved into another loft of straw, this time over a cow-shed, and one day the woman came up the step-ladder and saw Wiskar using a Primus-stove. Uttering a piercing shriek and jabbering in a high-pitched voice, she pounced upon the stove before the astonished Wiskar was aware of it, bore it down the ladder and carried it into the room where Captain Russell and the Quartermaster, Mr. Petersen, were billeted. She hoped to secure the prompt punishment of the offender, but received instead a severe lecture from the officers upon the sanctity of property and her heinous crime in running off with the belongings of a British soldier. There was enmity between us and the household after that. One groom gave vent to his feelings by throwing stones at the old woman's pigs, but this was rather a cruel form of warfare.

Our moving orders came towards the end of the month and it was a positive relief to feel we were going to the firing-line again, after such an unpleasant experience of rest billets. We packed our vehicles and kits with alacrity. Severe limitations were placed upon the extent of the drivers' kits, which in some instances had been found sufficient to fill half a limber. A driver's pack might be carried, but his blanket must be rolled with the others and taken by lorry. No other private kit was permitted, but the rule was made only to be broken. Every man was entitled to carry his rations, but owing to the difficulty of splitting them up, each mess put its food in a nosebag, which further contained any parcels from home and sometimes became unwieldy. Then every driver and groom was allowed to carry his grooming and harness-cleaning kit on the limbers. This also was put in nosebags or sacks, which became convenient receptacles for extra underclothing (professedly harness rag), mufflers or sweaters. Not content with this, each driver wore his overcoat with his pockets stuffed out and, instead of leaving the space for it in his pack, as company-men had to do, crammed his valise with personal effects so that it would have been impossible to march with it. His haversack would prove too heavy for his liking after the first halt and this, too, would disappear under the limber-cover ; some men had two haversacks. His mackintosh was fastened to his saddle—except in Flanders when it was usually worn; underneath the saddle was an extra blanket as well as the saddle one.

Altogether, each driver carried about twice as much kit as he ought, but to offset this he discarded his bayonet. Since we wore bandoliers we had nowhere to fix our bayonets and, as nobody ever looked at them, we decided to lose them. Most people had already done so, but it was a few weeks before I cast mine into a pond at Poperinghe. The N.C.O.s searched the limbers up to the very moment of our departure, but neither on this nor on any subsequent occasion during the War were they really successful in bringing the volume of personal belongings down to the regulation quantity. We were becoming " old soldiers " and " old soldiers " are really as adept at " losing " their own kit—temporarily—as they are at winning other people's property.

To my mind this was one of the great attractions of being a driver, since grooms and spare and pack-pony men with one horse naturally could not transgress to the same extent. Drivers would be most indignant at a groom suggesting the smuggling of some article or other unless that groom happened to be a member of their mess. For we became scrupulously careful to avoid our poor horses being burdened with excessive weights—when once our own pantechnicon-load was on board !

On that trek from Ryveldt we had sufficient surplus stores to fill two motor lorries, which had to be lent to us for the move—and we were supposed to be a self-contained, mobile unit !

CHAPTER XI.

YPRES AGAIN.

(*December, 1915–January, 1916.*)

Poperinghe—Taking rations " up the line "—A field of mud—First line transport work—A bombing raid—More leave—Building better quarters—Another limber journey—Exit Flanders.

OUR route to Poperinghe lay through Watou and we consequently approached the town from due west, instead of by the Hazelbrouck-Poperinghe road which we knew of old. For miles before we reached our destination there was a considerable amount of traffic on the road, a continuous stream passing in the opposite direction pointing to the relief of another division. Lorries passed between the two lines of convoys, spurting out mud and shaking themselves almost to pieces on the uneven surface of the much-used highway. Even this important road was in a very bad condition, having had many months of hard wear with heavy transport.

Very different were the back areas to what they had been in April. You could now tell you were approaching the battle zone some ten miles from the trenches, for huts and horse-lines, mobile veterinary sections and divisional dumps of various kinds occupied most of the billets and fields between Watou and Poperinghe. Soon we passed a signpost reading " Poperinghe : 2 kilos " and then, looming up over the crest of a small rise, we espied a church tower which called back memories. I recalled that tower distinctly ; we had seen it on our first visit to Poperinghe and again on that celebrated motor-bus ride. Here was that town once again and I remember the driver in front of me turning and saying, " Poperinghe ! " in a tone of awe.

When the town itself hove into view, however, there was nothing very awesome about it. On the outskirts there were a few rough shacks in which refugees were making a home and a living, one and all offering to sell coffee, eggs, chocolate and biscuits to the troops. We drew into a field on the right which had been allotted to us quite close to the main road through the town. Our billet was an empty building in the western end of Poperinghe, some two minutes' walk from the horse-lines, while the battalion was also accommodated near at hand.

One of the first things we enquired was whether the Germans still sent big shells over into the town, but we learnt that the only " strafeing " that was experienced was in the neighbourhood of the station. They seemed rather fond of shelling it, but as it was nearly a mile away from us, we thought we should be able to sleep quietly in our beds !

The town was comparatively full of troops. Apart from birds of passage such as ourselves, there were hospitals, concert parties, ordnance and salvage depots, and headquarters of all kinds. At the shops we could buy any extra food we required—at a price—and there were dozens of estaminets where even the thirstiest could get their fill. Some large emporiums were still carrying on business, and next to a house with its first floor kissing the street or a shop with shutters covering its broken windows you would find a first-class stationers or a picture shop where a little plaster off the walls and a shielding of lights were the only indication that there was anything unusual abroad.

We were only here for a day or so, for the battalion promptly made arrangements for taking over a muddy, miserable section of the line near St. Eloi. Here, as in other parts of the line, they would be overlooked from the German positions and it seemed pretty certain from all accounts that the beanfeasting of the previous winter at Ploegsteert would not be repeated.

On the afternoon when the battalion marched up to the trenches some half a dozen limbers were told off to accompany them, carrying rations, tools, &c., while the remainder of the transport was to trek to Reninghulst, a few miles nearer the line, but to the south, and pitch its horse-lines in a field there. The ration convoy was to make its way back from the line and discover the field as best it might in the darkness. Captain Russell, with Corporal Simmonds as N.C.O., set off with the six limbers about 3 o'clock, one of which I was driving, but the actual departure was postponed a few minutes owing to Tar deliberately walking backwards during a brief halt on the road and pitching the rear-half of my limber into a deep ditch beside me. Result : dragropes and eight men required to recover it, much cursing about Tar and his driver, and a pitying glance from the T.O. However, nothing untoward occurred after this and we followed the companies up the road to Reninghulst, feeling very sorry for the men having to carry their bulky packs. Both the road to Reninghulst and that we took after passing through the village were lined with tall poplars, as is usual in Flanders, and the muddy fields and isolated farmhouses and estaminets brought to mind an almost identical panorama in the same vicinity last April. Some of the fields were used for horse-lines and many contained huts and tents, intersected by numerous duckboards to keep the troops out of the morass of mud. Battalions resting in these atrocious " camps " after spells in the trenches, were drawing hot tea from their cook-houses as we passed, making our mouths water considerably. All I had to sustain me was a packet of chocolate and an Army biscuit.

At length we came to the road that runs south-east from Vlamertinghe to St. Eloi and the battalion proceeded ahead in companies while the transport halted until dusk, as the Germans held all the high ground, and from Hill 60 and the Messines Ridge the whole of the country for miles behind our lines could be observed. When darkness fell, we resumed our journey, Captain Russell leading the way, with my limber at the head of the vehicles in the immediate rear. Some little distance up this road the T.O. went into a house on the right to ascertain definitely our bearings, leaving word with me to " keep straight on."

This was a simple enough order to execute, but after a time I began to wonder when he would turn up again. We came to a main-road with a building at the corner, later found to be the famous " Café Belge," and crossed it. An Indian passed us on horseback, though what an Indian was doing in that part of the line I could not understand, and presently artillery limbers splashed by in the opposite direction. We were on a narrow road with a piece of " pavé " in the middle and very thick mud on either side, but we could see nothing in the darkness unless a flare went up, which happened frequently about two miles ahead of us and somewhat nearer on the right. It was the first time we had been so near the firing-line for over six months and it gave us an old-time feeling to be so near the flares once more. Going up this lane we were close to some of our own guns, but there was not much firing ; we could only trace their whereabouts by the artillery limbers and various ill-concealed lights in the fields to either side of us.

A little farther on we came to another cross-road at which there was the wreck of a village. I thought it might be Voormezeele, our destination, and wondered whether we ought to stop, but the flares still seemed a good way away and there was no reply from L.R.B. men when I continually shouted, " Are you the L.R.B ? " This tiny village was actually " Kruisstraathoek," an imposing name for such a small group of ruins : it lay on the Ypres-Kemmel road. On either side we could just make out reserve trenches with water in them, mazes of barbed wire. graveyards and lonely-looking pools of water with a couple of willow-trees beside them, the whole surroundings being very eerie. The flare-lights revealed some buildings a short distance ahead and a little light-railway-line beside the road, intended for pushing small trucks along, but rendered useless in several places by direct hits from shells.

Word came up from the rear of the column :

" Where are you taking us to ? "

" Straight on," I replied, but with a few qualms as to whether we were really right. Captain Russell had left us two miles back and the others possibly thought he was leading them all this while. I heaved a sigh of relief when, in the village of Voormezeele, a friendly answer came in reply to my enquiries for the L.R.B., and I learnt that head-quarters were in the place somewhere, but our further progress was prevented by the road forking to right and left. It was easy enough to keep straight on when there were no fork roads, but we obviously had to halt now. We looked around us. There were several houses in a tolerable state here ; on our left were the remains of a churchyard, with broken railings hanging over the pavement. Parties of infantry passed in various directions, some of them plodding back along our road, having been relieved from the trenches which, we were told, were eight hundred yards from this spot, at St. Eloi.

Someone had just volunteered to direct me to headquarters when Captain Russell appeared with Simmonds and led the convoy down the left fork road where an overhead wire lifted his hat off in the mud and had to be raised by each successive driver. There were two such wires in this village and they were always heralded by the shout, " Wire," from the foremost driver. A hundred yards along here we halted and dismounted while parties of men arrived to unload the limbers. We were glad to get off our horses and I must say that I felt particularly glad to be on the ground again. It was the first time I had ever driven up to the firing-line and on a horse's back it seemed such an exposed position for any enemy missiles that *might* find their way along the road. It was also a relief to get a short respite from the strain of peering into the darkness, endeavouring to dodge big shell-holes. The horses stood perfectly still, their ears stuck at absurd angles, their eyes perhaps a trifle frightened. No shells came over and everything was quiet except for a distant gun and the sounds of the unloading party as they came up and marched away with shovels and sandbags.

The surroundings were typical of those of a village a little way behind the trenches. Half-shielded electric torches flashed here and there as officers tried to find their way or Q.M.S.s tried to discover the rum. The flares revealed a sluggish stream on the right, the Bellaardbeek, over which stunted and shattered trees were hanging. In the ruins were dressing-stations, dumps and headquarters of the pioneers, signallers and so on, the entrances being covered by sacks or ground-sheets which, when lifted, revealed several huddled-up forms within, lighted by candles and possibly warmed by a coke brazier. As I paced up and down by my limber, I munched my biscuit and longed for some supper and a hot drink. A sip of rum from a bottle Simmonds had carried for our benefit, however, brought a little warmth to our veins.

When everything was unloaded we turned round and set off with Simmonds on our return journey. This time we had to give way to traffic coming in the direction of the trenches, since loaded limbers were liable to sink up to their axles if once they slipped off the " pavé," while empty vehicles could dash through the thick mud at the side. In and out of holes we went, sometimes going up on to the light-railway line, and at others nearly riding over infantry, of whose presence we were only aware when we were right upon them. The ride back was mono-tonous. Occasional convoys passed us on the way to the firing-line, artillery columns overtook us on our homeward route : artillery were allowed to trot, whereas infantry transports always were strictly forbidden to, except in justifiable circumstances. The desire to get home and go to sleep did not constitute such circumstances in the eyes of the Army.

How we found our new transport lines, I do not know. Simmonds had an idea where they were and continually shouted " L.R.B." until at last a picket-lamp moved in answer to our call and in a field on the right we distinguished a line of horses squelching in mud. Having drawn our limbers up a short distance away, we unhooked the traces and led the poor beasts to a portion of the line that had been reserved for them. We were treading in liquid mud and the field promised to be worse than the Ryveldt one. Having found a mackintosh sheet that was not mine, I dumped all my harness in an empty limber, since there was apparently no place for it, covered it over with the sheet, leaving to the blessed to-morrow all thoughts of building a rack and washing the leather-work. The horses were sending mud in all directions in their frantic pawing for food and at the cost of a face covered with dirty slime I reached Jack and Tar with the measly issue of hay that was left for them.

We then asked if there was any hot tea for us. No, the picket had definite orders not to touch the cook's scanty supply of fuel, else there would be no breakfast in the morning. Profuse swearing, relieved only by the echo of a limber passing down the road ! Was there anything to eat ? No, but our respective " messes " had had the following day's rations issued to them which we would find in the tents, but the picket

advised us not to touch them as the bread issue was very small.   More
cursing, tempered, in my case, by the knowledge that I had the remains
of a parcel in my valise which Trendell had carried to the camp on his
limber since it was not allowed on the ration wagon.   I fumbled in
the darkness for his S.A.A. limber and untied the covers of one after
another, but the pack was nowhere to be found ; evidently Trendell
had taken it to the tent with him.

The next thing was to find the tents.   There were five or six of
them, with a duckboard running along in front, reserved for transport,
headquarters (quartermaster-sergeants. storemen, company cooks, etc.)
occupying the remainder.   Owing to the difficulty of finding the
whereabouts of our various messes, who, of course, always slept in the
same tents, there were two tents allotted on this evening for the drivers
who got back from the line. and we could " sort ourselves out in the
morning." So we turned in these without parcels and some of us
minus valises. only too glad to drop off to sleep anywhere to be critical
of the hard and uneven floor-boards that had been provided.   Driving
up to the firing-line, even given complete absence of hostile shelling,
was a more trying and tiring experience than I had imagined.

Next morning, when we awoke, it was pouring with rain.   In places
the water was coming through the canvas and our blankets were
wet.   Outside it was dismal and wretched.   The field was a sea of
mud.   In order to reach our horses to take them to water we had to
step off the duckboard into a mass of literally liquid mud.   On this
morning it was not very deep, but since it rained without cessation
for the next week and the horses churned up the soil every time they
moved to and from the lines, it can be pictured what a morass had
developed after a day or so.   The authorities had been so convinced
that our September " Push " was going to alter the whole position of
the firing-line that they had not taken the first step towards building
stables in this quarter.   The transports and artillery of some twenty
to thirty British divisions were left, for the most part, without overhead cover or standing for their horses until the second winter of the
War had well set in : and then, under pressure, the authorities thought
about it and sanctioned building stables.

Much was written about mud during the War and I have seen many
realistic photographs of it.   But in four and a half years we never saw
such a picture of misery as was that open field on top of the hill by
Reninghulst Mill in December, 1915.   Since such an abode never fell
to our lot again, there is perhaps some justification for dwelling a little
upon our troubles there.   After the fifth day Leach, who had hitherto
written home a glowing account of life at the front, received a letter
saying : " So glad you are enjoying yourself out there."   In his state
of mind, amidst those appalling surroundings, he promptly sat down
and wrote home the truth !   I only gave vent to my feelings upon the
fourth day :

2/12/15.   " It is really wonderful to find some dry paper to
write on, considering everything else I possess is wet and muddy,
with the exception of my shirt.   You would think that with waterproof boots, leggings, overcoat and mackintosh on we should be
as dry as gunpowder, but actually the more things you put on the
more you get wet.   You see, from the moment we set foot outside
our tent we are treading in sloshy mud, which comes halfway
up to our knees, mud that is more water than otherwise and
spurts out in all directions as you squelch along : mud which looks

like one vast morass of slime and covers up treacherous big holes, down which your leg disappears : mud in which everything is sinking down more and more every day.

" Leggings do not prevent mud and water getting into the boots if you sink in ten inches or so, especially when the very leggings are so saturated when you put them on that they are like so much brown paper. As the boots are sopping wet to start the day with, it doesn't matter very much. What will no doubt be news to you is that your mackintosh and overcoat get saturated with mud, *both inside and out,* and your breeches are a sloppy mess and soaked through nearly to the top. The mac. and great-coat peel off one another like sticking-plaster and beneath them you are in as big a mess as if you hadn't worn them.

" You turn out and wade through this sea, with rain coming down, and visit your poor horses, who are stuck fast. You undo their head-ropes, all soaked with the sloppy mud : the ends are frayed and they flick a stream of mud into your face. After an effort you get the horses out and take them for a short walk, ending up at a stream, where you water them. Then you enter the morass again, where their hoofs splash your mackintosh right up to the neck. You tie them up and get a spray of mud again, put on their nosebags—which are more like wet mud swabs—and receive biffs in the face with them, leaving you with a face and neck of Flanders soil. Then you wade back and fall in to be dismissed, enter the tent and flop down somewhere—there are not many dry spots to choose—waiting for breakfast to be ready. You look in vain for a clean plate and, selecting the least dirty one, proceed to line up in a queue for your tea and bacon, standing a foot deep in mud and rained upon hard all the time.

" After breakfast you do your best to remove some of the mud on your face, but without proper washing arrangements this is a somewhat difficult matter. At nine o'clock it has probably left off raining for the moment and we set forth again to saddle up the horses for exercise. To do this, we first remove the horse-rugs, great heavy things which are quite a respectable weight to lift when walking on hard ground, let alone in such a field as this when the rugs themselves are sodden. The tabs and cords trail in the mud : you tread on them and probably drop your load. In stooping to pick it up your mac. and coat have a new mud bath, both inside and out, just to keep them wet and heavy. You get the saddle blanket which, needless to say, is dripping wet from the day before, and the saddle, which is caked with mud, and a pair of nice red rusty bits, and put these on your animals, finally filing out on to the road for a two hours' walk and trot. This is the best part of the day's routine.

" Midday ' stables ' mean, of course, a continual standing in and trudging through mud and it is such a difficult matter to extricate your feet that nearly everybody is suffering from sore heels, for the mud seems to drag the leather of the boots so that a ridge forms about an inch up the heel. You come in at dinner-time in an even bigger mess than before. Some of you have to leave for the trenches with rations and fuel limbers in the afternoon, which will return about ten o'clock at night. If you are luckier you possibly have to go out with a limber to a coal-dump or the brigade post-office : in either case you turn out soon, after a plateful of skilly, to put your harness on. Squelch, squelch, squelch go your socks. It may be raining, but off the horse-rugs have to come again ; you put them on some turnips—the driest spot. Then you lead your horses up to a limber, tie them up with their sopping head-ropes and carry your harness across to them, piece by piece. To hook in, you back one horse each side of the limber-pole and then, plunging your hands into the deep morass where you think the end of the pole may be, retrieve both pole and pole-bar from their submerged resting-place, lifting them up with the greatest difficulty. Harnessing up, hooking in, getting the horses' feeds ready to take with you, putting on your leg-iron, etc., take anything up to three-quarters of an hour under these conditions. Then you start off and, although the knees of your breeches feel wet and your hands are in a nice old state, you are glad at last to have your feet out of the mire. You probably get back after tea-time, in the dark, unharness, water the horses, search for the blankets, tie the horses on the line, give them their nosebags and finally flop into the tent again. It may be after six o'clock when you've finished tea and then you take off leggings, boots and socks, extracting from the latter two articles anything up to half a cupful of water. You remove what wet clothes you can and, putting down newspaper and blanket under you, proceed to scrape mud off your garments. However, they are quite wet when you put them on in the morning again. There is no cook-house to dry them in, our cooks using one of the companies' field-kitchens in the open field. The battalion is coming out of the trenches on Monday, when we shall leave this benighted spot and proceed to some other field (near Poperinghe). I hope we shall not return. . . ."

On the eighth day at Reninghulst I remained behind in the transport field with my limber, when the remainder of the section departed to their new lines, in order to pick up some stores, and it was amusing to watch poor Mr. Petersen, the quartermaster, going round the empty tents and observing how much equipment of all kinds had been left behind, almost submerged in the mud. Mess-tin lids, bayonets, spare pieces of harness and such things, which he knew we should be indenting for shortly, were here in abundance, peeping through the soil. Petersen shook his head sadly and passed on.

The new lines were comparatively dry, situated in a field on the outskirts of Poperinghe, while the section was split up into two billets, one close to the field and the other at the very edge of the town, some five minutes' walk from the horses. Both billets were barns and meant Heaven to us after our recent experiences. Trendell and I were billeted in the farther barn, along with Kimbo Vallentine and many other new members of the section. On the other side of the road was an estaminet, where the occupants were very kindly people who allowed us to have our meals at the tables, unknown to the military police, and washed up all our goods and chattels afterwards.

In the evenings there was plenty of singing and merrymaking in the estaminet, much of our jubilation being due to the fact that leave had started again and many of us hoped to go shortly. I found myself eleventh on the transport men's list and two were leaving every three days.

I saw something of Sergeants Fulkes, Gernat, Dennis, and other D Company friends, now that the battalion was back here in billets, and learnt that the trenches were in a very bad state. There was a little shelling, and in some places bombers were busy. Fortunately we did not suffer now from that inferiority in trench weapons which had meant such a trial to our troops during the preceding winter, in those parts of the line where trench mortars, hand-grenades and rifle grenades had been used by the Germans. We were continually adding to our equipment and did not have to remain passive under German provocation.

After a short rest, the battalion went " up the line " again on the 18th, and the transport should by rights have gone back to that cheerful spot at Reninghulst. However, after some trouble, we succeeded in stopping where we were while arrangements were made for us to build stables near Reninghulst Mill, and, although the journey to the firing-line from Poperinghe was inordinately long, we were quite prepared to put up with it under the circumstances.

Then we followed that very road whereon we had once marched from Poperinghe to the big field where the 11th Brigade had bivouacked for the night—now occupied by artillery lines and a wagon-park and scarcely recognisable. One muddy field after another was passed, nearly all filled with horse-transports and artillery, or else dotted with " resting-camps " for infantry, consisting of a handful of tents pitched in several acres of mud. It was again Flanders at its worst— dreary, bleak and wintry, with biting winds freezing our hands, ears, and noses as we sat perched on our horses' backs, covering mile after mile of monotonous roads. Towards dusk the braziers and cook-houses of various units would give a bright touch to the surroundings.

When we reached Dickebusch, about 5 p.m., we always halted for about half an hour's rest. Although only about two miles from the firing-line, there was nothing but a ruined church and a few shattered buildings to show its proximity, and there were civilians living here who supplied coffee while we left all the limbers in charge of one or two of the brakesmen. We had to time our departure from Dickebusch so that it would be dark when we reached the Café Belge, since we should not be allowed to pass that point until after dusk, and it was preferable to wait in Dickebusch than at the Café Belge cross-roads. The latter represented the only active danger-spot on our line of route, since the Germans were fond of sprinkling the neighbourhood with shells, there being many of our batteries in that quarter. The lot of the traffic corporal at the cross-roads was not at all a happy one !

Generally speaking, the back areas were unmolested to a remarkable extent at this period of the War (indeed, they only became really obnoxious in the spring of 1917), and the Germans appeared to expend what was available upon the trenches themselves to a greater extent than in later stages of the War. Our guns fired occasional salvoes, seeming to send over about ten to every German shell that came in reply. Except for a desire to get round the Café Belge corner as quickly as possible and to delay as little as possible in Voormezeele, where stray bullets hit the ruins, the thought of danger was almost entirely absent.

What worried us far more was the feeling that our limbers might stick in the mud down the Voormezeele road, where the morass at the side became a veritable quicksand. There were sometimes most irritating traffic delays on this road, due to some G.S. wagon mono-polising the cobbled pavé and causing a convoy to pass through the mud to avoid it. Sometimes one of these vehicles would stick, and the traffic would be blocked still more. At one period, there was a fresh abandoned vehicle in the mud near Kruisstraathoek every time one passed, sunk right in above the axles. When it became necessary to leave the pavé, as on one's return journey from the line, it was essential to keep one's horse on the move all the time ; if there were any load in the limber, one stop was fatal.

The procedure in Voormezeele was the same on all occasions. The ration party would meet us and unload, and well could I picture their journey from the dump to the trenches, stumbling along in the dark and losing touch, as we had done at Plug Street. When we had deposited our stores, the drivers made their way back home individually, unless there was anything to wait for in the shape of a bag of socks or an officer's kit, when there might be a few hours' delay in the village. We sometimes returned through Dickebusch at about 8 p.m., when the estaminets were closing and the road was full of very merry Tommies, singing and supporting one another, trying to stop the horses, patting them affectionately as they passed (and occasionally patting the air) and asking me why on earth I couldn't keep to the right or left, according to what part of the road they happened to be in at the moment.

Having been riding since two o'clock, we usually felt rather sleepy on these ration-trips, and sometimes I dozed off on Tar's back, waking up to find the sagacious brutes had successfully negotiated one or two corners and were still plodding on towards the transport lines. We had to go home *via* Ouderdom, owing to traffic regulations, and it was a very lonely trip. Occasional picket-fires or lamps flickered here and there, and a solitary vehicle might pass by, but most of the camps were sleeping soundly, and there was no succession of supply columns to keep the roads humming with traffic ; most of the front-line supply was negotiated within three hours of dusk.

Arriving back at the transport lines you would unhook your horses, unharness, put the animals' nighties on, and throw down some hay. This would be done with or without the co-operation of the men on picket, the degree of assistance offered depending entirely upon the individuals concerned. It was, however, a rare occurrence for the picket to sit tight over their brazier, leaving a driver to attend to everything alone. It was usual for the cooks to leave hot tea for the " men up the line " ; having swallowed some of the well-brewed liquid and bade the picket farewell, you would make your way down the road to the barn, kick against sleeping forms in your effort to reach your kit, light a candle, partially disrobe, and then fall asleep on the straw with your garments as a pillow.

On December 19th I woke from such a bed as that to hear rapid firing in the distance. The guns were so busy that the accumulation of their fire sounded like a mitrailleuse. Simultaneously we heard the swish of enemy missiles farther up the road, only a few in number and evidently chance shots. In a few seconds, bigger guns nearer at hand joined in the fun and the air was vibrating with the concussions. We turned up at our horse-lines, as usual, about seven o'clock, where we found the men in the other billet in a state of excitement. One shell had fallen in the middle of the transport field, close to their barn and to the horses, so frightening the latter that they had broken the picket line and one or two were wandering loose about the field. No other missiles had fallen in the immediate vicinity and it was evident that it had merely been one of those chance shells, such as the Germans threw about in such profusion when they were attacking, or else it was a bad aim for the railway line.

This incident furnished a topic for our breakfast tables in the estaminet and Bertha, the daughter of the establishment, expressed confidence that the bombardment up the line could in no event mean the advent of the Germans, with " les braves anglais " holding the trenches. I must say that we shared this confidence, for the backing of our artillery was now quite formidable, and there were more troops to man the trenches than there used to be.

Our ablutions after the meal were disturbed by a horrible swishing sound, quite unlike an approaching shell. It was followed by a crash just beyond the railway. Although this was the first time that most of us had heard a bomb, we instinctively knew it to be one and we then and there formed the opinion that a bomb was infinitely more gruesome than a shell, a distinction that we never had cause to amend in later days. One could at any rate judge the direction of the shells and get behind a bank or in a hole, but an aeroplane seemed to look right down into your refuge and have you at its mercy.

We entered the estaminet and endeavoured to give the appearance of nonchalance in the presence of Bertha and her mother. The proprietor of the estaminet and two Belgian soldiers who often frequented it suddenly found themselves called elsewhere at this critical moment, leaving the womenfolk to be comforted by the transport men. Another bomb fell a little distance away, its effect on various people being amusing; I continued to shave at the counter and cut myself, and several tried to disguise their feelings by telling Bertha that it was all right, while she smiled bravely and said she knew it was.

Suddenly there was a crash quite close to the house. Gunboat Smith made a dive for the door, this action alarming Bertha, who now, for the first time, showed signs of tears. Her army of comforters increased. I believe, though I could not swear to it, that Milcovich—one of our most popular drivers—had his arm round Bertha's neck to give more effect to the consolation. Her father did not return for half an hour.

However, the bombing was over. The three bombs had evidently been intended for the railway line, but the nearest had fallen some yards from its mark. This episode was a corollary to the excitement up the line, but we were not troubled any further. It transpired that the Germans had intended a considerable attack for that morning on the north-west of Ypres, preparatory to which they had sent over to our trenches thick clouds of gas. Our guns instantly got to work and their concentration was such that the Germans were pinned to their trenches by the severity of the fire. This lasted for a few hours and the attack was completely frustrated. It was the only effort by the enemy during our sojourn in this part of the firing-line.

After this events took their normal course, the only feature of note being an excessively convivial Christmas evening in the estaminet. Some Belgian troops appeared to consider that the premises should be monopolised by them on that occasion, and it was necessary for our fellows to get there early to secure some of the seats. The proprietor, having recovered from the bombing raid, was the most lively individual present and his efforts at singing a patriotic song were thoroughly applauded by the Belgian and, at first, by the British, in an " Entente " spirit. However, at the tenth verse enthusiasm waned; after a few more verses interruptions were constant; at the nineteenth one of the L.R.B. could stand it no longer and broke into " Any old night,"

I

accompanied by cat-calls and stamping of feet. At this the proprietor had to subside, showing his resentment unmistakably and emphasising it with the aid of a tankard.

On the evening of the 30th Chrisp and I went on leave—for seven days on this occasion—and we arrived at Victoria as the clocks were striking midnight on the last day of the old year. Quite a number of people were waiting round the barrier, smiling sweetly and wishing us a happy New Year. What a treat it was to see those dear English faces once more. I gazed at that bevy of pretty girls and, as I thought of the Flemish maidens, odious comparisons arose in my mind. Chrisp probably thought the same, but as he was going to get married he had no business to notice the girls at all.

There was no thought of a commission this time ; the colonels' letters had been relegated to the incinerators. I had made fast friends and was absolutely attached to the L.R.B., and could see quite well that I should not strike in any officers' mess a better set of companions than there were about me on the transport section. The section had resolved to stick together and I should " sink or swim " with it.

Space prevents any comments upon this all-too-short leave, but I might mention that when in London I resolved to buy some cavalry officer's boots, reaching up to my knees, in view of our experiences in Flanders mud ; I did not think it worth while getting gum-boots since there had for weeks been talk of a free issue which really seemed about to materialise. (The issue turned out to be one pair between three men, and they had nothing between 7's and 11's !)

I did not, however, bargain for my new boots causing quite such a sensation as they created when I put in an appearance on Victoria Station at the end of my leave. They were of the type that General French might have worn on a ceremonial parade, and, moreover, they attracted attention to the brand-new pair of nickel spurs I was wearing. The remarks from the troops on the platform soon made me regret my purchase.

" Party, 'shun ! " cried one of a group of artillerymen. " Here's Douglas Haig himself ! " (Haig had just taken over command of the Army in France.)

" Look at this, Bill ! What's 'e think 'e is ? "

" Mind yer don't trip up over them there spurs, mate. Yer might fall through yer boots." And so on.

Fortunately Chrisp came back with me wearing rather a daring pair of boots himself.

We guessed that by the time we returned to Poperinghe we should find that the section had removed to its new stables at Reninghulst, since pack-pony men and others had been engaged for weeks in making standings and overhead cover for the horses in a field there. We were not surprised, therefore, to find the old barn deserted when we reached it again.

Bertha was " up and about," and beamed when she saw us. Her estaminet had been placed " out of bounds " to the British troops, the L.R.B. custom of taking their meals there behind closed shutters having come to the notice of the military police. She had the Belgian soldiers all to herself now, but didn't seem to relish the idea.

We travelled to Reninghulst in A.S.C. lorries and walked up the hill and past our old muddy field. After our winter experiences with horse-lines, the new camp looked delightful. Brick standings had been covered in for the horses and a row of tents in a fairly dry field represented our living quarters. I could tell everyone was in the best of spirits from the hearty way in which they roared with laughter at my boots.

My party was in a tent with Figg, Collins, Wiskar and Lance-Corporal Main, whose fondness for sausages was proverbial and gave rise to many pleasantries. We were a very jolly tent-load and Collins and Figg soon became such friends with Trendell and myself that we resolved to form a little " mess " of our own when we moved elsewhere.

Every spare moment was being devoted to the improvement of the lines, including the building of neatly-laid brick paths all round the stables. Consequently, the ration convoys made a practice of stopping at Kruisstraathoek every night, on the way home, loading the limbers with bricks from the ruins. This poor little village seemed to cause the Germans great annoyance and they wasted many thousands of shells in smashing down the few remaining walls. Every time we passed the spot we could not help laughing at this wonderful disappearing trick, for there were soon only two ruins in the whole place much above the level of the ground. This trick of the enemy saved a lot of trouble by loosening the bricks for us.

Owing to the terrible state of the Voormezeele road, we now had extra pairs of " lead horses " lent to us by the artillery, so that there were four horses to each limber. This saved much anxiety as to sticking in the mud, but we nevertheless kept to what was left of the pavé whenever possible.

One night, when we reached Voormezeele, Captain Russell (now M.C.) gave me the pleasing information that I should have to bring back an officer's valise and a batman, who might not arrive from the trenches for another hour or so. There was no need for my artillery companion to stay, so I tied Jack and Tar to a broken lamp or signpost, gave them a feed and disappeared inside a ruin occupied by some friends of mine on the pioneers' section, under Cox of betting fame (at Caestre). Here I managed to secure a couple of biscuits and a sip of tea Rations were still poor, I am sorry to state, and when we set out on these ration journeys we had little or nothing to take with us to serve as tea or supper, unless we had received parcels from home. There were about six small shops in Reninghulst catering for neighbouring troops to the number of some thousands, and these places rarely possessed any small change, so that it was not easy to procure even such things as chocolate or *gateaux*. The Y.M.C.A. was very short of stores and there was no canteen.

In the centre of the "room" was a brazier, which looked cheerful, though the coke fumes were suffocating, and I spent an enjoyable hour or so there, chatting with one or another and going outside occasionally to see the horses had not been taken.

It was about midnight when the voice of our dear B.S.M. Adams could be heard enquiring for the driver.

" Where's the driver of this limber ? "

" Just coming ! "

" Aubrey Smith, you'd better disentangle your horse. A bullet just whizzed past his ear and struck the wall there and he nearly had a fit. He's trying to choke himself."

I rushed to the spot and found the terrified Tar struggling for all he was worth, with one front leg over the chain which fastened his head-collar to the signpost. In the end we got him free and then I turned to make arrangements to depart, for the valise had just arrived.

Valise ! Little did I know that it would be a huge affair, weighing nearly enough to warrant a motor-lorry being sent for it. However, it had to be taken, in addition to the batman, and I was instructed to deliver them at the doctor's tent in the battalion's rest camp near our transport lines. After a good search in the mud for my gloves, which I had lost as usual, but found eventually, we started off and Tar looked round inquisitively as if to know whether he was pulling the church away by mistake. I remembered in time that nasty overheard wire which usually lifted off drivers' hats and deposited them in the mud.

Voormezeele was a different place, it seemed, at this time of night ; the bustling of ration parties had ceased, all traffic had long since departed homewards and even the guns were comparatively inactive. The limber wheels rattled on the uneven surface of the road and the sound echoed and re-echoed in those deserted surroundings. That was the best time for being alone with one's reflections—which could then dwell on home and the life that had been and was to be again—instead of having the usual environment of the Army, which crushed such strains of thought.

When I got to my destination I found I couldn't drive in the field where the doctor's tent was, while, on the other hand, if I dumped the kit at the entrance it was impossible for the sickly-looking batman to drag it through the mud alone. It was a rule that a driver should never leave his horses in a limber unattended, but I foolishly broke the maxim on this occasion and set off to carry this load to the doctor's tent, first of all tying the horses' heads together as a futile precaution. No sooner had I reached the tent than I heard the two brutes break into a gentle trot, which soon increased in speed. I rushed at a gap in the hedge, only to get entangled with barbed wire. When I was on the road again at last, they were far away—the empty limber could be heard rattling along the Reninghulst road. Fortunately they passed our stables, where one of the picket, attracted by the trotting, ran out and soon brought the horses to a standstill. I resolved there and then that I'd never leave my horses again for all the officers' kits in the world, and the next time I had to deliver a valise at the camp I should leave it in the mud at the gate.

One night a mine exploded near the trenches occupied by the L.R.B., burying some men of another regiment. It was one of the largest mines exploded on this front, where the enemy displayed many signs of activity and frequently made small attacks ; during the night the guns on both sides were busy. On the following evening our men had to go up and dig a trench, bury cable wires, etc., and help to repair the damage. They were very glad to come out on rest on January 19th for a week at Reninghulst.

Their arrival in the neighbouring camp led to a calling-in of all blankets but one from the transport men, and a tent-to-tent collection was made, which yielded up two or three per man. Some of the " old soldiers," however, cunningly pushed their spare blankets out under the brailing of the tents when the corporal came round to purloin them, revealing only one each. They reckoned without Sergeant Gordon, who was also an " old soldier " and was prepared for smart work ; accordingly, as their blankets were pushed out in the open, Gordon, who was walking round outside the tents with a man from the Q.M. stores, simply collected them up and the transport boys saw them no more !

On the night of January 30th there was another terrific bombardment ; it was a very still night and sometimes we could hear machine-guns. From 3 a.m. onwards I lay awake listening to it, and it con-

tinued during the morning at intervals, but died down considerably
after midday. No doubt it was another minor German attack. We
were supposed to have the initiative, according to the papers, but
attacks were invariably made by the other side, who appeared to be
still very much alive. Most of the usual excitement around Ypres
began just north of the L.R.B. position.

In our lighter moments we got as much amusement as possible from
our efforts in laying brick paths. The staid Shropshire men in the
next lines to ours were amazed to see Corporal Chrisp shoving a little
handcart of bricks, pulled by four fellows, going at breakneck speed
down the path, swerving round corners, rushing through a small gap
between two harness-racks and knocking one over, and finally pitching
the contents on the ground amidst roars of applause and laughter.
What they thought of us, I don't know. Our method of doing fatigues
was in striking contrast to the stodgy way in which they carted bricks
under the supervision of a strict corporal, who wouldn't do a stroke of
work himself, let alone tear along with the cart. They looked extremely
annoyed when one of our trucks, dashing along and headed by four
howling dervishes, terrified two of their mules at the water-trough ;
the owners swore at our party, but their anger turned to blank
amazement when they saw Corporal Simmonds following in the rear,
pretending to be a traction engine. Words then failed them and
they merely looked at one another !

On January 31st the battalion came out once more, leaving two
companies in support up in Dickebusch ; this move was followed by
rumours of " rest," which presently became a certainty. We were
to be withdrawn from the 3rd Division and sent down to some back area
to be formed into an entirely new London division consisting of the
crack Territorial battalions who had come to France in 1914, and had
been, like us, attached to Regular divisions for the past year. This
news was hailed with satisfaction for, however sporting the " Ryal
Scats " might be, we naturally preferred to be brigaded with men who
spoke our own language. The London units—L.R.B., Q.W.R.,
Rangers, Q.V.R., London Scottish, etc., would all be under one
General and a second London division would be in existence.

The day for the move came at last. It was the 9th of February.
We surveyed our camp and stables, on which we had expended so
much labour—having worked up to the last moment perfecting them
for the benefit of those who took our place—and felt a momentary
pang at leaving such comfortable quarters for new surroundings
where we might have to do the same work over again. The limbers
were all loaded and drawn up in the mud beside the road, ready to
depart ; they were facing the wrong direction and each driver had to
turn round. Then something happened which might have been
expected. When it came to the turn of Jack and Tar, no sooner had
the wheels touched the pavé, which was on a higher level, than Tar
thought he had stuck and, in full view of Captain Russell and the
sergeant, backed, swung the front of the limber round and brought
the wheel with a crash against the pole of the rear half. . . .

The pole was smashed in half !

It was as though the sagacious animal had said, " Well, so long,
Flanders, *that's* my opinion of *you* ! " An emphatic denunciation,
appropriately timed. For after two winters and best part of a year
in Flanders we were at length leaving those mud flats for more
congenial climes.

CHAPTER XII.

WITH THE 56TH DIVISION.

(*February–March, 1916.*)

A change of scenery—The dud pair's final misfortune—Verdun begins—Snow and solitude—More moving—The damsel of Doullens—With 3rd Army H.Q.—Happy days at St. Pol.—The Australians arrive.

WHEN we quitted Flanders on February 9th, and entrained for the south, we brought to a close our life in Belgium, which, roughly speaking, had lasted for over a year. We were only to see that front once again, for a week or so in August, 1917, and the reader may almost obliterate all such places as Ypres and Poperinghe from his mind in the chapters which follow.

It is interesting to note that, in leaving St. Eloi when they did, the L.R.B. only just missed a succession of bitter local fights which centred round a piece of ground called " The Bluff," close to their old position. There was a severe German bombardment on February 13th, completely destroying our defences in this area, followed by the explosion of five mines, and the enemy succeeded in capturing the Bluff, which gave them a good position and almost imperilled the safety of Ypres. There were several attempts to dislodge them, but it was not before March 2nd that the ground was recaptured by the British.

1915 was our Flanders year. 1916 was to be our Somme year. And as we woke up and found our train had brought us to Abbeville our joy knew no bounds, for we were evidently destined for a part of the line where we had longed to be for some months. It was obvious that, if we were to be formed into a new division, it would take some time for the brigade and divisional headquarters, the signallers and auxiliary services to get into good working order and, in the meantime, there was a period of training before us to fit us for the spring offensive.

11/2/16. " . . . After an all-night train journey, we arrived yesterday at a big railway centre (Abbeville), far from the sound of guns, and at a little station a few miles farther on (Pont Remy) we got the order to detrain. We saw here the Queen's Westminsters who are to join us, and there were cheers and salutations from both sides. When we had got all the vehicles off the trucks and led the perturbed horses down the ramps, we set off in a southerly direction amidst most beautiful scenery

(The Valley of the Somme) ; it was a lovely day and the sun was shining. How different from Belgium !

" After climbing up gradually for miles we got a magnificent view, which might almost have been some part of the New Forest. There were no troops about other than London regiments just arriving like ourselves, and we went on for miles and miles without getting to any village or seeing signs of habitation. At midday we halted while billets were arranged, which took our Q.M.S.s until four o'clock. Where they expected to find billets in that wilderness we couldn't imagine, but it turned out that there was a small village (Huppy) close by, in which our own battalion managed to secure barns and farms, while our transport was taken to a big farm situated among trees in a valley about a kilometre away. The horses were put in a field which the authorities described as a ' sheltered spot,' but the soil was chalky and muddy and it rained hard during the night, so by daylight it had become a quagmire. The so-called ' sheltered spot ' turned out to be in a very exposed position, so arrangements were made to stable our horses in the various outhouses of the farm, where we erected head-lines and harness racks.

" On looking around we found that Huppy possessed two inns and one shop, the entire stock of the latter, amounting to some twenty loaves of bread, which were instantly bought up. Of course, the shop ran out of change because everyone tendered a five-franc note. The civilians dislike these five-franc notes immensely ; it is very difficult to get them changed and, as we are only paid in paper money, we find it awkward sometimes. As a rule, the only solution—after you have tried several shops in vain—is to enter a confectioner's and eat up jam tarts as fast as you can ; then tender a five-franc note in payment. You ought to see the angry look on the woman's face as she says ' No change.' You appear to look surprised and say that neither have you got change and then follows a waiting game, each expecting the other to do something to solve the difficulty. Of course, the soldier has the upper hand because he has eaten the tarts, and so he stands there fingering the note, knowing that she must do something eventually. Then she either calls in the aid of her husband or her mother or the next door neighbour and eventually gets the coins from somewhere—possibly from a box full of them—and hands them over in a sulky way. The soldier thanks her cheerfully, leaves the shop and calls in an estaminet up the road, where he drinks down three glasses of beer in succession and tenders another five-franc note. The same proceeding is followed and at last he finds himself in possession of several francs' worth of coins.

" The old lady at the shop yesterday was a wily person, for, when a fellow offered her a note in payment for a cup of coffee, she took the note from the unsuspecting purchaser and locked it in her drawer, remarking that he could have it back again when he paid her a penny (10 centimes) for the coffee. There have obviously not been many troops here before, because in one cottage some fellows got boiled eggs for a penny each, while the folk wanted them to have coffee for nothing. However, the cheapness does not benefit us much when there is so little to buy.

" There were some Indian cavalry here before us and they

evidently belonged to a caste who object to sleeping within brick or mud walls, for they took it into their heads to knock the outhouse walls down and substitute sacks, etc. This thoroughly annoyed the old man at the farm, who evidently doesn't appreciate the fact that it was merely a religious custom !

"The appearance of the countryside has changed since the advent of the rain, and it looks decidedly uninviting. The days are getting lighter now, but we are still called at 6.30 and start work at seven o'clock. A whistle is blown to warn us at five minutes to seven, before which nobody dreams of getting up ; then there is a scramble. Everyone is looking for matches, candles, gumboots and tunics. It is extraordinary how articles disappear ; you go to sleep with your hat and gum-boots in one place, your sweater and tunic in another, yet in the morning you find some articles in various corners and the remainder you cannot see at all. There is a mad scramble in the darkness, everything not claimed being piled on top of Wiskar, who insists on lying in bed until the seven o'clock whistle. Naturally, he turns up late, which involves the punishment of peeling carrots for the horses after breakfast, a job at which he is becoming quite adept. He has one consolation, however ; he has not time to peel carrots and wash himself too, and, since on a rainy day like this washing in the open is not pleasurable, he expresses himself as satisfied with this arrangement.

"*Later*. How like the Army ! We have just heard that the new divisional A.S.C. is coming to this farm and the transport may have to clear out to-morrow to another village. All the improvements we have made here are for someone else's benefit, while the limbers must be re-loaded. Wiskar says he is going to smash into a thousand pieces the saddle-rack he has erected, just out of sheer disgust.

" To-night we surveyed our half-tin of jam and wondered what we had better do for tea ; the remainder of our day's rations was exhausted. We had not been paid for some time, so that Collins had no money, Figg possessed half a franc, Main owed 25 francs, Wiskar boasted one halfpenny, while I had two francs. After a long tramp in the darkness and rain, Figg and I called at a farmhouse and, with our pooled resources, endeavoured to purchase bread. At first we thought it would be hopeless, but after commiserating with the old pair on the absence of their son at the front, we managed to induce them to sell us half their loaf for elevenpence ; this we carried back to our portion of the barn in triumph. At any rate we have had our tea, if supper be a minus quantity. However, Wiskar had just made some soup on his stove ; although Figg says it smells like dubbin and looks like cocoa, it is well worth trying as a nightcap."

The move preshadowed above duly took place, the transport removing to a tiny village called Wascherville and the battalion remaining at Huppy. Wascherville consisted of a collection of dwellings and outhouses, peopled by agriculturalists who kept the land under cultivation for miles and miles around. Most of the outbuildings, stables, etc., were mud-walled shanties, large enough to hold two horses here, four there, perhaps eight in the biggest ones. Our section, therefore, straggled from one end of the hamlet to the other and we worked more or less on our own, with occasional visits from N.C.O.s.

On February 13th, I drove one of two " G.S. waggons " which were to proceed, with Chrisp in charge, to a place ten miles away, involving a journey through one or two villages where the other units of our division were training. It was to be the 56th (London) Division and the L.R.B., 2nd Londons, Queen Victoria Rifles and Queen's Westminsters were to form the 169th Brigade. We passed the 4th Londons and London Scottish, and it was obvious that there was to be considerable rivalry between the various units. Already we had received special instructions about tidiness, cleaning boots (!), polishing badges, having our hair cut, etc., in order to show the other units that the L.R.B. was by far the smartest of the lot. This journey demonstrated that all the other battalions were proceeding on the same lines. We were most disgusted to note that some of the transports burnished all the steelwork on their harness—a wearisome, thankless and inane task—which boded ill for us.

Now we come to an incident which lost me my driver's job for one day, and relieved me permanently of those two arch-devils who had brought me so much misfortune. About six miles from Wascherville, Chrisp ordered us to trot in one place ; it was against regulations, but we were far from the madding crowd of brass-hats and military police. The ground was frosty, however, and Tar suddenly stumbled, fell on his knees and kissed the road, while I, retaining my seat on the saddle, found my feet on the earth. As Tar became hopelessly tangled up with the harness it was a long time before we were able to release him, and then we discovered that his knees were so badly cut that he could hardly walk. Fortunately there was a spare pair with us, who took my place and continued the journey while I led the lame hero and his companion to the Kensingtons' transport lines in the vicinity to wait for the return of the wagons.

It was late that night when we got back to Wascherville.

"Whatever you do, don't say we were trotting," said Chrisp. (He will not mind this being set to paper so long after the event.) The only excuse I had to offer Captain Russell, therefore, was that the horse fell under me, giving him the impression that I had allowed him to fall asleep. The logical consequence of so many misfortunes with that pair was that I was relieved of my driver's job and Jack and Tar were handed over to the custody of Bill Adams, who, much to my delight, fared no better with them than I did. My relief at being free of that pair at last can be imagined, but it was not comfortable to be under a cloud. However, perhaps to show me that the transfer was not intended as a punishment, I received the very next day a heavy " cooker " pair of horses, Jumbo and Ginger, whose driver had gone to hospital; they were a slow, steady-going pair who inspired affection and not bad language.

Three days later we were to be inspected by the Brigadier, and everyone went cleaning and polishing mad in consequence. We were to outshine all others in the 169th Brigade. However, these cleaning efforts were constantly interrupted by the numerous trips which the limber drivers had to make. For instance, one day I was out from ten until one o'clock, drawing stores; again at 2 p.m. I did a further two hours' driving, ending up with the delightful task of taking coal round to the various companies in Huppy until eight o'clock at night. The driving over, there was a picket to do until midnight.

When the day for the inspection arrived, we got up early, put the finishing touches to the harness and our personal appearance and were all prepared by half-past nine. As it was a pouring wet day, it was postponed until eleven o'clock, ready for which hour both the battalion and transport turned out looking very smart indeed. Although the rain fell in torrents none of the company men were allowed to put mackintosh capes on, so they got drenched to the skin; the horses who had looked so glossy now resembled drowned rats; everybody was grousing and cursing. Someone remarked sarcastically that it was all for the sake of little Belgium; another pointed out that this parade was an essential condition to the winning of the War. At last, after over half an hour's wait, we heard that the General would not inspect us that day, as it was so wet! At midday every man was sitting in his billet, wet through, with no change of clothes, thoroughly miserable and spluttering with wrath against red-hats!

It was in this village that the "Devils' Mess" was definitely instituted. Trendell and I had been thrown a good deal with Collins and Figg, and we decided to amalgamate our resources in parcels, etc., and form a little party under the above name. Conibeer, one of the original 1914 transport men, finding he had more in common with us than with his former party, decided to join the mess; this gave us four drivers—a sure guarantee that the "Devils" would never lack space on the limbers for their odds and ends.

On February 21st the great German attack on the French began at Verdun; we read about it in the *Continental Daily Mail* (no charge for the advertisement) and discussed it with the civilians in a cottage where we spent our evenings. These people were kindly simple folk who toiled hard in the fields and returned home to sit and dream by the fireside until bed-time. The War had taken the entire fit manhood from their tiny little village. Twenty of the sons and husbands had already been killed and a large number were wounded; every house had sent its males, and all that remained were the aged and the wives and children. The attack at Verdun alarmed them, for the latent fear of the Bosche which was inherited from 1870 prevented any blind optimism. They realised better than we did that the Germans were a powerful and terrible foe. The great Battle of Verdun, even in its initial stages, they knew to be the life-and-death struggle of France, but they accepted the conflict philosophically and rejoiced when the meagre French bulletins told of heavy German casualties.

For the next few days we witnessed a constant stream of French cavalry moving southwards on an adjacent road—a most inspiriting sight. They were in excellent spirits, exchanging pleasantries with the British, whom they regarded curiously and critically. Their uniforms were of a light blue colour and their equipment was excellent. It was the first time we had seen French soldiers *en masse* since the Second Battle of Ypres, when they had been either Territorials wearing red trousers, Algerians in khaki, or Spahis disguised as rainbows.

The cavalry passed in a seemingly endless stream along snowy roads —for a long spell of snowy weather had set in—and there was no doubt that they were intended for the Verdun front. The relief of the entire French force on the Arras front by the British was contemplated, which would unite the two sections of the British front and give us a continuous line from Ypres to the Somme. When we passed through Pont Remy a few days later we saw two trainloads of this French army, which showed that the scheme was already in operation.

It was on the 27th of February that we trekked away from Huppy and Wascherville, having received orders to change our area. We went over the same wilderness that we had traversed a fortnight before, but hardly recognised the surroundings now, for everything was covered with snow. With no houses in sight, it seemed as though we might be in Russia. It was the first brigade march we had ever undertaken, apart from an inspection, all four battalions with their transports moving off in succession. This method of transit is unsatisfactory as the pace is too slow for the horses, who find it most trying to be restrained at every step ; the companies also found the trek wearisome, for they had to cover fourteen miles in full equipment on roads inches deep in snow. When we at length reached our destination at the end of the day both men and horses were thoroughly exhausted.

Ergnies was as far from decent civilisation as Wascherville had been, and as it resembled it in most respects, there is no need to enter into a long description of either the village or our fortnight's stay there. Unfortunately there had been an Irish regiment here before us which had fallen foul of the civilians, who accordingly gave us an almost hostile reception. One woman, as soon as two of our fellows entered her yard on their way to purchase eggs, " shooed " them out in a very excited manner, as if they were cows or chickens wandering in there by mistake.

One day I called at the house of the mayor, who looked like a labourer, in order to heat some snow for shaving, and had a short conversation with him. He confirmed that the Irish had given a bad impression, but appeared to entertain a better opinion of the L.R.B. These folk were really very kind-hearted and only required to be treated decently.

The only incident worthy of record was the death of my late steed, Jack, owing to some internal trouble. There was general rejoicing at the event, but we wished the defunct one had been Tar. It took several men a day or so to dig a pit for him and the dragging of his corpse to the burial spot by a blindfolded horse was a ticklish job. Over his grave we erected a wooden board bearing the following epitaph, printed in ink :

" Here lies a steed, a gallant steed, whose Christian name was
    Jack.
How oft he lugged our limbers to the firing-line and back.
Although he's loth to leave us, he is happy on this score—
He won't be in this ————— rotten Army any more."

The next day Colonel Bates and some other officers happened to pass this way and we saw them laughing loud and long over the inscription. I wonder how long it remained there—firewood was at a premium !

We were thirty miles from the firing-line and it was impossible to realise that a war was in progress. We read daily accounts of the terrific struggle at Verdun, where two great armies were taking and re-taking the same pieces of ground again and again, involving terrible losses on both sides. The Germans in particular were spending their troops in mass formation just like water and breaking their heads against an impenetrable barrier, thanks to the dogged French infantry —whom we had already considered formidable in attack only—and to their artillery, which already had our unstinted admiration. It seemed impossible that these things should be happening " down south " while we, so free from strife, were snowed-up in this peaceful little village. Target practice for companies and transport, an examination of the edges and points of the companies' bayonets and an announcement that we were to be issued with shrapnel helmets were the only ominous signs of trouble ahead.

Even the next village—Gezaincourt—to which we trekked sixteen miles on March 12th, seemed to be no nearer to the War zone, although we heard the distant rumble of guns occasionally. We saw some of the R.B.s of the 4th Division here, who testified to the quietness of the firing-line south of Arras ; they had been in these parts for some months and called it a " holiday." We spoke to one or two men who had known us in the Ploegsteert days and who recalled the parcels in Elverdinghe Woods, but there were now very few of the originals left.

Gezaincourt was a village about two miles from Doullens, a town of which we had heard good accounts from our men who had visited it on lines of communications, consequently the majority of us applied for passes and went into the town the next evening. It was a treat to see such shops and hotels again ; the place was crowded out with men of the 15th Division, some of whom were lucky enough to be billeted in the town. Doullens reminded me of St. Omer, and if there were pianos in St. Omer, why should there not be here ?

After visiting an estaminet with the Devils' Mess, I left them to imbibe the refreshing liquor while I set off on a house search for a decent instrument. Three people in succession referred me to a rather imposing residence where they said the people possessed a piano, and besought me not to mention who had given me the directions. Having knocked boldly at the door, I pitched a tale of woe in my best French, upon which the lady, to my joy, admitted me to the drawing room and left me to amuse myself. She said that she would see whether her daughter could possibly direct me to a place where I could go and play at any time upon payment, the very thing I wanted, since I hated inconveniencing these good-hearted French souls. The daughter proved to be an extremely pretty, dainty, well-dressed demoiselle of the highest class, whose appearance put my old friend Zoé completely in the shade. " Oui, monsieur," she would take me herself, since the way was difficult, to the house of a blind piano-tuner who always had a piano available.

Only once, and then with Zoé, had I actually walked along in a big town with a female, since leaving England ; such a thing was not usually done. Imagine the honour I felt when this ethereal vision proposed to walk down the main street of Doullens in my company ; unconsciously I felt the place where my tie ought to be and almost flicked my boots with my handkerchief. Instead of attempting to disown her, as I had done to the landlady's daughter at Jarvis Brook, I hoped we should encounter everybody, and so we did. One transport man after another passed, staring in amazement at the superior " bit of fluff " and wondering how I could have made her acquaintance in the last hour. Being human, I noted their envious looks with satisfaction. When we reached the piano-tuner's house she said " Good-bye " and left me to enjoy an hour's music, but I confess that I should have preferred her company.

Unfortunately there was no opportunity to renew the acquaintanceship, for my stay at Gezaincourt was short. An extraordinary piece of luck came my way on March 16th. The 3rd Army Headquarters required a company of the L.R.B. temporarily for duties with them and it fell to the lot of A Company to depart forthwith on this mission. Now, they had to have a cooker with them, and the pair I had taken over were none other than A Company's cooker-horses. So, at a moment's notice, I left the section, taking all my kit and full feeds for the horses, and made my way to Beauquesne, a fair-sized village near Doullens.

The L.R.B. detachment were to furnish guards, orderlies, fatigue parties, etc., to Army H.Q., and from the start became extremely popular there, since one or two of the Staff were old 4th Division red-caps who remembered us at Ypres and had deliberately selected the L.R.B. out of all the battalions in the 3rd Army, an honour we were anxious to repay by giving satisfaction.

We relieved a company of a Scotch regiment which had not been in favour owing to their disinclination to keep sober; in fact, they celebrated their departure by getting dead drunk, and the hilarious and disorderly parades, as the various detachments "fell in," were the funniest sight we had seen in France.

Three days after this relief, the 3rd Army H.Q. moved to St. Pol (in connection with the handing over of the Arras front to the British) and we accordingly trekked with the cooker to that town, with one night's halt at Doullens on our way; the Headquarters moved in lorries. We found that the French were just vacating St. Pol, and, to our delight, we were the first British troops who had been there (other than occasional despatch riders, etc.). The town was *en fête*. The civilians had never seen a British field kitchen before and clustered round in curiosity as I drew it up in the playground of a big school where many of the men were to be billeted. French soldiers came up also and tasted Army tea for the first time.

We were pestered by little boys for souvenirs, ranging from pots of jam and cigarettes to trouser buttons; the only things they refused were haricot beans. They admired the horses, marvelled at my top-boots and split with laughter over the holes in the knees of my trousers. These breeches, I am ashamed to say, had been thoroughly worn out, with big gashes at the knees for three months, but Ordnance had been unable to supply me with another pair.

Having carted the cooker for them, there was now absolutely no driving to be done, so long as A Company remained at St. Pol; there were no T.O.s or N.C.O.s to interfere and set a time-table; no work to do except the care of my horses.

Our company provided the orderly on the forage lorry, which came round to the various stables in the town; consequently, the two L.R.B. horses got as much hay and oats as I cared to ask for and enjoyed the finest feeds they had ever known in the Army. I ventured to ask for bran in addition and received a whole sack. The absence of work, coupled with the liberal forage, soon made them as fat as butter, while they became so frisky that they kicked out sideways at passers-by when I exercised them in the mornings.

As far as we were concerned, too, the rations were on an exceedingly generous scale. Everyone connected with the Army Headquarters had more than enough to eat, vegetables such as peas, beans, etc., were provided, which we had never seen in our battalion; the bread issue was one between two. Anyone could come back for a second helping and get it; even then there was a great deal wasted. We had experienced such a surfeit only once before—when we were on lines of communications. Was it not significant that when we were behind the line, serving not as an infantry battalion but as "army troops," we invariably had too much food, whereas in a fighting division rations were, as often as not, insufficient? The unequal distribution of food was most marked and was freely commented upon by our men.

A further attraction of this place for me was that there were some British prisoners here—poor devils who had probably got drunk or sworn at a N.C.O. at some time or other—who had fatigues to do as part of their punishment, and A Company had a difficulty in finding work for them. There were an L.R.B. corporal and a guard in charge, and the former suggested that two of the prisoners—artillery drivers—should do all the work connected with my horses, while two others could be put on to cleaning harness. The two drivers were good fellows and took an interest in Jumbo and Ginger, who soon began to look glossier and fitter than they had ever been before. All the work I had to do then was to feed the horses and take them out for exercise, and it was such glorious weather that my spirits soared higher than they had yet done in France. Here at last we had realised ideal conditions. We had a decent town, a rainproof billet, plenty of food, hot baths, clean clothing, fine weather, a friendly populace, many a pretty face and very little work to do.

My greatest " find " in St. Pol was a house in which two middle-aged Polish ladies lived ; they spoke French like natives and taught music. I was able to play for hours each day on one of their three pianos, and, in addition to this boon, I got to know their pupils who were of a class that it would have been difficult for a mere Tommy to make friends with in the ordinary way. The " professors " would sometimes ask me into their teaching room to hear a pupil play, or a girl would be brought in and introduced as I was in the midst of breaking their instrument. In two days I met in this way the daughters of a judge and a French general, blondes and brunettes of about eighteen, delighted with my feeble efforts to talk French and gurgling with glee because I was the first *soldat anglais* with whom they had ever conversed. They thought it somewhat a pity that the British Army should allow me to go about with my breeches almost worn into two pieces, and I candidly felt thoroughly ashamed of my appearance. It led to my asking an embarrassed young dressmaker to patch me up, but my self-respect was not greatly enhanced even then.

A Company were as happy as I ; never had they fallen upon such times. Monotonous guards and such jobs were nothing when all about one were restaurants, shops, estaminets—the latter open all day long until the military police made themselves felt. A Company were, at any rate, going to enjoy these surroundings for a month, but my paradise was cut short on the 26th through an idiotic veterinary sergeant suspecting Ginger of mange and ordering her to be sent away to the nearest M.V.S. This left me with one horse and therefore powerless to move the cooker if required ; it was not surprising then that Greene—one of our drivers—should be sent over with his pair on the 27th to relieve me, bringing my stay in St. Pol to an untimely end.

I had to bid a hasty farewell to the professors and their pupils, to Captain Trevelyan (that sport who had been in the front-line trench on May 13th and now commanded A Company), and to my many friends in the company, my only consolation being that I might succeed in coming over one day on a flying visit.

The remainder of the battalion, with the transport, had left Gezain-court on the same day as I had set off to Army H.Q., the destination being the village of Magnicourt, about seven miles from St. Pol. It was for this spot that I had to make now with the aid of a map—not an easy matter on the back of a horse who pricked up his ears and listened every few paces for his beloved Ginger, resenting every step that took us farther from St. Pol.

On the way I came to a railway level crossing, where a train full of Australians passed ; they were fresh arrivals from Egypt. It would have been more correct to say that there *had* been a trainful, for, at most of the stations they had passed on their three-day railway journey from Marseilles, many of their number had alighted in search of food and about a third of them had been left behind to make their way up to the firing-line as best they could.

Truly we were accumulating a large army in France ; already the British Empire had furnished 5,000,000 volunteers for the services. The massing of reserves in men and munitions on the Western Front was steadily going forward, every week fresh munition factories started at home, every month the scheme for shells and guns set in motion by Lloyd George in 1915 was bearing fruit more and more. We had been too much out of touch with events during the past month or so to realise that this accumulation of troops and munitions was going on apace the whole time, but, for me at any rate, the sight of these Australians, freed from the Gallipoli Peninsular and now transported here, served as a reminder that our forces were growing. There was some big move ahead of us. Where and when should we strike and what would be the result ?

CHAPTER XIII.

Signs of an Offensive.

(*April–May,* 1916.)

An inspection—The French look to us—An ominous move—Discomforts at Halloy—
" Up the line " again—The ration trip to Hebuterne—Surrounded by guns—
A German " strafe "—More heavy guns arrive—The mysterious aeroplane.

In April, 1915, 1917 and 1918, the dates of the Second Battle of Ypres,
Battle of Arras and the German " Push," how willingly should we
have exchanged our environment for the placid little village of
Magnicourt, in which we spent the month of April, 1916 ! Situated
some seventeen miles from the trenches, in a direct line with the Vimy
Ridge, we might almost have been living in a quiet country district
at home but for the distant gunfire, which could be heard at night,
and the three " sausage " observation balloons that could be
distinguished upon a fine day. We were, of course, farther north
than we had been in the Doullens area.

When I rejoined the battalion, after my trip to St. Pol, I found the
Devils' Mess in excellent spirits ; they were about to participate in a
dinner to celebrate Trendell's birthday, the festive board for which was
the straw on the floor of a barn. The occasion was a great success,
enhanced by the kindly withdrawal of the remaining occupants of the
billet, who left the Devils to " guzzle in peace."

About this time, Conibeer, Figg and myself, intent on doing something to prevent brain-rust amidst our unintellectual pursuits and
occupations, conceived the idea of bringing out a transport magazine,
which would be written out once and passed round to everyone in turn.
It took us a week or two to prepare the first number, which proved to
be quite a success ; the personal nature of most of the contents seemed
to be much appreciated by all but two members of the section, who
disliked having their legs pulled. In view of this popularity, not
only among the section, but on headquarters and in the officers' messes,
it was obvious that " The Old Doings," as it was called, had come to
stay ; I think its production put the final piece of cement between the
" old " and " new " schools on the transport section and welded us
into one family. Corporal Simmonds assisted us with illustrations,
in return for services I rendered him in translating into French his
billets-doux to the daughter at the big farm where we had stayed at
Wascherville.

As an antidote to this attempt to keep our brains alive, there came a formidable inspection of the transport by the Brigadier and a few days beforehand we got the appalling announcement that all steelwork had got to be cleaned. It was as we had feared : the craze for " poshness " that had arisen in the division had resulted in one or two very smart turn-outs among other regiments and we had to dance to the same tune. Rivalry in dazzling effects is as ruinous as naval competition—there is no end to it. This lesson we were to learn thoroughly as time went on.

When we were attached to the 4th and 3rd Divisions, rusty steel-work was the order of the day. So long as one's horses and leatherwork were well looked after, that was all that was required. But Kitchener's Army divisions were arriving, all polished up to the hilt, with brass-capped hubs to their limber-wheels, burnished head-chains glittering in the sunlight, harness that could be seen a mile away. They were under the influence of the " Spit and Polish Brigade," the new school, and we were dragged into the mad competition. We would show the French people how smart we were ! When we broke through the German line, our division would be the most dazzling and imposing of them all !

The French soldiers held their sides with laughter and continued to use their agricultural harness and their ragtime collection of wagons. The civilians watched our expenditure of energy with a shrug of the shoulders and a smile. After a year's ingrained rust had eaten into the steelwork, it was a difficult task to remove it, but the Army made no attempt to supply us with cleaning materials : they had to be " scrounged." On a conservative estimate, the annual requirements of our section alone necessitated the tearing up, in the course of the year, of two hundred shirts, one hundred and fifty pairs of putties, perhaps thirty tunics and thirty pairs of breeches, and one hundred nosebags, not to mention miles of tape stolen from marked out football-grounds. Drivers would walk long distances in order to find the necessary rag and sand and, when once a supply was obtained, it was such a treasure that one had to plead with the owner for a handful. My people used to send out rag in parcels and I do not know how many home garments must have been destroyed to provide us with the wherewithal to clean our steel. As far as oil was concerned, the Q.M.S. frequently refused to part with any, yet the steelwork *had* to be kept clean ! What a colossal waste of time, energy, good clothing and rifle-oil, all for the sake of looking " posh."

Our inspection was not a success, although the horses and leather-work were irreproachable, for days of striving had failed to remove the year's rust and the drivers appeared for the most part with dirty steel as a protest, to the horror of the staff captain. The links were all he seemed to look at. His comment was terse and to the point : all steel-work was to be burnished and we were not to turn out in such a state in future. Our N.C.O.s, who were all sensible individuals, sympathised with us over the time and energy wasted daily in removing rust from thirty-two links, eight rings, eight D attachments and four awkward-shaped swivels, two bits and a pair of stirrup-irons. But brigade orders were brigade orders and that was an end to the matter.

Shortly afterwards there was an important change on our section. Captain Russell went home to England and Sergeant Gordon was given a commission in his place, which meant the elevation of Simmonds

K

to sergeant's rank, while Chrisp received his second stripe. The latter lost none of his geniality through his promotion and indeed became more of a clown than ever upon occasions.

There were other changes on our section, too. As the brigade was forming a machine gun corps, volunteers for its transport were required and the L.R.B. companies had to supply a certain number who took instruction from our transport N.C.O.s Every day they set out to learn riding, a sight which enabled me to understand better now what idiots we had looked when we had first taken lessons. One or two of these new men remained on our section in place of others willing to join the M.G.C., and in this way Clements and Williams, among others, came to us. In February, Morris and Frampton had come straight to the section from the 3rd Battalion. On the other hand, one cook had returned home as a time-expired territorial, the glorious life in France being insufficient inducement to him to deny himself office life any longer; others had got jobs with division or returned to their companies. so that, without casualties so far, there were changes of personnel, though the process was quite gradual.

Among the small events which went to make up the sum total of our existence at Halloy were a company concert, transport sports, brigade sports at Frevent, boxing matches, occasional trips into St. Pol and the measles scare The latter took from the Devils' Mess its popular member, L. C. Collins, who departed with an attack of measles which got him through to England, and reduced its number to four. Incidentally it placed me in an isolation billet where I had nothing to do but feel bored.

The battalion was doing a good deal of bayonet practice; this, together with the appearance of the much-talked of tin helmets, an issue of improved gas respirators and a frequent inspection of our iron rations, looked as though we meant business. The news from Verdun was exceedingly good, in so far as the German onslaughts were kept up without cessation and, far from gaining ground, were resulting in the annihilation of the flower of the German Army. For weeks they had had practically nothing to show for their repeated onslaughts, and their papers, which had been so jubilant, showed signs of unmistakable anxiety over the carnage. Perhaps the reader will excuse me if I quote from a German newspaper, the *Vossische Zeitung*, published about this time, which gives an interesting insight into the German mind when it became apparent that all their hopes of victory were doomed to disappointment :

"The Battle of Verdun is not a human battle at all. It is hell. A man needs a devil in him to be able to survive it. No human beings can be expected to tear away whole rows of barbed wire and escape the snares of all sorts and the pitiless machine-guns. The attacking forces have only death, carnage and horror before them. We are fighting against an enemy who is a match for us. In men and material—except for our 305s—he is our equal. No secret of modern warfare is unknown to the French."

Nevertheless, the battle that had been raging for two months was beginning to have its effect upon the French, who thought it was time we did something to help them. The civilians could not help comparing the quiet time we were having with the life-and-death struggle down south, where their husbands and sons were still fighting and falling. Fresh casualties were heard of almost every day and half the people in the village were in mourning.

There had been constant fighting round St. Eloi since March 27th, when we had captured some ground which was greatly prized by the Germans; it consisted chiefly of crater struggles of a desperate character. On April 19th the Germans attacked at four places on the Ypres salient and gained a little ground, which they were only allowed to occupy for two days. On the 27th they let loose clouds of poison gas near Loos, which brought them a temporary advantage, but the fumes reacted upon the attackers. On the 30th the Germans adopted the same means up at Messines, the volume of the gas being such that horses in fields miles behind the line fell stupefied. It was all very well for us to assure the inhabitants that our attack would come presently; the impression they got from our impassivity was that we were barely able to hold our own.

Nevertheless, the civilians were as kind as possible. They varied, of course. In a jerry-built stable, belonging to an old woman, I was housing Jumbo, who now had a companion resembling the caravan horse in "We Three and Troddles." Everything went well until I found Jumbo one morning protruding through what had been the wall before this baby elephant had kicked it to pieces. The good woman swore vengeance, in spite of all my efforts to appease her, but she wreaked it on the post-corporal whose clean socks and underclothing were hanging out in her yard to dry. She took forcible possession of them, and I do not think he ever saw them again.

The first ominous move for three months took place when A Company, having rejoined us from St. Pol, we left this area on May 6th and trekked southwards all day, ending up a short distance from Doullens once again; this brought us into one of the army corps holding the line south of Arras. It was a sort of "first step" to that very part of the firing-line of which the 1st R.B.s had given us such reassuring accounts.

The village in which we took up our abode was Halloy, where a few huts in an orchard were placed at the disposal of both battalion and transport. The floor of these huts was Mother Earth, while the roofs, instead of being waterproof, were made of thin sacking, through which the May showers poured as though it were not there. It is a pity that those responsible for building them had spoilt the ship for a ha'porth of tar. If only the roof had been waterproof, we should not have said so much about the floor.

When we arrived our thoughts naturally turned to watering the horses, but Hurford had a titbit of information on that point, to the effect that there was only one respectable well in the village, while the nearest water-troughs were two and a half miles away. What a delightful spot to be in! Fifteen miles a day to cover in going to and from the water-troughs, involving over five hours' riding and giving little time for our many other duties! Just for that night we drew off the water from the battalion's water-cart and then erected lines between trees in the orchard, some of which were stripped of their barks in the morning by ravenous and "cussed" animals such as Tar.

Next day we experienced the physical discomforts of our tedious watering-journey; no sooner had we returned from one trip than it seemed we were saddling for the next. As for the village well, the less said about it the better. It took three minutes to fetch up one pailful, so that the company men told off to fill cooks' dixies proceeded to line up in a queue early in the morning and appeared to wait there all day.

It was lovely hilly and wooded scenery through which we passed on our way to the drinking-troughs. In between the May showers the sun came out, making everything more delightful, and we all agreed that this part of the war zone entirely changed the aspect of war. The whole battalion seemed happy. When we got back to the camp we would hear "Way down in Tennessee" issuing from one of the huts, while the cheery remarks from the company men who flocked round the village were evidence of their spirits.

Two days after our arrival here I obtained a respite from riding for four days, having received a kick on the temple from Trendell's horse, which knocked me flat, raised a bump and necessitated my being lifted up and taken to the aid-post. However, by a great stroke of fortune, it turned out to be nothing serious, so I used the short holiday as a means of finishing off the magazine (No. 2). While on the sick list, who should arrive in our camp, as an officer in the 2nd Londons, but Whittle, whom I had last seen in our headquarters at St. Omer; naturally those of us who knew him were glad of a conversation. He told us he believed, from what he had heard at the Base, that quite a considerable portion of the British Army was concentrated between Arras and the Somme, and that all the back areas contained troops ; we had partial confirmation of the latter statement in the number of artillery units and others who made their way from far and near to use the watering-troughs. He believed, as we did, that there would shortly be a "Big Push," and that we, with our past experience and thorough training, would be regarded as a "shock" division.

Just after our arrival the Army called in *all* blankets, this order being followed by a succession of very cold nights. We on the transport had at least our saddle blankets and felt cold enough—sleeping on the bare earth, but the companies had nothing but their overcoats and felt so miserable at nights that our picket saw scores of men, in the very early hours of the morning, walking up and down in the fields to restore their circulation. This collection of blankets every May and redistribution in October became an annual pastime, the precious coverings being stored in a dump until late autumn. Red-tape ordained their removal according to the calendar, not to fluctuations in temperature. The Army said it must not, and could not, be cold before October, and—officially—it was not. The troops could therefore never remove their clothes at nights, even when temporarily resting behind the firing-line and we all know the condition of things that that led to, unfortunately.

On the 13th, in addition to the cold, we had a deluge of rain about two o'clock in the morning. Our ridiculous sacking roofs proved to be quite useless and some disparaging remarks were made about the mentality of the authorities who had erected huts without tops—for that is what it amounted to. Our saddle blankets, kits and clothes were soon soaking wet and the ground was covered with little lakes, so we all had to deny ourselves our groundsheets and mackintoshes, turning out in those early morning hours to lay such articles on the sloping roofs. It was a very patchy arrangement. This was neither our first nor last wet experience in these huts, but it is worthy of mention as being the occasion on which we came nearest to being drowned.

The definite forward move took place upon the night of the 20th, when the battalion set forth with quite a light heart and a swinging step over the downs that sloped towards Pas, a little country town sheltered in the heart of a valley, and up the hill beyond in the direction of St. Amand. The march was made under cover of darkness to hide all undue movement of troops from the watchful eyes in the German observation balloons. It certainly seemed a quiet part of the line as we plodded forward, for very few flashes were visible in the pitch darkness and only an occasional " boom " could be distinguished.

Our actual resting place for that night was the little village of St. Amand, where a guide indicated the field where we had to draw up our vehicles without the aid of lamps—how we carried this out without mishap was a marvel to me. The movements in the darkness, the groping after stables and huts and the shouts for the suppression of lights—quite needless, as it happened—were the usual phenomena of the firing-line and were sufficient proof that we were up there again, though the absence of gunfire would seem to belie it. Next day we found that the village was practically intact. A large British observation balloon was in the sky immediately above us, round which we once saw two British aeroplanes circling. The sky was cloudless and it was perfect weather.

In the afternoon the battalion " fell in " again and, passing out of St. Amand and through Souastre, continued in a direction almost parallel to the firing-line, they marched in platoons with a considerable gap in between each, since the road was either under observation from the German lines or from their " sausages," which seemed quite close to us, in a long line extending from north to south. The transport also had to make its way along with large gaps between the vehicles to escape detection, the dust raised by moving columns of troops and transport being, of course, a plain warning to the Germans.

Arrived at Bayencourt, we put our limbers and horse-lines in a field intended for our permanent quarters, since this was the first-line transport zone, about three and a half miles from the firing-line ; the companies carried on in order to move into the trenches at Hebuterne that night.

In Bayencourt there seemed to be a considerable amount of bustle. Every billet was full, long lines of artillery horses passed by on their way to water, sundry limbers passed also ; while motor-lorries arrived with R.E. stores. Fortunately the place was in a hollow and could be approached by such traffic from the west without risk of observation.

Our so called billet roused roars of merriment when we were introduced to it. It was a dilapidated barn with little roof, collapsing sides and an earth floor, the latter being full of ruts and holes. Gunboat said he would rather sleep on a midden. The Devils' Mess vowed they would build a bivvy in the open at the top of the field, a line of action taken by most of the others, who proceeded to collect their groundsheets, a few oatsacks, some wood for pegs and some wire. The impromptu bivvies erected in such a short space of time had many imperfections, but they were undoubtedly the most feasible dwellings for such weather.

Before the Devils' Mess could start on their bivvy, Conibeer and I were detailed to take company cookers up to Hebuterne with the ration convoy after tea. This *was* a peculiar part of the front, there could be no doubt of that ! The companies were to have their four cookers brought up and dumped in Hebuterne, where hot meals would be provided for the men in the trenches some two hundred yards away. Rumour said that when the French were on this front, there was such a complete truce that they and the Germans used to send orderlies in turn to use a pump in No Man's Land.   There were some of us, however, who discredited this story !

The convoy started off seemingly in the wrong direction, but its purpose was to work round in a semicircle on to the Hebuterne road, instead of passing along the sky-line on the more direct route.   The way was narrow and the little lane was bounded by hedges and trees, so that it was difficult in places for limbers coming in the opposite direction to pass us.   Brakesmen toiled and perspired in a vain endeavour to regulate the brakes to the satisfaction of the drivers, as we passed down the decline through the outskirts of the straggling place ; drivers held their horses back, but could not help occasionally nearly decapitating the brakesman of the limber in front, as the pole shot forward too far.

Just outside the village was a good-sized ammunition dump under a canvas roof, the largest one we had seen.   Here were shells of all sizes, bombs, S.A.A., wonderful looking aerial torpedoes and peculiar things like footballs on the end of short stumps, presumably trench mortar ammunition.   The notice " No smoking allowed " caused cigarettes to be extinguished as the convoy passed.   This dump was a cheering sight, but it looked as if it might be unpleasant if it suddenly blew up ; somehow it didn't seem as if there would be much of Bayen-court left if it did.

On the road we passed many of the Labour Corps, with picks and shovels, returning to their camp ; they might have been making up either the road or a new light railway under construction in the vicinity. Many of the old boys were between forty and fifty years old, and they looked as though they were dying for a pint of bitter at the end of their day's toil.

Halfway to our destination, or rather more, perhaps, our little country road led us into a village with scarcely a sign of damage—Sailly-au-Bois, —lying directly behind Hebuterne and about one and a half miles from the trenches.   Directly we emerged from the trees on the far side we should be under observation, so the convoy had to wait with many other limbers until it was dark, before we could pass that spot.

There were many troops about and, seeing an artilleryman standing at the entrance to a billet, I asked what the place was like.

" It's all right at the moment, but I shouldn't like to lay my chances on its being so for long. . . . This village is simply full of guns, but hardly any of them fire at all."

" Which artillery are you ? "

" Your division."

" Then you've never been in action ? "

" Oh, yes ! We're the London batteries who were in the 47th Division at Loos.   But I should say Loos won't be in it when we start in these parts."

Presently the policeman on point-duty allowed one limber at a time to go forward, with a hundred yards interval between each, and so, emerging from the wooded valley, we made our way individually across the Hebuterne plain, which was about a mile of rough moor and grass-land separating one village from the other.   At the entrance to Hebuterne, I came to a tunnel of trees which rendered it so dark momen-tarily that I could not see a yard in front or to either side of me—I simply left it to the horses to carry on, which they did as well as could be expected under the circumstances.   They chose the correct road out of five turnings which were indistinguishable to me and kept to the centre of the road to avoid branches hitting me in the face ! Nevertheless, I butted my head forward to avoid any such accident, for who could tell from one moment to another whether an overhead wire or branch would give one a nasty blow across the eyes ?

The overhanging trees became less dense and I could now distinguish the houses—many of them untouched—and barricades in the village : to my surprise two civilians passed me and a girl came out of a doorway.

I was met near here by a volley of questions in the gloom. Was I L.R.B. ? Whose cooker had I ? Had I seen D Company's cooker ? Where was the mess cart ? Then Idle, the A Company cook, came alongside me and, taking me round a corner by a pond, led the way up the main street of the village.

" What do you think ? " said he. " We've got to cook all the company's meals without showing any smoke ! The Germans are about five hundred yards away and we're not two hundred yards from the trenches."

I thanked him kindly and asked him to let me know when we got to the first-line trench.

" I'd walk beside your horses," he exclaimed. " They keep playing a machine gun on and off down this road. They turn it on every few minutes."

" Anything else ? " I asked. There was not much farther to go. I backed the cooker into the yard of one of the houses, took my horses out and then returned to the pond where the remaining cooker pairs met together, their evening's task performed.

As the Devils' Mess had not even chosen the site for their bivvy before I left that evening, I had to make a search for it with Conibeer upon our return. Under nearly every tree and along by the hedges our fellows had erected bivvies, most of the occupants of which had to be awakened before we found our proper abode, causing execrations to be poured down upon our heads. We then discovered the bivvy was only large enough for three men and, even so, our movements were so hampered and restricted that every time I went in and out I succeeded in uprooting some of the pegs. Everybody else seemed to manage all right, but somehow I was " all feet," and first someone's mug of tea would be knocked over, then my head would cause the roof to collapse or I would sit in Figg's dinner. In short, bivvy life did not come naturally to me and the Devils' Mess had a great deal to put up with in having me for a member.

When we were having our breakfast the next morning a burly R.G.A. corporal walked up to our bivvy and looked in at us.

" I say, mates, you might tell your pals not to build their shacks any further this way, and don't let any of your 'orses wander about t'other side of that 'edge. Don't want to give our position away, you know."

" Didn't know you had a position, old son," said Figg.

" Well, we've got hall our guns in that little wood there—nine point twos."

" What ! Do you mean to say that we've got our horse-lines bang on top of a battery of nine point twos ? By Jingo ! what fun there'll be when you fire ! "

" Won't be exactly an 'ealth resort."

" You might let us know when you're going to begin, will you ? "

' Can't say, old son. We've been 'ere a fortnight—come straight from England and ain't fired a blinkin' shell yet. Some surprise for

Fritz, I can tell you. We're all trained on to a wood over there and can let go any time we like. Jerry's got an observation post there what we can blow to blazes—give us the word."

" Well, I wish you luck. Only I can see our horses breaking their ropes and cantering off to Pas as soon as you start."

" You won't light any fires 'ere or move about out there, will you ? Tell your mates."

We looked at one another for a moment and then one or two of us went off to impart the news to the section. As a matter of fact, we were not first in the field with the information, some having done a little exploration on the previous evening ; the removal of our horse-lines was certainly a matter for consideration for, so long as we remained there, the danger of a panic among the horses was ever present.

The revelation of these hidden guns, however, acted like magic upon our spirits. The visual proof that we had something " up our sleeves "—a surprise in the shape of a really heavy bombardment— was the very thing we had wished for among all the vague rumours of an offensive that had been passed around. The mere knowledge that there was a battery of heavy guns in the wood was not in itself sufficient proof, for there had been a limited number of " heavies " out here for several months, but the fact that these had come straight from England and had been instantly put into position and trained on to a target, coupled with what the other artilleryman had told me in Sailly-au-Bois, implied that the front was probably bristling with artillery on a larger scale than ever before.

Our rising hour was now 5.30 a.m., for we had a full day's work before us, the watering of the horses here also being a lengthy business. We had to take them three times a day to a neighbouring village where so many other units used the troughs that there were interminable delays, necessitating our allowing one and a half hours for the journey. In addition to that, drivers were out nearly every day, as there were jobs of all kinds to be done.

Fortunately for the Devils' Mess, parcels from home arrived in plenty at this juncture—for rations were extremely short. On the 22nd we had a loaf between five, next day one between nine. Jam was issued in tins between thirteen men, there was practically no butter, while the cheese issue was laughable. Parcels containing cakes, biscuits and chocolate were always welcome, but had never been more so than at this time. Perhaps the transport fared worse than the companies ; at any rate, one of our men had annoyed the battalion Q.M.S., which was a fatal error. Mr. Gordon complained about the shortage, but it led to an improvement for one day only.

On the 23rd, when I went up with the ration convoy again, I found that Idle's machine-gun story had not been a myth and that the bullets did in fact whistle almost straight down the road, so it was more prudent to dismount and wait while the rations were unloaded than to remain in the saddle. The horses got very frightened at the " Pop-pop-pop," which sounded quite close, and when I tried to mount again they were so frantic to depart that it was a few moments before they would remain still enough for me to do so. There was a block in the traffic in Hebuterne, but it was not so serious as it was liable to be ; one night a passing limber caught the wheel of our mess-cart and smashed it at the corner by the pond.

I used the more direct route back to Bayencourt and noticed that, when we were nearly home again, there were eight newly-dug gunpits beside the road, placed so that no traffic could pass while the guns were firing from them. In such a case one might cross the Sailly-Soustre road off the maps, as far as transport was concerned.

Beyond them I branched off down a narrow side-lane, bounded by high hedges, which should have meant a short cut into our transport lines. I had not explored it, but had that morning observed a track near our orchard and guessed that it must lead out in that vicinity. It proved to be a lengthier route for me, however, for a hundred yards down the lane I distinguished something looming up out of the darkness just before me, impeding my progress. My horses pricked up their ears and stopped short. Ahead of me lamps were being flashed, revealing a huge gun with a tractor in front of it, one wheel being sunk in the ditch. Of course, it was a most difficult matter to negotiate the bends in the lane in pitch darkness, and it was obvious that, as I could move neither backwards nor forwards, I was doomed to stay there for a considerable time.

The officer came up and said I should be able to get by presently; he asked if there was any danger in flashing torches about as he had not been in the firing-line before ; none of his men had, he said, and they had been hurried out here with their training only half finished. . . . How the hell the Army expected . . . etc., etc.

While I was still sitting perched on my horses' back, watching with interest and yet some impatience the artillery-men's frantic efforts, supported by planks of wood, there arose in the firing-line what was commonly known as a " chimozzle." The sky became alive with flashes, and there was a considerable uproar. It was merely a German " strafe " of Hebuterne, hoping to catch convoys and troops and probably provoked by the enormous amount of digging that was being done up there ; I felt very glad I had escaped in time, but at that moment was unaware that Greene had his pair of greys up in Hebuterne on some R.E. job, or other, and was caught in the midst of it. Our field-guns were replying, but it was difficult to tell how much of the noise was our gunfire or theirs.

When I eventually got past the tractor, I found the transport picket wondering wherever I had been, and, when I told them, they thought it a huge joke that I should have been stuck about three hundred yards away for the past hour ; it didn't seem so funny to me, as it meant a reduction of my night's rest. As it turned out, however, my sleep was to be longer than that of most men on the section that night.

Shortly after I had turned " into bed," the picket came round flashing a torch in all the bivvies, ordering everybody except the men who had just come in from " the line," to turn out and scour the countryside for Greene's horses. He had been in the act of hooking them into a vehicle near the pond when the " strafe " had commenced and, being an exceedingly nervous pair, they had immediately bolted in terror, leaving Greene feeling very sorry for himself. The " strafe " had practically cut off the only exit from the town, but the horses nevertheless came through it unscathed and had been seen as far away as Sailly-au-Bois. Someone had ridden down to give the news, but no definite trace had been found as to where the pair might now be expected to be and there was nothing for it but to organise several small parties to set off in every direction. There is no space in which to record the amusing experiences of the search-parties, which " Spanny " Main described very wittily in the next number of the magazine. They scoured the country for miles, following false clues and losing their way ;

but Figg probably felt as disgusted as anybody when, thinking he was on the scent, he eventually hunted down a speckled cow! The two shame-faced runaways were discovered in the early morning tied to some artillery horse-lines at Coigneux.

On the 24th and 25th it rained hard on and off, revealing the fact that our bivvy had been built for fine weather. The water settled in the ground-sheets and we pushed it off at intervals, a stream pouring out each time at one place or another and wetting our kits. We got to know these places after a time and dodged a bucket or a couple of mugs about to catch the deluge where it was likely to appear. On the 25th, our rations being one loaf between seven stalwarts—all with healthy appetites—no butter and no jam whatever, in spite of Gordon's recent complaint, the Devils' Mess set out to see what they could buy! After visits to the neighbouring canteen, which only stocked soap, blacking and tooth-paste, and to two shops where nothing " filling " was obtainable, we came upon a farmhouse where a deaf, frowsy old woman was pottering about and asked her for " du pain." She first said she hadn't any, but when we told her we had only one loaf between seven she went to a hole in the wall which served as a cupboard and produced what was, apparently, a piece of wood. After hitting the cat with it she tendered it to us, alleging that it was bread; and bread it certainly was, or had been. She said it was good enough for her, so we bought if for 4d. and, when we had got back to our bivvy and cut all the mildewed bits out of it, we decided it would have to be good enough for us, too!

There was considerable aerial activity on the part of the R.F.C. for the next few days, but German machines rarely ventured near our lines—and when they made the attempt they either kept almost in the clouds or turned tail on receiving the attention of our anti-aircraft guns. Both our artillery and the German guns were more active, particularly to the right of us, opposite Serre. Fortunately no mishap occurred to the convoys, and on the 28th the battalion was relieved after its week in the trenches.

On that date we found that preparations were being made for bringing in some more howitzers beside the road which we took to the water-troughs and our brigade authorities at length realised that, beset as it was by artillery on all sides, Bayencourt was not the best spot to choose for its horse-lines. Accordingly we moved them about a mile to a sheltered valley near Coigneux, two days later ; the companies were close at hand and went up to " the line " each night to do digging and other fatigues.

On our second day here a British aeroplane that had been circling around in a queer manner, landed close to our horse lines. There was naturally a rush for the spot and a crowd arrived in time to see the pilot and the observer, both fresh-faced young fellows, alight and get out their maps.

They said they had just flown straight out from England and wanted to get to an aerodrome near Doullens, but had lost their way and for some time had been flying, as they thought, on the German side of the line. A Staff officer soon appeared, and hustled the crowd about, telling us to keep back. He then plied the pilot with questions. The other man never opened his mouth.

" It seems extraordinary, sending you out with a sort of *Daily Mail* map," said the Staff officer. " Do you mean to tell me that that inadequate thing is the only map you've got ? No wonder you can't find your way. Well, that's the direction of Doullens (pointing to the west), and it's about ten miles away."

The airmen started their engine again, got into their seats and whirled off, just skimming the horses' heads and causing a general panic among the animals—an incident they could have easily avoided. Then to our absolute amazement, after circling round once or twice, the aeroplane made off in a straight line, not for Doullens, but for the GERMAN LINES !

I understand that, in the House of Commons later, questions were asked relating to a new type of machine that had set forth from Farnborough to France upon that date, on a trial trip, and was reported to have landed in the German lines. The replies admitted that the aeroplane had never been traced. Thus, presumably, one of our secrets fell into the hands of the enemy, through the medium of a couple of clever spies.

I shall always remember this as the place where I took over one of Greene's horses from him to work with Jumbo. Greene had labelled them " Damn " and " Blast," but, though the latter was appropriate for the lazy brute whom he retained and then sent off to the M.V.S., " Damn " was an insult to the willing and lovable grey horse who now became mine. Although practically white, he came to be known as " The Grey," and was destined to have some exciting experiences on our section right up to within two months of the Armistice, when the faithful and affectionate old animal was fatally wounded by a German bomb.

CHAPTER XIV.

THE BATTLE OF GOMMECOURT.

(*June–July*, 1916.)

Preparations for the offensive—Congestion of traffic—The last week—Final activities—The Battle of the Somme opens—The great Bombardment—Waiting for news—The awful truth—Story of the attack—Consolation.

WE were at Halloy again. There were the sacking-roofed huts waiting for us when the battalion got there. Behold the same old well, nobody having taken any steps to improve the water supply.

The day after we arrived we were struck dumb by reading the account of the Battle of Jutland which, the reader will remember, was given out to the world as though we had suffered a serious defeat. The British report under-estimated the German losses, while the German official magnified our own. Certainly we got the impression that the British Navy had had a very nasty knock and it made everybody irritable for the whole day. After this we read that the Germans had made a strong attack at Hooge, near Ypres, capturing some ground and getting through nearly to Zillebeke. We did not at the time appreciate the severity of the battle that this led to, or the intensity of the German artillery fire, which was on the Verdun scale; but, nevertheless, it looked as though we were to have a Third Battle of Ypres and that our offensive down south would be nipped in the bud. This was no doubt the German's aim, since our offensive had been talked of so openly for months, that the enemy's natural policy was to interfere with our preparations. Many of our Ypres guns were on their way to the Somme, and had to be recalled in order to back up the inevitable counter-attack, which the Canadians carried out on the 13th, recapturing the lost ground.

Then the Italians were hard pressed in the Trentino and looked to us at that time likely to repeat the previous year's performance of the Russians. Of course, we had read before of the tragic fall of Kut, and when we turned to the Salonika expedition, we heard nothing but tales of Greek treachery and antagonism. On top of these events, which made the newspapers far from cheerful reading, the announcement that Kitchener and his staff had been drowned at sea came upon us like a bombshell. While, momentarily, it seemed as though the British Army would be lost without him, this news and the whole series of

reverses only made us more anxious than ever to carry on with the
" Big Push " to give the people at home something inspiriting to read
about for a change.

The papers began to talk about the coming offensive and to discuss
its chances ; it seemed to be accepted in some quarters as an open
fact that the thrust would be made south of Arras. Eventually it
became known that our division would be in the attack and that the
L.R.B. would advance in waves, the details of which were worked
out carefully. Indeed, it was clear that the battalion were to be
well versed in what they were expected to accomplish, for, in course
of time, shallow trenches were dug in neighbouring wheat-fields,
modelled exactly upon the German defences as revealed by aeroplane
photos. The British front line and the German first, second and third
lines were indicated by little flags, and time and again the whistles
would blow and the various waves, advancing through the corn,
would take the successive lines of imaginary trenches. Every battalion
that was attacking rehearsed on the same lines, each reproducing a
different section of German fortifications, and making itself thoroughly
conversant with them. If this went on throughout the attacking
divisions, as I have no doubt it did, it says much for the care that
was taken to make the advance a success.

Bomb-practice, signalling, Lewis-gun firing, rapid shooting, rifle
inspections, etc., were carried on, wet or fine, but we still found time
for an inspection by the Lord Mayor of London on the 10th of June.
After several days of this intensive training, the brigade moved up to
the firing-line again, taking over a section of trenches a little to the
left of their previous position, while the transport made their quarters
in Souastre. The road from there to Foncquevillers, where we dumped
the rations, could not be used in daylight, so the congestion of traffic
after dusk, with every gun receiving reserve supplies of ammunition,
was such that we were lucky to cover the three miles in two hours.
Not only were the artillery convoys as numerous as flies round jam,
but large quantities of stores of all kinds were being taken up behind
the trenches by infantry-transports, R.E.s and motor lorries. An
effort was made to relieve the congestion by making the return horse-
traffic use a track beside the road which, as the weather was so fine
and the surface of the ground so hard, was quite as good as the highway.

Tracks seemed to branch to right and left, to one battery and another,
which—in the absence of woods—had dug the guns into pits in the
open fields, and to which one ammunition convoy after another would
come up, deposit its shells and return to the rear for a further supply.
Then there were big guns being hauled up by tractors, which frequently
held up all the horse-traffic until they had branched off to right or
left. Fortunately these were moonlight nights, and one could see what
one was doing when traffic jams occurred and there was tricky driving
to be done.

I found the grey horse was exceedingly nervous and shied almost
at his own shadow. His pet aversion was an ordinary push-bike. He
scented these half a mile off in the daytime, then pricked up his ears,
dilated his eyes, snorted, and did his best to edge away from them ;
motor bicycles did not seem to trouble him so much. Lorries and
motor cars he disliked, broken trees he regarded with suspicion, limbers
he accepted with equanimity. But let him catch sight of a milestone
and watch the result ! I tried to make a mental note of where the
milestones (or rather " kilometrestones ") were placed, in order to be

prepared for any antics that might ensue.   Then again : wheelbarrows !
If I induced him to proceed past one it was only done with his head
twisting round, regarding it, and then a short trot to put distance
between himself and the object when once he had passed.   These
fads of his kept me on the " qui vive " the whole time, for he would
think nothing of shying to either side and attempting to scale the bank,.
limber and all, if he caught sight of anything unusual.   No doubt
the " strafeing " at Hebuterne, and his subsequent panic had made
his nerves particularly unsteady for a time.

I was up in Foncquevillers on the first night, but nevertheless, on
the second—after I had gone to bed—the sergeant awakened me and
shone his torch upon his pocket book.   Those gruesome words :
" Harness up at once," were not welcome to one just enjoying his.
beauty sleep.   The brigade required us to furnish a G.S. wagon at an
unknown dump at Bayencourt, to collect pit-props and take them to
Hebuterne with other vehicles from the brigade.   We had to be there
at an hour which was clearly impossible in view of the time when I
was awakened.

These journeys took so long on the crowded roads, while the traffic
regulations in some cases required you to return by such a devious
route, that we arrived back sometimes at 3 a.m., and then rose with
the others at the usual time next morning.   The daylight saving
scheme came into force here, but it penalised the poor drivers who
could not get up with supplies in daylight, for they had to start an hour
later every evening and yet rise at the same hour as before, thus losing
an hour's sleep !

The Germans were getting uneasy now.   A fleet of about seven or
eight aeroplanes would make an incursion over our lines and back again.
Their ugly sausage balloons were in position the first thing in the
morning and their guns were more active, turning their attention
first to one spot and then another, where they imagined troops or
batteries to be.

The men in the trenches had a rough time, too.   What with uprooting trees and hedges, digging new trenches, advanced gun pits,
etc., and making trench-mortar emplacements, they were furnishing
the enemy with ample evidence that an attack was in contem-
plation and he " strafed " the trenches accordingly.   At night
frequent bursts of machine-gun fire could be heard in the Gommecourt
region, where there were many casualties among the working parties
in our division.

The Germans were prepared for us—there was little doubt of that.
How could they help being so when we dug assembly trenches and
gun-pits under their very noses and advertised to the French and
to the world in general that we were about to take the offensive ?
The question was : Had we got sufficient weight of artillery and men
to break through their defences on which they had now worked for a
year and a half, and behind which they had concentrated a very
formidable artillery ?   Many of our own people and the majority of
German prisoners considered the positions impregnable.

Nearly every night now we were taking up stores of one kind and
another—barbed wire, tools, reserve ammunition, sandbags, etc.—
but we could not complain of any lack of sleep when there were front-
line men who worked all night long.   There was a sort of subdued
tension in the air, a general feeling of excitement and wondering
when the great day would come.   To feel that one had a part in its

preparation entirely compensated for headaches, disturbed nights and physical tiredness.

On the 22nd we trekked back to Halloy again to make our final preparations for the attack. While this meant more detailed battle orders for the companies, it affected us more by orders for the drastic curtailment of kit, and such things as attending to the horses with our respirators on and special attention to the condition of the animals and limbers. We made a final attempt to fit our horses with the absurd respirators which had been supplied for them, and terrified them out of their senses in our efforts to adjust them ; all these articles were the same size and had to be applied to heavy horses, pack-ponies, and mules alike. They were the most unpractical contrivance with which we were issued throughout the war. I made one attempt only to reconcile the grey to his respirator, but he loathed it more than fifty wheelbarrows, which is saying enough.

The next day I had a chat with my few remaining friends in D Company, which now, of course, bore practically no resemblance to its former self. West and Cooper, the two men who had tried to get on the transport with us, were quite cheerful and confident. They said the dummy trenches upon which they had rehearsed were a replica of the German line to the right of Gommecourt Wood, opposite Hébuterne. Our division was to attack at this point, while the 46th Division attacked the left (or north) of the wood. Certain platoons were told off to enter the wood at a later stage, but the main scheme was to capture in turn the second, third and fourth German trenches, after the front line had been mastered, and meet the 46th Division in Gommecourt village, thus squeezing out the wood. Such, in brief, was the plan of campaign that they were permitted to know, but it also leaked out that our attack was a subsidiary one to mask the main thrust on the Somme.

C. H. Hudson, Sweeting and Sergt.-Major Fulkes, all members of the old Q Company draft from Haywards Heath, were full of enthusiasm, and I had chats with them at different times. Then there were fellows like Dennis and Stapleton, old friends at Jarvis Brook ; Davis, poor fellow, who was the last person who ought to have been plunged into the diabolical atmosphere of war ; Gernat, of the signallers, Avery, an ex-transport man of D Company, and one or two others. I could almost count on my two hands the men who were old comrades and consequently very much in my thoughts. But there were many other acquaintances, especially in A Company, whose names I forget, but whose faces I still recall, men who, two years ago, had not thought of harming a fly—let alone killing their fellow-creatures. Now they realised that to terminate this never-ending deadlock of trench warfare there must be a fearful assault and that they must go with bomb or bayonet and engage in wholesale slaughter.

On the night of the 23rd the trial British bombardment started. It afforded such a marvellous display of flickerings and flashes in the heavens that nearly every man of us was walking about in the field in the small hours of the morning, watching the flashes and listening to the rumble, which was like a terrific thunder-storm. The men were intensely excited.

" Let 'em have it." . . . " Give them a dose of their own medicine." . . . " Keep it up, boys."

Fellows were laughing for joy as they contemplated the shaking this bombardment was giving to the Germans. The novelty wore off after

some minutes and many of us crept back to " bed." But what
man who had experienced the Second Battle of Ypres could help
lying awake, thrilled with joy, as he listened to such an impressive
revenge ?

We were told afterwards that the German defences had been
pulverised, but wherever there were signs of uncut wire or other
unbroken obstacles, additional bombardments would take place, while
a more or less continuous harassing fire would be kept up on and
behind the enemy's lines until the morning of the attack.

Everyone was now speculating upon the date which, I believe, was
originally fixed for June 28th, but was postponed owing to a serious
break in the weather. At any rate, we did not leave Halloy eventually
until the 27th, when the companies went into huts at Souastre, in the
neighbourhood of a twelve-inch gun, and the transport made for St.
Amand.

There was a narrow valley, which might almost be called a gully,
about a mile long, in the neighbourhood of this village, where every
transport section in the division took up its quarters. The bottom of
this valley may have been twenty or thirty yards across, this space
being available for the horses, and on either side were big slopes rising
to normal ground-level, the east one being somewhat steep and perhaps
a hundred feet high. It was covered with trees and undergrowth,
beneath the shelter of which we proceeded to erect a bivvy, since there
was no cover of any kind. The Devils' Mess suffered considerable
tortures from tree-stumps, stinging-nettles and earwigs, and it did not
promise to be a comfortable home. On arriving back from a " line "
trip we found that the only occupant who had remained behind that
night had slid down the slope right below the shelter of the roof, and
was only being saved from rolling into a prickly bush by a friendly tree-
stump. Nevertheless, he was fast asleep. In the morning we all
found ourselves outside the bivvy, having gradually obeyed natural
gravitation laws ; so we set to work to make a new home for about
nine men, using a tarpaulin with scores of little holes in it, covered with
mackintoshes and ground-sheets, and pitched it in the valley near the
horses. Others followed our example, and the valley was soon sprinkled
with weird-looking edifices from one end to the other.

We now learnt that we were to be put on fighting rations—that is,
bully beef and biscuits and about a fourth as much of everything else
as we normally received, with bread on one day in four. This was the
last diet upon which a man could feel pleased with himself and ready
to face the foe. One limber driver set out for a French baker's in Pas,
where he found a collection of men with vehicles from every unit for
miles around, all bent on the same errand as himself, waiting for the
next batch of loaves to be cooked. This congestion, however, very
soon caused the well-fed Town Major to prohibit the purchase of bread
from civilians, so we were perforce left to our dog-biscuits.

One morning I was sent as an interpreter to buy a barrel of beer in
Pas for the more thirsty portion of the section. You would have
smiled to see the faces of all the troops we passed on our return journey,
as they spied the barrel on the limber. Members of the Navvies'
Battalion ceased work, looked eagerly at it, and licked their moustaches
with glee, while the fellows in our own camp gave three rousing cheers,
which changed to a growl when they found I had forgotten to bring a
tap for it !

The guns were quite active now ; but it is curious that when one descended into the transport valley the noise abruptly ceased, unless the gunfire were specially heavy or the wind particularly favourable. By no means all the guns were firing, but there was sufficient of a rumble—particularly farther south—to cause general excitement, and on the 29th and 30th even the valley seemed to throb with the distant concussions. We were catching snatches of the great seven-day bombardment which was taking place all along our front, designed partly to fog the enemy as to the actual zone of our attack. There were many raids at various places on the British front during this last week, which met with varying degrees of success. These also were intended to baffle the enemy ; but, on the other hand, they kept him very alert and prepared.

We were still taking up stores of all kinds until Hebuterne had become a vast dump. My last journey was made in daylight, using a track which had been planned by the division to keep transports off the roads as much as possible. Wherever this track had been laid over ditches or through hedges such obstacles had already been overcome by parties of pioneers, and its only drawback was that it passed in front of the muzzles of many guns where alterations in route would be necessary. In following this track, which was indicated for the most part by little stumps of wood stuck in the ground, we had to cross the plain from Sailly-au-Bois to Hebuterne, where we were supposed to be under observation from the enemy on the right, and I was surprised to see the vast gunpits, earthworks and ramifications which stretched from north to south. Even if the Germans could not observe the spot, a single aeroplane photograph would have revealed it. The track passed between two of these gun-pits, and here again it would be quite impossible to get a pair of horses past while the guns were in action.

Hebuterne looked a different place in daylight. Gordon led the way down a back street with numerous barricades in it, a lane that would have to be used in place of the usual road in times of excitement, eventually emerging on the A Company road I knew so well. Our proceeding down the main street of Hebuterne with a limber and a pair of horses in broad daylight seemed to rouse consternation among the troops there, who besought us to return whence we had come as quickly as possible.

At length the preparations were complete. The blow that would relieve the pressure at Verdun was about to be delivered. On the 30th of June our speculations and conjectures were set at rest, for we learnt that the attack would be on the following morning at an hour known as " Zero," which would be revealed later.

I watched the companies have their final tea in the Souastre camp, I spoke to my friends again, took field-service post-cards to post for them, watched them put their kits together. Then I seemed lost in a dream for a moment and envisaged the whole of the front where similar preparations were going on, pictured the scores of units who would be tramping up as many roads and tracks in the next two hours, the tension up at the batteries and the nervousness of the Staff. Probably over 100,000 men would be " over the top " on the morrow, few of whom were likely to sleep a wink that night.

Suddenly the dream disappeared, as the individual element came to the fore, and laughter and songs echoed from one end of the ranks to the other. The companies were filing out on to the road, passing between several onlookers like myself, who gave them " God-speed " and final words of cheer. A few looked straight before them, but the

L

majority of faces were wreathed in smiles and there were all kinds of jokes and banter passing from one to another.

" Well, we're going to give it to them this time."

" Cheer-oh, Aubrey ! Dump our rations in Mons to-morrow night ! "

At length their last file had passed out on to the road, followed by the medical cart, mess cart and other vehicles ; then the rest of us who had nothing more to do that night made our way back to the lines.

*   *   *   *   *   *

July 1st dawned with a pale blue sky and the semblance of a mist. Having awakened several times, after dreams concerned with attacks and shells, to find the day had not yet broken, it is perhaps natural that I should have slept on in the end and missed the very early morning glow.   What I wished to hear was the big bombardment which we had imagined would be let loose at the first glimmer of dawn, as it had been in various Verdun and Ypres attacks.   To our surprise we could hear nothing but the birds singing in the trees, an aeroplane soaring overhead, and a picket driving a stake into the ground.   We began to think it had all been a wild rumour, or that the offensive had been postponed again, and every moment that passed seemed to confirm this view.   We went about our work with ears strained to the utmost, waiting for the sign that the great move had begun.

All of a sudden we heard some reports—one, two, three, four— probably emanating from some 9.2s we had seen in the neighbourhood of St. Amand.   These were followed by a rumbling sound and several smaller explosions in the direction of the line.   Then the big guns at Souastre, and on all sides joined in the chorus, and in a moment we were listening to the most tremendous bombardment that had been known upon the Western Front, or, for that matter, in the history of war.

The magic words : " It's started ! " called men from whatever work they were doing and from their bivvies ; shouts could be heard in other transport lines, where the personnel had gathered about in groups ; then there was a general exodus towards the slope of the valley in order to reach a point of vantage.   We were calling to one another in exultation as we clambered up the steep banks and, with every step higher, could hear the bombardment growing more distinct.   It took us a minute or so to reach the summit, but at length we were free of the trees and found ourselves in wheat fields near the outskirts of St. Amand.

Although trees, hedges and the contour of the land prevented us from gazing upon the trenches three miles away, we saw a wonderful panorama as we looked in their direction.   In the first place a battery of heavy guns was rapidly firing in our immediate vicinity, the flashes and smoke from which naturally attracted our attention at the outset ; then, looking beyond the trees we saw tremendous clouds of smoke from the bursts rising all along the firing-line to north and south as far as our vision enabled us to observe it.   All those guns in Bayencourt, Bienvillers, St. Amand and Souastre were now firing their hardest ; all those batteries on the Hebuterne plain, the masses of field guns round Sailly-au-Bois and Foncquevillers were contributing their share to the indescribable uproar that was going on.   Some reports were distinct in themselves, notably those of the siege-gun down in Souastre, which was firing on more distant objects, and the heavies around us hurling their 9.2s in profusion upon the German trenches.   But the remainder of the artillery hubbub was just like an orchestra playing at a climax, where all the individual instruments are merged into one great volume of sound ; the continuous throbbing and concussion caused a curious sensation of pressure about the ears, the earth seemed to be shaking beneath us and even the ants must have had headaches.

And what did all the smoke represent, where the shells were falling ? It meant that sandbags, planks, duck-boards, equipment and pieces of Germans were flying up in the air. Gommecourt Wood was being reduced to matchwood. I thought of what the R.G.A. man had told me at Bayencourt : " Jerry's got an observation post there what we can blow to blazes." Doubtless the German observer had made the acquaintance of a 9.2.

Overhead two aeroplanes made in a straight line for Gommecourt, while the St. Amand observation balloon towered above us, its occupant getting a splendid view of the battle area. There was not a German " sausage " in the sky. Within the last few days, principally on the preceding evening, our airmen had brought down one German balloon after another in flames. To-day the enemy was blind ; we had complete mastery of the air. We envied the R.F.C. men for their ability to see over those trees that just baulked our view.

For a quarter of an hour—half an hour—one hour—the pandemonium continued without showing signs of abatement. Surely by now the infantry must have advanced. Sweeting, Davis, Hudson, Cooper came into my thoughts and I fervently wished them back. Whittle was up there with the 2nd Londons : Gernat with the signallers. What were they experiencing ? Were they at that moment at grips with the Germans ?

This time we must assuredly win. After all, this was only a portion of the battle front ; the main thrust, we had heard, was being made near Albert. From north of Gommecourt all down the line to the Somme this colossal bombardment was in progress. If there was such a hubbub on this piece of front, how many thousands of tons of metal must be passing over the heads of our infantry all down the line ?

The white clouds continued to rise.

" Bong ! Bong ! " spake the guns in St. Amand.

" Boom ! " came from the direction of Souastre.

Further off, sounds like four exploding crackers told of a big battery endeavouring to make its voice heard above the prevalent din.

" Give them hell, boys," said one fellow.

" Well, if we don't get through this time we ought to," was a favourite comment.

We stood, some speechless, others more enthusiastic than I had ever seen them. After watching until nearly breakfast time, our numbers began to melt away as the men returned down the wooded slope to their horse lines. I felt too excited to eat much, and we were all athirst for news of our progress. The bombardment did not sound nearly so distinct at the bottom of the valley, where the pretty surroundings made it difficult to realise that a pitched battle was being fought with machine-guns, bombs and bayonets three miles away from us. Here were we, sitting in bivvies, eating bacon and dog-biscuits — what did they matter to-day ?—and doomed to inactivity.

Our contribution to July 1st had been made, such as it was. It was represented by the tons of R.E. stores, ammunition and reserve rations which had been carted up to the line in the weeks preceding the attack. If all went well, it would be continued by taking water, rations and ammunition over the captured territory that night. But it didn't seem much to be proud of, compared with the efforts of our company pals. Transport work had not yet reached that pitch where it meant carrying up supplies in daytime during the progress of an attack. Such adventures were, to say the least, exciting, whereas watching and waiting were positively riling.

What man could devote himself diligently to any work that morning with his mind full of the day's excitement ? Everyone wanted to know what had happened. An aeroplane came over near by, dropping a message at divisional (? or corps) headquarters, who presently issued its contents to us. It stated that the L.R.B. and London Scottish . . . were in the second German line and small parties had been seen in the German third line. Hurrah ! Then they had got across. So much of the trouble at Neuve Chapelle and in various attacks near La Bassée had been that the enemy's wire was uncut, but our observers had assured themselves of its demolition on this occasion. A subsequent message told that our men had been seen in Gommecourt village !

One of the 2nd Londons' drivers who had been out on duty said he had seen plenty of ambulances full of wounded coming down—L.R.B.s, Q.V.R.s, and the rest of them. But we were shut off from the world in this spot and no further information was forthcoming. The bombardment seemed to have died down, the St. Amand guns slackening off and finally giving up firing altogether. Surely they must be waiting for fear of firing on our men ; perhaps they were entirely out of range.

Morning changed to afternoon without anything but vague rumours being heard, rumours that varied from the capture of Cambrai to the most exaggerated estimates of prisoners. We knew that rations had got to be taken up on pack-ponies, from which we inferred that they would have to cross the pulverised No Man's Land and the captured German trenches, where no limber could pass, wandering on until they found the L.R.B. Gordon was busy studying his full-size map with the same thought in mind. It therefore fell to the lot of the pack-pony men on this occasion to provide the ration-party, this being the first time that the ponies had been used as a body for such work since the section had been re-formed. As water was being taken up in tins, several extra horses were put on to the work, for which purpose extra saddles had been drawn from brigade ; the grooms and spare men furnished the party to conduct these horses up and I did not envy them having to pass those batteries I referred to above. One bomb-limber was told off to accompany them to the farthest possible point.

Several of us accompanied the convoy to the Q.M. stores on the Henu road and helped to load. This being quite new work for us, it was not carried out as successfully as it might have been ; the saddles had to be held firmly on one side while the rations were being fastened on, but the majority of the loads slipped round underneath the horses before ever we had tightened the girths. Even those that seemed to be well fastened worked loose on the way to the firing-line, and more than one pony reached its destination with the rations almost scraping the ground. We watched them depart, and made a few bantering remarks about marching to Germany ; then we looked at the sunset and wondered what sort of a scene the old sun was setting on that night. Overhead the St. Amand " sausage " still remained on high to watch the flashes of the German batteries after dark—why had it not moved forward, by the way ? A solitary aeroplane was making its way back

from the enemy's lines. Evening had come on, but there had been
no further messages. A driver of ours said he had seen some German
prisoners; another had heard that all was going well, though heavy
casualties were mentioned. The only thing to do was to return to
our bivvies and wait for the return of the ration convoy.

*   *   *

The first stragglers of our ration party got back about 1 a.m. There
was a noise of horse chains and of footsteps out on the lines. Then a
voice—Simmonds' voice—sounded close to our bivvy, and those of
us who were awake strained our ears to hear what he said.

" . . . a failure. Back again where they started."

" What ! "

Some of us sat up, while Milcovich called to the sergeant to look
in at our bivvy.

" What's that, sergeant ? " asked Milky, huskily, in a tone of
incredulity.

" Awful news. The attack's a wash-out. From what I hear there's
precious little left of the L.R.B., and they're either back in our old
front line or lying out in No Man's Land."

" But who says so ? "

" Gordon has had it from Colonel Bates. Rations were left as
usual, in Hebuterne."

" But——"

A dozen questions and as many oaths occurred to us, but we couldn't
frame them; we were absolutely stupefied. The attack a failure !
Another Neuve Chapelle ! Another Loos ! Worse than that ! we
had come back to our starting point again ! And after all those months
of preparation, after that tremendous bombardment. It could not
bear thinking of—it was incredible. True, we only knew what had
happened on our portion of the front, but that meant everything to us.
The L.R.B. was cut up, with nothing to show for it. Gommecourt
was still German. Every fact that came to one's mind made the
picture more terrible. But the overwhelming tragedy was the cut-up
of the L.R.B.

Everybody naturally felt the disappointment most keenly and showed
it in their gloomy silence and irritability the next day. All of us had
friends about whom we were most anxious, but we got no further
news, for nobody could tell us anything. Even the people in England
were reading the accounts of the day's fighting and knew by now
roughly what had happened all along the front. We, up in the war
zone—three miles from the scene of the attack—knew nothing more
than I have set to paper.

I thought of that jolly battalion that had re-formed at Blendecques,
of the months spent by the division in training for this day of days,
of the practice attack carried out at Halloy and the hundred and one
preparations that had come to naught. We had advertised our intentions too much. How obvious had been the digging of the jumping-off
trenches out beyond the front line and the maze of earthworks on the
Hebuterne plain ! Apart from this, Germans who had deserted prior
to the attack had declared that they were quite prepared for us. In
one place the enemy had stuck up a notice to the effect that they were
waiting and invited us to " come on."

That afternoon the remnants of the battalion came down to St.
Amand, with a grim look on their faces of men who had been through
a furnace, as we had after the Second Battle of Ypres, dirty, unshaven

and pasty-faced, muddy and somewhat ragged. In feverish haste I sought out D Company, where I found Sergt.-Major Fulkes and Davis, both looking rather haggard, but otherwise safe and sound ; I asked for news of the others.

Cooper ? Killed—My God, poor old Cooper !
Dennis ? Killed.
Hudson ? Nobody could tell. He was missing.
Stapleton ? Wounded.
My three Jarvis Brook companions gone !
Sweeting ? Killed.
West ? Killed.
Avery ? Missing.

Whatever friends had I got left now ? It was as big a blow in one day as the Second Battle of Ypres had meant in a month. Fulkes and Davis agreed, however, that a short, sharp tragedy was less nerve-racking than a long-drawn-out one, and that plenty of artillery, gas-respirators, trench-mortars, and so on put Gommecourt in quite a different category to the former defensive struggle.

What had caused the failure, then ? Fulkes told me what he knew.

The bombardment had played havoc with the German lines, and, before attacking, our men had stood up and watched the wood being pulverised by our heavy shells, a sight which roused them to enthusiasm in spite of the return fire they received from the German guns. The enemy put down a protective barrage, but our attack started off in great style, under cover of numerous smoke bombs. The ground to be covered was from two to three hundred yards across, and the German machine-guns had a good field of fire before our boys reached their first trench. Many men fell from machine-gun bullets and others from shells, which the Germans were sprinkling about No Man's Land, but the waves reached the front-line where there was bomb-fighting with the garrison ; in the meantime the British were continuing to shell the wood itself. The front trench seemed to be smashed to atoms so the men passed on to the second objective, then to the third line, where Gommecourt was almost within their reach. Here they had to wait for reinforcements, reduced in numbers but quite full of fight. Time went on, however, and no fresh waves appeared, while on the other hand aggressive parties of Germans were bombing their way up communication trenches from behind them. They had been lurking in huge dug-outs under the ground which had survived the bombardment, and were now disgorging bombers by the hundred. The first and second lines had not been " cleaned out " by the captors who, it should be said, had never been led to anticipate such huge underground caverns, and therefore took less notice of their unpretentious openings than they would otherwise have done. The German bombers swarmed all round the advanced elements, who soon began to realise that they were surrounded and trapped as the hours went by. There was nothing to do but use their bombs sparingly and wait for reinforcements.

To the intense surprise of all, the reinforcements never came through, though they started to time from the 56th Division trenches. The German artillery barrage, strong at the outset, had now increased to such a curtain of fire that it was almost impossible to pass through unscathed. Here it is necessary to state a fact which was not known to Fulkes at that time. The 46th Division on our left, north of Gommecourt, only reached the front line and got turned out of it again ; the defeat was swift and took place while our division was still actually advancing, thus enabling German guns behind the Gommecourt salient to turn their full fury on to our divisional front. German machine-gunners and bombers, too, satisfied that the attack was definitely strangled north of the wood came to the assistance of the enemy in our quarter. The bombardment from our side had now lifted on to Gommecourt, consequently the Germans mounted their machine-guns on the parapets with a clear vision and perfect targets, while the wall of shells, cutting off the attackers from further supports, continued hour after hour. Again and again men started off carrying ammunition and bombs—the latter being a vital means of self-preservation in the captured trenches—but they were all annihilated. Prisoners with escorts started back from the German lines, but did not survive the barrage.

The small bodies of our infantry who were holding on, having run out of bombs, used German grenades for a time until these were exhausted. Presently the more advanced elements had to abandon their wounded and make a bolt to the rear. But the Germans were becoming more daring, knowing that our men were trapped, and they mounted their machine guns in the open while the bombers, drawing upon inexhaustible supplies, made it impossible for us to remain in their trenches. The run for life had to be attempted. From shell-hole to shell-hole the survivors darted, sniped at by Germans whenever they appeared, bombed when they remained in hiding. Third, second and, finally, first objectives had to be abandoned, leaving dead, wounded, equipment and tools behind, while the race across the two hundred yards of No Man's Land faced every man who lived until the afternoon. Through the intense artillery barrage and under heavy machine-gun fire men dropped right and left, until the ground between the trenches was an awful scene of carnage. The attack was over, and the best part of several battalions lay before our lines in this sector alone.

Perhaps I may anticipate a little here and record that Whittle told me later how he went up to the front-line with the 2nd Londons that evening. There were large numbers of stretcher-bearers out in No Man's Land, where the groaning and shouting were very agonising. Verey lights were constantly going up, while the Germans repeatedly sent over " whizz-bangs " to inconvenience us. It got light much too early, for there were many men still lying out there, calling for water. About 2 p.m. next day, a German doctor strolled towards our lines and was met half-way by the 2nd London's M.O. As a result of this, an armistice was concluded, enabling several stretcher-bearers to be sent out. The Germans deserve credit for this humane action, which was in such striking contrast to their usual conduct. A few of them came out to assist our stretcher-bearers and Whittle carried one of our wounded, with the assistance of a German, into the enemy's trench. At the same time he spotted a machine-gun position which he promptly reported. Some wounded casualties lay out there for days and on July 6th a man crawled into our lines, reporting the position of three more wounded whom he had assisted at nights by giving them food and water he found in neighbouring equipments. Another unusual act on the part of the Germans was the sending of a list of prisoners in their hands : whether this was dropped from an aeroplane or sent by a messenger, however, I do not remember. (I have since learned that this action was in reply to a similar list first furnished by the 56th Division.)

So much for details of the Battle of Gommecourt. On July 3rd we saw the first newspapers giving particulars of the opening of the Battle of the Somme, from which we learnt a good deal that compensated for the disaster that had overtaken our part in the battle. The British had attacked on a twenty-mile front, breaking through some of the Germans' defences down south, where we had captured Montauban, Mametz and Fricourt. Not only that, but the French had attacked on our right and done splendidly : the Germans had evidently been quite unprepared for them, suspecting their strength to have been sapped at Verdun. Their advance had been from two to four miles in depth south of the Somme, while our own amounted to between one and two. The British divisions north of the Ancre had apparently experienced the same set-back as we had, having made no progress, a fact that was explained by the Corps Commander when he addressed the L.R.B.

It transpired that the Germans had expected our attack would be made from Arras to the Ancre, with Gommecourt as its centre, so that their greatest concentration of artillery and their picked troops had faced us. The advertisement of our preparations had succeeded in confusing the enemy as to the actual front to be attacked. He had looked at Gommecourt all the time and the sector on either side of it. At Montauban and Mametz his concentration was not so great, and it was there that the thrust had been made. We had come in for the fury of his fiercest bombardment while others had made the vital blow.

Even such poor consolation as that must be accounted a mercy in war.

Our casualties in that one day amounted to 588 officers and men, made up as follows :—

	Officers.	O.R.
Killed or died of wounds	7	65
Missing (now presumed dead)	1	161
Wounded and missing (do.)	–	46
Wounded and prisoners	–	32
Prisoners	1	23
Wounded and brought into our lines ..	10	242
	19	569

CHAPTER XV.

From Gommecourt to the Somme.

(*July–August,* 1916.)

Up the line again—A harassing policy—The call of the Somme—August adventures —Back for a " rest "—Refitting and red-tape—First sight of the Tanks— Bound for the Somme—A panic move.

A MOTLEY collection of drafts from all regiments was ready to make the division up to strength immediately. What annoyed us was the persistency with which the authorities regarded all our units as " London Regiment," sending, say, sixteen L.R.B.s to the Q.W.R.s and at the same time sixteen Q.W.R. men to our battalion. With a little more thought a good deal of esprit de corps could have been retained.

Instead of getting a good rest, the battalion were sent up to Bienvillers again on the 6th, preparatory to going into the line to the north of Gommecourt. The transport were very busy, drivers being out almost every day. On the 7th, after making six short journeys during the day, I took up rations to the L.R.B. after dark, making the acquaintance of Bienvillers for the first time. Though there was great excitement in the neighbourhood of Hebuterne, there was an uncanny stillness about this place. One policeman cheered me up by saying it was usually a " hot shop " and telling me how many shells had come over on the previous night, with other interesting details. Another policeman shouted out a lot of nonsense in broad Scotch as I was nearing the village : honestly I could not understand a word he said and continued on my way without being any the wiser.

Having arrived home at 2 a.m., I turned in after breakfast to sleep for an hour, according to a new concession in force during our stay in the valley, but had not snoozed for long before I awoke to discover myself having a shower bath and lying in a pond. The rain was coming down in sheets, completely flooding us out. For the remainder of the day we were busy, either rescuing drowning horses or baling out our beds. In places the streams pouring through the roof filled a mug in thirty seconds, so that our clothes, rations and kits were very soon moist. In the evening the tide went out and we made a few alterations to the roof, such as stuffing up holes with frost-bite grease ; we also dug a network of canals. Three yards from our bivvy flowed a newly formed river, while a little farther away the horses were clustered together in the open sea, though no one seemed to have started building a boat. In the mud were a Primus stove, a water-bottle, two mugs and a looking-glass, peeping out above the slush, and eventually completely submerged knives and forks were rescued with some difficulty. Our little valley, amounting as it did almost to a gully, truly " came into its own " when the weather broke.

Every night on our ration journeys we were fascinated to watch the sky to the south of us flickering incessantly with the perpetual bombardment that was going on in that sector where we had " made good."

Almost daily attacks were being made, resulting in the capture of a piece of wood here or a small sector of trench there, but, attack or not, the guns kept up a continual bombardment, though we could only realise this after dusk, for, curiously enough, we usually did not hear a sound from that direction. It was only the vivid flashes at night that told us our hammering was being continued : these flashes were of all kinds, large and small, some sending a beam of light half-way across the heavens, others giving the impression of petrol being put on a bonfire. The cumulative effect of them was to give a permanent brilliance to the southern sky and to cause us to thank our lucky stars we were not " on the Somme."

Not that things were as they used to be, even on our sector. With the collapse of the northern end of the offensive it seemed to be the Army's policy to harass the enemy continually in our part of the line, keeping him uneasy and preventing him from transferring too many guns and troops to the Somme. Our corps artillery therefore had fits of strafeing and gave the Germans a terrible punishing every night : they would work up into a regular drum-fire and keep it up for hours. These choruses of hate became such a general occurrence that there was never any allusion to them in the newspapers.

In the trenches, too, our fellows kept up a harassing policy, making several bombing attacks and sending over doses of gas almost nightly. The L.R.B. took it in turns to occupy the right front (Foncquevillers) and the left sector (Hannescamps) where our experiences of German artillery shelling varied from time to time. The enemy could make Foncquevillers an exceedingly unhealthy spot when they chose and more than one of the L.R.B. ration convoys was caught in a German strafe of the village.

As for Hannescamps, it was more famous for bullets than for whizz-bangs or " five-point-nines." The enemy directed overhead machine-gun fire on to the road once every minute or so, terrifying The Grey to such an extent that on one occasion he tried to make a bolt up the road to the L.R.B. trench when we were dumping ammunition. Sometimes we were told to clear out of the village and make off home again without delay as a bombing raid, a gas attack or a gun-strafe was about to take place and instructions were issued that operations should not begin before the transport had got safely away, in case the enemy replied. Then the guns would start their chorus when we were half-way home and, turning round, we should behold Bienvillers—so calm when we passed through there—spitting fire for all it was worth. If, as sometimes happened, one of our drivers were delayed, he had the pleasure of driving right through the zone of the heavy guns while in action, which made the hair of even the calmest horse stand pretty well on end ! In a bombing raid we made one night, two of our parties bombed one another merrily for about ten minutes, much to the amusement of the Bosches who popped up their heads to watch them.

With little nightly adventures such as this we passed through July into August, during which time the battalion were not once farther from the trenches than a mile and a half. Fortunately rations improved after the first week in July, but even so, the companies missed the pokey shops and so-called canteens which were sometimes better than nothing when parcels were scarce. The Devils' Mess were particularly fortunate with parcels about this time, and with the better food, the improvement in the weather and the good news in the papers we were beginning to recover from the shock of July 1st, when so many old friends were taken from us.

" Down south," from all accounts, there had been some very severe fighting. We got newspapers every day and followed the progress on the Somme with enthusiasm, tempered by the realisation of the casualties it must involve. On the 11th of July Contalmaison had fallen ; on the 15th, in a set-piece attack, the German second line of defence had been captured with more villages, and a handful of cavalry had been used for reconnoitring. After that the fighting of the woods had developed. High Wood, Trones Wood, Delville Wood were the scenes of most bitter fighting. Our men would take a wood six times and lose it as many. each capture involving an immediate heavy bombardment from the vanquished, succeeded by a counter-attack. The woods were thus the scenes of some awful slaughter, but on balance the British were the gainers and our line was pushed gradually forward, though at heavy sacrifices. The Germans had a wholesome dread of our artillery, which admittedly far outweighed their own, and as for their air-service it was non-existent, their machines being afraid to venture over our lines. Of course, we had read such tales before and were inclined to discount a good deal of the newspaper reports, but, after all, we had evidence before us on our own front. The German gunfire could be extremely unpleasant, but its volume was nothing compared with our own, while our aeroplanes seemed to have the sky to themselves. The attacks were worrying them and they had transferred troops from the Verdun front, where the Germans seemed only too glad of an excuse to drop their offensive.

To the Somme we should go—we felt it in our bones. In spite of the nasty " cut-up " we had received we should be used again, for the British could not keep up such pressure on the Somme without continual reliefs of the divisions employed. Therefore we came to realise how comparatively well off we were during these August days and to regard Hannescamps, Bienvillers and St. Amand as " rest camps." The call of the Somme would come sooner or later and every night that passed we watched those flashes and wondered what conditions were like down there. Sometimes the sound of gun-fire from the Somme battle actually pierced the veil and we heard it in our valley. On the 8th of August. for instance, there was a terrific bombardment down south which increased at dawn and continued throughout the day.

We never met anyone who could give us a description of what life and transport work was like down there, though once, when taking a limber over to Doullens, I passed through Halloy where I spoke to a man who had helped to take Fricourt. However, beyond his allusion to it as " an 'ell," he was not discursive on the subject, though he waxed eloquent over some German souvenirs he possessed. I purchased a German forage-cap for two francs, which I subsequently sold to Eustace, the Q.M.'s batman, for ten.

The trivial incidents of our existence during our last week or so on this front are recorded in the following letter:

11/8/16. "Although we are only three miles from the line here, the Germans never shell the place, as they apparently reserve their ration of shells for the trenches and the village behind them. They did get rather annoyed with the next village (Souastre) last week, sending over one or two " chance " shells, but since then they have left it alone Hobson was on his way to the canteen there to buy some toothpaste at the time, but when he heard explosions in the direction of the village he thought better of it, retraced his steps and said his teeth could wait till to-morrow

" My grey horse is a cute sort of creature, for he knows very well when he gets within a couple of miles of the trenches that he isn't in too healthy a place. When a flare-light goes up he pricks up his ears, cocks his head on one side and regards it inquisitively, and if a machine-gun starts popping he gets very restless. Naturally our guns make him jump about pretty badly and shells affect him in the same way. Imagine his consternation when one night we met a ' caterpillar ' tractor hauling along one or two lorries with a gun on board! Fortunately I was not driving my limber, as I had left a field-kitchen up in (Hannescamps) returning with the two horses. At the sight of this monster approaching him. The Grey reared up on his hind legs, turned round two or three times and then rushed up a bank, while the other horse wondered what was the matter and resented following his lead, so that I nearly lost my hold of Jumbo. It ended in The Grey falling back in the road almost bang on top of the dreaded ' caterpillar ' which stopped for his benefit. However, on his second attempt to scale the bank, he succeeded, taking me for a wild gallop across potatoes, cabbages, corn and other crops, to the great annoyance of Jumbo, whom I was dragging along at the full length of his reins. When I eventually got them back to the road, another ' caterpillar ' came along and we went through the same performance over again. This time our canter was pulled up short by The Grey becoming entangled with some barbed wire. It took me twenty minutes to disentangle him for he won't lift his hind leg up and I had to dodge kicks and hold the two alarmed animals while I wrestled with the barbed wire. So we *do* have a little excitement, you see, just to relieve the monotony.

" This week has been an eventful one, for we have had two great inspections, one by a veterinary officer, the other by the G.O.C., who inspected everything from harness and horses down to clothes lines and rubbish boxes. Most of the harness looked beautiful, but I am not very accomplished in the art of cleaning it, as you know ; consequently my two sets always looked more or less moth-eaten, however hard I work. The officer and N.C.O.s arrived at my rack and suddenly exclaimed, ' Who the devil does this belong to ? ' Trendell remarks, ' Oh, that's Aubrey Smith's.' ' Oh ! ' A shrug of the shoulders, a half-smile, and they pass on. You will thus appreciate why they sent me out on a job on the day in question, so that my harness would escape the General's eye.

" I assisted in the general clear-up before he came round and did my best to observe the rules about cigarette ends and bits of string. The chief idea is to hide everything you possess when an inspection is on, and I crammed underclothes, muddy mackintoshes, wet sponge-bags and sundry eatables under my ground-sheet, in my effort to please him. By doing this it meant that the hour I had spent in washing a shirt the previous evening was completely wasted, as it got mixed up with a pair of boots while it was still damp, so it had to be washed again.

" I wish I had gleaned a few hints about washing shirts before I left home. I use a whole cake of soap over one shirt, take a very·long time to lather it, and in the end the washed article is covered with light and dark patches, principally dark ones. Even if ' Tommy ' is supposed to be so resourceful and handy, you see it isn't true of everyone ! Perhaps it is only by chance that my harness rack collapses about twice a week, but as mine is the only one that suffers in this way it is possible that the designer is not as resourceful as he might be.

" I suppose it is really a disgrace that my friends should decline my help in erecting bivvies or cooking the supper. After my first attempt at cooking they one and all declared I should never be allowed to touch the Primus stove again, so now I enjoy the luxury of eating boiled custard or tapioca, etc., without helping to make it. The reason is quite simple. I tried to fry six eggs, smashed one and served up the five as a yellow mess covering the bottom of the frying-pan ; following this by a terrible concoction made out of salt and flour in mistake for sugar and custard-powder. Since then I have done no cooking, so it is an ill wind that blows nobody any good ! "

On August 15th Colonel Bates, who had shepherded us through the Second Battle of Ypres and Gommecourt, went home on sick leave, much to our sorrow, and he was succeeded by Major Husey, with Captain Wallis as second-in-command. At length, on the 17th, we heard that our stay in the valley would shortly terminate, as the division was being withdrawn for a rest and refitting ; three days later the 17th Division transports arrived to relieve us, while our brigade set off upon a route march in a westerly direction. Then followed a three-day trek in broiling hot weather, along dusty roads and in full equipment. Towards the end of the second day men fell out in twos and threes by the wayside, and Captain Wallis and the M.O. had a very busy time in the rear of the battalion, though our unit did not suffer from stragglers to the same extent as others, while it is only fair to what was left of the pre-Gommecourt L.R.B. men to say that those stragglers were, almost without exception, draft men from other regiments who now made up most of our numbers. At the close of that day's march Major Husey delivered a smart lecture which resulted in better marching discipline upon the following day.

Our halting places were Sus St. Leger and Wavans, at which villages we rose at three or four o'clock to continue our journey. On the third day we arrived at a small place called Canchy, some five miles from Abbeville, which latter was out of bounds for us except on business. Not only that, but we were not allowed even to leave Canchy without obtaining a pass, a rather needless regulation as Abbeville was the only place outside our area to which anyone had the slightest desire to go.

The evidence of defective discipline—perhaps that is too strong a word—among the draft men led the officers to enforce very militaristic

ideas while undergoing our training here.   It was, of course, most
galling to the few old L.R.B. men left, who were accustomed to
being treated leniently as intelligent and trustworthy, and the C.O.
allowed his sympathy for them to be known.   They had to suffer for
the sins of the few, for there were among the new-comers certain types
of individuals who, if given an inch, would take a yard.

The red-tape flying around re-acted in part upon the transport,
who had to observe strict rules as to inspection of billets and kits,
clean hat badges and a score of other details.   After two days of this
sort of thing we were looking forward to being in the firing-line again,
even on the Somme.   The Army suddenly became lavish with clean
clothing and insisting on everyone who had a creased tunic being
promptly issued with a new one.   I gave in a very serviceable tunic
and many others were made to do the same; there was not even a
grease-spot on mine, the only fault being a tiny tear in one of the
pockets.   The only people to see me were French peasants, yet I had
to give in as useless a coat which the poor old English taxpayers had
stinted themselves to provide.   We should have to pay for this waste
after the War !

The companies went out trench-digging and manœuvring sometimes, and it fell to my lot to take A Company's cooker to supply
their dinner.   During my wait I allowed the horses to graze while I
sat down and wrote letters.

On the 31st of August, before setting out on one of these field days,
the C.O. addressed us and said that we were about to see a very
wonderful thing that day and that no reference was to be made to it
in any letters, as it was a secret, a statement which roused considerable
curiosity.   What with secret inventions, the entry of Portugal and
Roumania into the War, the Italian successes on the Isonzo and our
offensive in the West, things seemed to be really going in our favour
at last.

What I saw from a hillock that day was a number of black dots
giving forth smoke or steam, crawling across the plain where the
infantry were practising.   They were too far away for me to be able
to compare them with any known object and it was only when the
companies returned for their meal that I heard details of the prowess
of the " tanks."

"They'll run across any trench and tear up barbed wire like
paper."

" They'll run straight into any house and crush it flat."

" Any tree less than sixteen inches in diameter will bend like
matchwood when they run against it. . . ."

The powers credited to these monsters were far in excess of what
experience proved the earlier designs were capable of performing.
But the faith in them was there and there was tremendous enthusiasm
over this secret which was to be let loose upon Jerry.

The field day with the tanks practically completed our short training,
for on September 2nd the transport started off in the direction of
the line, the battalion entraining simultaneously for an unknown
destination.   We could make a pretty shrewd guess as to our goal ;
it was not a place where new tunics were of much avail.

We stayed for one night in La Chausee and on the following day
passed through the outskirts of Amiens, but unfortunately could not
see the centre of the town.   We caught here a glimpse of civilisation
once again and actually encountered a real live tramcar careering along ;

at this I had to add trams to the list of my grey's terrors, for he rushed across the road—I simply could not hold him—and nearly charged into a shop window.

On and on we went, meeting many fresh sights, such as Senegalese black troops making a railway line, French transport lines by the wayside, and a village full of French Algerian soldiers. The latter were about to be conveyed to the trenches ready to take part in an attack upon the next morning, and were standing about in groups or filling their flasks with wine preparatory to their departure. They expressed their camaraderie by various signs of friendship and words of good cheer.

The rumble of distant cannon grew ever closer, at first reaching us in occasional gusts, then becoming more continuous. Though we knew it not then, a great attack was being made at noon against Ginchy and the Waterlot and Falfemont Farms, gruesome bones of contention, all of them. At our destination, Corbie—where we found the battalion waiting for us—we were within fifteen miles of the scene of the "chimozzle."

Corbie was crowded out with the battalions of our brigade, who settled down in billets with a feeling that their training would be continued there for a few days All the familiar back area signs of battle were there : endless lorry convoys passing in both directions. French transport followed by British, then French lorries, French artillery, British ambulances, British heavy guns drawn by tractors. What colossal dumps, what myriads of horses, what scenes of bustle and confusion lay ahead of us up there ?

Early next morning the gunfire increased in volume—representing a French attack and a further British attempt against Ginchy. There was always some attack recorded in the papers, always some excitement "on the Somme."

We had our first taste of excitement almost immediately.

Harness up at once ! We leave the village in forty minutes !

The time is 1.20 p.m. I am relieving another man on line-orderly duty and have not had my dinner. All my kit is lying about in disorder in the billet, a few minutes away. Fresh feeds to draw ! Harness to put on ! Pack, grooming-kit, overcoat, buckets, nosebags, etc., to be taken to the cooker five minutes away down the street : two journeys necessary. General confusion on the horselines. Forage and a hundred and one other things to be packed. Requests that I shall assist the reloading of the limbers dismissed with appropriate language. Forty minutes' bustle in the midday heat. Forty minutes' cursing of the Army and all pertaining to it.

At 2 p.m. I reached the cooker and bundled my last piece of luggage on board. The brigade is lined up in the street and is moving off. A few minutes later I have charged through the marching ranks of fours, smashed the mudguard of a motor-lorry, overtaken the L.R.B. and squeezed into my allotted position in the convoy, which is heading up the Bray road for the battle area.

Yes, there is excitement on the Somme !

CHAPTER XVI.

THE BATTLE OF THE SOMME: FIRST IMPRESSIONS.

(*September 4th–9th*, 1916.)

"Happy" Valley—A miserable night—We encounter our Allies—Horses everywhere—Up into the inferno—A trip to Death Valley—Traffic congestion—Horselines among the guns—The day of the attack.

In vain do I search through my letters written during the next six weeks for any amusing anecdotes or comments which might help to enliven this account of our adventures on the Somme. Indeed, many of those little details which might serve to refresh my memory in recording events now five years old are missing, for several of our letters were at this period at the mercy of an unintelligent censorship, exercised by sundry subalterns who put up with the transport for a day or so, on their way from English training-camps to join the 1st L.R.B. It was the first time they had undertaken the job and they interpreted the regulations too literally. So it came to pass that, when I said I had been up the line with a water-cart over a very desolate area, necessitating the use of extra horses, finally returning to the lines at midnight, my people would receive a sort of jig-saw puzzle cut out of paper, from which they would probably glean the following:—

"I have been . . . with a . . . over a very . . . necessitating the use of . . . finally returning to the . . . at . . ."

Not very helpful data to one whose recollections of that period are in a somewhat jumbled state! Fortunately those letters censored by Mr. Gordon did not suffer to any extent, and their contents have helped me to remember other events.

Our panic departure from Corbie was followed by a long march, first up the Bray road and then across a muddy field track, which meant "hard going" for both companies and transport. When we reached Morlancourt we found some of the Guards there, looking very smart and soldierly; but we passed on, for our destination was not a habitable rest area, but that immortal spot, "The Happy Valley," known to a great many units in the British Army. Having covered another mile or so, passing a big aerodrome on our left, we crossed the main Bray-Albert road and struck off down a track leading into this valley, where we immediately found ourselves surrounded by horselines. The eastern slope up from the valley was dotted with hundreds of tents, into some of which the L.R.B. were being ushered.

" Cookers this way ! " shouted Simmonds.

Leaving the remainder of the section to carry on, we galloped up a slope between some tents and came upon the site for the cookers—a bare piece of ground in the middle of the camp. It was now dusk, so I hurried off with my horses to join the transport in order to dispose of the animals and find a home before dark. In the midst of all the other units it was rather hard to locate our own section, but, after passing hundreds of horses, I finally heard the welcome sound of Chilcott grousing.

" What's the trouble ? "

" Hurford says there are no tents for the transport. Fancy being stuck out without shelter in this —— spot. Everybody else has got tents. We're the onions every time."

Lance-Corporal Hurford always got all the kicks : he became a convenient football when anything went wrong. And the good-natured old girl took it all with a smiling countenance.

The site for our lines was in a wilderness where there was no shelter for man or beast. Rope had been put up between posts already in the ground, ready for the pony " Tommy " to windsuck upon, while the limbers had been drawn up close at hand and certain horses who usually had pegs to themselves were tied to the wheels. They thoroughly enjoyed nosing around under the limber covers and chewing up any rations or signalling apparatus they could find there.

The cooks had nowhere to make tea—when the cookers were serving the companies our transport cooks had to fend for themselves—nor was there a bivvy for the sergeant or the forage merchant. We were just dumped down in a barren valley with only the sky above our heads, sky which was just preparing to pull the trap out of the bath.

" Horses off to water."

We had to find the place where the horses would be able to get their liquid refreshment. Three-quarters of a mile away was a sea of mud ; in the middle of the sea, invisible except through a telescope, was a collection of " rocks," almost submerged ; and the rocks were water-troughs. When we reached them it was practically dark, but we could see picket-fires to right and left on neighbouring ridges which told of camps and horselines where enemy aeroplanes were apparently disregarded. This was curious after the fear of showing electric torches miles behind the line at Gommecourt ! Every other transport had watered by now, so we plunged through the liquid mud without encountering other queues. At the troughs we dismounted to take out the horses' bits and nearly disappeared up to our knees in muddy water ; before mounting again I had to run several yards beside my horses in my efforts to hop on to the saddle, getting splashed to the neck by Jumbo's dainty paws.

The wants of man are of secondary importance to those of beast. A driver's primary consideration was his horses, for on those poor dumb brutes fell the heavy burden of the day's work and they relied faithfully upon their masters giving them drink and oats as soon as possible at the end of their journey. Never in my experience did a transport man—however weary or hungry he might be—defer his horse's meal in order to satisfy his own wants, and these were pressing enough at times.

Having tied Jumbo and The Grey up to the line and fed them, I set off on foot to the cooker to get the remainder of my kit—not that I had any use for it that night, but things had a remarkable habit of simply disappearing—and to see if there was by any chance a cup of tea to be had there : our cooks had a fire under way, but it might be Doomsday before we got anything. As for rations, I felt precisely as though my diet that day had been a caraway seed, but there were the remains of a parcel (along with some harness-rag and boot-brushes) in my haversack, which would save me from starving that night.

A Company cooks were recognisable by emphatic language emanating from Edwards and King—there was a good deal of cursing floating around on this night—whom I discovered making an attempt to fix up ground-sheets to the cooker pole by means of bootlaces and haywire. The tents were crowded out and they were homeless as we were, but at least they would have nice red-hot cinders falling on them if they slept under the cooker, whereas we should feel decidedly chilly. I knew that. Yes, I might find a drop of tea left in the dixie. . . . Empty ? Oh, the company must have finished it up. No, there was no more.

It was pouring with rain now and I slid about in the mud as I made my way down to the lines again. Where were we going to sleep ? Must we simply lie in the mud and get rained on ? Rather than that we should walk about all night. The Army was considerate, we *didn't* think! No shelter, no blankets, no rations, no 'ope. The conversations of the next quarter of an hour would have made a Bolshevist see red.

At last, after a fruitless search for bivvy material, one of the Q.M. storemen brought along a huge tarpaulin which had been " won " at St. Amand and carried on one of the A.S.C. baggage wagons. Prior to its appearance at St. Amand I should imagine it had been used as a practice target at the Machine-gun School at Wisques and had then been passed on to the R.G.A. for artillery target work. At any rate, it was full of holes of varying shapes and sizes, but it would be better than nothing on a night like this. About twenty of us started to unroll it, draping it over one or two posts and limbers until it afforded a kind of roof varying in height from two to six feet. Under this we dragged several ammunition and bomb boxes, oatsacks and shovels to sit on—it was dangerous to lie down, for only one sickly lamp illumined the whole abode and there was a likelihood of faces getting smashed in by people's boots. The Devils' Mess quartette started off by sitting back to back in a little group, each helping to prop the other three up. One or two others got into the limbers or squatted against the wheels— some risked being stumbled over and lay on ground-sheets in the mud. Practically the entire section curled itself up into impossible and agonising positions, awaiting the inevitable deluge as the rain-water settled first in one part of the roof and then another.

What a night we spent ! " Happy Valley," indeed ! Outside the weather was stormy and tempestuous : the rain came down in torrents, pattering incessantly on the tarpaulin which almost touched our heads. The wind came up the valley with a roar, bringing us the battle echoes from a few miles away. At Neuve Chapelle or La Bassee or Loos, not to mention Ypres, such weather would promptly have put a stop to all operations, but here the guns were going incessantly, like a perpetual thunderclap. Even while we were bemoaning our discomforts we were in a palace compared with the men around Guillemont, for those guns meant that a night attack was being made up there, an attack in which our men pushed nearly a mile east of that village, which had just been captured. On this night, also, the 5th Division obtained a footing in Leuze Wood and captured the enemy's defensive system around Falfemont Farm. There was further fighting round Ginchy. Whatever the weather was like, the offensive was—rightly or wrongly—pushed incessantly in these parts.

And so we yawned on and swore and sat under spouts of water, got up to stretch, went out in the rain to relieve the monotony, talked to the picket, enquired the time, returned to find our place taken, cursed again, sat down in a pool, dozed off for another five minutes and continued this programme for hour after hour until the first glimmer

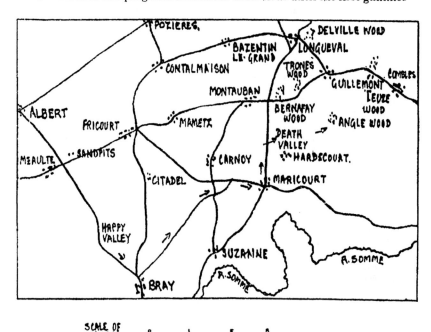

A Few Places upon the Somme mentioned in Chapters 16-18.

of a cheerless dawn. Not many men remained under that " roof " when they could see about them in the open on the horse-lines. An early morning· " Soviet " gathered round the site of the cooks' fire, commenting upon the delinquencies of the British Army and the drawbacks to offensives.

At dawn there was an even greater bombardment, which heralded not only a further attack at Leuze Wood but a big stroke by the French to the south of the Somme. With every day that passed the Germans stated that our artillery preparation was more intense than on any previous occasion. It was thoroughly alarming them, and Hindenburg and Ludendorff had just been brought to the Western Front to retrieve the situation. What upset them most was not the loss of land so much as the serious depletion of their artillery under our fire, the constant need of relieving divisions and the shortage of ammunition. They called a definite halt to the farce down at Verdun and set to work organising their man-power and munition work, also the construction of further lines of defence in the rear.

Six o'clock came at last. Soon afterwards we set off for the water-troughs, and on the way there were able to see about us much better than on the previous evening. The panorama remains vividly in my memory to this day. To right and left, on near ridges and distant hills, were horses, horses, horses. Horses and wagon-lines. Wagon-lines and horses. Wherever one looked there were long lines of animals being walked down to the horses' refreshment-bar. Quite half of them belonged to French units. Over one hill came a long stream of cavalry ; over another an endless queue of artillery mules ; one transport after another, English and French, was either on its way to or returning from the troughs. As for the troughs themselves, they were distinguishable at a great distance by the mass of animals waiting their turn to drink. There was apparently no private bar at this establishment and everyone was treated on an equality. It looked a most hopeless task as we headed for the congested area. Just as we approached it, an artillery section coming from another direction broke into a trot so that their leading pair caught up the tail of the preceding unit before ours did. Chrisp had something to say to the artillery sergeant on this point, but it was unavailing : we had to wait still longer for our turn until the whole of that unit had gone past. It took us well over an hour to get to those troughs and back, for when our horses had drunk their fill it was a difficult matter to get clear again, so fearful were the other units of being pushed out of their places.

It seemed as if the whole of the transports of the British and French armies must be congregated on these ridges above Bray ; never at Ypres had I seen a quarter of the number of horse and wagon-lines or the camps of tents and bivvies. The French soldiers were very friendly. We were apparently on the right of the British line where it joined the French and were evidently destined to see a good deal of our Allies. What pleased me was their freedom from outward show and eyewash. Their wagons were old and their harness did not appear ever to have been washed : it certainly might have been softened somewhat, but the fact that the steelwork was rusty spoke a great deal for their intelligence. Brasso would stand poor chances of sale in their canteens. Were they any wit the less useful as transport units because they did not care a rap about their brass and steel ? On the contrary—their transport work was magnificent.

Now we were up in these wilds where it was impossible to buy any food—canteens seemed to be non-existent—rations instantly became short again : on this day we had a loaf between six and our other rations were cut down. Oh, you who prated about parcels being unnecessary from the troops, come and join us in Happy Valley for the next few weeks of our existence ! Parcels *did* arrive for the Devils' Mess and we all wrote home for bread. What a difference they made to us ! It was a recognised custom on the part of the Q.M. stores, during trying periods for the companies, to cut the transport rations to a minimum for the sake of the trench rations—a policy we did not cavil at other than by grousing generally that the battalion rations were so meagre as to render this treatment necessary. In view of this fact parcels became a dire necessity for our boys and I do not know how ever we should have fared without them.

The Devils' Mess spent a great part of the 5th in building a bivvy up on the slope of the hill : to do this we picked to pieces a hut made of ammunition-boxes which we discovered some distance away. For the roof we used a pack-pony cover, as our supplies of bivvy-building material were inadequate, and as Conibeer now had charge of a pack-pony there was no trouble over our ability to use the cover in question. The Devils said they did not require my assistance and got rid of me during the afternoon by despatching me upon a canteen hunt. After half an hour's wandering I came across one and with eager eyes and longing looks approached the counter.

" Only the — Brigade, R.G.A., served here, mate," said the be-goggled, unshaven assistant behind the counter.

" Can't you let me have a packet of biscuits ? " I asked.

" No, I'm sorry. We've only got Soldiers' Friend, blacking, polishing brushes and Brasso, and I've only enough for the battery."

Soldiers' Friend and Brasso! All the accoutrements for going polishing-mad and not a scrap to fill an aching void in a man's tum !

Just as we were turning in that night we heard that we had to get up at 3 a.m. to be ready to move off at any time. This made my own rising hour twelve midnight, since I was to be on last picket from twelve till three—practically another night loafing around in the rain.

The guns were going hard again. My thought continually dwelt on the racket that was going on a little farther ahead. The capture of Leuze Wood was being completed and there was further fighting around Ginchy, but we did not know this at the time. We heard absolutely nothing of what was going on : we had not seen a paper since leaving Canchy, nor was any news given out to us by Brigade, though we knew from the drumfire that various attacks must be going on. As on the first day of the Somme Battle, the people at home knew all about the fighting long before we did : usually we never learnt anything even afterwards, unless we were lucky enough to get hold of a newspaper. The details of some attacks were absolutely a closed book to me until I read about them after the War. And yet how some of those communiqués would have cheered us up, if only they had been announced to us !

At 3 a.m. while it was still dark, I went from one new bivvy to another, rousing the section. In order to be well prepared, I took my kit up to the cooker, got my saddle blanket, etc., ready, and made final arrangements. Figg groused when I commenced to take our bivvy down before breakfast in order to dispose of the ground-sheets and harness covers which helped to make it waterproof.

" It's all right," said he. " The Army only gets you up in the dark because it wants you to leave at dinner time. My dear chap, there's no hurry. We shan't move till then."

It was, as he said, needless panic. The Army had ordered us to get up at 3 a.m. in order to move in the afternoon. We " stood by " all the morning, not knowing from one moment to another when the order to depart would come to us.

At last we set off with the battalion, passing camp after camp and horse-lines after horse-lines, eventually reaching the Bray-Carnoy road which was a mass of lorries and bustling French transports whose drivers seemed to be in a happy frame of mind.

" Bosche finish ! " they shouted.

" Allemagne caput ! Ha ! Ha ! "

We took their word for it, but felt we should like to see some evidence of this collapse on the part of the enemy.

" Seem awfully bucked with themselves," said Idle. " Anyone would think we'd won the War."

Presently we were diverted from the road to a track at the side, lorries alone being allowed to use the better route. A long British artillery ammunition column passed us, then came A.S.C. wagons, then French farm carts. At one place where we halted a French battalion commander was consulting maps with officers, while the light-blue clad infantry jabbered excitedly in groups. There was something about the enthusiasm of these Allies which kindled keenness in us. We had the greatest faith in their staff-work and every one of their soldiers looked as though he meant business.

Here was a British battalion on its way down from a scrap, laden with souvenirs : a few of the men were wearing German helmets. Their water-carts followed in the rear and I looked with amazement at their turn-out. The horses were caked with mud up to their necks, the harness was practically obliterated with it, the carts themselves looked as if they had been immersed in a mud-bath, while the drivers, with a few days' growth of beard, looked like prehistoric men with whips instead of cudgels. Some artillery limbers passed by in a similar state. Phew ! First-line transport work was a different game here to what it had been even in the previous winter !

We were drawing nearer to the devastated regions now and a terrific bombardment was going on. One or two twelve-inch pieces were getting into position to the south of the Maricourt-Fricourt road, from which eminence, lined by tall trees on either side of the roadway, other guns were visible in the valley upon the far side. They called to mind the July 1st bombardment, for flash followed flash in whatever part of the panorama one chose to look. No sooner had one flash drawn your attention to some big gun away beyond the valley than two more flashes to the right revealed long-muzzled monsters in another spot. The reports from all the guns mingled in a curious oppressive rumble, sufficient to warn The Grey that his old friend the firing-line had turned up again like a bad penny.

Carnoy lay in the valley, a little ruined village which had harboured the battalion headquarters and aid-posts of one or two units that had charged from near this spot on July 1st. Down the hill we went, with camps to the left, horse-lines to the right, nine-point-twos on one side, water-troughs on the other (the latter having a formidable queue of horses trailing away into the dim distance), and two lines of convoys splashing the mud up so that the men on foot had an unenviable march. The battalion had left us by now, carrying on towards the front in a different direction while we plodded on to the prescribed area for our horse-lines on the far side of the village.

We were dumped in a field with not the semblance of a bivvy or of posts for the horse-lines : on three sides were hedges and on the fourth a gun—no, by Gad, a collection of guns, six-inch naval monsters, two of which were firing on our arrival. Behind us were some 9.2's and ahead were numbers of other batteries—altogether a jolly spot for the horses.

" Lewis-gun limbers, cookers, water-carts, mess-cart and medical cart, don't unhook. You're leaving in half an hour," said Simmonds. So this very night we should pass over what had been No Man's Land and tread on territory that had been German. The thought was a thrilling one, for the idea that we should cross ground over which the July 1st attack had been pressed had a peculiar fascination about it. However, it was now almost dark and it was improbable we should be able to see much that night, though we expected an eventful journey, as a German counter-attack on Leuze Wood was in progress and the Ginchy front also was ablaze.

We were able to get a dixie of tea from one of the cookers, which greatly refreshed us, but there was nothing but Army biscuits to eat with it, two of which I put into my pocket, thinking they might be useful. Conibeer, who was remaining in the field, said he would do his best to find a canteen, but the first need was to rig up some kind of bivvy for the mess : this would probably take him an hour or so.

I think Mr. Gordon had followed the battalion in order to ascertain the destination for the transport and he must have rejoined us before our departure : Chrisp came along with us as well. We had to go by a roundabout route, thus going back out of the artillery zone for a short time : our horse-lines were behind a different portion of the front. The traffic on the Maricourt road was appalling and there were three stoppages before we reached Maricourt itself. Of the village little remained, but even the ruins were practically indistinguishable, as it was a pitch black night.

All of a sudden there was a blinding flash on my left, accompanied by a loud report—'twas but a British gun, but my grey shook from head to foot. My heart did a jump of several inches and I began to wish myself in my little bed in England. If only it had been light enough, I should have been prepared for the event and the gunners would probably have stopped us. The gun could not have been ten yards away and the concussion made me deaf in one ear for some hours. After that I was expecting a repetition of the occurrence and, sure enough, shortly afterwards a battery quite close to the road announced its presence by four vivid flashes and explosions, which caused a panic among some horses just ahead of us. My pair were wet with perspiration, caused more by fear than by work. After these dazzling displays, not an inch could I see in front of my pair except by such light as the other flashes afforded, and time and again, when there was a block in the traffic, I crashed into the vehicle in front. The road seemed to be in a very bad state and was barely wide enough for one line of traffic in each direction. Yet along it and one other the whole of the rations and ammunition for the army on the Longueval, High Wood, Ginchy, Guillemont and Leuze Wood fronts, as well as the left part of the French front, had to pass.

Suddenly Gordon called to us to halt and he himself wheeled back, for the head of the convoy had just passed the entrance to a track on the right which we should have taken. It was not too late for all the vehicles behind me to turn off, but my cooker and one other had passed the spot and would have to left-about-turn. My companion (? Harbord) attempted it and got cursed by an artillery officer whose convoy was passing in the opposite direction ; the downward traffic was never-ending, there was a high bank on either side and to turn round seemed an impossibility. Meanwhile, the remainder of our convoy was taking the plunge through a morass which separated the road from a track beyond, and one cooker stuck in the mud, necessitating a spare pair of horses coming to the rescue. In the end they all over-came the obstacle, however, and continued on their way, leaving Harbord and myself vainly endeavouring to turn our cookers round. The folk who were being held up behind us were furious.

" Get a move on there," they kept shouting. If they had had their way, Harbord and I would have been pushed into the German lines through pressure of traffic from behind us! We stuck our ground and referred the people behind to the person in charge of the downward convoy. A few minutes later there was a nasty swish and a Bosche shell landed among the batteries on the left of the road.

"For Hell's sake, get a move on!" they now shouted, with a few epithets thrown in, chiefly descriptive of someone's intelligence or lack of it. In desperation I made yet another attempt to turn, seeing about three yards of space between two passing lorries, with the result that Jumbo almost got run over: he backed and bashed in a dixie that was hanging behind the front half of the cooker. After about a quarter of an hour the opportunity came and we took it, I turning first followed by Harbord, making a three-quarter circle in the road and plunging on to the track the convoy had followed.

The question was: where had they gone? There was no path that we could follow. So far as I could see by the light of the gun-flashes we were in the midst of a sea of shell-holes, one almost joining the other, with wheel marks everywhere and yet no semblance of a track. It was like a picture I had once seen of Hell, with hundreds of people struggling in craters of liquid fire and similar horrors—only these craters were half full of water.

Artillery wagons were getting over the ground somehow on our left, so we could but try to do the same and it was quite possible to keep moving. First Jumbo would slip in a hole, then The Grey: one side of the cooker would tilt over and then the other, bringing cries of anguish from the cooks, whose dixies spilled some of their contents with every bad swoop.

We stopped and shouted. No L.R.B. man answered. However, we were evidently descending into a valley, and having heard the battalion were going to Death Valley, we were probably right in making for the bottom. We were shortly in an inferno, not of enemy-fire but of our own: here in Death Valley—for such it proved to be—guns of all calibres were massed in such numbers that one was fired almost every second in our vicinity. Each flash and bark was followed by a whirring noise in the heavens, as though the sound were being echoed up to the planets.

"Is that Smith?"

Oh, welcome sound! It was Gordon's voice. I do not mean to imply that there was anything extraordinarily musical and charming about his voice at that moment. But I was listening for it as one might wait for the sound of a policeman's tread when attacked by footpads.

"I thought I recognised the old grey. This way."

"I can't see an inch at the moment. Shall I trust to luck?"

"Well, I'll use my torch. It's rather a ticklish problem."

About fifteen yards ahead were the other cookers: the intervening space was one mass of craters with their lips touching one another, some three feet deep, some yawning chasms. Well, here goes!

"Mind the dixies," wailed Idle.

"Mind you don't get stuck. . . . Steady on, you fool. . . . Look out what you're doing. . . ."

Trust Jumbo and The Grey! A whip and a wild war-whoop did the trick. Bump—crash—clatter—bump—and we were alongside the other field-kitchens. A Company's cooker was delivered.

So this was where the companies were stationed—the poor devils were in trenches close at hand in the midst of all this pandemonium ! I unhooked my horses and joined the other animals and vehicles which were waiting to do the journey home together. If we had been able to go straight back to our lines then, it is possible that we should have been home before 1 a.m., but we had not yet learnt what traffic congestion meant on the Somme.

We had to wait nearly an hour before we could get off the track on to the Montauban road again, and then scarcely had we insinuated our way into the downward stream of traffic than a block occurred somewhere ahead, which brought all the vehicles to a standstill. For a quarter of an hour we waited, then half an hour. Nobody budged an inch, at least no vehicle moved. Exasperated French drivers came up from behind and walked forward to investigate. Officers and N.C.O.s passed by and disappeared into the darkness ahead ; we sat on our horses and shivered and munched dog biscuits, our sole diet for the past twelve hours.

The trouble was that a lorry and a gun had become locked, and various vehicles, not content with waiting in the queue, had attempted to pass the stationary vehicles so that a hopeless impasse had been reached, which seemed impossible to disentangle. True, French soldiers who returned from the scene of the deadlock declared that the situation only demanded commonsense and that, left to themselves, they would clear the whole thing up in five minutes. But we of the British Army liked to do things in our own way—time was no object and the queue of vehicles behind us might extend for a couple of miles for all we cared.

Two o'clock came. Two-thirty passed. I know it may seem incredible to the reader, but it is quite true. The French looked upon us as hopeless and passed by after their investigations, gesticulating and expectorating freely. All sorts of people came up from the rear of the column to ascertain what the trouble was. One officer said he had made his way up from the other side of Trones Wood and that there was a mile and a half of traffic behind. Three o'clock came. Presently German shells commenced to arrive. whizzing just over our heads and bursting about a hundred yards away. This was somewhat unsettling, for it is riling to remain perfectly still without cover, when strafeing is taking place. It clinched matters, so far as our Allies were concerned, and they would wait no longer for British ingenuity to free the roadway. They decided to skirt the road by passing through a neighbouring military cemetery and we accordingly saw. just as it was beginning to get light about 3.30 a.m., some scores of French limbers galloping past us *via* the cemetery on our left. The British preferred the road, the cold and the shells, and still waited ; we had got it into our heads that we were going home by road and nothing so unconventional as a drive through a graveyard would deflect us from our purpose.

Towards 4 a.m. our patience was rewarded, for the limbers ahead of us started to move and we followed suit, expressing our opinion of the lorry driver in no uncertain terms as we passed. We arrived home at 4.30 a.m., after which the six-inch naval guns kept us awake until it was time to rise. It should be understood that the guns near our horse-lines were firing on some part of the Martinpuich front, which accounts for the two artillery zones we encountered.

In daylight we were able to take stock of our surroundings. We were miles and miles from civilisation and everything was a shambles. The ground about us was scarred with trenches and pitted with shell-holes; just up the road was the old British front line.   As far as one could see there were horses, horses, horses and battery after battery of heavy guns.   The big guns near us, we heard, were trained on to a village behind the German lines and as soon as men from one battery had done twelve hours' work they knocked off, while the next-door battery immediately took up the target and fired for the next twelve hours, so that—day or night—one particular spot by which Fritz had to bring up his stores was kept under steady shell-fire.   These guns and others in the vicinity created a great din, but after a time we became so accustomed to the noise that each individual report ceased to arrest our attention.

Near by were one or two ruins, but they and the cellars were already being used by the artillery and we had to rely on bivvies—fortunately the weather had cleared up now.   We had long since lost all track of what day of the week it was, one day was exactly like another. On Sundays, if we were lucky, we might get an hour's rest in the afternoon, but there was no other way of distinguishing them.   Only Corporal Main had been to a church parade in the last twelve months— we were becoming fatalists, the rest of us, believing that if there were an all-loving, omnipotent Deity, He would not allow these horrors to be.   This was in contrast to the number that attended the Thanksgiving Service on Armistice Day.

Rations were very meagre indeed and we could buy nothing : most fellows were writing home for bread.   We got a post the next evening, but before that none had arrived for four days, so that any parcels that might have tided us over were not forthcoming.

The day passed quietly enough—save for the gunfire—and we spent an hour or so of it in the neighbourhood of the water-troughs, waiting our turn to swim to them : their surroundings looked as though the taps had been left running for at least a month.

On that evening some of the battalion moved up from Death Valley to the neighbourhood of the famous Falfemont Farm, leaving their packs in a dump by the cookers.   That meant that they were going to be put in an attack and my thoughts went out once again to the few A and D Company men that I knew.   I went up with a limber on this evening, but arrived too late to see my friends.

On September 8th there was an exceptionally heavy bombardment : the guns in our neighbourhood seemed to be able to fire without any hindrance from the enemy, either by shells or aeroplanes.   The fact of the matter was that the Germans were blind.   Our aeroplanes cruised about in the air the whole day long : we saw them heading straight for the German lines and coming and going at will.   A few German machines ventured up, but we rarely saw one, though on this day we watched three aeroplanes brought down—nationality unknown.   Our aeroplanes were superior, while artillery and ammunition were overwhelmingly more abundant.

I do not think that at any other period of the War I saw such a concentration as was massed on the Somme, partly because in this battle our guns stood boldly out in the open, for all the world to see. No better proof of our aerial supremacy was required.   There, drawn up on open ground, was the greater part of the heavy artillery of the British Army, pouring a ceaseless fire on the German positions until every portion of them was pounded out of recognition and receiving in reply only a comparative handful of shells, fired blindly from enemy batteries.   The latter, however, directed a more intense fire upon our front line than anywhere else, so that its local effect was sometimes very severe indeed.

That evening we got orders to move, so we dismantled our bivvies. Figg foretold that we should not leave that night—a shrewd judge of the Army and its ways, was Figg—and, sure enough, our staff shortly afterwards postponed the move until the following day, so that our homes had to be rebuilt. The reason given for moving was that we were too near the batteries and we were accordingly transferred to Happy Valley again.

During the next day it was whispered that the L.R.B. would attack that afternoon, but zero hour was unknown. I set out for Death Valley in daylight after dinner, driving a water-cart, while all the section except that day's ration convoy trekked to the Happy Valley in order to erect some homes before dark. Now I could see all those batteries which had startled me so upon the first night trip, 9.2's, 6-inch howitzers, 8-inch guns and French artillery. Going from Maricourt up the Montauban road we could see ahead of us, to the right, Bernafay and Trones Wood, and, in the distance, the heights about Ginchy. To the left lay Mametz and Fricourt. Nearer at hand were the old front line, the old No Man's Land, the second and third lines of trenches, barely distinguishable amidst the ocean of craters that extended to right and left. Amongst these trenches the concentration of our guns was incredible : and they were all " firing rapid " across the road we were using.

It was by no means pleasant, passing through that zone. Once or twice we came to a battery that signalled to us to halt and I had to do my utmost to keep the prancing Grey still, while a gun close by was elevated and fired. The noise of the explosion and the concussion made me feel thankful I was not a R.G.A. man. Either this was the preparation for the attack or it was actually being launched.

I looked half right in the direction in which the guns were pointing— a couple of shattered woods and a few mud-coloured ridges were distinguishable, but a pall of yellowish smoke hung over the battlefield and the air was dense with the fumes of our guns. Somewhere over there the L.R.B. were attacking : somewhere over there were those shattered villages of Guillemont and Ginchy, the latter still uncaptured in spite of repeated attempts. Somewhere over there was Leuze Wood, where our boys were.

However, I had to stop at Death Valley, for from that point water would have to be taken up in petrol cans on pack ponies. Whether this was done on that particular evening I do not know, but the whole of the water arrangements were under the control of Brigade throughout this battle, all the water-carts and pack-ponies required being drawn by them from the various transports. The ground beyond the valley was supposed to be impassable for limbers, but, as a matter of fact, Gordon, Macloughlin and Vallentine achieved the impossible on this or one other evening by taking two limbers forward over that ground for more than a mile. I believe they were the first vehicles to accomplish the journey on that particular route, for they had to bridge trenches in their efforts to get forward to Angle Wood.

The sun was low in the heavens as I stood in Death Valley and looked around at the scene of desolation. Dead horses, smashed limbers and numerous stray shells and shell-cases lay about. What courage it must have required to have stormed that further slope ! The dead had been removed, but other traces remained. Whose had been that half-buried haversack there, with its jagged edge where some piece of shrapnel had ripped it open ? Whose that blood-stained overcoat cast off in a shell-hole ? Four men passed by slowly bearing a stretcher along in the direction of a six-horse ambulance which was waiting close at hand. A few yards away was the pile of L.R.B. packs—I wondered how many would come back to claim them.

Death Valley indeed ! The whole place was ghoulish. The reek from the guns, the dead horses, the foul soil and the lachrymatory shells made the place repulsive and horrible. And yet, in the holes and trenches and dug-outs in this hill-side, hundreds of R.A.M.C., artillery and infantrymen slept, ate, scratched themselves and swore from morning till night, hoping for a slight wound to take them out of the line and, with luck, to England.

Anything to get out of that inferno !

CHAPTER XVII.

THE BATTLE OF THE SOMME: WATER-CART DUTY.

(*September*, 1916.)

The Leuze Wood affair—The transport and water problem—The attack of September 15th—Carting water to Angle Wood—The next attack—We move to the Citadel—Fall of Combles and relief of the L.R.B.

THE attack in which our boys took part on the 9th of September has been told so vividly by Captain Nobbs, who led the charge and was blinded within a few yards of the German trench, that no description seems necessary. His book, "Englishman, Kamerad!" has been read by all those who are interested in the L.R.B. and conveys the best pen picture of one's own personal feelings during an attack that I have ever read. This battle was Capt. Nobbs' first experience of warfare; he had to lead a company in a charge from Leuze Wood against a peculiar-shaped German trench, which had to be taken at all costs. The Germans, however, "got wind" of the attack and shelled our men unmercifully while they were assembling. Leuze Wood itself was a shambles and it is a wonder that anyone got through the barrage to take part in the attack on the farther side. Nevertheless, those that came through unscathed bravely started off at zero hour, raked by a concentrated machine-gun fire which absolutely decimated them. With remarkable vividness, Captain Nobbs describes how men laughed and cried during that advance, as one after another darted from shell-hole to shell-hole, cheating death at every bound.

With a bare handful of men he finally flung himself down within a few yards of the German parapet and endeavoured to send messages back to supports who, it transpired, had been so cut to pieces in the wood that they could render no assistance whatever. Captain Nobbs then led a forlorn little charge and was shot in the head and blinded; the enemy subsequently took him prisoner. From his book we learn that an entirely fresh set of orders was issued about an hour before the attack was due, resulting in a good deal of confusion at the last minute—altogether it would seem that some staff work was very much at fault.

The 4.45 attack, which took place on a three-and-a-half mile front, resulted elsewhere in the capture of Ginchy, some ground to the south of it, and a small advance east of High Wood. So that is what all

that bombardment had meant ! All this had been taking place while
I was going up to Death Valley with the water-cart, mentally observing
that our guns drew no return fire upon themselves. No, the infantry
got all the return fire.

By means of empty ammunition boxes won from an abandoned
group of bivvies about a mile away—all traces of our previous home
had disappeared—our fellows had arranged some kind of shelter at
the horse-lines in Happy Valley, which was a peaceful spot compared
with the field at Carnoy.

Its disadvantage lay in its long distance from the line. It was
over three miles from Carnoy and five miles from Death Valley, as the
crow flies and as we should like to have flown. This meant a six-
mile journey by the tracks and zigzagging roads we had to follow,
so that the pack-pony men who set off in the afternoons from the
transport-lines had a very tiring journey. When they went to Angle
Wood and beyond, they had an additional mile or so of " impassable
ground " to cover *on foot*, leading in many cases cantankerous ponies
or obstinate mules who had to be dragged every inch of the way,
persuaded from behind by a stick in the hand of the next pack man.
This meant that they were away sometimes for sixteen hours and more,
arriving back after daylight. Fortunately, nearly every one on the
section took a share in this work, so that men only had this experience
on alternate nights. Nobody could have led a pack-pony through
mud for sixteen hours out of twenty-four for several nights in succession.
And yet there were brilliant amateur newspaper critics who argued
that there was a needless train of transport behind the line and that
infantry transports could be drastically cut down. One delegation
of M.P.s had suggested that infantry transport work could be done
by C3 men ; the poor decrepit old buffers would have crocked up in
twenty-four hours. As it was, most of our fellows felt the strain very
much.

Four of us with heavy horses were exempted from this work, for
we had a special task of our own, viz., water-cart duty, a job on which
four horses had to be used for each cart owing to the mud and difficult
transport conditions. The water-supply on the Somme was a difficult
problem indeed, for hundreds of thousands of men and animals had
to be supplied in the devastated wastes, and there was only a limited
number of sources of supply, which had been opened up by R.E.s
and were surrounded all day long by carts from scores of units, waiting
in long lines for their turn to fill. Usually, when one load had been
emptied, it was necessary to return three or four miles to the refilling
point and bring a second one. Sometimes the water-supply gave out
before our turn came to fill, which meant that a trip had to be made,
perhaps, to Fricourt, two miles even farther away, where the queue
trouble arose all over again.

On the 10th Simmonds detailed the water-cart drivers for this
job and warned us that he did not know for how long we should be
away. The Devils' Mess surveyed their rations to see what titbits
they could spare me for my haversack ; their dinner was to be skilly,
which I obviously could not take with me, and the larder consisted
merely of a knob of cheese, a quarter of a tin of jam and four biscuits.
However, once again a parcel saved us and I was able to fortify myself
with a few Bovril lozenges and a piece of cake, a menu that had to
suffice from breakfast time until eleven o'clock that night. The
Army had to confess its inability to supply a man who had to go out

for twelve hours on end. Our battalion Q.M.S. did not encourage questions on the point.

I do not think I have described our Q.M.S. before. He was a burly man, one Hamilton to wit, who had a reputation for simply barking you out of the stores if you dared to put your head inside. As a matter of fact he was, at heart, a decent old boy and took all my parodies about him, in the magazine and elsewhere, in the best spirit. He bore me no grudge for them. Where he and I fell out was over the frequent indents I made for new breeches. For months on end I had to go about with my knee sticking through my breeches, partly through his obstinacy and partly through the inability of Ordnance to supply my size. Once he took compassion on me and lent me a spare pair of his own, which were the only pair he could find to fit me. Within half an hour I had stumbled in a ruin in Guemappe and slit his breeches in precisely the same place. Knowing Hamilton's reputation for slanging people, everybody commiserated with me on my misfortune and trembled for me as I approached the stores to explain matters. I myself was quivering like an asp. Men gathered outside the tent to watch me come flying through the door. The news spread to far and near and the Q.V.R.'s transport were on the *qui vive* for the outburst that was anticipated. Selecting my opportunity after he had just finished a specially good tea his batman had prepared, I walked up and explained my misfortune. To my utter astonishment his face relaxed into a smile. " Smith," said he, shaking his head, " I suppose you'll write another parody about this ! "

The next day I heard a few details of our boys' attack and was pleased to hear that, though Fulkes was wounded, he only had a " Blighty " wound in the elbow. Davis was all right, while Gernat (with brigade headquarters) and Whittle (with the trench mortars) had escaped the affair. I also heard rumours of a big set-piece attack that was to take place in a few days and, as if to confirm it, we saw the tanks arriving on railway trucks, camouflaged with painted canvas. The tanks were parked at a short distance from the Bray-Fricourt road and were surrounded by hundreds of amazed British and French troops, to whom this was the first glimpse of these new engines of war. We wondered what the Germans would think when they saw them : our French allies seemed delighted with the new toys and, shaking their heads wisely, remarked " Germany finish ! " with sincere conviction.

We had one or two false alarms about the new attack, for there were minor affairs on the preceding days when it sounded as though the whole front was ablaze. But on the evening of the 13th or 14th it was obvious that we meant business, for on my way back from a water-cart job, coming along the Maricourt road, I heard a clanking, snorting sound and the next instant recognised a tank worming its way slowly along with the upgoing traffic. Every pair of horses that saw it had varying degrees of fright. The road seemed to be a kind of circus. My own pair, erring in company with others for once, made a dive for the side of the road and ran among some tents. A little way behind me, Butt—one of our water-cart drivers—somehow or other got thrown from his horse, kicked by a mule and squashed flat by an empty limber which passed over him, He had to be taken to hospital, much to our grief, but fortunately rejoined us a few weeks later.

The big attack against the German third system of defence took place at 6.20 a.m. on the 15th, at which hour the bombardment attained a furious pitch. From the Happy Valley we could hear more distinctly the kettle-drum fire of the French .75's on their portion of the front, but the vibration in the air seemed to come from all directions. Twelve divisions were going over the top and forty tanks were being used. The 56th Division was again in the fray at the extreme right of the British army, attacking Bouleaux Wood and the ground to the right of it. At the close of the day, Courcelette, Martinpuich and Flers had been captured, High Wood finally cleared, and the Guards had advanced well between Delville Wood and Ginchy. It had been a day of hard fighting and unequal results, but of immense importance in driving our wedge still farther into the German line and threatening their stronghold at Thiepval.

We learnt all this long afterwards, as also the fact that, while the tanks had in one or two instances been a distinct success, their weakness for breaking down had incapacitated the majority of them at an early stage in the operations. The Germans had certainly been terrified at them, but the infantry, not the tanks, had won the success of the day. In fairness to the men who worked these machines, they would have to be given much more swift, powerful, easy-turning tanks before they could expect to score a big success.

The next day the water-cart drivers were to make their way to Angle Wood—which we were told we could not miss—over a mile past Death Valley, by means of that track which had hitherto been barred to them. Vallentine came as my lead driver, with his famous pair of horses, Gog and Magog, celebrated for their kicking propensities, which rather disturbed my peace of mind as I drove just behind them. It was a lovely morning and there was a freshness in the air which made me look on the bright side of things : moreover, I had just been able to procure some tinned rabbit at a canteen !

The back areas were infested with troops and horses, working like millions of ants, one and all concerned with the conveyance of supplies and the facilitating of the work. Parties of engineers and labour corps men were laying down broad-gauge railways and light tracks, making railheads and constructing bridges. Pioneer battalions and others were digging gulleys and huge wayside pits for the road mud to be swept into, filling up shell-holes and throwing down bricks. A battalion of West Indies negroes in Maricourt were widening the road ; farther on some more of them were assisting the R.G.A. men with their shells, rolling them from the wayside down planks of wood to the gun positions. The guns themselves were but moderately active, but lorries kept arriving with shells and yet more shells until it became quite a problem as to where to store them all. Artillery ammunition columns, working by day and by night, gave the road-menders no chance to put in any work, but the latter did not seem to worry very much. The majority of them were content to lean on their shovels and wait placidly for the convoys to end ; and then when they saw a lorry coming along a short distance away they would consider it useless resuming work until that also had passed.

Up the Montauban road there was a big dressing-station with several motor ambulances outside it and a group of some twenty to thirty slight cases was waiting for attention. The motor ambulances waited for a full load and then set off down the road to swell the number of vehicles already there.

The far slope of Death Valley was very steep and muddy and at one moment it seemed as if we should come to a standstill, but we urged the horses on with shouts and various unearthly noises and so reached the summit. There was no recognisable track and it was impossible to drive without one wheel or the other continually sinking into craters. The horses had to be constantly urged forward, half-trotting, half-walking. Over on our left was Trones Wood, with its shattered trees looking like so many clothes-props, while on the right were the remains of Hardicourt, now reduced to ground level and pounded into the earth with shell-fire.

We were struggling along on a plateau with a dip about three-quarters of a mile ahead and beyond was a big ridge with a fair-sized town upon its slope. Were the Germans there or not ? Surely they must be, in view of the fact that we were already in the neighbourhood of our field guns. And yet, if they were, they could see us coming over this sky-line as easily as we could distinguish the individual houses in the town.

While we were speculating upon this point, there was a big spurt of earth a little distance ahead of us, followed by the sound of the explosion a second afterwards. Then came another geyser of earth a little to our left. We broke into a full trot and the R.A.M.C. water man hopped on to the back of the cart. This was evidently an un-healthy neighbourhood ! We passed over a bridge over a deep trench, where we envied the occupants their snug retreat ; we dodged round a dead horse and a smashed gun-limber and continued helter-skelter through the maze of shell-holes till we came to the far edge of the plateau, where a very steep slope led us down to the valley. At the top of this slope two wagons and about six horses were lying in a heap and just before and after we reached the spot great geysers of earth rose close to the wreckage. In common parlance, we were " taped." Before you could say " Jack Robinson " we were rushing down the slope, the carts absolutely running away with us, and we were carried by the impetus right along a track beside a wood which indicated our destination. We were thankful to be off the skyline at last and started to breathe once more.

There were numbers of Argyll and Sutherland Highlanders about here who had recently provided reinforcements and a Scotch accent for the London Scottish. Beside the wood was a French battery—oh, age of miracles ! the Frenchmen were laughing over a hand of cards !

Death Valley was not nearly such a shambles as the spot we were in now : the shell-holes were so close together that we drove bodily through one crater after another until the poor horses were utterly fagged out and steaming with heat. Having passed about half a dozen dead mules we rounded a corner and drew up in a shell-hole close to some of our fellows who were in support. Here an R.A.M.C. man, detailed by the Brigade, appeared to be in charge of the Brigade water-supply and superintended the drawing-off of the water into petrol cans. The 2nd Londons and ourselves supplied the water on one day and the Q.V.R. and Q.W.R. the next.

In the meantime, Kimbo and I and the other drivers dismounted and looked round at the scene of desolation about us. French and British field-guns were concealed here and German howitzer shells were falling in the vicinity. The enemy seemed to have few shells to spare for the back areas during the Somme battle, as I have remarked, but up here we could hear plenty of " crumps " in the region of the front-line trenches (or rather lines of shell-holes) and the field-gun area was none too comfortable.

" How long are you up here for ? " I asked one fellow on the water fatigue.

" Goodness knows ! Looks like duration. They'll keep us up here till we're all wiped out, I expect."

" Where's Leuze Wood ? "

" Lousy Wood ? Just ahead, half left."

" And what's that town on the hill there ? "

" That, why, it's Combles. That's our objective."

So it was indeed in German hands ! No wonder they could control their fire from a vantage-point like that !

After waiting about half an hour, we were told the brigade wanted a further supply of water, so we should have to return to a place four miles away to fill up again. This meant that the gauntlet would have to be run three more times that day, but the most distressing part about it was the state of the " gee-gees," who were still panting and foaming after their exertions.

At dinner-time we reached the water-filling point and waited our turn behind thirty more water-carts, passing our time by munching biscuits. Owing to delays on the road and the necessity of resting the animals, it was nearly bedtime when we got back to the dinner-tea that was waiting for us in Happy Valley. Here I learnt that I was on last picket from 2 to 6 a.m., but I was able to take my tunic and boots off for a few hours. Last picket had its advantages, for it was possible to have a leisurely wash and shave, and sometimes a " bath," after daybreak before anyone else was astir in the camp. On this picket many of the pack-pony men straggled in individually and we kept tea hot for them. They then turned in and slept all the morning. Their nightmare journeys over those crater-lands meant real feats of human endurance.

The next night the weather changed, for I woke up to find my feet soaking wet as they were protruding from the bivvy in a downpour of rain. However, there was much to be thankful for in having a bivvy at all when the companies were wallowing in shell-holes, without even a saddle-blanket for warmth.

Henceforth I had an outing on at least alternate days, carrying water up to Angle Wood and doing a second journey when required. Coming under enemy observation as we did, we frequently received attention at his hands, but with the spell of wet weather we were now experiencing the mud became a much more trying enemy than the shell-bursts, and we occasionally used six horses. The lead driver got splashed to such an extent by the horses behind that not only his horses and harness but his overcoat, neck, ears and hat were smothered in slime and his hair was matted and caked with earth. Returning from these journeys, my appearance caused a considerable amount of merriment among the French soldiers, and, indeed, everyone who did not realise the condition of the advanced tracks looked in amazement at the state in which we emerged from our race through the craters.

No details of our adventures during the next week remain in my letters. Even when I wrote to my people saying that I shared their pleasure " in *reading* what our new tanks have done "—this was some days after they had been in action—some zealous censor cut it out of my letter.

On the 24th I was delighted at the arrival of my old friend Wood, whom I had last seen hobbling away from our trench following the gas-attack at St. Julien in 1915. He came now as an acting-corporal in charge of a draft of forty-five L.R.B. men, who had been lucky enough to get through to their own regiment instead of being drafted off to the 17th Hackney Harriers and such units. They put up at the transport lines, and Wood and I sat up till late at night, comparing experiences and exchanging titbits of information about the office staff. Farquharson had died of enteric in Mesopotamia. Truly there were compensations for being on the Western Front and the almost entire absence of contagious diseases was not the least among them.

Continuous fighting had been going on in the various sectors of the Somme battle-front during the past week, but on our sector the next attack of note was made on the 25th, when the 168th Brigade stormed Bouleaux Wood. At the same time fell Lesboeufs and Morval, two village sites on our left front where bitter fighting had been in progress.

We carried out the water-cart duty that day during the bombardment covering the attack, and the memory of that artillery zone shrouded in fumes is a distinct one. All those guns which seemed to have been working at half pressure during our recent trips were now in full chorus. We had to wait a couple of minutes while the fifteen-inch railway gun at Maricourt prepared to fire, and not once but many times were we halted by batteries when we got to the massed heavies about Death Valley. It must have been a veritable hell in the German lines. One or two newly destroyed limbers littered the track on this occasion. How awful it must be for a shell to strike my water-cart : what a mess there would be and shouldn't I get wet ! The thought was always present in my mind, but I had never *seen* such a thing happen—they always seem to have met with these accidents before I arrived. I began to take comfort from this and to imagine I had a charmed life, that my pair of horses was a lucky one, and that so long as I kept them my escape from dangerously near shells was assured.

Stretchers were being carried by weary little groups of men across the muddy waste : wounded men were coming down two at a time, limping along and supporting each other. Little knots of prisoners were assisting with the stretcher-bearing, and one bearded German, with a bandage round his head, staggered along unassisted, sitting down every few yards to hold his head.

Luck was against us at the refilling point when we were preparing for the second journey. The water was coming out in driblets, taking ten minutes to fill one cart—thus pointing to a four hour wait for us if no improvement was effected. So we decided to set off for Fricourt, where the next water-supply was situated. On our way we passed some Australian horse-transports and something caught our eye which made us green with envy. The Anzacs, with their usual common sense, had painted the steelwork of their harness black, so that no question of rust would ever arise : as for us, although we could not be expected to have clean steelwork under these conditions, we knew we should have to recover our old standard as soon as we emerged from our present surroundings. How we envied those Australians ! They seemed to be able to score successes, and pretty big ones too, in spite of their dirty harness !

While we were engaged in hunting for signs of drinking water, our transport section was moving its lines to the neighbourhood of the Citadel, the name given to several camps of tents and huts used by infantry, on the Bray-Fricourt road. Again it was a case of dumping them down beneath the canopy of the heavens and leaving them to scrounge. Half a mile away were some disused horse-lines with posts, bivvies and harness-racks, complete, but the Army did not order us to occupy them. Oh, dear, no ! the Army preferred us to walk over to the old camp, smash down all the racks and bivvies and carry them to the new site, necessitating one or two journeys for each man. Having erected our camp we then watched for the arrival of some other transport, and as a matter of fact one was dumped down the very next day at the site we had laid bare. When we left on the 27th the new arrivals came over to the camp we were deserting and proceeded to transfer all our " homes " to their original area, but yet another unit suffered for this smart work, for we in turn were followed by more wandering nomads. Such are the mysterious ways of the British Army.

This is slightly anticipatory, however, for the 26th of September was a red-letter day and cannot be passed over in a word. On this date the L.R.B. patrols worked their way into Combles where they met the French from the other side. The " pinching out " process had been successful, for the attack of the preceding day had forced the Germans to evacuate the town, leaving many houses almost intact and quantities of stores. It was the largest town yet captured and our fellows were in high spirits, which compensated somewhat for the disappointment of Leuze Wood.

Nor was this the only success of the day. Soon after noon we heard a terrific bombardment which heralded the capture of the Thiepval stronghold, which had resisted all attempts at storming since July 1st. The intense British shelling had told on the defenders, and the attackers carried the village and neighbouring fortifications with a bound, capturing a good haul of pungent prisoners.

The importance attached to the gains on this day was shown by the arrival in the afternoon of a division of Indian cavalry, who came trotting along the track next to our horse-lines. They made a very inspiriting sight, coming on and on in an endless stream, the men immaculate in appearance and immense in stature, the horses as superb as though they were entering for a horse-show. British squadrons passed by, too, and then came batteries of horse artillery all trotting along and disappearing over the Citadel ridge in the direction of the firing-line. I think they made the most imposing sight I had seen in France and the French onlookers were obviously impressed.

A cavalry track, marked out by signboards and flags, had been in existence for some time and had been used by horse transports, but exactly how near to the firing-line it stretched I was never able to discover. Knowing what we do now, it seems unlikely that the cavalry could have been used effectively, but at the time, when we found they had bivouacked at Fricourt for the night, we thought it was merely tardy arrival which had prevented them being of use. It was a disappointment to us to see the cavalry watering at Fricourt the next morning, but on the other hand the fact that they had been called up at the double seemed to indicate that the rupture of the line was imminent and we almost danced for joy on that account. To put a good finish on an exciting day we saw—and smelt—some hundreds of prisoners trooping along past the Citadel in the evening.

That night, as if in revenge for their reverses in the line, the enemy made a bombing raid near the Citadel, resulting in several hundred wood fires being extinguished in great haste in all parts of the back areas and a considerable amount of inward quaking at the thought that almost every square yard of countryside was inhabited by men or horses. We did not learn the result of the raid, for no bombs came very near us, but the crashes in the darkness sounded much closer than they really were and disturbed not a few sleepers.

On the 27th we learn that the battalion were coming down for a rest that day, as the squeezing out of Combles had reduced the length of front and the French had therefore taken over from the 56th Division. I had to meet them with a water-cart at Angle Wood, if possible, but owing to the breakdown of the water-supply I was considerably delayed and only succeeded in encountering two of the companies near the Montauban road, on their march down.

How the men rushed for the carts at the first halt and struggled for a drop of water!

" Where have the carts been to since we've been in these parts ? " asked one of them.

" Why, haven't you had enough to drink ? "

" We never had enough to drink, mate. Sometimes a water-bottle full had to last for forty-eight hours ! "

If every unit took up as much as we did, the brigade should have been adequately supplied, not only for drinking purposes, but for swimming baths as well. I do not know how the brigade apportioned it out, but it seems as if a good deal of our supply must have been purloined or used for other purposes in the vicinity of Angle Wood. At any rate, this much may be said : if the companies went short it was not the fault of the drivers who, from first to last, experienced all the joys that " water-cart duty " had to offer them. Many a parched straggler from another regiment used to crave a sip of water during our trips to Angle Wood, but to all such appeals we had to turn a deaf ear—to have heeded them would have meant depriving some L.R.B. fellow of the water we were supposed to be taking to HIM. And the motto of our section was, from first to last, " We deliver the goods ! "

CHAPTER XVIII.

Farewell to the Somme.

(*October*, 1916.)

Two days' respite—Farther into the desolation—At Bernafay Wood—Reflections—
The Guillemont battle-field—The L.R.B. attack at Lesboeufs—Explorations
at Mametz—From the Somme to Picquigny.

There was not a man in the regiment who did not yearn to leave the
Somme battle-field and there were few who did not honestly believe
the rumour that when the battalion came down through the Citadel
to Meaulte on the 27th it was the first stage in our journey towards
some rest area. It was most unusual for a division to be up on the
Somme for more than a few weeks and our sojourn there had already
entered upon its fourth week and had seen the division in three separate
important attacks. The sceptical few were those who put not their
faith in staff rumours, after their manifold disappointments of the
past two years, and among these enlightened people was our friend
Figg, whose opinions were always worth considering.

"My dear fellow," he said to me, as we set to work to build a bivvy
near the sandpits on the Albert-Bray road, "it's no good making
anything elaborate. We shan't be here more than two days."

"We ought to be back somewhere for a rest then," we urged.

"We *ought* to be," gurgled Figg; "but you may bet they've only
brought the battalion down here to get the mud off their boots and
polish their equipment. They aren't cut up enough yet."

We were to appreciate the truth of that remark.

At this place we were issued with a bivvy cover between each six
men and our mess was joined by Frank Greene, whose horses had once
run away from Hebuterne, and Volze—the latter becoming a temporary
and the former a permanent member of our party. I had felt very
sorry for Greene when we had been at the Citadel, for he had been
temporarily in a "mess" by himself, and on his return from a tiring
trip to the line in the early hours of the morning there was no bivvy
into which he could turn; so he had just thrown himself down on the
ground, too tired to rig up shelter until the morrow.

The people in Meaulte, where the battalion were in billets not far
from us, were extraordinarily hostile; they would not lift a finger
to help us, they profiteered most shamefully, and some said they would

prefer the German soldiers to be there. They had their wishes granted in 1918, when the enemy broke our line and Meaulte was razed to the ground ; but I must be charitable and hope that the old woman at Billet 48 managed to rescue her precious belongings.

We did not stay long to enjoy the inhabitants' disfavour, however, for things panned out as Figg had forecasted. On the 29th we wended our way back to the Citadel, where the battalion went into huts for the night ; there was another bombing raid, but beyond one horse getting killed no damage was done. The next day we all moved up farther and the transport found itself allotted a few yards square in an open space almost equidistant from Montauban, Maricourt and Carnoy.

We were growing accustomed to desolate places by now, but the drawback to this was that there were no disused camps at hand where we could scrounge materials ; there were horse-lines on all sides and everything that could possibly be used in the construction of a bivvy or harness-rack had long ago been utilised.

In France, whenever we arrived at new billets or a fresh site, there was rarely any provision for one's harness and yet a rack had always got to be built. Of course, the harness had to be left on the ground the first night, but work on the racks must be commenced the next day : these must appear at least by the following afternoon or else there was serious trouble. No wood was provided for this purpose and in most places we were strictly forbidden to cut down any trees or fences. In our new pitch there was not the least prospect of being able to fell trees, and our only hope lay in stealing racks from neighbouring horse-lines—a course which we dare not risk if their pickets showed signs of wakefulness. Yet, as I say, a new rack for everybody was expected miraculously to appear by the following afternoon. I think visits from the Staff Captain were feared.

Fear of criticism by higher authorities occasionally led lesser officers to extreme lengths of imbecility. Near our new horse-lines there was an artillery unit that was carrying about with it two wagon-loads of spare harness, all beautifully cleaned and saturated with oil, so that when an inspection was held after its withdrawal from the area it would be able to turn out at a moment's notice, dressed up like a ham-bone.

I said " Good-bye " to Wood, prior to his moving up with D Company ; Davis was the only other man in it whom I knew. It was rather depressing for Wood, coming out to a company where every man was a stranger to him ; nevertheless he moved off feeling very bloodthirsty and very much impressed by the signs of victory all around him.

The battalion bivouacked near Bernafay Wood, which was now almost a health resort. Big guns had moved much farther forward and a broad-gauge railway was being laid down nearly to Guillemont. It was not *absolutely* a health resort, however, for the road that ran past Bernafay and Trones Woods to Guillemont was ranged by German guns to a nicety. Moreover, the traffic blocks on this road were constant and serious. The French had complained that the British traffic police gave precedence to British convoys, and so now a French and English sentry, together with an A.P.M., regulated traffic at the Montauban cross-roads. But the delays on this route were so interminable and fraught with so much danger to transport—I once took over two hours to get from the cross-roads to the other side of Bernafay Wood, a matter of a few hundred yards—that new regulations were brought into force early in October, reserving that road for " down " traffic and diverting the upgoing vehicles on to a track that ran in the valley and through the woods. This eased matters somewhat, but, of course, it made no difference to the German shelling and we soon began to lament the fact that it was necessary to use the Guillemont road at all.

On all parts of the front the enemy shelling was growing more severe and the resistance stiffer : we were advancing over shell-pocked, desolate wastes, on which we had to lay railways and mend roads, while the enemy were falling back on to comparatively virgin soil, with billets and good roads behind them, served by a splendid network of railways. The better their conditions grew, the worse our own became.

Then he had altered his system of defence in places, using parties of machine-gunners as outposts instead of cramming his front trench full of men ; our system of attack was not suited to this system of defence and the number of unsuccessful attacks grew in number. Operations were hindered by the general break-up of the weather, which had heralded the stagnation of the past two winters, and it looked very much as though the British Army would be doomed to exist in these open, billetless wastes all the winter, while the Germans availed themselves of the French homesteads behind their lines. Yet the breaking of the line had seemed imminent a week ago. If only we could pierce that barrier and reach the land of milk and honey which our men had been gaining ridge after ridge in order to command !

" Only gain yonder ridge," said our Staff, " and the promised land will lie at your feet." Yet our men always discovered some other ridge which stood between them and the " trenchless open country where our cavalry would get their chance." About this time we received the news that the Roumanians had crossed the Danube and were invading Bulgaria, in conjunction with the Russian offensive : if only we could proceed at that pace, what enthusiasm it would arouse.

Our fellows furnished carrying fatigues from Bernafay Wood passing through Guillemont and Ginchy. On the 4th (?) they moved up into the front line where they only spent a day, but were heavily shelled in the afternoon and dug a fresh line about one hundred yards in front in the evening. They knew there was a shallow trench there and believed it to be held by the enemy, so they proceeded on the lines of a raiding party, but to their surprise there was no opposition. About midnight they were relieved by the London Scottish. Wood's platoon got mixed up in the relief and eventually emerged in two portions, Wood finding himself with about fifteen men of his own platoon and some fifty other people. They did not know in the least where they were and wandered aimlessly round No Man's Land for some hours until they eventually struck the French front-line. This gave them a guide to their whereabouts and they arrived back at Trones Wood about 8 a.m.

I saw Wood the next day looking very muddy and unkempt. He begged me for some chocolate and other canteen delicacies, but I had to inform him that I had been unable to get anything for him except a tin of cigarettes, which he thankfully accepted or purchased—I forget which ! The next night he went out on a digging fatigue, but owing to heavy shelling, soon after work had started the men were unable to carry on and so had to return.

While this was going on we were engaged in our trips with rations and water-supplies—a refilling point was now available in Montauban—but nothing of special interest occurred. Butt, the driver who had been run over by a limber, was put on a draft for another regiment when he left hospital, but, by a fluke, managed to get back to us.

One evening we felt we required a little enlivenment, so somebody suggested our getting the padre's harmonium out of the Q.M. stores. We dragged it into the open between the horse-lines and the bivvies and then I played rag-time ditties until a crowd gathered round. It reminded me of a minstrel troupe on the beach at the seaside, with the rumble of the guns serving as the murmuring of the sea. But oh, how we missed the sight of the girls in the audience, girls in their summer clothes with bathing costumes over their arms. . . . Would those days ever come again ?

What an unnatural life we were living ! Here were we, intelligent human beings (let us hope !), brought up to home comforts and decent, respectable pursuits and office life, living like savages—thinking only of our food and drink, our repose and safety. Here were we, presumably sane individuals all, going mad with delight over a cracked harmonium in the middle of a wilderness in the same way that some French Moroccan troops were dancing to some reed instruments farther down in the valley. Meanwhile our careers, our civilian prospects and what brains we once possessed were—to use a poetical phrase—being borne away on the wings of Time. Many of the men had lost their positions at the outbreak of the War : for two years they had not received a penny more than their army pay. They had got to start all over again when this Armageddon was over, like boys just leaving school, with whom they would be in competition. Some of them were married, their wives existing on the miserable army separation allowance at home. All sorts and conditions of men were here, some with little cause to worry and others with plenty of excuses for pessimism, yet all were rubbing along decidedly cheerfully. For our section was like one big family and in these months of close acquaintanceship we got to KNOW each other as men had never done before the War. Everyone's character, will-power, nerve, generosity, and general peculiarities came to be known little by little, and this deep understanding of other men was compensating a great deal for being deprived of business opportunities, though we did not appreciate this at the time. The War was revealing qualities in ourselves and others which we had not known to exist, and was building up character in everybody.

On one of these days I had to take a water-cart beyond Trones Wood, nearly to Guillemont. We had left the cookers there previously. The route took me through Trones Wood where, in spite of the efforts at clearance that had been made, traces of the severe fighting here were on every side. The wood was a vast cemetery and by no means all the bodies had been buried. It gave one an awed feeling to ride along the track through this undergrowth and these withered trees, realising the bitter fighting and terrible shelling that had taken place in that small area. Just inside the hedge on the far side were the remains of what had been a British front-line trench, when the wood had been won and consolidated. Beyond lay the stretch of country which confronted our men when they set out on those many fruitless attempts to attack Guillemont. Not a square yard of the ground had been left untouched by one artillery or the other. Only a few yards from the wood a tank had despaired of the task of bobbing up and down in these craters and had heeled over on its side in a vast shell-hole where it still lay, pointing its nose skyward.

The spot where I had to leave the water-cart was some distance past the wood. I had to wait there for some hours to replenish the dixies when required, so I tied the horses up to the wheels and set off on a little tour of exploration. When Bob Taylor was engaged on this particular job he spent hours in investigating the neighbourhood, but Bob revelled in horrors and his curiosity was unbounded. I saw certain gruesome sights in half an hour that I should not care to set on paper.

Among the memorable things I remember to have come across was Raymond Asquith's grave, marked by a wooden cross among a handful of other graves by the roadside. The piece of ground that surrounded me now had taken months to conquer. As I looked eastwards, Longueval, High Wood and Delville Wood were on my left : that piece of ground had seen the cut-up of ten divisions. The ground just ahead, including Guillemont and Ginchy, had cost us the greater part of eight more. On the right was Arrow Head Copse and, somewhere beyond, Angle Wood.

Guillemont had been a stumbling block to our advance and had only fallen on September 3rd, when we were moving up to Corbie. I found, in stepping from shell-hole to shell-hole, still unburied bodies which had evidently been mown down in lines from that trench ahead there : what would the trench itself be like ? I wandered on and jumped down into it. . . . It had been a trench once, but how wide it was ! It might almost have been a sunken road. Our artillery had evidently had the range accurately, but then they had plastered equally the ground in front and behind it so that not much could have been expected to escape. German overcoats, respirators and broken rifles were strewn all over the place. Here was a German machine-gun and beside it the dead bodies of the crew, still unburied. I peeped over the parapet in the direction from which the British had attacked and pictured the rush into the trench in the early hours of the morning. Here and there bits of field-grey uniform protruded through the soil.

I hastened away from this spot, clambering on in the direction of Guillemont. All the way along evidences of a hurried German departure were seen in the abandoned equipment, helmets, bombs and overcoats that littered the shell-holes. Guillemont itself was level with the ground : not a house remained. When I got there I felt I had had enough exploration to last me a lifetime and was very glad to get back to the water-cart again. There was quite enough to reflect upon in that spot.

On the afternoon of the 7th there was an attack on a fairly wide front, in conjunction with the French, with unequal results. Le Sars was captured and we advanced some hundreds of yards between Guedecourt and Lesboeufs. In the evening the enemy counter-attacked the new position north of Lesboeufs and regained some of the lost ground.

That same night the battalion retired to rest fairly early, being very tired after their successive nights of carrying and digging, but about eleven o'clock they were suddenly awakened and marched up to Lesboeufs. About 7 a.m. they took up a position in some trenches and then spent all the morning in bringing up ammunition and tools, as if to let the enemy know they were preparing an attack. The Germans were supposed to be eight hundred yards away.

A and B Companies, forming the first line, went over at zero hour—3 p.m., climbing over the front of the trench and then lying down and crawling up into line. Wood and Davis went over with the second line at 3.30 in irregular formation—two lines of sections in file per platoon—with their section in the last line. For the first four hundred yards everything went very smoothly, except for a few shells. Then they came under heavy machine-gun fire and casualties became rather serious. Wood got wounded in the leg and, having to lie down, handed over the section to Lance-Corporal Davis. The attacking lines eventually reached their objective but, owing to the supports failing to put in an appearance, it was necessary to abandon it and fall back : so about dusk the L.R.B. had retired to where Wood was lying. Wood then thought it expedient to crawl back, and he and another fellow, wounded in the arm, succeeded in making their way to a dressing-station at Ginchy, whence they got a wagon back to Trones Wood.

The Lesboeufs affair was another example of a hastily-conceived attack and what I should consider extraordinarily bad staff-work somewhere in the higher realms. The division was exhausted through its lengthy stay on the Somme, fed for five weeks principally on bully beef and biscuits ; the men were particularly fatigued during the few days preceding the attack, when the last ounce of effort had been extracted from them ; then they were panicked up without notice into a position they did not know and employed for hours in carrying ammunition and tools for their own attack. They were sent out in broad daylight to attack a position half a mile away, but with no idea where the enemy really were, and as soon as they got within machine-gun range they got knocked over by the dozen. Finally the objectives had to be given up owing to the failure of supports to appear and they reverted practically to the *status quo.* No mention was made of this attack in the official communique except the statement that we had advanced our line S.W. of Guedecourt. Of Wood's section—consisting of nine men—only one returned uninjured : the remainder were killed, wounded or captured. Poor Davis, my last friend in D Company, was killed.

We learnt what had befallen Wood and Davis, when the pack-ponies went up the same evening, though details of the affair only leaked out afterwards. It was clear that the division *must* be withdrawn now and we were not surprised when we moved our lines to Mametz on October 10th, preparatory to our departure.

As we were on the scene of the success of July 1st, we took the opportunity to explore the German trenches and vast dug-outs in the German front-line which, no doubt, were similar to those which had proved our division's undoing at Gommecourt. They were extraordinarily deep and well-constructed caverns, some of them being approached by thirty to fifty steps, at the foot of which you could walk about in underground chambers fitted up with bunks and furnished with tables and stools. How different from the British jumping-off trenches a little way off, with their small funk-holes scooped out of the earth ! No wonder the Germans were able to withstand the heavy bombardments. In some cases these caverns had proved to be death-traps, for the entrances were destroyed by bombs : however, there were two or three openings to each of the dug-outs. In the German trench at Guillemont there had been nothing like these. Deprived of their deep, safe dug-outs, where they had taken their meals and slept in safety for a year or more, the Germans were now experiencing British shell-fire under the conditions in which we had existed in the Second Battle of Ypres, hurriedly constructing new trenches which did not afford much shelter.

After spending a night in a big camp here, the brigade transports set off on a two-day trek, leaving the officers' chargers with the battalion. The companies were going by train or 'bus the following day, when the chargers would make their way down as best they could. The programme was upset, so far as the L.R.B. were concerned, by the horse Julia breaking loose the next night and eating up practically all the oats that had been left for the other horses. Julia was a decrepit old horse that had served with the regiment in the Boer War as the Colonel's mount, and had been brought over to France in 1914 as a mascot : she rarely had a stroke of work to do, but on certain occasions reverted to the position of officer's mount. The sudden disappearance of all the rations meant that the grooms would have to get back to the transport as soon as possible, and as we had already started our second day's trek, there was nothing for it but to trot the chargers for about thirty miles. The hungry ones did not experience much difficulty, but Julia, completely blown out and never, in the ordinary way, trotted even for a few yards, had the worst day of her life and almost succumbed at the end of it.

The two-day trek of the section was enjoyable. Gradually we emerged from the desolation of the Somme into habitable areas ; the two and three lines of traffic near Fricourt gave place to occasional lorries and vehicles : the countryside became green instead of brown. We took the Mericourt road to Corbie and at the entrance of one of the towns we passed about tea-time a battalion of French infantry lined the route. From them came the eternal remark " Allemagne caput," followed by signs of chopping off heads. But this time we said the same thing, we agreed with them, and there was a cordial exchange of greetings. Even if Germany's head were not yet in the dust, we had seen a good deal on the Somme to give us confidence for the future, and the fact that we were about to have a few months' respite from offensive operations gave everything a rosy hue. So in dumb show we chopped our own heads off, much to the delight of the French soldiers. They looked remarkably fit and all about twenty-two to twenty-five years old. Who said that France's manhood was exhausted ?

On the second night we reached Picquigny, a town in the Abbeville area, which had plenty of shops and estaminets. The last time I had stayed in a town of this size was in March at St. Pol. A delightful river ran past the house which furnished our transport billet. Compared with the Somme the conditions were ideal.

Leave—which had been non-existent for months—started again as soon as we got here, but the prospects of my getting home this winter were not hopeful. Although practically ten months had elapsed since I went on leave, I was one of the last transport men to go before leave stopped and consequently my name now appeared almost at the foot of the list. Most of the draft that had joined us after the battle of Gommecourt consisted of men back from one of the colonies, and they had all a claim to leave before the L.R.B. men, having been twenty months without it. The chances of the man who stood fortieth on the transport list were not yet worth considering, especially as leave was allotted in such a sparing fashion that only one man per battalion per day went home. I was infuriated at this, as my people had been eagerly looking for a further leave at the end of 1916. The French soldiers got it every four months.

There was a certain amount of cleaning up to be done here, and we were only too pleased to get ourselves and our belongings sweet and fresh once again. There was an impromptu inspection of transport, but we found it impossible to bring our steelwork and harness back to its pre-Somme state in the day or so at our disposal : consequently we incurred the condemnation of the Staff Captain. We ought, he said, to have kept our steelwork free from rust, even on the Somme ! Comment is superfluous.

Well, we had said farewell to the Somme, after passing nearly six weeks beyond the fringe of civilisation. As I looked back on that battle it seemed to be a nightmare—the product of a disordered brain following a surfeit of lobster mayonnaise.

CHAPTER XIX.

THE THIRD WINTER.

(*November, 1916–February, 1917.*)

Renewing acquaintanceships—The Neuve Chapelle sector—Truths about army baths—Fascinating females of La Gorgue—Peace talk and future prospects—Christmas and New Year celebrations—U-boat war begins—An inoculation parade—Beginning of German withdrawal.

A PLEASANT surprise was in store for us when we left Picquigny on the 21st. We trekked over the same ground we had covered when we had detrained on our arrival from Flanders in February—the reader will remember the snowy regions around Abbeville where we formed the 56th Division—and our destination was none other than the big farm between Huppy and Wascherville at which we had previously stayed for a night or so.

We got a holiday next day specially to walk into Wascherville, where the villagers remembered us at once, leaving off work in the fields to come and greet us. I made for the cottage where I used to discuss the Battle of Verdun with the old man in front of his fire and encountered him, leading his farm-cart, not far from his abode. He ran forward and shook hands, followed by the old girl and the infant daughter, beseeching me to come in and have some coffee. Every family in the place was equally hospitable. Many of the cottagers killed the fatted calf that night and asked the fellows who used to be billeted on them to come and share their supper. We had a great deal to tell them about in our broken French, while these good-hearted villagers expressed their joy over the Battle of the Somme and " les braves anglais." Unfortunately we had to leave on the 23rd, but those two days spent in renewing acquaintanceships were happy ones and proved that the villagers in Meaulte, with their dislike of British soldiers, were no criterion of French opinion.

We entrained that night in the dark at Pont Remy, putting eight horses in a wagon. It was my first experience of ushering The Grey into a railway truck and I hoped it would be my last. I had to sleep in the middle of the truck, just between the two rows of fore-feet, and got " pawed " not once but many times. One of the horses objected to the motion of the train to such an extent that he kicked a tremendous hole in the end of the waggon ! After an uneasy night, divided between swearing at the animals and dreaming of their " paws," we got to our unknown destination about breakfast time. It was none other place than Berguette, that station where Thomson and I had guarded an ammunition train when on lines of communications. Just before we reached it we passed over the canal where we had once bathed under difficulties.

The station and village looked much the same as before. There was the old R.E. dump where the officer had come round stealthily to surprise the sentries in the middle of the night. There was the house where Clarke, Scholefield and others had made the acquaintance of a delightful damsel just as I had been bundled off to the hospital at Aire. Chrisp, Conibeer and one or two others had been stationed at Berguette at odd times in 1915, so together with them I set off to renew the lady's acquaintanceship. It seemed as if our route had been specially selected by the Army in order to give some of us an opportunity to meet old friends. We took a second breakfast with the young lady, who was very pleased to see the L.R.B. again. She also was interested to hear of our adventures. As for her, she had a new ring. . . . Alas ! Alas ! (Why did our faces fall, I wonder ?) . . . she was married to a British Fusilier !

From Berguette we marched all the morning until we reached a place called Paradis, behind the Neuve Chapelle sector. We were still in France, but the surroundings indicated that we were not far from Flanders. The country was as flat as a pancake, with farmhouses here and there, muddy lanes with streams beside them, long lines of willow-trees, mud swamps, reeds and rushes and the dear old rain, which started as soon as we got there. I felt more than ever convinced that it rained in these regions when it was fine farther south.

The farmyard in which we took up our abode smelt like other yards. It had about it the national smell of Flanders : pigs, bad mud and mouldy middens. It would really be a punishment for the Germans to have these regions left on their hands after the War and to be compelled to live in them. It was what I had said the previous winter and I still stuck to the opinion. However, Paradis (what sarcastic puns were made upon that name !) was fortunately not our permanent abode, for the battalion moved up after a day or so, through Locon and Vielle Chapelle to Croix Barbee, near Festubert. This meant that they were taking over a sector south of Armentières which had the reputation of being a particularly calm portion of the line. I left a cooker at Croix Barbee and after much difficulty succeeded in finding the new transport lines.

Our winter quarters looked satisfactory, the most attractive features being half-finished stables for the horses, an empty barn for ourselves, which could be greatly improved, and the town of La Gorgue near at hand, inhabited by exceedingly hospitable French people. The town itself—which was about three miles from the firing-line—possessed the following attractions :—

A Y.M.C.A, which sold cocoa.
A divisional reading-room and library which gave away notepaper.
A theatre in which the " Bow Bells " performed.
Two cinemas, crowded out with British soldiers and French lasses.
Hundreds of estaminets, stocked with the best.
A " real live " canteen.
Shops where meals could be obtained ; and, last but not least,
Some really well-run divisional baths.

Horrible as it may sound, we were sometimes without a bath for a month or six weeks in the army. Unofficially we heated a little water ourselves and had a bathe in a bucket occasionally, but we had to steal fuel to heat it at bed-time ; this opportunity of an unofficial bathe was denied to the company men and we could never count upon it. Divisional baths were fitted out in all sorts of weird places, and, when at length we were allotted a certain hour at which to appear at them, one or more of the following seven announcements was sure to be made—you could absolutely count upon it :

    (1) Too many troops had been allotted : if we could wait until 5 p.m. we could take our chance.

    (2) The boiler had gone wrong but we could have cold baths.

    (3) The water-supply was either cut off or limited : if the latter, six men would have to get under one little trickle of water.

    (4) There was no clean clothing.

    (5) There were clean shirts but no clean pants or socks.

    (6) There were clean pants but no clean shirts or socks.

    (7) There were clean socks but no clean shirts or pants.

In regard to (1), we were many times marched miles to the nearest baths at great inconvenience to the work of the section and either turned away or else made to wait for hours. If a driver was out at the time it was sometimes difficult to get his bath subsequently.

As for (2) and (3) we seldom struck any well-run baths. The water was rarely hot enough and there was frequently not enough of it. In extenuation of this fact, it was sometimes remarked that, instead of having an efficient staff that understood boilers, some baths had as a personnel the halt, the weedy and the mentally deficient who were cast out of their battalions. Let us be fair and say that this was not invariably the case, but we did come across some places where this appeared to be the method of selection.

Nos. (4) to (7) reflect a bitter grievance. Unless a soldier cast off his old clothes entirely he could not turn over a new page and start again free from vermin, and he usually had to retain at least one of his old garments, through there not being enough to go round. I am speaking of divisional and similar baths, not of those at the base where, as always, there was plenty of everything for the permanent military staff. However, as it was a rare thing to receive " clean " clothing that really was clean, we were perhaps not so much worse off in retaining certain of our dirty garments. " Clean " clothing became such a questionable issue that in time a driver who was sent to fetch it from the baths, as we did occasionally, for the benefit of the battalion, would cover himself with vermin powder in the first place : then everyone on the section likely to be called upon to accompany him and load the limber would disappear ; while the wagoner who cleaned out the limber afterwards had the most unenviable job on the section. Frequently the rooms for the dirty and clean (?) clothes adjoined each other, so it is not surprising that the latter received such an evil reputation.

The baths at La Gorgue, however, were excellently run and we usually received brand-new garments whenever we went there. The only drawback was this : we had to undress in a big room and pass out into the open yard at the back, attired only in a towel—a chilly proceeding in winter weather. Then we had to ascend a long flight of steps to the bathing-room under the full gaze of hundreds of giggling girls who were employed to iron shirts in an adjacent portion of the building. Whenever we passed by, they were doing very little in the way of ironing our shirts, being apparently more concerned with criticising our legs—which made us blush.

The British soldiers stationed round here got on very well with the ladies of the town, some of whom were the objects of much adoration. There was one estaminet where you simply couldn't get inside the door after 6 p.m. owing to the swarms that went there to feast their eyes on the proprietor's charming daughter, who, to be frank, was remarkably pretty and unfortunately knew it. There were several slightly lesser stars who likewise drew crowds of worshippers to their estaminets, while many shops did a roaring trade by virtue of the attractiveness of the girls who served behind the counters.

My own tastes ran in the direction of some private family which included a topping daughter and, if possible, possessed a piano. Surely in La Gorgue such a house was to be found! On the fourth evening of our stay here, by judicious enquiry I found the place of my desires and, knocking at the door, commenced to introduce myself. There was a father—very unbending at first—a fat mamma, with a twinkle in her eye, and, yes, a fascinating daughter of about nineteen, who looked rather shy and embarrassed as I planted myself in the doorway and held forth in faulty French.

It was difficult to explain my mission. Of course I found it simple enough to say that I was a pianist and that it was rumoured they had a nice piano, but these two facts did not constitute a reason for my disturbing their family circle and seating myself on their piano-stool. They plainly thought as much, but I saw that they were more surprised than resentful and so proceeded to play upon their heart-strings in a most touching way, the result of the interview being that I was invited to come in after dinner on Sunday. The ice was broken . . . it only remained for me to plunge in.

On Sunday they were more affable; the daughter played the piano and I strummed; the father gave me a glass of wine, mother proffered me some marmalade tart. There were long conversations on war topics, in which I endeavoured to explain the humorous side of traffic congestion on the Somme. Finally, I asked the old lady if I could come again and she told me to ask Erma; Erma blushed and inclined her head, while my heart went pit-a-pat with excitement. Within two minutes I had received a standing invitation to come to the house on two evenings a week: they had only had one Englishman— an officer—billeted on them before and it was somewhat of a novelty to have a Tommy conversing with them. I could see an enjoyable winter for me, with the touch of civilisation which these friends afforded. Fellows on the section, however, viewed it in a different light; they foresaw wedding bells and confetti and strove, for my sake, to discourage my visits to the home of the nineteen-year old daughter, pouring ridicule on the boot-cleaning and badge-polishing propensities which began to manifest themselves on certain evenings in the week.

Our joy at being away from the Somme was enhanced by what we read in the papers now. Sir Douglas Haig referred to it as a " wilderness of mud." Every few days fresh attacks were made by us or the French, involving violent counter-attacks, amidst the most appalling conditions; very little progress had been made beyond Lesboeufs in the past month, but the French and ourselves were gradually extending the bite in the enemy's line. On the 14th of November we read of the Battle of the Ancre, apparently a well-carried-out attack, which naturally followed the fall of Thiepval and the resulting operations. Even on the very verge of winter our pressure was being maintained, and when the French in three successive blows recaptured two-thirds of the ground they had lost at Verdun we felt very pleased with affairs on the Western Front.

If only the same could have been said of events on the Russian front ! The German plan was obviously to hold us in the West, even at heavy sacrifice, in order to deal knock-out blows in the East, and they seemed to be succeeding. In 1915 they had fought Russia almost to a standstill and had overrun Serbia. Now they were again attacking the Russians heavily and forcing the Roumanians back into their own country, within a few months of their entering the War. In the middle of November they were heavily pressed, and shortly afterwards the retreat became a rout. Mackensen attacked from Bulgaria and crossed the Danube, menacing the Roumanian Army on its flank and early in December its capital had fallen. This meant that the bulk of Roumania, with its wealth of grain and cattle and oilfields, was in enemy hands ; thus they had gained more supplies in a month than our blockade had withheld in six. In nine days in December they had captured seventy-thousand prisoners on that front, as many as the French and ourselves had secured in four months on the Somme. The news in the papers was, on balance, very depressing, for what was the use of a gain of a hundred yards of trench and two hundred prisoners near Peronne when a thousand square miles of fertile land and ten thousand prisoners fell to the Germans simultaneously over on the other front ?

The Italians were attacking the Austrians again with success, while on the Salonika front the Serbians and Allies were conducting an offensive resulting in the re-entry into Serbia, but the attitude of the Greeks was hostile and constituted a very uncertain element in that quarter, where we could not hope for decisive events. About this time I learnt of the death of my best pal on that particular front, which depressed me more than ever for some days and I took very gloomy views. Just then it seemed as if the German Eastern Army, having annihilated Roumania, would be able to turn their attention to the Salonika Expedition and drive them into the sea with another succession of blows. We did not, however, give a true estimate of the frantic desire of the German staff to transfer more troops from those regions to the Western Front, about which they were really becoming alarmed. The Central Powers had gained a spectacular success by concentration of forces, but the hard hammering in the West was their predominant concern and they were intensely anxious to make peace while they held most of the trumps.

It was this desire that prompted their peace offer in December. The offer amounted to this : Germany was victorious all round and could not be beaten, but was magnanimously prepared to grant peace to the Allies in order to prevent further bloodshed. The German anxiety as to the Allies' reply was manifested by the crowds that waited in Berlin all night for news of our agreement to a Peace Conference. Had they only known the merriment the offer caused at the front ! It was true that we all longed for the War to be over, but we felt that 1917 would see such crushing attacks upon all fronts that the German resistance would crumble up. General Brusiloff had just assured the world that in 1917 the Russian Army would be larger and better equipped than it had ever been. Huge supplies of heavy artillery and ammunition were being despatched to them by Britain and France. So that, in spite of temporary reverses there, we believed that our position would be immeasurably improved during the coming year, and were very glad when first one Ally and then another gave emphatic replies to the German offer, exposing its insincerity.

An event which delighted the common or garden soldier above everything else about this period was the resignation of Mr. Asquith and the appointment of Lloyd George in his place. We had not had much sympathy with Asquith since he had announced that there was no shortage of shells at the time of the Second Battle of Ypres, and we now felt that a man was taking the place of a dear old woman. There were cheers in our barn at the announcement.

The routine work for both companies and transport went on in a more or less uninteresting manner, for there was little excitement of any kind in this part of the line. The companies divided their time between the right front, when they held the line not far from Neuve Chapelle, the left front, in the neighbourhood of Fauquisshart, and various hamlets and villages in the rear, e.g., Laventie, Lestrem, Merville and Croix Barbee. The transport dump on the right front was in an orchard near Richebourg, where the rations were loaded on to trucks and pushed up to the trenches. The journey had to be made at night, but it was quite straightforward, there being no shelling except an occasional " strafe " of the orchard.

The left front was more fascinating. The supporting troops occupied numerous posts and wired farms between Laventie and the front trenches, some of these positions being approachable in daylight, in spite of the panorama which the Germans on Aubers Ridge were able to command. A good deal of camouflage netting screened the roads and dumps around here, and even where the enemy were able to detect a solitary vehicle they never took the trouble to fire at it.

Early in December there was a great inspection of our transport and battalion at Lestrem, by about three or four Generals, and for days beforehand everyone was slaving away as though the very issue of the War depended on our smart turnout. To their extreme annoyance, many company men—instead of getting rest from the trenches—were sent over to La Gorgue to scrub our limbers, as we had more than enough work to do with our horses and harness on account of the high standard that was now expected by the Spit and Polish Brigade.

On the morning of the great event the horses looked in fine fettle and most of the harness was beautiful. Even my sets were satisfactory as I'd secured the services of two friends on the previous day and had worked by candle-light up till 10 p.m. Needless to say such a stupendous effort was made merely to save the regiment's reputation and to prevent Lieut. Gordon getting a complaint from the inspecting General. The men themselves looked smart enough for a Horse Guards' parade and the only things that might have been cleaner were the cookers which were away with the battalion until the last minute.

The authorities arranged that the transport inspection should be held, not at our horse-lines, but two miles away at Lestrem, which had to be reached by a muddy road and through a heavy mist which took the edge off the Brasso. The Generals kept us waiting, perched up on our horses for over an hour and then came round inspecting the nooks and crevices of the saddles and the brilliance of our spurs. Gordon was very pleased with the turnout, which was the best we had ever had, and congratulated us afterwards, giving us an afternoon's holiday as a reward. Imagine his and our own surprise and disappointment when next day the General's report said the turnout was " poor." I don't know what these big-bosses really did want. I wish they could have been made to clean links for a year. In the extent of the vocabulary that was invoked when we learnt this the transport surpassed themselves : it is a good thing the red-hats could not hear the remarks that were made about them.

The rest of the month rolled by quickly enough : we only wished that leave might have been doled out at the same rate. Soon it came to be twelve months since I had last been home, with the chances of getting leave this winter becoming more and more remote. Some of the Christmas parcels were delayed so that many men were driven for their celebrations to the various estaminets of La Gorgue. By this time I had become a regular visitor at my French friends' house and frequently had supper with them. The great day for French celebrations is, of course, January 1st, on which date I was invited there to dinner, tea and supper and so arranged that the transport should get along without me for a few hours. Erma was dressed in her best : Mother had brought to light some extra luxuries from a horde they kept secretly under their bed or in some such place : Father had unearthed some vin blanc and champagne, which he had evidently well sampled before my arrival. A somewhat merry friend was present also, exceedingly jubilant over the return of his wife and eight children from the German side of the line where he had believed some of them had died. These refugees confirmed that the enemy were short of food and in a bad plight—rather reassuring news to receive at first hand. They also reported that they were forcing civilians to work on defences, contrary to international law, deporting the males *en masse* from their homes.

The Devils' Mess celebrated Christmas over again on the arrival of my delayed parcels on January 13th, and as many others had by that time consumed their extra delicacies we felt we could not sit and gourmandise without sharing out with everybody in our section of the barn. What a repast there was ! Seventeen of us sat down at an impromptu table, illuminated by candles and a crazy lamp, to consume Mrs. Smith's dainties, and the flattering comments upon them would have rejoiced my people's hearts. We had washed our plates in hot water for the occasion and those who were short of a spoon or fork made a point of borrowing one and eating respectably for once. The menu proved to be too much for the majority of us, for our appetites had shrunk owing to the long-continued existence on meagre army rations. Conibeer gave up the attempt to get through as far as the dessert : Mears admitted that he had made a beast of himself.

In January the battalion was billeted for some days at Merville, where I had to spend my time with a limber, sleeping in a very draughty outhouse. The wind swept at a furious rate in the aperture where the door ought to have been, candles burnt away before you could say " knife," and the brazier smoked to its heart's content. Rats ran all over the place at nights, but as we had to sleep entirely under the blankets to avoid the wind, the heavier sleepers did not hear them. One night Cooper found one on his hand, which was evidently uncovered, so he flung the brute across the room, where it alighted on Trendell's head. What with rats, wind and rain we were not at all sorry to get to our old stable again.

The wet spell was followed by snow, and as the month drew to a close it became colder and colder. Even in the barn it was decidedly chilly : it was agony to potter about on the horse-lines. We walked the greater part of the way back from our ration trips beside our horses to avoid frostbite. Washing accessories and toothbrushes in our valises were frozen in the mornings, as were our boots and putties. What it must have been like in the trenches without blankets, only my memories of February, 1915, could bring home to me. Fellows spent longer in them now, however, and the *Telegraph* stated that many were dying of cold.

On February 3rd we moved our transport lines to stables near Laventie, less than two miles from the trenches. In the town itself, although certain houses were in ruins, most of the civilians " carried on," the estaminets and shops doing a roaring trade. It reminded one of Ploegsteert in its complete disregard of a war being in progress close at hand. We were not allowed to issue from one end of the town in daylight.

This move took me farther from my friends' house at La Gorgue, but I nevertheless continued the visits whenever possible. Figg, who had come with me once or twice, had now gone on leave. The French folk seemed rather relieved at this, for Figg sometimes sang at their house and they didn't understand the English style at all. They were amused and fascinated, but usually got up and went out of the room as soon as he opened his mouth. Playing the piano did not seem to annoy them at all ; in fact, as the daughter played too, we transformed the Entente Cordiale into action by learning duets. When I informed the section that these people left us alone to practice, there were cries of horror and the excitement grew to a great pitch as they speculated upon her charms. However, someone spread the false report that she had been seen cleaning the front step, with her hair in curlers, and after that the curiosity about the nineteen-year-old somewhat diminished.

Just at this time we received the bombshell of the German blockade announcement : all Allied and neutral shipping and all hospital boats were to be torpedoed at sight. Our supply routes were to become infested with submarines and a very serious state of affairs was threatened. It was Germany's last desperate throw : would it bring America into the War ? The French were extraordinarily optimistic about the whole affair. Nearly every French person I had met since the outbreak of war had given the War six months more to run, though the peasant at Wascherville had been dubious : they were still guaranteeing it would be over in six months. An old man in a Laventie estaminet who was always thanking his lucky stars he didn't live five miles away—i.e., in the German lines—went nearly frantic with joy over the threatened rupture of diplomatic relations between America and Germany. " Germany finish ! " said he.

The rupture of relations duly took place, giving us consolation for the unrestricted U-boat campaign : this had begun with the sinking of twelve merchant ships daily, which boded ill for the future of our supplies of all kinds. Leave was promptly stopped and we commenced to get less and less bread and fresh meat. Orders came out that we were to buy no more French bread. Simultaneously, the Army started to issue us with an American concoction called " Pork and Beans," originally intended, I should imagine, to supplement our bully beef issue, but actually distributed as the sole diet for dinner (our principal meal of the day) on several occasions. In case the reader is unaware of their nature, I will explain that " Pork and Beans " were really tinned beans with one tiny piece of gristle in them, the size of a lump of sugar ; this, presumably, was the pork. The beans varied in taste from tobacco-smoke to glue, and sat on one's chest for the afternoon. Very few fellows wasted time in opening the tins (which were issued one between two or three men) when it was possible to buy fried eggs at an estaminet. The day that the submarine campaign might force us to fall back on our reserve supplies of " Pork and Beans," Lord help our digestions !

Early in February there was an inoculation parade of those transport and company men who had not been done for over a year, and eight of the section, including Chrisp and myself, marched up to the L.R.B. aid post in Laventie. Four of us decided to refuse, as was our right, and I confess that I was among the number. The reader who knows the value of typhoid vaccine must be patient with me : the only occasion on which a private may defy an officer, knowing himself to be on sure ground, is when he has a conscientious objection to vaccination or inoculation.

That little bit of cussedness in all of us likes to come to the front sometimes, and there was a certain amount of fun to be got out of defying the M.O. and seeing what he would say. Captain Riddell had the reputation of being rather smart with his tongue and we therefore anticipated a little excitement.

Corporal Chrisp was the first to be called up. He had his tunic on.

" Take your tunic off."

" I object to being done, sir." The M.O. looked annoyed.

" What are your reasons for objecting ? "

" Well, I spent over twelve months in a fever hospital in London and got the views of several doctors and physicians on the subject and many of them were against it. I am content to go on the advice of medical friends and I don't wish to be done."

Captain Riddell got angry now.

" You don't know what you're talking about," said he. " This may save you dying of enteric fever. . . ."

" Well, I'm a bit of a fatalist," said Chrisp.

" What grounds have you for being a fatalist ? "

" The mere fact that I've lived for twenty-eight years is . . ."

At this the explosion came. Chrisp was told not to talk rot and to get outside, whereupon he saluted and cheerfully departed.

My turn came next.

" I object also, sir." A pitying glance from the M.O.

" Why ? "

" When I was done I was told it would last for three years."

" Well, the doctor was wrong. It only lasts twelve months."

" Also, I suffered from septic poisoning for some months after being done."

" You couldn't have been properly inoculated. I promise you'll have no ill effect from this dose."

" I took the risk evidently last year and had nothing the matter with me. I'll chance it this year."

" You are really stupid, you know. It's far better to have septic poisoning than to die of typhoid fever. Besides, you are not playing the game by the other fellows who might catch it."

" But I thought, sir, you were inoculating them so that they wouldn't catch it."

" They might get it, but it wouldn't affect them so badly. Come along, now, hold out your arm."

Silence.

" I know more about this than you. I'll take special care of you. Hold it out."

Poor Riddell! I feel a brute as I recall this conversation. It was pure cussedness that made me hold out. He was right and I was wrong. Yet I had put on a bold face in front of all the other men and could not climb down. So I still refused.

" All right," said he. " I'll give your names to the Colonel and see that you don't get leave."

When leave looked more hopeful in June and another parade took place, we cast our conscientious objections to the four winds and meekly fell in the queue with bared arms. We were opportunists where leave was concerned, for it was more precious than anything in the world.

During the winter we lost one or two fellows who left the section and went home " under age "—having been all through the Somme battle, suffering the same hardships as the older men. We might also have been affected by the request for names of all those who knew anything about railway work, as engine-drivers, plate-layers, joiners and dozens of grades of mechanics of one kind and another were required for the hundreds of miles of additional railway that were being laid down in France. However, none of our fellows were of a practical disposition and unless the Army wanted clerical work performed we should not be of any use to it.

One fellow—I cannot remember his name—put himself down as a stationmaster. Reading this, the officer asked him if he had been a stationmaster in civilian life.

" No, sir," he replied.

" Then why do you put yourself down as one ? "

" Oh, I just thought I could fancy myself strolling up and down Paddington Station, sir, in a top hat."

His name was struck off the list.

In the middle of February the L.R.B. made a raid on the German lines at Fauquisshart, resulting in the capture of a few prisoners and in some of our own men becoming missing. Unfortunately, I do not recall the details. These raids were becoming more frequent on either side, with the object of keeping the enemy in a constant state of nerves. Following a tranquil spell in the line, the entire artillery of one side or the other would suddenly be concentrated on a particular section of the trenches, blowing them to pieces and cutting off all support from the rear. Then the defending artillery would chime in with a barrage in No Man's Land and a counter-battery bombardment, and Hell would be let loose for half an hour or more. In the meantime the raiding party would follow their barrage, jump in the trench, blow up the dug-outs, capture a prisoner or two and a machine-gun, and return to their original line. It meant vigilant nights for those in the front posts and forward saps.

On the northern sector of the front this was the chief feature of the winter fighting, but down on the Ancre more serious matters were afoot. During January one trench after another had been taken, rendering the German position in the Gommecourt salient more and more precarious, and on February 7th the Germans had to evacuate Beaumont. On the 9th we advanced farther up the Ancre Valley and next day attacked at Serre. The cumulative effect of all these blows was manifested in a big German retirement down south to a depth of three miles on February 25th, involving the evacuation of Pys, Serre, Miraumont, Eaucourt and Warlincourt : a day or so later the enemy were found to have left Gommecourt and that memorable July 1st battlefield with its unburied dead fell into our hands. Oh ! the joy this caused in Laventie when someone brought us the *Continental Daily Mail* containing the news ! The Somme fighting had been worth while : the backward move of the Germans towards their own frontiers had begun ! The British had taken over the whole of the Somme battle front now and our line extended to Roye, a hundred and twenty miles from end to end. This meant that our heavy artillery must be far less concentrated than we had seen it in the autumn, and that many more divisions must have arrived. We saw one march through La Gorgue—the 57th Lancashire Territorial Division who had had over two years' training at home.

The time now came for us to leave the Neuve Chapelle sector. We had been there for four months and the battalion had had a most trying spell in the trenches, with only short breaks spent in barns behind the line. The ten days at Picquigny were really the only rest they had had since the Somme battle and they were now promised a period of rest and training a long way from the firing-line. Goodness knows they well deserved it : the cold had been intense and their conditions miserable and it was with thankful hearts that they marched away from Laventie on the 1st of March—destined to be thoroughly disillusioned. The transport did not feel so joyful for their own sakes, for it was not likely that they would be in clover like that again— nor were they until after the Armistice.

Before leaving, I hurried down to La Gorgue to take leave of my French friends and spent an evening with them. Nothing was too much trouble to them that night : they had prepared a sumptuous repast and toasted my health in the enthusiastic French fashion. Finally I departed with a packet of fruit and sweets they had done up for me and their final blessings and prayers ringing in my ears.

How glad I was to recall these signs of friendship in the next month or two when we encountered quite a number of people of a lower class who made themselves exceedingly unpleasant. There are kindly souls and sour dispositions in all races, so it is not fair to conjure up memories of the disobliging civilians and pass judgment accordingly on the French people as a whole, as some fellows are inclined to do. At Ploegsteert, St. Omer, Berguette, Huppy, Doullens, Picquigny and La Gorgue, to mention prominent instances, we had met with kindness and sympathy which many of us will never forget.

CHAPTER XX.

ADVENTURES AT ARRAS.

(*March–April*, 1917.)

An eight-day trek—Hut regulations—Arras—Hostile civilians—The Hindenburg Line—An air-fight at Achicourt—A.S.C. rations: an odious comparison—The attack imminent—A fatal traffic block.

THE thought that every pace you take carries you a pace farther from danger is a great incentive to march on and on, regardless of fatigue. The L.R.B. knew that they had a few days' tramp before them when they left Laventie, but the long trek was worth while, as they had been led to expect a period of rest and longed to be in some peaceful spot similar to the training areas of the preceding spring. We spent the first night at Vielle Chapelle, not far from Neuve Chapelle, and another day's march brought us to St. Venant. The third night saw us at Tangry and on the fourth we reached Fillievres. These names convey nothing to the reader and precious little to the writer. One day's tramp was like another. At nights he put up with A Company and endeavoured to find a decent stable and to purchase hay and straw for his horses. At first sight the advantages of being a driver were apparent on a long trek like this, as the pack-pony men, brakesmen, etc., tramped most of the way. But in view of the bitterly cold weather, the driving winds and sleet, every driver would have been only too glad to march most of the way and found a great difficulty in inducing those on foot to relieve him for a short time, to enable him to restore his circulation. Figg, Conibeer and Trendell, who were walking, refused to drive several men's pairs, though their " Devils' Mess " companions did not ask them in vain. The very time when the drivers should have reaped the reward of their looking after two horses and two sets of harness, they were in the most unenviable position of all.

March 5th found us continuing the interminable march with jubilant spirits at the promise of reaching our final destination that night. We had put some scores of miles between the firing-line and our skins and, with luck, it would be a month or more before we saw it again. At length we reached our goal, the village of Le Boisle, where, throwing our packs upon the ground and care to the four winds, we set out to explore the place.

Le Boisle could not have been a great distance from the sea, though it looked far from civilisation—judging by the sparsely-populated surroundings and the monotony of its jerry-built, mud-walled barns. There was scarcely a shop in the place and even in the general stores there was not enough food for anyone possessing fabulous wealth to buy sufficient to keep body and soul together for long. We were, and had been for five days, completely at the mercy of army rations, but the supply people did not come up to the scratch.

Whether or not it was because the old battlefields of Agincourt and Cressy were close at hand and the descendants of those who had suffered harboured resentment against the British, it is difficult to say : the civilians, however, regarded us as though we were their most bitter enemies. On the fifth day's trek we went into a yard to draw some water at one of our halting places. No sooner had we started using the pump than a fiery youth rushed up and removed a nail from the pump in an effort to put it out of order. However, we carried on with the assistance of a smithy's nail and when he discovered this he flew into a terrible rage, bringing a stick down hard on to Conibeer's knuckles, which were blue with cold. Conibeer, in retaliation, instantly chucked the contents of his bucket over the irate youth, to cool his temper.

The only person who beamed graciously upon us in Le Boisle was the village idiot, who jabbered up and down the one and only street, waving his hands. The woman at the transport billet was vitriolic. She objected to her stables being used for horses and her draughty tottering outhouses for troops. First one barn and then another she banned as our billet : then she had a strong objection to our using a certain door to get from her stable into the yard. I made my first acquaintance of her by using that door. Apparently I was about the tenth person to do so and the other nine men, together with several amused onlookers, were being treated to a maniacal effusion in the yard beyond. In the midst of this, in all innocence, the tenth offender came through the door and let it slam violently. My word, the screeching that ensued ! A hurried council of war thereupon decided upon reprisals and the opportunity came when her husband climbed up into a loft to get some hay. The ladder was deftly removed and hidden, its absence being discovered by the man only when his legs were dangling in the air. His wife, rushing out at this critical moment, was able to observe his plight and stormed and raved, clenched her fists and spat at us. Our revenge was complete. Pleasant people these, as neighbours, after our experiences at La Gorgue !

Next morning we were dumbfounded to receive the order to pack up kits and move in an hour. Colonel Husey was quite as astonished and disgusted as we were. The idea of moving again just after finishing a five days' trek ! Even Figg, who credited the Army with almost anything, was unprepared for this blow. Where could we be going to ? Were we in the wrong area ? Were we going down to the seaside ? The mystery was soon solved : our direction lay eastwards, which meant that we were bound for the firing-line again without any rest at all. There is no need to dwell on the intense disappointment this caused or the language that was used as the men tramped towards the line again. For three more days we pushed on, through snow and biting winds, until we reached Fosseux, a little village behind the Arras front, where the old familiar rumble of guns could be heard once more. Not a man had fallen out upon this march, truly a feat of which to be proud considering it was done in full kit and by men who were out of condition, through their winter in the firing-line. Instead of going half round the world to reach Fosseux it could have been reached in three days at the outside by a direct march from Laventie. Truly the ways of the Army were mysterious!

We were put in a camp of long Nissen huts where, owing to the fact that the companies shared the camp, we suddenly became involved in inspections of huts by "orderly officers" and all the usual paraphernalia of barrack life, from which the transport were usually immune. These huts, in common with all other billets with which we had come in contact, were not fitted with nails, pegs, shelves, stoves, ration-cupboards or anything that made for comfort, and so the transport followed their usual practice of driving in nails, extending wires to hang wet clothes or towels upon and effecting other improvements which made our lot a degree or so more civilised.

However, on the first morning the orderly officer who came round inspecting the entire camp appeared horrified at the "untidiness" of the transport huts. No article of clothing was to be left hanging up: ration boxes were to disappear: mackintoshes, food, blankets and other articles were to be arranged neatly in a pile and covered with a ground-sheet: on top of such pile were to be placed the packs with tin helmets resting on top: the bandoliers were to circle these like halos: on one side the water-bottle and on the other the haversacks were to be neatly arranged, while the respirator would repose in front: rifles should be leant against the wall, magazine pointing outwards.

These instructions left us stupefied, but the transport was nothing if not a loyal body of men and it should not be said that the old hands let the regiment down. So the next day, after breakfast, we had to take all our goods and chattels from the improvised pegs and clothes lines and bury them under our ground-sheets. It did not matter what rubbish one hid under them so long as nothing was left hanging up round the hut. Imagine the sleeping blankets, eatables, wet mackintoshes, plates and mugs, muddy overcoats, sooty galley-pots, extra pairs of breeches, cigarettes and wet towels, all jumbled up together and covered with a nice, smooth, innocent-looking ground-sheet! What cleanliness! What hygiene!

We did not see a paper during our stay here, but rumours reached us of the German retreat spreading southwards and of more village sites falling into our hands. The weather was bitterly cold, snow was on the ground and a more trying time for pursuing an advance could hardly be imagined.

To our great regret the Army plans for cutting down the strength of infantry transports resulted in four transport men being sent back to their companies here, and, incredible as it may seem, Conibeer—of the Devils' Mess—was among their number. Conibeer had been with the transport section before the War and came to France with it, but of late he had been speaking his mind pretty freely: in other words, certain individuals of varying ranks got into his bad books and they did not like it. It was therefore not altogether surprising that Conibeer was given his opportunity to vent his spleen upon others, but his departure caused considerable regret and we vowed we would have him back when the first vacancy occurred. He didn't feel the departure so much at the time and was rather anxious to go in the trenches, so, with a final "Cheerio!" he shouldered his pack, took his place in D Company and marched off with them when we left Fosseux on the 14th.

The battalion was marching up to " trench billets " in Arras, *via* the poplar-lined Warlus-Dainville road, accompanied by the bulk of the transport ; the remainder of the latter was making its way to the village of Simoncourt where the new transport lines were to be. We were pointed out the location of Simoncourt to the right of the road on our way up, so that we should be able to find the village on our return from Arras.

At Warlus the head of the column stopped for so long that I asked a passing R.E. what the trouble was

" You can't go past Warlus in daytime, chum ! " said he. " Fritz can see you."

" But it's a good way from the firing-line, isn't it ? "

" You bet ! It's about four miles. But Jerry can see all this country for miles around from the Vimy Ridge and, besides, his aeroplanes are busy. They want to keep all movements of troops in these parts a secret. And, take my word for it, there's going to be something doing up this way presently."

It was astonishing how far Warlus was from the line, for the remainder of the journey, which could not be performed in daylight, really seemed unending. We eventually reached the outskirts of Arras, a town which was to be the hub of our existence for most of the remainder of the War. What a size it was ! And what echoes the traffic made on the cobbled roads between the double lines of houses ! Scarcely a light could be seen in any building, but there was sufficient moonlight to make out their outlines and to distinguish a big edifice here, used as a hospital, or a barracks there, occupied by troops. As a matter of fact, Arras was teeming with troops—whose numbers increased in the next three weeks—but most of them lived underground. In preparation for a possible attack from this centre, R.E.s had been busy for months, joining up underground cellars and tunnelling out towards the firing-line, so that the town was capable of holding large numbers of troops without arousing the enemy's suspicions.

Some of the front-line trenches ran through the far outskirts of the city, the lines being only a few yards apart in places among the ruins. The bulk of Arras appeared on this and subsequent occasions to be untouched, but we heard that it was shelled daily and that the station and eastern quarters were badly knocked about—a fact we confirmed later. Many of the houses harboured guns and the whole town seemed to vibrate and echo when they were firing.

On this first night the companies went into a building close to the French cavalry barracks, the cookers, etc., being drawn up under some trees in an open space near at hand. Having unhooked the cooker horses and unloaded rations, we set off to find Simoncourt, but the journey proved to be an even longer one in the reverse direction. Fearful of approaching Arras by day, all the supplies and reinforcements were arriving by night, so that the roads were choked with traffic in both directions. An additional trouble was the fact that heavy artillery was arriving from other fronts, endeavouring to locate its prepared gun-positions (between Warlus and Arras) in the dark. A tractor-drawn gun would take half an hour to find its home and manœuvre into it, spending most of the time drawn up at right angles across the road, completely stopping all traffic.

Matters were made worse by what was known as " double-banking," that is, a convoy coming from the rear would discover a line of stationary vehicles on the right and, thinking they were waiting for ammunition or some such thing, proceed to pass them on the left. The second line would eventually halt as the first had done—owing to some break-down on the road—and then some crack-brained driver proceeding home on his own would attempt to pass the two lines of traffic on the wrong side of the road, until he was suddenly confronted with the opposite stream. A deadlock invariably ensued and such blockages became more frequent about this time than we had ever known before ; this may have been partly due to the large number of breakdowns and " ditchings " caused by the terribly dilapidated state of the roads behind the Arras front.

All roads converged on Arras. It was like a bicycle hub with numerous spokes forking out in every direction. As, for the last three miles to Arras, long convoys were unable to move in daytime, the congestion at night in the suburbs of the city led to some appalling fixes.

" This double-banking will cause trouble one of these nights," said Kimbo Vallentine to me, as we sat waiting for a Royal Marine Artillery unit to get its gun out of the way. " It's a mighty good job the Germans are not shelling the road."

We reached Simoncourt eventually after midnight and the ensuing experiences at that vile village are told in the following letter :—

17/3/17. " . . . I have often written to you about mud and there is no need to enlarge much on that subject. In this village it is of the watery, clayish variety and is most abundant in the streets and round the water-troughs. There are endless queues of horses on the way to water and they give all passers-by a free mud spray. Officers glare, privates grouse and civilians screech—positively screech. The inhabitants here are not so friendly as we usually find them. Perhaps the village of mud into which the British Army has transformed their once peaceful surroundings has made them a trifle short-tempered. Hardly anyone will serve you with a café and at one farm they tapped at the window, shouting ' No ! No ! ' before ever I had reached the door.

" There are a few wells available, but most people put them out of order or lock them up. By dint of a few pleasant remarks and a feeble attempt at wit, I persuaded one old French woman to unlock her well and let me use it on occasions, as a special favour. I had only been there a few times when a Scotch chap came up to draw water just as I had finished and, instead of lowering the bucket gently, let go the handle ! There was a terrible shaking and jolting as the bucket sped downwards at about sixty miles an hour. That roused the whole household. The old woman croaked and swore, while an old man rushed up, seized a bucket of water and hurled it at ME ! Fortunately I was not drowned and I was laughing too much to mind. At any rate the Scotch chap didn't get his water and the well is locked up once more.

" I had a wordy argument to-day with a Frenchman who tried to hit my horse because he imagined he was being forced into the mud beside the road. I also had trouble with a fat old wench who swore at me. One of her fowls flew through the mud, spraying my face with slosh ; as I was in a bad temper I gave vent to my wrath by chasing the offending chicken up the road. The owner happened to see the chase and ran after me, jabbering away nineteen-to-the-dozen and shaking her fist, which led to retorts in equally strong language conveying, however, nothing to her unreceptive mind.

" The first day we came here, a few of us arrived after midnight and I learnt that my party were in a billet half a mile away. It was no easy matter to find it in the darkness, but after looking in a dozen barns, I struck the right one at last, finding that the beds were arranged in tiers, one above the other, like bunks on a ship. They were made of wire-netting and the third ' storey ' was close to the roof, so that those on the top-floor had a difficulty in climbing up and down ; my party had reserved me a place in the middle storey and that was bad enough to scramble into. You have to keep all your equipment, blankets, overcoat, etc., on the ' bed ' and clamber up in muddy boots whenever you need a plate or mug. You eat your meals standing in the passage-way, resting your plates on the middle tier, and imagine you're at Pimms'. But if you're just passing along the gangway and someone climbs backwards out of his bed, sticking his foot in your face, you are rudely disillusioned.

" Another disadvantage of this system is that all the dust and odds and ends from the kit of the man above descend on you, on account of the wire-netting ! Last night I found an avalanche of bits of straw coming through : it was only the ' man upstairs ' getting into bed. The most unfortunate occurrence was when I spilt some tea on my bed. Poor Williams underneath was so annoyed that he promptly shifted his quarters and no one else will come to take his place, knowing my reputation. Whenever I want to get something from my bed, Figg insists on getting it for me to prevent half of the kit being kicked on the floor and the other half covered with mud.

" If you get in late and have to ' make ' your bed when the men on either side are asleep, it is an awkward task. This happened to me two nights ago : I couldn't kneel up properly and had to keep turning round in my own space to lay the blanket, kneeling on it all the while. By the time I had got the second blanket down and half undressed I was in a hopeless knot and both my next-door neighbours had been roused : worst of all, I had upset the sip of rum they had left for me in a mug. In desperation I put my valise, respirator, galley-pot, bandolier and water-bottle on the foot of a somewhat heavy sleeper, where they reposed in safety till the morning.

" The fall of Bagdad was good news and greatly rejoiced our hearts. We have just this minute heard the news of the Russian revolution, some receiving it dejectedly and others believing it is a ' win the war ' movement and that when a lot of the corrupt people are kicked out of high places Russia will stand a better chance. Many receive it with feigned enthusiasm and sing ' Pack up for ever ' to the tune of Tosti's ' Good-bye.' Another group are at the moment singing :

> ' We'll HAVE to sheath the sword, yes,
>   We'll have to sheath the sword,'

to the tune of the Hornpipe. The optimistic ones are singing :

> ' The Tsar's done a guy, yes,
>   The Tsar's done a guy,'

to the same melody. It remains to be seen how it will turn out.

" To-day it's finer and the aeroplanes on both sides are very busy. Very early this morning the guns were going ' hammer and tongs.' "

The German retirement was now taking place at a quicker rate, extending to north and south and involving our own front to a limited extent. We had been expecting it, as for one or two nights the sky behind the German lines had been red with burning villages. Arras and the Vimy Ridge were the northern pivot on which this vast backward movement hinged and, as the withdrawal reached a greater depth down south, so the line had to swing back a little at our end to conform with it. This meant evacuating the village of Beaurains which had been just behind the German front to the south of Arras, commanding every movement in the south-east suburbs and Achicourt. So about the 19th the L.R.B., who were in reserve, moved forward towards Beaurains. Another brigade in front had warily scotched up Fritz who had his new front before the village of Neuville Vitasse, in the valley beyond Beaurains. I say " warily " because it was by now common knowledge that the Germans had left booby-traps, trip wires, time-fuses and mined roads and houses where they had retired down south ; and no one knew whether a dug-out or ruin were safe until it had been certified as such by special parties of R.E.s.

Everybody had now heard of the Hindenburg Line, a vast series of outlying posts and fieldworks, protected by acres of barbed wire, themselves covering a main battle line miles in the rear, the whole having been prepared for months with prisoners' and civilians' forced labour.

The Somme successes had convinced Hindenburg of the necessity of having a shorter line to fall back upon, partly to economise in troops and partly because the tactical position on the Somme left him no option. We had first heard of these formidable fortifications a few months before and had despondently wondered what had been the good of forcing the enemy from one position and another at enormous sacrifices when he had an impregnable line of defence in the rear. In the north its outworks lay before us in Neuville Vitasse : behind that, line after line of heavily-wired trenches existed. Down south, Bapaume (the goal of the Somme battle) and Peronne had been evacuated—both being robbed of everything useful and blown to smithereens before the departure, as were all the other villages. But we had not yet reached there the outworks of the Hindenburg Line and the enemy were merely delaying us in those parts with bodies of machine gunners and small garrisons, to make our pursuit as costly as possible and to give time for the completion of his defence works. In view of the uninhabitable wilderness he left behind him, with all houses destroyed, trees cut down across the roads, orchards hacked to pieces, etc., we were thankful his retreat on our front only amounted to about a mile.

After a few nights of bitterly cold and very protracted ration journeys, in which we had to search high and low for the battalion, it was decided to move the transport lines to Achicourt, the next village to Beaurains, a move that had to be made at night owing to the Army's secrecy precautions. However, we waited until the early morning hours for instructions to depart and, although we set off in darkness, arrived at our destination after daybreak ! We put the whole of the brigade transports in the open beside the Aubigny-Arras railway line so that any German aeroplane coming over could note them as new arrivals ;

after several aeroplanes had in fact manifested themselves, it was decided to put the animals in various stables in the outskirts of Achicourt.

The next night I was on water-cart duty and spent hours on my own, trying to find the battalion, for I took a wrong fork-road by the railway bridge beyond Achicourt and, of course, roamed completely beyond the 50th Divisional area. In the end an officer gave me my bearings and I retraced my steps. On that trip I noticed what a concentration of artillery there was on this front : though it hardly rivalled what the Somme had been. After months of preparation of gun-pits, etc., most of it was now compelled to move forward in view of the German retirement, but no doubt all would be ranged on to the new targets by the time the Arras attack was desired. How cold it was ! The wind drove through whatever clothes one put on, and the long waits owing to traffic blocks caused many drivers' noses to take on a permanent purple hue.

The following morning, while we were in our barn eating biscuits and bacon for breakfast, listening to the sound of anti-aircraft guns and the whirring of aeroplanes, which did not in the ordinary way excite us, we heard a " pop-pop-pop-pop-pop-pop-pop ! " whereupon there was a precipitate rush for the door. Kicking over my mug of tea and seizing Figg's biscuit in my haste, I joined the crowd— some forty in number—who were all trying to get through the door at once.

" Pop-pop-pop-pop-pop ! "

Having kicked my way near the front and squeezed through the opening, I followed the rushing figures over a neighbouring cabbage patch and gazed upwards. Three aeroplanes were circling around, flying low down just over our heads—one German and two British. We were just in time to see one of the British ones, which was evidently winged, break away from the fight and make off to the rear ; meanwhile, the German turned its attention to the other machine. How anxiously we watched the duel ! We shouted in our excitement, in our anxiety to see the other man avenged, and worked ourselves into a frenzy as we realised the German machine was the faster. They were still flying around, firing machine-guns just above our heads. Then we saw a heartrending thing. A bullet had hit the British petrol tank which had caught fire ; from a little spurt of flame it grew into a regular blaze and, as the machine turned circles, we could see the two men quite distinctly. After some seconds which seemed hours of agony they set off in a straight line for Beaurains, a long trail of fire and smoke issuing from the tail of the aeroplane. About half a mile away it wavered, continued on its course a little farther and then crocked up : a moment later the whole paraphernalia became a mass of flame and the smoking debris fell to earth.

The German machine was by now making its way back to the enemy lines, no doubt feeling very pleased with itself, and we watched anxiously for some fast aeroplane of ours or our anti-aeroplane guns to bring it to earth. For a time it seemed as if no one would take any notice, but our anti-aircraft gunners in Arras had seen the fight and were going to make sure of their man. Suddenly the batteries spoke out and the machine was literally surrounded with puffs of smoke. Never had we seen such good shooting : it could not fail to do some damage. Sure enough, the conqueror who had just put two of our machines out of action was himself hit and fell to earth to the accompaniment of the cheers of many hundreds — probably thousands—of onlookers.

A few people I spoke to were inclined to whimper as though we had lost the mastery of the air, just because one or two of their crack men ventured out occasionally in specially fast machines and attacked our observing planes. Just for a few months about this time their Fokkers certainly gave us something to think about, but on balance there was no doubt as to which side was " top dog " in the air. When it was all over we had a short argument with the owner of the field where we had been standing : he was far more concerned about his cabbages than the air fight.

On March 25th, Kimbo, Harbord and I had to take our horses to the A.S.C. Divisional train in order to assist in carting the division dump down to Frevent, midway between Doullens and St. Pol. I only mention the trip as it was noteworthy as revealing the incongruous system of apportioning out rations. Our transport and company men were existing for the most part on bully beef and biscuits, with a shortage of all other issues. In spite of every local effort to supplement our rations, we had to rely on our parcels to prevent the tightening of our belts. The Russian revolution had been precipitated by food shortage and absence of bread and we were really able to understand how empty stomachs had driven those people to extremes. The months of March and April, 1917, were the leanest of the whole War, as far as the transport food went. Before some of us visited the A.S.C. we resignedly attributed the shortage to the submarine campaign : the British soldier is a remarkably long-suffering, philosophical individual and treated the shortage as a joke in his lighter moments, but the wit had a tinge of sarcasm in it.

The nearest Expeditionary Force canteen was some miles away, and in order to get any supplies there, limbers had to line up at 4 and 5 a.m. If we sent one away even at daybreak it got there too late to get any food worth mentioning, and we could not spare horses for non-essential all night jobs. We got some peculiar ration issues about this time ; sometimes four dates per man would be given out in lieu of a butter issue. At others, we got about twenty raisins per man, only to learn that they were in place of our jam. No flour was provided for making date or raisin roll, and it was not explained how these non-essentials were to help down dry bread or biscuit for our meals. Other weird issues that made their appearance on occasions were five-sixths or two-thirds of an orange per man and a handful of chestnuts. What we required was bread, bread, and still more bread.

When we got to the A.S.C., however, on the evening of the 25th, we were asked if we had had tea. No ! Then, without questioning whether we had brought the remains of our day's rations—which had long ago been eaten—they placed before us a box filled with slices of bread and told us to help ourselves. Beside the box were two or three opened tins of jam and butter. It seemed too good to be true and I felt like a kid at a party. All the curbed hunger of the past week seemed to be suddenly craving for satisfaction, so that after swallowing three huge slices I was as ravenous as before.

" What's the limit of the ration ? " I asked.

" No limit," said the cook. " Take as much as you want."

Our appetites were not satisfied that night under five slices per man ! It was the same all the while we were with them and they kept us six days. Never did we descend to consuming biscuits. Never were we refused a second helping of anything.

When the Frevent job was over they used. us for easing their own men's burden somewhat—I admit they had long hours and plenty of work to do—so we were employed in drawing our own brigade rations from the railhead and depositing them at the A.S.C. dump—an open field.

We then learnt the riddle of the five-sixths-of-an-orange-per-man issue and the box-of-matches-between-seven mystery. All the drivers engaged in drawing rations from the railhead—A.S.C. and ourselves—were surreptitiously handed an orange and a box of matches each by the N.C.O. in charge ! We only got this one glimpse of things behind the lines, but we learnt much in that short time. When we returned to the section we found the Devils' Mess still pondering the question whether to start on the next day's rations or go supperless to bed. A loaf, which the A.S.C. sergeant had presented to me on my departure, solved the problem for that night.

The next day the L.R.B. went a few miles farther back for a week in that mucky mud-heap, Monchiet, the village in which the three of us had just been quartered with the A.S.C., but the transport section remained at Achicourt, that is, in advance of the battalion. Our chief objection to Achicourt was that we could get no baths there. It was now early April, whereas my last bath had been at La Gorgue on February 7th : the uncleanliness did not, however, appear to perturb the Army authorities. Perhaps they thought we were getting wet enough without them, with all the rain that continued intermittently.

In spite of the weather, it was now practically certain that the attack was imminent. Reports from various parts of the front down south indicated that the German resistance was stiffening and the advanced elements of the Hindenburg system appeared to have been reached all along the line. Just south-east of our own front, a further bending-back of their line had taken place, Henin and Croisilles having just been occupied. This might mean an alteration of our plans on the extreme right of the front to be attacked, but on the greater part of it everything was now in readiness. We heard reports of tanks coming up by train. I was struck by the great increase in the number of light railways being laid down behind the front, ready to cope with some of the ammunition supply.

At last April 7th arrived, on which day the companies were due to leave their huts at Monchiet and take up their battle position in reserve for the attack. I rode over with several drivers to take back the cookers, water-carts and stores, reaching the village after the battalion had finished tea. Jumbo had a trick that was becoming positively riling of late—he was apt to hang back and allow The Grey to take the entire weight of the cooker in starting off, though once the vehicles were on the move, he would work like a Trojan. If the limber were in mud and it was beyond the power of The Grey to take all the weight alone, I sometimes had great difficulty in getting away at all. On this occasion, when I was attempting to start the cooker on a muddy incline, the trouble became acute and there was some delay while the rest of the convoy waited for me. Afterwards I bitterly cursed that delay, for an earlier departure might have made all the difference to our trip that night. Even when I joined them there was a further wait, for some unknown reason, so one or two of us dismounted and had a talk. Kimbo had just purchased a few biscuits from a French shop where he had had to pay an outrageous price.

" It doesn't do to consider the price out here," he said. " What is the use of a hundred francs in notes in your pocket-case if your stomach's empty ? Why keep the money and go hungry ? We only live once and might as well make ourselves as comfortable as possible."

Then, in his generous way, he offered the precious fancy biscuits round the group of drivers.

" Get mounted," cried Gordon, riding up at a gallop.

Hastening back to our vehicles, we scrambled into the saddles ; then the convoy set off for the Doullens-Arras main road which we joined at Beaumetz. It will be remembered that Achicourt lay quite close to the line not far from Arras, so that the vehicles returning to the transport lines and those accompanying the battalion to their destination all moved together. At Achicourt, some would make for the wagon-lines and the others would keep straight on.

For three days the British guns had kept up a severe bombardment of the German lines and the sky flickered with thousands of flashes. On the main road there was a good deal of traffic moving up, under cover of darkness, the volume growing greater as we drew near to Arras,

After several halts, short moves forward and further halts, we got to within a few hundred yards of the Achicourt-Dainville cross-roads where we should turn to the right and be free of most of the congestion ; but at this spot we stuck. The whole of the upgoing traffic was apparently 'suspended and it was indeed tantalising to be within a stone's throw of a quieter road and yet have to sit still on the horses, perishing with cold, waiting for an unintelligent traffic corporal to interpret impossible traffic regulations.

In spite of a lot of stationary ambulances on our right, a double-banking convoy came alongside us on the left, receiving curses from everybody. Of course, this, too, was brought to a standstill, leaving three lines of vehicles facing Arras and pretty well filling the entire road. All of a sudden we heard the report of a German howitzer on the right—that distinct pop which tells you very clearly that the muzzle is in a line with you and enables you to distinguish its sound above all the British guns firing in the other direction. The familiar " swish " followed it and, a second or so later, the shell whizzed over our heads and burst in a field, a hundred yards or so to the left.

" Get a move on," came in an exasperated tone from several people in the convoys. What *could* all the delay be about ? Surely they were not deliberately holding up all this traffic when shells were about, just for the sake of some rule about intervals between convoys ? Those who were on foot could easily find a ditch if need be, but the back of a horse seemed such an elevated and exposed position. The animals were nervous, too, standing with ears alert for a repetition of the sound.

At this juncture downward traffic proceeded to push its way past, amidst much colliding of limber hubs, with language to suit the occasion: beyond it, forming a fifth stream, the 169th Infantry Brigade battalions were wending their way towards the firing-line in single file beside the path, thus completing a good old muddle which seemed farther from a solution than ever.

Would the gun fire again ? Might it not hit the road next time ? What a target we presented for it—perhaps the news of the traffic block was being telephoned through to the enemy by spies in one of the cottages ahead there, as such things had been done at the Second Battle of Ypres.

" Bang !   Wh-z-z-z-z-t !—Crump ! "

The second one had landed a few yards off the road on the left : we could see the smoke rising beyond the poplar trees which lined the path.   The single lines of infantry had momentarily flopped down and were now continuing on their way again with quickened step.

" For God's sake get a move on there."

There was absolutely no escape from the tangle.   No L.R.B. vehicle could move to right or left, owing to these idiots who had " double-banked."   The " down " convoy was wisely trotting past as quickly as possible ; some of the infantry were doubling to put distance between them and the line of the howitzer.

" If they shorten the range again, it might land just here," remarked Rayner.   No need to dwell upon that fact !   It was so patent that we simply waited our fate with pattering hearts, wishing it were permissible to seek shelter in the empty dug-outs close at hand—places that had been erected for an artillery headquarters by the roadside before the German retirement had rendered them obsolete.   But to leave your horses is a crime in the army : the best thing to be done was to dismount and stand by their heads in case they took fright.

" They won't learn a lesson till someone gets hit," shouted Coombs. the R.A.M.C. water-cart man, making off in haste for the nearest dug-out in company with the cooks.   " I'm not taking any chances."

Still our shouts from the rear and the proximity of the shells had no effect on the blockage, whatever the cause was.   For the next minute everyone was on the " qui vive," listening intently for the dreaded " pop."   I shall not forget the scene : Jumbo and The Grey, impatient and nervy, their noses almost touching the cooker in front in their desire to get as far forward as possible ; the jammed vehicles, the convoy passing by and the L.R.B. single files plodding along at the edge of the road : the distant firing-line rumble, the noise of passing vehicles, the curses from one and another and, near at hand, the horses' heavy breathing.

Then it came.   Gun report, rush of air and shell-burst came practically together.   There was a cloud of smoke ten yards ahead, shouts could be heard, and " awky pieces " fell all around.   It had landed in the middle of the road !

The downward convoy seemed to melt away, the cooker ahead of me backed into my horses who in turn backed and then ineffectually attempted to turn round and bolt.   All happened in a second.

Who was hit ?   It must be the next vehicle but one to mine : in the confusion I could not think whose it was.   It was as much as I could do to pacify my pair and straighten out the locked wheels of the cooker.

" What's happened ? " I shouted to Harbord.

" Kimbo's hit," snapped Harbord, who was in charge of the vehicle in front.

Kimbo—practically the most popular man on the section !   And all through this cursed traffic block.   When *would* we learn to control traffic as the French did ?

" Get a move on," everyone shouted again.   In another minute perhaps a second shell would fall in the road.   Surely the head of our column would break through somehow, now.   Ah ! There was a move-ment in the convoy parallel to us.   A few seconds later Harbord had seized an opportunity and, as I leapt into the saddle, my pair also moved forward behind him. When Harbord's emotions were aroused he cared not two pins for any man Butting his way between two vehicles of the upward convoy, he compelled the rear driver to pull up short and let him pass through, thereby calling down all the oaths that can be imagined on to his head I followed so close behind that there was no time for the gap to be closed and Rayner, behind me, was " old soldier " enough to let not an inch separate him from my cooker, so that the other convoy was completely cut in two. We got right over to the side of the road and were immediately on a level with the spot where the shell had burst. In the middle of the road stood D Company's cooker with the shaft smashed and all that remained of Gog and Magog strewn about on the ground. A water-cart was drawn up beside the road with the horses removed. Where was Kimbo ?

The horses, who were sweating with fright, needed no persuasion to break into a trot. With a clear field before them, for the traffic seemed to have melted away, they hastened down the Achicourt Road, from which we heard another shell go over and land in nearly the same spot as the last. Chrisp came alongside when we had slowed down to a walk and were drawing near to Achicourt.

" What news ? " I asked him.

" Poor old Kimbo's done for." Chrisp could hardly frame the words.

Kimbo was killed ! We could not grasp it for the moment. Many a jolly evening had we spent with him ; many a parcel and billet had we shared ; I had known him since recruiting days at Bunhill Row. His cheery disposition when anything was going wrong and we were suffering from waves of depression had often put our hearts in the right place ; and now the worst had happened.

" What about the water-cart ? " I asked.

" Bob Taylor's all right. His grey horse has got a leg off, and he's stopping there with him—won't leave him. Gordon'll go back and shoot it."

Kimbo had been carried to the side of the road at the time of the disaster, but, being wounded in the head, was practically unconscious until he passed away. Next day there was a burial service in the morning at the cemetery at Agny—near Achicourt—whither Vallentine's body had been carried, and many of the section were in attendance.

Even then it seemed incredible. Our long immunity from transport casualties had given us an absurd faith in our good fortune and this had come to shatter it. What a matter of chance it was, whether one got hit or not ! Who should say when one was in danger and when in safety ? On his horse's back—for Kimbo had not dismounted— he had been in far greater peril than the men in the trenches at Beaurains. In the Second Battle of Ypres he had been through everything with me : the Gravenstafel trenches, the gas-attack, the 13th May bombardment, all these he had survived, narrowly missing hits, not dozens, but hundreds of times. Yet, two years later, on a road miles from the firing-line, a chance shell had burst under his horses. At what moment could you feel safe on any road ? Demobilisation seemed a futile dream, for what must inevitably happen before that were possible ! How many unsafe roads were we still to traverse ?

One thought was uppermost in every man's mind. Five words summed up the outlook of hundreds of thousands of men on the Western Front. What we all asked ourselves was : " When will my turn come ? "

CHAPTER XXI.

THE BATTLE OF ARRAS : THE INITIAL "PUSH."

(*April 8th–16th*, 1917.)

Achicourt blows up—The battle-eve—The attack opens—The first day's achievements—Discomforts of the infantry—Moving the ammunition forward—A pack-pony stunt—An account of one attack.

NEARLY every house in the heart of Achicourt had been crammed full of ammunition, forming a reserve dump for the attack : shells were now arriving at such a rate that we had to commandeer villages to house them ! And still there seemed to be no end to the convoys which passed our billet at the outskirts of the village, on their way to the batteries and various ammunition dumps further forward.

The attack was fixed for the 9th, and on the 8th convoys of lorries—disregarding all the regulations hitherto in force about daylight movements—passed us continually during the morning. Achicourt, in fact, presented as busy a spot as could be seen anywhere on the Western Front. R.F.A. convoys and infantry transport limbers added to the bustle : in between all these motor and horse vehicles moved despatch-riders, groups of officers on horseback (with maps open as usual) accompanied by orderlies, and batches of infantry in reserve wandering about the village. Civilians stood at their doors watching all this unwonted bustle and excitement. Needless to say, there were delays, collisions and breakdowns ; traffic regulations to be complied with ; pauses while some lorry or lorries turned to right and left or performed acrobatic evolutions in the square.

About dinner time a long line of these ammunition lorries stretched from one end of the village to the other, held up by a traffic muddle of some magnitude. We were in our billet wrestling with bully-beef tins at the time and consequently did not observe either the blockage or the appearance of German aeroplanes which flew over the village, noticed the congested state of the main street and promptly signalled to their guns.

The first we knew of it was when a loud explosion occurred—the biggest we had ever heard—which violently shook the ground and brought various bricks down from the roof into our dinner plates— or thereabouts. The speed with which we had rushed out of this same billet to watch the air fight was excelled by the rate at which we now strove to get outside to see what the present trouble was ; no doubt, the loose portions of roof, etc., which were falling around spurred us on in this effort ! Less than half a mile away an enormous pillar of grey smoke had arisen high in the air, and this was followed by another, the sound of the second explosion being even greater than the first.

We guessed the trouble : it was either bombs or shells, hitting the lorries in the main street. What an uncomfortable position for the lorry drivers and others in the village ! How well we could appreciate their predicament with the memory of last night's tragedy on the Arras road fresh in our minds.

Boom ! Another sudden upheaval of bricks, masonry and lorries, lost in great clouds of smoke !

" Good heavens ! " said Hobson—Hobson loved to be dramatic— " the village is simply crammed full of shells. If it catches fire, the whole place may go up."

What was happening behind that row of houses ? What of the troops in billets, the sentries at the dumps, the transport men and lorry drivers ? One of the latter was earning a decoration by driving his flaming lorry into a pond. Two A.S.C. men, dishevelled and very much out of breath, ran down the road and hardly paused to speak when we questioned them.

" For Gawd's sake, —— well hop it," said one.

" The —— village is being blown to —— Hell ! " gasped the other.

So saying, they commenced to run again, their long coats flying behind them in the wind. In another minute they were out of sight.

Crash ! The pall hanging over Achicourt from the previous ex-plosions had hardly begun to be disseminated when another geyser of black smoke shot upwards, carrying with it doubtless many luckless individuals apart from countless thousands of pounds' worth of shells. All this ammunition that was being wasted represented weeks of toil for bands of munition workers at home ; fatigue parties of unfit men had spent days laboriously loading all those shells on to steamers, trains and lorries ; our own folks across the Channel were stinting themselves in many ways in order to pay for them. Here they were, exploded in a flash, the only damage caused by them being to Allied life and property.

Some of our fellows whose stables were nearer the scene of the explosions had already made off in that direction to remove their horses to a place of less danger, Gunboat Smith strolling off in the first tin helmet he could lay his hands on and with a borrowed field dressing in his pocket. Presently we all got the order to lead the animals off to some slopes beyond the village where we squatted down, each holding two horses. The animals, taking no account of the fact that their guardians desired to squat in one place, proceeded to graze at the extreme length of their head-ropes, regardless of the fact that there was perfectly appetising grass at their very feet. I spent most of the afternoon in an extremely uncomfortable position, with arms outstretched, being torn asunder by Jumbo and The Grey who sought their refreshments in opposite directions.

All through the afternoon one big explosion followed another until it hardly seemed possible that there could be any portion of the dumps untouched. Nothing could save the ammunition now. Down in the village those who were still alive were having a terrible time of it. People would rush out to attend to wounded and the next instant a building close at hand would blow up. . . . One fellow whom I met afterwards told me he spent hours imprisoned in a cellar trying to pacify two women of the billet ; whenever the danger seemed to have passed he started to emerge, but another holocaust would take place and he would have to retire underground again. Fellows passed us on their way down the road, with bandages on them, in such numbers that the offensive might well have begun.

To the left of the village, over in Arras, big enemy shells fell at intervals. The British artillery which had been so active for days was now comparatively tranquil and this seemed to be the German's field-day. Their aeroplanes, too, were very busy—though our airmen were doing all they could to prevent their observation The enemy knew the attack was coming, but our tranquillity on this day may temporarily have put them off their guard as to the actual date of it.

Towards evening the outbreaks in Achicourt became more spasmodic, but Gordon naturally did not like the idea of resuming occupation of our old stables, so we fixed up horse-lines in the open by the railway line where we had settled when we first came here We transferred our kits to the same spot, as nobody felt at all anxious to sleep in any part of Achicourt that night.

About 6.30 that evening there was a shout of laughter from a group of our fellows who had just had an interesting announcement. When I enquired the cause of this hilarity, I learnt that some driver had got to take a limber of hand-grenades to a dump in Agny, which meant passing through a portion of Achicourt. Ha ! ha ! Some blighter had got to go through Achicourt. One hoped he would wear his identification disc and send a note to mamma ! The sergeant was turning up his note-book to see whose turn it was for duty, and all of us were watching him anxiously. At last he looked up with a grin.
" Aubrey Smith, harness up."
This order provoked everyone to greater mirth than ever, though as I got ready to depart my face was no doubt as long as a fiddle. Amidst the quips and jests of all the others I eventually set off down the only possible road to my destination, praying that a further explosion might not take place and turn me into mincemeat. There had not been any disturbance for half an hour and, at the spot where I passed closest to the scene of the recent trouble, several people were going quickly to and fro. With a sigh of relief I turned off to the right, avoiding the centre of the village, and had hardly done so when there was another of these unearthly reports behind me, followed by a sound as of a cart shooting bricks into the street. Looking round, I found I was almost on the fringe of one of these smoke eruptions—another houseful of ammunition had been blown to smithereens a hundred yards away. People bolted and scattered in all directions and, needless to say, I broke into a canter which lasted until I was clear of the village.

At Agny, where I stopped to unload, there was hardly a soul to be seen, though it was less than two miles from the line. What with the deserted appearance of this place and the quietness of our guns, it was so unlike the eve of an offensive that I had doubts as to the correctness of the rumour that the great day was fixed for to-morrow.

My return journey was all serene and it appeared as though the danger were past. Our end of Achicourt had escaped intact except for odd tiles and bricks which were strewn about the road. There were few of the section about to welcome me back ; it was quite dark and raining and most of the fellows had sought cover. The forsaking of

the billet had meant a sudden return to sleeping on the earth in hastily
rigged up bivvies, which might almost have not existed at all for all
the good they did. The previous summer we had gradually accumulated
bivvy materials and just as the campaigning season was over the

THE BATTLE OF ARRAS

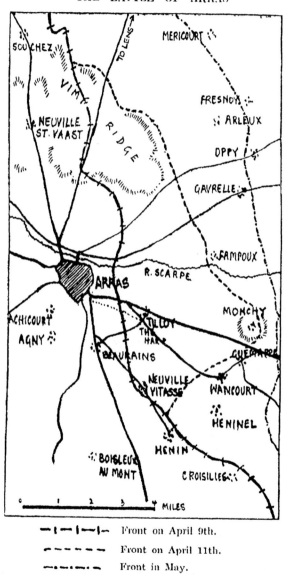

—ı—ı—ı— Front on April 9th.

━ ━ ━ ━ ━ Front on April 11th.

—·—·—·— Front in May.

Army had issued out canvas sheets : in the winter, however, the former
had been discarded and the latter " called in " for storage in a dump—
where they would no doubt repose until the summer of 1917 was well
advanced and the need of them had gone.

With the rain, the weather had suddenly turned cold and windy and during that night we were forcibly reminded that spring had not yet arrived. We had anticipated a sleepless night through a regular drumfire of preliminary shelling, but the guns continued to display little or no activity and our wakefulness was caused more by the anticipation of excitement coupled with the temperature and the utter inadequacy of our " roof," " walls " and " door."

There was no bombardment actually at dawn. As at the Battle of Gommecourt, we thought the attack would not take place that day after all, probably postponed on account of the squally weather, the wind, rain and low-flying clouds. However, at 5.30 a.m., with a sudden roar, the whole of our artillery opened fire suddenly, heralding the attack itself. From our lines we could see Verey lights of all colours being fired from the German trenches, signalling their distress to the artillery ; near the suburbs of Arras these lights seemed very close to us indeed. Red, yellow and green ones were sent up in succession and there was a deadly rattle of machine-guns which could be heard quite distinctly.

How many German hearts were palpitating now as our fellows went forward in the rain ? How many of our boys would get well " under way " before the German protective barrage fell ? As was the case with previous attacks, our aeroplanes were out early flying low over the trenches and some were soon returning to report progress. The guns kept up a perpetual rumble and evidently suffered from no shortage of ammunition.

About breakfast time we saw the first prisoners arriving down the road, evidence that someone had got across somewhere, and from that time onwards they continued to pass by in driblets. One of our fellows saw a German doctor and his complete aid post.

Although we got no particulars of how the attack was progressing, things seemed to be going very well judging by the comparative absence of shelling on the slopes of the Vimy Ridge later in the day. In the early morning the crest had been wreathed in smoke : in the afternoon the flashes of our guns were visible just below the summit. The slopes which had defied the French in 1914 and 1915 had now fallen to the Canadians. The spell of Arras was broken. No more would we have to wait at Warlus until nightfall or creep about Achicourt as though we were intending burglars. The camouflage could now be removed from the surrounding roads and moved forward if need be.

Seeing that life in what remained of Achicourt was resuming its normal round, we returned to our old billet during the day. The centre of the village was absolutely unrecognisable : in some places not a vestige remained of buildings we knew well. The square looked as though the earth had completely swallowed it up and no corner of Ypres could be more forlorn and devastated. All that remained of the lorries was a piece of mangled axle here or a section of distorted framework there. At a greater distance we found sections of limbers that had been blown many yards ; all the other transports in our brigade had suffered, the L.R.B. being the only unit that had not a vehicle in the heart of the village at the time.

Small batches of prisoners and considerable bodies of our own wounded continued to pass through Achicourt and we learned from the latter later in the day that the 167th Brigade had been heavily engaged, but that our own brigade was still in support. Neuville Vitasse had fallen. It was quite amusing to watch the prisoners coming down unescorted, looking for their cage, some assisting wounded on their way.

Towards the end of the afternoon some of us made for a point of vantage near by and scanned the Vimy Ridge through a borrowed pair of field glasses. It was then that we confirmed that the Ridge had been captured. Away to the left, making for Dainville, was a long line of prisoners, numbering more than a thousand—a sight which so rejoiced us that we required confirmation through the field-glasses before we could believe our eyes. Never on the Somme had we seen a quarter of the number of prisoners in one batch. As a matter of fact, there were so many collected in the prisoners of war cage that they had to stand up. One of the prisoners was found after some hours to be missing, but they discovered him calmly walking up and down outside the Town Major's office, trying to keep warm.

Although we did not see a paper nor glean any important news until the 14th, it may be as well to indicate briefly what happened during the day. The River Scarpe, running through Arras, divided the battlefield into two parts : north of the river we had gained the outstanding success, advancing two or three miles along the Vimy Ridge. To the south of it, the British had got well clear of the Arras suburbs and on towards the Monchy Hill, while Tilloy—the pivot on which the German retirement hinged—had been captured, together with other important points. To the south of that village the attack had been a frontal assault against the Hindenburg Line and the 167th Brigade had done well although, after capturing Neuville Vitasse, the 1st Londons came upon barbed wire and suffered heavily. However, the 7th Middlesex came to their assistance and eventually carried the line farther forward. On our right the next division, flanking the attack, also came upon uncut wire and made little or no progress. It was known that we had captured over ten thousand prisoners and one hundred guns—quite a good result for one day's work.

The crowning joy of the day was the appearance of cavalry who came up at a trot that evening through Achicourt and passed on over the hills to the south of Arras. The few remaining inhabitants of the village were wild with joy and it was with pride that we watched the units trotting past as they had done once before on the Somme. The stream seemed never-ending and before they had all passed by I had to make my way back to the horse-lines and prepare for my night journey to the battalion. Rations were going up on pack-ponies to minimise traffic on the roads, but the two water-carts were required : we were now short of two heavy pairs which meant more work for the few remaining ones.

While we carried through our ration journey, the troops on the left were making further attempts to advance, but it transpired that the attacks were unsuccessful and the losses severe. On our own front, not only were our guns very busy, but the German artillery was getting annoyed with Beaurains. The Kimbo incident was too fresh in one's memory for one to feel at ease when stuck in the traffic on this evening and it was with considerable relief that I turned out of that village again, not, however, before receiving a nasty shock near the cross-roads. All traffic " doubled " over the last-named spot and Jumbo and The Grey were as fast as any pair that passed over it ! On my way back I was delayed about an hour by a cavalry regiment who had lost their bearings on the Achicourt-Arras road ; but it was well worth the wait in the cold to listen to the clattering of hoofs

and jangling of swords, for it gave one a feeling of enthusiasm to see
all these fresh mounted troops.

Next morning at 8 a.m. our division attacked again, some of the
168th Brigade being brought into action; the L.R.B. were still in
support. The advance was also resumed on the left where we closed
in on Monchy. The weather now changed from rain and hail to rain
and snow—most appalling conditions for an offensive. The men in
the trenches were of course soaked through to the skin. Conibeer
had sent down an urgent appeal for food and cigarettes and by paying
fabulous prices in a small shop, and adding to these purchases the
greater part of a parcel just received from home, we were able to
make up for him a useful packet, which the pack-pony men took up
in the evening. Our own rations were bully, tea, sugar and biscuits—
nothing else whatever: the company men had the same, but no fuel
to heat water for the tea, so their lot must have been miserable indeed
in those sodden, icy-cold trenches. I could picture their feelings
only too well; they were probably as wretched as I had been on
May 14th, 1915, after the great German attack. . . . So ran my
thoughts.

When Figg went up with a pack-pony that night he met an L.R.B.
man at the dump whose cheery spirits seemed to indicate that, instead
of being depressed, he—at any rate—was enthusiastic. To Figg's
astonishment he said:

" Isn't it a jolly fine war, eh? *Isn't* it fine? You should just see
all the cavalry and the tanks. And you should see them rushing the
guns up."

Figg gasped. The feelings of 1915 and the spring of 1917 were
not the same. In the Second Battle of Ypres we were all suffering from
disillusionment and too long a retention in the front line; we were a
defensive army, hopelessly outclassed in artillery, machine-guns and
other important matters, outnumbered in men, and at the mercy of
poison gas without efficient respirators. Now the fellows had an
admirable backing in artillery, tanks, cavalry in action and cheering
sights to keep their spirits up, with something to show for their efforts
in the way of captured territory, guns and prisoners.

The cavalry had not really been engaged, as machine-gun fire had
kept them at a distance. Their great effort was made on the third
morning, when Monchy—a village on a commanding hill, five miles
from Arras—was taken by assault. The cavalry advanced at the gallop
but strong lines of wire to either side of the hill forced them to close
in on the centre, where they tried to get into the village itself: the
result was rather a bad slaughter, over five hundred horses being hit.
However, the Germans were driven from the height which gave us a
splendid position, overlooking the Scarpe valley, Douai and numerous
other places in the German lines. Some of our brigade went into
action that day and the L.R.B. moved forward.

I was on first picket that evening, congratulating myself on not
having been " up the line "' for two nights in succession, as we were
getting heavy snowstorms. My comforting reflections were somewhat
premature, however, as I was awakened at midnight, together with a
couple of others, for the purpose of carrying out a brigade ammunition
stunt. Our task was to remove a dump from Achicourt to the captured
village of Neuville Vitasse, completing the journey under cover of
darkness. Had the heads instructed us to leave at 8 p.m. this would
perhaps have been successfully accomplished, but to expect us to

cover the three miles to Neuville Vitasse and back in four hours with traffic in its present state was, to say the least, a trifle over-optimistic.

In company with several drivers from other units we waited for an hour while some person unknown looked for an elusive loading-party, which was ultimately discovered asleep in a barn. While they were being given time to don their overcoats, etc., we stamped our feet in a few inches of snow for a further half-hour. Their arrival was denoted by a volume of grousing surging up out of the darkness, but if anyone was entitled to grouse I think we drivers were. At about 2 a.m. we eventually left the dump, loaded with S.A.A. boxes, and set off towards Beaurains, pinching our ears occasionally to make sure they had not dropped in the road and allowing our legs to swing to and fro in an effort to regain circulation. I had been wearing a big pair of lined leather gloves, wet inside and out, but nevertheless most useful. However, one had gone the way of most gloves—having been dropped and lost in the darkness at the dump : the other lasted a few days more and was then eaten by a horse. But that is by the way.

Between Achicourt and Beaurains, we found that the heavy guns were being moved forward, bringing the horse traffic to a complete standstill. The particular obstacle holding up the convoy ahead of us was the friendly embrace of a lorry and a tractor, which kept us marking time for over two hours—this being the chilliest, bitterest, windiest wait that I ever had in France. We could not feel our stirrup irons when we remounted and the reins slipped several times from numbed fingers as the journey proceeded. The Bosches were shelling Beaurains before and during our flight through the village, which was not conducive either to dignified bearing or good temper : but we all got past the cross-roads without mishap and, proceeding up the slope on the far side of the village, emerged on territory where we had not driven limbers before.

Neuville Vitasse, as I said previously, had been a part of the Hindenburg Line. In various parts of it the Germans had left a large " R.E." dump and considerable quantities of ammunition which they were now endeavouring to destroy by continual heavy shell-fire; consequently our own folk thought it would be a splendid idea to deposit our brigade dump in practically the same spot. It was only good fortune that prevented our new store from being blown to smithereens at its very inception : the locality was unhealthy and Fritz knew every feature of it. On the other hand, the new dump may have enjoyed long life, for all I know—I never had occasion to go there again.

It was daylight when we dropped our loads in the captured village where we could see all the signs of recent battle—dead Londoners and Germans, abandoned machine-guns and equipment, a trench full of shovels and rifles. The earth about here was very much churned up by the heavy bombardment, but a thick coating of snow lay over everything, half-burying those objects that we were able to distinguish. Ahead of us the L.R.B. and the other regiments were attacking at Wancourt and Heninel—how comparatively simple this ammunition job was to what our ration convoy would have to perform the next night, carrying their loads perhaps a mile or so ahead of this spot if the attack went well !

On returning from the dump on my own, I gazed round from the hill leading up to Beaurains, surveying the countryside forming the battle area. No big action was in progress that morning, covering the entire front, for the guns were evidently advancing and units were being relieved. Everything was white with snow, against which the gun flashes showed up more distinctly : the atmosphere was somewhat misty, but every report sounded particularly loud.

Suddenly The Grey shied and broke into a series of lurches forward which Jumbo could hardly comprehend. I looked round for the cause of this fright and found it was not the artillery fire, nor the moan of a 5.9 bent on destruction at the cross-roads, nor yet the sudden appearance of a motor-car : 'twas merely the presence beside the road of a dead cavalry horse which the snow was endeavouring to hide from the passer-by, but whose stench would have defied the deadliest of German stink-bombs.

At seven o'clock in the morning we were back at the transport lines again, ready for a tempting breakfast of bully beef with biscuits and a cup of tea without milk. This was the fourth successive day of this iron ration diet and I felt so inclined to vomit at the thought of it that it mattered little now whether I ate or not. Fortunately a parcel arrived once again at a critical moment.

That evening Figg and Trendell went up with the pack-pony contingent under Lance-Corporal Main, commonly called " 'Arry-'Arry " and vulgarly called other things. The battalion, it was understood, had advanced considerably and no one knew where they were—least of all 'Arry-'Arry, who took the convoy to a spot somewhere on the far side of Neuville Vitasse and then halted them, waiting, Micawber-like, for something to turn up. It was thought that the " something " might be either a guide or the transport officer, but the chances seemed to be in favour of it being a five-point-nine ! The spot was one of the unhealthiest he could have chosen and what annoyed Figg was the fact that, after that particular section of the road had been badly strafed for some time, 'Arry-'Arry still refused to budge an inch from the spot. They waited here for hours without any sign of Lieut. Gordon or a guide and it became increasingly certain that for the first time on record rations would not reach the battalion before daybreak. (In Second Ypres, on May 3rd, they had been dumped successfully and it was because the Lancs' carrying party had not discovered the right rations that some of us went short.)

Finally, when the enemy artillery fire became really too obnoxious, the representations of the entire party of sufferers began to have some effect, and 'Arry-'Arry instructed Figg to take the convoy to a quieter spot farther back, at the same time, for some reason or other, handing him a flask of rum. Presumably 'Arry-'Arry remained at the danger spot faithful to orders. Although the rum was intended for *all* the pack-pony men, Figg and one or two others had a very good share of its contents, so that before daybreak this little party was in that state of mind that sets itself on one particular purpose and is willing to go cheerily through Hell to achieve it. In other words, the rum on their empty interiors acted as a galvanising force, making them determined to take the rations right up to the front line if need be, even if it meant wandering about all the next day. In this very desirable frame of mind they eventually went forward to the neighbourhood of Wancourt and dumped their loads, arriving back in our lines at midday on the 13th, having been out since the previous tea-time with nothing to eat. The reason for the inability to discover the battalion was explained later by Conibeer.

While 'Arry-'Arry was thus having the time of his life, another local attack was taking place, but the L.R.B. and the other units could

not get much past the line of the Wancourt Tower on the hill beyond
the village, being enfiladed from Guemappe on the left. On the 14th
the British attacked at that place and east of Monchy, but it was
an unsuccessful day owing to the strength of the enemy's counter-
attacks.

On this day there was a pretty little incident at our cookhouse,
admirably illustrating the " greenness " of the Labour Corps, that
collection of dear old Johnnies—some of them on the wrong side of
fifty—who toiled at road-making and similar jobs, usually getting
little credit for their toil. No doubt the reader has heard the
unauthentic tale of the staff officer who was held up in a traffic
block and, leaning out of his stationary car, snorted and roared :
" Where's the delay ? Where's the delay ? "

" Waal, sir," said a Labour Corps road-mender, anxious to be of
service and thinking the officer meant " du lait," " oi can't be shure
but oi think you can get some at that there farm on the roight 'and
side o' the road."

But here is a true tale of what happened at Achicourt. In going
through some Q.V.R.'s casualty kits which had been sorted out in
their stores, some fellow had found a bundle of restaurant bills such
as you get at Lockharts, or Lyons : " Egg on Toast, 6d." " Tea and
Scone, 4d.," " Steak · and Kidney Pudding, 10d.," etc. Goodness
knows why they were in this man's kit, but the fact remains that they
were there and one of the fellows—unknown to our cooks—stuck
them up on the cookhouse door. Now there was a labour battalion
stationed near by, consisting of C 2 men who had just come out from
England and were extremely " green." One of these poor old Johnnies
came up, read the advertisements, licked his moustache, felt in his
trouser pocket and then went in the cookhouse and calmly asked
for a steak and kidney pudding. Thinking the request was made for
a joke, Waters—always ready to play up to anybody when there was
fun to be poked—replied that he was sorry they would not be ready
until half-past six that night. And, do you know, at half-past six
that night there was a queue of some dozen of these C2 men lined
up outside our cookhouse door waiting to buy their precious puddings !

On the 15th we took cookers and limbers up to the Wancourt Road
to meet the battalion who had been relieved, and on the following day,
to our great joy, Conibeer returned from D Company to the section,
owing to the vacancy caused by poor old Kimbo's death. We hardly
recognised him until he had had thirty-six hours' rest and taken the
ten days' growth off his face. Since the 7th he had spent his life in
open trenches, most of the time soaked to the skin : he had not had
his boots off for a fortnight and one of his feet was quite lifeless. He
had been without sleep for seven nights and lived all the time on bully-
beef and biscuits as his staple diet—the parcel we had sent up to him
had " just saved his life." These were the miserable conditions that
the infantryman had to put up with for 1s. a day : a short while
previously the civilian engineer trade-unionists, who were sleeping in
beds and eating decent food, had threatened to strike and hold up
the output of munitions in order to grasp another increase in their
already inflated incomes.

Conibeer had been in two attacks and of the second he had much
to say. It is necessary to state here that he naturally said nothing in
the way of self-glorification and his outlook was necessarily very
restricted, so that his remarks were not meant to imply that the L.R.B.

were not deserving of the highest praise for all they accomplished. The gist of his accounts was as follows :—

On the night of the 12th (the same evening that Main was in charge of the rations) D Company of the L.R.B. were relieved about midnight. That day they had captured Wancourt and held it against two counter-attacks. After stumbling back along communicating trenches for about a couple of miles they were halted and instructed to dig funk-holes, which Conibeer proceeded to do with the aid of entrenching tool and finger-nails. He had dug out a hole of sufficient size to contain his body when the order to retrace their steps came upon everybody as a bombshell, and before anyone realised what had happened they were all filing back towards Wancourt, without any idea of what they were to do, and protesting volubly the while.

At daybreak they reached Wancourt—no wonder nobody could instruct the transport where to drop the rations !—in which village absolute pandemonium reigned. As the L.R.B. filed out from the sunken road into the open, they were met by machine-gun fire from everywhere, at which there was a general scattering, but Conibeer could not remember what the rest of the battalion did : he had quite enough to think about himself. The next thing he recalled was that he was in the midst of a battalion of Durhams who were just fixing bayonets, preparatory to " going over." D Company had vanished and he was laden with three Lewis-gun panniers belonging to them, in addition to his rifle, a spade and an axe, which he came to the conclusion was too big a load to carry any further. So, dumping all " spare kit," he fixed his bayonet and went over with the best of luck with the Durhams ! Eventually he came upon Captain Hancock of D Company and a few others about three-quarters of a mile ahead—what they were doing or where they were he had not the faintest idea. Part of the battalion were mixed up in a brawl with some Germans over a factory on the Arras-Cambrai road. Ahead of him were supposed to be all sorts of attacking waves, but, curiously enough, there were Germans very close to them and it appeared that these waves had vanished into thin air. That is to say, Conibeer and his companions suddenly found that they formed the first-line which had to be speedily put into a state of defence to meet counter-attacks.

That night they used their little remaining strength—they had been rationless all day—to dig their hardest and form a kind of front-line. However, the ground was chalky, it was impossible to make an impression and they had to move about 2 a.m. to another place where the earth was softer, leaving them about two and a half hours in which to get under cover. However, it never rains but it pours, and in this new position they struck water about eighteen inches below the surface so they had to lie practically at full length in this miserable trench the whole of the next day. This meant their second day without rations for, although the latter were taken up again and dumped where brigade instructed them to be, no arrangements apparently were made for a carrying-party by the infantry or, if they were, the fatigue party was wrongly directed.

That evening they moved on a few yards and, to everyone's astonishment, found a small party of Queen's Westminsters who were lost. Later on the L.R.B. were relieved by the London Scottish and search parties were sent out for rations, which they found being guarded in a shell-hole by Bryer, one of the storemen.

" Nobody knew anything and the organisation was hopeless," said

Conibeer, summing up the attack. " I think it's marvellous that the men, through sheer dogged pluck, have done as well as they have, with such management. . . . If that was a fair sample of the way our staffs usually work, I don't wonder there is such a clamour for reinforcements. Let's hope the time will never come when they'll badly need the men they squander in fiascos like that."

The Devils' Mess was once again up to strength and very glad were we to have our Magazine co-editor back with us. He admitted that, of two evils, the transport section was preferable to the company, for he had no enthusiasm for the trenches after his recent experiences. But what he felt he would most like at that moment was a job with the Railway Transport Officer at Rouen, the Town Major of St. Pol or the Inland Water Transport at St. Omer. Such billets should not be monopolised by the favoured few : everyone should get an opportunity of a change of work occasionally so that all might do their share. But that was not the way of the Army. Those who had the foresight to snap up the cushiest jobs should stay in them for the duration of the War at special rates of pay : those that were foolish enough to get tangled up with infantry divisions, content with 1s. a day, should be irrevocably condemned to remain with them until wounds, sickness, or death should carry them away !

CHAPTER XXII.

THE BATTLE OF ARRAS : SUBSEQUENT OPERATIONS.

(*April–May*, 1917.)

Visit to an old battleground—Necessity for continued British attacks—We move east of Arras—Attack of May 3rd—Exciting ration trips—Open-air sick parades —We get the wind up—An eventful picket—Shelled out.

ONE or two fellows had been suffering from blood trouble as a result of the poor diet of the past few weeks (vegetables had been impossible to obtain and it was two months since we had tasted a potato); for this reason, on April 18th, our tenth successive day without bread, I had to parade sick at a dressing-station in Achicourt in order to have boils treated. At the parade there were dozens of men of sundry units suffering from the same complaint ; the members of the labour battalions also flocked there in scores, with bad legs, boils, rheumatism, gout and senile decay, these representing the bulk of all those parading sick. Still, if they *would* insist on gathering all the halt, the maimed and the blind into the army, leaving thousands of fit young men out of it, what could they expect ? This blood trouble had come to stay for a long time and, in my own case, prevented my riding a horse on and off for six weeks ; Conibeer therefore took over my pair while I was marked for light duties and had to get along as best I could.

Three days later, when the battalion left Achicourt, I drove the officers' mess cart : it was the first time I had tried single-horse driving and, though in theory nothing could be simpler, the wheels seemed to collide with everything and more than once we nearly got ditched.

Our destination was no other place than Bienvillers, which lay behind the line slightly south of Arras. It was a place that had many associations for us, since in the previous July and August we had passed through it many times on our ration trips to Hannescamps from our horse-lines in St. Amand, though in those days we only saw the village at nights and it was miled with troops and guns.

22/4/17. " . . . How different now ! When the Bosches retired south of Arras they abandoned all their positions in these parts and (Bienvillers) has now been far from the firing-line for two months. In those days flare lights went up a little distance beyond the village and we only distinguished its features by moonlight as we hurriedly passed down its streets. Now we can examine it in daylight and the aspect of everything is changed. About half the houses are standing and those civilians who were refugees are now returning or contemplating doing so : there are still a good many empty cottages about, though, and, generally speaking, the surroundings are sad and silent.

"You can wander over fields that seem any man's property, coming across disused gun-pits, old trenches, crumbling dug-outs ; everything that seemed to throb with life in those summer evenings as we passed by appears all the more deserted and lonely now, owing to the disappearance of the troops and guns. You can pass from orchard to field, field to orchard, without encountering a soul and over everything there hangs quite an uncanny silence. Now and then you may find an old civilian searching among the debris of a fallen-in dug-out for anything worth having, or a few small boys collecting faggots. Away on a hill, formerly observed by the Germans, a Frenchman will be ploughing in between our wire barriers.

"I went into a field where I used to notice the dark forms of our big guns, hoping they wouldn't fire until my horses were a bit further away, and examined in daylight the spots where they had been. The elaborate dug-outs, with many steps, dug out by the artillerymen, are now under water and the walls are falling in. The sandbags are dark green with lichen and rotting with the damp.

"Round by the church there was an unpleasant sickly smell of shell-gas whenever we used to pass. It hangs about there still—has eaten its way into the houses, the ground and the foliage. Round this quarter it still looks as if the Germans might be a mile away. It is very much knocked about and no civilian is yet to be seen there."

On the evening of the 22nd I walked with one or two others over to see Foncquevillers, where we used to dump rations last year. The change here was even more extraordinary. So far as I could see there was not a soul living in the place—military or civilian. All the houses were damaged to some extent and apparently anyone could enter them with a view to burglary. For over two years there had been very little movement there by day, but the place had buzzed with life at nights. Now, robbed of their human element, the ghostly surroundings gave the impression of an excavated city of the dead or the scene of an earthquake where every soul had perished. Thick undergrowth grew up everywhere, dank pools stood in shell-holes and portions of the street, disused wells were almost choked up, lamp-posts leant over at extraordinary angles, walls had crumbled and toppled into the street. The old signboards : "Gas Alarm," "Batt. H.Q.," etc.. seemed truly relics of bygone days.

In wandering up a muddy shell-torn sunken road at the outskirts of the place, near the old British front-line, we came across a wooden shack which served as a sentry-box for the first soldier we had seen. As we approached he took a step or two forward, his rifle slung over his shoulder in most unorthodox fashion, and informed us that no one was allowed to pass. He stood between the old territory and the new, the long established British area and the recently-evacuated regions.

This refusal was rather disconcerting, and we enquired the reason.

"They're now searching all these parts for booby-traps and mines, so this is a prohibited area," said he. " But still, I see you're L.R.B. and as I've let your Colonel and a lot more through to-day, I shan't say anything. You'll find some more of your chaps ahead there looking for their pals' graves by the wood" (Gommecourt Wood).

Thanking him kindly and proffering him " Three Castles " and " Arf-a-mos "—the latter being those insults to the British soldier which we had to smoke in times of necessity—we walked on to the crest of a little ridge where we saw just before us the fatal wood—dark and silent—with its belt of rusty wire in front of it. From this spot the 46th Division on our flank had attacked the left of the wood on the memorable first of July; we were now treading on the very ground where so many of the Midland men had fallen, and a moment later entered the wood itself, to survey the damage caused by our artillery.

From one side to the other the vast craters showed how our 9.2's had peppered the place, but large numbers of trees with splintered branches and torn barks still remained standing. Spring was already bringing out the leaves and undergrowth, endeavouring to cover up the traces of war. Making our way across the wood, dodging unexploded shells and piles of German hand-grenades, we eventually came upon the old enemy front-line just within its borders. On the very parapet was a cross denoting the grave of an L.R.B. man; the trench was fairly intact, so that the entrances to at least two deep dug-outs met our gaze—the dug-outs which had meant our boys' destruction. There on the left, facing the British line, were the trenches we had taken and given up; before us was the No Man's Land in which it was easy to imagine what a splendid target had been presented to the Germans as our men debouched from their positions on the opposite slope. In the space before the trenches was the grave of forty-two unknown soldiers, while round about were a few graves of our battalion but not those of anyone I knew, as I had fondly hoped. To our surprise, the battlefield debris, equipments, rifles, etc., were lying about just as they had been for the past ten months. Everything was quiet and still, save for the distant rumble of guns, and the only folk in sight were a few other L.R.B.s visiting the scene of their misfortune.

As it was now sunset, we had to think about making our way back to Bienvillers, so there was no time to look round carefully, or else we might have discovered one or two of the graves we were seeking. On our way back we passed through Hebuterne, where we tried to work out the trajectory of the machine-gun bullets that used to annoy us on the road.

Next day I felt very glad that I had taken this early opportunity of exploring the neighbourhood, for we moved back two miles to Souastre (where our horse-lines had been for a short while the previous summer) and, after spending only one night there, got orders to move forward immediately behind the Arras front again. In other words, our brief sojourn in this land of memories was over and we never returned to the spot. We were about to join in the fray once more and our hopes of getting our first hot bath for eleven weeks were dashed to the ground.

The Arras Battle should have stopped at the point it had now reached; as such it would have been a good example of the success of attacks with a limited objective. In the first three days the captures had been twelve thousand prisoners and one hundred and fifty guns, as against thirty-eight thousand prisoners and one hundred and twenty-five guns in three-and-a-half months on the Somme. But the great French attack on the 16th April against the south end of the Hindenburg Line was a comparative failure, due to Nivelle ambitiously attempting the " big stroke " on a wide front, with the result that the real objectives were not gained and the losses incurred were very severe. Of course, it was hailed at the time as a big success, and we were elated at the capture of terrain and booty, but the resignation of General Nivelle soon put a damper on our enthusiasm. This left the French Army in a very weakened condition, and it became imperative for the British to keep up the pressure in the north, all the more so as the Italians would not be able to attack for another month, while fighting on the Russian front had almost ceased as a result of the revolution. The whole scheme of a combined Allied spring offensive crumpling Germany up took on a different aspect. To hold the enemy's reserves, then, all the Allies looked to the poor old British to go on battering their heads against the strong German lines east of Arras, incurring heavy losses with little to show for them, for the enemy had brought up important reserves with plenty of artillery. Moreover, Haig had to weaken his artillery in this area for his preparations in the Ypres zone, where his main assault of the year was to be delivered.

The next blow at Arras was given on the 23rd of April, the day that we moved to Souastre. For three days in succession we had heard a tremendous bombardment up the line, which had aroused enthusiasm, for we imagined that a strategic success must be within our grasp at the northern end of the Hindenburg Line, while the French " victory " down south would probably " turn " the other end of it.

The results were disappointing. On the front we had just left, the artillery preparation was insufficient, and two-and-a-half divisions could make little progress against wire and machine-guns, and finally fell back to their starting point. To the left some ground was captured at Guemappe, but the enemy counter-attacks were heavy and furious and the village had to be given up until the evening. The troops further north still were unable to get forward. Beyond the Scarpe, Gavrelle was captured, but both sides suffered heavy losses in a day of continual fighting. Counter-attacks proceeded all next day. The policy of hitting our heads against a brick wall was now in full swing ; we were calling down all the Teutonic venom upon us because we were the only Allied army capable of maintaining an offensive for the next month. Fine fellows, we ! But we did wish our heads would show their appreciation by giving us baths, clean clothes, adequate food and a reasonable amount of leave !

On the 28th, another day of attempted advances, we entered Arras, having spent a couple of days each at Wanquetin and Bernaville. The town was bustling with life and simply full of hospitals, depots and camps. The streets were alive with lorries and limbers, the pavements crowded with troops : shops had opened by the dozen and estaminets were plying their usual trade, administering to the proverbial thirst of the British soldiers. No longer were the enemy in the suburbs, overlooking most portions of the town : the nearest Bosche was now five miles away, so that all the inhabitants had to fear was long-range guns and aeroplane bombs. Both day and night air-raids in one portion of the town or another were already common occurrences and it was not long before a big ammunition dump blew up.

The weather was now perfect and for the first time that year it was possible to sit with our coats off after tea. From our point of vantage near the racecourse we could see the myriads of flashes from our guns supporting an attack that night on the German positions over by Roeux and Oppy. Such a widespread panorama had seldom been excelled on the Somme.

For the past few days I had paraded sick at our own aid post, but now that the battalion had moved up the line again I had to go to a field ambulance in Arras, where, instead of giving time to hot fomentations—the only cure for my trouble—they dismissed me in a few moments with a touch of picric acid, an utterly futile treatment. I was still unable to ride, but found a means of assisting the transport when, on the 30th, we received orders to move our horse-lines to Tilloy on the following day. It was decided to send forward at once a limber containing five tents, which had just been drawn from ordnance, and " stake our claim " to a particular site by pitching the wigwams : I suggested going with the advance party and lying down like a faithful watchdog until the arrival of the section next day, which scheme was adopted. So, having loaded my multitudinous belongings on the limber—Coni now had the right, of course, of carrying his kit on A Company's cooker in lieu of mine—together with rations and a bag of completely inedible dog-biscuits which made excellent fuel for picket braziers, I myself jumped in on top of them and we set off towards Tilloy.

Beyond Arras the Labour Corps were perspiring in an attempt to lay a track to Tilloy, consisting of planks of beech-wood placed one beside the other with more or less mathematical precision—chiefly less. They were also filling in shell-holes, laying bridges over trenches and removing obstacles, such tasks being accomplished in the intervals between leaning on their spades and staring at passers-by. They were on a real battlefield and had not yet ceased talking about it.

We passed the old evacuated front-line and, as we sloped down from there, could see Tilloy on the left and Beaurains on the right, while, between the two in the distance, were the hills by Wancourt and Guemappe—the ground gained in the past fortnight. At the spot where the projected track struck the Tilloy-Beaurains road there was an enormous crater, blown by the Germans when they retired to the Hindenburg Line, a hole of such depth that it would easily have accommodated several horses and G.S. wagons. Close to this spot was the site selected for the transport lines and it was just as well that we arrived to claim it when we did. Horse-lines and camps of tents were already here in abundance, stretching north and south, while units were arriving to scrounge whatever available space was to be had.

One or two others had come along with me to help with the tents and before dark we had erected these, " won " some posts for the horse-lines and scrounged enough corrugated iron for a cook-house. Then the inevitable officer with a map came along with the assertion that we were occupying ground reserved for his unit. We knew full well that it had been allotted to us, so we told him—indirectly and politely, of course—that we had been out long enough not to get caught like that. We said if he wanted a site for his horse-lines, he might find one over towards Telegraph Hill or Wancourt, whereat he departed in a great huff, threatening to interview everybody from Haig downwards, but we never saw him again. Next day the brigade transports arrived and definitely secured the site against any further attempted thefts.

We did not at all like the sound of the shells that came over in the night. True, they fell some distance ahead, seeking for batteries, but there were such delightful targets in our area that it seemed probable some enterprising enemy airman might suggest tickling the camps and horse-lines up a bit. Then again, there were six-inch naval guns not far off, between our lines and Tilloy, hitherto probably unlocated, but always in danger of being spotted. A tent seemed such poor shelter, too : cover of other kinds was non-existent unless one walked two-hundred yards to The Harp trench—which had fallen on April 9th—but since that would not accommodate horses it had to be ruled out as impracticable. For the moment, however, we comforted ourselves with the delusion that the crowded nature of the area between Tilloy and Beaurains had not been revealed to the enemy and that, in any case, he had not enough shells to spare for promiscuous back-area strafeing.

At dawn on the 3rd there was a tremendous bombardment on a fairly wide front which, we knew, heralded the next sacrificial attempt, in which our own boys were this time engaged. Except for a few H.Q. signallers, the aid post men, an officer or two and several chance

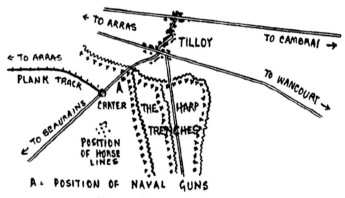

Memory Sketch of " The Harp."

acquaintances, there was nobody up with the battalion whom I knew, but I nevertheless waited as eagerly for news of the regiment as on other occasions. The gunfire continued all day long, among the sounds being a good proportion of enemy " crumps " which confirmed the strength of their artillery. A few dilapidated prisoners passed by, but we were really off the beaten track. Most of the wounded were picked up by ambulances in Tilloy and taken straight to Arras, Agnez or Aubigny, *via* the Cambrai road, since our plank track was hardly an ideal road for stretcher-cases. Of course, the dear old labourites would have been pleased if the ambulances had used their road : they were highly delighted a few days later when a heavy gun was drawn along it.

The pack-pony convoy that night brought back heart-breaking news. Our boys were back where they had started, through absolutely no fault of their own : they had re-captured Cavalry Farm, lost a few days previously, and gone beyond it, making good their objectives. They had captured prisoners and were in the best of spirits until— the 14th Division on the right fell back before midday, leaving our flank exposed.

In order to appreciate the position, it is necessary to start on the right of the line and, although it is really beyond the scope of this narrative to enter into details concerning other divisions, it is just as well to emphasise the extent of the British sacrifices in order to keep the ball rolling at this period, as the cumulative effect of such experiences naturally accounted for much of the grousing that distinguished our thoughts and utterances later in the year.

On the extreme right the Australians had got into the Hindenburg Line, but the 62nd Division was held, thereby leaving them in an awkward salient. The 18th Division found the enemy counter-attacks so heavy and their artillery fire so severe that they had to give up most of the conquered territory ; their withdrawal involved the 14th Division, who in turn abandoned the greater part of their gains. Then came our own brigade, near the St. Rohart factory on the Cambrai road, confident that they could hold on to their captures and doing so until almost cut off : they then had the galling experience of calmly walking back to their starting-point with nothing to show for all the casualties. On our left flank the 167th Brigade had suffered terribly through being hung up by uncut wire, which for some unknown reason had scarcely been touched by our artillery. The enemy artillery fire was especially severe on our portion of the front and it appeared that they possessed the same unlimited supply of explosives as ourselves. To their left the 3rd Division hardly got forward at all, and north of them the 12th Division met with such strong counter-attacks that the entire right half were driven back to their original trench. North of the Scarpe there seems to have been hopeless confusion in the darkness preceding the attack at Oppy—units got completely mixed up and the attack failed. There were small gains of ground and heavy losses further north, but the Canadians captured Fresnoy. Altogether this was a fruitless, disheartening day. All along the front our losses had been severe and there was little to show for them.

The pack-pony trips on that night and the following were sheer nightmares. As I was now incapacitated, both as regards walking and riding—a useless ornament that limped about the camp and travelled in an empty limber each morning to attend a farcical sick-parade in Arras—I cannot speak from any experience of these line journeys. I merely woke up and listened to adventures when the transport men returned. I only know that the Germans had intensified their hatred of the roads behind the line and now seemed to have a prolific amount of ammunition to expend upon them. On the Somme they had experienced a shortage : in the first week of the Arras Battle they were too busy withdrawing their guns to be very objectionable ; now, however, they proceeded to prove that the area within three miles of the front-line was uninhabitable and you only passed across it at your peril. Now, also, they commenced to use gas rather freely upon the back areas.

On the second night shells were falling either side of the Wancourt road and shrapnel was bursting overhead. Figg, stumbling along with an obstinate mule named Salmon—partner to one Shrimp of that ilk—suddenly found his eyes smarting and realised that gas-shells were also bursting around   It was a toss-up between taking his tin-hat off in order to put his mask on, thereby risking a shrapnel wound in his head, or else carrying on and chancing being poisoned. He chose the latter course, for the shrapnel bursts were unpleasantly close and frequent, but although the gas-shells were drenching the valley he does not appear ever to have suffered for his action. A big Verey-light dump blew up on his right, sending rockets in all directions.

To add to the excitement, a number of artillery wagons cantered by, taking up the whole of the road regardless of its other occupants. Many are the times that we may have been cursed by infantry for the very same act. (The Royal Scots on the Voormezeele road used to imagine that to shout out " Clear oot. We're the Rile Scats ! " was sufficient to halt convoys. But they were mistaken. Many times I have seen them scatter at the very last moment as Jack and Tar loomed up out of the darkness !) There is a morass beside every road that it is the lot of all infantry to plunge into when a wagon passes by, but the boot is on the other leg when the erstwhile driver leads a pony and is nearly crushed underfoot by some other convoy. At Wancourt, these passers-by, who were in as great a hurry as the frequent shell-bursts entitled them to be, careered down the road, colliding with the pack-saddles as they dashed past, ripping open the sandbags of rations and in some cases entirely dragging off the loads. In other words, Figg suddenly found his cargo of dog-biscuits hurled into the mud and trampled underfoot. In between gasps for breath amidst the fumes he passed word up the convoy that the saddles were coming off ; how far the message went forward is doubtful, but he got a prompt reply from the man who was in front :

" Let them ——— well stay off, then."

When one is inconvenienced by gas-fumes and suffering from bad temper and wind-up, one is not too particular about one's language.

After searching all night for the battalion it was eventually discovered that they had been relieved and had taken up their abode in Harp Trench, a stone's throw from our lines ! What was left of the rations was therefore brought back to the starting-point. There were luckily no casualties on this trip.

The companies settled down in this spot for some days and although some of the brigade were in an attack near Cavalry Farm on the 11th, our fellows were not called upon to take part. The 168th and 167th Brigades then held the front, making further attacks on the 12th, 18th and 19th, while our own was kept in reserve, licking its sores and patching itself up.

Most of the L.R.B. patching-up was done at the M.O.'s sick-parades held amidst the shell-holes between the Harp Trench and the old German wire. These took place every morning at seven o'clock, by which hour every participant was expected to have washed, shaved, properly dressed and duly informed the orderly corporal of his regimental number and his religion. (N.B.—It was of the utmost importance that a man's religion be specified on the sick list—his ailment was added as an after-thought by the doctor.) Having neither orderly nor disorderly cor-porals on our Bohemian section, I used to wander over to the sick parade unattended, as soon as I saw the various contingents collecting together and divesting themselves of their garments ready for a good hour's dilly-dallying, half-naked, in the most exposed spot that could possibly have been found for them.

Captain Riddell presently arrived looking as spick and span as though conducting a sick-parade at Aldershot. He surveyed the motley throng while his acolytes, Sergts. Hammond, Koester and Humphreys of the aid post, waited at his right hand, ready to flourish iodine bottles. count out pills and dangle bandages in the breeze : then he beckoned to me first. For some reason or other this very militaristic M.O. made no fuss about my presenting myself without a sick-report or an orderly corporal. A great deal of latitude was allowed the transport on account of their being " old hands " and every new officer that came received the tip from battalion headquarters as to how to pick them up the right way. As he marked me down for hospital, I explained that I should prefer light duties with the transport, doing extra pickets for the men on ration jobs if need be, so he acceded to my request and told me to come every day.

While I was awaiting treatment at the hands of Koester, Riddell went round the various cases of skin-trouble, boils, impetigo, toothache, internal pains, etc., accusing fifty per cent. of the men of not having shaved for the occasion. His policy was a sound one. He was out to discourage malingering, and to do this he had to make sick-parade as unpleasant a job as possible. Men attending it had to wake up in the dark to perform their ablutions, while their fit comrades snored on. They then had to squat in the cold wind for probably an hour, waiting for treatment, finally returning to a spoiled breakfast in the trench with " Medicine and Duty " marked against their names. I feel convinced that nobody went on those sick parades at Tilloy unless he was absolutely obliged to do so. The regulations were, of course, a hardship to genuinely sick men.

Our food improved about this time, but, nevertheless, indignation had full rein when a letter appeared in the *Times* of May 8th, signed by " Army Officer," stating that it was a preposterous waste of food to send parcels to soldiers in France " where there was already a waste of food and the grub was excellent." Unfortunately, though everyone was up in arms about it and eager to reply, we feared the censorship would prevent us from adequately voicing our feelings and, since no one in our division was getting any leave at all, it seemed impossible to carry to the other side of the Channel an exposure of the statements made by the " Army Officer " in question, who was probably in the A.S.C. Among other of his statements were the following, and in view of various particulars of shortages already given in this book, the effect of the letter on us can well be imagined :—

" I allude to the tons of unnecessary food sent daily to soldiers in France."

" I write with absolute knowledge of my subject." (He might have been in the Base Post Office !)

" The Government ration is excellent and ample."

" It is notorious that men actually in the trenches often do not eat the whole ration." (After a time a diet of " pork " and beans and bully becomes so nauseating that hunger is preferable.)

" I am not alluding to small luxuries, though most of these can be got at the excellent canteens now established."

In spite of the censorship, certain comments of ours got through. One of our drivers had just been sent to one of these " excellent canteens "—a wholesale one, too—on behalf of the section, endeavouring to buy some forty tins of fruit, twenty tins of milk, six tins of cocoa, six tins of cafe-au-lait, two dozen packets of chocolate, thirty tins of cigarettes and goodness knows what else. He returned with six tins of fruit and some cocoa : that was all. However, he could have bought nail-brushes, bootlaces and matches if required, for the canteens would have made excellent Ludgate Hill hawkers. A full commentary on this passed the censor, resulting in a letter to *John Bull*, one of the only two periodicals that ventilated soldiers' grievances.

One morning we were astonished to hear a tremendous gun report, seemingly close at hand, followed instantaneously by an equally loud explosion in Arras. Both concussions were so great that the air quivered and it seemed as though the earth shook. It transpired that this was a British railway-gun captured from the Russians and now turned against ourselves : any amount of heavy artillery had been denied our front in order to supply these " gallant " allies, who had lost many hundreds of guns the previous autumn. Now matters were worse, for there was fraternising on the Russian front and we had not the least doubt that in some quarters the Germans were calmly collecting " souvenirs." No real debacle had taken place so far—the Bosches were merely marking time, letting Russia crumble internally, meanwhile a few German divisions and some artillery had been transferred to the West, which partly explaned the serious resistance we were encountering at Arras. The fact that we were paying for the Russian Army's inactivity and folly made our blood boil. The long-range bombardment of Arras now became a regular performance. " Saucy Susan " was not particular where she aimed so long as her missiles fell somewhere near the hospital or the station, and a large number of the town residents promptly reverted to underground life. Particularly was this the case at night when air-raids were regularly anticipated and the populace were rarely disappointed.

The number of aeroplanes flying around by day also alarmed the authorities, who ordered us to have our wigwams painted brown : but by this time the enemy surely possessed all the photos he required. The six-inch naval guns near Tilloy were particularly sought out by the Germans, who started ranging for them during the last day or so of our sojourn in their vicinity. Had they located them accurately we should not have minded so much, but Brother Bosche was not at all sure of their position—a fact which gave rise to a considerable amount of wind-up among the transport units, the occupants of Harp Trench and the Labour Corps camps situated fifty yards from the monsters.

The ranging took the form of indiscriminate shelling while German aeroplanes hovered above and our anti-aircraft guns engaged in a competition as to which should kill the largest number of British men and horses with empty shell-cases and falling shrapnel bullets, hurling down like bolts from the blue. Gunboat Smith now lived in his tin-helmet while the saddler spent most of his time in a trench.

Gordon thought we ought to take steps to meet an emergency and accordingly instructions were given that :

(1) Every man should keep on such clothes at night as would enable him to turn out at a moment's notice.

(2) Everyone should take his horses' bit to bed with him (in lieu of a hot-water bottle), while his respirator should always be kept close at hand, since gas shells seemed to be all the rage.

(3) In the event of shells falling uncomfortably close, the picket —using their discretion in the matter—should blow three short sharp whistles, whereat every man would spring through the tent door, take a flying leap at his horse and insert the bit, ready to lead him off to calmer regions when the order was given.

(4) Those men who did not possess a horse should take to bed with them the second bit of someone who was inflicted with two animals, so that all could be rushed away from the danger-zone in the quickest possible time.

From the moment such orders were issued there was an electric atmosphere about the camp. As soon as it got dark and thoughts turned from writing letters and games of " up the line " to such reflections as usually occupy the minds of soldiers who sleep under tents on a moonlight night listening to aeroplanes, our ears were tuned up to the least noise. When a shell came over someone would be sure to say " Where was that ? " Calm and placid individuals like Conibeer assured the audience that it had fallen at Wancourt ; rumour-mongers like Hobson preferred to consider it this side of Tilloy ; while Volze was convinced it was just outside his tent. Most fellows slept with their breeches on, respirators and bits by their heads and boots in a handy spot ; while the saddler, who did not take his turn at line jobs, decided to sit up all night by the picket fire. However, morning came and all the pickets reported that nothing came near enough to warrant raising the alarm, so a good deal less was thought about it.

The only disquieting news next day was that the Bosches were using fair quantities of percussion shells for horse-lines, which made very small holes and scattered hundreds of fragments along the ground for a matter of fifty yards radius. Thus several horses could be wounded by one such shell, while men sleeping in tents were placed in a particularly exposed position. It was said that bombs also were being used which burst with similar effects.

The next night Figg and I had to conduct the second picket, during which we sat for a long time by the brazier which we had to hide once in the early hours owing to a Taube overhead. Upon it we were endeavouring to boil a mess-tin of water for cocoa. Now and again we got up to inspect the horses and make sure the kicking we had heard emanated from the 2nd London's transport and not our own. Their picket was probably asleep, but at any rate it was no business of ours to interfere. The Grey got loose and wandered off in a vain search for grass ; as I followed him he broke into a trot, tripped up over a tent guide rope, thoroughly frightened the inmates whose nerves were already on edge, then came to a complete standstill and waited for my arrival. When I got him again I tied him up very securely, inwardly remarking that Conibeer was more careless than I had been in that respect and vowing that the knot I had now tied would teach him a lesson in the morning.

Then, dodging a kick from Salmon, I crossed over to Beattie and Babs, whose hindquarters were facing the rope with their head-chains entangled with their front legs. Finally we sat down once more to discuss the usual subjects : prospects of rest, chances of leave, latest rumours, the good old days at home, Conscientious Objectors, the everlasting toll of merchantmen, the Russian fiasco and the great topic of peace and when it would come.

" I can see Russia chucking up the sponge and leaving the poor old British and French to fight it out by themselves," said Figg. " Where is this smashing general offensive we've been bragging about, that was to crumple the Germans up and bring peace by the autumn ? Here we are, nearly half-way through 1917, and all we've got to show for it is twenty thousand prisoners (i.e., taken by the British) and a few —— miles of —— ground. The French push seems to be a bit of a wash-out and the Italians haven't done a thing so far this year. How long will it take them to dictate terms at this rate ? "

To emphasise his point he kicked against one of the bricks supporting the brazier, upset some of the hot water and then told me to be more careful.

" Did you hear that one ? " he asked, alluding to a solitary shell that had just fallen about six hundred yards away.

" Yes," I assented surlily.

" I hope it won't fall to our lot to turn the men out. They'll never let us hear the end of it if we give a false alarm."

" They were falling over there last night. I daresay there will be no cause to use our whistle. But we might as well make the cocoa now ! "

However, very shortly afterwards another shell came over, this time somewhere near the Harp Trench. It seemed as though we ought to make provisional arrangements for rousing the camp so we agreed that if the next was appreciably nearer Figg should give the three blasts and run along the tents, adding his lusty voice to the musical alarm, while I should deal with the bivvies where several men were sleeping.

Directly we had fixed on this plan and before we had time to consume the coveted cocoa, the third arrival landed uncomfortably close to the horse-lines : the 'awky-bits could be heard swishing around.

One ! Two ! Three ! The short sharp blasts rang out and then I hurried to the first bivvy which harboured Clements and Williams, notoriously heavy sleepers, who greeted my shouts with grunts.

" Turn out. The whistle's blown," I said, peering round their ground-sheet doorway.

" 'Tisn't time to get up yet," said Williams, without showing the least sign of stirring.

" You panicky bleater ! " remarked "Aggy " (Clements' nickname). " Just because you hear a gun go off somewhere about a mile away you expect us to turn out——"

" They're quite close, you idiot. Come along."

On the horse-lines one or two were aleady bitting-up their steeds. Volze had sprung up with a bound, fully dressed, and had flopped clean through the tent door, sending guide ropes to the four winds. But most fellows thought they were being turned out on a fool's errand and some absolutely refused to move.

" Go to Hell," said Joe Wiskar, thoroughly incensed at being awakened.

In another minute they were converted to my way of thinking. The next shell landed with a crash seemingly in the middle of the horse-lines : from where I stood by the bivvies the lines appeared to be lost in smoke and pieces of mud and metal fell in a shower on our tin helmets.

" Horses off the line," rang out the Sergeant's voice, and no further bidding was necessary. There was a moment's suspense in which we wondered how many people had been hit, but nobody seemed to have been wounded, not a horse was on the ground ; most of the fellows were going about their business with more bustle than they had ever exhibited before. Coni, however, always refused to hurry on such occasions and came up in a most casual manner to lead away Jumbo. Only then did I realise that I had promised to take charge of The Grey in the event of panic and it flashed upon me that it would fall to my lot to unravel the difficult knot I had made in the head-chain for Coni's benefit, a knot that was now more firmly secured than ever, as the horses had reared up with fright when the shell had burst.

I tugged at the chain, cut my fingers and swore copiously at my folly. Only twice before had I worked with such frenzy : on that first night at Ypres when we dug in not knowing whether British or Germans were before us, and on the second night when I had only an hour or so to get below the surface before daylight in chalky soil. Everyone else was leaving the horse-lines and another shell might come over at any moment.

It seemed as if a couple of minutes passed before Simmonds came up and requested me in blankety terms not to take all night over it. Finally I hit the knot with one of the smithy's implements, a blow which had the effect of unravelling some of the links and " putting the wind up " The Grey : then, following up my advantage, before the links had time to recover from the shock, I unfastened the chain and quickly fled from the spot, threading my way along in the darkness guided by the moon, dodging shell-holes and—farther on—artillery bivvies. All of a sudden The Grey stumbled, having trodden on an innocent looking ground-sheet stretched across the top of a trench. Beneath this roof evidently dwelt at least a couple of artillery drivers, though the streams of purple language that poured forth suggested a greater number than that. The Grey's forefeet had crashed right through on top of them, bringing in the side of the trench and ruining their home.

" Who the —— ? What the —— —— Hell ? Wait till I —— well catch you, you blankety blank blank ! "

In view of these dire threats that issued forth from the bowels of the earth, I did not wait to apologise : as soon as The Grey had recovered his balance, I hastened on again and succeeded in effecting a complete disappearance before the irate drivers could emerge from the trench and deal with me as suggested. I am not surprised that their tempers were not of the best, for the day before I had seen these hidebound wretches being made to dress their nosebags by the right in a line on the ground behind the horses, preparatory to putting the feeds on. While the horses neighed, pawed the ground and kicked each other in their impatience, some eighteen-year-old brainless subaltern was standing in line with the nosebags making one man move his a little forward and another backward. " And yet we wonder why we're taking so long to win the War," was Mac's very audible comment as we had passed this exhibition on our way to water.

Just as I reached the plank-track beyond the crater Gordon hurried up, recognising The Grey's form.

" What happened ? Is anyone hurt ? " he asked anxiously.

" A shell came over somewhere in the horse-lines. No one's hurt, so far as I know. They're all off the lines now, I think."

" Thank God for that," said he. " My tent, as you know, is some way away, and when I heard that shell come over I was afraid it might have made a mess of things."

We caught up the others who had been proceeding in single file up the plank-track towards Arras and had now reached a spot some hundreds of yards from the crater. Here it had been decided that they should squat down on the bank beside the track, holding the horses by their reins, until the strafeing had ceased. Other units from the vicinity of Harp Trench also trooped along with their animals, much to the astonishment of the artillery pickets in the neighbourhood of our resting-place, who had not had any shells near enough to disturb them and wondered what all the panic was about.

The shells continued to fall in the distance and it looked as though we should have to sit up all night. To some this was a chilly prospect as, contrary to advice, several had gone to bed the previous evening in a more disrobed state than was suited to the occasion and a few had rushed out attired in little more than an overcoat and boots. The horses, restless at first, presently fell into a state of coma, dropping their lower jaws, commenced to dribble and became unsteady about the front knees—to the alarm of their guardians who squatted immediately in front of them. Meanwhile, the object of all this strafeing— the six-inch naval gun at Tilloy—remained undisturbed, laughing to itself over the inconvenience caused to the transports. In Harp Trench itself the companies, who nearly received some of these unpleasant missiles, were for the most part safely lodged in the spacious German dug-outs, but we were destined to spend a night out. I certainly dozed off once or twice, but for the greater part of the time it was a weary vigil. For hour after hour we waited, but not until dawn was there any surety that the German gun had ceased its unwelcome attentions.

Just when the aeroplanes were starting their early morning cruises, when the artillery pickets were having their wash in buckets of refreshing-looking water, when their horses were just peering round to see how much chewed wood lay scattered around the picket-line posts, the weary band of refugees set off to resume occupation of their abandoned horse-lines. A bombardment was in progress on the right, but the naval gun was lying low : if it did not feel ashamed of itself it ought to, was the general verdict.

Naturally we were very anxious to see where the shell had fallen and whether any other damage had been done during the night. The shell-hole was immediately discovered, some six yards from the end of the horse-lines and five yards from the nearest tent, which now had several holes in it. Fortunately the shell had not been one of the new " spreading " kind, nor a very big explosive : the hole it had made was comparatively small and its effect was very local. By a miracle the only remaining occupant of the tent had escaped unhurt and the sole damage was caused to the nearest horses which had sustained a few wounds and cuts that were noticeable only by daylight.

This fortunate escape of ours, coupled with the immunity of our convoys on the Wancourt road, did much to revive our faith in the good luck that seemed to attend our section's adventures, at any rate as far as casualties were concerned. There was a legend that Julia—the old Boer War horse—was our lucky mascot, and that so long as she remained with the section good fortune would attend us. Certainly we frequently saw and heard about the misfortunes of other transports and artillery convoys, yet our only casualty since the Second Battle of Ypres had been Kimbo.

As if to confirm this belief of ours, orders were given to us next day to accompany the battalion to Duisans for a rest, and another collection of transports came up to relieve our brigade of its unhealthy site. Shortly afterwards we heard that within three days—in the course of experiences similar to our own—the newcomers suffered several casualties in men and horses and had to shift their lines. At which, doubtless, the naval gun, still undetected, thrust its long muzzle through the camouflage and grinned !

CHAPTER XXIII.

A Hospital Interlude.

(*June*, 1917.)

A short respite—News of Messines—More strafeing of horse-lines—A " sick slight " case—From field ambulance to C.C.S.—At a base hospital—Curious characters —What the L.R.B. represented—Convalescent camp—Leave at last !

Only two things worthy of note occurred during our five days' stay at Duisans : leave started again and we got a swim. Two men who had been without leave for nineteen and eighteen months respectively were promptly warned and departed the next evening, the rate at which it continued thereafter gave me strong hopes of seeing Blighty once more about the end of June.

At Duisans it turned out that we were in our wrong area, so the authorities pitchforked us into a neighbouring village, Agnez-les-Duisans, generally alluded to by the traffic corporals as " Agnidweesins." Here the battalion occupied huts round the four sides of a bare field, while the transport were rejoiced to discover that half a mile separated their hut from the " orderly officer " paraphernalia of the companies, so that we were left very much to our own devices.

Agnez-les-Duisans was about four miles north-west of Arras, but from its appearance it might have been situated many miles from the war zone, for life went on here in a placid sort of way. There was a stream where fair numbers of fellows went for a swim every evening, undressing in an enclosure which the beneficent Army had actually rigged up for the purpose ; there were tiny rivulets where watercress grew wild and we went round collecting it for tea ; the cottage folk welcomed us into their kitchens where they were prepared to make coffee or cook omelettes whenever required.

Down in a hollow, about three-quarters of a mile from our camp, was a C.C.S., consisting of numbers of white marquees ; motor ambulances made their way along the dusty roads at all hours of the day and night and disappeared amongst the tents with their freight of wounded, while occasionally a beautifully painted British hospital train came alongside the hospital to take on board the latest batch of evacuated cases and carry them off to the base or Blighty. As I watched the sad little encampment, little did I think that I should shortly be passing through it with one of the slightest ailments imaginable.

At nights life was sometimes less serene than by day, as the droning and buzzing of German aeroplanes bent on bomb-dropping were scarcely conducive to sleep. Many were the " packets " dropped in the distance, most of the targets being nearer the line, but occasionally the machines passed right over us in quest of railway junctions or more conspicuous camps than our own. One night we lay quaking in our blankets, listening to the steady drone of a low-flying 'plane above us when there were half a dozen loud reports not far away which shook the hut. It was the C.C.S. that was hit—the C.C.S., which was perfectly well-known to the Germans as a hospital and was accordingly supposed to be immune from such attacks. The enemy could easily excuse themselves by saying they were trying to hit the railway line, but later events proved that this form of frightfulness was considered clever.

In view of the perfect weather, the inevitable inspection was no hardship to us ; there was plenty of time in which to go mad, everything looked smart and glittering, and so the General was delighted. For days the stables resembled a Brasso shop and the number of shirts and nosebags torn up for harness-rag beat all records. The Brasso was purchased on this occasion by the T.O. instead of the men, but there was little diminution in the amount of grousing, in return for the gift. Harness cleaning had become an infernal monotony and one or two of the old drivers were giving up the job in disgust, contenting themselves with a single horse job (officers' horses and pack ponies) which were gradually developing from the most despised to the most coveted positions on the section.

The next item on the programme was a battalion concert held on an impromptu stage rigged up in an open field by the pioneers. At this the Q.M. was to supply free white wine and whisky for the artistes, which caused such a number of performers to offer their services that the arrangement of the concert became a difficult matter. At length a programme was drawn up which was estimated to last three hours without encores ; needless to say, the transport had secured a very full share of the places. There is no space to describe fully the farce that followed. The L.R.B. now consisted of a great variety of individuals from all walks of life, so that Figg's baritone solo was followed by a " comic " song given by someone who sang without music or even intelligible sounds—a song that made even the C.O. blush with shame, yet called forth lusty applause from a little knot of the performer's sympathisers who had probably arrived in his draft. Meanwhile the consumption of liquor proceeded apace behind the scenes and, when I came away from the outskirts of the audience (where I had taken my stand after assisting with sundry accompaniments), I found on looking into the artistes' quarters that not only the performers but many intruders were sharing in the refreshments. So much so that those who were not on the official programme set up a concert on their own account at the back of the stage.

The T.O. twisted the muscles in his leg when playing football one evening and was taken away on a stretcher ; he did not rejoin us for several days. On the same evening we all had to be inoculated, the conscientious objectors putting their leave in the foreground on this occasion and calmly submitting to be spiked. I do not think Riddell remembered my previous obstinacy and, at any rate, he was so attentive to me with my ailments that I feel sure he bore me no malice. Under his care I had now got practically well again and on 3rd of June I took over my pair of horses from Conibeer, becoming a full-fledged driver

R

once more. A hot bath on the 5th completed my joy ; in fact, I went into such ecstasies on a post-card over getting my first hot bath for four months that the censor got to work with his blue pencil and took all the enthusiasm away from the announcement !

About this time we got rumours of our going up to the Arras front yet again, but it was stated that it was only to hold the line ; in fact our attacks up there had now died down, except at Lens, and ordinary trench warfare had been resumed. That is to say, the great Arras offensive had drawn to a close and there was very little of interest in the papers. German attacks at Champagne, a German air raid on Folkestone, hospital ship and transport torpedoed in the Mediterranean— all such items we were long since accustomed to ; we could almost anticipate the news in the papers before we opened them.

Yet one thing we were not prepared for, and that was the Battle of Messines. Of the explosion of the twenty-four huge mines, charged with over a million pounds of ammonal, we heard nothing. Of the terrific bombardment that followed them and kept up all day long on the 7th, not a rumble reached our ears. This must have been accounted for by the lie of the land, for Mr. Lloyd George in London is said to have waited for the vibration at zero-hour and, wizard that he was, imagined that he felt it ; moreover, at other times gun fire had sounded quite distinctly at a much greater distance than that which now separated us from the Messines Ridge. In one day the whole ridge, which had dominated the British line from Armentieres and Ploegsteert up to Ypres, fell to the British, who advanced two and a half miles on a ten mile front and captured over five thousand prisoners. It was the smartest piece of work yet performed on the Western Front and was all the more creditable as the preparations for it must have been made right under the Bosches' noses.

To be sure we got no official announcement of it at the front and thrived on rumours for a day or so, but papers soon arrived which revealed the extent of the success. It meant, among other things, that Hill 60 had fallen, so that it would now be possible to leave Dickebusch in daylight, travel up the Voormezeele Road and even visit St. Eloi without waiting for darkness. The prisoners had increased to 7,200 with 67 guns. The line at our old haunt, Plug Street, was advanced in a day or so, also, since the Germans had to retire from their positions opposite the old Essex and L.R.B. trenches. Once the Messines Ridge had been captured, together with its farther slopes, it became evident that there were to be no "battering ram" tactics as there had been at Arras. We had got all our objectives and were content with them. Let the next blow be made elsewhere !

Our return to the firing-line was made on June 9th, when we were discomfited to find our new transport-lines rather close to the home of an observation balloon at Beaurains. The lorry which formed the anchor for an O.B. was a particular enemy of Fritz, and if the latter gentleman had any idea where that lorry usually resided he made it his business to cause as much inconvenience in the neighbourhood as possible. Accordingly we disliked our new site intensely. As in the case of the six-inch guns at Tilloy, which were now about a mile away from us, it turned out that Fritz had but the haziest notions of where the lorry was domiciled, and though he put several shells over into its back-yard, a considerable number fell, so to speak, in the front garden. Some came unpleasantly close to our horse-lines at night and in the morning we would find a couple of new holes just beyond the old trench that formed one of our boundaries. Three or four times we had to panic off with our horses, as at Tilloy, when an unpleasant dose of " hate " was being administered, and everybody got " wind-up " rather badly. Living in bivvies, as we were, above the surface of the ground, we always wondered if the next shell would land on top of us, and when once a light sleeper realised that shells were falling within half a mile, his peace of mind for that night was irrevocably disturbed. The companies, who occupied the deep dug-outs at Telegraph Hill for the next few days, were in a distinctly enviable position.

Application was made to brigade for permission to move our lines, and whilst anxiously awaiting the result, a runner was seen approaching : everyone expected the request would be granted and was almost packing up his goods and chattels in anticipation. However, on perusing the document delivered by the runner, we found that it required particulars as to how many limbers we had painted and what steps were being taken to paint the remainder ! The next chit from brigade required a lecture to be addressed to the section on the subject of " Poison Gas." For this purpose Corporal Watkins was advertised as the star turn, he having been recently appointed " Gas Corporal " with responsibility for the good condition of all our respirators : but when he got on his feet to speak it was evident that he didn't know any more about gas—of the poison variety—than ourselves. Nevertheless, he spoke for three-quarters of an hour, amidst ironical cheers and applause, fitting on his respirator at times and continuing his lecture inside it without anybody in the audience being able to distinguish a syllable that was uttered. He was like some wandering conjurer who holds an audience spellbound at a street corner : but the unfortunate part about it was that there was so much leg-pulling that no one was at the end any the wiser, though the subject was becoming a very important one for us.

A malady known as trench fever took hold of one or two men here, and Figg, whose presence was badly needed in connection with the next magazine, had to go into hospital for a few days. Lance-Corporal Milcovich followed him. Watkins was brought up in both these cases to pronounce an expert opinion as to whether the men were gassed by German green-cross shells ; and that gentleman solemnly pronounced an opinion—little suspecting leg-pulling—though his views were quite valueless ! Trench fever was a sort of condition of high temperature which rendered you incapable of work : I think it was brought on by sleeping on the ground.

One or two others started to get boils, probably traceable, as I said before, to the nature of our diet. It looked as if the health of the section was beginning to " crock up," which would not be surprising since it was, for many of us, our third summer in France. For my part, you may imagine my chagrin when, just as I thought I had recovered from my troubles, my eye commenced to close up. Although it was somewhat difficult to see out of it, there was no pain, and so, as I could not bear the idea of becoming useless once more, I " carried on." When driving up a limber in the ration convoy to Guemappe on the 16th, however, the vehicles in front raised such clouds of dust that the eye watered copiously and had to be kept shut tight. In the morning it was impossible to see out of it at all and I had the appearance of giving a long-sustained, doleful wink after shedding crocodile tears on the decease of a wealthy aunt. Simmonds insisted that I should parade sick, so I had to hand over my horses, walk about a mile to the field ambulance at Tilloy, present my sick-report and sit down in disgust to await the M.O.'s pleasure.

This is how I came to go to hospital. My kit, or, rather, such of it as I could conveniently carry, was sent over from the transport, the "Devils' Mess" taking charge of sundry superfluous articles which were of a communal rather than private character. Assuring me that I should only be in hospital a few days and that all I needed was rest, the R.A.M.C. corporal affixed a ticket to my tunic marked :—

BATTLE CASUALTY
ACCIDENTALLY WOUNDED   SLIGHT
SICK   SEVERE

from which the unwanted words were erased. A friend of mine had recently been reported as having gone into hospital with an attack of "sick slight" which had so puzzled his people that they had written to ask me what it was !

Then I clambered into a motor ambulance with a few other men from different regiments and by dinner-time was whirling down the Cambrai road, regarding from my seat of luxury the lorries, transport-limbers, working parties and all the battle area around that would be but a memory in a few hours. They deposited me at one of our own divisional ambulances in Arras, where I had already paraded sick on certain occasions : the building was a large hospital in peace time and therefore made a very spacious abode for the F.A., for there were several wards.

After providing a really ideal dinner they left us to our own devices until the doctor was ready to hold his reception. At this parade the words "Conjunctivitis" and "Foreign Service : 2 yrs. 5 mos." were added to my label, making me feel exactly like a packing-case being marked and labelled for despatch by rail. Finally I was allotted a bed where I lay ruminating on the delights of straw pillows and sheets, even though the latter were coarse calico.

But when evening came we were ordered below into the vaults on account of the nightly air-raids, so my dream of a comfortable bed was shattered. The vaults were long dark cellars, illuminated at infrequent intervals by electric lights, and against either wall were long rows of stretchers, each with a couple of dubious blankets folded upon them. The place smelt fusty and must have been rat-ridden, but it was decidedly better to sleep there than to lie in a nice bed listening all night to the droning of German bombing machines. As a matter of fact, free from the fear of shelling that had exercised our minds lately, I slept more soundly than I had done for a week.

Early the next morning there was a German attack on Infantry Hill, east of Monchy, which had been captured on the 14th, and at breakfast time wounded cases commenced to arrive, including several L.R.B.s, who had incurred the barrage in their front line. This fact made the doctor rather more inclined to evacuate certain sick cases than he would otherwise have been, for they had to cater for wounded here much as a London restaurant-keeper caters for larger numbers on days of celebrations. He did not ask what was the matter with me or how I felt : a casual glance at the card was enough. Seeing that I had been in France two and a half years, he shook his fountain pen and wrote "C.C.S." on my label. At that I must say I somewhat quaked, for I happened to know what a splendid target the marquee hospital at Agnez offered to night bombers.

" There will be rather a rush on to-day and with luck you may go right through to the base," said he, with a twinkling eye. " Good luck to you."

I could scarcely believe my ears. Go right through to the base with a petty little complaint like that ! Why, such a chance was more than I dared to hope for ! Yet it was with mixed feelings that I regarded the prospect. If I stayed in the C.C.S. until I was better I should be sent back to my unit, but once I reached the base, my individuality would be lost : the 17th Hackney Gurkhas might require a draft and I might have to give up all hope of rejoining my L.R.B. pals again. It was only by a fluke that Butt got back to us on the Somme. On the other hand, hospital trains had been known to go alongside the quay at Boulogne and Calais and discharge their contents on to a homeward-bound hospital-ship : the mere possibility of such a contingency made me hope for a speedy trip to the base.

Things panned out as the M.O. had predicted. Motor ambulances arrived in the afternoon and conveyed many of us to Agnez-les-Duisans, where hundreds of wounded cases, including German prisoners, from the Infantry Hill scrap were awaiting attention. After considerable delay, all those who could walk went before a doctor, who regarded us cursorily just as specimens being handed on from one hospital to another ; on our cards he wrote the letters " E.S." (Evacuation Sitting) and then we passed on to the " dressing hut." From there I was ushered into one of the marquees where a long queue of fellows was lining up for tea. German prisoners were standing in the queue, absolutely dumbfounded at being treated on equal terms with all the British soldiers. What British Tommy, passing through a German hospital, would have been lent a mug, thrust into the middle of a queue of sick and wounded German soldiers and then allowed to sit among them as an equal at the tea-table ? Some artillerymen were cracking jokes with the grey-clad creatures, who could scarcely credit their good fortune and hardly knew whether to smile or not. They gazed in amazement at the slices of bread and butter that were handed to them. This sight made many of the British furious, recalling, no doubt, a meagre bread issue on the preceding day.

In the midst of tea a burly sergeant stuck his head in at the door and shouted : " Done none of you go losin' yerselves. Stand by for the amblince train. When yer goes, take hall yer kit with yer. Rashins will be issued in an-arf-ower."

A chorus of satisfaction followed this announcement. It *was* true, then. We were going straight through to the base ! Good-bye Agnez ! Good-bye Arras ! Farewell to the firing-line and all the villages behind it ! Farewell (alas !), all my pals in the L.R.B. ! We were off to the sea, far from the rumble of guns and the smell of barns and horses and gas-shells ! With a far less serious ailment than a " cushy " wound, I was being swept through by the tide, if not to the goal of most infantrymen's ambitions, then considerably more than half-way there. Many would have gladly endured a bullet wound in the arm or leg for a seat in the train that was waiting now.

*　　　　*　　　　*　　　　*

The railway at Etaples runs along parallel to the sea, some mile inland. On either side of this for a considerable distance were innumerable depots, hospitals and convalescent camps, consisting of huge camps of marquees, huts and tents, placed so close together that the boundary between the various establishments was impossible to distinguish. Most of the hospitals were on the mainland side of the railway line, where the ground rose to quite a fair height, and the slope was therefore studded with little white dots, reminiscent of a large training camp in England. Parade grounds and rifle ranges were here also ; beside the line extended one of the largest cemeteries in France, containing the bodies of the wounded who had come to the base to die.

It was in the midst of this vast seaside settlement that our hospital train drew up early next morning ; the stretcher cases were removed first and then the " Evacuation Sitting " filed into a long hut belonging to the No. 1 Canadian General Hospital where they were relieved of every particle of clothing but their hats, boots and belt, thrust into delicious hot baths and then fitted out in hospital " blues." It was like stepping into another world : there was such an atmosphere of comfort and leisurely procedure about the place. Whether this was the impression gained on entering a British hospital, I cannot say, but the Canadians were delightful folk with a " go-as-you-please " attitude about them, a " live-and-let-live " spirit that contrasted with British discipline.

We next passed before a very overworked M.O., who told the various orderlies what our treatment was to be and what wards we were to occupy. Finally we made our way to our new abodes. As I was the only new arrival in " Chalk " ward, there was a good deal of attention focused upon me, which was somewhat embarrassing. To my disappointment there were no " sisters " in this ward and so my heart had been palpitating in vain. There were not even any R.A.M.C. men about. But at a table by the door sat what appeared to be a " Soldiers' and Workmen's Soviet " who were apparently in sole charge of the establishment. Timidly gazing round as I stood within the portal, I was greeted by something like the following :

FAT FUSILIER : " Well, whacherwant ? Oh, you're a new Johnny, are yer ? Well, I'm sorry, mate, but we're fullup."

GINGER JOCK : " Tae hell. Why, there's the wee bed at t'end there. Number thirty-seven."

FAT FUSILIER : " Wot old Worters 'ad ? Oh, yus. . . . Just come darn the line ? Woppart ? . . . Arras ! . . . That's where I copped it."

GINGER JOCK : " Gie us yer card." (Perusing it.) " What's this the matter wi' ye ? Con-con-con-con-junc-ti-vitis. What the . . . hell's that ? "

LANCASHIRE LAD : " Loondun Rarfle Brigeed ? What mob's that, choom ? Ar 'aven't 'eerd o' that crowd, 'ave you, Jock ? "

FAT FUSILIER (perusing card) : " Been out 'ere long enough, mate ! My 'at ! Two years an' five munse. You'll get to Blighty right enough, son."

GINGER JOCK : " Twa yeers and feeve moonths ! Why, there's na mon in this ward wi' more thun fifteen moonths' furren seervice."

FAT FUSILIER : " Yus, there is. There's ole Tubby o' the East Yorks. 'E's bin out eighteen munse."

" My dear chap," I said, " my eye is already nearly well. There's no chance of getting across with a little thing like this."

FAT FUSILIER : " Ain't there ! Why, the ole doc., the fust thing 'e looks at is yer furren service. If you bin art about three munse there's —— all 'opes of you gettin' acrorst. But if 'e thinks it's 'bout time you 'ad a rest 'e'll mark you Blighty, sure."

LANCASHIRE LAD : " Oo, aye."

" Well, anyway," I said, " show me this bed of yours."

FAT FUSILIER : " There yar. Chuck yer 'at darn there, chum. Make yerself at 'ome. No one'll worry about you 'ere. You can lose yerself orl day, ony come back punshal meal-times else yer won't get yer grub. We're very strick on that pint, ain't we, George ? "

Gurgling with inward amusement at this strange committee, I could not help realising that, having lost the 56th Division atmosphere of London and the little circle of friends that made life pleasanter on the transport, I was transplanted to a different world where everyone spoke a different dialect, and, to say the least, I did not feel at home. All the concessions that were made by Battalion H.Q. to the transport section, recognising that *esprit de corps* could take the place of regulations, the latitude that was allowed to certain of us on account of individual temperaments disappeared the moment one got outside the L.R.B. sphere of influence. Then you became just one of a million and had to conform to the standard of discipline laid down for the million. On the L.R.B. transport there were still some half a dozen 1914 men who would be eligible for lance-corporal's rank before the 1915 men would be considered, but that worried nobody in the least ; there was no disgrace in being a private in the L.R.B. Once you got outside the unit, however, you discovered that ex-navvies who had joined up in 1916 had become corporals, imbued with authority to shout at you because your boots wanted cleaning or because you were making too much noise. Not that the worthy Fusilier, who was a lance-corporal, attempted to become nasty ; on the contrary, he and his two satellites seemed to regard me as an old soldier, albeit a bit of an old fossil, who was worthy of a certain amount of respect ! I was to learn the other lesson after leaving hospital.

It transpired that, to economise in R.A.M.C. men, the wardenship of certain wards was entrusted to a private or N.C.O. in the convalescent stage who performed the work for a month, or perhaps two, before going up the line again. Two or three men served with him on similar terms, their duty being to draw meals from the cookhouse and take the food round to all the patients. This accounted for the important position held by the Fusilier, who would no doubt have been content with such a job for the duration of the War.

For the first day or so the comforts of the hospital, the good food and the attractions of a reading hut and a piano made life very enjoyable. Everything was so peaceful and calm and there was nothing to worry about—no horses, no pickets, no ration journeys. What would not poor old Figg and Coni give for an undisturbed night in these beds, with no fear of the picket giving three shrill whistles, and no need to keep their respirators and tin hats close at hand ! It was certainly like heaven to sit on the verandah of the recreation hut watching the sun set upon the water.

Only now could I realise the extent of the tension at which we had been working. I had come back from leave nearly eighteen months ago, and we had worked without holidays for seven days a week ever since, always liable for ration journeys at nights when the battalion were in the line and pickets whether they were or not. From May, 1916, onwards we had lived up to a high pitch of excitement ; the work had got more strenuous, our surroundings noisier ; recently there had been far more trouble on the roads, and Fritz had become so obstreperous that at no hour of the day or night could you feel certain that a shell would not arrive in the horse-lines. Continued apprehension had taken the place of mere excitement, and it was that apprehension that was suddenly lifted from one's mind in being suddenly transported from the racket of the firing-line to the idyllic surroundings of the Etaples hospital where there was nothing to fear.

Yet, after a day or so, I began to miss the transport fellows terribly. Although there were papers to read and fellows to talk to (including two L.R.B. men who had come down with scratches incurred in the bombardment), my thoughts continually harked back to the section, wondering what they were doing and whether I should see them again. I was so accustomed to being among a circle who knew me that it gave one a sense of loneliness to wander the whole length and breadth of the hospital area and be recognised by no one.

A few days before my leaving the section, the Devils' Mess had planned to have custard for dinner as a great treat. Figg and Greene were out, so Trendell made a little fire, while Conibeer carefully mixed the custard in a mug. They would not trust me to perform these tasks but, as I wanted to do my share, consented to my pouring in the custard when the diluted Nestlé's milk reached boiling point.

" He can't go wrong there," they remarked. " There's only one way to pour it in."

" Take it off as soon as you've stirred it round," said Coni, " and for goodness' sake don't spill it."

" Right-o, you get the plates ready."

Immediately they had departed, I accidentally kicked the iron bar supporting the gallipot, the whole of its contents being pitched into the fire. It meant tragedy for the Devils' Mess. Figg had gone miles to buy the milk and custard, Trendell had been at great pains to steal the fuel, and Coni had quitted " stables " early to prepare the fire ; all I had done was to suggest the meal. I deserved every curse imaginable.

Conibeer returned in a couple of minutes in a state of ecstasy at the thought that all these efforts were about to be consummated : our official meal was " pork " and beans, hence the custard was going to be a luxury. Suddenly he stopped short. The wreckage of all his hopes lay in the smouldering remains over which I stooped ; they couldn't leave me alone for two minutes without my doing something idiotic ! Yet not a syllable passed his lips. He just wheeled round and returned to the bivvy, whistling. After three minutes' hesitation I made my way there also, the empty gallipot trembling in my hand as I peered within the abode. But not a curse descended on my head ; instead of that I found the two of them lying back on their kits, absolutely helpless with laughter !

This little incident shows the extent of the friendship I missed. Had the same thing happened at the hospital, there would have been a storm of angry protest and thereafter everyone in the ward would have borne me malice and referred to me as that " blinkin' idiot that spoilt our grub."

From the moment of my arrival my eye rapidly got better under the care of a Canadian sister, who squirted drops in both eyes with a fountain-pen filler at 11 a.m. daily. In the ward where I attended for this purpose were dozens of serious cases, most of them too severe to be moved across the Channel, but I was told that the gas cases were the worst. The Germans were using a gas that burnt out the eyes, and the number of men afflicted in this way was growing daily.

Every morning a doctor came to our hut and examined the patients, those who could walk lining up in a queue and passing before him one by one. The fat Fusilier stood by in attendance. One fellow, who was obviously malingering, started to shiver and shake as soon as he took his place in the queue and, by the time he reached the doctor, this had developed into a kind of St. Vitus' dance. His case was described as "shell-shock," and the kindly old doctor was most perturbed; but, as soon as the latter gentleman had left the hut, the malingerer returned to his bed and doubled up with laughter. On the second day I discovered him playing the piano in a hut, yet on the following sick-parade he acted his part so well that the doctor marked him for England, and when I left the hospital he was waiting for the very next boat !

At first I had hoped that there might be something in what the Fusilier said about getting across to England, and I conjured up visions of ten days' leave, followed by training at Fovant with a lot of the old first battalion men who had gone home from the Second Battle of Ypres and had never come out again since, though quite recovered from their wounds. I might be able to stop in England for another twelve months, with occasional week-ends at home.

But it was only a dream. On the third morning the M.O. shook his head and said : " I'm sorry I can't mark you ' Blighty,' lad, with your thirty months' foreign service, but I'm afraid your eye's not bad enough. If I did so, the Commandant wouldn't pass you out."

That was, after all, what might have been expected. Passages on hospital ships were not given to men who had the appearance of being able to carry on longer in the firing-line. The men marked for the next boat home were, for the most part, wounded cases, the balance being made up of sickly men of B and C categories, who had been conscripted regardless of their health or bodily and mental infirmities ; in " Chalk " ward there were cases of men with one eye, crippled legs, bad sight, no teeth, frail physique, etc., who had been passed as fit for foreign service, and who were now being shipped back in large numbers after about three months' futile effort to make good. Our man-power scheme had come to a pretty pass when we were reduced to conscripting such specimens for foreign service, while thousands of fit young men were still masquerading as indispensables at home.

The Fusilier expressed his sympathy at the shattering of my hopes, but offered to " lay a wager that the doc. 'ud keep me 'anging around at the 'orspital for another two or three weeks." Unfortunately, " 'anging around " would mean postponing leave, which was due as soon as I returned to the battalion. The Lancashire lad then volunteered the priceless information that, if anyone had been eighteen months without leave he would get it at the base before rejoining his unit. It was, therefore, only natural that my enthusiasm for kicking my heels about at Etaples straightway diminished, and a frantic desire to get to Havre and then home seized me instead.

The sister seemed very upset when I informed her of the doctor's remarks and, after asking for full particulars of my period of service, stated that she would see the M.O. herself. The next day, although her mission had been fruitless, she offered me the choice of assisting in her ward for at least two months or taking up clerical work in the orderly-room for an indefinite period. I think that without difficulty I could have obtained the post of cook-house warden, bath-house steward, dressing-room assistant or canteen merchant, but where was

the inducement in even the most respectable of jobs unless I got my
leave first ? I thanked her kindly, but said that even the post of
barber-in-chief could not appeal to me under the circumstances, which
she quite understood.

On the 24th I asked the M.O. to mark me for the base, much to the
astonishment of the Soldiers' and Workmen's Soviet in " Chalk "
ward, where the same inmates that had been there when I arrived
showed every sign of remaining on long after my departure. Certainly nothing but the prospect of leave would have induced anyone to
curtail that holiday and hasten the rigours of discipline at the base
depot, especially with a Third Battle of Ypres looming up in the background. (Two or three men down from the salient had expressed the
opinion that the Messines affair was but a prelude to the big attack
that would take place shortly at Ypres, where all the signs of an
offensive were accumulating.)

The doctor acceded to my request and marked me " Convalescent
Camp," where I had to go whether I wanted to or not. Then followed
a twenty-four hours' process of inspections, baths, drawing clothing,etc.,
which brought my departure to the 25th, when a batch of us fell in
and waited about an hour for the arrival of a sergt.-major who
endeavoured to form us into two ranks, called the roll, and then gave
the order to " right turn." Nothing could be more slovenly than a
conglomeration of individuals from sundry units sauntering along
together—whether they were trooping down to the leave boat at
Boulogne or filing from one hospital to another at the base. Away
from one's unit, all smartness and desire to present a good appearance
vanished and it was difficult for those in charge of details to get much
marching or any other discipline out of the men.

This they endeavoured to do at the No. 6 Convalescent Camp,
which we reached after wandering through the precincts of a Portuguese
hospital and one or two other camps. It was the first step towards
the iron discipline of the base depot at Havre, for the attitude of
the authorities towards the troops changed immediately they got you
out of hospital " blues " and invested you with khaki.

To begin with we were put immediately on to a diet that is registered
for ever in a letter I wrote on the spot —

For Breakfast : One slice of bread and jam and a knob of cheese.

For Dinner : Bully and maconachie, followed by a filthy concoction of soppy biscuits and dates.

For Tea : One slice of bread and jam.

True, there were a Y.M.C.A. and a canteen where those with funds
could buy the remainder of their food, but the Army ought to have
provided convalescent troops with better nutrition than that. Every
one commenced to get " fed up " from the moment they got here.

Before breakfast we were taken for a march by a R.B. sergt.-
major, who led us out of the area of camps along some beautiful
wooded lanes. Here we caught one or two glimpses of wandering
couples—officers and nurses—who endeavoured to escape our notice.
But a party of details, with no respect for anybody, could hardly be
expected to look the other way and pretend they had noticed nothing.
Immediately they spotted one of these couples strolling along in the
thicket they raised a terrific, long drawn out " O-o-o-o-oh ! " followed
by the refrain of " Hullo ! who's your lady friend ? "

In the ordinary way one would stay on at this camp for ten days,
but the inadequate food and the way it was served up were enough

to make anyone ask to be sent on to the base : I think it was part of a deliberate plan to make one's return to the firing-line less bitter. I was not the only one that demanded to be sent straight to Havre ; the two men before me at any rate were expressing their sentiments in no uncertain terms and the doctor made no objection to our speedy transition ; this would take place on the following day.

After this parade there were physical drill and children's games, the latter being an innovation to bring an element of interest into the problem of getting fit and tough again. They were quite good fun, but to see " Old Bills " playing " Twos and Threes," " Passing the Skittle " and " Touched you Last," was simply ludicrous. I do declare they would have given us marbles if there had been time.

Next afternoon I amused myself on a new Broadwood piano in a privately-run recreation hut where a couple of dear old English dames, who evidently were in charge, came up when I had finished and wheezed : " Now you've got to give us your name and regiment and all your particulars. The Commandant said that when we found a pianist he would allow him to stay on at the camp."

What a tempting bait ! But what a one-eyed camp ! What friends should I ever make in that place where, week in and week out, new faces would come and others would disappear ? And by now I realised acutely that I should be like a fish out of water until I was back again with the section.

The two dear old dames at first thought me disobliging : and as I pitched a tale of woe saying that only a few days separated me from the realisation of my hopes of leave, their faces changed and they wished me " God speed " from the bottom of their melted hearts.

That night I crossed the railway line and entered the Base Details Camp, a collection of tents pitched on the sand-dunes. Next day our sole occupation was watching trainloads of French troops going north-wards, thereby confirming the rumours of a coming Flanders offensive. Finally they allocated the details to their respective bases—Havre, Rouen, etc.—and at 7 p.m. on the 27th, only ten days after leaving the L.R.B., I found myself in a cattle truck embarking on a sixteen hours' journey to the infantry base depot, my mind confused with memories of Arras, hospitals, convalescent and details camps, nurses, doctors and thousands of " Old Bills," all jumbled up together owing to the quick succession of events.

After spending a few days at the base depot, of which there will be something to record in the following chapter, my application for leave was granted, but owing to the proximity of submarines at Havre the route lay via Paris and Boulogne. One other fellow travelled with me—both of us blessed with first-class passenger train tickets—and after being jostled about for three days we eventually set foot on Blighty's shores. Folkestone was in a feverish state of excitement, trains were delayed and telegraphic communication interrupted. 'Twas the 7th of July, the occasion of a severe daylight bombing raid on London ! From a blissful seaside holiday I had been transferred into the midst of war's alarms and, paradoxical though it seemed, the farther I got from the firing-line the nearer came the sound of guns. For the home front got a bit of excitement too, and at the moment it was ablaze

CHAPTER XXIV.

BEHIND THE FRONT.

(*July–August, 1917.*)

Optimism and other things at home—Asinine antics at Abbeville—The infantry base depot—Discipline and training—How I left the base—Back again with the L.R.B.—The Third Battle of Ypres begins—We move into reserve.

A FEW days' leave from the front acted on one's spirits like a dose of Alpine air. Everyone at home seemed to possess such confidence in an early victory, such optimism in regard to even the most discouraging events, that after a few hours of their inspiriting talk one was apt to become as cheerful and unreasoning as they.

The folk on the home front may have had doubters in their midst, but they were not much in evidence in London or Kent, at any rate. It seemed as if the majority had been served out with rose-coloured spectacles through which every cloud appeared as blue-sky, every reverse a victory. To the cynic just returned from the Western Front this was at first rather riling (and nearly everyone was a cynic by now, at least if he had been in France a good time). The cynic knew that a fruitless attack by several divisions, relieved only by a small gain of ground at X, would be described as a " successful attack at X," with scant reference to the remainder of the front. The optimist at home merely read in the communique that there had been a " successful attack at X," put down his paper and beamed with delight.

Or the optimist might read : " Our pilots destroyed five enemy aeroplanes and forced ten to descend. Two of our machines are missing." At which he would make a simple calculation and joyfully exclaim that we were thirteen machines to the good on the day. The cynic had perhaps himself seen three of our machines brought down on the British side of the line, but he knew that as these were not " missing " they were not included in the reckoning : in other words, he drew no conclusions from the official announcement, which was misleading.

Likewise the man on the home front sometimes read that we had exploded an enemy dump at C, but he heard nothing of the many British dumps blown up. An incident like that at Achicourt was never reported in the papers, but the soldier in France knew all about it. Therefore he took our communiques with quite a bucketful of salt.

When I got home I found the optimists highly delighted with both the Arras and the French offensives : they believed that a smashing blow was about to be delivered which would break clean through the German line, making a gap for the cavalry who would gallop through and surround the bulk of the German Army. On July 11th, standing in our garden at home, we could hear a distant drum-fire which indicated an attack of some kind : it might be the next British offensive ! People said that the rumble had never been so distinct. It transpired that this was a German attack on the sand-dune positions recently taken over by the British on the coast, but the optimists—nothing daunted —found considerable consolation in the losses we must have inflicted on the enemy before retiring ! A great deal of the ever-cheerful attitude was due to the manipulation of the war news by the ingenious Press correspondents, who dwelt eternally on the slight losses incurred by our side and the appalling slaughter of the enemy : on the adroit success of every British trench-raid and the complete failure of every German attempt ; on the utter demoralisation of the enemy when it only existed in their perverted imaginations.

But after I had been home a few days I came to the conclusion that it was better so. It was preferable to have a hopeful, cheerful populace than a world of weeping Jeremiahs : it enabled them to endure their privations with less grumbling and goodness knows they had enough to harass them, with their air-raids, food queues and lighting restrictions. It was a good thing that the jaded warrior should return to find the folk at home still smiling : he preferred his friends to be happy than to see them depressed and glum.

Perhaps they were more elated than usual just at this moment. They had read of the arrival of a few boatloads of American soldiers in France, of the defeat of a strong German attack against the French ; and, above all, of the resumption of fighting on the Russian Front, where, after superhuman efforts, Kerensky had inspired the best troops to make an offensive. By the 14th of July they had captured 30,000 prisoners in a fortnight's fighting and the optimists regarded this flash in the pan as proof that the Steam-roller had emerged stronger than ever from the Revolution and was joining us in the culminating blow of the War. As a matter of fact, that day's paper contained the last piece of good news that was to come from that quarter.

Except for the occasional firing of anti-aircraft guns and the cruising of aeroplanes, the countryside surroundings were much the same as they had been in pre-war days. No Army lorries passed the little Kentish lane where we lived ; but for a few cyclists, billeted in the cottages around and enjoying years of training at home, you might have forgotten the existence of an army. Labourers worked in the fields, the baker came round with his bread as of yore, little children played with their tops and their skipping ropes. Was I not back in the summer of 1914, the victim of a hideous nightmare ?

No ! Several things told me I wasn't. In the first place, I could hardly frame a dozen sentences without wishing to introduce some word that would have offended the civilian ear. Conversation had not been such a strain in 1914 ! Then, again, it was rather a trial to attend a dinner party. The natural inclination was to reach out for whatever you wanted, take your plate on to your lap, peel potatoes with your hands and call out " Chuck us the bread " to your hostess. In 1914

I fancy I behaved rather better than that. As a civilian I had been a law-abiding citizen, but now I noticed a tendency to cross railway-lines contrary to regulations, to jump on the back of a milk-cart without permission if it meant getting to my destination quicker, and to regard all the neighbouring fields and woods as public property if they looked tempting for a stroll. There was also an inclination to feast one's eyes on every pretty girl one saw, almost to the extent of being impolite.

I called at the office as usual, to find them getting on splendidly without me : profits were better with their staff of girls and over-age men than they had been in pre-war days. This, as the manager said to me with a smile, was scarcely an incentive to the company to be impatient for the demobilisation of its young men. I also saw Wood, who had recovered from his Somme wound, and bid fair to instruct recruits in musketry until the end of the War.

Before returning once more to France, there were the usual purchases to make, *e.g.*, khaki shirts, black rifleman's buttons (which were not provided by the Q.M.S.), Fox's putties, nickle spurs, etc. I also bought a pair of knutty whipcord riding-breeches, knowing that if I got back to the battalion it would take the Q.M.S. at least two months to replace the trousers I had received at hospital. Finally, I provided myself with ample funds to place between myself and starvation at the base when I got back.

It was a terrible wrench to quit home again and a great temptation to over-stay my leave seized me. But base A.P.M.s had an awkward way of enforcing the strict letter of Army law to the extent of shooting you at dawn for desertion, and it was not worth while running such a risk for the sake of a few hours' fleeting pleasure.

In the blazing heat on the afternoon of the 17th, I climbed up the steep hill to the leave camp at Boulogne with thousands of others as silent as myself. It was very different to the time when we had sung popular songs amidst a throng of onlookers at Rouen in January, 1915. Even as far back as that the cavalrymen had laughed when we had shouted, " Are we downhearted ? " " But you —— well soon will be," they had replied. Now, nobody raised the cry, nobody sang, no crowd gathered to watch us ; processions like ours passed to and fro every day and we were not particularly beautiful.

My train started at ten o'clock that night, but after a few hours journey all those for Rouen, Havre and such places had to alight at Abbeville. Here we shouldered our packs and were marched off by an unknown person to an unknown destination. First we turned north, then east, then south across the railway, continuing for nearly a mile at the double, and finally bent back until we got to Abbeville station again. It was merely an Army device for taking us to a Y.M.C.A. hut without crossing six sets of metals in an unofficial place !

Our next train was not due to leave until the following night and for this reason we were confined to the hut for the whole day, not being allowed to stroll outside on any pretext lest we miss the train. Most of the time was spent in queues at the counter, where a brown fluid which might have been tea or cocoa was served out at a penny (10 cents) per mug.

Would that the same supervision had been extended to us when the time came to resume our journey that night ! I was lying on my kit on the dirty floor about ten o'clock, when everyone jumped up and started putting on his equipment. Apparently somebody had ordered a move, for there was a general exodus on the railway line, whither I followed the contingent in the darkness. After crossing several sets of metals we came alongside a train that loomed up out of the night and the next thing I discerned was men clambering on to the footboards and getting in wherever they could ; where the train was going to or who gave the order to entrain not a soul knew. Following suit, I hopped on to the footboard and, after falling over my rifle, swung a carriage door open. Immediately a chorus of sleepy voices shouted out with one accord :

"There's no room in 'ere. We ain't got room for you 'ere ! Then the door was pulled to and firmly held.

My next attempt was not more fortunate.

"Get out of-it. Ain't we got enough —— men and kits in 'ere already ? "

"Well, I must get in somewhere."

"Then troi the froont," another chimed in. "There's plenty room oop there."

By this time nearly everyone seemed to be aboard. One or two were scurrying along, but the rest had evidently found seats. At this moment fortune guided my steps to a carriage full of Anzacs of whom I enquired if there was any space. To my astonishment one of them opened the door.

"Well, we're pretty full up. There's eleven of us in here. But, damn it all, we'll make room for you somehow. Hand us your kit and rifle, chum. Mind Jim's legs. Hey there, Sammy, we can make room for one more on this side, eh ? Move up a bit."

Thereafter I was absolutely in clover until we got to Havre.

* * * *

The population of Havre infantry base depot seemed to be equally divided between the reinforcements (anxious to stay away from the firing-line as long as possible when they arrived from hospital), and the permanent base-wallahs who shared that desire but seemed intent on converting the others to a different frame of mind. The object they sought to attain was to convince the details that life at the base depot was a far more unbearable hell than the firing-line could ever be. The means used to achieve this object were the strictest discipline, the maximum of work, the minimum of freedom, and an extraordinary low scale of rations.

The discipline was of the good old Aldershot type, with special corporals' messes to prevent infection from the ranks, big orderly room staffs for dealing with everything from religion returns to toe-nail parades, and strict orders against doing most things one would like to do. If one had the time or energy to go into Havre, one had to apply for a pass three days beforehand, and on arrival there one could scarcely get out of sight of military policemen who enforced the letter of the law in regard to correctness of dress, boundaries, estaminets, etc.

Breakfast was at 5.45 a.m., and at 7 or 7.30 all those eligible for infantry drill were fallen in and marched to the Pimple, a vast training ground where everything from platoon work to open order skirmishing and bayonet fighting was practised daily in the blazing heat by thousands and thousands of men. Two biscuits and a piece of cheese were carried by each man, this being the sole nourishment afforded him until 5.30 or 6 o'clock at night, when he returned. I cannot be certain of the latter hour, but remember that a tea-supper was provided. Every convalescent man was supposed to go through a three weeks' course of this drill before returning to his unit, and by the end of that time he was usually very thankful to leave. It was this drastic treatment that led to the troops getting out of hand a month or two later at one or two base depots, resulting, among other damage, in the destruction of their training grounds. These incidents led to a considerable amelioration of their conditions, including better food.

It was necessary to spend most of the evening waiting in a queue outside the Expeditionary Force Canteen, where no foodstuffs could be obtained before 4 p.m. The first few hundred men in the line consisted of those who, for countless reasons, were not included in the Pimple contingent and these started to form up at three o'clock, so great was the rush for food. The average wait in the evening was an hour from the moment you took your place in the queue, which gives some idea of the necessity for amplifying the Army issue : most fellows were bent on procuring tinned stuffs and packets of chocolate and biscuits to keep them from practically starving the next day between 6 a.m. and eventide. There was scarcely a private in the camp who was not spending the whole of his meagre earnings in this endeavour to procure enough to live upon, though the N.C.O.s in their messes were not, I believe, in a similar plight.

There was a special London Division base camp, in which each battalion had its particular line of tents : incidentally, I found myself placed in charge of a tent, being senior rifleman present, a position which involved a great deal of extra work without any compensations. Nearly all the L.R.B. men in the camp were from the 2nd Battalion, and I recognised several I had known at Hayward's Heath. They had not come out to France until the previous January, but had very soon tasted something of war in the various battles that had raged on our right around Bullecourt : here they had had a bad time of it, most of those in the L.R.B. lines now being recovered wounded cases from that affair. One or two 1st Battalion men had come down here also, and I learnt from them that the division was undergoing training.

One of the first persons I met here was " Elsie " Collins, the old Devils' Mess member, who had left us at Magnicourt, in April, 1916, and got to Blighty with measles. He was now on his way out again with a draft, hoping to get to the 1st Battalion, though no special pleading would induce the Authorities to grant a man's request if it meant departing from red-tape regulations. The recruiting promise that a man should join up and serve with his pals had long since been repudiated, and they split up parties of friends in a most ruthless manner when it could easily have been avoided. A few days before, I was informed, about sixteen L.R.B. men had their badges removed and been drafted to various other battalions, principally the Westminsters ; at the same time, several Westminsters had to give in their badges, many of them ending up in the L.R.B.

Fortunately for me, it transpired that a regulation was now in force whereby a man, returned from hospital, should remain on the roll of his unit. Evidently the Army Records were getting rather irritated at the enormous amount of transferring entailed by the brainless behaviour at the base. I therefore donned my new riding breeches and applied to return to the regiment as a driver. This promptly brought a hornets' nest about my ears. Within half an hour the Sergt.-Major had marched me into the Q.M. Store, awakened the Q.M.S. and pointed out Army Order XYZ 1746837, Sub-section K 10, which stated that any man, infantry, found wearing breeches, riding, was to hand them in at once—this order was to be read out at reveillé, after breakfast, just before lights out and at other stated times. Having read this to me, he ordered me to strip forthwith. My statement that I was a transport driver left him cold : they didn't recognise drivers at the base and were disinclined to believe those who said their jobs were being kept open for them. Very likely it was only an L.R.B. man who could make such a statement with confidence ! However, when they realised that the breeches were private property and had brought themselves to realise also that I might possibly be telling the truth, they retired as gracefully as they could from the scene, enabling me to make a dignified exit down the steps.

My application to leave the base was, however, hung up and it now seemed worth making an attempt to escape the three weeks' course of drill at the Pimple by a little bit of bamboozling. As Figg had once remarked to me : " The way to get on most comfortably in the Army is to appear a fool. It will get you out of all sorts of trouble." Self-respect forbade this course in the battalion, but at the base I was one of a million, so I determined to appear unconversant with drill and got the first opportunity when on guard the night after our arrival. As regards appearance, what with brilliantly polished boots, Fox's putties, new breeches and tunic and a badge on which nearly a tin of cleaning powder had been expended, I determined to outshine even the Sergeant-Major. But when it came to changing guard I proceeded to make an ass of myself, not that this was a difficult matter, since I had done no ceremonial drill for two years ; had I tried my hardest to prove efficient no doubt my efforts would have justified a reprimand. As it was, the guard turned out a fiasco. The smartly-dressed man nearly poked the officer's eye out when " porting arms." He took a step forward when he ought to have gone to the rear. He shouldered arms instead of sloping them. He presented arms to a lieutenant and came to attention for the Camp Commandant. Finally, he called out the guard by mistake and omitted to do so when the General passed.

The result was a feverish enquiry by the O.C. Camp, as the result of complaints received, from which he gleaned that the miscreant was a driver to whom all such ceremonial was Double Dutch ; that he would require weeks of special drilling before he could be fitted for the more complicated gyrations on the Pimple ; that the L.R.B. were pining for his return ; and that the simplest policy would be to pack him off with the very next divisional draft. This decision was speedily made, much to the delight of Collins, who had hatched the plot. Figg's maxim was undoubtedly a good one ; but I preferred the motto : " Nothing venture, nothing have."

The newspapers which arrived every day were readily bought, in order to see whether the expected push in the north had yet taken place. But we only learnt that there had been a tactical Russian withdrawal, followed by rioting in Petrograd. On the 20th we read that the Germans had pierced the Russian positions and next day that certain troops had refused to fight. On the 23rd the enemy were at the gates of Tarnopol. The Russian communique itself said the troops were " on the whole not showing the necessary stability whilst elsewhere they were not fulfilling the military commands." In other words, some of them had laid down their arms, walked away from the front and abandoned their artillery and military stores to the Germans. Cheerful news ! What hopes of peace being signed before the fourth winter of the War ? What would not Germany be able to do with all her Russian prisoners and guns and the products of the territories she would occupy ? It could not bear thinking of for long : it left us grousing and irritable.

Then came the call for reinforcements for our division, when some hundreds of infantry and artillerymen were warned for draft. There were some, no doubt, who required a further three weeks' course to make them so nauseated with these surroundings that they were glad to depart ; but the permanent base-wallahs had succeeded in converting the majority of them into the required frame of mind— sheer relief to get away at last ! Before going, I said " Good-bye " to Collins, who was destined to go to the 2nd Battalion (his plea that he was an original 1914 1st Battalion man having been treated with disdain). Then we fell in, listened to the admonitions of the base Chaplain and the Commandant for a quarter of an hour, and finally set off on a march of some four miles to the Havre Docks with the Sergeant-Major's " Up you go and the best of luck ! " ringing in our ears.

*   *   *   *

After three days of wandering, during which we were taken past Dunkirk and to all sorts of weird places in an endeavour to locate our division, whose whereabouts nobody knew, we at length reached the 56th Divisional Reinforcement Camp, situated between Audruicq and St. Omer. Here I met Major Burnell, who, after spending a couple of months as O.C. L.R.B. during Col. Husey's temporary absence, had now assumed command of this depot. He allowed me to leave the next morning, and after a three or four mile walk I eventually found myself in the midst of the good old L.R.B. at the village of Bayenghem.

Howls of laughter greeted my arrival at the transport lines, the reason being apparently that I was so smart as to be almost unrecognisable. Accustomed to seeing my boots and putties a mass of mud, my knees sticking through my breeches and several grease-spots on my tunic, they now peered at my new rig-out in sheer amazement. Having heard that I was in England, they assumed that I had gone across from hospital and would not rejoin them. Consequently a new man had been taken on in my place, who was, however, retained as the section was short-handed now that leave was progressing. Nearly all my possessions had been thrown away, owing to the difficulty of carrying them about and the impossibility of commandeering a motor lorry for the purpose, and among other things I lost underclothes, sweater, handkerchiefs, grooming kit and my entire chemist's shop. However, the Devils' Mess had done what they could to smuggle along my blanket, mackintosh and " British Warm," which they now unearthed from odd corners.

Mr. Gordon was away for a few days, which I considered fortunate, since he had taken advantage of one or two drivers going on leave to give their pairs to someone else and put them on to other jobs, stating that everyone had got into a groove and he thought the change would be beneficial. Most of the drivers affected also thought it beneficial since, as I mentioned before, their job was becoming less popular as the " Spit and Polish " standard became more exacting. At the moment my feelings had not got to that stage owing to the special kindergarten standard that was laid down in my own particular case, hence my joy to receive my pair back again. In Gordon's absence Sergt. Simmonds was not making any changes and so I took over The

Grey and Jumbo, thereby giving an extra lease of life to Conibeer's prediction that we should always remain " a ridiculous and senseless trio."

On picket the next night Figg gave me an account of the section's experiences since I had left the lines near the observation balloon at Beaurains. Eventually they had obtained permission to move their camp further back and took up a position at Achicourt, indulging in sports of various kinds in the evening when the battalion had come out of the line. After this the battalion had gone in for hard training at Sombrin, where brigade sports were held. Our section did very well, winning the N.C.O.s' turn-out and coming second in the mules and Maltese cart entries ; whilst our variety friend, Trooper Shelley, came third in the mule race. When the magnificent prize-money was given out there was an evening of great revelry ; even Eustace, the Q.M.'s batman, opened his heart and gave away a pair of leggings. From there they had gone to Le Souich, entrained for Wizernes, spent a night at St. Martin's, a suburb of St. Omer, and eventually reached their present abode, where they had now been four days.

Bayenghem was situated about thirty miles from the Ypres front and nobody had the least doubt but what the great offensive was imminent and we were to take part in it at an early date. There were all the familier signs of preparing for the fray. Limbers had been painted and repaired, respirators examined, equipment polished, iron rations replenished, new identity discs reindented for ; the divisional band came to play in the village street to make glad the heart of man. The only question was, When would we take part and how long should we be kept up there ?

To the east there was a perpetual rumble which had been going on for some days. No reference was made to it in the British communiqués, but the German ones had plenty to say :

    23/7/17 " . . . The artillery battle in Flanders continues with undiminished intensity."

    24/7/17 " . . . intensity never hitherto reached."

    25/7/17 " . . . most extreme intensity."

    27/7/17 " Artillery battle continues."

    28/7/17 " Drumfire again commenced."

    28/7/17 " The development of intensity represents the highest degree of massed effect in the War."

It was the preparatory drumfire for the great attack. All day long as we rode to the watering-place or attended to our work the dull rumble kept our thoughts continually on what was happening in the Ypres salient. I wondered if the place where we had buried our ammunition on May 3rd, 1915, had remained undisturbed by all this shell-fire, whether the little crucifix remained on the Weiltje-Passchendaele road and the graves of Pepper, Tucker, and many others would be found again as we had once left them. No doubt all those places would be in our hands again and we might see the spot where we had first dug in. . . . But our taste of the battle was destined to be a short sharp one and the thrill of returning to the north-east of Ypres was never to be ours.

At dawn on July 31st the bombardment reopened with such intensity that there was no doubt it signified the commencement of the battle. The weather did not seem propitious for it, as the sky had recently been overcast and there had been showers the night before. In the afternoon the rain started in real earnest and continued to fall in sheets throughout the evening. We waited eagerly for news of the operations, but only learnt that the British and French had attacked north and east of Ypres. There were many disgusted comments upon the break in the weather, for, knowing the Ypres neighbourhood as we did, it was obvious that any attack would be dislocated and held up by mud after several hours' rain. It was the most unfortunate thing that could have occurred and it really seemed that the weather controllers were invariably on the enemy's side. When August 1st broke also a miserable soaking wet day, everyone's disappointment was intense. Thereafter it proceeded to rain without ceasing for four days and nights, thus effectively damning the whole of the operations at the outset. Everyone swore hard. We had to move our own horse-lines on the 2nd to the next village, Monnecove, as our field was flooded out. (My smartness had disappeared already and I was recognisable as my muddy self once again.)

The papers of the 3rd showed that, with the French on our left, we had captured Langemarck, Pilkem, and had advanced to the outskirts of St. Julien, with three thousand five hundred prisoners. In fact our front line was now somewhere beyond the hamlet of Fortuin, where we had dug in upon that first night at Ypres. The position where our enfiladed trench had been on the second, third and fourth nights was still in German hands. Further south, by the Menin road, progress had been difficult. Hooge and Sanctuary Wood were captured, but Glencorse Wood and Inverness Copse on the heights by the Menin road had proved insuperable barriers and there we had not gone as far forward as in the north.

It was evident without reading the papers that the whole of this area would now be a gigantic marsh, moving guns and ammunition a terrible task, and ration trips a most trying experience. Artillery observation and flying were almost impossible. Meanwhile the roads through the salient were no doubt choked with traffic and liberally sprinkled with high explosives. The British and French were holding an irregular line consisting of shell-holes nearly full of water.

For a day or so we carried on the work of the section in a state of preparedness for a sudden order to move, only taking certain necessaries off the vehicles and reducing our impedimenta as much as possible. We got our instructions on the 5th, on which day the bulk of the transport trekked eastwards, while the cookers moved down to St. Omer station in the early morning hours of the 6th in order to entrain there with the companies at nine o'clock.

It was like old times to see the town again. There was the site of the camp that had been our H.Q. in lines of communication days. We passed the hospital I had once visited, the canal where some of us had unloaded coal, the siding we had guarded. We saw the estaminets with the same girls at the doors—two years older and by now fluent speakers of English—the familiar storekeepers with the same old wares—also two years older and double the price ! Finally we came to the station yard itself, now more active than in bygone days when we had left there by a sleepy old passenger train to go on leave and on sundry other missions in June, 1915.

After getting the horses and vehicles on board the train, we rushed to a hostel for refreshment and then started off three hours late, sitting at the open doors of the cattle-trucks, thoroughly fascinated with the whole itinerary. For what regiment in the British Army has not that little bit of railway line to Ypres the most vivid associations ? St.

Omer, Ebblinghem and Hazebrouck, the big junction where we had seen
the motor ambulances passing down in an endless procession from the
Second Battle of Ypres ; Caestre, where Chrisp, Trendell, Harbord and I
had spent August, 1915, cleaning up the station yard and having rows
with the R.A.M.C. corporal—where also Zoé, of tender memories, used
to take the morning train to Hazebrouck, arrayed in her best ;
Godearsvelde, the station where we had entrained in February, 1916,
when we had last left the salient, hoping it would be for good ; the Mont
des Cats on the right of the railway, with the monastery on top, from
which I had once looked down on Ypres, Kemmel, Bailleul and Armentières. Another mile or so would have brought us to Poperinghe, but
since our last visit to these parts a new railhead had been erected
a mile west of the town, to relieve the traffic and probably to avoid
shelling. To our great relief—since Poperinghe was, after all, Poperinghe !—our train pulled up at a siding here and we were invited to hop
out. The station was appropriately named " Hopoutre," but whether
this was a Flemish jaw-breaker or an army witticism we were never
able to discover. A heavily laden hospital train passed us on its way
down, bearing the inevitable wastage from the salient and striking
something of a chill to our hearts. The future was hidden for us.
If only we could draw the curtain aside for a moment !

In the middle of the afternoon we were all clear and formed up
on the cinder-paved platform, ready to depart. Shortly afterwards
we filed off on to the famed Poperinghe road where, to our joy (although
it was only postponing the evil hour), the column moved to the left,
that is, in the opposite direction to Ypres. We continued down the
road for a mile or so, yet not one fraction of it could I recognise as the
same highway we had traversed in 1915, when motor-'buses had
hurried us over this same ground in the direction of St. Omer. Now,
there were hundreds of wooden shanties lining the road, occupied
by Belgian refugees, every one of whom was advertising " Cocolate,"
" Egs," and " Cafce " for the troops.

When we got to Abeele we struck northwards on the Watou road
and turned off down a muddy track, galloping through seas of slush
where the A.S.C. wagons inevitably got stuck, sent up the S.O.S. and
settled down to drown. We were in a typical Flanders area where the
billets were farms—miles from any shops or canteens and surrounded by
an almost impassable flooded waste. This was the place where we
joined the remainder of the transport upon August 6th, the section
sharing a barn with about two dozen fowls. From the noise they
kicked up it would appear that they were the original and lawful
owners and their protests became so loud in the early morning that
nearly everyone hurled mugs, boots and other missiles at the rowdy
roosters. The civilian owners of the farm, as one might expect in these
parts, were surly and resentful. As if we were out here for a bean-
feast, deliberately choosing to live with their live-stock and sleep on
their smelly straw ! As if we were occupying their filthy barn for the
love of the thing ! We were no happier than they—we, who were far
from our homes and would shortly be enduring Hell at Ypres. The
least these mercenary old peasants could do was to be grateful to the
British for keeping the Germans from their doors.

Colonel Husey came up in a day or so and called an immediate
parade, at which there was much speculation as to what was in the
air. It turned out to be gas, or rather the probability of it, for the
Colonel—after a few warm words of greeting to the section for whom

he always had a kind spot in his heart—proceeded to deliver a lecture upon the dangers of a new form of German devilry. I think he referred to mustard gas or else a specially diabolical form of it, which the enemy were using with great liberality upon the back areas. It burnt the lungs, it burnt under the arms and in other parts of the body, it rendered your eyes temporarily useless if slight and completely blind if severe. The chief danger was that you could come into contact with it without suspecting it, for the effects might not be noticeable for hours. For instance, an unsuspecting platoon might come along and sit down near the spot where these shells had burst, with the result that a few hours afterwards every man in the platoon would find nothing left of the seat of his breeches and the ability to sit down would be denied him for many a long day! The number of casualties the Army had suffered from the effects of gas in the last few months had rendered it necessary to warn the troops of its dangers and insist upon proper precautions. The advice was probably prompted by the large number of men who became slightly affected and seriously reduced the trench strength of battalions for weeks at a time; some of these cases, it was thought, might be deliberately incurred to obtain a few weeks' rest from the firing-line, and the authorities evidently wanted to " put the wind up " us. They succeeded quite well, and our general state of perturbation was not diminished by a series of nightly air-raids on the Abeele aerodrome, one of the side-shows of the neighbourhood at no great distance from our farm.

The weather was warm now, and, though it rained a bit on the 8th and 9th, there were fine spells in between. Distant rumblings came from the Ypres direction, but, with the exception of a local battle on the 10th, there was nothing to indicate any renewal of the general offensive. It would now take weeks of this weather to make the ground as it should be, and, according to the papers, everything was at a standstill. Haig's disappointment must have been extreme. The opportunity that he had been preparing for all these months was snatched out of his hand by the caprice of the weather; instead of having a sultry August, as in the three previous years, the month was as abnormal as it possibly could be, and in another three months the campaigning season would be over. Already the Germans were stiffening their defences, bringing reinforcements and large quantities of captured artillery from the Russian front, where our gallant allies had walked or run back from fifty to eighty miles in three weeks. In Flanders, if we were going to make a success of our offensive, no time must be lost. . . . We should be in the next stage of it. This juncture was the exact equivalent to our halt at Corbie on our way to the Somme : we were in army (or corps ?) reserve. The move when it came might be another sudden one, but we were not well prepared for it. Cookers were in widely separated billets, Lewis-gun limbers were similarly distributed, other vehicles were unloaded, our own kit was scattered broadcast.

This was the position on the 11th of August. And at 1 p.m., just as we were about to begin our dinner, Colonel Husey calmly walked up and announced that we were to be on the Abeele road in half an hour !

CHAPTER XXV.

THE THIRD BATTLE OF YPRES.

(*August*, 1917.)

Remarkable changes—A warm reception—Transport work at Ypres—A trip to Sanctuary Wood—Casualties—Unwelcome aerial activity—The attack of August 16th—A pack-pony trip—A succession of disappointments and the result.

IT was just such a panic move as that at Corbie. But then, at least, there was time to finish dinner, while this time our sumptuous repast had to be abandoned, which was heartbreaking in the extreme. As it was, all the cookers were half an hour late and a regular scramble ensued. With the utmost difficulty we waded through the flooded areas, passed through Abeele, and then followed an unfamiliar route to the right of the Poperinghe Road.

Presently we struck a track which was in a deplorable condition, but we managed to keep going, and eventually crossed the main Poperinghe-Reninghulst road, trekking over the same ground where we had spent the winter of 1915. The change was really remarkable. In place of the old muddy transport fields and narrow roads there were railway-sidings, dumps, stables and wide tracks, while the number of camps had increased considerably. The amount of traffic was always large in this sector, but now there seemed to be thousands more lorries : light railways crossed the roads in several places. At one spot where I remembered an open field, there was an enormous R.E. dump with a railway line where dozens of Chinese coolies were unloading planks of wood, duck-boards, etc. Even at Ouderdom, which had once been a comparatively quiet village on our firing-line trips, there was now a big railway siding with a camouflaged railway gun waiting in it, while the whole area had been completely transformed by vast camps of Nissen huts extending up to the La Clytte-Dickebusch road. All these preparations must have been made during June and July, and there had admittedly been no attempt to conceal them, for it would have been a hopeless task. To concentrate the attacking divisions with their supplies in the exposed flat country around Ypres necessitated using every available square yard of space, regardless of German shelling and aerial activity.

The battalion entered a huge farm near Ouderdom where the trans-

port pitched wagon- and horse-lines in the open ; as there was no
official billet for the transport section, we chanced the consequences and
appropriated an empty loft to our use. Here Greene and I were
detailed for picket and, losing the toss, incurred the middle shift from
ten o'clock, and when I turned out discovered the first pair without
a picket lamp.

" The shout, ' All lights out ! ' came along an hour ago," they said.
" There are Fritzes about." This was our first experience of intensified
aerial warfare, hardly a minute passing during the four hours' vigil
without the sound of whirring in the heavens around us, most of which
came from our own squadrons, while the peculiar note of the German
type could frequently be heard. Bombs were dropped over by Dickebusch, Vlamertinghe and Ypres, foretelling a nervy and sleepless
existence during our sojourn up here. The gunfire was continuous and
the whole sky was bright with flashes.

This stage in the game was the exact counterpart of the Happy
Valley on our move to the Battle of the Somme. In precisely the same
way as formerly we hung about all day on the 12th waiting to move
off in the evening. The chaplain announced a communion service and,
looking through a window in the farm, I caught a glimpse of it—
there was only one communicant there, his batman. When evening
came on the move took place, the brigade moving up to the vicinity
of a white chateau nearer Ypres, whither many of the transport
journeyed with Lewis-guns, medical stores, rations, water and tools.
They made the acquaintance of Dickebusch and the Café Belge cross-
roads on the way and found the neighbourhood beyond there thickly
dotted with big guns, sufficient proof for the poor horses that their
masters never intended to keep them away permanently from these
regions of flashes and bangs. Having no forward lines to go to,
the section continued to occupy the same field, passing a somewhat
disturbed night in the pilfered loft.

The following morning, however, another transport arrived and
claimed our pitch, whereas we had no orders to move, and the rival
units groused, swore and raved at one another for an hour or so. Possession was nine points of the law, but eventually our moving order
arrived, so the prize had to be given up, to the huge delight of the
Scotties who had disputed it. With as good a grace as possible we
packed up our belongings and followed Sergt. Simmonds, who was not
looking at all confident that he would find our new site, but nevertheless led us serenely down the La Clytte-Dichebusch road. On either
side of this dozens of artillery and other horse-lines occupied every
patch of land, while Dickebusch itself was thronged with a continuous
stream of horse and motor traffic going in both directions, but, as it had
been heavily shelled, the shops and civilians had disappeared. No
doubt the old lady who used to serve us here with coffee, while we were
waiting for darkness to fall, was now sitting by the stove in the house
of her daughter's second cousin's great-stepfather whose family was
now sharing a room with others in one of the dwellings on the
Poperinghe road.

Suddenly a low-flying aeroplane opened machine-gun fire on the
traffic, so we had to duck and make ourselves as small as possible on
our horses' backs. Then a British Lewis-gun started firing almost at
my elbow, alarming The Grey even more than the first disturbance.
The German hit someone of another unit and there was a good deal
of confusion. In the midst of it, Simmonds, whose directions had not

been of the explicit order, became convinced that we should have turned off to the left in the village, so we joyfully wheeled round at the first available opportunity.

No wonder our new site was difficult to find! It consisted of a few score square yards of bare field, sandwiched in between dozens of other transports about half a mile west of Dickebusch, and could only be approached by a track across two crowded fields. In this space, where there was scarcely room to swing a cat, the whole brigade had to draw up its limbers, rig up its horse-lines and build Q.M. stores, forage huts, cook-houses and bivvies. There were no trenches to occupy—had there been we should have been happier—and the frail bivvies we erected, consisting merely of our groundsheets, were not only useless in the event of bomb-dropping, but hopeless for keeping out rain; in the next day or so there were violent thunderstorms, during which spouts of water poured in upon us.

On the afternoon of the 14th I went with Lieut. Pocock (an L.R.B. company officer temporarily attached to Brigade H.Q.) in search of a divisional ammunition column on the Dickebusch road, from which a supply of hand-grenades had to be drawn and taken to our brigade horse-lines. The job was quite straightforward when we succeeded in finding the place, but this took so long that I returned at the end of the third journey too late to join the ration convoy. When I was loading for the third time a German aeroplane dropped bombs on the artillery lines in the next field, although it was still daylight, and I began to think Pocock had had designs on my life in sending me there! After this the Bosches, determined to give us no peace, commenced shelling on our left. Evidently a thoroughly unhealthy neighbourhood!

Drivers were taking their turns with the pack-men to lead ponies, as very few limber jobs were required, and for the next few days everybody had a very uncomfortable time. All the roads were shelled incessantly when you got east of Ypres and in places plank tracks had been constructed across the muddy wastes, but these were registered perfectly by the German guns which were sufficiently numerous to keep them also under continual harassing fire. Going across country was out of the question, owing to the number of shell-holes, and you could only trust to chance on the recognised routes. Certain localities —*e.g.*, Hell Fire Corner, Hooge, Dead Man's Corner, etc., were particularly strafed, and the Menin road was a sheer nightmare to every man that passed upon it. I only wish that in this record of our adventures it were possible to mention what every man individually performed, but the detailed experiences of each N.C.O. and man are unrecorded. If everyone on the section could put down the events he remembered, each would reveal something fresh in the way of excitement. Macloughlin, who was acting N.C.O., could give a perfectly true account of some adventurous trips up the Menin road that would make his people's hair stand on end; he subsequently got the M.M., as did Sergt. Simmonds. Conibeer, I know, had had some excitement that day in collecting empty Lewis-gun panniers from Sanctuary Wood, whither the battalion had proceeded. He had to load them himself under heavy shell-fire, leaving his mules three or four times in the process, and then cantered down Derby Track where the limbers in front and behind received direct hits and were lifted skywards while Coni was unscathed. But the worst of such stories is that people think you're "telling the tale" and letting your imagination run away from you in a craving for cheap glory; consequently these individual experiences remain untold, and it devolves on me to record soberly the brief adventures of Jumbo and The Grey and the happenings of our transport field.

The night of the 14th was a most disturbed one. We lay trembling half the time, listening to the leisurely drone of the enemy bombing-planes hovering above us as though they were searching for a particular target and did not mean to release their missiles of destruction until they had made sure of it. Suddenly a series of violent concussions would shake the earth, and the raider would make off, only to be followed by another one on a similar errand. Some fellows found it preferable to sit down outside their bivvies or wander about—to do something, anything, rather than lie still and wait in suspense. It was a sleepless night for everybody, but fortunately nothing worse.

The pack-pony convoy of the previous night had returned without hurt, but Lane, who had been acting as a guide to the rum dump, had not returned. It was suggested that he might be found at the rum dump itself, but we were most concerned about him, and two men were therefore sent off the next morning to scour the country astride the Menin road where he had last been seen.

At 7 a.m. one driver from each battalion was detailed to form part of a convoy of four limbers under Lieut. Pocock, the object being to carry hand-grenades to some place beyond Zillebeke in readiness for the offensive which was to be resumed on the morrow. Two Queen's Westminsters were to act as spare men, and an N.C.O. was detailed. The convoy set off after breakfast, and, after passing the Dickebusch Lake, called at a dump near the Café Belge for further supplies, as we were not fully loaded; this gave me ninety-six boxes for my limber— a fairly substantial load.

We followed the Ypres road farther than I had ever been before and soon took a well-constructed track to the right, passing one or two artillery convoys coming back from their umpty-umpth journey. We were now in the region of the "heavies," some of which were firing, but the gunners took more pains to conceal their whereabouts here than they had on the Somme, which accounted for the seemingly greater concentration in the former battle. The numerical strength here, though less obvious, was undoubtedly great, but as the German counter-battery and observation work was far more efficient on the present occasion it behoved the batteries to camouflage as much as possible.

We passed through two distinct heavy artillery zones and then, crossing the Comines Canal and the Kemmel road, struck eastward along the road to Hill 60.

Never on the Somme had I seen such an abomination of desolation as there was here. On all sides was the rack and ruin—not of three months'—but of two-and-a-half years' shelling. Only a mile ahead of us was the Hill 60 mound, the scene of countless struggles, from which point the enemy had looked down on Ypres (except for one brief spell in April, 1915) from November, 1914, till the recent Battle of Messines. It was the first time I had seen it. How on earth any living being existed between this priceless observation post and the shell of Ypres was incredible; how the British field guns massed here under the very noses of the Bosches and carried on their bombardment was even more of a mystery. Why, from the hill there the salient had been scourged with directed fire from the flank! A position more tactfully difficult to defend could not be imagined—yet the Germans had never set foot in Ypres.

On our left was the Zillebeke Lake and some little way beyond it on slightly higher ground ran the Menin road practically parallel with us. To the left rear was Ypres itself, a mass of ruins, while ahead was the battered village of Zillebeke, half a mile away. Little puffs of smoke on the rising ground beyond it denoted either our field guns firing or small shells bursting, but we were not left long in doubt, for it was soon obvious that most of our field guns had taken a morning off, and the Germans, who were fully aware that our attack was about to take place, were searching the whole of the artillery zone for their position. At the same time, this effective barrage was designed, of course, to hinder the transport of ammunition.

To either side were myriads of deep shell-holes, filled with water ; no tree existed that stood more than a few feet in height ; no five yards of the road but showed traces of recently filled-in shell-holes or pits that had not been touched. Everywhere there was a vile battle-field stench, chiefly caused by the bodies of dead horses ; in one spot a mule had apparently had a twelve-inch all to himself—we came across his head farther up the road ! One or two shells fell in the lake and some crumps landed on the Menin road.

Gradually the space between us and the strafed area diminished, and when we had passed through Zillebeke and were mounting the hill towards Hell Fire Corner, we were on its very fringe. One's legs began to tingle, and a longing to turn back, or, at any rate, abandon the horses and fall in the ditch, was no doubt present in every man's mind. We clapped our helmets on tighter and had trouble with the digestion of our breakfasts ; a tight feeling gripped one round the chest and a craving for a stimulant arose, varying according to different tastes.

Pocock, however, calmly led the way up on to the high ground and struck off across a track to the right, leading to Sanctuary Wood, which was a little way ahead. Here we found ourselves in a most exposed position in the very heart of the strafe ; not a sunken road nor a mound was there to afford us cover. In fact, far away in the distance we could clearly see some woods which must have been the Glencorse and Polygon positions in German hands. The shells were not heavy stuff—merely those jolly little fellows that came singing past one's ear and made holes the size of a packing-case, but they were nevertheless exceedingly unpleasant, for no sooner had one whine concluded with its inevitable " Pop " than another whistle came out of the Beyond. The fact that my load was bombs was of more consequence to me than the size of the Jennies. A subject for a Bairns-father cartoon might have been two drivers waiting by their limbers under shell-fire, one looking reasonably cheerful ; the other terrified out of his wits. Cheery One : " Whatcher lookin' so blinkin' un'appy about, Bill ? " Bill : " Yus, you can ——— well stand there an' laugh wiv a load er warty-cans. Moi limber's full of ——— bombs ! "

The track we were following was not only muddy, but dotted with shell-holes, and only the fact that we kept moving prevented us from sinking dangerously and perhaps getting stuck. However, Pocock unfortunately had to halt us while he located the exact spot for dumping the bombs, and the limbers before me suddenly pulled up short, leaving my back wheel in a shell-hole. Knowing Jumbo's failing, my heart sank within me as rapidly as the rear-half sank into the ground ;

the mischief was done. When the two front limbers moved on again, sure enough Jumbo's heart failed him, and he leant back hard in his breeching while The Grey, finding it impossible to shift the load, just stood rooted to the spot, petrified with fright. The Queen Vic.'s man was in a similar dilemma several yards behind, but I couldn't see him.

Endeavouring to coax the horses forward with endearing names and tugs at their nose-bands was no more efficacious than sitting on top of them—using spurs and whip. Standing broadside on to the firing-line, they preferred to offer themselves up as a sacrifice and resigned themselves to their fate. Their driver was not so heroic, his one desire being to get back home again, and the wild swear-words he used revealed the full extent of his wind-up. His heart now left his boots and leapt to his mouth; would that the phlegmatic horses had shown such animation! The Grey, instead of putting forward a supreme effort, inspired by panic, had gone right past that stage to one of utter helplessness, terror-struck with the noise.

The most obvious solution is not necessarily the first that comes to one's mind when excited, which possibly explains why for the moment I took the idiotic course of trying to dig the wheel out. The spare-men had gone on, but I borrowed a shovel from a man behind a barricade and frantically worked at clearing away the sticky mud round the axle of the wheel, knowing that the horses could not run away in the meantime. But its futility was soon apparent, for after a few minutes' labour the wheel looked as firmly embedded as ever. Just then, the other two limbers cantered by, empty, on their way home, the drivers grinning at my plight and shouting advice to unhook the horses and depart. The dump was a hundred yards ahead.

Only then did the saner course of unhooking the rear-half and taking the front half forward alone suggest itself to me; relieved of the incubus, the horses leapt forward with delight and reached the dump in a series of mad plunges, The Grey setting the pace of the war-dance to which Jumbo somewhat reluctantly conformed. There was not a soul at the dump. In various dug-outs ahead, some poor wretched infantry were crouching, awaiting a dead-hit on their thin roofing, but they could hardly be expected to come out and assist a driver who was, after all, but a temporary visitor up there; they had got to endure it for the rest of the day. The two Q.W.R. men were nowhere to be seen, and as for the N.C.O. of the convoy, it transpired that he had already been packed off to the rear with an attack of nerves. Lieut. Pocock, it is only fair to add, had his hands full elsewhere—helping the Q.V.R. driver, I believe. Therefore, down with the tail-board and out with the forty-five boxes of bombs into the nearest shell-hole, "beaucoup" wind-up on the part of the unloader, who had never worked so frantically before, and many curses directed at the heads of the fatigue men who had quitted the scene so abruptly.

The horses cantered back gladly to the rear-half, but it turned out to be a sheer impossibility to hook it on again without assistance, though Jumbo and The Grey consented to be " backed " several times in making this attempt. It therefore became necessary to dump the remaining boxes by the shell-hole where we had stuck, and although the horses could easily have bolted with the empty front-half during this process, by a lucky chance they stood perfectly still. One or two shells had come very close to us, and as soon as the unloading was complete I went round to look at the horses, both of whom, I was sick to find, had been wounded. Jumbo's wound was slight, but The Grey was smothered in blood from his shoulder to his foot ; the blood gushing out so quickly that it became imperative to get him away at once to a place where the wound could be bound up. A minute later, fortunately, Pocock arrived, and I was therefore able to get the rear-half hooked on. It was his first transport trip up the line and he prayed God it would be his last, but this in no way implied that he wished to be struck dead on the spot. He bade me flee from the benighted place, and, needless to say, I fled.

The Grey, in spite of his wound, cantered with Jumbo over the rough track to the road, and not until we started to descend to Zillebeke did he give any sign of trouble. Then the poor old beast started to limp badly, and it was a cruelty to ride him a moment longer than necessary. As soon as we got through the village, therefore, I drew the limber up at the side of the road and endeavoured to bandage him up, which was a difficult matter, while he watched me reproachfully with his great big eyes. Then I changed the horses round, putting the saddle on Jumbo's back, which was only slightly scratched ; his harness was broken, but it had saved him from a bad wound.

For the remainder of the journey home Jumbo pulled the weight of the empty limber, enabling The Grey to limp along beside him without working. It was a pathetic sight to see the old horse, of whom I had grown to be very fond, bleeding profusely and suffering pain, and my conscience smote me for having spurred and sworn at the poor creature when he had stood petrified with fright a quarter of an hour before. Jumbo, too, in spite of his previous jibbing, was at any rate working hard now and seemed to know that something had happened to his companion, who required his assistance.

The sight of the old grey was hardly a good advertisement for the state of the roads ahead of the artillery convoys that passed by on their way up the line, as a good many drivers' faces testified. The officers' faces were set, and the men looked fed up to the hilt, for shells had to be taken up by day and night, while by some miraculous means time was found, at the expense of sleep, to keep the drivers' links free of rust. Many passed remarks such as " You'll lose 'im, mate," " He's going fast, chum," " Much shelling up there ? " etc.

But the query I remember most clearly was that of a Labour Corps man in Dickebusch, where I watered the horses.

" 'As 'e bin 'it, choom ? " asked the idiot.

" No, he's had a tooth out," was the only reply I could frame on the spur of the moment.

The Grey gave signs of being unable to carry on much farther, but we arrived back at the horse-lines without mishap. Most of the section gathered round the " ridiculous and senseless trio," examined the horses and harness, and commiserated with me on the loss of my mac., which had slipped from the saddle in the melée. They also taunted me with the ruination of my new breeches with bloodstains, many bets having been made as to how long this garment would remain respectable.

I was rejoiced to learn that Lane had been discovered, though he had a very bad wound in the shoulder from a piece of shell. He had been taken down to a big C.C.S. close to our lines and had sent over a message to Simmonds, enabling him to go to see the patient before evacuation.

Throughout the afternoon the rumble continued up the line where several divisions were getting ready for to-morrow's attack, living every minute of the interval under conditions as bad as those of which, after all, I had only had a taste that morning. To be up there with our batteries or in the trenches subjected to an unceasing bombardment like that was enough to shatter anybody's nerves in a few days. Yet thousands of men were enduring the endless racket as I had seen them that morning, huddled here and there behind mud banks or crouching in shallow dug-outs and shell-holes, fully expecting a wound of some sort before next evening. What our casualties must be, in the course of an ordinary day's happenings in the salient, I couldn't imagine. On no part of the Western Front was the destruction of life more ruthless.

Not content with hindering the transport of ammunition in the neighbourhood of the guns, the enemy sent over aeroplanes late in the afternoon to bomb the roads further to the rear. They came over with great daring and made direct hits in Dickebusch where the road was crowded with traffic, a pack-pony convoy of one battalion being nearly wiped out.

The observers in our balloons immediately acted on the principle that "discretion is the better part of valour," seized their parachutes and leapt into the void. One after another they jumped out all along the line, gliding slowly to earth with their huge white umbrellas. Immediately afterwards the balloon nearest to us was attacked by an aeroplane, bursting into flames and falling rapidly to the ground : at one moment it seemed that it would overtake and envelop the two little figures who were still in mid-air, but a kind breeze carried them out of the line of danger.

Our next excitement was the sight of a British machine making rapidly earthwards, apparently heading for our field. It was evidently making a forced descent, being either damaged or driven by a wounded man. The throbbing drew nearer and the plane whirred over us at no great distance from our heads, then skimmed the top of the C.C.S., struck an overhead wire, buckled up and crashed to the ground. The fall of twenty feet looked ghastly, but to everyone's surprise the observer clambered out and walked in an unconcerned way to the nearest marquee to have some cuts dressed ! The pilot had been shot in the air. The incident had a tragic touch, for the aeroplane's machine-gun let off a few rounds of ammunition when it crashed which killed one of the wounded in the nearest ward.

Before nightfall two of our observation balloons were brought down in flames in the Ypres direction, so that the aerial activity was carried on right up to the close of this eventful day. Our pack-pony convoy that night had a very trying experience ; however, Sergt. Simmonds, who was still acting as T.O., succeeded in bringing it back without mishap.

Next morning we were awakened by the crashing bombardment which heralded the second great blow of the Flanders offensive. The L.R.B. were going over the top for the eighth time in a full-dress attack, on this occasion under the command of Major Wallis, since Colonel Husey had been wounded for the fourth time two days before.

Angerer and one other transport man departed in the very early morning hours to take part in a brigade pack-pony stunt, intending to follow up the advance with bombs and ammunition, taking them as near as possible to the new front line. This was the first daylight expedition of its kind we had attempted, but it developed into a regular scheme which was eventually extended to ammunition and trench-mortar limbers.

Our own activities during the morning were much the same as they had been in previous offensives. There was no thought for a moment that we should be in readiness to move off suddenly and follow victorious infantry on an advance of several miles. It was not in the minds of commanders. These were sledge-hammer tactics where battalions and brigades were wiped out in a struggle for a copse here or certain portions of trench there. There was not much element of surprise in these attacks ; the enemy knew more or less where we were going to attack and had a pretty shrewd idea as to the time fixed. For twenty-four hours preceding zero-hour he did his utmost to cripple our batteries and to cause heavy losses to our assembling infantry by concentrated gusts of fire on the foremost trenches. But his artillery fire was not as strong as our own, and the scenes behind his own lines where our big shells were falling must have baffled description. Our destructive fire on the 16th, in spite of Fritz's efforts, was indeed an example of what massed artillery meant.

On the left that day we captured Langemarck, but in the centre and south of the battlefield we received such a set-back that it was over a month before the British attack could be resumed. On the whole front south of St. Julien our attack was held before our old Zevenkote position (Ypres II., April 27-29), Zonnebeke and the heights around the Menin road, where the German resistance was stiffest, resulting in the virtual annihilation of the greater part of the 16th, 36th, 8th and 56th Divisions. We had come up against a new system of defence which we had as yet no scheme for circumventing. Briefly, the Bosches had abandoned the strongly-held front line system, substituting thinly-garrisoned outposts intended to be a hindrance to the attack and nothing more. Behind these were innumerable concrete " pill-boxes " which nothing but a direct hit from a six-inch gun could destroy, and, owing to their being sunk into the ground, they easily escaped detection. Further back still there were reserve divisions available for prompt counter-attacks.

The experiences on most parts of the front were identical. Our men, advancing behind a powerful barrage, came up against the machine-gun fire from the pill-boxes, which were hardly touched by our shells. Then the barrage went on ahead, leaving the infantry struggling amidst the concrete redoubts, where isolated encounters took place for hours. A certain number of these pill-boxes was reduced, and fortified farms were captured. Our own brigade advanced to the far side of Glencorse Wood, but the machine-guns did such deadly work that here, as in other places, our ranks got thinner and thinner until the few srvivors, left to face strong German counter-attacks, were driven back practically to their starting-point.

We learnt nothing of all this at the time, but then we very rarely did know what was going on. Some time during the afternoon when I was giving the old grey a little walk up and down for the edification of a veterinary officer, Angerer arrived back at our lines, minus his horse. Immediately a crowd gathered round him to learn the news, and we were upset to find he was wounded in the back. Having handed over his horse, he had ridden down in an empty limber, and was now on his way to the C.C.S. He said we were " getting as good as we gave " up there and that our casualties were very heavy. He didn't think we had gone forward at all. Having said farewell to the section, he crossed over to the hospital, after which we saw him no more. When he recovered he was sent to the 2nd Battalion, and afterwards, owing to the consideration shown by the authorities, was transferred to the R.I.R.s, with whom he was again badly wounded. Angerer had done very good work with us, especially at Arras, for which he was recommended for the M.M.

Soon after this incident Simmonds called an impromptu parade at which he read out the names of the pack-pony men for that night and the animals they were to lead. None of those detailed received the announcement exactly with enthusiasm, least of all the driver with the bluggy trousers. I was to lead the " Brat," a one-time colonel's mount—now one of the pack-pony fraternity, and therefore treated with disdain by all the haughty officers' chargers. But, even if it had been the most valuable thoroughbred in existence, it could hardly have made me cheerful.

We had tea, donned our helmets and respirators, fastened pack-saddles on our steeds and led them to the Q.M. stores, a patch of open ground piled up with boxes of bully and biscuits. The convoy then set off, long before nightfall, but had to wait farther up for brigade orders as to where the rations were to be dumped. After we had spent about an hour, squatting in the same field as a twelve-inch gun which, in common with several other heavies in the vicinity, was sending over messages to the Hun transports, Captain Mackenzie of the Q.V.R. rode up and said the brigade was coming down to Sanctuary Wood that night. In other words, rations had to be dumped in practically the same spot where my limber had stuck the previous day. The route we took was new to me, however, as we struck off up the wooden track which passed north of Zillebeke Lake ; somehow a track seemed safer than a road, but considering parties of men were already repairing numerous new shell-holes and there was not a square yard on either side of the track that did not form a crater or the lip of one, this comfort was illusory. Looking down into these vast holes full of water, we could see men, horses and wagons that had been pitched over the side of the track to clear it for traffic in moments of stress.

Something was restraining the Bosche at sunset that night : his guns were having a rest, while the whole of our artillery was taking a turn at strafeing the territory that should now have been ours. We chose the psychological moment for our ration-trip. Even the barrage zone at Zillebeke was silent, and we dropped our loads at the specified point without molestation.

" Unload and make your own way home," said Simmonds to the convoy. " Don't hang about here."

It was sound advice, and we acted on it promptly, not knowing when Fritz would consider it time to get to work again. I decided to go home by road, since trotting was easier than on the track, and the Brat and I beat a hasty retreat through Zillebeke, after which we proceeded at a more dignified gait, and finally relapsed into a walk. Sitting on an empty pack-saddle was hardly comfortable for trotting, but none of us ever regretted that hasty departure, for the London Scottish pack-ponies, arriving at the Zillebeke end of the track five minutes afterwards, received a salvo of shells in their midst which killed and wounded both men and horses.

Arriving back at the lines, we found all lights out and searchlights very busy, so every movement had to be conducted in pitch darkness, from feeding the ponies to crawling into the bivvies and putting our fists in other fellows' faces. The nightly bombing raids had begun again, and we lay for the sixth night in succession in fear and trembling for the safety of our skins. Exactly what had happened that day in the salient we did not know, but we had learnt this much since our arrival a week ago : that the so-called advantage for transport men of being able to return to a billet and a night's rest after a ration journey was an utter delusion. The best punishment for the Kaiser would have been to be placed for a week in an area where neither dug-outs nor trenches were available and to be bombed regularly from dusk till daybreak.

Very early next morning we were awakened and told we were moving off after breakfast. Our dose of the Third Battle of Ypres was over already : the division was so cut up that it had to be withdrawn immediately from the line. Of course, we were overjoyed to leave those parts so soon, but were stupefied to learn that the whole division had to be withdrawn after one day's attack. Why, after Gommecourt, they had carried on for seven weeks ; after Leuze Wood, for a month ; at Arras they had fought for over a week on end. Something like a feeling of indignation came over us that whole divisions should be squandered as though we had an unlimited reserve of men and human life counted for nothing. One attack after another had produced disappointment, heavy losses, limited gains. What had happened to us at Gommecourt ? Inadequate artillery preparation and no reserves. We had come back to our starting-point. What had happened at Leuze Wood ? Inadequate artillery preparation, no reserves, change of orders at the last moment. The attack failed. What had happened at Lesboeufs ? Inadequate artillery preparation, supports did not appear, general muddle. The position had to be given up. What had happened at St. Rohart on May 3rd ? Inadequate artillery preparation, flanks in the air. We had come back to the starting-point. Now we had had the biggest cutting-up of all. The bulk of the L.R.B. who had left Abeele in the prime of health six days ago were helping to fill the hospitals at the moment or else lying out among the stumps of Glencorse Wood.

How could all these dashed hopes fail to dishearten us ? After seeing the pitiful remains of the battalion when we got back that day to Abeele, something like disgust with the British tactics made itself felt. That this feeling was not confined to our unit may be gleaned from the following extract from Nelson's History of the War, apropos of this attack :—

"The Fifth Army had fought with the most splendid gallantry, but their courage had been largely fruitless. We had no doubt caused the enemy serious losses, but he had taken a heavier toll of our own ranks. Fine brigades had been hurled in succession against a concrete wall, and had been sorely battered. For almost the first time in the campaign there was a sense of discouragement abroad on our front. Men felt that they were being sacrificed blindly ; that every fight was a soldiers' fight, and that such sledge-hammer tactics were too crude to meet the problem. For a moment there was a real ebb of confidence in British leadership. That such a feeling should exist among journalists and politicians matters nothing ; but it matters much if it is found among troops in the field."

And again :

"At Third Ypres he (the Commander of the Fifth Army) had been given the chief part, and his army had borne the brunt of the heavy fighting in the first month of that action. But there he had somewhat failed in resource and had squandered fine divisions

т

against the enemy's defences without attaining his object. Hence his old reputation had become a little dimmed, and among his soldiers he had acquired the name of a general who tried his troops too high and used them blindly as battering-rams against the stoutest part of the wall. The criticism was not wholly just, but it was widely made."

We ourselves laid the blame at nobody's door in particular. God knows it was not the fault of the regimental command, nor, I suppose —since other divisions suffered similarly—was our brigade or division to be censured. We were really not in the least interested as to who our army or corps commander might be, since we were continually being transferred from one to another, and it is far from me to criticise anyone in particular. But I am giving a true reflection of our state of mind at all periods, and, after the Third Battle of Ypres, in August, it was certainly the feeling of the rank and file that the Passchendaele Ridge was not worth the sacrifice involved.

Alternative suggestions from the rank and file were numerous— some merely impracticable, others idiotic. Strategy and tactics were not our province. We were not paid 1s. 6d. per day and fed luxuriously by the Army in return for our views on military science. Thinking was not required of us; common sense not expected. All our energies and intellect would have been devoted to the problem of how to clean harness and burnish links without rag or polish, if we had let the Army have its way. They paid us to grin and bear our lot without questioning the " why " and " wherefore " of any-thing, to camouflage a lousy shirt with a shiny bandolier and clean tunic, to write home and say we were enjoying the life and would soon be in Berlin. But fortunately some regimental commanders gave rankers credit for more intelligence, otherwise many of us would have ended the War in a lunatic asylum !

CHAPTER XXVI.

In the Evacuated Regions.

(*September–October*, 1917.)

Retracing our steps—Transferred to the Cambrai front—Petersen's light railway—
Extraordinary ration journeys—The Div. Horse Show : a candid opinion—
Changes on the section—The Italian débacle.

ABEELE may have been a " rest " area for divisions that were destined
to return to Ypres, but for us it was only a half-way house—or rather
barn. We were placed upon our return visit in a farm close to the
aerodrome, and about nine o'clock every night searchlights, anti-
aircraft guns, whistles, and a nasty drone would signify that a cargo
of bombs for the Abeele aerodrome was on its way. It was bad
enough to sit and conjecture where a machine was going to drop its
load, but when you KNEW that every night it would pass over such
tempting targets as batteries, dumps, hospitals, and railheads for
the express purpose of bombing the aerodrome next door to you, it
was a sheer impossibility to sleep. The R.F.C. men possessed deep
dug-outs, but we had merely a barn-roof and some fowl-perches over
our heads. Every night, when we ought to have been snoozing, we
stood outside the billet waiting and watching for the Fritzes who never
failed to put in an appearance, and sometimes a further detachment
would arrive after midnight, so that the combined gun-firing and
bomb-dropping became practically an all-night diversion. We were
therefore very thankful to leave this spot on the 23rd and turn our
backs on Flanders for the last time.

The Grey was led by a spare man on the trek, but he succeeded in
keeping up with the convoy ; Jumbo, having in vain swung the lead
with his slight cut, pulled a cooker as of yore with a different companion in draft. After dark we reached a small village, Ledringhem,
where we made a temporary horse-line in a field, having to turn out
again at 1 a.m. to resume our journey. Then we marched on again
in the darkness, passed through the suburbs of St. Omer at breakfast-
time, and finally came to our new quarters at a place called Moulle.

We learnt that we were shortly going to be put in a quiet sector of
the front opposite the Hindenburg Line towards Cambrai, a part where
everything was supposed to be as serene as was Hebuterne before we
made it lively last year. This announcement was most welcome,

and the fact that our numbers were not made up to strength before departure was comforting, for we were obviously not intended for another " binge " ; no doubt all the reinforcements were being drafted to the Ypres front, where, from all appearances, they would be needed. The battalion soon got over the shock of its Ypres adventure and the rank and file naturally fell into the old routine of drills, inspections. and sick-parades once more. We felt rather disillusioned—that was all.

The French had carried out an attack at Verdun, on August 20th, which resulted in important captures of ground, together with ten thousand prisoners. This served to restore the moral of the French Army, which had been in a bad way after its April offensive, and at the same time increased our admiration for the dogged determination of this Ally. However, two months elapsed before they struck again, showing that France had by no means an inexhaustible man-power and that the Aisne Battle must have hit her hard. The Italians also had resumed the offensive—after a lull of over two months—and by August 24th had taken over twenty thousand prisoners in six days. The three Western Allies were retaining the initiative. but in the East the enemy had everything his own way. Roumania, still fighting bravely with hostile armies on one side and a treacherous " ally " on the other, presented as sorry a spectacle as had been seen in the War, and our Salonika force was not strong enough to relieve the pressure upon her. It was increasingly apparent that Germany intended to subject Russia and Roumania while holding her Western fronts, and her gains of ground, prisoners, and supplies in the East certainly took the gilt off our hard-won trophies on this side.

We entrained for the evacuated Somme regions at the station of Wizernes on the 30th of August, making our way *via* St. Pol, Mont St. Eloi, and Achicourt, to Arras, where we stayed for a while about tea-time, observing many familiar landmarks. Unfortunately, just before we got here Hobson insisted that he could race the train, and jumped out to prove it, but he chose a bad landing-place, twisting his ankle so badly that he nearly had to be left behind.

Arras Station was still subjected to long-range fire, we learnt, but it was not unpleasant enough to prevent us using it in moderation. When Gunboat learnt this he was about to make immediate representations to the engine-driver to "aller vite" when a roar of laughter from several of the section diverted his thoughts to another channel. The object of this mirth was a South-Eastern and Chatham Railway engine which came into view at this moment; it was one mass of bright paint and glittering steel and brass, looking as if it had just taken first prize at a Railway Exhibition at Olympia. Everything from the brass fittings to the rivets and steelwork looked as if it had been cleaned for a week on end, and the shining dome alone was enough to attract half a dozen aeroplanes from afar. Nothing could have been more inappropriate in the yard of a station five miles from the enemy, a station where the buildings were shattered and scarcely a pane of glass remained in the roof. A filthy old French engine puffed alongside about the same time, the grimy driver of which gazed at the show-piece with as much amusement as ourselves.

" Say, that's the way to win the War," shouted Chrisp. " Who pays for your Brasso ? "

But the British engine-driver merely grinned. It was only another form of the same lunacy—" Spit and Polish " in the Railway Operating Department !

Eventually an engine was shunted on the back of our train so that we could be taken down the renovated track to the Somme, which the Germans had thoroughly destroyed when evacuating those regions. This part of our journey was most interesting, for soon after leaving Arras we passed through the old front lines towards Boisleux and thereafter traversed the territory that had been laid waste. The fields between the villages were wild and untended, all the wayside trees and orchards had been hacked down, all the crossroads had been blown up and some only partially repaired, the townships themselves had been fired. These were the places whose burning had been reflected in the sky before the Battle of Arras in March. As we travelled onwards into the desolation with this immense plain on either side of us, the firing-line got farther away as it bent south-eastwards, but we passed several back area hutments and camps. One of the latter was occupied by Americans, who clustered round when we happened to stop and an exchange of pleasantries followed, each army summing up the other's characteristics. These Yanks wore forage caps, smart khaki uniforms and green canvas gaiters, utterly unsuitable for mud ; still, they would live and learn. It was rumoured that their first division would not be fit to put in the trenches till about the end of the year, and, in view of their considerable distance from the firing-line, Mac imitated an American twang and called out :

" Waal, I guess there's no war on at all ! "

The Yanks laughed and seemed to appreciate the thrust.

After several delays we reached Miraumont after dark, where we detrained with some difficulty, having no lights, and lined up in the village street. It was an eerie place, particularly at midnight, for there were no human beings or illuminations to be seen and yet a number of houses seemed almost intact.

We then set out on an eastward trek to Bapaume, leaving a cooker by the wayside in the course of the march, as it succumbed to the effects of being detrained. Every house in Bapaume had been deliberately damaged by the Germans, but it was astonishing how many substantial edifices remained standing. We could not see much at 3 a.m., but a divisional cinema, baths and a fumigating depot caught our eye, and we were rather glad to find our camp was only half a mile from town. At half-past four we turned in to sleep in very over-crowded tents, thankful to rest after our twenty-four hours journey, but such are the demands that horses make on their masters that we were up and about again two hours later.

This camp formed our quarters for a few days while the necessary arrangements were made for taking over our new section of front. These included a visit by several officers to the firing-line, and, as usual on these occasions, we waited eagerly for their return in order to question the least excitable of their mounted orderlies on the quietness or otherwise of our sector. From their accounts this was a most extraordinary part of the front. The Hindenburg Line was known to consist of various outposts and subsidiary trenches covering a main battle position, heavily protected by wire : the British facing it seemed to have adopted the same tactics with the exception that the battle position could not be compared in strength or echelon to the enemy's structure. Our grooms had ridden up to Battalion Headquarters in daylight and had hardly met any troops or experienced any shellfire. Shell holes were few and far between, and there were delightful cross-country tracks where one could canter for a mile or more. There were, of course, no civilians

about—a fact that appeared to upset Rifleman ———— and ————
who always had an eye for a pretty wench and an estaminet bar.
Altogether it sounded a most desirable neighbourhood, and, though the
battalion would never get far away from the line when they rested from
the trenches, at least they would be in calmer surroundings than the
populated regions behind Ypres. Also, there was a good E.F.C. in
Bapaume, which would supply our regimental canteen with slightly
more than toothbrushes and blacking.

After dark on the 4th of September we moved forward to our new
transport quarters which stood beside the Fremicourt-Lebucquiere
road. These consisted of covered stables with brick flooring, huts for
our billet and rooms for harness, picket. etc.—altogether an ideal
home, situated in the midst of acres of grazing land scarcely scarred with
shell-holes, yet only three or four miles from our front line.

The transport decided to make a really good job of the camp and
lay down brick paths in all directions in preparation for winter quarters,
for which purpose scrounging parties were organised every night to
proceed to the ruined village of Beaumetz, select timber, whole bricks
and other materials, and stack them in readiness for the empty ration
limbers on their return from the line. A great deal of fun was got out
of these parties, chiefly on account of the witticisms of Chrisp, who
frequently went with them, and from first to last they consisted solely
of volunteers who made scrounging a pastime on the nights when they
were off duty.

Life promised to be so quiet for Petersen. the Quartermaster, however, together with his satellites, that he hit on a brilliant scheme for
amusing himself and at the same time making work for the various
details. It is described in the following letter which he himself
censored :—

12.9.17. " The Quartermaster, Petersen, has secured the
services of several of our buglers, storemen and others in order to
construct a light railway from the stores to the cookers—a matter
of about forty yards. There is absolutely no need for anything of
the kind, as the only traffic which it will be used for is the conveyance of meat and stores once a day. Nevertheless, the dear old
man has thrown himself into the scheme with the greatest zeal, and
has purloined several lengths of old German light railway line and
a truck.

" The entire staff seem to be in their second childhood, judging
by the first day's results. Apart from the railway itself being
totally unnecessary, there are all sorts of useless platforms and
bridges in course of construction. Stations have been started at
the stores, the sergeants' mess hut, the post corporal's hut and
the cookers, while by Simmonds' tent there is a bridge of duck-
boards that cannot possibly be used except by a cat.

" There are notices such as ' Whistle,' ' To the Trains.'
' Beware of the Trains,' ' Petersen's Patent Pneumatic Puffer.'
etc., and a red flag is hanging from the window of the terminus. To
give a further semblance of reality to this wonderful scheme, there
is a confounded station-bell that has turned up from somewhere,
which one of the buglers rings at intervals. The bootmakers' shop
has been turned into an R.T.O.'s office, with a notice outside it, and
the stores look rather like Clapham Junction with signals that move
up and down.

" As I am writing the Q.M. has hit on the brilliant idea of

running a switch-line round to his tent, a matter of twenty yards off the main track, and so the entire line is being relaid to make room for the points. He will never have the slightest use for this line, but he is rushing round, measuring first one thing and then another, as excited as a kid with a new toy, while most of the transport look on in a pitying sort of way.

" Wallis came down from the trenches to-day and he has been looking at the work accomplished while Petersen has explained the scheme minutely. The Major has not yet noticed the signboard reading, ' Petersen's Patent Pneumatic Puffer.' It has been creating much mirth, and we're wondering what he will say when he sees it.

" The Grey's wound is better and he hardly limps at all now. However, he cannot be worked yet, so I'm taking out another horse with Jumbo."

Although a few riders might trot up to Battalion H.Q. in daylight the ration trips to the firing-line were made at night, as the enemy overlooked the country and we didn't want him to know whether we were eating bully or pork and beans. Bourlon Height, a wooded prominence inside the German lines, was the one landmark in all this featureless region ; it overlooked us to such an extent that we could almost pick out the trees on its slopes as we stood in our horse-lines, and we were under observation the whole way up the line and even by the water-troughs miles to the rear. So close did it seem that for a long time we could not credit this hill being in German hands ; we could scarcely put a new battery in position without the enemy being perfectly well aware of it, and we used to joke about our toy railway being mistaken for a railhead.

When travelling up with rations we passed through Lebucquiere and followed a hard, dry track across undulating grass-land to Beaumetz, which had been the scene of much hand-to-hand fighting when we had brushed up against the Hindenburg Line on the German retreat. It was in an advanced state of ruin, but many walls were standing, and in some cases roofs were perched on insecure-looking beams which lent a little excitement to the brick fatigues. On the far side of the village there was a further stretch of track, and then a short, sharp climb brought us on to the Bapaume-Cambrai road. There were so few troops in these parts that beyond an occasional limber or an artillery convoy we never passed anything on this thoroughfare. In fact, one means of returning home was to follow the road for about four miles to Beugny, but the monotony of the journey and the interminable cobbles—unrelieved by the jostle and rumble of other traffic—made a solitary driver feel so lonely that he usually chose the Beaumetz route if only for the comfort of the homely lights in Brigade H.Q. and the camps at Lebucquiere.

After we grew accustomed to the outpost positions of the various companies the limbers parted company by the Sugar Refinery on the Cambrai road and made their way separately to their destinations. H.Q. rations would be taken straight on, while the other limbers eventually found themselves flirting with the German star-shells. Where our actual front-line was I could never make out. I always took it to be a sunken road near Boursies, lined with sand-bagged dug-outs and fire-steps. But the ramifications of the outpost positions were so complex that we would pass right on into what was virtually No Man's Land and drop No. 1 Platoon's rations beside a line of willow trees and No. 2 Platoon's beside a ruined farm farther to the left, etc. The limbers always made more noise than we cared about, but Slade had the most unpleasant task of anybody when he was told to take his mules up a new road by Louverval "to see if the Germans would shell it or not." His remarks on receipt of these instructions are unrecorded.

The chief thing the isolated platoons feared was German raids, for the enemy could approach by night on every side, and our patrols frequently encountered Germans when wandering about. However, the jangling water-carts had to be taken round to each post in turn where the R.A.M.C. man would draw off the water in petrol-cans, banging them about, dropping them, and generally kicking up enough noise to put the wind up the local garrison. If the horses neighed, loud denunciation emanated from the dug-outs close at hand. Meanwhile, the drivers stood in breathless anticipation of beating a hasty retreat with their vehicles or assisting in a hand-to-hand scrap—we had to take our rifles with us on these trips.

Macloughlin was now made Lance-Corporal, in place of our dear friend 'Arry-'Arry, who had left us with trench fever at Abeele, and got home to England on the strength of his foreign service. Macloughlin, having received the M.M., was one of those fêted at the Military Medal dinner, held by the transport in one of their huts, on September 15th, and no one deserved the stripe or decoration more than he. In the absence of Mr. Gordon, Peterson took the chair, and, after the meal, speeches and general merry-making ensued. Hebblewhite, the T.O.'s batman, sang " Down by the Gas-works in the Old Kent Road," a Gladstonian ditty which he had given at every concert since mobilisation, while others obliged with similarly stale musical items. However, as there was no piano, the concert was less successful than the refreshments—liquid and otherwise—which undoubtedly made the evening what it was. As the audience became livelier, the Q.M. was treated to cries of " Puff-puff," " Right away," and " Good old light railway," but it did not perturb him, for he was shortly going home to be demobilised.

Just after these celebrations Gordon returned from hospital, and Figg arrived back from a corps rest station, whither he had been sent, much against his will, ten days before. A " rest " station, instead of being a place where the sick might recover amidst cheerful surroundings, with lenience and amusements abounding, was only too often noted for red tape, poor food, and uninteresting routine. Our section regarded the prospect of being sent to one just as though it were a prison. Figg had received very superficial treatment and had concealed part of his trouble—boils—in order to get out of the place as soon as possible. With us, he secured a supply of bandages, etc., from home, and speedily cured himself with hot fomentations. Parcels were not delivered at the corps rest station, so that Figg subsisted on army rations, about which he had an amusing tale to tell. One day it was announced that a certain R.A.M.C. Colonel was coming to inspect the place, and the O.C. (who apparently could have indented for hospital delicacies for the patients) got the wind up at the extremely poor rations in evidence. Consequently he caused a fictitious menu to be posted up for the Colonel's edification, mentioning soup, pudding, and various imaginary dishes. The visitor, however, was a wary old bird, and decided to visit the kitchen to see things for himself ; he accordingly asked the cook to show him the pudding, at which he was told the truth—the real meal was to be bully beef and biscuits !

Fortunately for us, the Army at last realised that we needed vegetables. Not only did they grant a small sum daily for the purchase of them, but they started a collection of vegetable gardens where we dug and planted cabbages and potatoes under Brigade orders. So long as we were to benefit by the product when it grew, we did not begrudge the time given to enterprises of this nature. But, as the reader knows only too well by now, only a portion of our time could be said to be profitably employed.

The culminating event of the month was the Divisional Horse Show, at which there were to be prizes for the smartest turn-outs ; this brought Spit and Polish to a stage where it and I definitely parted company. The frantic polishing efforts at Magnicourt, La Gorgue, and Agnez were quite sane by comparison with the exhibition which we got now. This was really the maximum effort yet made by the authorities to win the War (for presumably it was intended to assist towards that end, otherwise the energy expended could well have been diverted to more useful channels, such as digging lines of defence). The strength of our feeling over the matter may be gauged from the following letter :—

26/9/17. " . . . There are several competitions for various kinds of horses and mules in limbers, cookers, etc., all with harness. We sent in two or three entries to-day, but none of them got anything. You simply can't imagine the extreme lengths of idiocy to which the poshing-up craze will go. For weeks certain men, mostly details, have been engaged in painting vehicles and burnishing all possible bright parts, polishing screws, whitening cords and drag-ropes, burnishing brakes and the rims of the wheels, and shining up brass hubs, until the whole turn-out makes you almost shed tears of rage at the waste of energy, time, labour and money, not to mention material. Things have come to a pass when men file brakes, swivels and hooks for days, clean them with emery cloth, finish them off with Brasso and keep them carefully wrapped up each night. The very axes and shovels have been painted for the occasion, while the cooker coal-shovel has a burnished knob and stem ! Then you go in the show with dozens of other equally maniacal turn-outs and perhaps get ' turned down ' straightaway because your horses are a bit too ' heavy ' for that particular entry. Conibeer went in for the competition and I was glad to see he didn't go daft over his stuff. It was nice and clean—as respectable as possible without going ' poshing mad '—but Coni took quite a back seat. This takes place a few miles from the firing-line. And people wonder why we are so slow in winning the War ! "

Of course, the burnished coal-shovel simply delighted the judge. The staff officers chortled with glee over the new paint, the bright lids and the whitewashed rope on the prize cooker, and though other vehicles approached this in drivelling idiocy, the burnished poker carried the day. I'm thankful this took place in uninhabited regions so that there were no French soldiers or civilians there to see it.

After this I allowed my blood to boil for about three weeks, and then, finding Clements would be quite willing to take over my pair, told Simmonds that I was positively fed-up with the thankless job of link-cleaning and that a change of work would be welcome. I didn't mind whether I took up pack animals or rode a galloper or drove other men's pairs when required, but I candidly confessed my inability to keep two horses and two sets of harness clean. The Sergeant said he had known that for two years and wondered I had not discovered it sooner. My turn-out had worried him more than anything else on the section, and he was always having to send me on night instead of day jobs for fear the Brigadier should see it. Then I mentioned that there were only Barnett and Butt, beside myself, who had retained their driving job for two years, and that the position ceased to be held in such esteem from the moment steelwork had had to be kept free of rust. Simmonds agreed that I was entitled to a change, so Jumbo and The Grey went to their new master, who soon improved their appearance. I wanted a rider to look after, more than anything having visions of mounted orderly, " galloping " and exploration work; accordingly Simmonds handed over to me a decrepit mount called " Ben," officially allotted to Captain Hancocks. This gentleman, however, practically never rode the beast, and Ben therefore became my special appurtenance.

In the middle of October Petersen and Gordon (now Captain) were called back to England, the former for demobilisation, the latter in response to a wire from the War Office intended for someone else. The popular Q.M.S. Denny then became Q.M., while Captain Rose was sent down from A Company as our T.O. We were somewhat afraid that this change would mean the introduction of stricter discipline than our section cared about, for Rose had been very stern and military with his company. However, his first address to us entirely dispelled that fear. After saying what great pleasure it gave him to take charge of the transport, most of whom he had known since he came out, he said :—

" I know you all think that, coming from a company, I am going to ginger things up, to ' woof ' you and to make alterations all round, but you're wrong. I'm going to leave you to yourselves. You know what your work is and know more about transport and horses than I do. So I leave it to you."

Three cheers for Rose and all officers like him !

His first piece of excitement came when the Lord Mayor of London visited our palatial camp. Much was done in preparation for this visit, but we might have spared ourselves the trouble, for the Mayor passed round the stables and huts as quickly as possible and with an air of complete indifference. He was much too near the front line to please him and was in no mood to comment on our equipment or speak words of encouragement. In fact the only syllables that passed his lips were directed to ascertaining what the observation balloons were for, and rumour has it that when our Old Kent Road friend told him they were canteens for aeroplanes he was quite satisfied.

During these two months things had been busy elsewhere. On September 19th the offensive at Ypres had been renewed, and thereafter, in successive attacks, the Menin Road Heights, Zonnebeke and the Gravenstafel Ridge had fallen to us, in spite of appalling conditions of rain and mud. The artillery had now devised more efficient means of dealing with " pill-boxes," and the infantry also had methods for tackling them. Each " push " brought us a few thousand prisoners and a little more ground, but our own casualties could only be surmised.

We must definitely make up our minds to face a fourth winter : for, we thought, nothing unforeseen could now occur. The French attack on October 23rd had a limited objective, and it was as plain as a pike-staff to us that no decisive thrust was coming off this season. The

Germans had Riga and were capturing cities, populaces that could be converted into slaves, military prisoners, guns, stores and food, while we were literally blasting our way forward with a few square miles of mud swamp as our final reward.

Then, towards the end of October, came the sudden news of the Italian disaster at Caporetto. The Germans and Austrians had broken through, and in a few days captured a hundred thousand prisoners and seven hundred guns, later increased to two hundred thousand men and eighteen hundred guns. And yet our war correspondents had for two years been issuing diatribes on the loss of the enemy's morale. Loss of morale, indeed ! What victories had we on a par with this to cheer us up ? We had to be content with nibbles at their Western line, whereas every autumn the Germans did some big thing that would have sent us into ecstasies had it been our victory. In 1915 it was Serbia, in 1916 Roumania, in 1917 they had broken through on the Russian and Italian fronts.

Imagine our feelings when we read of the " insufficient resistance " on the part of certain Italian units and the old, old story of our line retiring " according to plan " and munition stores being blown up before retreating. There was no mistaking the import of this communique : it spelt rout. While our hearts hardened still more against those Russian scoundrels who had made this possible, very few of us, in the stress of the moment, had any sympathy for the Italians either, because many of them had deliberately laid down their arms and we knew perfectly well that, if British troops had been there, that treachery would never have happened.

After a few days of suspense word came round that British troops were to be despatched to Italy and that our division was to stand by, ready to depart. Instead of this rumour depressing us further, however, it gave Chrisp the opportunity of making one of the happiest orations he had uttered for a long time.

" How jolly," said he. " We shall have oranges galore ! Luscious wines and lovely Italian girls—they're hot stuff, I can tell you ! Gondola rides at a franc each and mountain air for nothing. Barrel organs for Aubrey to grind and monkeys for transport work. . . . But, my word, when we get there, *won't* we give those ice-cream men the ' bird ' ! "

But there were to be no gondolas or ice-cream for the 56th Division. The order to stand by led to nothing. For we were ear-marked for yet another affray on the Western Front, the secret of which was so well kept that at the end of October nothing was further from our thoughts. The Battle of Cambrai was in the wind, and, since we knew our front thoroughly, we were to be engaged once again, notwithstanding our full share in the year's offensives and our appalling shortage of men.

CHAPTER XXVII.

THE BATTLE OF CAMBRAI.

(*November*, 1917.)

Secret preparations—Hopes run high—The surprise attack—A first night adventure
—The battle develops.—The German counter blow—Transport casualties
and misfortunes—Good-bye to Jumbo.

THE first indication we had that our quiet sector was to be the scene of
unusual happenings was the arrival of a staff officer who wanted an
estimate of the maximum number of men each building in our camp
would hold at a pinch. To our surprise and amidst general subdued
protest, he put down about fifty for the Nissen huts, fourteen for the
sergeant's tent, forty for the harness room and twenty for the wash-
house. It was confidentially whispered that there was to be a secret
concentration of troops on this front, and that, as the erection of fresh
camps would arouse suspicions on Bourlon Hill, the existing buildings
had got to harbour everybody.

The Staff Officer looked askance at our toy railway. This, in itself,
said he, was sufficient to make the enemy think we were a munition
depot instead of a harmless transport camp. I wish Petersen had been
there to hear these remarks, but he had bequeathed this legacy to his
successor, Denny, who had to bear all the ridicule attaching to it. He
must have felt uncomfortable as the Staff Officer looked pityingly upon
the signals, station bell, R.T.O.'s office, and all the signboards scattered
around. Even thirty yards away from the track there was now a
notice, " To Bedlam Junction," stuck on the outer wall of the harness-
room.

After this visitation the matter dropped, as nothing more was heard,
and we continued to carry on with our line work, devoting also great
attention to improvements in our camp, ready for the winter. The
Devils' Mess gave up their spare time to preparing a souvenir number
of the " Old Doings " for publication in London.

On November 5th there was a hilarious dinner and concert in a hut at
Lebucquiere for all those who had come out with the original battalion
three years before, amounting to some twenty-six men on the transport,
a bunch of cooks, signallers and details, a few officers and various
N.C.O.s and men in the companies who had turned up in the battalion
again. Although not of their number, I was invited to the affair, and

was amused to find that all distinctions of rank disappeared when the
"originals" got together, and officers, B.S.M. and sergeants made
bigger asses of themselves than the men. Six of the officers delivered
an old Crowborough song of 1914 when some of them were rankers,
while a merry batch of sergeants gave us "Old Roger Rum."

Gordon was on his way back to us by now. The War Office, noting
his amazement when told to proceed direct to Russia, discovered they
wanted a different person, so he was given ten days' leave and a ticket
back to France. His return meant that Captain Rose had to take over
his company again, which was certainly rough luck on him, as he had
been ordering comforts and gifts for the section and had quite made
up his mind that the post was a permanency. It is not derogatory to
Gordon to say that we were very sorry indeed to lose Rose, who was a
real sportsman.

Day after day went by without hearing further news of the coming
battle, but one night we noticed some guns coming up the Cambrai
road to take up positions which our astute camouflage brigade evidently
considered well-concealed, in spite of Bourlon observers and German
aeroplanes. In order to disarm suspicion it was impossible to concentrate more than a few extra guns or to allow them to register on
targets before the battle began, since surprise seemed the essence of
our preparations.

Presently the battalion, who were in camp at Lebucquiere, were told
that the surprise attack would shortly take place without any artillery
preparation, the way being prepared for the infantry and cavalry by
masses of tanks. The most ambitious objectives were attributed to the
scheme. They spoke of advancing six miles the first day, making the
gap we had so often heard about, passing cavalry through to surround
all the garrisons of the Hindenburg Line and then marching on, un-
obstructed, into the heart of Belgium. Of course, the announcement
and rumours were received with derision and many sarcastic comments.
We had learnt in a very bitter school the folly of expecting too much
and under-estimating our opponents' strength.

On the other hand, the more we heard about the scheme the more
plausible did it sound, in spite of our conviction that nothing much
could be done before the winter. It was the news about the tanks
that cheered us. These engines of war, which had been improved
within the last twelve months, had never been given a real chance, as
the mud up at Ypres had been so serious as to restrict them to the roads.
Here there was hard, dry ground and their chief role was to plough lanes
through the vast fields of wire that protected the Hindenburg Line,
destroy the machine-gun posts and clear a way for the infantry and
cavalry, the latter having a splendid terrain before them, practically
free of shell-holes. It certainly seemed feasible, but we must have a
good number of divisions that could be poured through the gap.
Would they be forthcoming, or should we find ourselves pushing on
with only our initial impetus to send us forward without any supports?
Passchendaele had only just been taken and there could be very few
divisions fresh enough for another major operation this year. Besides,
as far as we could see, there was no intention of even making our
numbers up to strength; the L.R.B. had received only a small draft
or so since the cutting-up at Ypres and other units were doubtless in a
similar plight. These were our misgivings, but some of us were really
inclined to modify the cynical impressions formed during the spell at
Ypres, conceding that this might be the Big Thing.

We were told to see that our horses were well shod and limbers in good order, as we might have to carry out long treks ; we were to travel as light as possible, throwing away surplus personal kit, dumping at Lebucquiere all non-essential stores and packing up our limbers as far as possible in readiness to march forward at a moment's notice. Rumours grew wilder and wilder. People talked of getting to Namur in less than a week and more and more persons became infected by the optimism, especially when three days' iron rations and extra ammunition were issued to the transport. Bryer, the storeman, in particular, was convinced that the only opposition between us and the German frontier was the Hindenburg Line, which would be completely over-run on the first day : he made several bets of five francs that we should then march forward several miles a day and indulge in open warfare.

On the other hand, we had the opinion of Figg, who had almost invariably been right in his prognostications, and on this occasion spoke his mind freely on the folly of expecting we could do anything on the same scale as the enemy had just accomplished in their coup in Italy.

" Take my word for it, we shan't move from this camp," said he. " I don't mind betting that three days after this wonderful break-through we shall still be taking up rations from these jolly old lines. Something will go wrong somewhere. I'm hanged if I'm going to throw away any of my kit—we'll be unloading all these limbers again shortly and laughing at ourselves for being such blinking fools."

" Z " day was kept a secret, but was felt to be imminent. The extra troops duly arrived at our camp and spent a night there, sleeping wherever they could get a scrap of cover ; then they passed on to the front. One of our drivers reported about the same time that scores of tanks were arriving by train at Ypres and being camouflaged in Havrincourt Forest.

Trendell and Harbord were detailed to attend at Brigade H.Q. with their mounts—for " galloping " purposes between there and Battalion H.Q., transport lines, or wherever else they were required to go. This was the job I coveted, but all of us could not be on it at once. I had recently been on several mounted-orderly trips with Rose and Chrisp, and had found out some alternate routes in case things got too lively.

Then, on November 19th we heard that " Z " day was the morrow. On returning from their jobs that day the limbers had to be loaded with tools, ammunition and stores ready for the great move forward, and we went to bed wondering what the following day would bring forth. Some there were, as usual, who would not credit the attack was coming off at all, especially as the neighbourhood had retained its serenity up to the last moment. But at 6.20 the next morning one big gun fired and then all the others joined in with a deafening roar, disillusioning even the most dubious in our midst. The whole arc from Bullecourt, just north of us, to beyond Havrincourt to the south-east was illuminated with big flashes, for it was not yet light ; at that very moment hundreds of tanks were creeping forward behind the barrage, giving the Bosches the biggest fright of their lives. . . . The Cambria Battle had begun.

It was a very misty morning, so that the aeroplanes which flew just over our heads in order to get their bearings were considerably hampered, but, on the other hand, the fog undoubtedly assisted the tanks and added to the initial confusion of the Bosche. Towards ten o'clock the mist cleared to some extent and we caught sight of an endless stream of cavalry proceeding at the trot up the Havrincourt road. Evidently the main thrust was being made to the south and the Bullecourt attack north of us was only a feint.

Presently we received word that the tanks had broken through and that all was going well, this being followed by a second optimistic message. Havrincourt, Graincourt, Marcoing and other places had fallen with thousands of prisoners and many guns; before evening we had penetrated to Anneux, Neuf Wood and Noyelles. Flesquieres, which held firm, was the one fly in the ointment. North of the Cambrai road our own division had formed a flank, their task being to occupy the bulk of No Man's Land, advance to the German outposts near Moeuvres and wait for the 36th Division on the right to reach their objectives. A dummy tank, consisting of a man on a bicycle with a huge framework attached, had bravely journeyed down the Inchy road to draw fire from the infantry: let us hope he came through unscathed.

In the evening I went up with the brigade ammunition pack-pony convoy, working under an unknown officer, with Lance-Corporal Milcovich as N.C.O. We had to collect bombs in the sunken road near Boursies and make one or two journeys to the new dump that would be found near a huge crater on the Inchy road, out in the old No Man's Land. The Germans had been so surprised that there was little shelling and we had no trouble before reaching the first dump, but soon after setting off with our loads we came to a wide and very deep trench that looked like an insurmountable obstacle. The unknown officer evidently expected to find a bridge, but the men in the trench said the only crossing they knew was a duckboard farther on. A 5.9 landing not far away at this moment made up our leader's mind for him, and he decided that we should cross the duckboard although Milky said it couldn't be done, while I, being the foremost man in the convoy, echoed his sentiments heartily. However, the officer said we must proceed and the obvious thing happened: the board broke in two and the pony disappeared into the abyss to the consternation of the officer and the amusement of all the men except myself. It took me a quarter of an hour to get the bomb-boxes unloaded, for they were wedged against the sides of the trench, and in the meantime the pony was kicking and struggling furiously, having poked his leg through a hole in the floor-board at the bottom of it. When he was free we had a great game getting him out of the trench, the occupants lifting up the duckboards for a matter of fifty yards or so, but eventually I pulled, while Milky pushed, the perspiring brute up a sloping gully on to terra-firma once again. The remainder of the convoy had long since disappeared, but we discovered a proper bridge eventually, reloaded the boxes we had left on the parapet and set off to find the dump, wandering about for some time among the long grass and hedges that made this captured territory so different from any we had yet known.

When we reached the dump at last we found the London Scottish (I think), who seemed to be on the *qui vive* behind a bank; there was a good deal of machine-gun fire and, according to them, only one line of troops in front of them. The division had not suffered much as they were still waiting for the 36th Division, who had not yet taken Moeuvres. For the rest of the night Milky and I worked together on our own, returning to Lebucquiere together and wondering whether we were following up our advantage down south. It must take the

Germans a day or so to bring up troops to this area, and with all that cavalry handy really something ought to be accomplished.

The day's work had been very successful and the enemy had been simply terrified at the tanks looming up out of the darkness. The Hindenburg Reserve System had been breached and in one place we had advanced 4½ miles. All honour to the Tank Corps, who had enabled us to pounce this surprise upon Fritz! The employment of our cavalry in large numbers, however, had depended on their crossing the canal at Masnieres, but the Germans had damaged the bridge and the first tank that tried to cross it crashed through, completing the destruction. Instead of the great " mop-up " by the cavalry, therefore, the mounted troops had hardly got into action at all. The hold up at Flesquieres also had upset calculations, and in spite of this place falling on the following morning and various other advances being made, it was generally felt at the end of the second day that all was not well. We had not yet captured Bourlon Wood on the hill that overlooked the whole battlefield, and so long as that remained in German hands our present positions might prove as awkward as the Ypres salient.

On the third night I drove another man's pair when we took limbers up to the dump, and it was at once obvious that the Germans had brought up reserves and were becoming more aggressive. We found it necessary to canter down the Cambrai road from one end of Boursies to the other, as the village was being severely strafed and houses were toppling down in quick succession. The excitement was increased by the Westminsters attacking and capturing Tadpole Copse, not very far from the dump. The L.R.B.s were in support. Gradually this region was developing into a battlefield of the recognised type. Big guns were coming up in fair numbers : blazing oil-drums, gas shells and other devilries landed in profusion in the German lines, the Cambrai road was completely transformed. The operation was becoming a major one and every hour reduced the chances of our complete success, which had depended on surprise and the capture of Bourlon within forty-eight hours.

During the fourth and fifth days fierce struggles took place on the Bourlon height, which was wreathed in smoke : we watched the big bursts from our horse-lines, speculating as to whether they were our own shells or the enemy's. Although we gained the wood, however, it was not until the 27th that the bulk of the ridge was in our hands, for the Germans made incessant attacks with powerful new forces, considerably reducing the strength of our divisions. Incredible though it may seem, in view of the highly ambitious scheme mooted, on the six miles of active front from Moeuvres to Fontaine only four divisions (including ours) kept up the attack from the 20th till the 27th, which gives an idea of the lack of reserves when this operation started. The number of prisoners was about ten thousand, and over a hundred guns had been taken. The Guards and the 47th London Division which marched past our lines on the way to the battleground were elated at the unlooked-for success in these parts. Perhaps we had got a lot of reserves after all, and in spite of their late appearance they would be able to do something wonderful ! But we were short of bread and, as we had noticed as far back as Ryveldt, a shortage or surfeit of rations changes one's outlook considerably. For six days every scrap of bread that arrived at our stores was sent up to the companies and we contented ourselves with biscuit and bacon for breakfast. When we got back from our all-night trips we had appetites for a six-course dinner, and the fact that only dog biscuits were available did not help to improve our tempers. Figg placed no faith in a favourable outcome of the whole affair and we agreed with him. Allusions were made to the fact that over a week had passed and we were still in the same old camp, as he had forecasted; the limbers had been unloaded again; those who had thrown away surplus kit were grousing; the march to Namur was off! Thank goodness we had not done any premature bell-ringing at the end of the first day like the idiots at home!

Idiots? No, poor folk, was it not natural, after all the talk of impending victory and after a succession of disappointments throughout the year, that they should have been joyful over one success amidst so much that made for depression? Your mother, my mother, all our folk at home, watching and waiting with brave hearts, sending inspiring messages and keeping up a stout heart amidst adversity, must have felt that the gods had indeed forsaken them when they heard of the awful disaster in Italy. The air raids on England were becoming intolerable and the prospect of a fourth war winter was a depressing thought. How natural that they should prematurely rejoice over the Cambrai Battle, and yet how sad! For the greater would be their disappointment over what was to follow.

On the 30th liveliness up the lines reached its zenith, and we first of all wondered whether, with our reinforcements, the wonderful "something" was taking place. All the guns were firing rapid and Bourlon height was simply enveloped in smoke. As time went on, however, it was clear from the nature of the fire and the state of Bourlon Wood that the Bosches were making a serious attack on us, although we did not think for a moment there was any cause for alarm. Then, to our great surprise, we got orders during the morning to harness up at once and be ready for a move. Whether this move would be backward or forward was not mentioned, but nine-tenths of us guessed correctly. To say that you could have knocked us down with a feather is to describe our condition mildly. This was the first time since the Second Battle of Ypres that we had ever had to prepare for the contingency of a backward move under compulsion. Whatever were we coming to? Had we under-estimated the enemy's strength? How different to the position ten days before.

Our Cambrai offensive had left us with a big salient in the enemy's line and that morning the Bosches had attacked at the two extreme corners with the intention of cutting off the troops at the head of it. In the south they were only too successful, for they effected a surprise and overwhelmed our line, so that by 9 a.m. they had reached a spot three miles west of the front from which we had originally started our offensive. The situation was extremely serious, for the Germans were outside our Brigade H.Q. before the staff knew what had happened and one divisional general was nearly captured. Only a counter-stroke by the Guards and tanks saved the break through from having the most unpleasant consequences in the south, but in the north the Bosches received at Bourlon one of the biggest hidings that had ever been administered to them. Owing to the magnificent defence of the 56th, 47th and 2nd Divisions (two of them London Territorials) the Germans battered themselves all day long against a stout wall, leaving Bourlon Wood in our hands and their dead thick in front of it. In the afternoon the L.R.B. relieved the Westminsters, who had had rather a rough time of it.

I spoke to a few of our L.R.B.s who, for some reason or other, came down that night and found them delirious with joy; in fact, they were suffering from blood-lust. They roared with laughter as they told of one battered-in part of a trench, past which the Germans kept trying to creep, but each one appearing received a bullet. They said that our machine-guns had mown down the enemy wholesale. This affair resulted in many gas casualties, including Sergt. Robinson and Gernat of the Signallers, my office friend Whittle of the T.M.B.s, and other old pals. They had worn masks as long as possible, but when they felt the pangs of hunger, prudence had been cast aside together with their respirators. Headquarters suffered very badly.

We spent December 1st in recovering from the surprise of the day before, while the 2nd was devoted to preparations for our departure next morning. The division was being withdrawn immediately and those who were to take over from us arrived on the evening prior to our departure, pitching temporary lines close at hand. The L.R.B. picket, of course, had to keep an ever-watchful eye on our harness, forage and loaded limbers, lest our belongings mysteriously disappear before the dawn. The winter quarters we had taken three months to perfect were to be handed over to others, and the new-comers expressed amazement at the really model camp as we showed them, with reluctance and yet pride, the vegetable garden, washing place, incinerators, brick paths and wagon lines—monuments to months of labour. What interested them most was the light railway, for which we would accept no responsibility.

That night, while those of us in camp were making final preparations for leaving or turning in to sleep amidst the arguments in various quarters of the hut, certain members of the section were doing their last journey up the line. The vehicles detailed for the occasion had to wait for the battalion to be relieved and collect their Lewis-guns and stores—a most unenviable job, for the dump near Moeuvres had earned a horrible reputation. On this night Gordon, who had been up on several evenings in succession, asked Simmonds to take charge instead, and it was curious that on the very night they changed over the transport had its worst experience of this Cambrai Battle.

The journey up the line was quite fair, but when the convoy got within a mile of the dump, Fritz's attention caused it to take to a track, and at their destination there was a warm welcome in store for the men. There never had been any cover at this spot, where the German wire could be plainly seen, and the assembled drivers consequently got no protection when a salvo of high explosives came over not far from them. Sergt. Simmonds and Greene, who were standing together, got wounds in the thigh from pieces of shell that came under the horses and the former promptly told Greene to clear off, whereat he mounted and commenced to gallop away. He had not gone fifty yards, however, before his off-horse dropped down, having been badly wounded, and after trying to carry on by unhooking his traces he had finally to abandon the limber, depositing the poor old animal in a shell-hole. Greene then remounted his remaining steed, whom he rode on for a short distance, but another driver in a fix caused him to stop again. This was O'Hanlan, whose horses had bolted when the shells came over and who now found one of his sets of harness completely broken by shell-splinters. He and Greene then effected a change, leaving the latter with a single horse to ride home bareback; not a word did Greene utter about his wound and it was not until three-quarters of an hour afterwards that he got someone to bind him up—like many more on the section, his own field-dressing had long since been used on a horse. Every pace the horse took must have meant agony to him, but he carried on and delivered the beast at the transport lines, where he almost collapsed. His arrival caused some excitement, as the news spread round the camp and many friends turned out in their weird attire to say good-bye before a motor ambulance arrived for him. Had we known then that he would be awarded the M.M. for his conduct there would have been many congratulations to offer him ; as it was, we all rejoiced that his wound was a " Blighty " one.

We saw Simmonds no more, as his case was also a "Blighty" one, and he went down from a dressing station on the Inchy road to the base, crossed the Channel and took up his abode in England for the remainder of the War. Chrisp therefore became our sergeant, while the vacant N.C.O.'s place was filled by yet another 1914 man, Charles. We were sorry indeed to lose both Simmonds and Greene ; they had come out with the battalion and every old hand that departed left a gap that no new-comer could adequately fill.

The list of misfortunes on that evening is not yet complete, for a shell landed near the water-cart, which Clements was about to draw away with Jumbo and The Grey, slightly wounding Coombs, the R.A.M.C. man, and knocking Jumbo about pretty badly in the leg. Just as on the previous occasion The Grey had been pulled home by Jumbo, so now it was The Grey's turn to help his limping companion. He pulled the whole weight of the loaded limber from the dump to the transport lines, seeming to know there was something the matter with his comrade, who was in such a bad condition that it was obvious he would be unable to accompany us on the morrow. In other words, we should have to hand him over to the relieving unit for veterinary treatment and would see him no more.

Very early the next morning I went out on to the lines to see the old horse who had been my mainstay for over a year and a half. There he stood, with his mutilated leg swathed in the rough and ready bandages that had been applied by lamplight, his brown eyes looking sadly at me, as much as to say : " What have I done to deserve this ? " Chrisp had said that he would be of no further use and would probably have to be shot ; did he instinctively know this as he rubbed his old nose against me ?

I thought of his good points, not his jibbing qualities, in that moment ; how he had taken me all through the mud and squalor of the Somme at the expense of the flesh he had put on in the blessed days at Third Army Headquarters at St. Pol, and how the third winter, the Battle of Arras and Ypres had all seen Jumbo ready at any time to pull his share even though it was sometimes such a bore to start off !

After I had handed over my pair I had watched them with a fatherly interest, even to the extent of putting down more than their fair share of hay while on picket ! Now, I was really upset at the thought of parting with Jumbo.

After an early breakfast, the other horses were taken off the lines and hooked in their limbers. Leaving Ben in someone's charge I crossed over to my old friend again and stood by him until the last moment, a lump rising in my throat.

" Good-bye, Jum ! You've been a faithful old pal and I shan't forget you. Yes, the old Grey's leaving you. So am I. Let's stroke your nose for the last time."

" Get mounted."

" Good-bye, Jum ! "

He begins to fret and whimper. Gordon rides past, the Lewis-gun limbers are moving off down the brick-laid slope into the road, brakesmen are already waiting their opportunity to slip half their impediments on to the limbers. Taking a last look round, I see the other unit preparing to take possession of the deserted lines. I also see a solitary horse, head erect as far as his chain will permit, plunging against the rope and prancing to and fro—on three legs.

CHAPTER XXVIII.

The Fourth Winter.

(*December, 1917–March, 1918.*)

Reverting to the defensive—The Vimy Ridge sector—An imaginary speech by Lloyd George—Deferred Christmas celebrations—In a good old grousing mood —Two incidents at Caucourt—February speculations: tense expectancy— My last leave.

" Well, they say the first seven years of a war are always the worst, that's one consolation ! "

This time-worn phrase was uttered at least half a dozen times a day by Mears in a well-meant endeavour to keep up the spirits of the grousers in the hut and harness-room ; he never wearied of it and others took it up until it came to be the recognised answer to every complaint. reasonable or otherwise.

We were back at Arras once more, in a part hitherto unexplored by us. North of the city runs the great Arras-Lens road, about which had sprung up a large collection of camps of all kinds set out on Ideal Home Garden City lines. Nobody was driven to building bivvies or keeping horses in the open. The Army had now realised the necessity for huts and stables, sufficient of which were erected to house every unit that could possibly be required, at any rate in these regions. The whole area made a delightful mark for German guns and aeroplanes, but the winter lull had descended upon Vimy Ridge and surroundings and there was not much annoyance from the enemy.

After our trek from the Cambrai front, involving two nights at Bernaville, we had taken up quarters on December 5th in Nissen huts near Ecurie, not far from the Lens road. Here we found water laid on, troughs only a few yards away, and a divisional canteen, cinema and the Bow Bells close at hand, altogether a better home for spending the winter in than we had yet experienced.

But it was our *fourth* winter, a fact that led many people to think gloomily of the Thirty Years' War and wonder whether we were just at the beginning of a life-time struggle. The omens were certainly less favourable than they had seemed at the end of previous years. In the 1914-15 winter we were under the impression that some such battle as Neuve Chapelle would bring the War to a victorious conclusion. When a year's marking time had proved that the offensive must be postponed, we lived during the second winter on the deferred hopes of the first. Then the Battle of the Somme took place, leaving us at the end of 1916 on the high tide of success. Everything had looked favourable for 1917 and the Kaiser's peace offer had been treated with derision.

Now we were faced with very different prospects. On December 2nd hostilities had ceased on the Russian front, our allies welcoming their German " brothers " with open arms ; the Russian General Staff had surrendered to the Bolsheviks. Already Germany had stiffened her ranks at Ypres and Cambrai with drafts from Russia and had even brought complete divisions across. Now it appeared that she would be able to hold the Eastern front with a mere handful of troops and turn her whole weight upon our line in the West. We even got official instructions early in December that we were to revert to the defensive, in other words, to " mark time " and wait and see what would develop. It was such a reversal of roles that it took us a month or more really to appreciate that our people were in earnest.

What the next year would bring forth was more a matter of uncertainty than had ever been the case before. Though our confidence in the ultimate defeat of the Germans was undiminished, it nevertheless looked as though there were stern times ahead in the near future and it would therefore be foolish to pretend our spirits soared as high as they had done months before. The Cambrai Battle had put a final stopper on the optimists. A few days after leaving there we had had to evacuate the whole of Bourlon Wood owing to enemy gas shelling, which had in turn necessitated giving up other ground, so that the major part of our Cambrai gains was lost to us. The Germans claimed six thousand prisoners and a hundred guns. From the outset it had been an operation dependent for its success upon a great weight of numbers, which were not forthcoming owing to the terrible casualties up at Ypres. Not even Bill Bryer was now prepared to bet that we could do much before America had thrown her weight into the scale. That great " Associate " power—she did not wish to be called an " Ally "—was no doubt making big preparations, but her thoughts seemed to be set upon 1919 and so far the number of Yanks in France was only four divisions while not one was yet in the firing-line. What odds had we to fight against in the meantime ? That it was too early to judge.

In view of this none-too-hopeful outlook, it is surprising that we were not more depressed than we were ; but there was plenty of beer to be had and the effect of imbibing it is the same the world over, even with the hundred per cent. diluted French variety. This was supplied in various canteens, there being no civilians at Écurie. We had seen French people at Bernaville when we passed through, this being our first glimpse of civilians since the end of August, but the type that met our eyes was not such that we bemoaned our fate in passing out " beyond the pale " once more. Arras, of course, harboured them, but there was no point in walking a mile and a half down into that ghost-like town when refreshing, comfort-giving liquor could be obtained at a more reasonable price close at hand.

Those that preferred cocoa could line up in the queue at the Y.M.C.A. marquee, which was a well-patronised establishment just off the Lens road. Figg and I paid it a visit one evening, hearing that a piano was to be found there and being anxious to try over one or two songs for the next dinner or concert. In order to spare the feelings of those present, I played with the soft pedal down while Figg, bending over me, hummed or whistled the tunes " pianissimo " for my benefit. But it appeared to get on the nerves of the assembly, who would have preferred some choruses, and after about ten minutes Figg whispered that we were " getting the bird."

" Play us something cheerful." " Jolly well sung." " B—— fine song," came from various quarters of the marquee.

" Don't let's knuckle under," said Figg. " Try the last one."

We made the attempt, but it was greeted with shouts of " Horatio Bottomley at the front singing to the troops," and similar remarks, so we finally made our departure midst sighs of relief and requests for someone to get up and PLAY. That was our first and last visit to the place.

The battalion had taken over the line near Gavrelle, about five miles east-north-east of Arras, this being the limit reached in the spring " Push " when the Vimy Ridge had been taken. Between the front line and Arras lay the southern portion of the Ridge, the bulk of which was still being defended by the Canadians to the north of us. It was therefore a very vital sector of the line, for the British Command prized the Vimy Ridge above all other vantage points, even Passchendaele itself.

The ration trips were monotonous and cold, the journey being long, while the wind and snow blew fiercely across the heights that we had to traverse. Starting off before dusk, we made our way by a circuitous route through the battered suburb of St. Nicolas until we reached the Gavrelle road, running east-north-eastwards from the city, after which our journey continued in a perfectly straight line. There was a stiff hill to climb until we got to the famous railway cutting that had figured in the April fighting. The bridge across this was vital, as it was the sole means of road communication with all the batteries and troops east of it. In the event of a German shell blowing it up, all the guns and vehicles forward would be caught like rats in a trap unless they were taken by a circuitous route across other divisional areas, which would no doubt require special permits from at least twenty different officials. Recognising its importance, the Army stationed a military policeman to count the vehicles which crossed over and frighten away German shells.

This spot we were not allowed to pass in daylight; east of it the road was rather exposed and all the time we trod it there was ever present an eerie feeling that our retreat lay through the neck of a bottle while, on the road itself, there was no protection from shells or bullets. The latter whizzed past much too frequently from the line to the right of us, which curved back around Greenland Hill. German overhead machine-gun fire could be brought to bear on us for the last mile of our journey and at the dump itself we were glad to dismount in order to stand behind our animals.

We came upon the dump unexpectedly, our progress being barred by a trench dug right across the road just before we got to Gavrelle. This was known as Marine Trench, where Gordon went along to talk with H.Q., leaving his mounted orderly to mind the two horses until his return. The limbers turned round here, deposited their loads and made their way home separately, but the lot of the drivers was an unhappy one as, according to regulations, they had to go at a walking pace in the cold for mile after mile until they reached Ecurie again, with not a soul to speak to on their way. In this matter I was glad to have a single mount for a change. The wait on the Gavrelle road was cold and lonely, of course, for Gordon frequently spent an hour or more at H.Q., taking instructions and telling stories, but once we were mounted, with our horses' heads turned to home, we trotted the greater part of the way back. Gordon chatted from first to last and frequently warmed the cockles of his orderly's heart with a sip from his flask.

One night Major Wallis was coming down to the transport lines on his way for leave, and I had the tedious task of holding three impatient horses for over two hours in a blinding snowstorm. What with the horses' peevishness at the snow, their irritation with one another and their wind-up at the machine-gun fire, which even the worst of weather did not silence, the vigil was worse than any sentry duty or picket I had ever done. An occasional star-light threw into relief the ruined village just ahead and once a company man came out of his dug-out to draw some water from the cart ; otherwise there was not a single incident to divert my brain from the slough of despond in which it was wallowing. I was thinking of the Russian armistice and the German divisions hurrying West. When the Major and the T.O. did arrive, they mounted their steeds and in another moment were trotting off in the homeward direction, Ben following in their wake as fast as his fat legs would carry him. But even trotting was not pleasant on a slippery road in pitch darkness, in the midst of blinding snowstorms, and when we got to the lines Wallis remarked to me :

" Smith, I wouldn't be on the transport for a thousand a year."

I told him it was nice to have a hut to come back to, in these days of decent camps, but he replied that on a dark night he thought the discomforts of the transport worse than the perils of a company.

Unfortunately the companies had to spend Christmas in the trenches, but the transport men who did not happen to be on duty on Christmas night were able to have a feed in their huts, with songs and revelry to follow. A few days before we had shifted our quarters to Nelson Camp, situated right on the Lens road, where we were thrown into close contact with the remainder of our brigade. This afforded the merrier members of the section an opportunity to serenade a large number of acquaintances on Christmas night, among whom was the Wesleyan padre, outside whose abode the carol singers made their most magnificent effort. The reverend gentleman, who came to the door of his tent, summed up the condition of the choristers well when he said in a whisper, " I'm sorry there's no whisky left." He then jingled money in his pocket, but one of the party told him that nothing was farther from their thoughts ! Another person to be serenaded was Q.M.S. Hamilton, from whom they got precisely what they expected : sticking a fierce face out of his door he shouted grumpily, " Nothing doing ! " and disappeared again.

Nelson Camp, and indeed all these camps on the Lens road, could be rendered untenable if the enemy commanded observation from Monchy and made any appreciable advance up the Cambrai road, or if any portion of the Ridge fell to him. Only our hold on these places enabled us to turn the whole neighbourhood into a kind of suburb of London ! Emerging from St. Catherine's (Arras) and following the great wide road up the hill until it reached the level of the spur on which it ran towards Lens, you would first come upon a huge ammunition dump on the right. Woe betide any driver or pedestrian who passed by smoking a cigarette ! On the opposite side of the road were an artillery camp and a salvage depot. Farther on came one or two groups of huts for infantry, then our divisional horse-lines and camps, followed by artillery lines, Y.M.C.A. and other divisional stables. On the right were the 62nd Divisional concert party, then an infantry camp, then the "Bow Bells." And so on, right down the Lens road, nothing but homes for troops and horses, huts, head-quarters, light-railways and dumps.

After a few more days of toil we saw the old year out and welcomed the new—in lukewarm fashion, 'tis true, for it brought with it no stereo-typed "Dawn of Victory" speeches such has had characterised previous New Years. Lloyd George made a speech on January 5th, of which Conibeer, who first read it in a paper, said that he was "positively grovelling in the dust." His speech set forth what we were *not* fighting for and was evidently influenced by the desire for peace that was daily becoming more insistent. It was a distinctly mild utterance compared with the inspiriting orations of former times, which were sometimes rather exasperating to the man at the front, who, more often than not, had no love for politicians with their fine phrases about "not sheathing the sword." His usual comment was : "They ought to come and have a taste of it themselves." We were beginning to think that if our orators did less boasting about what we should do to our fallen enemies and concentrate more on helping us to conquer we should make far better progress.

Just at this time we drafted for the next transport magazine an imaginary speech delivered by Mr. Lloyd George at the Albert Hall on August 4th, 1920, that is, at the beginning of the seventh year of War, which sums up our feelings at this time so much better than I can describe them that I make no apology for inserting it in full. A copy was sent home in a censored letter, but Gordon referred it first to Colonel Husey, thinking that it did not tend to the maintenance of good order and discipline. The Colonel, however, merely had a good laugh and let it pass. It next found its way to a newspaper in England which announced publication of it, but through the zeal of the Editor it was first referred to the Censor. It never appeared in print !

FORECAST OF A SPEECH DELIVERED BY MR. LLOYD GEORGE AT THE ALBERT HALL, AUGUST 4TH, 1920.

" Gentlemen,—On this sixth anniversary of the commencement of the greatest War that has ever afflicted our tortured humanity, I have been asked to reiterate the aims which we set out to accomplish and to review the military and economic situation as it stands at this moment.

" You are all aware of the causes of this conflagration and the success which has all along attended the efforts of the Allies to crush German militarism and establish for ever a comity of nations whose watchword shall be freedom.

" With the entry into the War of Norway, Sweden, Switzerland, Spain, Denmark, Holland and Greenland on the side of Germany. and the active support which the Central Empires have derived from the rejuvenated Russian Army, our difficulties have been great and the way has sometimes been tortuous and thorny. But with the advent of Costa Rica on our side, this addition to our enemies' strength has been more than neutralised, and we hope soon to see our new allies fighting side by side with the Americans and ourselves in our efforts to free the world. (Applause.)

" On all fronts our arms are still scoring extraordinary successes. The Germans and Russians certainly got through the Indian Passes in the earlier part of the year, but the heroic defence and self-sacrifice of our troops have for the time being brought the invaders to a standstill. In the Egyptian theatre of war our troops have carried out a masterly retirement into the East African forests, severely harassing the pursuing Turks and Bulgarians. Although Egypt is temporarily in the hands of the enemy, it has no influence whatever on the ultimate result of the War.

" Our withdrawal from Salonika was a wise step, necessitated by the growing importance of the Western Front, and although the Germans and Russians have since overrun Greece, our Army took all the necessary steps to prevent them doing so by destroying roads and bridges. The establishment of German naval bases at Salonika and round the coasts of Italy and Spain has rendered sea-journeys in the Mediterranean somewhat hazardous, but since we lost the Suez Canal and Gibraltar, it has not been necessary for us to use that route, so the enemies' energies in that direction have been wasted. (Hear ! hear !)

" On the Algerian and Moroccan fronts the invading German and Spanish armies are meeting with energetic resistance from tribes of nomads and Sudanese irregulars, who are withdrawing in order and in accordance with plan.

" The landing of Japanese in Canada and the United States is certainly an unwelcome diversion, but several regiments of Red Indians and Jamaica negroes have been hurried to the threatened districts and we shall soon drive the invaders into the sea.

" On the Western Front the most colossal battle of the War is proceeding. Twenty-five million German, Austrian, Russian, Scandinavian, Swiss and Dutch soldiers are hurling themselves against the stone-wall barrier of the Allies. Ten million British and American oppose them, together with some hundred thousand Frenchmen, fifty thousand Indians, two hundred Portuguese and ten Belgians. (Cheers.) It has been necessary to withdraw our line to X—— and Z—— and by this smart ruse we have caused considerable inconvenience and losses to the enemy, who will have to bring up men and guns over muddy country, hindered by our barbed wire and twenty-inch guns. Our air service has been doing most excellent work during this strategical retirement. Yesterday we brought two enemy machines down and forced four to descend : only twelve of ours are missing."

VOICE : " What about the Battle of H—— ? "

" What about the Battle of H—— ? That was merely an experiment. We never expected to break through. We withdrew to our original line after capturing and holding the enemy's trenches for forty-eight hours. The Germans claim to have captured nine thousand prisoners and forty guns. As a matter of fact, WE captured nine thousand and one Germans, four machine guns, twenty duckboards and several tin buckets. Altogether it was a nasty blow for the Hun and a distinct success for the British Army. I might add that the spirit of the troops is excellent.

" If we turn to our mighty Fleet, the same reassuring facts stare us in the face. During the past week, enemy submarines sank fifty large vessels and seventy-two small ones, while the number of boats unsuccessfully attacked was two. These figures show a decrease on the previous week's returns and I can state with absolute confidence that we have the submarine peril in hand. During the last five and a half weeks we have sunk nearly twice the number of U-boats sunk during the four weeks in February and the first week and a half in March. (Cheers.) That excludes last Thursday and the second Sunday in February.

" There is one difficulty which the Allies have to face and that is this. No ships are available to supply the vast American Army with its needs, as ships have been sunk at a greater rate than they have been built and their Army is thus placed in a serious predicament. Some of them are abandoning the trenches and raiding the British A.S.C. depots for stores. To remedy this I have appealed to the Irish People's Government to allow the work in the Belfast yards to proceed and negotiations are taking place to lessen the number of enemy submarine bases on the coast of Cork. I am consulting the Minister of National Service as to the possibility of freeing certain skilled men from the army, to speed up the shipbuilding work on the Clyde. I am also prohibiting the import of Grape Nuts, watches and perambulators, and hope that the tonnage thus saved will enable more raw materials to be brought to this country.

" I appeal to those at home to do without many of the necessaries of life : they will soon be unobtainable. We want ten million more acres put under the plough. I appeal to the farmers and farm-hands to settle their disputes. We want more guns and aeroplanes. I adjure the engineers and aircraft workers now on strike to return to work. Let the army at home do its bit behind the army in the field. Railwaymen ! patch up your disputes and come off strike : it's all for the sake of little Belgium. 'Bus conductors and bootmakers, the lads at the front are waiting eagerly for 'buses and boots. These strikes give encouragement to the enemy and cripple our output.

" Food is scarce—we must eat less and still less. Adopt the voluntary rations—bully beef, biscuits, swedes and parsnips, and we shall yet frustrate the designs of our enemies. Subscribe to the Fifteenth War Loan more generously. Make the total ten billions in place of the paltry £50 so far subscribed and you will further strengthen our remarkable staying power. Wear less clothes ! Our ancestors wore fig leaves and bear skins : let us emulate their example. Let us present to the world such a picture of self-denial that the fame of Britain shall ever be enshrined in the annals of posterity.

" And now we come to the question of man power. We want men, more men and still more men. We want them for shipbuilding, munitions, agriculture, railways, mines, the House of Commons, the music halls and the pulpit——"

VOICES : " *And* the infantry."

"——and the infantry. Where are we to draw them from ? I have just arranged with the Minister of National Service for the release of all imbeciles, criminals and enemy aliens, and for a revision of the starred occupations. Barbers, waiters, farm-hands,

railwaymen, miners, munition workers and candlestick makers
are to have their exemptions revised. Women will take the
place of men in such jobs as night-watchmen, road orderlies,
artillery drivers and officers' batmen. We must cast aside con-
ventionality and old shibboleths in this hour of Victory. Believe
me, we've won the War and when I say this I'm not speaking
idly. We've won the War—and the Huns know it. In a short
time all will be well."

Voice : "What about the air raids ? "

"What about the air raids ? Well, we are coping with that
problem. Yesterday morning several hundred machines came
over London, but many were turned away by the accurate firing
of our guns. Two were brought down in flames and others were
riddled with bullets. Our machines flew up and gave chase on
the return journey and all except twelve landed safely. The
casualties, so far as I can ascertain, are believed to be lighter
than the day before. They were four thousand eight hundred
killed and sixteen thousand wounded, including ten babies and
an invalid. We must look at these things in their proper perspec-
tive. The population of London, in spite of the War, is quite
three millions, so it is truly surprising that so few casualties
occurred. We shall certainly carry out reprisals on a large scale,
but the growing demands of the Western and Egyptian fronts
necessitate our sending aeroplanes there faster than they're being
built.

"What stands in the way of Peace ? Why, since we are victorious, can we not impose our peace terms to-morrow ? What
stands in the way of a just settlement ? Why, the *enemy.* Blind
and prostrate with rage, they will not listen to our terms. They
mock at and ridicule our War Aims.

"Our War Aims, gentlemen, may be summed up in three
words : Reparation, Restitution and Guarantees. To him who
prates about peace at this juncture, I address these words :
Remember Belgium ! Remember that fair land still in the foul
hands of the Hun, her peasants petrified, their poultry pilfered.
Let us win back by force of arms what has been taken from her.
Remember France ! We shall not sheath the sword until Alsace-
Lorraine, Westphalia, Baden and Wurtemburg are handed over
to our faithful Ally. Remember Montenegro, whose great monarch
is sitting on the platform here with me. Remember Serbia and
Roumania ! We shall not rest until Bulgaria and the greater
part of Austria-Hungary be handed over to these poor little nations.
Think of Nurse Thomson, put into irons and shot at dawn. Think
of Lieut. Jones and Private Bill Smith ! What of Portugal,
overrun by Spaniards and robbed of her oranges ? What shall
I say of Italy, trampled under the Austrian heel, with all her
mandolines commandeered ? We demand that Italy shall have
the whole of Switzerland and a large part of Austria and Albania.
Think of poor Greece, invaded by the Russians : we shall not sheath
the sword until Constantinople is handed over to M. Venizelos.
The map of Europe must be entirely re-drawn. Persia and
Afghanistan must be freed of the enemy and he must evacuate
Egypt, Palestine and Mesopotamia before we will discuss peace.
Remember America ! Remember China ! Remember Cuba,
Liberia, Brazil and Ecuador ! Think of Nicaragua, Paraguay

and Abyssinia ! These countries cry aloud for salvation. Shall we be deaf to their cries ? Never ! ! ! (Loud applause.)

"The armies of the Central Empires must be demobilised and sent to St. Helena. Their navies must be handed over to us. The Kaiser must be delivered to Scotland Yard. An indemnity of £2,000,000,000,000,000 must be paid to Belgium and £1,000 to Nurse Thomson's uncle. We are in a position to demand these terms. Failing acceptance of them, we shall fight on to the last drop of our blood, to the last farthing of our money. (Loud cheers.) Only hang on a little longer and I have no hesitation in saying that we shall have all the remains of our gallant menfolk back on our own shores. (Cheers.)

"With the vast armies which Costa Rica is preparing to place by our side, we shall break through on the Western Front and shall then be on the high road to Berlin. Brethren, bright as the road to Victory has so far been, that road will be brighter ! ! ! " (Loud and prolonged applause.)

* * * *

The companies' deferred Christmas celebrations did not take place until we were settled in the dirty village of Frevillers, some thirteen miles from Arras, with nothing of interest in the place except an estaminet or two. It was a second edition of Wascherville or Fosseux, with mud-walled stables for the horses, snow all around and not a place within many miles that was worth a visit—the sort of village where one was completely dependent upon Army rations and the humorous contents of the regimental canteen. Judge of our chagrin, therefore, when a five per cent. decrease was effected in our rations as the result of an order from some of the higher authorities, who probably had no conception of the quantity that got lost or " won " on the way to us. As a result of this curtailment of our already insufficient diet, the Q.M.S.s. in our brigade one day held a meeting at which it was resolved that our new rations were quite insufficient to keep us fit. They then made strong representations to the D.A.Q.M.G., who eventually effected some improvement. A little while afterwards an unknown officer arrived from some staff headquarters or other to lecture our Q.M.S.s. on waste !

The officers held their belated festivities in one of the rooms of the best estaminet in the village. The programme consisted of dinner, champagne and whisky, and a sing-song, but, having little talent in the entertainment line, the Colonel requisitioned two transport men to sing one or two parodies which had been delivered in recent concerts. I was to " win " the padre's harmonium, bring it into the dining room on a given signal, and strike up the first accompaniment. As a reward we received a piece of ham and potato salad to start off, but the two vocalists, who had only come on the understanding that there was to be liquid refreshment, were thinking far more of the drink to follow. They each sang a song, their turns being much appreciated, but to their disgust the only reward was a single glass of champagne. Therefore, while the officers continued the musical programme, the two vocalists had to fortify themselves for the next effort at their own expense by purchasing champagne in the kitchen, where a host of batmen were busy with plates and dishes and looking upon the intruders as infernal nuisances. Presently A came in and gave another turn, followed by B, and it was evident from their performance that they found the flowing bowl a begetter of self-confidence, not to mention an aid to brilliant voice-production. In short, each was anxious to give a recital on his own and they presently got to the stage where, as soon as one had finished a song, the other would thrust him out into the kitchen regions and start another turn without any invitation whatever from the long-suffering audience who were, however, too happy to mind.

" Order, please, gentlemen," shouted A at the top of his voice. " Give your kind attention for a minute." Then followed his fifth song.

In the kitchen I believe these two were " jolly good turns." They had been joined by at least three other transport men, always sure to be on the spot if there was any chance of a refresher, and the party caused quite an obstruction to the batmen, whose futile requests to leave the premises were received with buffoonery or cordial toasts. Now and again an officer, happening to come outside, would be fervently gripped by the hand.

" Cheerio, old man," or " Tata, old chap," said A, patting him affectionately.

One of these officers happened to be Captain Gordon, whose surprise may be imagined when he saw half a dozen of his section imbibing in the kitchen, among whom was the picket (lamp and all) who should have been patrolling the stables.

" What are you doing with that lamp ? " asked Gordon.

" Which lamp, sir ? " asked the picket, hedging while he thought of an excuse.

" Come, come, I'm not so far gone as that," said Gordon.

" I'm the picket, sir."

" Then why aren't you going round the stables ? "

" I'm looking for a missing horse, sir."

" Well, you won't find it in that glass. Get back on the lines."

Next day the miscreant heard a great deal more about that missing horse, not to mention a broken picket lamp, but his punishment, like his name, shall remain unrecorded.

After this the companies had their dinners on separate evenings. Our vocalists, A and B, far from having made nuisances of themselves on the occasion above, now found they were the idols of the hour in the eyes of everyone but the batmen, so that each company invited them to be present to enliven the proceedings. We wrote some more parodies, getting a knock at the rations, at our short rests, at Q.M.S. Hamilton and sundry celebrities, which added to the gaiety of the entertainments.

But the gaiety was superficial. It was a means of forgetting cares for an hour or so. Occasionally the boom of a gun would remind you that the firing-line was at hand, that the men who were merrymaking here a fortnight ago were now up there and that you would soon be following in their footsteps. Only two of the four company dinners had taken place in the estaminet " dining saloon " before the peremptory order to move up again reached the battalion. The authorities were bent on improving our defences and required us for wiring fatigues up on the Vimy Ridge, but we were promised the remainder of our rest after another week.

This sudden departure took place on the 16th January, the battalion moving up to a camp east of the Lens road, while the transport were allotted the cellars of ruined houses in the suburb of St. Catherine's, not far away. The animals were tied among the ruins wherever space could be found and the picket were responsible for such an extended area that they could not prevent the thieving of all kinds of harness and materials from outlying "stables." From here I took on a pair for a very short time and had one or two interesting trips through Roclincourt to the Ridge.

On the 20th an old first battalion man named Gill, who had just come out again with a draft, walked down to the transport billets to visit Conibeer and other friends. We found him dubious as to the possibility of a German attack and very optimistic as to its outcome if it took place, being convinced that if the Germans couldn't break through at the Second Battle of Ypres they would never be able to do so now.

I may say at once that we shared this conviction and confidence, but to tease him we assumed an air of utter disbelief in anything, an attitude that was fast becoming the most fashionable feature of the British soldier's inevitable grouse. It quite infuriated Gill, who came to the front again after years spent in England amidst decent surroundings, in the same frame of mind as I had had when setting out from Southampton four years ago almost to the very day. Gill now felt as I had done when we arrived at Rouen to find the regulars " fed to the wide " and cynical over our enthusiasm.

" I'm sorry to see you're all feeling fed up," said he.

" Isn't it enough to make anyone fed up," said Mac, " when we're crying out for more men after four years of war, not to carry out an offensive, but to hold our own blessed line ? "

The whole fact of the matter was that we could not yet swallow the bitter pill of acting on the defensive when our whole training and outlook for three years had been aggressive. Words fail to describe our feelings towards the Russians ; we were impatient with the Italians and peevish with the French, who were forcing us to take over more of their line. No less was our resentment against the Government, whose fear of the workmen at home prevented strong action when it was needed.

Our battles in 1917 had given the British some 800,000 casualities against 650,000 for the Somme year. Whether these would have been minimised by different strategy or tactics is not a matter for argument here. The fact had to be faced and so had the future. In face of these losses most urgent steps should have been taken to ensure the Army being kept up to strength in 1918. Shipbuilding, agriculture, mines, munitions, railways, not to mention non-essential industries, were employing millions of men of whom large numbers were not indispensable ; but the claims of the poor infantry were met with a " non possumus." Our numbers were so low that one battalion in every four was disbanded to provide drafts for the others and we thought at one time that we ourselves were to be treated like this ; but it was our second battalion that was broken up, while in our brigade the poor old Q.V.R.s were selected for this treatment.

We resumed our rest in the village of Caucourt, not far from Aubigny, at which the greater part of the Rangers, who had been eliminated from the 168th Brigade, came to us as reinforcements. It was a shame that old-established Territorial battalions like the Rangers, Q.V.R.s and others should be swept out of existence, considering all their traditions and the splendid esprit de corps that existed in them. The men were furious over it and it was only the good tact of Colonel Husey in welcoming the Rangers as fellow-riflemen, that reconciled them to the change of badge. We soon made friends with the new-comers, who quickly merged into the battalions, becoming indistinguishable from our fellows.

I remember the village of Caucourt for two outstanding reasons. The first was my trouble with the M.O., and the second was the momentary cloud under which I passed when I was conducted to the orderly room as a prisoner. The tiff with the doctor arose from the fact that I, like many others on the transport, had been treating I.C.T. myself with lint and bandages sent from home. We found that a good hot fomentation put on four times a day by an obliging pal was more efficacious than a lukewarm one applied, at the outside, twice daily by an overworked aid-post ; so we doctored ourselves instead of making a lot of fuss over a sick report. But one day when we attended baths an officious R.A.M.C. man had the effrontery to look us up and down as we emerged from the bath-house clad in nature's garb, making a note of everyone who had a blemish on his body. That evening my name appeared among others who had to see the M.O. next day and the way in which Captain Riddell cursed me for presuming to be my own doctor will live in my memory until my dying days. Truly I was sorry to have fallen out with him as he had been very good to me in the past and he seemed to take my action very much to heart. He looked contemptuously at me for a week after that, while I inwardly cursed him for a similar period. Sick parades became once more the bane of my life ; and I am almost tempted to say that the I.C.T. got worse !

The other incident came upon me like a bombshell. One night the Sergeant told me that I had to attend at the orderly room at half-past nine next day and that Captain Gordon was to be present. For the life of me I had no idea what it could be about and, having nothing on my conscience, it was with perfect serenity that I waited for the dawn. Three men had to assist me to clean my bandolier, boots, hat-badge, etc., in order to get respectable in time for the appointment ; Cornford lent me his new tunic, someone else loaned his putties. At the last minute I appeared on the scene immaculate, full of excitement as to what was in the wind. The B.S.M., orderly sergeants and other signs of officialdom were present outside Headquarters. Gordon was looking distinctly ill at ease.

" What have you been up to ? " said he.

" I'm sure I don't know." I looked round at all the faces and thought I detected the shadow of a twinkle in B.S.M. Adams' eye. The exact orders which followed are dim in my memory. The guard fell in on either side while, speechless with amazement, I complied with the S.M.'s instruction : " Prisoner, remove your hat. Right turn ! "

In one minute everyone had clicked into his regulation position in different parts of the orderly room, leaving me facing Colonel Husey and Major Wallis, who sat at an imposing table doing their utmost to hide a smile. Wallis looked up perplexedly and said, " Good morning."

The Colonel instantly got to work, reading out from a document in front of him something to the following effect :

" Private and confidential.

" Secret Intelligence Dept.,

" Rifleman A. M. Smith, 300281, 1/5 London Rgt.

" It has been ascertained that this rifleman is a subscriber to the
. . . ' and inasmuch as this paper is a pacifist journal circulation of which is expressly forbidden in France you are

requested to investigate the matter, watch this man closely and take the necessary steps if he is found to be carrying on any propaganda among the troops.

"(Signed) Captain NOSEYPARKER."

It is doubtful whether there was a single man in the room (except, of course, the S.M.) whose face had not broadened into a grin during the reading of the communication. Colonel Husey asked what I had got to say about it.

"Only this, sir. At Frevillers, some of us found a copy of the ' . . . ' which contained part of the contents of the secret treaties with Russia, which have now been published by the Bolsheviks. No other paper has printed them, and since we were interested we thought we'd like to see further numbers. I sent a subscription, but they have now returned the money because they're not allowed to post copies to the Front. Here is their reply."

"That settles it then," said the Colonel.

"As for stirring up trouble among the troops . . ."

Colonel Husey laughed. "My dear Smith, you needn't say anything about that. They don't know you like I do. The paper was for your private edification only and I shall tell them so. Perhaps it is just as well they didn't open that Lloyd George's speech ! "

A minute later I was a free man once more and Captain Gordon walked off with me to the transport lines.

"When they told me to appear last night," said he, " I got a fright. I made sure you'd put some military information in your letters. They must have steamed that one open and then allowed it to go to its destination. I've never seen the ' . . . '."

"It's a rag," I admitted, " a rag of the rottenest type. But it's the only paper that has published the details of our treaties with Russia, and as they are known in all enemy and neutral countries we have a perfect right to know them too."

"It certainly looks as if our people were ashamed of them," he agreed.

President Wilson's Fourteen Points had been issued on January 8th. They were endorsed in the main by the Allied Governments. And first on the list was : " Open covenants of peace and no secret diplomacy " !

* * * *

February was a month of tense expectation. A succession of trench raids took place on both sides, but the enemy was noticeably more aggressive than he used to be. In Jaunary alone he had carried out 75, as against 14 made by the British and 84 by the French. Some of them failed, but in many cases he succeeded in capturing prisoners. Quite a number of these raids took place in our neighbourhood and they were frequently attended by heavy gas-shelling of our back areas, our batteries in particular receiving a deluge, calculated to place the teams hors de combat or, at any rate, seriously disorganise our protective barrage.

War correspondents told us that the Germans were undergoing intensive training behind their lines, sometimes with engineers, sometimes with tanks, across mimic canals. Dumps and gun positions were being established and, furthermore, leave had been stopped in the German Army. Troops were now pouring across from Russia and the artillery coming West included Austrian batteries.

But it was not likely that the enemy could make any real progress if we had failed to do so in 1916 and 1917 with our then superiority of guns and man-power. At the worst Fritz would only outnumber us slightly on the whole of the Western Front and our people ought to be aware in good time of the portion that was likely to be attacked by overwhelming forces and take steps to meet them. From bitter experience we knew that barbed wire and trenches were terrible obstacles to the attack, and we were now at the right end of the machine-gun. It made us almost hope that the Germans would make such an attempt, so that we could exact vengeance for Glencorse Wood. All talk of them breaking through left us cold. The utmost we expected was a good hammering until the cream of the German army, their storm troops, was destroyed. Some there were who didn't " think Jerry 'ud be sich a fool." At any rate weeks passed without the fears of an attack being realised and when the cold month of February gave place to the bright, spring-like days of March, the incredulous ones took a certain amount of credit on themselves at the vindication of their beliefs. Verdun had started on February 21st, said they. Sure, Fritz wasn't going to be such a fool again !

We made our home once more in Nelson Camp, whither we had gone on February 7th, while the companies carried on with ordinary trench warfare routine, occasionally coming to Roclincourt or Maroeuil for a few days. We had quiet, moderately " warm " and occasional exciting ration trips with no incidents worth special mention. The Grey received a slight wound one night, while being driven by Volze.

One of the chief occupations during the day in Nelson Camp was to make our huts and stables splinter-proof by building up banks of earth around them, according to a definite formula laid down by corps or division. The annoying part about this scheme was that the Army's idea as to thickness, height, and so on, varied from day to day.· A hut was made splinter-proof one day and next morning someone would come round with a new idea, so that another pattern had to be done . . . yet even another . . . Of course, the G.O.C. made his periodical inspection and we came through the ordeal quite satisfactorily though our pack-saddles were adversely criticised.

Leave had been going much better for the last few months, so that my turn came round again on February 23rd. This time each man got fourteen clear days at home, a boon that must have made those in Salonika and Egypt very envious. The food question was getting serious at home and I actually took with me butter, lard, tea, &c., purchased in the E.F.C. at Arras, in order to eke out the rations on which our folk were subsisting. What an example our people at home still afforded us who were for ever grumbling and grousing. They were putting up with more privations than they told us about, without swearing nearly as much as we did. They were all " fed up," of course, but their faith in the Tommies was as strong as it ever had been.

While home I met an infantry officer friend who was on leave from the front opposite St. Quentin. He declared that the Germans could break through opposite him as easily as anything—there was nobody to stop them, for we had taken over a very extended front from the French. Each division in those regions held an average line of about four miles for a stretch of over forty miles, brigades were reduced as elsewhere to three battalions, reserves were scanty and defences were in a bad state. What was even more worrying was that my friend was confident that his was the portion of the front where the blow would fall.

Daily we opened the papers anxiously to learn if this had happened, but they were merely witness to the signing of the Russian peace and the concluding of treaties between the Central Powers and Roumania and Finland. These events overshadowed such incidents as the fall of Jericho on the Palestine front, where we had been doing remarkably well since the capture of Jerusalem in December. It was a pity that these side-shows were allowed to eat up our man-power when more divisions were so badly needed on the most decisive front of the war.

Once more I called at the office. By now the firm had suffered the further loss of " Elsie " Thomson (of Ploegsteert days), killed in the Third Battle of Ypres, Coupland (R.F.C.) also was killed. So was Pugh (Indian R.F.A.). Of those now serving, Tyler was in Italy, two were in Egypt, three in France and seven in England.

There were large numbers of soldiers at home and it puzzled me why more could not be sent out to thicken the front in view of the impending attack. They still kept a good sized army for coast defence, just because it was thought possible for the Germans to effect a surprise landing, notwithstanding that their communications would be cut as soon as the Navy came on the scene. Really we should have given the enemy credit for more common sense than to have attempted such a forlorn hope.

But if the number of troops on the wrong side of the Channel came as a surprise, the swarms of civilians still sheltering as " indispensables " amazed me still more. I recognise that many were doing vital work, but it was riling to see men—to all intents and purposes fitter than many who were in the trenches—leaving their banks and offices or shopwalking or driving 'buses, taxis and carts. The engineers' trade union was on the verge of a strike because the Government's dilution proposals meant that more of them would have to join the army : why should they have the right to threaten the paralysis of our munitions while the soldier would be shot for the same offence ?

Threats of strikes by tyrannous unions, swarms of indispensables who were not indispensable, thousands upon thousands of troops who might easily have been on the French side of the Channel, still more countless thousands ear-marked for Salonika, Mesopotamia and so forth ! Yet down by St. Quentin " the enemy could break through as easily as anything : there was nobody to stop them ! "

My subaltern friend's fears were justified. Within three weeks his battalion was overrun and thereafter he eked out the remainder of the war as a prisoner in Germany. Had we had the misfortune to be in that part of the line on March 21st, the rest of this narrative might have dealt solely with German barbarities or British operating chambers—perhaps the book would never have been written at all !

CHAPTER XXIX.

The Big German Offensive : First Week's Events

(*March, 1918.*)

The calm before the storm—Opening of the offensive—Thriving on rumours—Fall of Monchy and Wancourt—Open warfare on our right—A spy incident—What the papers said—Things become rackety on the Ridge—Disquieting news from the south.

March 9.—Left Folkestone, feeling this was perhaps really the last time I'd see dear old Blighty's shores unless it be from a hospital ship. Crossing was perfect. Everyone fed up as usual, especially at Boulogne, where the M.P.s tried to form us into fours and the entire leave party "struck," calling the police all sorts of nice names and asking them when they had last heard a shell. Put up in camp for the night. Air-raid in the distance : great excitement amongst the Chinese in a neighbouring encampment. It is said that during one air-raid they suffered casualties, which so incensed them that they broke bounds, entered a German prisoners' reservation close by and vented their wrath upon the inmates !

March 10.—Met Jim Green, one of our drivers, also returning from leave. Had to hang about all day, not allowed to leave the camp. A fair number of men, including Green, broke bounds by climbing through the barbed-wire fence and striking off across fields towards the town. These daring ones spent a happy day in Boulogne, while the disciplinarians, cooped up in their depressing enclosure, had little to do but curse at their own timidity.

March 11.—Took the train to Maroeuil, at which place we were expected to enter a details camp and spend yet more hours in idleness, but Green and I gave the party the slip and got in a lorry bound for Arras. I sat beside the driver, who was very chatty and offered me a cigarette. While he was lighting his own, he removed his hands from the steering wheel, at which—fearful lest the wheel be jerked by a bump in the road—I put my hands out to steady it. The driver, however, thought I must have some knowledge of driving, and, assuming the vehicle was in safe hands, took his time over getting a light. Unfortunately the road happened to curve, and at my wits' end as to what to do, I tried to negotiate the bend by turning the steering wheel in the wrong direction. That was my first and last attempt to drive a lorry !

Having alighted at Anzin, we were making our way across country when we met two members of the section who had heard where to get " vin blanc " and were acting on the information. They told us that the Germans took it into their heads sometimes to shell the camps beside the Lens road and that the section were living in perpetual fear of a missile exploding in their huts. They left it to us to infer that, Anzin being a safer place, they proposed seeking liquid refreshment within its precincts rather than patronise the canteen at Nelson Camp. We also learnt from them that men who had been in France for more than two years could put their names down for going home for six months—in exchange for someone in England, though why that " someone " was not out in France in any case was not explained. What did I think of it ? Not much ! From what I knew of the Army Practical Joke Department, we should find our connection with the L.R.B. severed, the six months would probably amount to two—passed under Havre training conditions—and then incorporation in the next draft for the umpteenth Fusiliers.

Found the section bright and jolly, in spite of shelling distractions. The records I brought out for the transport gramophone were much admired, some thirty people crowding into one hut to listen to them. The enjoyment of the lawful occupants was, however, somewhat tempered by the sight of the audience sprawling over their kits and blankets in muddy boots.

March 12-15.—Up the jolly old line once or twice more. Germans rather more aggressive, flinging plenty of stuff round the " red " and " green " lines. We seemed to be taking up plenty of ammunition and bombs. Great feeling of excitement : pretty certain Germans about to attack. Supposed to be huge enemy dumps everywhere, which our aeroplanes were busy bombing. Weather really delightful and spring-like with dry ground and nice sunny days. Difficult to realise a sword was hanging over our heads.

March 16.—Harbord and I started to receive the *Times* each day, as I paid a subscription while on leave. Every evening we were to get the copy of the day before, sometimes as early as mid-day. The paper of 15th—I think—contained the following announcement by Ludendorff : " We can now think of attack. We are entirely confident that the battle that is bursting forth will be successful for us." He would not talk like that unless he meant business, but let him try it on, that's all !

March 17.—Spent our Sunday afternoon " holiday " in preparing turns for a transport section concert party, which had been in course of formation since early in November. The rehearsal took place in the empty " Bow Bells " theatre and everything went well. It was, however, to be a long time before we gave a public performance. Moreover, it had not yet won the approval and sympathy of Sergt. Chrisp, without whose co-operation we felt we should fall flat. At the present stage he withheld assistance on the ground that we bid fair to become a laughing stock and he objected to having the section held up to ridicule. Perhaps he was right. At any rate I'm glad the Bow Bells were not there to witness our first rehearsal.

March 18.—The battalion went down to rest at St. Aubin, not far from Anzin (about two miles from Nelson Camp). A few of the transport, with officers' chargers, etc., joined them, but the remainder of the section stopped on the Lens road. St. Aubin had a delightful river running through it and the surroundings were similar to those at Agnez-les-Duisans, which was not far away. Among its war-time features were a huge railhead, ammunition dump, C.C.S., motor repair depot and a coal dump. Although the latter was carefully guarded by a sentry and protected by several strands of barbed wire, it was a great nocturnal amusement to fill sandbags and buckets with coal to feed the braziers in our wind-swept billet, timing our arrival and departure with the sentry's disappearance round the far side of the dump.

March 19.—A very wet morning. Officers' horses were required at an early hour. All of them set off for Vimy Ridge, with Harbord and myself on so-called chargers following in the rear. Not far from Chantaclier (the light-railway station on the Bailleul road) the C.O. halted and he and the others proceeded on foot, evidently exploring a different part of the divisional front. Had a good look round all this high ground. What a value they set on it ! To our left it was held by Canadians—four divisions of them in line, I believe—then came the 56th Division with the L.R.B.'s old friends, the veteran 4th Division, on their immediate right. Beyond them again was the famous 15th Scottish Division of Kitchener's Army, then the good old 3rd—another regular formation, at any rate in name—relic of the Voormezeele days. Somewhere in reserve near them were the Guards. A batch of divisions, as good as any in the British Army, all clustered round the Vimy Ridge and Arras—did not this show there could be no retirement here ? With the Ridge lost we should be situated as we were before April 1917, but if the town of Arras went with it, all our battle-line would have to be reorganised.

March 20.—Weather fine once more. German aeroplanes rather active. The battalion taking things easily. My old cooker—A Company's—was stationed near my billet and the same old cooks (Idle, Edwards and King), who had catered for me at St. Pol, allowed me to partake of special afternoon tea with them for old times' sake. Many were the talks we had over the machine-gun that tattooed the cooker at Hebuterne, the long treks of the previous summers, Jumbo's idiosyncrasies, the fatal night on the Arras road and so on. Most of these reminiscences seemed to belong to some dim and distant age, so many were the fresh incidents, the vividness and variety of which blotted out the countless tragedies and humorous interludes that were, after all, only events of yesterday. If only we could feel a reasonable certainty of the War being over before next winter ! But no ! It looked more than ever as though it would drag on and on as the years rolled by. The whole of our civilisation was probably in the melting pot. We, poor little nonentities, were indistinguishable among the bubbles on the top. Even the smallest bubble was an army division, perhaps a corps.

March 21.—Awakened shortly after 5 a.m. by the sound of a terrific bombardment, bigger than anything we had heard. Seemed to be principally in the Bullecourt direction, though this was difficult to determine. Lay awake until six o'clock, listening to the furies let loose up the line, and then got up. The only comments took the form of " some chimmozzle over at Bullecourt this morning," or " some raid in progress, eh ? " But when the bombardment increased in intensity, lasting throughout breakfast and continuing without respite as the morning wore on, it became clear that it was something very much more than a raid. In fact there was little doubt that the much talked of German offensive had materialised. However, down at St. Aubin things went on as usual and no news filtered through.

In blissful ignorance of the seriousness of affairs, we carried out our ordinary routine and went for a ride in the delightful country between St. Aubin and Maroeuil. Every now and then a gigantic crash, just like the firing of a 15-inch, sounded at some distance from the line : some of our railway guns seemed to be making more than their accustomed noise. Apart from these there was an incessant rumble and roaring, greater than the opening of any of the offensives we had experienced. However, so far as one could see, nobody seemed in the least perturbed.

In the afternoon the battalion got orders to move up the line at dusk by light railway, and so for the next hour or so we were busy preparing for departure. Limbers and horses came over from the section to take back blankets, cookers, etc. The drivers found themselves much sought after for news of the day's happenings, for though information might be very scarce, you could always rely on transport men for rumours " straight from the horses' nose-bags." The best-informed and most imaginative driver, Hobson, who came along with the mess-cart, knew " all about it." The Germans had attacked that morning on our right (that is, to the south of the Scarpe) on a very wide front : result, unrumoured. They were shelling places miles behind our lines—villages and railheads that had never previously been touched by the long-range guns. Aubigny, St. Pol and other well-known peaceful places were receiving huge shells at intervals and the train service was somewhat disorganised. So the big bangs we were hearing were these enormous shell-bursts, not railway guns ! Well, thank goodness they had left St. Aubin alone !

Returned to Nelson Camp after dark, where I learnt that I was on second picket. The guns were fairly active, so were German aeroplanes, the latter causing us to extinguish our lamp just as we had begun to write letters by the light of its flickering flame.

What was happening down south there, where occasional big flashes illuminated the sky ? How had the day gone with the troops who had received the full force of the German attack ? Were the scenes of Gommecourt and Glencorse Wood being repeated, with the British this time at the right end of the machine-gun, firing on discomfited Germans ? Hobson's rumour that that day the Germans and British had come to death grips just on our right evidently had a certain amount of justification, for it was the common possession of all units around Nelson Camp. But nothing more was to be ascertained at the moment and so we turned into bed at 2 a.m., little realising that in at least one place near St. Quentin the enemy had got right past our outpost and forward lines into our battle-zone itself.

March 22.—A very misty morning such as yesterday had been. Heavy firing down south ; our front moderately quiet. Still no news during the first half of the day.

In the afternoon the A.S.C. brought up rations, together with a pack of rumours of back-area shelling. This or that divisional ration train had been blown up, this or that part of the railway was impassable. Here shells fell every ten minutes or so on a certain junction, there aeroplanes were bombing such and such a road. Someone said the enemy were attacking with stupendous forces and had gained some ground. The battle covered a fifty mile front. . . .

Great excitement in the evening. Gordon received instructions that limbers were to be loaded in case of having to retire and that those which were used at night to take up rations, etc., were to be loaded with their ordinary complement of tools, ammunition, etc. on their return from the trenches. This meant that about midnight the whole section turned out to load wagons, amidst an atmosphere of sarcastic utterances which eclipsed anything that had gone before.

March 23.—Dawn of practically the most critical day of the whole battle, though we knew it not. Rose at 5 a.m. according to new "standing to" instructions. In the night the 3rd Division had moved west of Monchy, on account of the Bosches having captured Henin Hill the day before ; this step meant giving the enemy observation over all the ground between Monchy and Arras and exposing all our camps to view. The retirement, as a matter of fact, anticipated a very heavy German attack which took place on this morning, but the enemy's bombardment was rather superfluous under the circumstances. When we heard that the Germans were in Monchy and Wancourt—that village Conibeer had helped to capture a year before—no one could believe it. It meant that it would surely be only a matter of days before we said farewell to Nelson Camp, for theoretically Lens road was no longer an ideal garden city for transports !

In the afternoon our *Times* of 22nd arrived and Harbord and I eagerly tearing open the wrapper, spread the paper upon the ground where quite a crowd fell over us in a frantic endeavour to catch a glimpse of the news. The enemy had "broken through our outposts and succeeded in penetrating into our battle positions on certain portions of the front."

"Whew ! Not bad for the first day," commented Harbord.

"That means anything up to six thousand yards advance," said another, "perhaps more."

"I'd like to know how many men they've lost doing it," said Tubby Butt.

"And what we've lost, too," remarked a hardened pessimist at the rear.

"Hullo ! Announcement by the Right Hon. Mr. Bonar Law, M.P."

"B.F. ! " added the assembly with one accord. (B.F. means many things, e.g., bright fellow, banana fritters, etc.)

"Read it out," cried Milky.

" ' I should like to say there is absolutely nothing in the nature of a surprise in connection with what has happened. I may tell the House that this attack has been launched upon the very part of our line which we were informed would be attacked by the enemy if any attack were undertaken at all. Three days ago we learnt from Headquarters that they had now definitely come to the conclusion that an attack was going to be launched immediately.' "

"Well, if they knew when and where it was coming off, how is it the Germans got into our battle-positions the first day ? " cried Harbord.

One of the storemen assured us they would soon be driven out again. That statement was born of confidence in the bravery of the British infantrymen. But I could not help thinking of my subaltern friend who had said that there was no one to stop the Germans down there.

At dusk I rode up the line with Gordon, at the head of the ration convoy. The battalion were right up in the trenches again, and we followed the good old Gavrelle road, with every feature of which I was familiar, even on dark nights. On the sector over on the right of us both our artillery and the German were very active, for there were but two divisions between us and the 3rd, who had met severe attacks and were, therefore, at the moment, the pivot of the great offensive. Our own front was, however, not unduly boisterous ; the limbers deposited their loads, the water-cart was changed and all drivers got away without mishap.

Gordon was gone about an hour and when he reappeared he seized the reins, mounted and galloped for some distance before speaking.

" Things are pretty serious," he said at length, slowing Chrissy down to a walking pace.

" Is that true about Wancourt ? " I asked.

" Quite true. Wancourt is in German hands."

There was silence for a little time.

" Which means ? "

" It means that if they get much farther our position here will be impossible. But it's down south that affairs are most serious. It looks as if they've broken through."

" No ! " Another silence.

" Do you know where they've got to ? "

" No, I've got no details. But the front extends from here to La Fere. The attack has fallen entirely on the British, particularly heavily in the sector we recently took over from the French."

" I've heard that it was very thinly held," I said.

" Everyone says the same," Gordon replied.

" And yet they knew that if the attack came off that was where it would be. Bonar Law got up in the House and said so."

Ben probably guessed something of my feelings when I spurred him into a trot again. Here were we, well on in the fourth year of the War, and never had we been able to break through the German front. (I know there are some who say we never tried ; we never entertained such a thought. To that the answer is what I saw of the cavalry on the Somme, at Arras and at Cambrai.) Yet now the army whose morale, according to the war correspondents, had sunk to nothing, had accomplished what we had never achieved—a break-through.

" They expect an attack here," said Gordon. " We've got to get up at 5 a.m. until further notice and continue loading our limbers in readiness every night."

A shivery feeling went down my spine. Shortly we should be in the fray once more. If they didn't attack here we should no doubt be sent to the scene of action. The Devil's dance had begun early this year. There were at least eight months of horrors, eight months of living in fear of death, before the next quiet spell could come. And this year the horrors would be intensified, while the odds would be greater. If only a cushy wound would settle for me the question of what the next few months would bring forth ! That " exchange " arrangement, with six months at home, might not be so bad after all— but now everybody would be needed out here, even the men who had just gone back for the six months' rest. The Army Practical Joke Department would have an excellent excuse to incorporate them in the next draft for the umpteenth Fusiliers, with all this scrapping going on.

When we got back to the lines I did not have to take part in the loading that was going on in the darkness and so turned in to sleep. What good fortune to have a peaceful night when so many thousands away on the right were fighting for their lives ! In France what a vast

difference a matter of a few miles meant to one's comfort and safety !
But we all got our share of troubles in due course.   Perhaps there were
not many divisions down south who had been plunged into *three*
offensives in 1917.   Every division's turn came sooner or later and
so would the turn of every individual and every horse if they were only
kept in the firing-line long enough !

March 24.—Another morning of thick mist, very helpful to the
enemy.   Learnt at breakfast that an order had come out the night
before stating that a spy was wandering about behind the front dressed
in British officer's uniform and that any suspicious person was to be
watched.

A.S.C. rumours included a tale of open warfare in the south and
onslaughts by forces equal to four times ours in numbers.   This was
borne out by my paper when it arrived : about forty German divisions
had been used in the first wave alone.   The enemy claimed sixteen
thousand prisoners and two hundred guns in the first two days,   The
most interesting news in the paper was the description of the opening
of the attack, especially where it told of events upon the old Cambrai
front, for, although experiences were much the same on all parts of the
front attacked, we were able to visualise so well the happenings in
places that were familiar to us.   As we read of the doings of the 6th
and 51st Divisions on the Cambrai road sector, our minds went back
to the outposts near Boursies where we used to dump rations, expecting
to be surprised by the enemy at any moment.   True, the line had been
advanced to Moeuvres in the Cambrai Battle, but it had been somewhat
withdrawn afterwards and doubtless these strong points we knew had
still been manned.   How easy to picture the sudden arrival of Germans
out of the mist when a crushing bombardment of gas-shells and high
explosives had been forcing our men to keep as low as possible and at
the same time decimating their numbers.   The machine-gun system
of defence on which we depended so much was absolutely useless in
the thick mist that hid everything from view on that fatal morning.
In a short while the little groups of survivors down among the willow-
trees had been completely submerged : the troops in the sunken road
we used to take to be our front line, evidently defended it to the last
after it had doubtless been pulverised to atoms in the tremendous
bombardment.   Small groups of isolated men hung on all day taking
toll of the myriads of grey figures that swarmed round them in the mist,
fighting to the last cartridge and often to the last man.   The outposts
being for the greater part overcome, the enemy then rushed on and
seized Louverval and Boursies and evidently swarmed down the
Cambrai road to that sugar refinery we knew so well.   Doignies also
fell and many battery positions must have been overrun if struggles
were taking place at Beaumetz as reported.   Beaumetz !   The home
of our brigade H.Q. last autumn, the scene of our celebrated brick-
scrounging jaunts.   If that fell there was no line of defence between
the Germans and our previous model camp at Lebucquiere ; moreover,
there was only one system of defence anywhere near that neighbourhood
and behind that I knew of none.   True, had the Army cared to use our
services for constructing defences instead of insisting on three hours a
day being spent on useless harness cleaning, had they armed us daily
with a shovel instead of encouraging brainless polishing efforts for
horse shows and inspections, there might have been better positions
to fall back upon.   Consider the number of men in every transport
and artillery unit in the Third and Fifth Armies who could have given

on an average three hours a day all the winter to constructing defences instead of removing rust from steel, and it is not difficult to imagine the vast difference this would have made to our capacity for resistance when the crisis came. I think it was the French General commanding in Salonika who was one day shown round a British mounted unit whose dazzling display of glittering brass and steel was the pride of the British general who accompanied him. The French soldier was visibly unimpressed and at last the British staff officer asked him if he did not think the turn-out was magnificent. " Umph," said the French general quietly, " but don't you think they would be much better employed in making roads ? "

In the afternoon a suspicious-looking R.E. officer came through our transport lines and asked Pat and a few others what routes we were to follow up to the Ridge in the event of heavy shelling of the roads. From our camp he passed on to the Westminsters' lines and, after speaking to a few of their men, made off towards still another unit. Instantly we thought of the German spy warning : a man masquerading as an officer and wandering behind our lines. Two or three of us went immediately to the Westminsters and asked what they thought of the person. The questions he had asked them were not the same as those he had put to us, but they seemed highly suspicious and so two of the fellows set off in the wake of the spy, visions of special leave and promotion swimming before their eyes.

We had almost forgotten about the incident when the audacious officer turned up in our lines again and put to the line orderly the same question about transport tracks. The orderly replied that he couldn't tell him, but that he thought our T.O. could, and asked him to step down into Gordon's dug-out. The officer objected, but the line orderly was most persuasive in the way he held out hopes of the priceless information obtainable there. Once in Gordon's dug-out, the man was cornered. In spite of furious protests, Gordon said the officer would have to come along with him to Divisional H.Q. at Roclincourt, and word soon got round the camps that the famous spy was shortly to appear.

The result was that, by the time Gordon had finished his tea, quite a crowd had collected outside to watch the daring spy emerge from the dug-out. His appearance was rather slovenly, and he walked with an ambling gait, his head down and looking neither to right nor left. One or two people were with him as an escort. Gordon was away for over an hour, and finally came back looking very disgusted, while a small army of men, eager for news, noted his demeanour with displeasure. It was Chrisp who tactfully ascertained what had happened and enlightened the assembled multitude.

" Wash-out ! " he cried. " They've let the blighter go."

" What ! ! ! " We could not believe our ears.

" He's an R.E. officer from a camp at Roclincourt, been in the Army umpteen years and Div. know him quite well."

It was difficult to express our disappointment.

" Well, I thought all the time," said Figg, " that if he wasn't a spy, he was completely loopy, and if he's been in the Army umpteen years—what can you expect ? "

March 25.—Towards early morning shells fell in a camp a few hundred yards up the road. Learnt soon after dressing that one hut had received a shell in the middle of it. All the occupants but one had fled when the shelling commenced, but the fellow who refused to move (on the grounds that he was just as safe there as outside) was killed instantaneously.

This day we received an order that anyone heard spreading rumours about reverses to our arms would be court-martialled. This, in effect, prevented any discussion of the news in the papers and restricted our remarks to comments upon how excellently we were faring in the south. In other words, each fellow had to say exactly what he didn't mean, and he said it in such a way as to convey his true meaning. Immediately after this order came out, you might have heard conversations like this in any part of the camp :

" Doing well down south, they say. Completely disorganised the German plans, this strategic retirement of ours."

" The paper says Fritz has got Boursies, but I don't suppose he has."

" Oh, no, couldn't have. But even if he has, what's the use of that waste land to him ? "

" Besides, Bonar Law says that's where we expected him to attack. You bet we were all ready for him."

" Fritz says he's captured two hundred guns, but that's all bunkum."

" Oh, he means machine-guns, of course. Poor old Fritz, he always gets the worst of it, doesn't he ? "

No Sunday papers came to hand, nor did we glean any further news of note. Once more we loaded limbers at night ; once more we lay down to sleep wondering whether the morning would find us packing our personal belongings and carrying out a strategical retirement ourselves. Above all, would a shell land in *our* hut this time ? I was on picket again, last shift.

March 26.—Rumours arrived surreptitiously all the morning to the effect that we had retreated to the Somme, losing an enormous amount of equipment in the process. The mounted orderly of the night before learnt that Peronne and probably Bapaume had fallen, which meant that not only Beaumetz but Lebucquiere, our old transport camp, the vegetable gardens, Petersen's light railway—all were in German hands. It was unheard of, incredible ! Bapaume was seven miles, Peronne eleven miles, behind our old front. All our defence lines had been penetrated. Whenever had we been able to achieve a like feat ? When had we captured stables and camps and got past all the German defence systems into towns several miles behind the German lines ? We boiled with inward fury at the treachery of the Russians who had doubled our burden because they no longer wished to continue the War : they alone had made this thing possible. It was sheer weight of numbers on a weak and attenuated line that had rolled up our defences. What could stop them now ? Only the indomitable pluck of the British infantryman, who would cause such terrific casualties among the picked German troops that when our reserves hastened to the point of danger most of the ginger would be taken out of the enemy's stupendous effort. When our reserves hastened up ! Where were our reserves and why were they not packed behind the front where we knew the attack was coming off ?

The next rumour came from the divisional train, whose drivers said that numerous transports had been captured near Bapaume. When the retreat became general, the Bapaume-Cambrai road became choked with lorries, motors, and horse-transport of all kinds, all endeavouring to make an exit through the town. Thereupon German aeroplanes came over and dropped bombs on the splendid targets that were offered, causing an entire blockage ; the tale went that the

Germans arrived before they had time to get away. There was one story of a unit that shot its horses rather than let the enemy seize them ; another rumour told of a staff officer in a car who, in his impatience to retire, left his car in the blockage and proceeded on foot. Vast quantities of stores in Bapaume had fallen undamaged into the enemy's hands, including railway stock and the huge E.F.C. Oh, it was enough to make one shed tears of rage at the thought of the hundreds of camps, the railway material, hospitals, and other stores that must have been lost on this retirement.

I felt almost too disgusted to open the paper and read about it. But there were clamourings for official news from the men assembled at tea, so I found the middle page and appealed for silence.

" Back to the Somme . . ."

" It's true, then," said Mac.

" It's here in black and white : ' Back to the Somme.' Not only that, but the Germans have crossed it."

Someone or other's sanguinary aunt was here appealed to for sympathy.

" Well, let's hear all about the German defeat," said Rayner.

" British Official . . ."

" Let's have the German Official first and see what's happened."

" Righto. German Official . . . uninterrupted forward movement . . . 25,000 prisoners and 400 guns."

" My hat ! "

" That was Saturday's Official ; quite half a column of it. Here's the Sunday bulletin. . . . The battle has been won. . . . A gigantic struggle is taking place for Bapaume. . . . Booty in war material is enormous. . . . 30,000 prisoners and 600 guns."

A few exclamations of surprise went up from the listeners. These were three days' captures. In the Battle of Arras, spread over a whole month, we had captured but 20,000 prisoners and about 250 guns, thinking this a great feat. In the Third Battle of Ypres, spread over three months, our takings were only 24,000 prisoners and 74 guns. Consequently, the new announcement left us simply flabbergasted.

It was indeed a blow to us at the time—this return to the old battle-fields of 1916, when we ourselves had seen evidences of the price paid for all that dearly-bought land. Was the Battle of the Somme to count as though it had never been fought ; was all that blood shed in vain ? In our disillusionment at the vast strength of the German army that had been revealed, we lost sight of the fact that, whereas all our troops were splendid, the Germans consisted of picked troops and inferior ones, the picked ones being those who must pay a heavy toll in this attack and whose supply was not inexhaustible. Only the certainty of speedy victory justified the sacrifice of them. But such consolations hardly weighed with us at the moment. The leading article of the paper said there was no disguising the fact that the Germans had broken clean through our defensive zone—that was enough for us to swallow for the time being. As to how they could do it ? how they could keep up the pace ? where we should bring them to a standstill ?—these questions remained unanswered. We merely listened to the roar of battle away on our right, and, fatalists that we all were, waited for whatever should befall.

That evening Figg and I, with two others, had to take limbers up the Bailleul road on the Ridge to drop loads of ammunition at a certain spot not far from the village of Bailleul. This represented the left front of our division, and I had not been to that destination before, though the familiar Chantaclier light-railway station was but three-quarters of a mile short of it. Close to this railhead a traffic corporal warned us that the enemy had been drenching the batteries ahead of us with gas, and as it was so appalling to attempt to drive in our masks and so difficult to fix the horses' respirators, we decided to draw up on a piece of open ground for a short rest. This was an opportunity to examine our respirators once more, leaving them hanging out of their cases, ready for immediate adjustment.

Presently a limber driver, coming from the direction of the line, reported that most of the gas had blown away and that it was safe to proceed, so we mounted again, drew out on to the highway and resumed our journey up the long straight road, just as dusk had fallen. Very soon we came to the region of our heavies, which, having submitted to a gas strafe a short while before, were now engaged in a violent bombardment of the German positions, several batteries firing continually all around us. Doubtless their targets were the numerous new gun positions which had lately been observed by our aeroplanes. At this spot, although we started to ascend a spur of the ridge, the ground on either side rose more suddenly, with the result that we found ourselves in a sunken road where the banks hid the guns from view and incidentally minimised our animals' discomfiture. Here the gas from the previous shelling still hung about rather badly, and we passed some men with masks on, in the act of unloading shells from a convoy of lorries. However, we hurried by, holding our breath as best we could, until we had ascended the hill farther and reached our destination some few hundred yards ahead, where no gas traces remained. The pack-ponies were waiting somewhere here in readiness to take the ammunition forward to the front-line (or else they came up behind us. My memory is very hazy as to what did occur that night, and better informed readers can doubtless correct me). So we emptied our limbers, drew close in to the side of the road and stood by our horses, awaiting orders.

" Ph-ew-ew-ew-ew-ew-flop."

" Ph-ew-ew-ew-ew-Ph-ew-ew-flop-ew-ew-flop."

Above our heads a slow whistling sound came from out of the beyond and ended up in a languid way over by the batteries behind us. Then came a dull " flop." Before the first sound had finished another droning noise could be heard, then another, then another.

" Gas shells," commented Figg, putting both hands on his opened respirator in readiness to don it.

" Evidently."

In such quick succession did they come that there was not a second when we could not hear one of them careering through the air, while the weird flops with which they burst followed one after another. Immediately this gas shelling started our batteries ceased their strafe. What an effectual way of crushing artillery fire ! That is just what the Germans had done in the south when they attacked ; the British batteries were deluged with gas for hours on end, and the inconvenience caused can well be imagined. It really was a serious problem, for the feeling of assurance which the presence of so many batteries on the front gave to one was diminished when it was proved how easily they could be disorganised. When occasion warranted, of course, they could give a good account of themselves even though the gunners had to work in their masks, but there was always a danger of half the team becoming incapacitated.

For five minutes the deluge of gas shells continued without intermission, and the thought of all the fumes hanging about between us and the bottom of the sunken road caused both Figg and me to consider the advisability of staying where we were indefinitely. But orders came down to us to return to the Chantaclier dump and wait there, on the assumption that we were not in a healthy spot. And our minds were finally made up by the arrival of a five-point-nine beside the road just ahead of us.

" I'm off," cried Figg. " Let's make a dash for it."

" Better put respirators on ! "

" I can't see an inch ahead of me in those ——— things. Let's canter and chance it."

There was a good deal in what he said. Blinded by a respirator, it would be impossible in the darkness to dodge the wheels of those lorries back there which were taking up most of the road. So I mounted and, turning round immediately after Figg, allowed the horses to canter for all they were worth down the hill. In ten seconds we were inhaling the fumes, and in five more were passing through a veritable cloud of them. A kind-hearted driver in one of the stationary lorries evidently lifted his mask to shout " Gas ! Gas ! " as we dashed past, but it would have been as impossible to don our respirators at that moment as to halt, turn round and retrace our steps. We must go through with it.

After holding my breath as long as possible, I had to take in another whiff, though instinctively I raised my handkerchief to my nose while doing so. It smelt rather like chlorine, but there was also something lachrymatory about it which made the eyes run. In about a minute the banks on either side levelled out into flat plain, and another quarter of a mile or so brought us completely out of the foul area, but we did not leave off trotting until we reached Chantaclier, where we dismounted.

" Phew ! I got mouthfuls of it," said Figg. " I suppose we shan't know whether we're gassed until to-morrow." (Most of the Cambrai gas cases only felt the effects some hours after inhaling.)

One of the other drivers came up and shook hands enthusiastically all round.

" We've clicked all right this time, boys. To-morrow night we may be at the base. It'll probably be slight, thank God, but it'll mean we'll miss this damned attack."

" What about the court-martial on slightly gassed cases ? "

" My dear chap, no one can fix a respirator when he's trying to keep a pair of cantering horses under control."

" Don't you rejoice too soon, anyway," said Figg. " I know enough about gas cases not to want to be one myself."

" Oh, if it catches you slightly, you'll only lose your voice for a little time and perhaps be unable to see. The effects won't be permanent."

" Personally," said a fourth driver, " I wish that five-point-nine had sent a splinter into my arm or smashed my foot. I can see unadulterated blue hell ahead of us, and I'd give a limb to be out of it ! "

March 27.—Effects of the gas made themselves felt. None of us could speak above a whisper, our eyes were red, and we felt sick. Stayed in " bed " to breakfast.

The attack did not take place at dawn as we thought it might, and we were getting rather tired of five o'clock reveilles with their accompanying midnight loading parties. However, Batt. H.Q., Gordon said, were convinced an attack was imminent. Some of our boys were in the outpost positions, others in Marine Trench and the Red Line. I didn't know many of them, especially as they consisted largely of ex-Rangers, but Colonel Husey, Major Wallis, Captains Rose, Slade, Burroughs, Hancocks, etc., were a few of the popular and familiar figures that came to my mind, also the aid post and signalling staffs. The best of luck to them if the blow fell. We knew that they would inspire in our reinforcements the best traditions of the regiment.

During the morning I got up and wrote a letter, then wandered round the camp feeling rather unlike work, but the clear air was very refreshing and it was not now so difficult to speak. I badly wanted to know what was happening down south, and just as I was on the point of bewailing the absence of rumours, a heaven-sent motor despatch-rider drew up alongside our hut on the Lens road, beckoned to me and asked me to direct him to his destination. This was too good an opportunity to miss, so I asked him if he knew anything.

He drew himself up with the air of an important personage who has important secrets locked within him.

" The Fifth Army," said he, " is *na poo*. Wiped clean out. I don't see how the devil we're going to stop 'em. About ten to one against us."

" How far have the Germans got ? "

" Right past our old Somme trenches. Somewhere round Bray and Albert, I should say. Territory they've never trod before. Capturing aerodromes, hospitals, tanks, lorry-parks, ordnance, stores, horses, God knows what all."

" Don't let anyone hear you saying so, at any rate," I warned him. " I suppose you've heard the order about spreading panicky rumours."

" Bah ! It's in the papers. We admit it ourselves. Bleating cheerful, eh ? "

After a few more encouraging remarks, he replaced his maps and continued his journey, leaving a very perplexed and dejected person on the footpath.

On territory they'd never trod before ! Montauban, Trones Wood, Guillemont, Leuze Wood, Death Valley—all those places overrun in a day or so, after taking sixteen weeks of horrible slaughter to capture but eighteen months ago. It was impossible to visualise the wonderful rearguard actions fought by weary men who had been retiring and killing for a whole week, holding the thinnest imaginable line against divisions that outnumbered them by four to one, and receiving only one division to help them during all those days. What a commentary on the disposition of our reserves ! The thousands of men whom I had seen on my last leave were now being packed off across the Channel—three months too late. Divisions were hastening down from the north to the part of the line where we had known the attack was coming off, but it took them over a week to reach the danger spot. Not only were our infantry hopelessly under strength owing to the Government's truckling to Labour, but the reserves, such as they were, were placed everywhere but in the part of the line that required them. Perhaps this would force the Government to " weed out " more drastically. Of what use was it to employ men on building ships that would not be completed before 1920 or 1921, when there were not enough men in the field to save us from defeat in the meantime ?

The German communique published in the *Times* of the 26th, which reached us this day, was the most bombastic one they had published. It reported that fresh British forces had been brought up and numerous tanks had flung themselves against the attacking Germans, but that by the evening they had been completely defeated and were streaming back westwards. They said there was hot fighting for Combles and the heights to the west (where oft we had hauled water-carts through muddy crater-fields in the days of the Somme). More than 45,000 prisoners and many more than 600 guns were claimed, together with thousands of machine-guns, tremendous quantities of ammunition and implements, great stores of supplies, etc. The British report confirmed that the losses in material had been heavy and included tanks.

45,000 prisoners ! More than we had taken at the Battles of Arras and Third Ypres combined. More guns than we had captured in the whole of 1917 !

It was indeed a depressing moment for everybody—for the men in France as well as for the people at home. In a little Kentish house two anxious pairs of eyes scanned the news columns for some ray of hope, or, perchance, some reference to the L.R.B. in action ; two pairs of ears listened in dread for the arrival of a telegraph boy or a postman with a letter from the front in an unknown handwriting ; two minds cast loving thoughts across that narrow strip of Channel and pictured the absent one enduring a thousand torments. It might have done them good to see him sitting calmly in a hut scanning his shirt or open-ing a home parcel. They would have been relieved to see him placidly surveying a sock minus toes or heel as he put his boots on or smiling grimly as he beheld fifty rounds of mildewed ammunition in his seldom-used bandolier. These sights would have removed their fears for his immediate peace of mind, though doubtless the good folk would have been shocked if, in addition to seeing, they had been enabled to *hear* their offspring. Not that he cursed more than anybody else. But the fact of the matter was that recent events had not only added consider-ably to the number of epithets in the section's vocabulary, but had intensified the virulence of our normal expressive adjectives, with the result that Gordon had to express a mild remonstrance, while the horses positively blushed for shame !

The first piece of really good news we had received for days came from Sergt. Chrisp when he arrived with orders on that evening of March 27th.

" The section will *not* turn out to load the limbers to-night," he announced amidst cheers. " It's a lot of tommy-rot, for it can easily be done very quickly if the occasion arises. Reveillé will be at six o'clock once more until further orders."

Yet even as he spoke the Germans a few miles away were making final preparations for a colossal attack on our front—their famous effort of March 28th against the Vimy Ridge and Arras. The very night when we relaxed our precautions they should have been carried out in their entirety. For in the event of an attack we had got to abandon Nelson Camp and it might have to be done in a hurry !

CHAPTER XXX.

The Big German Offensive : The Attack on Arras.

(*March 28th*, 1918.)

The Germans attack—Preparations for departure—The transports retire—We bivouac and wait for news—The battle progresses—Ammunition required—That night, up the line—A revelation—Result of the day's battle.

THE night of March 27th was disturbed by a phenomenal series of double explosions, so unlike anything we had heard before that we may be forgiven for mistaking their origin. Every few minutes we heard what seemed to be the firing of a gigantic gun, which we assumed had been brought up by rail to Arras, and the curious feature about it was that each crash was followed a second later by another one, equally loud. The incessant Bang-Bangs, each of which shook our hut to its very dubious foundations, wove themselves into our dreams until our disturbed sleep became a veritable nightmare. Those who were sufficiently wide-awake to reason things out thought the second explosion must be the echo on the far side of the Roclincourt valley, but the apparent close proximity of the gun when there was no wide-gauge railway within a mile puzzled them exceedingly. The idea that this double explosion might emanate from German sources occurred to very few of us, notwithstanding that on March 21st several high-velocity enemy shells had similarly deluded us, owing to their burst being so similar to the firing of a gun. The double report, unless it be an echo, was an entirely new feature, and it kept us so wakeful that when the second picket came off duty, several questioners asked him for an explanation.

"It must be a big gun of ours," he said. "We've been listening to it for the last hour. Seems to be just down in the valley across the road. We thought it must be shells once or twice, but there isn't any swishing row. You don't get any warning at all."

Even as he spoke there was another "Bang-Bang," which awakened practically everybody in the hut. The second concussion seemed even louder than the first.

"But is it the same gun all the time ?"

"Seems to be. There are some other rows in Arras that might be either shells or guns."

After this the nightmare continued throughout the early morning hours and we grew quite accustomed to it, but before the last picket called us at six o'clock there arose such a babel that there were very few drowsy ones to be awakened at that hour. The violent artillery preparation of March 21st was being repeated, and this time the line was not so far away as it had been then. A few of the blanketed forms stirred uneasily, a remark was passed somewhere at the end of the hut, here and there a hand stretched out for a cigarette tin and a box of matches. The thought that this might mean a renewal of the attack on Arras was, of course, present in every man's mind. It was for this contingency that we had loaded limbers as a precaution every night except the previous one. The very ground trembled and seemed to be trying to convey to us an idea of the weight of metal with which its surface was being pulverised a few miles away.

Bang-Bang !

" I'll swear that's not a railway gun," said Corporal Watkins.

" Go outside and see if there's any gas, Watty," suggested the facetious Gunboat Smith. " And for the Lord's sake examine my respirator. I bet you what you like there's a hole in it."

" What is it if it's not a gun, corporal ? Someone bursting a paper bag ? "

" Shells, of course. And not so very far away either."

This was confirmed by the last picket when they called us.

" High velocity shells falling on the light railway down in the hollow there. The first report must be the gun firing in a direct line with us. . . . Show a leg ! Show a leg ! Germans knocking at the door ! Fritzes flying overhead. Cheer up, my hearties, we'll soon be in Germany. Show a leg ! "

" What's all this damned noise about ? " asked Conibeer, just awakening.

" Come out on the lines and jolly well see. Seems as if all the artillery in the whole blessed German army has been massed on this front."

It certainly seemed so. When we turned out in our quaint early-morning attire and gazed over towards Gavrelle, Monchy and Wancourt, we were facing such a crashing bombardment as it had never been our lot to behold. In a semicircle around us the massed German artillery was showering missiles of all sizes and descriptions upon our trenches, batteries, roads and tracks, including, doubtless, large quantities of gas shells to disorganise our defensive fire. We could not see the spurts of earth and clouds of smoke in such detail as we had on that memorable 13th of May in the Second Battle of Ypres, when it seemed as if every single landmark had a separate battery assigned to it. But the cumulative effect of all those shells bursting and batteries firing round the broad arc from Vimy to Neuville Vitasse gave us probably a better conception of its awfulness than a closer view of one part of the front only. At any moment, of course, a huge coal-box could be seen sending up its geyser of earth somewhere on that elusive horizon, while nearer at hand many individual bursts arrested the attention. In front of us these were particularly severe in the neighbourhood of the St. Nicolas-Bailleul road, while to the left Roclincourt and Ecurie were receiving missiles intended for the main thoroughfares. To our right, in Arras, big crashes told of destruction in the town and suburbs. Our own Lens road was within the zone of excitement, a trifle to the north of us, while far to the rear at Acq. Mareouil and Aubigny the long-range bombardment was resumed. Several bursts of " Archies " in the air drew our attention to German aeroplanes hovering over the battlefield. The furies were let loose with a vengeance. Just such an assault as this, upon March 21st, had led to the enemy breaking through.

Gordon was on the lines early that morning. Certain single-horse men had to attend to two animals, those who were freed by this means being told to load limbers with everything in preparation for departure. As soon as possible we all lent a hand, and by half-past seven the vehicles were in readiness except for a few eleventh-hour loads such as forage and cooks' belongings. Then we sorted out the day's rations, swallowed our breakfasts, and set about washing and shaving with perhaps a little more promptitude than we usually displayed.

While I was still searching for the broken bit of glass that served as a shaving-mirror and arguing with Trendell as to how many had already dipped their brushes in my mug of hot water, Dixon, the smithy, looked in and informed us that the brigade R.E. signalling limber was coming down the road. Five minutes before it had been seen dashing through Roclincourt at a furious pace, with shells bursting in apparent close proximity, and even now it was still trundling along as though the drivers were anxious to put a good distance between them and the line. This limber, together with sundry horses, had always been kept at brigade headquarters near Chantaclier and had evidently had rather a warm time of it.

" Have they attacked yet ? " we asked the drivers as they passed.

" No, not yet," was the reply, " but they're shelling some."

As a matter of fact, the infantry attack had been launched some little time before, but they could not be expected to know that. After watching them scamper down the road, evidently intending to turn off towards Anzin, we returned to our ablutions. Men seemed to be putting a good many things away in their packs, though at first few would have admitted they were preparing for departure. Cigarettes were slipped into overcoat pockets, macs were strapped on to the saddles, grooming kit was collected in nose-bags and stowed away on the limbers—little actions that revealed as well as words could do what was in every man's mind. The Devils' Mess packed up their rations and gradually got everything in readiness to depart. What was the use of blinking at facts ?

" Harness up at once. We've got to be clear of the camp in half an hour."

It was the voice of Chrisp—Chrisp with a surly scowl and a fed-up expression well suited to the occasion.

" Where are we going to, Sergeant ? "

" Mind your own damned business."

The Westminsters and the Machine-gun Corps, we noticed, also were harnessing up. It was a general order affecting the camps on the Lens road : perhaps the authorities wanted to minimise the chances of our being captured or merely feared the stables were now too dangerously situated to be occupied. A few had been abandoned for that reason a few days before. At any rate, the fact of having to effect a retirement was riling in the extreme and Chrisp was no worse tempered than the rest of us.

Various instructions came round in the next quarter of an hour or so. Each hut was to be cleaned out by two orderlies who had to burn anything that might be of service to the Bosches ; every man had got to keep his rifle handy and carry fifty rounds of ammunition on his person (this was too often put with one's grooming kit on a limber). Then came the final order to " get mounted," and upon the tick of 10 a.m. we started off from the camp under circumstances as depressing as any that had attended the section's movements during its three-and-a-half years of war.

Our route lay over the waste ground between our camp and Anzin, across hurriedly dug reserve systems with no one to man them, past old transport camps as deserted as ours now was. Behind us was a mighty armed force, ready with its cavalry, tanks, infantry and artillery, to smash its way through and roll up the British Army. Between it and the fulfilment of its desires were a thin line of British infantry, an odd transport or two, and an artillery zone drenched with gas. Reserves farther back were non-existent. As we passed on to the Anzin road we realised even more fully how marooned were the fighting divisions up in this stricken area. Everyone else had cleared out days before and made for safer climes. The village of Anzin was deserted. The motor repair depot had been transferred elsewhere and was completely empty. Not a lorry passed us in either direction : we were the sole unit on the road. Thoroughfares humming with traffic and camps crowded with troops lying alongside each other give one a sense of companionship and a feeling of security : empty camps, deserted roads, backs turned to the enemy, and a pandemonium at the rear have exactly the opposite effect. We had practically been abandoned, we and all the other component parts of the fighting divisions up here. Chinese Labour Corps, A.S.C. supply columns, road-mending battalions, the thousand and one transport limbers and G.S. wagons—usual sights on any of these back roads—all these seemed to have vanished into thin air.

Our westward journey did not cease until we reached a spot somewhere between St. Aubin and Maroeuil, where it had been arranged that we should wait until further orders. Here we drew up in a vast expanse of uncultivated grass-land, pitched temporary wagon and horse lines in the open, and surveyed our surroundings.

" It's a good job we're winning," said Williams, whose naturally pale face and cold red nose, coupled with an expression of utter lack of interest in anything, gave him the appearance of being the most unhappy martyr of the whole contingent.

" Oh, the first seven years, you know . . ." replied Mears in a more cheerful vein. " There's a jolly old silver lining somewhere."

" Someone must have chucked it into the incinerator," said Arthur Smith.

Not far from us, a freshly-dug trench of no great depth scarred the surface of the field. If the Germans were held this would have to be our temporary " home," while if they broke through there was no knowing whether we should man it or withdraw our transport farther westwards. Before us, facing the firing-line, the ground sloped upwards slightly so that we could not see far in the direction of the Ridge, but from over the brow of the hill came all the noises of the Pit. The stupendous effort of March 21st was being repeated, this time without the aid of a morning mist—what would be the result ? How far did the battle-front extend ? Perhaps if they failed opposite our front they would succeed elsewhere in the south, where the line had not had a chance to become stabilised ? (It was so. Near Amiens they were pushing on to within five miles of the Amiens-Paris railway.)

The gunfire continued without intermission, sending a chill to the heart at the thought of the Hell which certain friends were enduring and of the scenes of the Second Battle of Ypres being repeated at that moment. Rain started to fall, putting an additional damper on our spirits and practically nullifying the cooks' efforts to start a fire in the open with the aid of a few pieces of wood and a match. To be suddenly ejected from the princely cook-house at Nelson Camp and dumped down with their dixies in a barren, wind-swept field was enough to tax the resource and adaptability of the most professional of cooks, let alone an ex-bank clerk such as our worthy friend, Spanny Main. But still they struggled on and we helped them to the best of our ability, so that eventually a dixie of tea and hot tins of " pork " and beans were assured for a one o'clock meal.

When the A.S.C. brought up rations from the rear, it was quite a treat to see the vehicles and realise that there were some other folk about besides ourselves. Their arrival represented an attempt to make things look as if we were carrying on as usual when everything else was disorganised. Naturally, their talk was, as usual, chiefly concerned with the frequent arrivals of high velocity shells on back areas, particularly on the villages round us ; they even advised which was the safest route for us to take in our next retirement.

But fortunately it was intended to hold this front at all costs. In the afternoon orders came along to send up to the trenches every available man from surplus personnel, stores, details, cooks and transport, and altogether some fifty men were fitted out and held in readiness to depart. It was impossible to spare anyone from the section, for both ration and ammunition pack-pony convoys had got to be supplied and there would hardly be enough men left on the lines to move the remainder of the transport in case of emergency. Names for both transport convoys were read out and I found myself detailed to accompany the brigade ammunition pack-ponies, which would be starting off about 5 p.m.

In the meantime the Devils' Mess made rather feeble efforts to erect ground-sheets across a portion of the trench, which seemed to be the occupation of most of the others also, until four tents were miraculously scrounged from somewhere and utilised. Nobody had a thought for the cleanliness of horses or harness, and even hardened link-cleaners like Volze gazed in a bored way at their steelwork rusting on the open ground without making any attempt to rescue it. A worried-looking Staff Officer, map in hand, came over the brow of the hill and walked up and down the new trench where we were encamped. Then after frowning at the spot where the barbed wire ought to have been, he walked on again with such a perturbed expression on his face that it was quite disconcerting to watch him. Heavens ! If the Germans should just as suddenly appear over the rise ! What if a Hun tank bobbed up and started firing at our little encampment ! Or if German cavalry should approach us from the rear, owing to a break-through on our right !

The post limber had located the brigade post office all right and brought me the *Times* as usual, but we had little opportunity or inclination to read it. The number of captured guns had gone up to over nine hundred. Better news came from Gordon, who had been in touch with Brigade over the question of the ammunition convoy. He said that the Germans were being held before the Red Line, where a magnificent stand was being made. The enemy's losses were appalling, but they were still attacking. To the right also they were not having things all their own way and the day looked like being a great disappointment to them. Good old L.R.B! Good old 56th! To halt the Germans before they had gone a mile and nip their Arras offensive in the bud— that was something to be proud of! Of course it was premature as yet to judge : there might be other severe attacks by fresh divisions ; the rupture of the line to the right near Amiens might force a retirement. But somehow things seemed much more hopeful : even the details going up to join the companies were now in a cheerful state of mind. It was rumoured that the battalion would be relieved that night and the report was presently confirmed by the fact that the battalion's rations had to be dumped that night not far from Chantaclier.

In order to find the full complement of pack-ponies required, some of the lighter draft pairs were to be fitted with pack-saddles (which we obtained from the brigade dump), so that a portion of the transport left behind was rendered immobile until the pony stunt was over. It was rather comical to see draft horses which had never made the acquaintance of a pack-saddle before, launching forth with their hind feet and biting all within reach as the clumsy-looking mass of leather and straps was placed on their backs, particularly when boxes and sandbags were piled high on top of them. At four o'clock these animals were tied out to various limbers, devouring their evening feed, while those who were to lead them clustered round the open-air cookhouse and likewise " stoked up " for the journey or else searched amidst the debris from half-unloaded limbers for respirators, water-bottles, and so on.

With the adventures of the ration party I am unfamiliar, being only able to write of the ammunition pack convoy which was to load up somewhere near the line. We started off amidst lowering clouds and a semblance of rain about an hour later, wending our way across country in the direction of that scarred and desolate area of tortures known as the " firing-line." The guns were still creating a pandemonium ahead of us—oh, welcome sound—telling that, in spite of all Fritz's gas-shelling, our batteries were still able to give a good account of themselves : proving that the Germans had not made that smashing break-through they had counted upon. That was the great feeling of relief which was uppermost in our minds as we trudged back over ground we had feared would shortly be no longer within our lines.

After a lengthy inexplicable halt somewhere near Ecurie we led the animals on in a long straggling line up the Roclincourt road which had more traffic upon it than we expected after our observations that morning. Although it was almost dark, the twilight enabled us to distinguish a great many vehicles ahead, and in places the roads were positively choked. A Canadian division—infantry, artillery and all—had sprung up from nowhere and was now going straight up to relieve the 56th, and when their troops and transport came to a halt we hurried by on the outskirts of the traffic, for we were due to move bombs up the line as quickly as possible. On we went, across the Lens road, down into Roclincourt, up the ridge on the other side— occasionally colliding with artillery wagons and ambulances coming from the opposite direction—until all of the stragglers congregated amid the shell-holes at Chantaclier dump. Here there was further presumably unavoidable delay and we must have stood for nearly an hour, watching and listening to the guns. Very few star-shells were falling, but it was clear from the gun-flashes that there was no possibility whatever of the front line having been radically altered.

It might be a thousand yards or perhaps even a mile nearer, but what was that compared with the tremendous effort put forth ?

When we resumed our tramp we followed a track that was new to me, an excellent plank road that turned and twisted across the rugged country, crossed the railway cutting by a substantial wooden bridge and continued its winding route for some distance to the east. No longer were we jumbled together with bustling transports and relieving troops, holding us up or else dividing our little party into numerous detachments, each consisting of a man and a pony. Apart from various stretchers being brought down from the shambles ahead of us, we had the track to ourselves and there was no local rumbling of wheels or clanking of lorries to deaden the sound of gun reports and whining shells which caused nine-tenths of the commotion around us. The inky darkness that had now descended on the Ridge was filled with these sounds and, as this was new territory to us and we had somewhat lost our sense of direction, we knew not where to expect the next gun-flash nor whence the enemy's fire might come.

Presently the track led us out on to a road where we turned to the left and halted beside some sandbagged dug-outs, which represented the brigade bomb store. An L.R.B. sergeant attached to brigade was in charge of our convoy and he promptly roused the occupants of the dug-outs for the purpose of loading our ponies—apparently much to the men's annoyance, for they had obviously had a very trying day of it up here. A salvo of five-point-nines, screaming through the air from the right, caused us to crouch down, but they landed slightly beyond the road. Curious how convoys always seemed to come to a stop in unpleasant places ! Around the dug-outs, on the road, were several brand-new shell-holes, bits of trees were lying about, and one had fallen nearly across the road. Apart from the loading party there was no one about : the road was not being used by traffic or troops. It was rather annoying not being able to get my bearings. Gavrelle, I thought, must be somewhere on the right : those flashes down there must come from our divisional artillery : this road must run parallel to the Red Line and lead to Bailleul.

At long last we moved forward, threading our way among shell-holes and inducing the horses to step over branches and tree trunks that were strewn about. Nine-tenths of the damage had been caused that day. Although it was so dark, it was possible to see the fresh earth strewn all about and the clear-cut nature of the crater-lips. What a deluge of shells this road had received ! Every patch of it was the same. It would have been impossible to withdraw guns under such a barrage as must have fallen here. Under the circumstances our progress was somewhat slow, the horses dodging and shying, and their masters continually tripping or pausing to adjust the girths of the pack saddles. Fritz's enthusiasm for the road had very luckily cooled down by nightfall, although there were moments during our presence on it which reminded me forcibly of our march to the Ypres salient in 1915. Compared with the bombardment that had recently shattered this region to pieces, the surroundings were, of course, tranquil and no one could complain of a few crumps when it was quite justifiable to expect thousands. Jerry seemed to have spent himself that day and indeed he must have had a nasty knock. Crump ! Crump ! went two of his H.E.s to the left of us, messages from some disappointed battery over in the German lines. Bang ! Bang ! replied a couple of our field-guns not far from where the shells had fallen, just to show that in spite of hard knocks we had still got some kick in us. Such was the only display of which either side now seemed capable.

Neither the fellow in front nor the one behind knew what the road was, where we were going or what the time might be. A rough calculation told us that, allowing for our devious journey, we had already tramped eight miles and had stood still for some two hours. How much farther had we got to continue with this obnoxious obstacle race ?

The question was answered when, having progressed rather more than a mile from the grenade store, our convoy turned up a little sunken lane where quite a number of our division (I forget the regiment) were manning improvised fire-steps or squatting down inside substantially-built dug-outs that must surely once have been a luxurious H.Q. Here we were requested to drop our loads, " about turn " and retrace our steps to the ammunition store, evidently for the purpose of obtaining a further supply. A brief interrogation revealed the fact that the Germans had got nearly as far as this during the day, but since my geography was all at sea it conveyed very little to me. One of the men said the road led to Gavrelle, but this only perplexed me more, for I did not see how it could ever reach that village if it continued in such a straight line : the man must be misinformed.

Over the ground we went again, our ponies stepping out more briskly on this occasion—encouraged by the thought of that open field down by St. Aubin with its collection of hay-nets awaiting their return. The obstacles did not perturb them in the least, the approach of shells merely caused them to look inquisitive without slacking the pace. It was always so on a homeward journey. " But what is this ? " they seemed to say when, after a good mile's tramp, we halted by the grenade store and turned their heads round again. More ammunition ! Not going home yet ! In an instant their renewed vigour abated. They submitted to the loading of further boxes on their backs with sighs of resignation. And when they started off once more up the shell-pocked road their nervousness at noises and their fastidiousness about stepping over branches or dodging shell-holes returned with increased intensity. They knew something had happened here : this road was not deserted for nothing, this damage was of very recent origin. They knew this as well as we did.

And then, on that second journey, a revelation came to me, shattering all my previous conceptions about our direction and the position of the firing-line. Yes, certainly this road led to Gavrelle. It was none other than *the* Gavrelle road with which I had become familiar through months of ration journeys from Nelson Camp to Marine Trench. This was the very road whereon time and again I had ruminated on our way of retreat being through the neck of a bottle. Behind us, quite close to the ammunition store, must be the railway bridge guarded by the policeman who counted vehicles, while the spot where we had so often unloaded the battalion's rations was ahead of us, now in German hands.

The spot where we had deposited our grenade boxes was very near the Red Line. In a flash, as it were, all was made clear. But no wonder we could not recognise the road ! Five days before Gordon and I had positively galloped down here on our way back from the line, with scarcely a shell-hole to mar our progress. Now it was so altered that I had twice covered a considerable part of it without even suspecting that the ground was familiar, and the others

had done the same.   Only the horses had known it (intelligent brutes !)
and that was why they were so afraid !

Our second visit to the precincts of the Red Line was a somewhat
livelier one, but its excitement led to a general speeding-up of the
unloading and we were scurrying away down the road again within a
very short time.   We had landed the boxes this time on the parados of
a trench held, I think, by some of the 167th Brigade, and the arrival of
a shell caused my horse to break away and canter off in terror, but
fortunately someone stopped him on the road.   After this, the sergeant
in charge happened to be walking alongside me, so I asked if he had
any news of the day's happenings.   What he told me can be condensed
into a few words.   The initial bombardment had been carried out with
an enormous concentration of guns of every conceivable size, gas-shells
being scattered about profusely, especially among the batteries—as we
had assumed.   As for the forward posts, they were subjected for hours
to a terrifying bombardment from trench-mortars, minenwerfer and
high explosive which must have almost blotted them out before any
advance was attempted.   Two of our companies must have been
exterminated, but, doubtless, some of the men were prisoners.   At
any rate, they were overrun and masses of Germans, all wearing packs
(also, it afterwards transpired, carrying six days' supplies and extra
boots), stormed onwards and entered into a desperate fight for Marine
Trench where H.Q. had been.   It was finally necessary to retire to the
battle zone (Red Line), where orders were given that it must be held at
all costs.   For the rest of the day, the remainder of the L.R.B. with the
Westminsters on one side of them had fired continuously on the masses
of Germans that came on against them, and the ground before the
trench was thickly strewn with dead.   So confident were the enemy
that they would break through that about 9 a.m. a German battery
had been seen beyond Gavrelle, drawn up on the road ready to gallop
forward : our artillery had promptly directed fire on it and made a
nice mess of things.

" It's the finest day in the history of the regiment," said the sergeant.
" There's not many of 'em left, but they've killed simply thousands
with bombs and rifle-fire and Lewis guns.   Fritz hasn't got a kick left
in him."

So this was the outcome of the colossal attempt on Arras, the
extension of the front of the German offensive to the north !   We were
still traversing the Ridge, still walking along the Gavrelle road !   Later
we learnt that the stalwart 4th, 15th and 3rd Divisions on our right
had done equally well.   At least five German divisions had been flung
against the 4th and 56th Divisions, and the capture of Arras had been
assigned to the enemy on our right as the first day's objective—yet,
although we had had to withdraw from Neuville Vitasse in the Wancourt
neighbourhood, the enemy were not so near to Arras as they had been
two years before.

Of this fight Ludendorff wrote in his Memoirs, long afterwards :—

" The 17th Army had already attacked in the last days of March
in the direction of Arras, making its principal effort on the north
bank of the Scarpe [*i.e.* against 4th and 56th Divisions].   It was to
capture the decisive heights east and north of Arras ; the next day
the 6th Army was to prolong the attack from about Lens and carry
the high ground in that area.   I attached the greatest importance
to both these attacks.   To have the high ground in our possession
was bound to be decisive in any fighting in the plain of the Lys.

In spite of employing extraordinary masses of artillery and ammunition, the attack of the 17th Army on both banks of the Scarpe was a failure ; it fought under an unlucky star."

Up the Red Line, Canadians were advancing to reoccupy Marine Trench, which had been evacuated by the enemy as the result of their failure ; while the L.R.B. were on their way down to a reserve position at the rear. The few of them that were left (about ninety in all) were worn out with killing, Colonel Husey himself having fired three hundred rounds at close range. He was the heart and soul of the defence and received a well-merited D.S.O. for his conduct. Major Wallis was as usual magnificent and we should have liked to see him gain another distinction on this occasion. The aid post we never saw again ; the doctor, Sergt. Hammond, Humphreys and Koester were all prisoners. Cooks and H.Q. had been brought into the fray, my poor friend Idle being amongst the killed. But the greatest tragedy of that day— keenly felt by all the section—was the death of our beloved Captain Rose, who had been T.O. for such a short while a few months before. If ever there were a sportsman and a gentleman, he was one, and we felt that yet another link with the past had snapped when he, too, passed into the beyond. Practically no one remained even in H.Q. to remind one even of 1916, let alone 1914. Among the rank and file, the transport section was now absolutely the last remnant of the old battalion.

CHAPTER XXXI.

On the Defensive.

(*April–July,* 1918.)

Reinforcements—Back in the line—Germans attack in the north—Exciting transport trips—Life at Bernaville—Old figureheads depart—Aerial activity on
both sides—Another offensive—Taken for spies—Influenza sweeps the
battalion—The position in July.

After spending two nights at Chantaclier the remains of the L.R.B.
were withdrawn from the front and sent to Le Pendu camp near Mont
St. Eloi, a quaint collection of reinforcements (some eight hundred in
number) joining them en route and marching, or rather slouching, to the
destination. The new-comers came from a battalion of miners which,
in common with many other units at home, had been disbanded to
furnish drafts in the present emergency, and their marching discipline
was, to say the least of it, unlike the L.R.B. standard. The men had a
mutinous air about them, doubtless engendered by the fact of their
being rushed out, not to one of their " Doorham Divisions," but to an
unknown " blinkin' Cockney mob." But Colonel Husey soon changed
all that. On arrival at the camp he gave them a short lecture on their
disgraceful marching and said that they had come to a distinguished
regiment where such slackness would not be tolerated for an instant.
And thereafter the Doorham lads changed for the better, though
nothing could alter their brogue. The name " London Division " was
rather a farce now.

We spent a week in this camp, a week of pouring rain and slimy
mud, refitting and generally recovering from the tension of the last
days in March. Our spirits were distinctly hopeful after the rebuff
the enemy had received on our front and the more reassuring news
that came to hand from other quarters. The German onward tide
had come very nearly to a standstill, even in the most fluid part of the
front, and though there would doubtless be further anxious moments,
it appeared that sufficient reserves had been scraped together from all
quarters to repair the rent in the line. Above all, Foch had been
declared Generalissimo, an appointment that was hailed with universal
satisfaction.

It was therefore with lighter hearts that we returned to the line
again on April 8th to take over a sector just south of that we had

previously left. The section was not at all surprised to find a sea of mud allotted to them as a transport field, with a dark gloomy barn, fitted out with tiers of wire beds as a billet. This was in no other place than Bernaville, where we had once or twice stopped for a day or so on our way from one vile part of the line to the other. To think that after all our wanderings we should have come back to this spot—this dirty, profiteering, flea-ridden village of all places in the universe! Well, well! It was a decidedly better spot than the Harp and other trenches at Tilloy to which the " Doorhams " were consigned for the next few weeks, and this in spite of the perpetual nightly drone of Fritz 'planes which kept the section in a constant state of " wind-up."

From this time onwards the Huns developed a mania for bombing villages behind the front, and the sight of figures clad in shirts and very little else scurrying for the open country became not the least of a picket's many diversions. Some there were who simply could not lie down and sleep or pretend to sleep while bombing 'planes were about, and for weeks on end they became highly-strung as darkness fell. At about nine o'clock, with unfailing regularity, searchlights would appear in the sky, the drone of the heavily-laden machines would reach the ear and our anti-aircraft guns would open fire at the heavens above. The majority of the troops in the back villages would stand outside their billets, watching and waiting, expecting each minute to hear either the dull muffled boom which told of bombs being dropped in the distance or that unearthly swishing noise which indicated that their abodes were a likely target. These were almost nightly occurrences, and if I dismiss most of the bombing scares of the next few months in these two or three lines it is because the full record of them would make unbearably monotonous reading.

Two days after our arrival at Bernaville we were in the midst of our painstaking efforts to evolve order out of chaos on our new lines when Mac came into our midst and said that the Germans had attacked north of us above Bethune the day before, advancing to the River Lys. We were thunderstruck with this news, for, with the slowing-down of the advance on our right, we had foolishly imagined the German effort was spent. An attack to the north, if successful, would—by outflanking us and cutting our communications—cause us to fall back and abandon the Vimy Ridge, thereby giving to the enemy what their direct assaults had failed to achieve. If it came to the worst, it would mean that we should be entirely cut off.

For the next few days we again thrived on unhealthy rumours, which were more or less confirmed by the papers when they arrived. On the 11th we heard that the enemy had crossed the Lys at Estaires, which meant that the whole of the Neuve Chapelle region where we had spent our third winter was in German hands. La Gorgue, that town where we had found such friendship, was now in the firing-line. Every man's thoughts flew to some damsel or other in that once happy little township. Some went to Madeline, the girl at our billet there; some recalled the saucy puss at the favourite estaminet, and other scintillating beauties. What had happened to the inquisitive females whose glances had disturbed us at the baths ? My own thoughts flew to Erma, my especial favourite, wondering whether she had got away safely and picturing her delightful piano buried in a room full of debris. She wrote afterwards to say that she and many others fled a day or so before, when the town was heavily shelled.

Then the attack was extended to the north, and our old haunt,

Ploegsteert, became involved. They had attacked the famous wood. All the fortified posts were captured—London Farm, Mountain Gun Farm, Artillery Farm, full of mixed memories for some of us. Details were lacking, but we conjured up visions of the fights that must have taken place round such places. The trenches where we had first experienced warfare, the Demi-lune road which had swarmed with rifle bullets, the turnip field where we had wallowed at nights filling sandbags, the breastworks in the wood where we used to " stand-to " and drink our rum before dawn—how little did we think early in 1915 that the Germans would one day overrun all this territory ! They claimed in the three days ten thousand prisoners and a hundred guns, and loudly did we curse the Portuguese !

Matters got more gloomy every day. Ploegsteert itself fell. Armentières, filled with gas and practically surrounded, became untenable. Merville, situated miles behind our old La Gorgue transport lines, fell to the enemy. Bailleul was captured. And, worst of all, we were driven from the Messines Ridge : this meant that our hard-won gains of the Third Battle of Ypres, Zonnebeke, Passchaendaele, Langemarck, St. Julien, etc., were simply handed over to the Germans once again. Our line was drawn closer to Ypres than ever before, and now all that had been captured not only at the Third Battle of Ypres, but in the Battles of the Somme, Messines and Cambrai was lost : only the Vimy Ridge—the fruit of the Battle of Arras—remained. It was heartbreaking in the extreme. Haig's order to the troops to fight with their backs to the wall showed the seriousness of affairs. Meantime we could but look to our duties on our own sector and hope that those elsewhere might be able to hold the enemy.

Things were far from quiet on the Arras front. On the 11th the Germans made strong attacks round about Tilloy and Neuville Vitasse, and not only on this but on other occasions caused us considerable apprehension and excitement. On our transport journeys we had to pass up the main Doullens-Arras road, past the dread spot near Dainville where Kimbo had been killed, through the town of Arras itself and out beyond the station, now quiet and deserted again as it had been when we had first seen it. What a brief return to bustle and activity it had known : just long enough to repair the railway tracks, the bridges and the signalling system ! And now it was untenanted once more—and transports hurried past the level crossing in obedience to instinct which told one it was an unhealthy spot.

The *bête noir* of our journey was, however, the celebrated plank track along which we had passed so often from Arras to Tilloy when our horse-lines were near the Harp Trench in 1917. As the front line had been withdrawn to the Harp Trench itself on March 28th, it can be imagined that the area which used to be crowded out with horse-lines was now a deserted, desolate waste, passable only by night. The familiar region, however, was barely recognisable, for hundreds of Nissen huts had been erected all around here since our departure in the previous summer, and these were still standing in various stages of disrepair, even within a few hundred yards of the front line. The dumping of rations amidst deserted huts was quite a novelty for us, but the queerest sensation was to wait with one's horse under the shelter of the very gun-pit which had once harboured that highly annoying six-inch gun. There was something unutterably sad about that empty pit : it seemed to be the symbol of disappointed hopes. The camouflage remained, as though departure had been hurried ; the gunners' dug-outs were deserted ; the spot which the enemy had once found so difficult to locate was now within a few hundred yards of our front line. We grew to dread that plank track, especially the Tilloy end of it where we turned to the left near the crater. A battery or two seemed to be detailed to sprinkle shells at uncertain intervals along the whole length of it, but especially at its eastern end, and on some nights it was essential to halt the convoy for a time before running the gauntlet. The cross-roads at Beaurains, the Café Belge corner, the track to Angle Wood and the main road of Boursies had all been danger spots at different times, but not one of them was a driver or a mounted orderly more relieved to get past than the much-strafed surroundings of the track to Tilloy in the spring of 1918. (The Menin road and various spots at Ypres have been omitted from this comparison : nothing could eclipse *them !*)

There was very little in the way of entertainment to be had in Bernaville. Certainly we had a canteen which boasted a piano, but half the notes did not sound and the first time I attempted to thump out some sort of tune a wire flew out of the top and hit me on the nose. A coster-gentleman who had been standing by in rapt attention begged me, however, to proceed.

" But I can really only play classical stuff," I said, by way of an excuse. " The people in the canteen here won't like it."

" Garn ! That don't matter," said he, " so long as you an' me unnerstand it."

Then there was a cinema where somewhat illuminating remarks were frequently shouted out with reference to the conduct of the War, particularly if staff officers were present in the audience.

Later on we tried to get up a cricket team and challenged the artillery to a match, but they declared for six wickets after making 150 runs, while we got " all out " for 12. Thereafter our enthusiasm waned.

This was the sum total of our amusements.

There was nowhere for a man to go in his spare time except to the estaminets, which frequently contained a very rowdy element. A party of American railway engineers were stationed here, and when a burly Yorkshireman started telling one of these fellows across an estaminet table that they didn't know what war was and asking when they proposed to start fighting, it was always advisable for a peace-loving Londoner to quit the establishment. These Yanks, as a matter of fact, were not a bad set of fellows. Some of them quite frankly admitted that they didn't know how we'd stuck it for three-and-a-half years and they were heartily fed up after a few months of it. One or two, however, had arrogant ways, and a remark that they had come out to win the War for us once led to the speaker receiving a punch on the nose from an irate Highlander. It was rather amusing watching the Yanks doing sentry-duty in gum-boots, sauntering aimlessly along and kicking stones about. When the time came for changing guard, an N.C.O. came along and merely told the sentry to " Get ! "

On the 17th Captain Gordon went to hospital with a temperature and was destined to get to England, where he stayed until after the Armstice. Having been with the transport since mobilisation and fulfilled the duties of T.O. for two years, his departure was a loss to the battalion ; his capacity as T.O. was all that could be desired and up the line he showed coolness and initiative. Both he and Simmonds had done excellent work and we missed them very much. In Gordon's place, Major

Wallis, M.C., came down as O.C. transport for a few days, but he also
was on his way to England, a compulsory exchange having been
effected for his health's sake, much against his will. He needed a rest,
if anyone did, but had consistently refused to take it. There is no
need for me to say what his farewell meant to him and to us. At a
parade of the section he came round and shook hands with each man ;
his words caught in his throat and there were almost tears in his eyes.
" Good-bye, Aubrey," he said to me. " Write to me sometimes."
He had a few words for everybody. Some remembered him as a
pre-War colour-sergeant, but I associated him with May 13th at the
Second Battle of Ypres. In his eyes we alone were the regiment.
Now . . . yet another good friend was lost to us.

All the figureheads seemed to be departing at once. Colonel Husey,
D.S.O., M.C., who had been our C.O. since September, 1916, received a
promotion to Brigadier-General about the end of the month and was
appointed to the 50th Division which was holding a quiet part of the
line on the Chemin des Dames. This should have meant another
farewell parade, but when we fell in he simply could not bring himself to
say " Good-bye." How hateful these departures were ! In Colonel
Husey's case, unfortunately, he was going to his death. In his place
Major Burnell took charge : he had done so for a short time once before
and we liked him very much.

On April 30th, and again on May 21st, the battalion came down for a
few days' rest at Dainville, midway between Bernaville and Arras, a
place where there was nothing for men to do but clean equipment and
meditate upon the likelihood of a Fritz attack. This uncertainty as to
what the next move would be—the blow in the north had been held and
another attack at Villers-Bretonneux had been squashed—was at the
back of everyone's mind, morning, noon and night, whether he were
riding, digging, eating or even sleeping. The *Times* said the offensive
was going to begin again, but no one could guess where ; and the more
one thought about it or read about the terrible fighting up at Mount
Kemmel, the more did one's eventual maiming or extinction develop
into a practical certainty. Nobody could go on and on, whether
holding redoubts, or scouting in aeroplanes, or carrying up ammunition,
without encountering at some time a shell with his name and address on
it. Fresh faces—always fresh faces came to the fore. Some of the old
ones stayed longer than others, but fate claimed first one and then
another. . . .

Our section, however, continued to have extraordinary luck. During
the battalion's second visit to Dainville, in the midst of a regular
orgy of air-raids, a few bombs actually landed in the transport's
camp at Bernaville without injuring any of the L.R.B. (The section
had recently changed its barn for some Nissen huts in a big camp there.)
One bomb fell in the centre of a hut next to that occupied by the
Devils' Mess, bringing casualties to another unit, but the ranks of
earth erected round the L.R.B. hut saved everybody from the splinters.
Naturally there was much bustle and hurrying for the doorways, in the
midst of which Coni—who slept nearest to where the bomb had burst—
woke up and asked in his usual nonchalant manner what all the noise
was about. Farther down the road a bomb severed the legs of an
artilleryman who was sleeping in the open near our Q.M. stores, and
there were many other casualties. Undoubtedly one was safest lying
flat down in a well protected hut, but it required some will-power to lie
still in this belief when the raider was hovering near at hand ; every

instinct within you urged immediate flight, and there were many who scattered over the fields towards Warlus.

But if German aerial activity was causing disquietude in the villages at the back of the British lines, we got proof just about this time that this was child's play compared with what the Germans had to put up with at our hands. The proof was furnished by two L.R.B.s who had been taken prisoner on March 28th and had escaped through to our lines, having experienced life behind the German front for nearly eight weeks. Curiously enough, they had come back through the trenches in our sector and had been sent straight to the transport lines for a good meal and a rest. We could scarcely believe our ears when they told us they were escaped prisoners. It transpired that they, together with a number of other L.R.B.s had been sent down to Douai on the night of the Gavrelle attack and had there been deliberately stationed in a building close to the station, which was a favourite target for our night squadrons. That night the captives had tasted a bigger bombing raid than they had ever known before. The Germans, they said, lived in mortal terror of our bombing squadrons, far more than we dreaded the German ones, nearly everyone on the German side living underground at nights. We were told that we dropped about ten bombs on their back areas to every one they dropped on ours. This information was extremely comforting and thereafter we looked more kindly than ever towards the busy bombing squadrons of ours that set out and returned from their missions at all hours of the night.

Nor was this the only comfort we gained from these men's statements. They had been sent with a party of others to clear the old battlefield near Bourlon Wood and testified to the avidity with which the enemy salved everything they could lay their fingers on. Our boys had nothing but a plate of mangel-wurzel or turnip soup, a piece of bread and some coffee for their entire day's meal, but the Germans fed the prisoners badly partly because they were so hard up for food themselves. They even dug up the old British cook-houses and made use of the decaying food they discovered there, in order to feed the hundred thousand odd prisoners they had recently taken. Under these conditions, life had become so intolerable that these two men decided to escape, and, slipping away from their working-party, hid in an old trench until it was dark. The old British territory between Bourlon and the present firing-line was fairly familiar to them, but, in any case, they had only to keep close to the Arras-Bapaume road in order to come through the lines at Tilloy. For two or three nights they travelled stealthily onwards and hid as soon as dawn began to break, finally succeeding, by some miraculous means, in crossing No Man's Land and regaining our lines. In a few days they were sent back to England as a reward, after giving our divisional staff a lot of acceptable information.

Towards the end of May the preparations for meeting another German smash were at their height. Arrangements were made whereby certain mounted orderlies, pack-ponies, and Lewis-gun limbers should remain in attendance on battalion H.Q. in the event of open warfare being probable, while the remainder of the section was to effect a graceful *sauve qui peut*. These plans were evidently based upon experience during the March retreat. The men who were detailed for " A " Echelon, as the " forlorn hope " body was called, were naturally subjected to a good deal of good-humoured banter, for their chances were not of the rosiest description. But the scheme never matured, for the enemy struck this time upon the French front, where four very weak British divisions, sent there for a rest, bore the brunt of yet another blow. Wherever they struck, the Germans seemed to hit upon a weak spot in our line. In this new attack they advanced twelve miles the first day, and penetrated to a maximum depth of thirty miles within four days. What congestion of transport, what bombing of roads there must have been on a break-through like that! Did they have Echelon "A's" down there? If so, as Baker said : " What 'opes ? " It was in this affair that Colonel Husey was reported wounded and missing ; four times before had he recovered from wounds, but this time, alas! they were fatal.

The battalion went into the line again on June 1st, and there followed eighteen most exciting ration trips up the plank track, Sergt. Chrisp acting as transport officer on each occasion. Casey, the famous charger of Captain Russell, was so badly wounded that he had to be shot, whilst three draft-horses also received wounds. One of these adventures led to a rather amusing experience, when Bob Taylor and myself were taken for spies.

5/6/18.—" . . . The day before yesterday when I turned out at 2 a.m. to do four-hour picket, I found, to my surprise, that the drivers on our convoy had not yet returned from the line, nor did they reach our horse-lines until an hour later. It transpired that they had scarcely commenced unloading rations when the Germans attempted a raid on the trenches close by (occupied by the L.R.B.), and the neighbourhood, of course, instantly became an inferno. The unloading party disappeared ; two limbers were promptly driven off at breakneck speed to a safer spot ; a third driver rode away with his mules and left his limber ; and a fourth one in an attempt to pass it had a smash-up. The N.C.O.'s horse took fright, leapt into the air, as he was walking along with it, knocked him over and galloped off in the direction of home. The N.C.O. (Milcovich) walked all the way back to the transport lines, but as the animal had not turned up, he thought a couple of men should ride off and scour the neighbourhood. Accordingly, at 4 a.m., in obedience to instructions, I awakened Bob Taylor and informed him that we were to start off at once in search of The Harp, as the animal was called. However, we had reckoned without Taylor's methodical preparations, for it took him at least an hour and a half to get up, eat a slice of bread and butter and saddle up his horse !

" The most obvious place to look for a stray horse is on the lines of another unit—preferably an artillery unit. When we set off, therefore, we made a tour of all the horse-lines for miles around, watching the artillery at (Dainville) on their way to the troughs and gradually working our way up towards (Arras). Combining pleasure with business, we made a thorough tour of the interesting parts of that city and saw many things we had not noticed before ; then we continued as far as the plank track (beyond which no one could venture on horseback), but our quest was in vain. The Harp was nowhere to be seen. And five hours had passed.

" Taylor thought perhaps the beast might have gone off across country, grazing, and met with an accident in a shell-hole or on some barbed wire, in which case it would be hopeless to try and find him while we were encumbered with our steeds. We therefore trotted back to (Dainville), put the horses up at a Y.M.C.A., and resolved to retrace our steps to the firing-line—after dinner. But here was a problem. We had no rations with us. Both Taylor and I were ravenously hungry, and yet nobody had any food to give away. The Y.M.C.A. man had no change and it was impossible to get any. In the end he allowed me to pay 10 centimes, instead of 20, for two cups of cocoa and made it quits by borrowing Taylor's pencil and not returning it.

"Apart from the drink and some biscuits, we therefore went without dinner, which makes our subsequent drowsiness somewhat inexplicable ; both of us dropped asleep, if you please, while resting on a seat in (Arras) and only awakened after threequarters of an hour's doze !

"Our afternoon's investigations on foot covered a good deal of ground in the neighbourhood of the Cambrai road, but though we asked questions of everyone we met, nobody remembered seeing a stray horse. In one instance we asked two men if they had been about between midnight and 4 a.m., and, finding that they had not, did not question them further or enlighten them as to the object of our inquiries.

"This left a vague doubt in their minds—one of them being evidently possessed with the spy mania—and their suspicions were aroused when they saw us questioning other people—so much so that they followed us. What more likely than that we were two spies who had got through during last night's raid and were looking round behind the British lines ? Knowing that the L.R.B. were in the trenches, we no doubt looked to them rather questionable persons, wandering aimlessly around, pointing to various places and pursuing inquiries here, there, and everywhere.

"An irregularity in our dress probably loomed large in their eyes : we were not wearing any equipment except a haversack and a respirator—quite an unorthodox procedure—and the absence of bandoliers and spurs disguised the fact that we were transport men.

"Taylor and I soon noticed that these enthusiasts were watching us. In one case they spoke to a man we had questioned, but since we had only asked him whether he had been up there the night before, they were no wiser as to our intentions. Sometimes we lost trace of them, but they would always turn up again, either waiting for our arrival or following in our wake. Once, on the way from the plank track to (Achicourt), they overtook and passed us. This was an opportunity of which Taylor promptly availed himself. Sinking his voice practically to a whisper, yet taking care that our amateur detectives caught his words, he asked me : " Wo werden wir gehen ? " Thereafter we expected them to turn round at any moment and close with us, but as a matter of fact they disappeared.

"Our wanderings led us eventually into an obscure street at the top of the hill at (Achicourt), where we found a tumbledown cottage advertising coffee for sale. Chancing the occupants possessing change for our five-franc notes, we went in to rest from our labours, which we had now given up as futile, and ordered " deux tasses " and " des gateaux " from the old dame in charge. It was in this shop that our pursuers ran their prey to earth. In they came, within two minutes of arrival, and taking encouragement from the glance that Bob exchanged with me, seated themselves at our table.

" ' Your chaps were raided last night, weren't they ? ' one of them asked.

" ' I think so. It was rather too hot up there, I believe,' I answered.

" ' Were you up there ? '

" ' No.'

" The men looked at each other.

" ' Where are you going to now ? '

" ' To the transport lines,' said Bob.

" ' What ! Are you *transport* men ? '

" ' Yes. For the last twelve hours we've been looking for a missing horse, but we don't intend to waste any more time on him.'

" The look of disappointment on their faces was amusing to behold, but we pretended not to notice anything. Even now the truth dawned on them very slowly, so obsessed were they with their own idea, but after asking a few more questions they became convinced in the end that they had been on a fool's errand and watched our departure with sickly-looking faces. No doubt they were wondering whether it could possibly be April 1st.

" We had to report failure on our return to the lines, but we could hardly complain that the day had been dull. Our own regret was that it should have been possible for us to be mistaken for Huns, but when we surveyed ourselves carefully in a looking-glass it had to be admitted that beauty was not a strong point with either of us."

It was only a matter of time before Sergt. Chrisp got his commission when it was once established that Gordon had got to England, and it can be imagined what satisfaction this gave the section. As a ranker he had known most of us intimately and his demeanour had not changed in the least with his successive promotions. His sympathy with us may be gauged from a chronicle of the section's wanderings which he wrote for the June number of the Transport Magazine, only six days before his commission came through :—

" General ——— paid an impromptu visit to our lines," he wrote apropos of a recent event, " and informed us that the division he had left were very posh : even the chains on the *stable* head collars were like silver ! Perhaps that is the reason why his division was swallowed up, who knows ?

" Very shortly afterwards we had the Brigadier's inspection, which I suppose we may consider passed off satisfactorily. No matter how good a show is, the policy of the Army heads is to give as little credit as possible. WE DELIVER THE GOODS is our first thought ; whether the head chain is rusty or like silver makes no difference to us, so long as we deliver the goods."

Coming from the pen of an acting T.O. who knew that it would be read by the C.O. and possibly Brigade H.Q., I cannot help thinking that those remarks were rather daring, and it says much for the section that, far from prejudicing discipline, they had precisely the opposite effect, as Chrisp knew they would. We would have gone anywhere and done anything for " Crip," and for his sake we maintained a very fair standard in our turn-outs.

The printed souvenir number of the " Old Doings," our Transport Magazine, arrived from London about this time. It had been written in 1917, but censorship and other difficulties had delayed publication for some months, and now we had several hundred copies to dispose of at a franc apiece after most of the likely purchasers had become casualties at Gavrelle.

Fearing lack of interest on the part of the miners who now comprised most of the battalion, we had solicited orders of half a dozen copies per man on the section, but we need not have entertained any fears. The edition was sold out within twenty-four hours and all the officers' messes and the other transports were clamouring for more. So far as Watkins (now Sergt.) was concerned they were, I think, welcome to his six copies, for as soon as he discovered Conibeer's parody on his gas lecture, he appeared anxious to cancel his order. The publication was, of course, rather personal, and nobody came in for more leg-pulling than Q.M.S. Hamilton. Consequently when I touted with copies at the stores, I only waited for the money before disappearing like a streak of lightning round the door!

After the exciting eighteen days the battalion came down to a camp in Bernaville, where the majority of men promptly got laid up with influenza. We had heard there was a great deal of this about and that it was seriously inconveniencing the Germans themselves in their offensives, but so far, as a unit, we had been remarkably free from the germs. Then they assailed us all at once. On the section, first one man and then another developed a high temperature, while in the camp where the companies were stationed whole hutfuls succumbed to the illness so rapidly that within about two days the bulk of the regiment was temporarily *hors de combat*. The camp was like a field hospital, for, owing to the C.C.S. and F.A. being overflowing with similar cases from all quarters, it was decided to treat most of them on the spot. Nevertheless quite a number of serious cases were carried off in motor ambulances, and we heard many of them proved fatal. So this was what warfare was bringing in its train! It was really remarkable that some kind of plague had not raged through the armies long ago in view of the unnatural conditions reigning everywhere.

There was something quite uncanny about the rapidity with which the 'flu seized its victims. But those who did not get it really badly were able to carry on again after a few days. The battalion, reduced though it was in numbers, managed to return to the line before the end of June, and on the transport, too, we were able to carry on work. By the 4th of July I was one of the few left who had not caught it, over a hutful of 'flu cases representing the toll of our section. The cooks were busy day and night preparing invalids' diet, and I must say the sight of the convalescents taking special food and sitting up reading papers on the third or fourth day of their illness made the fit men somewhat envious. As it was, a few of us felt as limp as pieces of chewed string, but, having no temperatures, were able to attend to the horses, otherwise the animals would have had to water and feed themselves and find their own way to the firing-line.

The " left " sector, on the other side of Tilloy, in which the companies spent their next spell in the trenches, will ever be memorable to the section on account of the last stretch of the journey from Blangy Cemetery to the trenches. It was here that, for practically the first time, the ration convoy as a whole had to don respirators one night for a considerable period. A shower of gas-shells was falling around the track, and we had to drive onward, scarcely able to see the vehicle in front, let alone all the holes in which the place abounded. Arrived at what we believed to be our destination, we found nobody there to take delivery of the rations. Eventually a party of men wearing gas-masks arrived and unloaded, but for all I know they may have been London Scottish!

Another night when I was acting as a mounted guide to take a limber round by a different route, so as to avoid the cemetery, the horse I was riding suddenly reared up on his hind legs and refused to advance when he realised this was only another way of approaching the same track. Foolishly I pulled him over on top of me, and we crashed together on the cobbles of the Arras-Cambrai road.

Now that I was engaged chiefly as a mounted orderly, transport work became more interesting than before, because it frequently happened that a message had to be taken somewhere by galloper, or a convoy wanted a guide, or perhaps Brigade wanted a runner, and in this way one not only got a good deal of riding and trotting but was able to act much more independently than in any other capacity. Of course, I still drove a limber occasionally, as it turned out that drivers who were up the line more often were passing through a rather strenuous period, and it was only fair that they should have their places in the ration convoy filled by others sometimes, so that all bore a more or less equal burden. Many of the ex-drivers, however, couldn't help wishing that this system had been in force in the olden days when it was an unheard-of thing for a pack-pony man or a groom to drive a pair of horses, in spite of the amount of strain on the limber men.

By July 7th all the section having recovered from the 'flu, we held a transport dinner to celebrate Chrisp's commission coming through, the affair being financed from the profit on the magazines. It was a great occasion, and it seemed to commemorate the successful termination of our arduous spell in the Tilloy sector. For it was whispered in confidence that we were shortly to be drawn out for a rest, and this rumour soon developed into a certainty.

World-stirring events had happened since the offensive in March had died down, and, though we had had quite as lively a time as we wished for, it might indeed have been much worse if we had had the misfortune to be on a different part of the front. Quite a number of divisions had been involved in both the March and the April fighting, while the unfortunate 19th, 21st, 25th and 50th Divisions had, I believe, been engaged in each of the three big offensives to date. Truly we might have fared far worse, and we could thank our lucky stars that the enemy had not dared to attack at Arras a second time.

The third offensive had come to a standstill about the middle of June, with a further loss of about 40,000 British and French prisoners and some 400 guns and the Germans within fifty miles of Paris. Simultaneously a great attack had been launched in Italy, in which the enemy claimed at the outset 30,000 prisoners and 120 guns. But it turned out to be an ignominious failure, and the Austrians had had to withdraw almost as quickly as they had advanced, at a cost to them of some 20,000 prisoners and at least 150,000 casualties. There was plainly nothing more to fear from that quarter for a long while, but the great question was : " What would the enemy do next ? " Time was slipping through his fingers. Our own losses in material and, to a large extent, in men had been made good, while Americans were arriving in incredible numbers. On the other hand, the cream of Ludendorff's officers and storm troops were already wiped out. But we only realised these things at the back of our minds and pinned our hopes on 1919. The all-important fact was that the enemy had the initiative, that he was contemplating another stroke, and that this time it might mean Paris, Amiens or Calais.

We marched away from the Arras front on July 15th. Miles behind the firing-line we passed a little village filled with American troops, who hurried to the roadside to watch us pass. Men fresh from the States, who had never been nearer to the war zone than they were at present, were drilling in these back areas, and it was inspiring to our men to see them. They had British rifles, British limbers and cookers, British water-carts, British harness—everything about them was British except their uniforms, their accent and their hideous Harold Lloyd spectacles. At any rate they formed reserves on paper, and it was comforting to feel that there was someone between our troops in the trenches and the deep blue sea. If there was another attack on the Ridge they might or might not be called upon to take a hand in the defence, but our boys most certainly would, even if their rest had only lasted a day.

But we need not have worried on our own account. The next blow had fallen—that very morning—upon the French in the direction of Paris.

CHAPTER XXXII.

The British Offensive : Arras Sector.

(*July–August*, 1918.)

A change of fortune—Good news from the south—Preparations for the Third Army offensive—We miss the opening attack—Night treks—A brigade runner job—The attack at Bullecourt—Reconnaissances with a Red Hat—The following day—and night—Reflections.

For three days we rested in the wooded village of La Thieuloye, where the relief from not having to worry over air-raids was most marked, it being the first time most of us had had a really satisfactory night's rest since March. It was here that Conibeer and Jim Greene, thoroughly fed-up with the rotting of intellect and cherishing hopes of several months' respite from the war zone, applied for commissions and received the C.O.'s approval on the usual terms : each must pass a fortnight in the trenches as a platoon commander prior to going before the Brigadier. They were both to receive corporal's stripes when we went up the line again and do their probationary period in command of two platoons. This action on their part revived the old commission discussion, and many of us came near to breaking our vow that we should all stick together as long as possible.

On July 18th we shifted our abode to Beugen, a village some long way back from the line opposite Lens, yet near enough to the coal area to be a mining place. It was surrounded by open country, of which the C.O. took full advantage for training purposes, and the companies proceeded to go for long marches and carry out dummy attacks in which good use was made of the officers' chargers. On the first field day the Colonel read out a telegram to the effect that the French and Americans had attacked the right flank of the Germans in the Marne salient and captured 15,000 prisoners—an announcement that was received in lukewarm fashion, since two-thirds of the men obviously did not believe it. There had been too many exaggerated reports at different times for troops to accept as truth everything that was read out to them. But this time the news was, of course, true, and as it gradually sank into men's minds when they saw the communique in the papers, a new feeling of hope inspired them and the cultivated stories about Foch's great " mass of manœuvre " took a great hold on the imagination. Little realising that the stroke was a gamble and that it was carried out by a handful of worn divisions, we were deluded, as most other people were, into believing that Foch had been deliberately holding back reserves to strike when the enemy's strength was exhausted. The stroke was successful, and day after day we read of the Germans trying to extricate themselves from the big salient they had recently created, without losing too many prisoners. They had been too clever for once. They were on the run. How eagerly we waited for the papers, and how greedily we devoured the incredible news! Accustomed to reverse after reverse as we were, the change of fortune overwhelmed us at first. It put everyone in good spirits. A parcel which arrived for me a month overdue with all the contents mouldy, merely provoked mirth instead of tears. Sarcastic remarks lost some of their bitterness and sting : there was a marked diminution in the amount of cursing : even Williams wore a smile on his face, and Eustace actually gave away another pair of leggings !

Our light-headedness was reflected in our decision to give a public performance of the transport concert party, which had been in embryo for six months without showing any signs of maturing. The C.O., beaming with satisfaction, gave orders that every possible assistance should be rendered to us, and our limbers made countless journeys with planks, etc., for staging purposes which some neighbouring R.E.s, in a similar fit of enthusiasm, had presented to us without demur. French civilians lent us clothes for certain of the turns, while Frank Little from H.Q., who was to be one of the flappers, had a regular " bottom drawer " of unmentionables sent out from home. The vocalists spent the evenings rehearsing their parts in an empty school, while other willing workers erected the stage. A damper was thrown on our enthusiasm when the " Bow Bells " announced their intention of performing at Beugen on the afternoon of the very day fixed for our concert ; and when the Colonel said they might have our stage for their entertainment we felt inclined to " chuck up the sponge " in despair. An amateur performance following a professional one on the very same stage within a few hours would be a hopeless fiasco. Eventually our show was postponed until the next day, and as it was well advertised in battalion orders, we got an even greater audience than we anticipated. This included, by the way, a host of gaping Chinese coolies who, bird-cages in hand, broke bounds from their camp and clustered round the outskirts of the crowd, gazing with particular interest at Sharpe's conjuring tricks. The entertainment was an unqualified success, and ever after we felt grateful to the companies for their sporting attitude in remaining seated in the uncovered auditorium while sharp showers of rain fell and drenched them to the skin.

Our brigade's rest was terminated about the end of the month by an order to return to the Arras front, with a short break at Cambigneul. At this place we came once more within a zone which received the special attention of Fritz' planes, and they disturbed our peace of mind for two nights ; and upon our return to the same old camp at Berna-ville our study of astronomy began once again in real earnest. It was just like coming " home " again to take possession of the same old lines and the same old huts, though there was a slight variation in our nightly itinerary and we saw the plank track no more. The battalion took over the front to the right of the Harp Trench, holding prac-tically the same trenches at Beaurains as they had before the 1917 Battle of Arras, and we went over very familiar ground as we took forward supplies. Conibeer and Green were now acting as platoon commanders in the trenches, and most of our conversation was divided between discussions as to whether we should go and do likewise and forecasts of the evening's aerial activities.

Then came August 8th, the "black day in the history of the German Army," as Ludendorff termed it, the occasion of the great surprise attack by the Canadians and Australians at Amiens. So well had the secret been kept that we had not heard a word of what was afoot : for all we knew the Canadians were still holding Vimy Ridge. Not until the papers announced the news did we know that the German Army had had the surprise of its life. In three days its lines had been penetrated to a depth of twelve miles, and 21,000 prisoners with 400 guns had been taken.

The effect upon us was electrical. The determination to " stick it," which had been our creed for the past few months, now became a conviction that we were not so hopelessly outmatched as we had thought. In fact, it flashed upon us that here we had the Germans on the run ; and just as August 8th convinced Ludendorff that Germany could not win the War, so it inspired us with confidence that the end might really be in sight—within, say, twelve months.

It was the surprise of the victory both to ourselves and to the enemy that held out the greatest hope for future success. Hitherto, with the single exception of Cambrai, all our preparations had been made more or less ostentatiously, and days of preliminary range-finding and destructive fire had made the enemy fully aware of our intentions. But now it had been found possible to break through their defences by the use of tanks in such numbers that the long preparatory bombardment was dispensed with. The tanks had come into their own ; there was no comparison between the slow-turning lumbering monsters we had seen on the Somme and the fast " whippets " which so thoroughly demoralised the Germans on August 8th. They might almost be said to have taken us as much by surprise as the Germans. Four hundred of them had been used in the attack, and, considering two hundred had been lost in the March retreat and we had seen very little of the Tank Corps, we had no idea until then that there were as many as four hundred in France—let alone in one sector of the British line.

Undoubtedly a good deal of the surprise had been due to the manner in which the Canadian Corps had been transferred south just before the attack had taken place. Now they came back from the Amiens front just as rapidly. About the 15th of August, a couple of Canadian battalions, which had been in the fighting but a week before, had occupied a number of empty huts in the same camp as ourselves ! The greater part of the camp had not been used for months, and the sight of all these sturdy Canadians completely transformed its appearance. They were a fine lot of men, and their attitude of complete confidence gave one an optimistic feeling similar to that inspired by the old regulars of the 4th Division. From the new-comers we heard details of the Amiens affair ; every one of which served to prove that the newspaper accounts had been no exaggeration. And now, so these men vowed with quiet determination, they had come back here to take Monchy. Monchy had been German long enough, they said. It was the one fly in the ointment so far as the holding of Vimy Ridge was concerned ; the Germans had no business to occupy a commanding site like that just to the south of it ; and so the Germans had just " got to come off it."

But something more than the mere capture of Monchy was in the wind. It was now the turn of the Third Army to send the Germans reeling, and, though details were lacking, there were rumours that a general offensive on our front was imminent. More Canadians arrived, and at the same time we were taken back into corps reserve at Lignereuil on the 17th, where we lost touch with the preparations that were being made.

Then followed a couple of treks that seemed very puzzling. The 169th Brigade moved forward into billets at Arras on the 19th, while the transports were sent to an open field at Wagonlieu (near Dainville) and had to make themselves as comfortable as possible without a scrap of bivvy material to utilise. Most of the evening was spent in searching far and near for raw material, and finally several of the section slept half a mile away from the horses in some empty roadside dug-outs which afforded the most satisfactory cover from aeroplanes that we had yet enjoyed.

But scarcely had we settled ourselves in these new surroundings and the companies occupied their billets at Arras, than the brigade got the order next day to move back again—this time to Hauteville. One must expect these puzzling orders when operations are in full swing; it is necessary to "shelve" a brigade sometimes for twenty-four hours at a time when divisions are being moved about like halma men. We did not know whether to be glad or sorry ; the sudden order had something behind it, and yet we felt we were deliberately turning our backs on the firing-line on the eve of a momentous attack. It was rumoured that the offensive would start the very next morning, yet here were we embarking on a night march, every mile of which took us farther from Arras and the firing-line !

It was a wonderful trek, carried out on familiar roads in full moonlight. The men were not allowed to smoke, and there was very little talking. Behind us—up the line—the guns were comparatively silent. Occasionally, in the distance, bombs would be dropped and swarms of our own aeroplanes would pass overhead on their nightly expeditions. It seemed impossible that the attack was coming off ; where were the hosts of lorries, the battalions moving up and the congestion on the roads ? When we halted just beyond Dainville not a vehicle passed us ; we had the thoroughfare to ourselves.

The battalion reached Hauteville in the early morning hours, and the Q.M.S.s, who had preceded us, were waiting to show the companies into their billets, while the transport were allotted an orchard, where a big French army hut, with uneven earth as a floor and a swarm of vermin already in possession, served as an abode for the 2nd Londons and ourselves. We did not trouble much about our surroundings at three o'clock that morning, however, and it was not long before all except the luckless picket were fast asleep in various attitudes and stages of attire among the hopeless confusion of kits and boots that littered the "floor" of the hut.

There *was* an early bombardment—the picket said so. But I, for one, did not hear it, being fast asleep until Figg shook my shoulder and said that most of the men were already out in the orchard. When I got outside and looked around I heaved a sigh of satisfaction. Here we were in idyllic surroundings, far from the roar of guns, when we might reasonably have expected to be up in the rowdy battlefield. Why, we could make ourselves comfortable here for a long time with certain alterations to the billet.

The village was quite a passable one, as it conformed with the standard desired by most of the troops, viz., plenty of beer, a few shops and a suitable distance from the front line. But its serenity was disturbed on this day by the multitude of lorries filled with wounded that passed through it. Most of them belonged to the 15th Scottish Division, which had made a feint at Arras, while the main thrust had been farther south, but of the extent of the front attacked and the whereabouts of the rest of our division we were completely ignorant.

Perhaps it was instinct that told us it was useless to unpack our kits, unload the limbers or set to work erecting harness-racks. All the harness rested in heaps on the dewy grass, already so rusty that the staff would have had serious misgivings as to our military fitness, had they seen it. The lumps and ruts remained in the French hut—unlevelled. The cooks were using a trench fire under the obvious impression that it was waste of energy erecting a cook-house. And our prognostications were right. We had got to leave at eventide. Men were allowed the afternoon off in order to snatch a few winks of sleep and then aroused almost as soon as they had commenced to snore, in order to receive rations, load forage, water horses and draw extra feeds. Soon after tea we were quite ready to depart, and before sun-down the battalion was marching off again—in a more or less southerly direction which would take us a shade nearer the firing-line, and perhaps meant that we were on our way to join a different corps. Thus we carried out another night trek which was in all essential features similar to the first, but our destination this time was the wooded grounds of a big chateau at Saulty, where we were carefully tucked away under trees and undergrowth so that by dawn no trace of our whereabouts could be seen by wandering airmen. But the tucking-away process left us very little time to settle down before dawn, and the tremendous bombardment which took place about 4 a.m. effectively roused us in spite of our fatigue.

We found in these woods many other units besides ourselves, all bivouacked under the trees and leading their horses to water down shaded avenues. In four years of war many little incidents repeated themselves, and the day we spent at Saulty, hiding among the foliage and caterpillars and listening to the roar of battle, was almost a repetition of a similar bivouac at Vlamertinghe Chateau during the Second Battle of Ypres. Confined to the precincts of the grounds and only allowed to venture forth if one's limber was required for some job, we were completely cut off from the world. Nothing was known of what was happening and no attempt was made to enlighten us. But the very fact that great events were pending and that one attack was following another so as to give the Germans no rest was enough to keep everyone's spirits buoyant.

That night we got a complete rest, but we were again awakened by a crashing bombardment on the morning of the 23rd. What had actually happened was that the Third Army had attacked from Moyen-ville (six miles south of Arras) down to the Ancre upon the 21st and, in spite of hard fighting, had advanced anything up to three miles. The drumfire we had heard at dawn the next morning was really a German counter-attack, but the Fourth Army had struck simultaneously farther south, capturing Albert. Then on the morning of the 23rd the two armies had again resumed the offensive on a thirty-three mile front. Though we did not know it, our division, represented by the 168th Brigade, were at that moment in the attack. As for our brigade, Corps H.Q. probably knew roughly its movements for the next two or three days, but for us they were a closed book and our most immediate concern was whether the post would arrive in good time and when it would be possible to get a clean change of under-clothing.

Our orders to prepare for departure came along in the afternoon : and again we marched off just before nightfall so as to reach our destination under cover of darkness. Within our limited sphere of observation, divisions and brigades were coming and going, relieving one another with the automatic precision of a railway time-table, for regiments which had been in action on the 21st were arriving to take over our bivouac even as we left the chateau grounds. It was reassuring to note that they still bore some resemblance to battalions— a very different impression to that gained after the offensives of old.

On the Doullens-Arras road there were two orderly parallel lines of traffic moving towards the line, one representing our brigade on the march and the other a line of cavalry jostling past and raising clouds of dust in our faces. All the bustle of previous offensives was present and the constant flickering of gun-flashes in the dark sky ahead told its own story. At one place we halted alongside some of the Guards who had fallen out for a rest on their way down from the battle. It was they who had been counter-attacked on the previous morning, but a little group of them that spoke to us were in good spirits. They said all was going well.

On arrival at the village of Bailleulval about 11 p.m. we bivouacked in an open field, where Chrisp told us to snatch what sleep we could, as reveillé would be at 2.45. The horses were simply tied to the limbers and though some of the company-men found huts, the transport lay down anywhere, with a cold wind blowing all around and the canopy of the heavens above them. " Up there " the guns continued to rumble, but in that brief three hours' rest very few men other than the picket heard them. Then on again—first in darkness, then in mist, making our way through Basseux, Riviere and Wailly and turning off towards Ficheux, until, well after daybreak, we stopped at a spot called Blamont Mill. Near by was a prisoners of war cage, where we noticed with glee some fifty or sixty dirty prisoners gazing sullenly at the reinforcements appearing on the scene. The country was scarred with old trenches, relics of the firing-line of the first two years of war, before the Germans carried out their retirement in the spring of 1917, and the sight of artillery lines in the open, queues of horses at the water-troughs and scrounged bivvies on all sides, brought back to mind scenes in the Battle of the Somme. The same congestion of space, preponderance of horses, perpetual flow of traffic and abandon-ment to the open-air life existed. The British Army was on the move again and we had no home we could call our own for more than an hour at a time ; yet wherever we might be, however indistinguishable one's " place in the sun " was from another amidst all this shambles, the A.S.C. supply columns invariably arrived from somewhere with food and forage and succeeded in ferreting out the Q.M. store for which their loads were intended.

Next day a 2nd London man and myself were attached as mounted runners to brigade H.Q., which was split up into two sections : rear brigade in Blairville and forward H.Q. in a railway-cutting near Boyelles. One of us had to remain at each station, ready at any hour of the day or night to gallop with messages and yet unprovided with any site for our horses or ourselves to occupy while waiting. Since the Boyelles pitch was very much in the war zone and being drenched with gas, it was with relief that I found " the other fellow " had been detailed to wait there while my functions were to act as a guide and take messages with Blairville as my headquarters ! Beyond trotting up to Boyelles to learn the route and guiding the transport up to the L.R.B., who were in trenches in Boisleux, there was little to do upon the 25th.

Most of the roads were camouflaged owing to the fact that Monchy overlooked all this country, but at 3 a.m. on the 26th the Canadians were given their chance and a huge attack broke out to the left of us. Before breakfast time the hill was captured and, as the day wore on. Neuville Vitasse and Wancourt Ridge became ours again : in other words, the firing-line was pushed forward to where it had been before the German offensive. This breathing space on our left enabled all the horse-lines to be brought a couple of miles or so forward and later on the same day our section encamped by the Cojeul stream close to Boisleux-St. Marc. Simultaneously rear brigade was moved to the same neighbourhood and, to my joy, the brigade horse-lines where I had to keep my gallant steed were pitched beside those of the L.R.B. Consequently, I was able to live with the Devils' Mess and together we erected our home in a serviceable trench. After the bombing of the past two nights, which had been wretchedly nerve-racking, nothing short of a six-foot trench suited our requirements and, once inside it at night, we stayed there if possible. The Fritz machines were very active and there were so many bivouacs and horse-lines about that every missile was almost bound to do damage : why should it not be our horse-lines as much as anybody else's ?

On the morning of the 28th, under instructions of acting brigade T.O., I went forward on Ben with the Q.M.S., whose object was to point out to me the route to the new brigade H.Q. on Henin Hill. This meant rather an interesting trip, as we passed through the recently captured village of Boyelles very soon after leaving the lines. Several walls of houses were standing here, and there was no destruction that could compare with the ground-level village sites of the Somme.

" I'm afraid we'll just run into the attack," said the Q.M.S. " Croisilles fell first thing this morning and the next thing is to attack Bullecourt. Our brigade is going over about midday and our H.Q. may move forward this afternoon."

Just after leaving the village we passed a wrecked German wagon and team which had evidently encountered a nine-point-two a few days previously. It was the first German transport outfit of any kind we had seen all through the War and it astonished us to note that the harness was civilian and the wagon itself had been a most ramshackle affair : we had pictured the German vehicles as being modern like our own, and of course some of them must have been. Near here were some nine-point-two's in action, drawn up in the open country to the north-east, without any semblance of cover for guns or gunners. Likewise the six-inch batteries near the Boiry road were firing continuously and when we got to the region of the field guns it was clear that the barrage for the attack was already being put up. On the hill here we had the unusual spectacle of field-guns drawn up in the open and firing rapid and it was with considerable difficulty that we got our horses past this zone. To the east, on the far slope, lay Bullecourt, although it appeared to us like a hill of white chalk with a few stumps of trees showing up against the sky-line. There it was that the L.R.B. were attacking the Hindenburg Line at that moment, in the same place as the 2nd Battalion had suffered when they first came to France. . . . What portion of the front, excluding the Ypres salient, had meant so much bloodshed and struggle as that ridge beyond there, indispensable to British and Germans alike ?

Brigade H.Q. was stationed in a series of trenches and dug-outs on the top of Henin Hill, from which one could look back upon the valley of the Cojeul, which had been the scene of such struggles in the fizzling-out stage of the 1917 Battle of Arras and the first German offensive and now once more in the recent British attack. The very field works which the brigade telegraphists and others were now occupying had been a German strong-point two days before. I dismounted and, after looking round among the knots of people who were hanging about as if in readiness for departure, discovered a few L.R.B. pack-ponies saddled up close by. Much grousing was taking place on account of there being no water for the horses, for the pack-pony men found they were attached to H.Q., and would go forward in the afternoon without any certainty of a supply of water reaching them. I promised to let Chrisp know their predicament on my return to the lines, but further conversation was cut short by a terrific rushing of air and a great explosion about thirty yards away. The shell landed close to the R.E. signalling wagon, wounding a driver and a mule, but this was very slight damage considering the many groups of men and horses standing about. Fritz was reminding us that it was rather presumptuous to stroll round in the open and he certainly succeeded in effecting a clearance. Ben and I took refuge behind a bank and the Brigadier, who had been walking about a moment before, prudently descended into his dug-out once more.

A few more missiles came over, probably intended for some of the batteries of field-guns near by, but I do not think much further damage was inflicted on Brigade. Presently, wounded from the Bullecourt attack commenced to arrive, finding, to their relief, horse ambulances waiting below the brow of the hill, and we saw several L.R.B.'s with arm and head wounds. The battle was going well, according to their statements, but we could not learn anything of importance. The Staff Captain eagerly questioned the wounded, official news evidently being somewhat scanty—and one or two prisoners who had made their way down in safety found themselves vigorously cross-examined by an interpreter, who was awaiting them outside the Brigadier's dug-out.

During the afternoon, there being no sign of our moving forward, I began to search about for a convenient spot for pegging out my horse, with a crevice near at hand in which I could pass the night. But it seemed that a brigade mounted runner was expected to be at hand outside the Staff Captain's dug-out at all hours, for it happened that this gentleman wanted me at the very moment when I was conducting the search for quarters and I received a short lecture for forsaking my " post "—a beastly post it was, too, viz., an open road next to the spot where the shell had burst !

I had to accompany him on what he termed a reconnaissance and our route lay eastwards across Henin Hill, which was really several hundred yards of plateau-land dividing the valleys of the Cojeul and Sensee. Some of the field-guns were galloping forward and were coming under direct observation of the enemy, who were shelling them unmercifully. Relics of gun teams and broken limbers already littered the track, and since it was still being strafed everybody was moving at full speed. Every now and then a spurt of earth would rise at one portion of the track or another, and we spurred our horses on in order to get the unsavoury journey over as quickly as possible. On the eastern face of the ridge the Staff Captain stopped and proceeded on foot, leaving a quaking orderly to mind two rather restive steeds, who were much excited by the galloping gun-teams that passed by towards a wood close to Croisilles, but after half an hour's wait the officer returned to find us still in the land of the living and took over his horse as he might have done on the barrack-square.

As soon as we returned to brigade H.Q. I was ordered to proceed to the transport lines at Boisleux and bring up two G.S. wagons whose drivers did not know the way—altogether a better way of spending one's time than standing with one's arm through Ben's reins waiting all day long for orders. Besides, I felt like a glorified T.O. and rode with great pride in front of the two wagons, feeling my importance intensely until the foremost driver told me to "wake that blinkin' nag up, else this pole'll make 'im 'op."

When the miniature convoy reached Henin Hill we learnt that, although the L.R.B. were in Bullecourt, Brigade would not move until to-morrow morning. Simultaneously another runner appeared to relieve me for twelve hours, and I therefore got as much sleep as aeroplanes would allow in company with the transport, though several of the section were away all night long searching for the battalion with ration ponies. (I believe this was the second and last occasion on which the companies could not be located.)

Daybreak next day found me back again at brigade H.Q., where a certain amount of news was available. It was not altogether favourable. The Germans, who well knew what the loss of Bullecourt meant, were contesting every inch of the ground and the village was far from clear: some said we had given it up. The 167th Brigade on the right had had a very rough time of it. Down south things were going well: Trones Wood and Maricourt had been taken and fighting was going on all over that devastated area—Death Valley, Guillemont, Combles, names that were only too familiar with us. To our left the Canadians were well east of Monchy. In our sector the defence was stiffer than anywhere, for we were assaulting the Hindenburg Line, whereas to the south the British were still a long way from it. Ludendorff wanted a leisurely withdrawal similar to that of the 1917 spring, but it was obvious that our advance was more than a brushing of scouts and rearguards, judging from the prisoners that were being taken every day. We were forcing the Germans back much faster than they wished to go.

"Orderly!"

In other words, the man with the torn breeches. It was the Staff Captain speaking.

"I want you to come with me and I'll show you where the brigade ammunition dump is and also where the ration convoy is to go to-night. You'll have to guide the brigade transports up."

In civilian life I should have adjusted my tie, coughed appreciatively, and had my boots cleaned to celebrate the event: in actual fact I gave myself an extra scratch and covered up a grease-spot on my tunic with my bandolier.

We set off over the same track we had covered yesterday, surveying the litter we had seen on the previous afternoon. The enemy were still strafeing and ammunition columns were clattering along at e furious canter, so that when we reached the dump (a trench behind a thick belt of barbed wire), the Staff Captain hardly paused to indicate it with a sweep of his arm. Having signified the spot, he galloped on, following the relics of a road towards Croisilles and then striking off across the Sensee Valley, where a practically dry water-course indicated the River Sensee. On the far side the ground rose steeply and we came at once upon the Hindenburg Line at the first spot where it had been pierced. Somewhere within its ramifications was the new brigade H.Q., which the Staff Captain proceeded to inspect, leaving his orderly in fear and trembling upon the Fontaine-Croisilles road.

I wasn't happy : there were too many "'awky bits" flying around. And a dead mule was giving off diabolical odours in the ditch near by. Across the valley, on the Henin Hill, an artillery convoy was running the gauntlet of the directed German fire we ourselves had experienced. So small did it appear that I thought it must be crawling along, yet, as it came broadside on and began to descend the eastern slope of the plateau, it could be seen that its pace was a canter. Nearer and nearer it came, across the stream, up the slope and on to the road where I was waiting, and in another minute the sweating teams, with their drivers crouching low in their saddles, clattered past in the direction of Fontaine. Not one, but a score of shell-bursts had all but landed in the midst of the convoy in those few short minutes, yet it had got through unscathed. How many times would it repeat the journey with equal immunity ?

Ah ! there comes another convoy over the brow of the hill. . . . More bursts. . . . Pop-pop-pop-pop-pop-pop. . . . A German aeroplane, damn it, potting at the road. Ben cocks one ear forward and the other back. . . . Crash ! A five-point-nine near the road. . . . When is that perishing captain coming ? . . . The rations have got to be brought up here to-night, oh ! miserable thought ! And what a benighted place for the pack-ponies to be moved forward to ! Pop-pop-pop-pop. Come over, Ben, and stand quiet while I squat in this ditch : never mind the damned mule. Come over, I say. That's better : now for Heaven's sake don't fidget any more. You want to get back and so do I, but you won't do any good by pawing me with that perishing hoof. . . . What about my breakfast ? Why can't Brigade provide a meal for a miserable mounted orderly ? I expect the Staff Captain's batman got him a decent feed before he came out. . . . Crump ! Nice place to leave a Johnny with two horses, I *don't* think. . . . Damn ! I left my shell-dressing in the bivvy. And so on—a train of thoughts of the " fed-up and far from home " variety, a half hour wait with the two impatient steeds and a succession of false alarms, as first one man and then another emerged from the trench wherein the Staff Captain had disappeared.

He arrived at last, took his charger and galloped back across the valley.

" Note the landmarks," said he. " Will you know the place by night ? "

With the whiff of putrefying mule still pervading my nostrils, I grunted an affirmative. Would there be a to-night ? was the question. But so far as our second journey over the track was concerned, there was every reason to suppose there would be. Brigade H.Q. were really going to move forward this time and Winslow, who was with the pack-ponies, enquired as to the extent of wind-up justified by the liveliness

AA

ahead of them : he also asked if there was any water where they were going.

"Give my kindest regards to Chrisp," said "Winny," "and tell him that the water he's sent up is not sufficient for a louse to swim in, and we want at least ten petrol-cans full as soon as he can oblige."

I was able to deliver the message, my instructions being to take a chit to the transport lines and await orders. But "the kindest regards" did not mitigate in the least the virulence of "Crip's" comments when I got back to Boisleux.

"We haven't a single pony to spare," said he. "Tiny will have to go, that's all." (Tiny was an obstreperous dink who had gained quite a reputation for his reluctance to be led.)

I laughed, a good hearty laugh. Tiny, indeed ! Someone was going to have his arm lugged out of its socket.

"Where is Brigade now ? " asked Chrisp.

"Just moved forward to the Hindenburg Line, near Croisilles."

"Do you know the place ? "

"Yes. I've been up there this morning."

"Well, since you know the place you'd better take the water-cans up. No one else knows where to go."

"Well, I'm . . ."

"I dare say you are. But can you suggest anyone else we could send ? "

There was obviously no help for it. I was the only "onion" who had the misfortune to know the way.

"Well, you get a bite of dinner," said Chrisp. "When you've finished the drink'll be all ready. You might as well ride up on Ben and lead Tiny beside you."

It sounded easy enough, but never was there a more fatiguing job than the literal tugging of that obstinate mule at the full extremity of his reins over every yard of that four mile route from Boisleux St. Marc to the road where I had waited that morning. The mount I was riding really pulled Tiny the whole way there, the connecting link being the mule's taut reins and my arm, which was dragged backwards and nearly wrenched off. At times my temper got the upper hand and I hit the obstinate beast on the nose with his reins, resulting in his standing absolutely like a rock and even backing, the nearer I tried to get to him. I cursed hard and implored every passer-by to "whip up behind," but the pedestrians on the track were all wounded men, and passing drivers were in such a confounded hurry that they scarcely had time enough to emit war-whoops, which only had a momentary effect. Fair numbers of our division were among the wounded, for the battle was in full swing again.

The brigade pack-ponies which had moved forward in the morning were tucked away in portions of trench and various excavations which denoted the old front-line system of the Hindenburg Line between the Sensee and the Fontaine-Croisilles road, and it was as great a juggling feat as I ever wish to perform to lead both my rider and the shrinking mule in single file along the crumbling parapets that led to our destination. One of the brigade staff directed me to the exact spot, otherwise I should never have distinguished either men or horses, for they were well below the surface of the ground. Naturally the spot was now even livelier than it had been in the morning, since the attack was progressing again, and it was with considerable relief that I found a protected nook amidst the maze of earthworks, for both animals, not to mention myself. One of the pony men enlarged on the delinquencies of the staff in expecting the animals to keep fit in so confined an area, parched with thirst which even the newly arrived water-supply would not quench, and packed so closely that they continually kicked one another with annoyance. His indignation was probably caused not so much by the material discomfort of the animals as by the strafeing of the neighbourhood, which necessitated cursing somebody or something in order to calm ruffled nerves. It was, however, rather more comfortable to sit and munch dog-biscuits with Jarvis and the other men in the bowels of the Hindenburg Line than to emerge from it, skip over trenches and parapets with a horse and a mule, and set about dragging the latter every inch of the way over that hateful Henin Hill. What were the brigade pony-men's adventures in between my casual glimpses of them, I do not know : when I left them at four o'clock that afternoon they were still awaiting orders—killing time by commenting upon the duration of the War and on the comeliness of their bristling beards.

It was nearly dark when I got back to the horse-lines. The pairs detailed for the night trip were already harnessed up, ready to be hooked into the limbers, while one or two drivers stood by smoking cigarettes, their shrapnel-helmets and respirators indicating that they had " clicked " for the ration-convoy. " Milky," who was now full corporal, said they were leaving at dusk and asked me if I should know the way in the dark. Know the way ! What fool could miss it when he had done the journey four times in one day !

The L.R.B. convoy included cookers which were to be parked behind a bank where I had waited for the Staff Captain that morning, near which spot the brigade were expected to concentrate after their relief by daybreak, and it was, of course, my special privilege to show the drivers where the bank was. But it soon became evident that the route was not so very plain after all. In other words, recognised landmarks such as hills, cross-roads, telegraph poles, etc., were either invisible by night, or else easily missed, whereas fork roads and corners appeared one after another, which I had omitted to note by daylight. Once or twice it seemed as if we were on the wrong road, but I put my faith in Ben and a loose rein : *he* knew the way well enough and I found him turning corners and even skirting shell-holes which he had noted by day and instinctively recollected as he returned to them in the darkness. Ben, in fact, pulled us through nearly as far as the Sensee Valley, after which we proceeded on foot and lost ground while the head of the convoy, plunging blindly ahead and outpacing Chrisp and myself, passed both crossings of the Sensee and very nearly reached Croisilles before it could be brought to a standstill. However, after wandering round for some time, we discovered a new route, which enabled the convoy to reach its destination without mishap, and for an hour or so the Fontaine road was illuminated by dozens of electric torches, intended to assist in manœuvring of field-kitchens into concealed positions and to enable everyone to scrutinise everybody else. Originally only officers carried torchlights, but now every driver and runner and cook seemed to possess one which he flashed in the faces of all and sundry, regardless of his surroundings. My recollections of that night's events are very dim : I only know from a letter written next day that I got back to Boisleux at 6.30 a.m. At dawn there was a big German attack on Bullecourt just after the relief was effected, but fortunately the companies, although delayed, were not required again, and they spent the day in the system of trenches not far from the cookers, which supplied their needs under rather difficult conditions.

The next night we took up officers' chargers in case any of the company commanders wished to ride back with the battalion, who were to drag themselves down to an improvised camp at Boisleux the following morning: it was daybreak before the company-men, in a very worn state, emerged on the Fontaine road, and even there they had to take refuge hurriedly from a low-flying German aeroplane, which "machine-gunned" them without opposition. Although the L.R.B. had not had the satisfaction of completely retaining Bullecourt, they had taken part in much of the preparatory spadework and not suffered so badly as in certain other offensives. Their efforts can be appreciated from the fact that they had made five attacks in four days !

This account of the opening of the British offensive is necessarily greatly restricted in scope, for it is the ordinary soldier's lot in battle to be aware only of those things which are happening in his immediate vicinity and even then to be completely in the dark as to the why and wherefore of them. How forcibly this truth came home to one when crouching behind those banks of earth at Fontaine, where I had found the pack-pony men and their steeds, listening to the confused jumble of explosions and whining shells without the slightest notion of what was happening outside a radius of some twenty yards or so ! The battle might be on a two-mile or a thirty-mile front ; we might still be advancing or the enemy might be counter-attacking ; a convoy might be suffering untold tortures a quarter of a mile to either side of us ; a platoon of reinforcements might have just been blown to pieces three hundred yards ahead. But what could men know of these things, sandwiched in between walls of chalk—waiting until they should be required to do their next little bit ? Even when one clambered up and surveyed the immediate surroundings, what could one see ? Trenches in front, behind and to either side, half a dozen puffs of smoke from shell-bursts scattered about, Fontaine Wood to the left—now a mass of splintered trees—a few men with shovels walking along a neighbouring parapet, and, up in the sky, three or four British aeroplanes cruising serenely up and down. A few more isolated details, perhaps, but they conveyed nothing. How much wiser was anyone as to the magnitude and fortune of the big battle ? Even Hobson, the famous disseminator of news, would have been at a loss to concoct a story of the attack from the scanty material afforded by such surroundings.

Our recollections are therefore concerned mainly with the most trivial things, but we had a good deal to occupy our minds, for an empty stomach or a verminous shirt is a matter of utmost concern to any man when directly affected. There is a good deal of truth in that saying : "They say a reasonable amount o' fleas is good for a dog—keeps him from broodin' over bein' a dog, mebbe."

CHAPTER XXXIII.

THE BRITISH OFFENSIVE : ASTRIDE THE CAMBRAI ROAD.

(*September*, 1918.)

The Drocourt-Queant switch broken—More Brigade running—Recollections of a trip to Dury—With the section at Guemappe—A chapter of accidents— Preparations for Armageddon—Echelon "A" moves forward—The worst bombing raid of all—Chrisp wounded.

THE march of events had been so rapid that it already seemed ages since the British offensive had opened. Up in the north the Germans were evacuating the Lys Salient, and from Arras to below the Somme the British had driven them back to the outposts of the Hindenburg Line, which was already partly captured near Bullecourt. Since August 8th the British alone had captured over 60,000 prisoners and 700 guns, while the French also had been exceedingly active. Yet only six weeks before, on July 15th, we had left the line in fear and trembling lest our promised rest should be cut short by a big German offensive !

Accustomed as we were in recent months to depressing news from all quarters, it was difficult to assimilate the good tidings that now came to hand. What impressed us most was the efficiency of the Army's organisation and the marvellous control of all the services in the rear. The British had often been blamed for maintaining a costly mechanism behind the line, for it had never before been used to advantage. But now that a battle was being waged, and the line was moving forward, on a front of forty miles, the wonderful organisation that had gradually been built up justified itself and worked like clockwork. Not a unit possessed a horse, a vehicle or a lorry which was not put to good use in the next few months. All the light and heavy railway material needed in the advance was not only handy but provided with men to lay it. Wherever a captured road needed rapid repairing a Labour battalion mysteriously appeared for the purpose. Whenever a sausage balloon was brought down in flames, there was another on the spot with observation officers to man it. And so on, right through the branches of the service. Even rations were better than they had been in far quieter times than these. Oh, that everything had run so smoothly in those Somme days when the traffic problem appeared insurmountable, although the offensive

was carried on on a much shorter front ! It had taken four years to
get to this pitch, but it was consoling to have lived to witness it.

No longer did we turn to the German communiques to find out
what had really happened. For the German staff found it difficult
to disillusion their people as to the efficiency of the British Army.
at which they were far more astonished than ourselves. Their greatest
surprise came on September 2nd, when the Canadians broke through
the famous Drocourt-Queant switch, which was regarded as impregnable and was, in fact, the key to their whole front. It caused them
to retire precipitately over the Canal du Nord on our front and it is
necessary to recall the exact situation this brought about in order
to understand our own movements up to the day when the big attack
on Cambrai began. Our front now bulged out in a sharp salient
in which our line faced northwards along the marshes of the Sensee
and then swung suddenly south and south-west to the Hindenburg
Line and it was within the angle that most of our forthcoming activities
were centred. The strategy of the Army for the next week or so was
to mark time in this Cambrai sector, while in the south the Battle
of Epchy was fought and a good jumping-off ground was obtained
ready for the final onslaught upon the Hindenburg Line.

During the battalion's few days' stay near Boisleux-aux-Mont I
returned to the transport section at Boisleux-St. Marc, which had
now become quite a back area. A squadron of tanks was stationed
there. and we caught sight for the first time of whippets careering up
and down in a field for the sake of exercise. The railway had now
been put in order and trains arrived from Arras with large quantities
of R.E. material for the further extension of the repaired track. On
the 5th the battalion and transport had orders to move up to Bullecourt and the march was accomplished, only for the orders to be
cancelled later in the day, so that everyone had to come back to the
starting point. The real move was made on the 7th, when we set off
down the Cojeul Valley, through the villages (?) of Henin, Heninel
and Wancourt, and pitched our lines in that old centre of struggle,
Guemappe, which had marked almost the limit of our 1917 Arras
offensive. Monchy lay nearly level with us to the north of the Cambrai
road, and it said much for the distance we had advanced when we saw
British sausage balloons ascending even farther east than we were.
Like all the ground just east of Arras, it was scared with trenches
and our site appeared no worse, if no better, than every other unit's
surroundings. Q.M.S.s and other favoured beings took up their abode
in the cellars of ruined houses, etc., while the common or garden
transport men took possession of a fairly serviceable trench beside
the horses. Lieutenant Chrisp and Sergt. Watkins, however, erected
a couple of scrounged tents—being satisfied with the proximity of
our trench in case of emergencies.

It did not appear as if our lines would come in for any hostile shelling.
but we cast many ominous glances, within the first hour or so of our
arrival, at a hill about a mile away over which it would be necessary
to pass on our journeys eastward. We could see the straight white
Cambrai road wending its way up to the summit, whereon stood the
half-destroyed village of Vis-en-Artois and every minute or so a
familiar sound drew our attention to a cloud of smoke and dust against
the sky-line. Vis-en-Artois was going the way of many another
village, while its cross-roads were rapidly gaining a reputation. The
companies were occupying dug-outs east of the village for one night

and that same evening some of our drivers made a closer acquaintance with the place.

For the first day or so I again had to be absent from the section as brigade runner, for I found myself upon the first evening detailed. with a Q.W.R. man, to report at once to brigade H.Q. in an unknown spot somewhere ahead of us. After many wanderings, we at last discovered our goal in some trenches near the Cojeul river, but nobody seemed to know anything about us ; all the H.Q. staff were far too busy preparing homes to sleep in before dark to worry about two men standing in the rain with their chargers. Repeated messages to the Staff Captain eventually brought some officer on the scene, but he appeared to think that we had merely to peg out our horses in wet soil and leave them to their own devices, while we could fling ourselves down anywhere for the night. When we pointed out, however. that there was not the faintest chance of their being there in the morning, he bestirred himself somewhat and gave us permission to occupy a sheltered spot right beside the river, with a splendidly-built block-house for our own abode. He didn't seem to know anything about rations, so we retired empty to our slumbers. There was one consolation ; no one but this officer knew our whereabouts, so, even if we were wanted, there was little need to worry about being awakened.

In the morning, however, the Staff Captain soon ferreted us out and bade us accompany him on one of his unhealthy jaunts. The L.R.B. were moving into trenches facing north along the marshes and brigade H.Q. were going to shift forward to the Drocourt-Queant switch, so that our ride would introduce us to the " impregnable " line which had been stormed six days before. The Q.W.R. man and I breathed again when we found it was possible for single mounts to skirt Vis-en-Artois itself by using a track to the left of the village ; it took us past a sunken road where the L.R.B. were stationed preparatory for their move, but we found the thoroughfare so narrowed by substantial German " bivvies " that it would be impossible for wheeled traffic to use the route in both directions. No rules appeared to be in force, for on a subsequent journey I actually encountered a hopeless impasse at this point. Rather than pass through Vis-en-Artois, it was perhaps an excusable route to take, but it was unavoidable, in any case. joining the Cambrai road again on the far side of the hill.

The Staff Captain was rather more talkative on this occasion.

" Remember to take this track here," he said, as we branched off the main road again near Haucourt. " There is a German R.E. dump a little farther up which is receiving a good deal of attention from the Boche. and this is the only way to avoid it."

And again, when we had struck off to the left, along a road to Dury. " This is St. Servin's Farm, which meant a good deal of scrapping for the Canadians."

The farm appeared to be fairly intact, while in its grounds were some German army huts—the first we had seen in the course of the War—and it can be understood that the sight of buildings still standing upon ground recently captured made quite an impression on our minds. All the familiar traces of war were on every hand, and yet we moved in an environment suggestive of back-area surroundings. The ground had been well shelled and debris lay about, yet there were large stretches of green grass in places.

In another minute or so we reached the terrain where the Drocourt-Queant line could be seen. Less than a mile away on a ridge, forming almost a semicircle around us, was the famous "switch," with the practically untouched village of Dury, marking the most prominent part of the hill, just in front of us. In the dip between us and the ridge was an extraordinarily thick belt of wire, several yards deep, through which the Canadians had managed to force their way, while near the trench line was another belt scarcely less formidable. Close by us were several of the outlying man-holes defended to the last by devoted German machine-gunners, as could be seen from their corpses lying each beside the shell-hole from which their deadly fire had been directed upon the advancing Canadians until the inevitable end had come. What a story each one of those dead Germans conveyed to the minds of those who followed in the wake of the attack!

It was by the thick belt of wire that we had to wait with our horses, while the Staff Captain ascended the ridge on foot and inspected the trenches to be occupied by Brigade. Several six-inch howitzers were firing close at hand and we realised for the first time the peculiar position of the firing-line, for some were firing in almost a north-westerly direction while others, close by, were facing due east. Unlike the informed readers of newspapers at home, we were quite unfamiliar with maps or the present state of the firing-line, so that the behaviour of our batteries was most puzzling at the time. (I had ceased to subscribe to the *Times* owing to half the numbers not arriving at all, and the remainder coming to hand irregularly and in any sort of order, presumably the fault of the Practical Joke Department at the Base!)

It seemed to us, as we waited there, that we had taken a very roundabout route, and that the quickest way home lay through the village of Eterpigny just behind us, but when the Staff Captain returned he advised us to give it as wide a berth as possible. It appeared to be crammed with dead horses, and it was probable that any convoy passing through would add to their number. The Q.W.R. and I thereupon vowed that we would follow the route by which we had come that morning, whate'er befell; yet within three days I had to break the vow and choose ten Eterpignys in preference to one St. Servin's Farm! Such are the idiosyncrasies of the Boche!

In the afternoon brigade H.Q. moved up to their new position—a trench system close to the Etaing-Dury road, at a point nearer the latter village. The quarters for the men were superb, consisting of deep German dug-outs in the heart of the Drocourt-Queant switch, but accommodation for horses and runners was another matter, and appeared to have received the usual scant consideration. After waiting with our horses near the parados, and shouting in vain the old, old query: "Well, what abart it?" for about ten minutes, the arrival of a couple of crumps settled the matter for us. About a hundred yards away in an exposed position close to the road was a wooden German stable, big enough for six horses, and we promptly made a dive for the shelter of its hospitable roof—one inch thick!

Ben and the other horse seemed delighted, especially when they received a feed to keep them quiet, but the place was too near our guns for our liking. Only twenty yards across the road in an orchard was a battery of field guns which, we promptly discovered, divided its time between strafeing the Germans a mile away, and submitting to a fairly accurate fire from the enemy in return. In fact it seemed that our men had scarcely time to fire a round or so and clear off before the answering swish came from the blue beyond.

The Westminster and I looked at one another; had we been Charlie Chaplins our hats would have come clean off our heads and settled themselves in place again. Ben ceased to eat his hay within five minutes, and started his old game of exercising his ears; the other horse reared up and pulled his iron staple out of the wall.

" What a palace ! " said the Westminster. " I'm going over to see the Staff Captain about this."

At that moment a crouching figure arrayed in tin helmet, with respirator at the alert, scurried across the road and came towards us.

" Take them ——— horses away. We're under obsivashun 'ere. Them didn't ought to be up 'ere at all."

I assured him with a heartful fervour that we wouldn't keep there a moment longer than necessary, and it was not long before I was searching about for a healthier site, while my companion had gone off to interview the Staff. But neither of us was successful. I discovered that to the left, as well as just behind me, were further batteries, which practically pinned us down to our present spot as the only possible abode near at hand, and since dusk was falling it was impossible to go further afield. As for the Staff, they insisted that we must stay close by, and seemed to think we must just make the best of a bad job.

The arrival of gas-shells shortly after this, coupled with the attentions which a most obnoxious German battery paid to the British guns just behind and in front of us, made us determine that—whatever befell the horses—we, at any rate, should find a better place than the stable to sleep in, but our responsibility for the animals prevented our going so far away as the brigade trench. Just beneath the road, close at hand, were some excavations which showed that our R.E.s were about to build a dug-out, probably for the use of the artillery officers, and it was in the hollow already scooped out that we decided to lie down for the night. This intention necessitated our hurling out several boards, picks and shovels which had been left there, at the risk of incurring wrath at the hands of the R.E.s, but it was an artillery sergeant, not an engineer, who first opened his mouth on the subject. He came on the scene just as we were spreading sandbags over the " floor " to take off some of its roughness, and cast a fierce glance upon us, mingled with pity.

" And what the blazes are you doing here ? " he asked, expectorating freely on our doorstep.

" That's just what we want to know," said the Q.W.R. " We're not here for our health."

" You've got two horses here, haven't you ? Well, d'you think you're going to move 'em about in daylight with the Germans eighteen hundred yards away and our battery only just across the road ? "

" All depends on our Staff Captain ; you'd better see him. If there's a message to take anywhere, I've got to move my horse, but I'll take damned good care I don't come back," rejoined my companion.

" Well, I shall report it to our captain. . . . But I might tell you your nags won't be there long if Fritz keeps it up to-night like he has to-day. And I advise you to keep your respirators handy. We had to wear ours for an hour last night."

The periodical one-minute interval between the German shells having nearly expired, the N.C.O. then departed as suddenly as he had come. With such regularity did the shells arrive, in fact, that as soon as one salvo had landed—and most of them fell in the orchard—it was reasonably safe to cross over to the stable and back, or to scurry to the brigade trench before the next arrival. This regular strafeing, however, slackened off somewhat later on and the intervals became longer and rather spasmodic during the night. My companion and I lay upon the sandbags, wedged together, yet wretchedly cold in spite of wearing overcoats, and fell off eventually into a more or less comatose state, from which we were constantly roused by noises without. Three or four times, after a particularly noisy crump, one or the other would clamber out, convinced that the stable had been blown sky high—only to find the place still standing and a new hole not many yards away, while the poor animals were perfectly still, their evening feed of hay left untouched before them. It was raining outside and, to add to our troubles, water and mud started to fall upon us from the roof until by daybreak we were nearly saturated from head to foot and our " funk-hole " had become an impossible abode.

When the first glimmer of a cheerless dawn appeared in the sky, we crawled out for the last time and made an examination of the chargers who, marvellous to relate, were unhurt. Several new shell-holes lay in the vicinity and one side of the stable had given way to its feelings during the melée, so that Ben had really had a lucky escape. The enemy were rather quieter now and it was possible for us to view the surroundings with greater care than on the previous evening. We even paid an early morning visit to our friends the artillery, who were occupying trenches a little way up the road. After a great deal of difficulty we succeeded in finding a pump and filled buckets for our horses, but our efforts were wasted, as they refused to drink. The most interesting occupation for the next hour was watching the brigade cooks prepare breakfast in their deep German trench, where we finally enjoyed a good mug of hot tea and a morsel of frizzly bacon.

By this time Fritz had started his favourite occupation, but since he consistently kept the orchard as his target or else strafed a battery behind us, we remained in the centre of the happy hunting-ground and only heard the noise. The only inconvenience we got was stray whiffs of sneezing gas, which, though harmless, was annoying. Ben, the grand old knock-kneed cab horse, was thoroughly angry and obviously pining to get away from the spot ; and about nine o'clock his opportunity came, for a message had to be taken to the transport lines. The Westminster lost the toss as to who should go and so, with great glee, I led Ben forth from the stable, outside which I slipped in the mud trying to mount and nearly lost my hold of him, so anxious was he to depart. Never had he moved as he did that morning. The difficulty was to prevent him from cantering all the way home. Across the valley, past St. Servin's Farm and the R.E. dump, down on to the Cambrai road, past Haucourt, through the sunken road, across the Sensee and back on to the Cambrai road we went, trotting most of the way. But Ben wasn't satisfied until he had reached the section at Guemappe and been tied up on a line with his old friends once more.

Chrisp announced his intention of sending up Gunboat Smith to relieve me and I thought it only fair to Gunboat to give him my opinion of the place. Chrisp promised that Gunboat in turn would be relieved next day and, after saying some nasty things about the Staff, decided to use only second-rate chargers for the job. In the meantime my successor started to collect his kit together, amidst the jibes of his companions, who were seldom kind on such occasions, and about midday we were ready to start off from the lines. It was, of course, necessary for me to accompany him as he did not know the way, and when Ben was saddled up again the disappointed steed developed a fit of the sulks. which increased in intensity the nearer we got to Dury, so that our journey was a slow and tedious one. But I had no intention of putting him in the stable again ! When once we hove in sight of that little wooden shack. I pointed an arm in its direction, indicated the brigade trench to the right, bade Gunboat a hasty farewell and then administered an immediate restorative to Ben's nerves by wheeling round on to a homeward course.

I should have liked to hear Gunboat's remarks when he made a proper acquaintance with the mounted runners' quarters, for they must have been emphatic. All we know is that, after tying up his horse. he withdrew to the brigade trench to await developments and witnessed enough in the next half hour to make his fiery Ulsterman's nature boil with indignation. Firmly convinced that " something had got to be done about it," he brought the Staff Captain on to the scene and bade him poke his head over the trench and watch the display. How much of it came as a revelation to the officer I do not know, but in a short while he had decided that no runners would be needed there at all and, in one of those minute intervals, our friend Gunboat dragged out his horse and fled for his life. Our best thanks are due to Gunboat for his timely and effective protest, for it ended once and for all the brigade orderly stunts on that sector, at any rate so far as housing horses at brigade H.Q. was concerned. We had, of course, several messages to take up from our lines on later occasions.

The Devils' Mess had in my absence erected a comfortable bivvy in the trench by the horse-lines in Guemappe, where they had fortunately provided sufficient space for me to share it on my return. Coni was with us, for, after serving his qualifying period in the trenches and staying on surplus personnel during the Bullecourt affair, he returned to the section until such time as his interview with the Brigadier, etc., would result in his commission papers arriving. He had spent an afternoon wandering round the scenes of his trench adventures in the old Battle of Arras and said he could scarcely recognise the trenches he had once occupied. In one place he came upon a grave on which the inscription ran :---

R. I. P.
S. V. P.
Here lie the bodies of a Sergeant
And a Private of the Imperial German
Army who attempted to raid the
Lines of the Canadian Scottish.
NUFF SAID

I took the first available opportunity to wander over to the famous hill of Monchy, round which so much fighting had raged. On the way we came across one or two disabled tanks and a maze of old overgrown trenches which must have been relics of the 1917 struggle. How the cavalry had then been cut up was very simple to understand when one saw the serried ranks of trenches which not only encircled the base of the hill but also its upper regions. Of the village itself practically nothing remained. The street climbed sharply to the summit where we obtained a magnificent view of the Douai and Lens district (in German hands) as we gazed north ; of the Drocourt-Queant switch to the east, Arras to the west and Henin Hill to the south. There was an official observation post up there, the occupants of which requested us to move on, as they were not at all anxious that attention be called to their locality, which was doubtless under careful observation from the German Scarpe defences that seemed to lie at our feet. No wonder this hill had been such a bone of contention ! No wonder the Canadians had said, " Fritz must come off it." He had " come off it " now. It lay in peaceful solitude in the glow of the evening sunset. its crumbling ruins nearly hidden with grass, its streets almost deserted. The ravage of war had finally passed beyond it, eastwards, leaving merely crumbling walls, ruined palings and similar inanimate relics to testify silently to the tragic fate of many souls hereabouts. All human traces were removed . . . but if ghosts frequent places of the dead, surely that summit must have been thick with them.

The trenches occupied by the battalion until the 12th were beyond Dury Wood, and on that date they came back to Dury for six days, so that the route followed by the ration convoys from our lines at Guemappe was, until the 18th, practically the same as that leading to brigade H.Q. Not content with bombing the horse-line area. which was still a recognised nightly performance, the Bosche planes provided a diversion in the shape of a systematic bombing of the Cambrai road itself, while Dury and Dury Wood came in for frequent visitations. Our thoughts throughout these journeys were therefore centred as much on the searchlights around us as on the likely artillery targets. The one consolation was that our squadrons were continually at work giving the Germans ten times as much bombing as we were suffering at their hands, but we had to admit that at this time a few of the German airmen were extremely daring. One afternoon a plane calmly circled round three of our observation balloons in succession. bringing them down in flames. A new one had scarcely ascended in one place. near Guemappe, when the airman returned and brought that down also !

The heavy casualties caused by night bombing to horses had led to an order that each unit should erect separate short lines so as to spread the animals out and localise the effects of bombs. But at Guemappe even this was considered insufficient and we were told to dig pits as far as possible in order to keep the animals beneath ground level. This was all very well, but digging pits took a considerable time, even when fashioned out of shell holes, and since harness had to be kept so clean drivers really had little time to give to affording protection to their horses. At the end of a week, by dint of working hard until dark. we dug enough cover for eight out of our fifty to sixty horses, and then came a colossal thunderstorm which flooded them out and rendered all our labour futile.

The thunderstorm, which visited us in the middle of the night. was accompanied by the heaviest rain I had ever experienced and it kept on for hours. The roof over the trench stood it pretty well, but suddenly Trendell and Conibeer, whose funk-hole was at least a foot deeper than mine, uttered howls of agony ; the foot of their bed was a lake and upon striking a light they found a torrent rushing into our home. which was throughout lower than the normal trench level, owing to our desire to be as far below the surface as possible. The stream was swamping the end of my blankets en route and, of course, finding its way into the still lower level of their " bed," so that everything they possessed was soaked through before they had time to rescue it. The only remedy was to dig a gulley away from our " doorway " and carry it on indefinitely down the trench, an operation which would mean getting soaked through, boots and all. We stood for a time, putting whatever was salvable up at my end of the bivvy and throwing everything that was soaked on to the parapet, seeing that it could get no worse. This included half the blankets and the ration sack. At last I began to have fears for the safety of my own bed, since the water kept rising, and, taking the largest mug I could find, I attempted to catch the incoming stream and hurl it back into the trench again—obviously the action of a lunatic. When its futility dawned upon me I took off all my clothes in desperation, covered Nature with a mackintosh and, seizing a shovel, squelched barefooted out into six or eight inches of sloshy mud. It was necessary to make up one's mind that one was going to get wet and dirty and so I revelled in the adventure, delving like fury by the aid of frequent flashes of lightning. After a few minutes I succeeded in digging a deep enough gulley to drain the water away, which naturally diverted it into another man's bivvy and within a short while he was nearly drowning! Next day we baled the place out and, so far as our bivvy was concerned, we had no more trouble.

An accident of a different nature befell the bivvy occupied by Chilcott's party. One of our horses, when let loose to graze, tried to cross over the trench by means of their roof, with the result that the animal, the roof, and the sides of the trench collapsed on top of their entire belongings.

Even this does not complete the record of misfortunes in our trench, for one afternoon Baker attempted to light a fire with cordite in his bivvy and nearly blew his party into "the end of next week." There was plenty of artillery ammunition scattered about and the cooks had discovered that a few sticks of cordite were very useful for imparting a blaze to their fire—so, profiting by their experience, Baker took a 60-pounder charge into the trench, extracted a small portion, and did the needful. Unfortunately a light fell upon the charge itself with the result that Baker was in a few minutes being conveyed on a stretcher to the nearest ambulance. His burns kept him in hospital for some months, but fortunately he grew a new face, which some people think has considerably improved his appearance. Another bad casualty was Long, who also left us, while dear old Lance-Corporal Hurford, our transport "Q.M.S." (who had been indenting for four years for some theft thoap, but without success), got a nasty burn on his hand. About this time we lost another friend, Winslow, who took a well-deserved trip to Blighty on account of his age.

On the 18th the battalion moved to an area just north of us, and two days later went into some old German positions south of Vis-en-Artois, where they remained until the 25th. One evening Chrisp took me as orderly a good distance up the Cambrai road, farther than I had been before, striking off ultimately not far from a place called Villers-les-Cagnicourt, where he wanted to investigate the possible site of horse-lines in the event of an advance. According to the statements of a man I spoke to while waiting at our destination, nobody could move about Villers in the daytime, while at night the wood there became a favourite target for bombs owing to the German belief that we had a headquarters there. Little did I think at the time that we should have to occupy such an advanced place as the wood with our horses two days before the British attack began.

As the month wore on we received excellent news from the various fronts. The offensive in Salonika was crumbling up the Bulgarian

Army, the final rout in Palestine had begun, and the Americans had, with French assistance, captured the partly-evacuated salient at St. Mihiel. With the Battle of Epehy, just to the south of us, Foch's preliminary punches had come to an end and the stage was now set for the final drama—the great knock-out blow from one end of the line to the other. In front of the British was the greater part of the Hindenburg Line, still uncaptured, the fortifications of which afforded the dejected German people their last hope of keeping us at bay, while on our portion of the front, although the Hindenburg Line and the Drocourt-Queant switch were breached, there were canal defences and the massive Bourlon height, which was now threatened mainly from the west and north-west. (In the Battle of Cambrai it had been attacked from the south.)

The first sign of the preparation for Armageddon came when the transport was ordered to split up into A and B Echelons. Echelon B comprised the bulk of the transport section under Hosking—a second transport officer who had just been attached to us—and its task was to carry out the ordinary functions of the section, supplying both the battalion and Echelon A with rations, water, post, etc. Echelon A, which consisted of trench mortar and Lewis gun limbers, eight ammunition ponies, an N.C.O., mounted runner, spare man and cook under Chrisp, had to operate in close touch with the companies and bivouac as far forward as possible.

On the day of the first move I was sent off to the neighbourhood of Upton Wood, on the far side of Vis-en-Artois, to stake our claim to a certain piece of land on which to bivouac and mount guard until the arrival of Echelon A in the afternoon. Unfortunately the only clue that was given me as to its whereabouts was the proximity of some telegraph poles, and in blissful ignorance I scrounged the wrong site. The long wait was rendered more tedious by the fact that some Canadian artillery sent me a message to come off the skyline, as the horse would draw attention to their headquarters, and so I had to keep Ben in a big shell-hole, where he got hopelessly tangled with some barbed wire. It did not seem as if we had much chance of pitching our lines there if the Canadians objected to the presence of even one horse, and it presently dawned on me that as there were thousands of other telegraph poles about I was probably waiting in the wrong place. Just as I had decided to try my luck elsewhere, however, Gunboat arrived on the scene, having been sent to call me back to the lines owing to our move being cancelled.

It was when our echelon actually moved on the 24th that I found our real goal was about a mile away from the scene of my previous vigil, on a flat piece of country not far from Hendecourt. We were very glad to be such a small party on our own, particularly under Chrisp, who had not changed one iota since his private's days, and on such occasions as this became absolutely one of the party. Unfortunately on this day an incident happened which separated him from us for the rest of the War.

To-morrow we were to go still farther ahead and Chrisp rode back to Guemappe after dusk to see if more detailed orders as to our future movements were to hand, while we rigged up very improvised bivvies in one of the many deserted German trenches which ran in every direction, and finally settled down to sleep. The bombers were busy as usual and we heard several " packets " being dropped back there in the direction of Guemappe and Monchy. Of one load in particular someone remarked : " Sounds as if it's not far from the section," but little did we realise at the time that it was indeed the psychological moment of which we had all been living in dread for months past. " Someone's lines are almost sure to be hit—why should they not be ours ? " When Echelon A left Guemappe that afternoon they were, by a singular stroke of fate, marching away just in time to avoid the calamity. When Chrisp rode back to the lines, by a still stranger decree of fate he was not only just in time to experience the raid, but was to be badly wounded by a bomb-splinter. We were awakened about eleven o'clock by someone who had ridden up from Guemappe with the news that four bombs had fallen actually in the L.R.B. lines, that Chrisp was wounded in the throat, Dennison in the mouth, and Spanny Main in the leg, also that several horses were killed and wounded. With the exception of the announcement about the Battle of Gomme-court, nothing perhaps had rendered us so speechless since we had been in France. Chrisp, who had been with us a few hours before, Chrisp, the figure-head of the section, was nearly dying from a throat wound.

The Devils' Mess fortunately escaped. Figg and Trendell were in fact down in the Q.M.S.'s dug-out at the time, trying to " wangle " a bottle of *vin blanc* from Q.M.S. Skeats. Four terrific explosions practically simultaneously, followed by two others, caused them to forget the liquid refreshment and hurry on to the horse-lines, where they heard shouting and groaning in the darkness, coupled with wild shrieks from the horses. Owing to the danger of showing a light in the open, it was exceedingly difficult to ascertain the extent of the damage : all that could be discovered was that many of the horses were on the ground, either dead or wounded. Word soon went round that Chrisp, who had been in his tent, was hit, then that Spanny Main was wounded, then that Dennison was struck. Chrisp was the worst casualty, owing to his throat being torn, and if it had not been for the prompt action of the Echelon B-officer, Hosking, and Sergt. Watkins, he most surely would have died. While he was being attended to, with the assistance of an electric torch used surreptitiously in the tent, all those who knew anything about veterinary work did their best for the horses in the moonlight, while others set off to the surrounding units in search of veterinary officers and sergeants. Our own brigade veterinary sergeant was unfortunately hit by one of the bombs.

The adventures of the next half-hour baffle description : Figg afterwards endeavoured to give me an idea of them and they must have been a nightmare. Several horses had to be shot, but it was a long time before some could be put out of their misery. Figg rushed to his pair and found Beattie absolutely dead and Babs kicking a little, but through my absence I was spared the sight of the old grey lying horribly mangled and yet alive for some half hour after the occurrence. In all, twelve were killed or shot on the spot, five were shot later and another five were slightly wounded, among the casualties being some of our best animals, who had been with us since the days of Blendecques. All the living horses were moved to a separate place and the old lines were naturally left untouched until next morning, when their appearance was such that it is better left to the imagination.

It was very fortunate that the raiders did not come five minutes earlier, otherwise all the section would have been haying up their horses and many more casualties would have occurred. As it was, the fact that all the men were in the deep trench—"clinging to the bottom of it with their eyebrows," so to speak—was the salvation of the section. Chrisp got to England with his wound and. though it permanently inconveniences him, he is fortunately hale and hearty, and a familiar figure at transport re-unions. Spanny Main and Dennison also recovered eventually from their wounds.

Small though the casualties were, this raid was a severe blow to the old section, which, so long as Chrisp was in charge, had still been the relic of bygone days in spite of the gradual wastage. The casualties of 1917, the men who had gone home sick or over-age, the recent victims of the burning episode—all represented a gradual diminution in the old ranks, and the advent of strangers in their place, but the change had not been so noticeable while Chrisp remained. Now that he was gone, the diminished strength of the older hands was more obvious and with the advent of a new officer, a stranger to the section. things would never be the same again.

The effect of the raid, as can be well understood, intensified our dread of air-raids and our desire to be well below ground-level : fellows' nerves became more on edge, as evidenced by peevishness and irritability over even the slightest incidents : and the hour of dusk was charged with more tension and foreboding than ever before. Every time we heard bombs falling we conjured up more vividly pictures of all they might mean and the sound of our swarms of bombing machines became increasingly pleasing to the ear in our thirst for revenge, even if it be upon poor innocent German horses.

One person in whose destiny the raid played an important part was Lieut. Finch, a platoon officer who had recently arrived from England, though he had been in France before, both with the Essex Yeomanry and the Essex Regiment. On the 25th he found himself suddenly promoted to the position of transport officer with Echelon A. though he himself was the first to admit that he knew nothing about transport work. Fortunately he was a real sport and when he realised that the N.C.O.s and drivers were adepts at the game he very tactfully left matters in their hands. Had he endeavoured to institute innovations under the circumstances he would have trodden on dangerous ground : but he allowed things to go on exactly as they had done before. with the exception that he occasionally led the convoy by riding at the rear ! This procedure, though unusual, had the merit of being inspired by common-sense, and it worked with complete success. I feel sure that if all my old pals were with me as I write and if I called for " three cheers " for Lieut. Finch they would heartily respond.

CHAPTER XXXIV.

THE BRITISH OFFENSIVE : THE BATTLE FOR CAMBRAI.

(*September–October*, 1918.)

In concealment at Villers-les-Cagnicourt — The attack of September 27th— Adventures of Echelon A—Life at Cagnicourt—Splendid news—Back for a short spell—Germans in full retreat—We move up to the Valenciennes front—Three days' interesting trek.

LIEUT. FINCH joined us on the 25th and Corporal Milcovich showed him round the horses, in which he appeared to be much interested. I do not know whether he had seen a regimental transport before, though, of course, he understood horses. We took quite a fancy to him from the start for the absolute candour with which he confessed his ignorance of the work ahead of him and the utter indifference with which he regarded the harness.

"That's all right, sir," Milcovich assured him. "All you have to do is to come up with the convoys. The men know their job."

He naturally found us in rather a morose state on account of the previous night's affair, and it was probably with the intention of cheering us up that he seated himself on a biscuit tin and recounted his recent adventures in the Strand.

In the morning, in the course of a scrounging expedition, we found a German propaganda leaflet, evidently dropped from an aeroplane, which exhorted us in very bad English to pay heed to Austria's peace offer. It asked if we did not want to be home by Christmas, adding that it rested with us. "Do you want to charge any more the Hindenburg Line ? " Then followed a description of the enormous strength of their defences. "Will these torrents of blood cease to flow ? Its about time, one should think." Altogether an amusing pamphlet.

Ours was not the only Echelon A which had been sent forward to Upton Wood. The Q.W.R.s and 2nd Londons also provided contingents, each regiment being under its own officer, but as the 2nd London T.O. was senior (in rank, though not in years) he took charge of our general movements. Later in the day I had to accompany him to Villers, to point out the horse-line site Chrisp had inspected with me a few nights before, as the A Echelons were to occupy it that very evening. The village was about two miles away and to reach it we had to ride through a maze of captured trenches from one end of the journey to the other, which gave one a better idea of the defences of the Drocourt-Queant switch than those around Dury.

We set off that evening at dusk, the three echelons moving together with the transport officers in the van. At the same time, though we did not know it, the L.R.B. relieved the Canadians opposite the canal at Marquion. Shortly before our arrival at Villers-les-Cagnicourt. Lieut. X. announced his intention of riding forward to see whether the site was still there and asked me to accompany him, which I did willingly, secretly hoping that I should be able to secure the best end of the field for the L.R.B. The entrance to the field was through a gap in a hedge running beside a rough track, and it was difficult to discover it in the darkness : in fact, we very nearly mistook some camouflage over a trench for a bridge, which would have had disastrous results. The search took so long that, even by cantering back to the spot where the track left the road, we were unable to intercept the head of the transport column which, in blissful ignorance, had passed the place where it should have turned off and was continuing its course gaily towards the firing-line. The turning of the vehicles in the narrow sunken road was no easy matter, but was accomplished with less cursing than might have been expected, owing to the fact that we were " winning the War."

The next hour was spent in erecting horse-lines as close to the hedge as possible, for concealment purposes, a procedure which delighted the horses, who promptly set about eating their way through the foliage. Then the men took possession of a trench intersecting the field, and as, owing to the weather being fine, there was no need to erect shelters, it was not long before some of us were asleep. Those who lay awake listening for the arrival of German aeroplanes were relieved to find that they did not put in an appearance in our vicinity.

The next morning we got up very early to camouflage our limbers with branches and take a general survey of the surroundings. It was with a feeling of novelty that we set about our work, seeing that our horse-lines were pitched in a spot where enemy observation was possible. However, the staff knew more about the enemy's ability to see us than we did at the time, though it transpired that it was the Bourlon Height which dominated the Villers region, just as it had overlooked the Lebucquiere lines in 1917. We had instructions not to move the horses off the line and so buckets of water had to be carried to them from a filling point some three hundred yards through the wood. All day long we remained practically in the one spot, varying the monotony by strolling up and down in the sunken road, where a number of R.E. signallers who were occupying German sand-bagged bivvies kept a vigilant watch upon their belongings in view of the scrounging propensities for which transport men were renowned.

In the evening Lieut. Finch received orders for the following day's operations, which showed the reason for our having been sent as far forward as possible. That very day the French and Americans had struck on a forty-mile front down south and on the morrow the British were to attack on the Cambrai sector at dawn. The 56th Division, however, was not to come into the fray until 2.30 in the afternoon, when its task was to extend the attack to the left, striking from south to north and clearing the space between the Canal du Nord and the River Agache, also capturing Sauchy-Lestree and Sauchy-Cauchy. The A Echelons were to provide three pack-pony parties, which would leave Villers at half-hour intervals from about one o'clock onwards, to take ammunition and bombs to a spot called Wancourt Farm on the far side of both the canal and the river, assuming the said farm to be captured in the first place by the infantry. (This stipulation was noted by the echelon with much relief.) It was later learnt that Lieut. X. would go with the first party and Lieut. Finch with the third, my humble function being to accompany the latter and to keep up communication on Ben with the party ahead of us.

That night the British bombardment started, not only on our sector, but right away down south, where the attack was not to be launched until the 29th. In that sector the great Siegfried Lines confronted them and · there followed two days of preliminary bombardment, reminiscent of Somme days, in order to smash down the defences. It was the greatest massed effect in the War, and its rumblings were borne up to us at all hours of the day and night.

It was difficult to believe that a fierce battle was in progress on this very front, for there were not many troops in sight. About half a mile ahead of the second party were some dug-outs occupied by a brigade H.Q., and some way beyond them were some Canadian machine-gunners in a trench, dressed in battle order. But the general impression one gained was that of stretches of green grass, of woods, of charming landscape, with just a few soldiers here and there who might have been manœuvring at Aldershot. It was now possible to get a close view of the Bourlon Height, which a machine-gunner told me had been captured by the Canadians that morning. I had not realised it was so close and that only a mile or so on the right were the old landmarks of the " Cambrai " front, the Inchy road, the villages of Boursies and Beaumetz, and the Houndsditch dump, where Greene and Simmonds had been wounded in the previous November. The hill was barely recognisable when viewed from a different direction : moreover, we were so much closer now than we had been before that it seemed double the height as it towered above us. The Canadian said that the village just ahead of me was Baralle and that the canal was " down among the trees " ; on the all-important matter of missing pack-ponies, however, he was as uninformed as myself. Down in the village of Baralle there were actually entire buildings standing as at Dury and Villers. Yet only two men—Canadians—were to be seen in the whole length of the street. The place was in the peculiar position of being miles behind the Canadian front line, which passed over Bourlon in that morning's attack, and yet close to the canal where, on the left, the attack was not being launched until the afternoon. From the gunfire it sounded as though it had started now, however, and down by the canal several " crumps " disturbed the hitherto tranquil nature of the surroundings.

It therefore appeared that there was no time to waste in further search, since the second party was over a mile farther back, and it might have to be making its way forward now. Fortunately word had travelled down that the attack was in progress, so that the men were already on the move when I encountered them, and in a short while Finch's convoy had likewise quitted the triangular field, leaving the drivers in charge of our belongings.

Finch was rather concerned as to whether we should reach our destination. The instructions and directions read like Double-Dutch, and the only point upon which he felt clear was that we had got to make our way to a wood on the left of the Cambrai road. It was therefore only natural that the trees surrounding

Saudemont should attract his attention, but to my dismay he became convinced that they were our goal, whereas they must be miles from our destination, seeing that they were away to our left rear. We were therefore placed in the exceedingly uncomfortable position of insisting that he was wrong, with the result that we continued our course towards Baralle, while he kept looking longingly back at Saudemont as though a magnet were drawing him there. We followed, as far as I could remember, the direction in which some platoons of one of the London regiments had been marching towards the canal half an hour before, a route that led us across the Cambrai road very near Baralle. There was undoubtedly scrapping going on somewhere here; our guns were busy, and some three hundred or so prisoners were formed up not far away.

Just then, to Finch's relief (not to mention ours), a line of ponies sped towards us which, on close acquaintance, proved to be the first party, now on its homeward journey. As the foremost men came up to us, they slowed down, and one of them gave us directions. Yes, we were on the right track.

"Just round the corner of that little wood there, over a railway, across the canal, and keep straight on."

"Is it lively up there?" we asked.

"Not so bad as it was," was the reply, given with a twinkling of the eye. "We didn't know the attack was postponed, and were carrying on merrily past the wood there when a machine-gun started. We didn't half 'aller vite,' I can tell you."

After this we carried on with more confidence. Ammunition columns were halted near the wood, and we saw also an R.F.A. battery limbered up ready to cross the canal when a pontoon bridge had been erected; apparently the ponies were to use a footbridge that had already been constructed. The Germans in Oisy-le-Verger, a village on a hill not far away, were being given the chance of their life to shell the assembled columns in the valley, and yet the strafeing was of a most spasmodic kind; no doubt the enemy were hastily withdrawing their batteries to the north of the Sensee marshes and were confining what guns were in action to shelling the crossings of the canal and the " river." At the latter spot the crossing was most difficult, as it consisted of a newly-constructed isthmus of earth from bank to bank, across which we had to lead the ponies in single file while the enemy's guns were proving the old adage : " Time, tide, and German artillery wait for no man or mule." We had a most unpleasant time of it for a few moments, and on the far side I raced ahead, ostensibly to look for Wancourt Farm, but actually to put a few hundred yards between me and the stream.

Wancourt Farm was empty, though I made every effort to discover the proprietor of the ammunition dump, but on rejoining the convoy I found that that gentleman had already come forward to welcome them, and was even then conducting Finch to the spot where the other parties had dropped their loads.

Our mission was accomplished. Lieut. Finch breathed again. So did I—after we had re-crossed the brook.

* * * *

The battalion had fought a most successful action with light casualties. No big advance was contemplated at this point, as that afternoon's operations were really a " mopping up " expedition to clear the flank of the big Canadian attack. On the following evening they were allotted the task of holding the front reached by the 2nd Londons near Bailleul, for further operations at this point depended on the result of the big battle that was pending in the south.

A Echelon spent the whole of the 28th on their own, having little to do, but on the following morning it was announced that B Echelon would shortly be coming up to that neighbourhood, when the two portions of each transport section would once more be united. In preparation for their coming and before Echelon A left their field, I was sent to the intended site by the Staff Captain with strict instructions to allow nobody else to claim it. In this way I lost my dinner, but the advantage of having first pick of the bivvies for the Devils' Mess compensated for my loss, and I spent two or three hours improving a splendid little dug-out which would just hold our party. Two men of another regiment came up and took possession of the site by orders of the Colonel, which was certainly rather disquieting, but since my instructions came from a staff captain, it did not worry me very much. Late in the afternoon, however, Williams came over from our echelon to say that they had been moved to a spot about a mile away, and that I need not mount guard any longer, as my site would not, after all, be required !

The place that had actually been decided upon was in the open stretch of country between Cagnicourt and Villers, rather nearer the outskirts of the former village, and we found accommodation in some old German artillery shelters and gun-pits, one of which I reserved for the Devils' Mess. On the 30th I rode over to Upton Wood (to which Echelon B had moved during the recent affair) in order to guide them to our new lines at Cagnicourt, where I felt sure my mess-mates would be pleased with the bivvy I had selected for them. However, I had underrated the effects of the bombing-raid upon my pals whom I had not seen since the fatal night of the 24th, for they wouldn't look at my bivvy when there was a chance of living in a thirty-foot deep German dug-out at the edge of the village. Personally, I thought there was far less likelihood of a bomb striking an invisible bivvy in open country than of landing in a prominent place like Cagnicourt, but there was no dissuading them, and the German dug-outs carried the day—until the Q.M. allocated them to the host of bandmen, bootmakers, and others who followed us around.

Eventually we discovered a good cellar in Cagnicourt, which we converted into a respectable living quarters, with tables, chairs, etc. Frank Little, an H.Q. batman who had now joined the section as cook in place of Spanny Main, had been welcomed into the Devils' Mess in view of Conibeer's impending departure, and his enthusiasm for a decent mode of living, the regular washing up of plates and cutlery and an orderly larder, brought all of us to a keen realisation of the slovenly methods to which we had grown accustomed. As a transport cook he was a great success, and his culinary gifts were a valuable acquisition to the Devils' Mess in the preparation of suppers from time to time.

On the 28th, the day following the Canadian attack on our front and the capture of Bourlon, the British and Belgians on the Ypres sector struck the Germans an unexpected blow on a twenty-mile front, carrying all before them, and passing in one bound the farthest limits reached in the Third Battle of Ypres. Over 10,000 prisoners, and some hundreds of guns were taken. The only part of the line that was disengaged on that date was that to the south of us, where the two days' preliminary bombardment had been in progress, and on the 29th the hardest blow of all was struck by St. Quentin. It heralded the famous breaking of the Hindenburg defences, a battle which lasted ten days, and finally convinced Ludendorff that the end had come.

Armageddon was going on all around us, and yet signs of it were less visible to us than they had been on the Somme or at Ypres or Arras. Our division's part in this, the greatest battle, was not a conspicuous one, the biggest efforts being demanded of it in August and November. But this did not detract from the excitement we all felt at the incredible news that came to hand almost every day. On October 2nd we read that Bulgaria had capitulated; Turkey was cut off. Next day we learnt that the British captures in August and September amounted to 123,000 prisoners and 1,400 guns—figures that were difficult to comprehend. Then came the retreat on Lille, the freeing of Rheims, and, above all, the German plea for an armistice. Prospects of seeing home again grew rosier, whilst the desire to protect one's skin and carry through to the end naturally increased. What extra bad luck it would be to get killed or mutilated now—having carried on so far! How wretched to be " snuffed out " without hearing what the final outcome might be ! The American reply took the wind out of our sails, though we quite sympathised with its tone. It said that there could be no discussion until Belgium was evacuated, a stipulation that caused us to discount some of the extravagant forecasts we had been making. But then came another big British advance with several thousand more prisoners; Cambrai fell; and then Le Cateau. Civilians had been reached ; the British had at last effected that thrilling release of crushed French folk which we had always had at the back of our minds in other offensives. The German retreat grew more pronounced, and our spirits soared higher and higher. We might get the Germans back to the Rhine by next spring after all, if things went on like this !

Captain Hosking, who had been with Echelon B, returned to the battalion here to take charge of a company, but it was decided to keep two transport officers in future, and another officer was therefore posted to us from the companies—a Lieut. Bradley, who had arrived from England a few weeks before. He had been an A.S.C. officer at home, and we had qualms as to the standard he would exact from us ; but somebody had whispered something in his ear, with the result that he might almost have been described as docile. It was very clear that he would not interfere with the established customs of the section, and we were therefore fortunate in having two new officers who got on well with us. Finch and Bradley took it in turns to come up with the convoys, and they certainly had a good introduction to first-line transport work in the trips that were made to Bailleul and, later, to Epinoy.

For the first few days of October the companies remained in the trenches, and we took rations up nightly from Cagnicourt. Then, after two days in support at Sauchy-Cauchy, they came down to Saudemont, where they were allotted " rest-billets " in some dirty little funk-holes in a field. Colonel Burnell insisted on the men having blankets drawn for them, as the nights were exceedingly cold—a request which doubtless caused some flutter down at the D.A.Q.M.G.'s, since the official mind would not admit the fall in temperature until such date as had already been decided on. As mentioned before, the same thing happened every year. It was while the companies were stationed there that the Hindenburg Line was finally pierced on October 8th.

On the 10th I rode up the line as mounted orderly to Colonel Burnell, who went up to visit the present H.Q. of the unit the L.R.B. were about to relieve, and our route took us through Sauchy-Cauchy and Sauchy-Lestree, where the recent canal scrapping had taken place. It was extraordinary that these villages should be so intact, considering that the tide of war had flowed over them. All the houses had German notices posted on the walls, and, with characteristic German thoroughness, large signs were painted at the cross-roads indicating each route. There were no civilians left—these evidently having been evacuated by the enemy. Colonel Burnell was in an exceedingly good temper until he found that his mac, which I had strapped to his saddle, had fallen off and was irretrievably lost. On our return through Sauchy-Cauchy he called at a bath-house and arranged a hot dip for both of us. As it was my first bath for two months, it can be imagined that it was not only appreciated but needed.

On the following day the troops whom we were to relieve had advanced to a point over two miles north-east of Epinoy, which involved a nightly ration journey of over ten miles in each direction when our battalion entered the line. Fortunately this only lasted for three nights, for, on the 14th, the L.R.B. were taken back by light railway to Haute Avesnes, a village west of Arras, and over twenty miles from the firing-line. The transport travelled by road on the 15th, and a very memorable trek it was. As a matter of fact, it was the last occasion in the War on which we journeyed *away* from the firing-line, and all the details of the familiar, desolate landscape over which we passed for mile after mile were like a panorama of past incidents being brought before our eyes. Cherisy, Wancourt, Neuville Vitesse—it was the first time I had been in the village since April, 1917—Beaurains, Achicourt, Arras—all these places filled one with melancholy and gave plenty of scope for philosophising. Overgrown trenches, almost obliterated German and British graves, relics of barbed wire, scenes of old horse-lines and memorable dumps once visited by night, passed by us as though the Kaiser were taking us for a tour of inspection from end to end of this abhorrent wilderness and saying : " See what I have accomplished." Arras was regaining its self-confidence now that it was out of big-gun range, and many of the civilians were returning, but the station end of the town was as forlorn as ever.

We had never stayed in Haute Avesnes in our many wanderings around Arras, but it was not far from familiar villages such as Aubigny, Marœuil, and Agnez-les-Duisans. Both companies and transport were put in huts, and since the section were able to rent a piano from a neighbouring village and install it in the centre of their abode it can be imagined that those who resided close by were constantly reminded of its existence. We were promised a fortnight's rest, and so officers, companies, sergeants, headquarters, and transport set about organising dinners and concerts, which were, as usual, rendered highly successful by an adequate supply of liquid refreshment !

To our delight, Major Wallis, who had bidden us such a heartfelt farewell earlier in the year, rejoined the L.R.B. on the 21st, and became Second-in-Command. He was present at the transport dinner, and it was a great treat to see him among us once more. If only Colonel Bates could have put in an appearance, too, along with Major Ducat and others, the regiment would indeed have recovered some of its Plug Street associations. As it was, our evening's entertainment was carried out in quite the old L.R.B. style, with plenty of attention being paid to the final touches ; each man carried away with him as a souvenir a menu card with a pretty girl's face on it, and Colonel Burnell made me feel a fool by publicly inquiring why a particularly spicy drawing had been presented to Aubrey Smith.

While we were here we received encouraging news from Chrisp, who had passed the very dangerous stage ; and the other cases also sent cheery messages. Personally, I was somewhat upset to learn of one or two friends being killed about this time, including Tyler and Pugh, from my department at the office, which made one realise how conditions would be changed if we returned to civilian life, and how those good old 1912–1913 days could never be again. Another event which affected the Devils' Mess in particular was Coni's return to England for his commission ; the papers came through during our stay here, and one evening, after most of the " Good-byes " had been said, a few of us accompanied him towards the railway. He looked upon his adventure as a means of getting away from the firing-line for six months or so, and then, when it was time to be drafted out, he would apply for a commission in the R.A.F. This was his original intention, but for some reason or other he went to the infantry first. " Lucky man ! " we thought now ; for, with luck, the War might be over within a year and he would probably never come out to France again.

But events soon began to move so rapidly that hopes of a much earlier settlement did not seem so extravagant as they had done. The evening that Harbord rushed in with a paper announcing the fall of Ostend, Lille and Douai, we began to feel somewhat optimistic. and the further capture of Tourcoing, Roubaix and Bruges showed pretty plainly that we had now arrived at semi-open warfare. On the 24th we read of another big British attack south of Valenciennes ; then the Italians struck, then Ludendorff resigned. Aleppo and the whole of Syria were conquered. Austria sent in a request for peace. Of course we had been so beguiled by hopes of victory in the past and so steeled to face the prospect of another two years of war, that our feelings erred on the side of incredulity rather than over-exuberance. Nevertheless the next two months must witness important events, and somehow we began to feel that in Haute Avesnes we were rusticating in a one-eyed village when we might be sharing in the culminating triumph. Thoughts of that kind came to us—some had them more than others—and for once we were rather keen to return to the firing-line : we wanted to know the thrill of going forward, day after day, liberating civilians as they had done at Bruges and elsewhere : we wanted to know the joy of being welcomed by the French population and showing them our pretty harness. The whole Allied line was advancing, and we were kicking our heels so far from the madding crowd that we longed for the sight of a railway gun or an R.E. dump.

At last the movement orders arrived, and we made preparations for departure. So light-hearted were we that, when the hired piano was loaded on a G.S. wagon and driven over to the residence of its owner, the unloading party, with one man seated at the piano, sang ditties to all and sundry as they passed through the village, and before they reached their destination quite a crowd of civilians had crowded round to listen to the novel concert-party.

We were going back to the Cambrai sector, but no longer could it be given that name. For the line was now close to Valenciennes, and beyond that, the distance getting shorter every day, was the town we wanted to reach more than all others—Mons !

*　　*　　*　　*

Although the battalions went straight to the village of Lieu St. Amand by 'bus on October 31st, it was necessary for the brigade transports to do this journey in two stages, and we ended up our first day's trek at Marquion. Right up the Arras-Cambrai road we trekked, past Tilloy, Monchy and Vis-en-Artois, which we reached after dark, and then along that final stretch which we had come to know quite well during October. But instead of approaching Marquion with misgivings as of yore, we were considerably surprised to find that a huge aerodrome had been erected on its outskirts ; marquees and lorry parks could be distinguished on either side, for the R.A.F. men were not in the least particular about exposing their lights. In the village itself we were shown into a kind of factory, which had escaped damage, and erected horse-lines in the outbuildings. Since we arrived fairly late and were awakened before dawn, however, there was not much opportunity of inspecting our billet or the village. After a hasty breakfast we set forth again full of excitement, for our journey was bound to be most fascinating, and from its very commencement we seemed to move in a dream, so unusual were the circumstances and surroundings.

From the earliest days of trench warfare we had all imagined some dim and distant occasion on which we should move forward over captured territory, through villages that were standing, past woods that were unscathed and along ground that was unscarred by war. But it was not until the autumn of 1916 that we saw a captured front line and passed beyond on to captured ground—only to find shattered ruins, splintered trees and a wilderness of shell-holes. In the spring of 1917 we found the same thing, and at Cambrai the troops had only had a momentary glimpse of the " open beyond." It had grown into an idea to be ridiculed, and the more cynical had remarked that the War would be fought out within a mile or so of the old trench systems.

With this fact appreciated, our impressions of the daylight trip of some fifteen miles to Lieu St. Amand, north-east of Marquion, will be better realised, for we passed through green and wooded country from which the Germans had precipitately retired or been driven in the Battle of the Selle during the past two weeks. We tramped for miles beside a canal, the pretty woods on the farther bank giving no indication of active warfare. The villages, in spite of being more or less intact, were deserted, however, though in one we did see a woman in the far distance working the pump outside her house. She was probably too broken-hearted to wave to us, which could be readily understood since practically the entire population must have been evacuated and the hundreds of deserted barges moored alongside the bank testified to the activity that should have been in evidence there. At one halting place we entered an empty estaminet which had already been searched by troops, and we got some amusement from a cracked musical-box, while other hilarious spirits evoked smiles by pretending to serve drinks behind the counter. But in a far room we came upon the ruin of a home, signs of hurried departure, all the home treasures left to the mercy of whoever came after, a cupboard filled with garments, an abandoned baby's cot—and the ribald laughter soon faded away.

We had one or two long halts, and it was towards the end of the afternoon that we reached Lieu St. Amand, of which the companies had been in occupation since the previous evening. It was a village of no mean size, and I believe some half a dozen civilians were to be found there, but few of us saw any and most of the houses were occupied solely by troops. We secured a splendid billet, an abandoned private house, where the Devils' Mess made themselves comfortable in one of the rooms and began to feel less keen after all about " scotching up Fritz," feeling that it would be nice to remain where we were. On arrival we found a notice posted up announcing that Turkey had surrendered and that the Italian and British offensive on the Piave had brought in 50,000 prisoners and absolutely routed the Austrian Army. This put us in excellent humour, which was by no means diminished when Hurford announced the impending distribution of a double issue of rum.

" Ha ! Ha ! This portends something," said Figg ominously. He was still apt to distrust any action of the Army authorities which outwardly appeared to be considerate and thoughtful.

" It portends a damned good sleep," said Trendell. " ———— aeroplanes, ———— bombs, ———— everybody. Cheero ! "

It was indeed the best night's sleep we had for some days.

Next morning, after being awakened by the familiar sound of drumfire at dawn, both companies and transport set off on the next stage of their journey, a tramp which took us seven miles or more still nearer to the firing-line. The Colonel and some other officers rode on ahead, with a few of us in attendance, through similar scenery to that we had seen on the previous day, but now there were unmistakable signs that we were reaching the war-zone. Yesterday we had seen scarcely a wagon and very few soldiers : not a camp seemed to be in existence between Marquion and Lieu St. Amand. But as we rode onwards this morning we came across lorries and horse-lines, the latter being specially in evidence in a valley near Maing where, it was pointed out to us, our own transport lines would be pitched. It was not possible to use roads all the way, and part of our route lay over an already well-used track. From one point in the journey we could see chimneys rising from the huge town of Valenciennes in the distance on the left. At that very moment the Canadians were in the suburbs of the place, its fate depending upon the success of the outflanking operations just south-east of it—on the sector for which we were destined.

We found the section eventually between Maing and Mancheux, where they had erected their lines in the open—their elated spirits of that morning now changed to an orgy of cursing as they contemplated spending the night in the rain. Brigade would not let them scrounge billets in Mancheux on account of bombing, and the prospect of a night like the first one in Happy Valley was not alluring, especially after the pampering of the last week or so at Avesnes. Attempts were made to build bivvies, but as we had depended chiefly on trenches for the past few months, there was absolutely no material available on the section.

As matters turned out, I was not destined to pass a night with my pals there. About seven o'clock Sergt. Watkins' voice rang out, calling my name in a tone which implied " Saddle up." Guessing that this meant a brigade orderly stunt and considering that somebody else might have a turn at it, I slipped out of the bivvy in the dark and proceeded to search on a limber for something that wasn't there. It rejoiced my heart to hear Watkins calling my name in vain, and I cherished the false hope that he would shortly tire of the search. But Watkins was a wily bird !

After a few minutes Barnett's figure loomed up in the darkness.

" Is that Aubrey ? The Sergeant has been calling you. You're wanted as a brigade orderly."

" Well, he can jolly well want. Let someone else go for a change."

" You don't catch Watty like that. He's left word with your party that you're to pack up your things as soon as they find you. The sooner you put in an appearance the better for you."

" ———— ———— ———— ———— ———— ! ! "

Two hours later a mounted scarecrow, loaded up with pack, equipment. overcoat, mackintosh, tin-hat, bucket, picketing peg, horseshoes. grooming kit and horse feed, drew up in the street at Maing and enquired for brigade H.Q. At first nobody knew anything about them—as usual—but after being referred in turn to the cooks' billet and the lodging of a trooper in the Australian Mounted Horse, who did not thank him for disturbing his slumbers, he at length discovered the whereabouts of a Westminster and a 2nd London runner who, with their horses. had been sent on the same errand as himself.

We were on the eve of our last " binge," but little did we realise that the Armistice would be signed in nine days !

CHAPTER XXXV.

THE BRITISH OFFENSIVE: THE LAST BLOWS.

(November, 1918.)

Officers' chargers wanted at the canter—Another early morning move—The civilians of Saultain—A trench mortar convoy—More moving forward—Sebourg—Two night trips to L.R.B. headquarters—More attacks—Excitement at Angreau—The German withdrawal more rapid—Effect of their mine-craters.

ON November 3rd there was further drum-fire at dawn, which revealed how much closer we were to the firing-line. After an early breakfast, brigade H.Q. details—telegraphists, bombers, batmen, cyclists. R.E. limbers, mess-cart, and, of course, mounted runners—got orders to fall in in half an hour, and presently we moved forward to the farm whereat the officers had halted on their reconnoitring expedition of the previous day. Situated about two miles from the firing-line on the Querenaing-Famars road, it was rather close to some eighteen-pounders, and the fact that the imposing-looking building was quite untouched by shell-fire was rather remarkable. The substantial outhouses were as luxurious as any we had seen, and there was room for at least twelve horses in the stable where the runners put their steeds. We took possession of this stable at once, but relieving of the staff occupied over an hour to accomplish, during which time the signallers and others lounged about in the yard or sought billets among the barns and cellars.

Some time after our arrival the Westminster was despatched to the transport lines at Maing with instructions to send forward Echelon A's that afternoon, and about midday the Staff Captain rushed up with a further order in writing. It required all L.R.B. officers' chargers to be brought up at once.

" You must be as quick as ever you can," said he. " Are you saddled up ? "

It savoured of a German withdrawal, and Ben, to whom I confided this information, beat all records in his canter to the transport lines, two and a half miles back, where the message was delivered. One or two of the grooms knew the way to the farm, and there was therefore no need to wait for them ; so, seeing that they were still searching for a saddle blanket here or a bit-head stall there, I rode back alone to brigade H.Q., reporting the message as delivered.

There was an air of excitement about the farm when I returned. The 2nd London man said Valenciennes had fallen and the Germans were retiring on our front—which doubtless explained the Staff Captain's impatience for the chargers to arrive. The idea of scouting on horseback was a new one for infantry officers, though a small body of cavalry was already operating on our sector. Presently the Staff Captain fumed at the non-appearance of the grooms to such an extent that I hastened off again to meet them, warn them of the " wrath to come " and urge them to canter for all they were worth. The delay had been caused by a traffic block, but the head of the column was continuing serenely on its way when I met it and explained the Staff's displeasure. The tidings galvanised everyone into action, and in a moment we were racing helter-skelter through Querenaing as though the bogeys were after us. On and on we galloped, everyone turning to watch the approach of the "cavalry," until the tiny speck in the middle of the road—representing the Staff Captain—grew bigger and bigger and we finally pulled up at the farm gates, the horses steaming with heat. A few cuss-words fell from the officer's lips, but there was not time for an oration, and he soon gave the men their orders to proceed to the battalion, while I led the exhausted Ben into his stable once more.

Rumour had it that brigade H.Q. would move forward that evening. but our dinners—which the cooks succeeded in preparing by four o'clock—consisted solely of boiled rice and tins of pork and beans, and it would have been impossible to shift the brigade details in the midst of the indigestion which followed. Fortunately the Staff either realised this fact or else other equally good reasons weighed with them, for they decided not to move until the following morning. In the meantime the Echelon A's arrived at Caumont Farm and put up in various parts of the grounds, and since they happened to be so close to brigade. it made it more jolly for me. The L.R.B. party consisted of Lieut. Finch and Corporal Milcovich, with Rayner, Clements, Williams, Gerrish and Heyward as drivers, as well as a few pack-pony men—more or less the same fellows it had comprised before. The question again arose as to whether three shifts of two men each, involving pickets on alternate nights, was preferable to three shifts with only one man on at a time which. though lonely and monotonous, spread them out so that everyone did a picket once in four nights, and the latter scheme was adopted. The three brigade runners were not liable to do the echelon pickets, of course, but in a fit of commiseration for Williams I offered to keep him company on his shift, a step that was regarded with indignation by the other two runners, whose old-soldier instincts told them it might form a precedent. The echelon men looked upon it as further proof that I was " not all there." Only Williams understood the offer : we liked to have chats together, and it was a long time since we had discussed the War. So, from 10 p.m. until 2 a.m., we talked about the present advance, future prospects, rations, red-hats, leave, love affairs and lice ; and even though we turned in eventually heavy with sleep, I considered the four hours well spent.

But within two hours the brigade details had been called again, breakfast was ready for us at 4.30, and an hour afterwards, just as drum-fire broke out along the front, the men fell in on the road ready to move forward to Saultain. That village had been occupied by the L.R.B. on the previous afternoon, and, even as we moved onwards in the early morning hours of the 4th, the Q.W.R.s—with the L.R.B. in support—were attacking the village three miles beyond it—Sebourg.

It was the occasion of the final great general attack on the British front when the German resistance definitely crumpled up.

The Staff Captain, evidently considering that the mounted runners' existence must be justified, detailed me to ride ahead and see that the road was passable for the vehicles, returning every few minutes like a good dog to its master—a job that certainly had the merit of enabling one to keep warm. Not many other troops were about, a great change from the areas immediately behind the front in stationary warfare. In fact Famars was almost deserted, but we met here a French civilian, the first one I had seen at close quarters. He was an old man who was hobbling along the pavement and turned to gaze at us.

" Vive les anglais ! Vive les anglais," cried he, waving an old handkerchief somewhat feebly.

" Ah *oui*, but a good many die, old son," answered one of the details.

From Famars we went down a steep hill—there had been a heavy German counter-attack at this point—then over a river by a rough-and-ready bridge where artillery columns came into evidence with all their usual bustle, past some trenches, up a slope and straight on for a long way across flat country without much sign of it having been a battlefield. And then we were forcibly reminded once again of the horrors of war, as we had been on many another scene of battle, though this momentary glimpse impressed itself on my mind perhaps more than any other. We suddenly descended a small slope so as to cross a sunken road, the banks of which were perhaps five feet high ; then we passed straight across, up another slope and continued our course in the direction of Saultain. But in the momentary glance to right and left, as we passed from one side of that road to the other, was enough material for any artist who cared to portray what warfare really meant. Strewn all about the road—as far as the mist would allow one to see—in all kinds of attitudes, lying with their faces downwards, huddled up in funk-holes, flung backwards with hands raised as if to avert a blow, were scores of dead bodies, British and German. In addition there were rifles, equipment, overcoats and stretchers in profusion. . . . It was the Preseau-Marly road, the scene of bitter fighting, attack and counter-attack, on November 1st and 2nd, and nothing had been touched since the battle. The spot was now behind us, but its impression was on our minds and caused us to shudder. Were not hundreds of wives and mothers waiting for news of those who had fallen there ? Was not the whole of the Western Front a similar scene of butchery ? Come, put such thoughts aside. Think of the glorious peace to be achieved by all this sacrifice ! Think of the land we shall return to, " fit for heroes to live in." Over there is a German aerodrome, hangars and sheds complete. Just ahead is the village of Saultain, captured yesterday afternoon, probably full of civilians ready to welcome you. Forget all about that sunken road and live in the present. . . .

As we surmised, there were many civilians in Saultain who watched our arrival, in some cases with joyous smiles, in others with wistful looks on faces that seemed as if they would never smile again. Old women came to their doors wiping their eyes, old men attempted to give a feeble cheer. Mothers and daughters stood on the pavement exchanging approving nods and remarks, while youngsters fell in beside us and marched in the gutter. There were no young men to be seen.

Brigade naturally entered into possession of the chateau, where we found the L.R.B. grooms who had gone forward to the battalion the

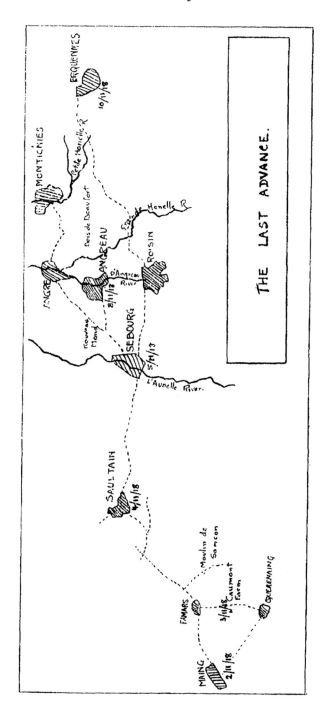

THE LAST ADVANCE.

previous day and ended up at Saultain. They must have been practically the first mounted people to arrive there. The village was in an excellent condition and we three runners soon found good accommodation for the horses close to Brigade, leaving us free to speak to some of the French people. We were most anxious to ascertain the state of minds of the German troops and to confirm the reports as to the poor state of their rations, and for this reason some of us passed an hour or so in conversation with the open-mouthed bystanders or with folk in their cottages.

The state of their larders was appalling. They had practically nothing to eat, just a little bread, vegetables and coffee, and yet we were offered cups of coffee from their scanty supplies, which most of us, I believe, refused to accept. On the contrary, we felt impelled to give them some of our own measly rations, at the sight of which they nearly wept for joy. The German soldiers, they said, were gluttons for the first two years, but after that their rations had gradually become less and less, and now they were nearly always hungry. We might have added that we were frequently in that state, too, a fact that is doubtless even now being related by many French civilians who had at various times held up their hands in surprise when they heard what rations we had for the next day. But the Germans were certainly very badly off, from all accounts, their usual diet of late being bread, coffee and soup and the latter being frequently thrown away as uneatable. If they ever got meat in the evening it was a tiny piece of horseflesh : in these days they never knew what it was to lick their lips over beef or mutton. This meagre diet must have been that of the men on lines of communication, as it is certain that their fighting troops could not have subsisted on such fare.

One fairly young Frenchman with whom I spoke had hidden in a cellar until the fighting was over and had thus escaped being carried off by the retiring Germans, a fate that had befallen most of the fit manhood. He said the Germans realised they were beaten and told the civilians so. They had admitted that the " English " would be along in two or three days and that they (the Germans) would retire and put their hands up at a favourable moment. This man testified to the brutal treatment of our prisoners who looked so bad that they could hardly drag themselves along to work, and sometimes their appearance was so pitiful that the French used to give them a slice of their own poor ration of bread. He pointed out a field where a British soldier, under extreme provocation, had shaken his fist at a German officer, whereupon the sentry came up, brought the butt-end of his rifle down on the prisoner's leg and broke his knee.

In the midst of this narrative three German prisoners, who had been marched down from the line, were halted outside brigade H.Q. and at the sight of them the Frenchman's face became livid.

" Don't give them anything to eat ! Don't give them anything to eat ! " he bawled in his loquacious native tongue, emphasising his injunction with much expectoration and waving of arms. " They have starved us and our women and children ! Let them starve ! " I really believe he would have rushed up and torn their hair out by the roots if there had not been a sentry in charge. It gave one an insight into the sufferings of these folk and their detestation of the German soldiers.

His next remarks would probably have been a discourse on German brutalities, but what they were I have no idea, for suddenly there was a crash close at hand, followed by the sound of falling masonry. The Germans were shelling the village and a house had been hit in the main street. Filled as it was with troops and civilians, all hanging around out of doors watching artillery pass by, it was only natural that the road should immediately become a scene of panic, everyone scurrying in one direction or another, yet uncertain as to where a refuge might be sought. The Frenchman I had been speaking to disappeared—so did the German prisoners—and the next thing I knew was that the R.A.M.C. were tending two wounded civilians and lifting up a small boy who had been killed.

Crash! came another shell in the roadway a little farther up the street. Traffic was stopped and the civilians retired into their houses, terror-stricken and perhaps rudely disillusioned after rejoicing that the War had passed their doors.

Having no underground place in which to take shelter, I crossed over to a field on the other side of the street, where the A Echelons had drawn up their vehicles, and sought the sympathetic company of Williams & Co., who were standing under a brick-wall—of all places! I also sought a cup of tea from Barnett, who had brewed a small quantity, since it was now past twelve o'clock and we had breakfasted at 4.30, but unfortunately there was barely enough for the members of the echelon and I was placed at the mercy of the cooks at brigade, from whom the runners were now drawing rations. Everyone was discussing a report of Austria's capitulation, which was said to be an absolute fact, and the effect this would have on the War. In ten minutes not more than two references to the fact that the shells were making a mess of the main street came to my ears; it was evidently the philosophy of Milcovich's party that it was time enough to discuss five-point-nines and their propinquity when they knocked down our brick wall, and so those who had no wish to argue about Austria remained silent.

Not very long after I had joined the congenial company of the transport boys, the sight of the 2nd London runner crossing the field in my direction caused some misgiving, for I wondered what he could want with me. Was Ben wounded? Had we got to find a different stable?

"You're wanted," said the runner laconically, as he approached.

"Who by?" was the ungrammatical reply.

"Brigade Intelligence Officer wants to go up the line and says he must have your horse as the others are too light. . . ."—Curse him! Riding Ben to a shadow!—"He wants an orderly, too. You can ride my horse. . . ."

"But it is the Westminster's turn . . . ."

"Can't find him. And this bloke's in a hurry. I've been guiding the rest of the transports up to the aerodrome all the morning, so it's not my turn to go."

In other words, the dinner for which I was pining and which must be nearly ready would have to be sacrificed. A thousand curses on that Westminster! I'd let the officer see I was annoyed. . . . I'd mutter to myself as I put his saddle on and make his stirrup leathers too short. . . . I'd . . . But it transpired that the Intelligence Officer was in an equally bad temper and I quickly decided to do none of these things—lest he wax exceeding wrath and put me in the guard room. Poor Ben! When I espied the officer's immense stature it was clear that he ought to have had a heavy draft, not a mere cab-horse, to ride, and the state of perspiration to which Ben was soon reduced necessitated an altogether slower pace. The 2nd London's horse I was riding was a bit jumpy and shied at everything from a great burly German, dead as a doornail, who lay beside the lane on the outskirts of the village, to the batteries drawn up and firing in the open on either side of us as we trotted over open country in a north-easterly direction.

" It's a quicker way than continuing on the main road through Saultain," said the officer, alluding to the by-lane we were following. " We're going to Sebourg, which was captured by the Westminsters a few hours ago. I believe the Bosche is still in the far side of the village, so I may have to end up the journey on foot."

After that he became quite chatty, pointing out this spot and that and remarking on the German retreat. It was a good three miles to Sebourg and yet not a single shell came over in the course of the journey : so quiet was it in fact—except for our own artillery—that he had no compunction about descending the hill into the village where we turned to the right down a sunken road, skirted a derelict German tank, and pulled up beside a trench occupied by some L.R.B. men. Here the officer dismounted and said farewell, apologising for the exhausted state of his charger and stating that he would not require him again. My antagonistic feelings had by this time vanished, for there was some consolation in having been shown in daylight the route one might have to follow by night.

Arriving back in Saultain, my first business was transacted in the cook-house, where the relics of dinner were obtainable and where the Staff Captain, seeing me lapping up skilly, took the opportunity to fire off a list of questions. Was the road suitable for transport ? Could transport enter Sebourg ? Could limbers pass the tank ? Was there much shelling ? Had I come back the same way ? Then which way had I come ? Which was the better road ? And so on. He did not ask how I enjoyed my late dinner, but that was probably an oversight.

The next item on the programme was to clean down the horse and then there were letters that must be written at all costs, since every day's delay meant additional worry for those ever-anxious ones at home, to whom the news of continued " successes " did not necessarily convey unalloyed joy. All the evening long convoys passed through the village to the exhilaration of the inhabitants, who gazed in admiration upon the field artillery and larger guns, the splendid horses and equipment, which evidently compared favourably with the German. For my part, after finishing off writing letters and digesting a home mail, I settled down to read a newspaper which had just arrived. But in the midst of an account of Turkey's surrender the paper slipped from my fingers and I fell off into a deep sleep.

The next thing I remembered was being shaken roughly out of my slumbers by a fellow who grasped my shoulder with one hand and tilted a guttering candle over my overcoat with the other. It was one of the echelon men.

" Wake up," said he. " You've got to turn out."

With this remark he handed me a chit, but I was far too sleepy to read its contents and it was with the utmost difficulty that I succeeded in half opening one eye and recognising the intruder.

" But what do you wake *me* for ? There's the Westminster man, there. He's agreed to do the next job."

" It was you that went up to Sebourg with an officer yesterday, wasn't it ? Well, you've got to guide three trench mortar limbers up there before dawn. You'll find Corporal Milcovich over in the field. He'll give you the orders."

" Hell! Blankety-blank-blank Hell! Who are the drivers ? "

" Rayner's harnessing up now. The other two limbers are Westminster and 2nd London."

" What's the time ? "

" Three o'clock. You'll have to look sharp."

Thereupon the picket disappeared, leaving his candle to light my movements and to reveal a score or so of lucky snorers still enjoying their slumbers in peace.

The village seemed deserted in those early morning hours : all the troops had passed through, most of the inhabitants and troops were asleep and the picket lamps in the field were the only signs of wakefulness. Not a German gun or aeroplane disturbed the silence. Milcovich, who was squatting down on a truss of hay, thought it a huge joke having to turn me out because I had boasted the day before that mounted runners took orders from brigade H.Q., not from the echelons.

" All we have to do," said Milky, " is to ask brigade for a guide and they say we can have one of you. None of our fellows have been to Sebourg yet."

Milcovich then explained that I had to take three limbers to a certain cross-roads close to Sebourg, pick up some trench mortar ammunition, proceed into the village and leave each limber at the headquarters of its unit before five o'clock, which was said to be zero hour. Considering, however, that not only the cross-roads, but the position of all three headquarters were as unknown to me as they were to Milky or anyone else, it looked as if we'd be lucky if we delivered the goods by midday. And when one driver took so long to put in an appearance that we finally set off from Saultain after four o'clock, the misgivings as to our arriving in time were, if anything, increased.

" Hi ! " called the 2nd London driver, after we had covered about two miles of the journey. " You ain't goin' the right way for our 'eadquarters."

" We're going the right way for Sebourg and that's all I can tell you."

" Nao. Our 'eadquarters is back there somewheres. We was at 'em yesterday."

" Well, damned well go to them then," Rayner called back irritably. I think he suspected me of leading them all astray, but, being kind enough not to say so, disguised his feelings by cursing someone else.

" But you want to load up with ammunition, don't you ? " I asked the 2nd London man as I rode beside him.

" Nao. My limber's full a'ready. You're going all wrong. We ought to be staying back there."

This was too much for my self-respect. If he thought he knew his jolly old headquarters, let him take himself off there, by all means, but I couldn't stand being told I was an idiot in front of everybody. So I said the best thing he could do was to " hop it," and thereafter our convoy continued its course with two limbers only.

We discovered the cross-roads all right and also a store of ammunition, which the three of us loaded up as quickly as possible. But before we got to Sebourg the British barrage or preliminary fire started. All the guns opened fire simultaneously and in a moment we were in the midst of a Somme or an Ypres inferno which brought the inevitable

German reply. A few shells dropped not far away on the right and our convoy automatically broke into a trot, overtaking some platoons of the London Scottish who were marching up the road. A rather loud burst accelerated our pace at the edge of the village and we positively charged down the hill, so that when I swerved Ben round a lane to the right the limber-drivers—unable to pull up, went careering onwards for about a hundred yards.

"*Some* convoy," I remarked as the drivers turned back again.

"*Some* guide," retorted Rayner, being unable to conceal his disgust any longer.

The sunken lane was full of troops and we found some L.R.B. in battle order filing out of the trench where the officer had stopped yesterday and lining up in the road ready to move onwards. Over our heads the British shells whizzed without cessation and the morning was still sufficiently dark for the flashes to light up the heavens around us. The noise was terrific. We could hear rapid rifle fire in the distance.

When the infantry moved forward the limbers followed in their wake until we came to a house which was pointed out as L.R.B. headquarters, where Rayner and the Westminster waited while I went in to see the C.O. The passages were crowded with men just putting on their equipment and there was a general air of subdued excitement, increased by the pandemonium outside. Down in the cellar, sitting at a table strewn with papers, were Colonel Burnell and Major Wallis, and buzzing around them were various satellites through whom I pushed my way and gave a brilliant salute. This was intended to make up for the lateness of our arrival, but we needn't have worried as they did not appear to be expecting us. Major Wallis conjured up one of his sweetest smiles, thanked me for coming and asked how many limbers there were, at which with a qualm of conscience I explained that two were outside, but a third had made its way to the 2nd Londons, whose whereabouts I should be interested to know. This led to five minutes' conversation on the telephone between the brigade signalling officer and some ignoramus at the other end who eventually supplied the reference number and enabled us to turn up the spot on the map. The third driver had evidently talked sense—the Londons were miles away. Having thus disorganised the routine of our headquarters for several minutes, I asked permission for the drivers to put their horses in a neighbouring barn till wanted, saluted again, knocked a chair over as I about-turned, and bustled out of the room.

Outside it was a little lighter now and the drivers easily found a shack for their horses. They were to have a terribly hard day's work, galloping about with their limbers absolutely in the face of the enemy's infantry and co-operating with our own battalions, and Rayner was recommended for the M.M. on account of it. The guide's work was finished, however, and having wished them the best of luck I hopped on Ben and returned to Saultain, visiting en route the 2nd London driver to make sure he had reached his goal.

In Saultain, both brigade H.Q. and Echelon A were having breakfast and making preparations for yet another move. Rumour had it that at nine o'clock we should all march on to Sebourg—a rumour which a year before would have been received with well-merited contempt. But now things were different : the attack went well and in due course definite movement orders arrived. It already seemed many hours since I had been called that morning, such a number of

Impressions having been gained between that first awakening and the return to Saultain : and by the time the brigade details fell in and set off on the same route in daylight the trench-mortar trip seemed an affair of last week.

Sebourg itself looked a different place as we entered it—now no longer a village crammed with troops moving up to battle in the half light, the streets echoing with the noise of gun-fire, but a comparatively peaceful hamlet, the inhabitants of which came timidly to their gateways in the rain to watch " les braves anglais." Brigade H.Q. occupied a big building, the three mounted runners secured a good stable close by, and Echelon A—still keeping close to brigade—moved into outhouses and barns belonging to the same farm. The Germans were still shelling the corner by the church and the eastern outskirts of the village beyond the River Aunelle, but this did not deter the civilians from coming out of their cellars : They did not realise that their danger was not past. For twenty-four hours they had crouched underground, with the British in part of their village and the Germans in the outskirts, and now that the morning's attack had pushed the enemy a bit farther away they considered, as the Saultain civvies had done, that peace was as good as achieved.

About midday the 2nd London runner was lucky enough to be sent on a long journey back to Maing or thereabouts, but the Westminster was not so fortunate, his job being to take a message forward to a battalion H.Q., which entailed crossing the Aunelle by a bridge that was expected to blow up at any minute by a delay action mine ! The catastrophe did not occur, but, once the rumour had been circulated, everyone waited for it to happen and even that evening it was with qualms that we crossed the river. On his return, the Westminster drew a rough sketch of the route to L.R.B. H.Q., which I kept for future reference. He reported that the attack was going on well and that Angreau was captured, that being the first village over the Belgian frontier.

After dinner he and I received from the delightful folk at the farmhouse the offer of a mattress to sleep on down in their cellar which, though it may sound an unpleasant abode, was a cleaner room than might have been expected. Having no billet, we accepted with gratitude and carried our kits as unostentatiously as possible through the room over the cellar lest the brigade bombers who slept there should consider they had first claim on the generosity of the house owners and usurp our place down below. Having dumped our kits in a corner we sat down to talk with the civilians, who numbered more than we had imagined, and amused ourselves with the kiddies, whose pinched little faces told of underfeeding and malnutrition. There was a doorway leading from the cellar into another apartment in which we thought the civilians would take up their abode at night, but the family appeared to be so large that we began to view with suspicion the two beds in our own room. Finally my companion asked if any of the residents intended to sleep there and our confusion may be imagined when they replied in the affirmative. Ah, *oui !* Mother and father slept in one bed and their eighteen year old daughter in the other : as a rule the little boy slept on the mattress, but to-night he would keep his sister company. The occupants of the second cellar were an entirely different family, a band of refugees to whom hospitality had been offered !

Our mirth puzzled them exceedingly and they thought us extraordinary folk when we asked that a screen might be put up between their portion of the room and ours, but they readily complied and had soon rigged up a sheet so that the shy soldiers should not feel they were perceived. It was all to no purpose, however, for when the time came to "turn in" the brigade sergeant descended the stairs and kicked up no end of fuss. He was sleeping on a hard floor in the room above and it was easy to understand his feelings : but there was a good deal of justification for what he said, for if the Staff Captain had discovered us there is no knowing how many Army rules we might be held to have transgressed.

Some time before this tiff took place I was warned that I should have to take two limbers of trench mortar ammunition up to the new L.R.B. headquarters that night, but as the limbers in question were only just setting off for Famars to draw their loads they would probably not be back before ten or eleven o'clock. I was therefore to "hold myself in readiness" for their return, tack myself on to them and act as guide to a place I didn't know. The description given by the West-minster was the only data to work upon and since the nights were pitch black I sent in a request to brigade for an electric torch, explaining to the brigade sergeant that it was not reasonable to suppose we should get to our destination without one. Half an hour's enquiry on his part, however, elicited the fact that there was not a torch available on the whole of brigade and, in growing alarm, I put my plea before Milcovich. He was likewise unable to help. A month or so before nearly every man Jack of us had wielded a torch—now there was not one to be found on Echelon A, unless Lieut. Finch possessed one.

After darkness had fallen and it was evident that one would not be able to see an arm's length in front of one's face, I set out in desperation for Finch's billet. It was pouring with rain, the road was muddy and I stumbled on down the street towards the church, cursing wildly and determined not to leave Finch's abode until I had borrowed his torch for the evening. Passing limbers liberally sprinkled all pedestrians in mud from head to foot and as the horses loomed out of the inky blackness of the night without any warning, I clung to the side of the road for safety : it did mounted troops good sometimes to realise the annoyance they caused to the poor foot-sloggers ! At last the street opened out into a small square by the church and when Finch's billet was located, not without difficulty, I was directed by his batman into the dining room of a respectable house where he sat alone censoring letters. With the rain pouring off my mackintosh and tin-hat. it was hardly an appropriate condition in which to enter an officer's sanctum, but these were not times when one stood on ceremony. He listened to my wail sympathetically, but the torch I asked for was not forth-coming for the simple reason that he'd broken it. Nor could he offer a solution of the difficulty. He said if he knew where H.Q. was he might come himself, but since he didn't—well, what was the use of two of us losing our way ? It was perfectly sound logic, impossible to refute. So I simply did a despondent salute, clicked my muddy boots and went out into the street, leaving a pond of rain-water on the dining room floor.

It was soon after this that we fell foul of the brigade sergeant. for the Westminster had decided to go to bed while I thought it a good idea to lie down for a few hours, until the two limbers appeared and leave word with the echelon's picket as to where I slept. Just as we were rolling up our great-coats to use as pillows, the N.C.O. came downstairs with dilated nostrils and launched forth. In vain did we point to the screen, and his emphatic remarks resulted in our taking leave of the civilians, who were very astonished and showed their hostility to the sergeant. At the time we were most resentful, as we had no billet to go to, but the echelon found room for us in an outhouse and the little storm blew over. It was a difficult matter to explain to the mystified civilians next day the reason for our sudden expulsion. *Quel droles, ces anglais !*

Convoys of various kinds were now passing down the street in an endless line, for the British had advanced a good distance and those guns which had not gone forward during the day were now being moved east of the village with all their ammunition. It was a repetition of the endless stream we had watched the day before in Saultain. A few of our fellows stood in the gateway to our yard waiting for the arrival of a limber from Echelon B with rations and post, but one or two of us grew weary of this after some time and lay down to doze in the barn. The more patient ones, however, were rewarded about eight o'clock by the sound of Lance-Corporal Charles' high-pitched voice : " Are you L.R.B. ? " He and Lieut. Bradley were leading the Echelon B ration convoy up to battalion H.Q. and had brought with them the rations for our echelon on a separate limber, which was detached from the main body and ushered into our yard. Immediately afterwards Bradley and Charles were " carrying on," keeping their allotted place in the regular procession " going-up," and the L.R.B. vehicles followed them without more than a word of greeting being exchanged between the bystanders and the drivers. A few minutes later Clements, seized with a sudden brain-wave, hastened to my barn and planked his great foot with deliberate intent upon my back.

" Get up ! Quick ! " he shouted. " Echelon B's convoy's outside. Now's your chance if you want to know where battalion H.Q.s are."

Mechanically, not knowing exactly whose orders I was obeying, or whether they were orders at all, I groped for tin-hat and respirator, crossed over to Ben's stable, put in his bit, tightened his girth and clambered into the saddle. The horse was asleep, like his master, and if a searchlight had been flashed on us we must have looked a decrepit, drunken pair. " Outside," Clements had said, but there was no sign of L.R.B.s among the vehicles passing onwards. Scotch accents, Northumbrian dialect and Devonshire drawls came from one and another, but the good old London voice of Figg or Frampton, in response to my questions, was silent. The convoy must have gone on for some distance and the only thing to be done was to trot past all these other vehicles until a friendly voice came out of the darkness.

It was only gradually and in a sub-conscious way that I realised even what I was on the horse's back for at all, or why I wanted the L.R.B. convoy. Days crowded with events and excitement are liable to render one a trifle dull-witted and when one is suddenly awakened with a boot the dawn of intelligence is slow in making its appearance. Presently I realised that German shell-bursts which had been crumping all day beyond the river were still to be heard and that we were getting nearer to them. Then it became clear that the convoy had come to a dead stop. For hundreds of yards Ben and I groped our way past the stationary line of vehicles, amidst the flashes of officers' torches and the curses of dismounted drivers, without any sign of Echelon B. Over the bridge—which was still foolishly thought to be dangerous—and up a hill through the western outskirts we passed, without any break in the

long stretch of waiting limbers. It must be just about here that the
shells had been falling.

"Are you L.R.B. ? " I asked for about the fiftieth time.

"You can't get past there, mate. There's a team bin 'it."

A flashing of lights revealed movements somewhere about two
limbers ahead and Ben pushed his way forward gingerly between two
vehicles. A second later, visions of the Doullens-Arras road on the
night Kimbo was killed came back to me like a flash—of a sudden I
was wide awake.

The same stationary transports, the same chafing at the delay,
brought back the electric atmosphere of the former scene and the
central feature was almost a repetition of the cooker tragedy. A
shell had made a dead hit on a team of artillery horses at a fork-roads
and the animals were strewn all over the ground, completely blocking
the lane for traffic. An officer and N.C.O. were flashing torches and
superintending the removal of the dead and wounded drivers to a
cottage garden close by and at that very moment another shell came
close at hand to add to the tension. By keeping to the gutter, Ben
succeeded in getting past the wreckage and hastened up the right fork
road, only too glad to be clear of the spot : but we seemed to be no
nearer our goal, for even after riding on for some hundreds of yards
there was no sign of a convoy. The road was deserted. Had the
Westminster indicated a fork-road ? No, there had been no .such
thing on his sketch. It might equally well be the left turning.

While I was still lingering in doubt, a convoy approached from the
opposite direction. Nearer and nearer it came, passing within a yard
or so of Ben, who suddenly got excited. Could it possibly be——?

"Are you L.R.B. ? "

"Yes," came the voice of Leach. "Is that Aubrey ? "

"Thank God ! What are you coming this way for ? "

"On the wrong track, I think. We've just turned back."

"Were you anywhere near the fork roads when the shell fell ? "

"We'd just got past. And now we're coming to the —— place
again."

At the head of the column were Bradley and Charles, who had likewise mistaken the turning and were now hurrying past the dreaded spot
and hastening up the left fork road. Briefly, I explained to them why I
was wandering alone over the face of the earth and then rode in their
company for the remainder of the trip. For three-quarters of a mile
we continued, past a battalion or so occupying funk-holes in the right
bank of the road and then onwards in pitch darkness and rain, until
a light in a building on the left indicated the house we were looking for—
"the first of a scattered group of buildings called Nouveau Monde,"
which the L.R.B. had mopped up that morning. Our arrival was
greeted by a whizz-bang which landed about ten yards away and
caused Bradley, Charles and myself and the leading driver to perform
a series of evolutions which resulted in the loss of a tin-hat, a pair of
gloves and an acid drop.

"Half left," shouted Charles—and leading the way behind the
welcome shelter of the substantial-looking house which harboured
headquarters, we dismounted our steeds, alighted in twelve inches of
thick mud soup and then proceeded to disentangle yards of German
telegraph wire from the horses' hoofs and legs.

"Do you mind going back to the road and picking up my gloves ? "
asked Leach, who, being a driver, could not leave his horses for the

purpose. "They're just near the place where the shell came just now. I'll hold your horse."

"A damned good joke," thought I, but there was not much to be said, because Leach had recently washed a shirt for me : besides he owed me ten francs. So he took Ben's reins, while I hastened out in the direction of the so-called road and kicked about in the slime, fearing that the whizz-bang would repeat its performance at any moment. It was so dark that the scene of the mishap could not be located and it was, of course, by the merest fluke that in groping about my hand touched two slimy lumps held together by a long piece of tape—Leach's gloves, by all the saints !

"Er—er—excuse me," said a drawly voice in the darkness. "Can—er—ai want to know if—er—you could direct me to the—er—road."

"You're standing on it now," I answered very shortly, for I itched to get away.

"Oh—er—how strange ! It's very muddy, isn't it ? " came in sweet-toned accents, obviously from a padre.

" I shouldn't hang about here . . ."

" Ai want to get to, er—ha ! ha !—to Sebourg. Could you—er—be good enough——— ? "

"Keep straight on. You can't miss it. Good-night."

" But ai don't know what you mean — ' straight on.' Which direction ought I to—er—face ? "

Whizzt—Bang ! !

It was about thirty yards away. No longer was the padre in any doubt as to which direction he ought to face, and with a " Bless my soul ! " he was gone. Let us hope he did not hear the voluble swearing which came from the transport man as he blundered back to Leach's limber with the gloves !

There was nothing more to be done up there, so I left the convoy to its unloading and set off homewards in company with one driver, who returned to Sebourg to draw some stores.

Rayner had made his way back to Echelon A during the evening, after a strenuous day's work with the battalion. Much had happened since I had last seen him outside battalion H.Q. that morning, and though he was never one to pitch yarns, it was easy to see that he had had a " very thick time of it." He and the Westminster driver, having left their trench mortar limbers at the end of the day in a sunken road near Angreau, were sent down to their echelons with instructions that two more drivers with fresh horses should relieve them and be ready at dawn to co-operate in the next day's infantry advance. This was semi-open warfare with a vengeance ! Attacks every morning and shifts forward each day : trench mortar limbers co-operating with the infantry ! Incidentally, the echelon pack-pony men were doing sterling work in keeping the battalions supplied with ammunition even in advanced positions. It was exhilarating to say the least of it—far better than the usual consolidation of a captured position, the usual shift-forward of the transport lines and then—deadlock !

The two limbers which had been sent back to Famars to draw ammunition drew up at our gateway somewhere about eleven o'clock, the drivers, Williams and a Westminster, being chilled to the marrow, soaked to the skin, horribly hungry and utterly miserable. When I joined them with Ben they were practically asleep. Gerrish and another driver were detailed to accompany us with their pairs of horses, these two men being sent up to the trench mortar battery H.Q., who would instruct them what to do in the morning and where the limbers would be found.

" You will show them to the T.M.B. H.Q.," the brigade sergeant had said, quite ignoring the fact that I was as ignorant of its whereabouts as he was. " Oh, you'll find it somewhere in the houses at Nouveau Monde."

So we set off, the two limbers and the spare pairs of horses making quite a respectable-sized convoy, and to our joy found ourselves almost the only transport people on the road. All through the village and its outskirts, instead of the waiting line of vehicles, the roads were deserted : everything was silent. The darkness was still intense, so that picking one's way forward was like riding along with one's eyes shut, and the only illumination on the route was a big lamp hanging on a barricade at the fork road, where the relics of the team tragedy had been fenced off on one side. However, no untoward incidents marred the journey and before long I was picking my way over dozens of sleeping forms in order to ferret out Colonel Burnell and Major Wallis, who were again in a cellar, sitting over a table just as they had been at five o'clock that morning.

After a somewhat unconventional salute I put my hand in my pocket and produced what I believed to be the chit advising the quantity of ammunition to be received.

" I've brought this, sir," I said, handing it to Major Wallis.

The next instant Wallis' face changed from a puzzled expression to an enormous grin, while I felt like falling through the floor. He was holding the fortnight-old menu of the transport dinner, with a picture of a very pretty girl, upon the outside, staring him in the face !

After explanations, the mirth subsided and he told me where the trench mortar people would be found. So while the limber drivers were unloading outside the L.R.B. H.Q., the rest of us made our way along to a house farther up the road, where Gerrish and his companion actually found a stable for their horses, and were then welcomed by one of the T.M.B. staff, who said they could sleep in the front room for an hour or so until they were wanted. That was the last I saw of either of them, for in a few hours they were both gassed.

The operations on the next day (November 6th) were hardly successful, but it was not to be wondered at, considering the battalions, wet and cold and hungry, got the order every night to go over the top on the following day and the forward movement was so continual that there was no time to make extensive preparations for an attack, as in the past. Besides this, the division's front was so extended that in the L.R.B. attacking waves the men were twenty to thirty paces apart and nobody knew what was happening on the right or left. The inevitable result was that the Germans—realising the weakness of the attack—counter-attacked in the Bois de Beaufort and by 8.30 a.m. had driven the 169th Brigade back to their starting point. The amount of gas used by the enemy in that morning's attack may be guessed from the fact that from dawn onwards it was so strong back at Sebourg that men's eyes were running and about breakfast time some were to be seen in respirators.

The noise of the battle was, if possible, louder than on the previous mornings, but it died down considerably during the forenoon. Word came down later in the day that Gerrish had been badly gassed and had passed through as a casualty, while the poor driver who had gone up with him had been found completely blinded, yet trying to bring his horses back to the lines. Owing to the failure of the attack there was no occasion for further trench mortar limber horses to be sent up that day, and as our brigade was to be relieved by the 167th that night it developed upon the latter to make its own transport arrangements.

That day we saw the papers of November 4th, in which the news of Austria's capitulation was confirmed in black and white, so that even the most sceptical were convinced. All three of Germany's allies had collapsed and the way was open for a big attack on Germany through Austria. In fact our aeroplanes could now go right up to the Bavarian frontier and carry out wholesale raids and the enemy were panic-stricken. From all quarters dazzling news was coming to hand which even two months ago would have been considered fantastic. So great was our excitement that we hardly knew whether we were standing on our heads or on our feet. The Germans were trying to get back over the Rhine through the neck of a bottle and a great coup was possible on the Western Front if only the American part of the operations were up to time.

On the morning of the 7th there was no drum-fire—a welcome sign to Clements and myself who had to go up and fetch Gerrish's horses from their stable, then bring back the limber from the sunken road where it had been left by Rayner on the 5th. We were to start at nine o'clock and the absence of gunfire made us hope for a quiet journey; but at the very moment that we left the billet the artillery chorus crashed forth once more, zero hour having been fixed for 9 a.m. for a change— a circumstance that altered the outlook for our trip, not to mention the smiles on our faces. Many new batteries had taken up positions in the open between Sebourg and Angreau and, of course, we found them firing merrily when we got up there. Considering the offensive was being waged on the entire front, it was very impressive to observe how many guns of all calibres were concentrated on just one tiny portion of the line. It was a misty morning and not much was visible, but we saw, alas, a great many bodies lying just as they had fallen two days before— poor fellows who had met their death at the eleventh hour of the War. There must be thousands more who, like ourselves, were commiserating with these recent casualties and who, nevertheless, would themselves fall before the last shot was fired. But the dead did not grieve over their fate : it was the man who was maimed at this stage of the War who deserved most sympathy, since he would live to curse his ill-luck for the rest of his days. It was my last trip in the artillery zone, for when we moved up to Angreau on the following day all the guns had gone still farther forward and we never caught them up again.

On the 8th, when the move to Angreau took place, not only brigade H.Q. and the A echelons, but the L.R.B. companies—who had been resting for thirty-six hours or so at Sebourg—went forward to occupy the village, which had now become almost a rest area, so quickly were the Germans retiring. The civilians in this place had had a terrible time, for, apart from the house-to-house fighting, there had been two days of revengeful strafeing from the German artillery, which had put shells of all calibres into the village, including gas shells, and not a building had entirely escaped. The villagers' feelings were divided between profound gratitude to the British and overwhelming grief at the ruin of their homes, the casualties among their friends and the disappearance of their boys and young men who had been dragged off by the Germans. Many of the old folk stood in the street and discussed excitedly the fate that had befallen their homesteads, while groups of L.R.B.s sauntered up and down visiting the scenes of their recent scrapping. It was said that, when they were taking the village, many of them were offered coffee by the inhabitants while fighting still went on in the street !

The old man in the farm where I tied up my charger was in tears because the Germans had taken his horse, his stock of hay and all sorts of private belongings, including two sons, without paying for them ; and he found it impossible to turn his eyes towards his ruined barn without fresh tears bursting forth. We witnessed a touching reunion between this old fellow and the two missing sons whom he had been mourning for ten days. Just as we thought we had cheered him up and taken his mind temporarily off his grief, a boy of sixteen rushed up and kissed him on both cheeks. " Mon garçon ! " said the old man, and then the handkerchief came out again and more tears fell. The boy then went in and greeted his mother, who also blubbed copiously. It appeared that in the " sauve qui peut " of their hasty retirement the Germans could not possibly attend to all their civilian prisoners and had dumped them in a certain place from which they had walked back through the German rearguards and the British scouting parties. A few minutes later the elder son also returned and fell on his parents' necks. He spoke at the rate of two hundred words a minute for the next half-hour, but we judged from certain phrases here and there that some of his companions had been shot.

Since seeing the paper of the 4th no news of the War had come to hand : all that we knew was that the attack of that date had sent the Germans reeling so fast that it was a somewhat difficult matter to overtake them, a fact I realised better a few hours later. We had been hoping for some really good peace news for days and now a rumour came round which, although difficult to believe, was confirmed by several people at brigade. General Hull, who paid H.Q. a visit during the afternoon, said that German delegates had come through the French lines to receive the Allied Armistice terms and he gave the War two more days to run. While we were prepared to accept the news about the delegates as truth, nobody, so far as I know, had much respect for the General's opinion as to the duration of the War. We had heard optimistic staff utterances before and, with all due respect to the General, we thought he was somewhat extravagant in his talk of the War being over in two days. Two *months* perhaps—if we were lucky ! We therefore fell to discussing the looks on the delegates' faces when they read the terms which Foch would present to them.

At dusk the Staff Captain requested the most intelligent runner to report to him, which was rather an absurd message to send, since each of us started a long oration to prove his own intelligence was nil. After five minutes another messenger arrived, repeating the request, but being still in the midst of a heated discussion, and each having failed to convince the other two of his idiocy, we were unable to comply with the Staff Captain's demand. Finally, we agreed to toss for it and I lost the throw ; it consequently fell to me to report at H.Q., and I'm sure that a muddier, more unkempt, ragged and dirty-looking specimen never posed as an intelligent human being.

The task was to ride through the next village, Angre, and carry on to some place beyond that, report on the state of the roads for horse transport, the size and strength (!) of the bridge over the River Grand Honnelle and any other feature of interest. The answer was *not* a lemon, as one of the irreverent runners was kind enough to suggest. So far as I was instructed to proceed, it was quite possible for horse transport to use the thoroughfare, but this was only because other vehicles—mostly artillery, no doubt—had already used the route and made other tracks where necessary. Considering every cross-road had a huge crater blown in it, twenty or thirty feet and more deep, it was obvious that horse traffic was going to have a difficult time and that motor lorries would be held up entirely.

Later the same night I had to ride back to Sebourg with a message for Echelon B, who had just moved up there, and the full extent of the disorganisation caused by these obstructions was then apparent. Losing my way on the way back to Angreau through taking a new route which was supposed to be more direct, I wandered miles out of my course along roads over which endless convoys were journeying and meeting with accident after accident at various huge mine craters. It was so dark that the leading horses, coming upon them without warning, tumbled right in. At one cross-road, in a village of which no one knew the name, lanterns were being frantically hurried to an enormous crater in which a whole wagon and team had disappeared and the drivers, pinned under numerous horses, were supposed to be drowning. Some of the cross-roads were impassable and vehicles had to turn back.

Nobody could tell anyone else what road he was on, what village lay ahead, or how to reach his destination. Even officers I spoke to hadn't the least idea where they were, and if a civilian gave them the name of the next village it conveyed nothing to them. Here and there a group of officers could be seen trying to read maps by torchlight in the pouring rain. Never before had my sense of direction so far deserted me as it did that night, for, coming to cross-roads, I had not the least idea which of the four would be most likely to lead me to Angreau. Bitterly did I curse myself for experimenting with a new route on such an occasion !

It was quite by luck that I came at last to some houses which proved to be on the outskirts of Angreau, and on turning in eventually I found there was very little time left in which to snooze before the break of dawn. But on this morning there was no drum-fire. The batteries were miles away and it was extremely doubtful whether they knew where our own infantry were, much less the Germans. Our infantry were "away forward" right enough, but all the services they depended upon for their food and ammunition were falling out by the wayside one by one, like "also rans" in a cross-country race. The foremost rail-heads were getting farther from the front, the roads available for lorries were becoming scarcer and scarcer, and the distances to be covered by horse transport had been extended to four times the normal. In other words, the War had run away from us and only a small band of skirmishers was able to keep touch with it. First-line transport limbers had given way to pack-ponies and on the afternoon of the 9th these also were given tasks that promised to be too much for them. Then, and then only, did the Staff turn to the good old R.A.F. And on that day the 168th Brigade's rations were delivered by aeroplane !

CHAPTER XXXVI.

THE ARMISTICE AND AFTER.

(*November, 1918–January, 1919.*)

Rumours of an Armistice—Armistice Day—Living for demobilisation—Life at Harmignies—Our last Christmas dinner—The transport section's last "Fling" —Farewell to the L.R.B.—The journey home—Demobilised at last.

On the 9th of November the arrival of a relief terminated the brigade running job so far as I was concerned, and I rejoined the transport section, which was now reunited owing to Echelon B's appearance in Angreau. The whole battalion was therefore together again, both companies and transport occupying the village. Twenty-four tedious hours followed, tedious because we could learn no news of the progress of the War from any source. We were cut off from the outside world and depended for everything upon the ability of the A.S.C. to tide over their transport difficulties. Not only were newspapers delayed, but rations were rottener than ever, while canteens had closed down apparently for good.

Next day the whole brigade marched forward over appallingly bad roads and past intact houses where the civilians turned out to give us a good welcome. Obstacles such as barricades and craters had been circumvented sufficiently well to enable motor traffic to use the road, but the way was narrow and the ground bad so that those lorries which had ventured forward were in great difficulties and many were ditched. Our march was so devious that we began to wonder if we should ever reach the firing-line, and by dusk it seemed to be as far away as ever. Just as we were drawing close to our destination—Erquennes—a temporary blockage caused us to halt beside a long line of lorries facing eastwards like ourselves and a few of us, thirsty for news, got into conversation with the drivers.

"The War's over to-morrow at eleven o'clock," said the one nearest to me

What a typical A.S.C. rumour !

Seeing the cynical look on our faces, the driver proceeded to state that he had come straight from corps H.Q., where he had heard that the delegates had accepted the terms.

"You see if I ain't right," was his parting remark as we moved on again. Nobody believed him, but it gave us an excuse for feeling optimistic, and that night we lay down to sleep in a civilian cottage with rather lighter hearts than we had had for some time.

Early next morning one of the section came along with the statement that the rumour was true. He had heard it from another L.R.B. man, who had spoken to an R.A.M.C. corporal, who said——

Smiles greeted the credulous man's statement and seeing that he was unable to convince anyone of its truth he departed on his mission elsewhere. Meanwhile we turned out on to the lines to attend to our horses.

But the rumour was persistent. Hobson, the great rumour-monger who could be trusted to trot out some fresh item of gossip at a time like this, came up and asserted that a notice had been posted up at brigade H.Q. to that effect. Where he had heard the news I don't know, but he was so convinced of its truth that he offered to take any odds on it. We really did not know what to believe, but thought it best to carry on our work with disbelieving hearts, for the statement was really too absurd for serious discussion! And in this frame of mind we returned to our billets for breakfast after morning "stables," anxiously waiting for a definite statement to be made one way or the other, to relieve the uncertainty.

It came at last and the bearer of the news must indeed have felt proud at becoming suddenly such a centre of interest. The courier was Harbord, who had relieved me on the orderly job two days before, and he had come straight from brigade H.Q., where the news was to be seen in black and white on the notice board.

"Cease fire at eleven o'clock this morning, boys. I've *seen* it— brigade headquarters—yes, with my own . . . eyes. Armistice comes into force in another three hours. It's posted up there, I tell you. All right, go and . . . see for yourself. Do you think I'd go off my bally head for nothing?" He then departed to take the tidings to other billets.

Well, we must believe that there was an announcement about the Armistice, anyway. Most of us grinned rather sheepishly, and then remarks such as, " I'd like to see it myself all the same," " Wonder how long the Armistice will last," &c., came from one and another, as we continued with our ablutions.

Trendell tried to create an atmosphere of rejoicing by throwing his hat across the room and hitting Sharpe in the eye ; Dixon bemoaned the fact that there was no beer in the place with which to celebrate the event, while Greene declared that he would end up the day " blind " if he had to steal rum for the purpose. The astounding piece of news had left Figg speechless at first, but it was not long before he recovered his articulation and pronounced it to be a staff dodge to cheer the brigade up preparatory to being ordered " over the top "; and his facetious question : " What's the betting we shan't hear a gun fire at five past eleven ? " put rather a damper on the assembly. We could only wait and see and, in the meantime, try to obtain news from other sources.

What happened during the next few hours it is difficult to remember. Who could do an ounce of work or look at harness when every man who passed down the road had some remark to make about " keeping his head low for the next hour or so," or " being in Berlin within a week " ? Everyone had got hold of the news : even Major Wallis said it was true. And at last we accepted it as an incontrovertible fact, like the statement that rations would be short for the next few weeks owing to the British feeding liberated Belgium.

Towards eleven o'clock we constantly looked at our watches to see how much longer the War had got to last and it was a difficult task for Watkins to walk up and down the lines urging men to erect harness racks in breathless moments like that. At about ten minutes to eleven a gun sounded in the far distance and we wondered whether any poor devil had " gone West " as a result of that shot.

Then the minutes ticked on and a clock struck eleven. Immediately the bells of the village church rang out and women came to their door-steps literally weeping for joy ; a feeble cheer went up from the section and men gathered in knots to discuss the turn of events. We were really too stunned for much gesticulation. To think there would be no more shells, no more bombs, no more gas, no more cold nights to be spent on picket through fear of lighting a fire. Of all the incredible announcements that had ever been made to us, this left us the most staggered. It must be only a dream ! Surely we should hear the distant sound of guns in a minute or so, which would prove we had been deluded ! We strained our ears for distant gunfire. . . . Silence ! Only the sound of church bells in other villages proclaiming the event.

Armistice signed ! If only we were in England now ! Just picture the enthusiastic crowds in London, in the offices and restaurants and streets ! Just picture the shouting and singing and waving of flags ! What celebrations ! What lovely girls would be blowing kisses to all and sundry ! What crowds there would be round the bars !

Erquennes ! Fellows repeated the word contemptuously, as though there existed in the universe no more benighted spot in which to celebrate the occasion.

" To think of being stuck here," wailed Rayner. " No champagne, no *vin blanc*—only about ten widows and a cow."

By some of the men the fact of our being sent to Erquennes was regarded as a deliberate move on the part of the Army authorities to deny them their wish to get dead drunk. Now if we had been a few miles farther ahead in Mons ! Later in the day we learnt that the Canadians had entered Mons that morning. " Just our rotten luck," was the comment. " There would have been some jolly decent girls there who would have given us a fine old time."

Twice during the afternoon our hearts sank to our feet at the sound of a distant report like the firing of a big gun, but word came along presently that it was either blasting or else the exploding of some German mines under the roads ! Everyone, troops and civilians, had knocked off work for the day, and we were welcomed into the cottages, where the good folk made cups of coffee out of the scanty supplies they had, and told us many tales of suffering and hardships. The Devils' Mess " palled up " with a peasant and his family in a small cottage near our field, and we listened to stories which were a replica of those we had heard during the past week.

In the evening large numbers attended a thanksgiving service, held by a padre in the village school, after which there was nothing to be done but return to our billets or sit in the cottages once again, writing letters. What joyous scenes we missed that night can only be judged by those who celebrated the Armistice in royal fashion in the big towns, either at home or in France. Of our rejoicing there is unfortunately nothing to record. That night the picket kept up a glorious fire, and were able to flash their lamp about freely without fear of Hun aeroplanes, occasionally pinching themselves to make sure they were living in a world of reality. The civilian rooms in which we prepared for a good night's rest were filled with talk about one subject only : Demobilisation. And when we lay down on the floor eventually, the last thought before we dropped off to sleep was not the eternal " When will my turn come ? " but : " When shall I be in civvies again ? "

From that moment we simply lived for news of the demobilisation scheme. Every day we spent in uniform now counted more than ever as a day wasted, and we were more impatient to get away from France, even though we should now be able to find more joy in life than in the bad old days of bombs and " bust-ups." The news of the Kaiser's abdication and the publication of the severe Armistice terms did not arouse such enthusiasm as the announcement, a few days later, that employers could apply for men previously in their service. How feverishly did we write home, one and all, drawing attention to this scheme and requesting our employers to urge our claims, or, in the case of unlucky ones who had no jobs, beseeching friends to pretend they had employment for them ! What enthusiasm could the companies put into road-mending or the drivers into harness-cleaning when such duties were regarded as an objectionable means of passing the time until one's papers " came through " and one was finished with such manual labour for ever. The pettifogging attempt at " poshing up " made everybody " fed up " to the hilt. The inspiration for this came from higher quarters than battalion, for we received notice that we were to be exceedingly smart, as we should shortly be marching proudly into Germany.

On the 15th three officers and seventy-seven men went into Mons to march past a General who was inspecting the units supposed to be included in the projected Army of Occupation. But after being told to hold ourselves in readiness, it transpired some days later that our division would remain in Belgium after all. This was rather disappointing, but when we heard about the terrible rations received by those troops who did move forward, we felt pretty thankful we were nearer the base. It was all very well for people to express the opinion that we should have carried on in ruthless pursuit to the Rhine. We knew ourselves how impossible conditions had become for all the supply services in the last four days of the War, and we should, in any event, have had to call a halt while we built railways and roads. If, after waiting a week before advancing, it was necessary to call more than one halt to our unopposed march forward, because of the impossibility of feeding even a portion of our army, how much worse should we have fared if the whole front had tried to push onwards in active warfare ?

Even at Erquennes rations were atrociously bad, and we scoured the countryside in vain in search of civilians who could sell us potatoes for the battalion. One exploration took us to a fair-sized town, Dour, where everything except food was to be found in the shops. At one big emporium there we were astonished to find a piano department, where I seated myself at a beautiful new German instrument, and played for an hour, while my pals—pretending to be listening attentively—took the opportunity to flirt with a fair assistant behind my back. I explained that I had not enough money to buy the piano but purchased a handkerchief instead, and the shopkeeper appeared to be quite satisfied.

During our stay here we heard that Lance-Corporal Charles had received the M.M., and later the same award came through for

Corporal Milcovich, which showed that the recent work of the section had been appreciated.   Looking back on it now, it was all one hideous nightmare, carried on under a strain which could not be realised at the time.   As we had noticed before, it was only when one got down to the quietude of a base hospital or saw those splendid old cliffs of Kent from a leave boat that one realised the tension under which life had been carried on,   Now the quietude of the base hospital was obtainable at Erquennes, the strain had suddenly snapped, and, able at last to banish thoughts of ration trips, shelled roads, and gas respirators from our minds, we could at last think freely of our future prospects.   We should shortly be picking up the threads of business where we had dropped them, and it should certainly not be long before we returned finally to our homes, where mothers and fathers, wives, sweethearts, cats and canaries all waited anxiously for our return.

On the 26th the battalion moved onwards to Harmignics, about four miles from Mons, and therefore four miles from the place where the war ended on November 11th.   Harmignics itself had, I think, been captured on the afternoon of the 10th.   As it was to be our winter quarters, we were told to make ourselves as comfortable as possible, and many of the men secured billets in private houses. Needless to say, these included all the transport who scrounged the greater part of three residences, leaving the house-owners little more than a kitchen and cupboard in which to eat and sleep.   Most of the inhabitants did everything to make the L.R.B. comfortable, but there were some who preferred the Germans to ourselves, and emphatically declared their preference.   Others there were, again, who had become mentally deficient through years of worry, but as these lived the life of hermits we did not have much to do with them.

At Harmignies the mania for " poshing up " developed with redoubled fury, and matters reached a climax when, on December 3rd, Frampton won the much-talked-of money prize from Division for the smartest transport turn-out.   The gift proved to be a five-franc note, which was only rivalled in generosity by the bottle of pickles presented by Lieut. Russell at Ryveldt.   It is rumoured that after standing drinks all round, Frampton invested the balance in War Bonds.

The necessity for extra hands to enable us to bring our vehicles and harness back to ceremonial state caused the transference of several men from the companies to the transport.   Our own numbers were below strength, and we should in any case have to get extra men if leave started shortly.   So one fine day a contingent of some twenty to thirty men, mostly recently recruited miners, found their way to the section, with whom they had not even language in common, let alone any other bonds of sympathy.   From the moment they joined they bore the older hands a grudge, partly owing to their being put on to the dirtiest work, and partly on account of our amusement at the way in which they lined up at the cookhouse with their mess-tins quite twenty minutes before the meals were ready.   Accustomed as we were to " rolling up " with our mugs when word was passed round that tea was being given out, it was rather funny to find the approach to the transport cookhouse a scene of seething humanity, waving plates and mugs and arguing as to who got there first.   Frank Little and Barnett treated them as greedy little puppy dogs, yelping for their food, and sometimes became helpless with laughter as the hungry ones thrust their mess-tins forward over each other's heads in their eagerness. We used to wait until the bun-fight was over before we came up for our food, a fact which still further accentuated the circumstance that there were now really two transport sections, not one. With such an accession to the transport strength as these new-comers represented, the small muster of old hands became more pronounced, and it was reasonable to suppose that as soon as demoblisation started our little band would practically cease to exist, since our claims to rapid demobilisation were assuredly paramount.

But exactly the reverse was the case. Foremost among the starred occupations was that of mining, and it was laid down that the miners should be sent home before anybody else, irrespective of their period of service. It was incredible that these men, who had been conscripted for the most part at the fifty-ninth minute of the War, thrust into khaki and sent out as reinforcements in September or October, should be the first to go home, while men who had volunteered in the first months of the War and seen years of active service remained in France to watch their departure. The troops in France had the additional grievance that men in camps at home who had not even left England's shores were reported as being demobilised in big batches because they were at a convenient distance from the various demobilising depots. Conibeer reported this early in the month when he and numerous other cadets—good luck to them !—were sent back to civilian life. Can it be wondered at that the temper of the older soldiers was at boiling point ? Was it not natural that there should be rioting and turbulent scenes in various quarters owing to this very unfair treatment ? The feeling was so strong that the demobilisation authorities had perforce to give way to a certain extent, and we received the assurance that only one man at home should be discharged for every half man sent home from France. Tubby Butt, however, expressed the opinion that this was all " my eye."

In order to equip us for civilian life and to put an end to the intellectual rot which had set in during these four wasted years, the battalion started a series of school classes under directions from the Practical Joke Department. There were, however, very few qualified teachers and the remainder had to be recruited from volunteers, who undertook to teach such subjects as arithmetic, French and English for an hour or so each day. The scheme promised well at the outset, judging by the number of pupils who desired to attend the classes, but when it came to putting the scheme in force unforeseen difficulties arose. One transport man who turned up at the mathematics class, hoping to refresh his memory in regard to decimals, declared that he found the master engaged in an argument with a Doorham lad as to whether twice two made four or five. This was no doubt an exaggerated way of describing the situation, but the fact remained that if we were all to receive instruction of real value we should require about twenty different classes in each subject, and even then there was the language difficulty ! The battalion school therefore became an effete institution. Fortunately for fellows who were interested enough, a special class was started at brigade H.Q. on a matriculation level and so, having obtained permission to attend, I gave up my transport duties for more congenial work at a desk for the remainder of my life in the Army. This did not prevent my keeping in touch with the Devils' Mess, who had decided to make great celebrations at Christmas time.

For weeks before Christmas it was dinned into our ears what a splendid feed was to be given us : extra special Army rations, **turkeys,** nuts, oranges, figs, wines and, above all—a real surprise, which was kept a guarded secret. D.A.Q.M.G.s announced the glad tidings to supply officers, who in turn passed it on to the quartermasters, who trumpeted the news abroad in the battalions, and, as the time approached, we at one time contemplated writing home to say it was not necessary to send Christmas parcels this year. At last the great day arrived and everyone waited eagerly for Hurford's return from the Q.M. store, bringing with him the good cheer and, above all—the great surprise. Nobody took much heed of Figg's timely warning that the Army had never yet given something for nothing and that we should not utter thanksgivings before the glorious repast was set before us. We were all so confident that the grateful Army would surely not disappoint us now the submarine peril was past. But our dear friend Figg was, as usual, right in his attitude towards Army pronouncements. As he said, "Once a . . . ., always a . . . ." and our Christmas repast went far to confirm the truth of this dictum. The following is an accurate list of the special Christmas rations served out to each man on the transport section, specially noted by everybody at the time and afterwards mentioned in our letters :—

One-eighteenth part of a scraggy Turkey (No gravy).

Beef.	Potatoes.
Three and a half ounces of Pudding.	Unsweetened Custard.
Three-quarters of a Fig.	One-third of a rotten Apple.

One-eleventh part of a Chestnut. (In other words, six for the section.) And the great surprise turned out to be—PAPER CHAINS !

Aye, it was a fine thing to remember about the Army, that Christmas dinner. As someone remarked at the time, they seemed to be doing their best to cover up the bad impressions of the past and send us away from the service with a kindly feeling towards all those who had been responsible for our comfort and welfare.

After this, the bad feeling over the miners began in earnest. The demobilisation scheme, which had been coming into force gradually for some weeks past among the non-combatant elements of the service, at last flung its tentacles far enough afield to fasten even on little units like infantry battalions, and on the 26th an application was received by the L.R.B. for *one* man to proceed home at once. He was to be a pivotal man and he *must* be bound for the Leeds district— consequently a miner, who had recently been roped in and served two months on active service, paraded on the following evening in full kit, received his papers from the orderly room and departed for England.

Once, in the Happy Valley, on the Somme, after the impossible night of September 3rd, 1916, a " Bolshevik " assembly had gathered round the site of the cooks' fire in the early morning light and steadily cursed the Army and all connected with it for a solid hour. But the feeling did not run nearly so high as now and with each fresh departure of miners which took place henceforth about every other night the billets became filled with mutterings which would have sent the Secret Intelligence Department into blue fits.

Something of the disorderly element—which, let me say, for the credit of the L.R.B. was kept in such a magnificent check that the honour of the regiment was not tarnished for one moment—was reflected at a performance of the " Battalion Concert Party," given early in January, when the transport formed part of the audience. Both because it was the last occasion on which the transport section, as a body, came well into the limelight, and also because it is the last incident I remember about my life in the L.R.B., I make special reference to this entertainment : otherwise it would be my bounden duty to close forthwith a narrative which has already covered many more reams of paper than I care to contemplate.

The concert party was composed chiefly of officers, including the Adjutant, Von Berg, the doctor, and two or three recently joined lieutenants, together with Barnett and Stainer (of the old transport party) : other of the section's concert troupe had been invited to join, but had declined as a protest against the preference shown in demobilising the miners first.

The opening performance was given to two of the companies, who received it somewhat apathetically, but at the next show the transport were invited as part of the audience and the terrific laughter they poured forth at the feeblest jokes, coupled with thunderous clapping after each song, gave quite a spark of life to the proceedings. This uproarious applause was, curiously enough, taken to be genuine by certain of the new officers in the party, and although they certainly thought the transport noisy, they put it down to ignorance on our part. Consequently, when it was decided to give a third performance to all the officers of the L.R.B. and 2nd Londons, the transport section were specially invited to attend once more, in order to infuse the audience with the right spirit. It was thought that if company men were invited to fill up the hall they would be afraid to cheer with so many officers present, while it was certain the transport would make it into a rousing evening. Von Berg asked me to be the pianist at this performance, and although I knew the concert party would, in Army language, receive the " order of the bird," it would have been tactless to refuse at a time when the orderly room was brandishing discharge papers about.

As soon as the transport received the invitation to attend the performance a second time there were loud declarations, accompanied by much laughter, that if the party couldn't see they'd been " getting the bird " before, they would damned well be made to see it on this occasion. Accordingly several men went off in search of combs and paper, while bells, whistles, hooters and various other noise-producing instruments made their appearance from different quarters. Jim Greene busied himself with filling a tin with broken glass, an idea that was acted upon by others, so that by the time the section took their place among the back rows of the small concert-hall everybody was equipped with something capable of adding to the unearthly din.

At the back of the stage the three transport performers could hardly contain themselves with excitement, for they were in the peculiar position of thoroughly sympathising with the reception about to be accorded to the " officers' " concert party of which they were humble members. The only good things about the troupe were the costumes —hired from the Mons Theatre—and the make-up, which was put on in double-quick time by a professional who, in civilian life, put the finishing touches to Oscar Asche.

Even before the concert commenced the weird orchestra started at the back of the hall, to the intense amusement of the officers in the audience, who anticipated a lively evening. But when the curtain went up a perfectly appalling pandemonium started, all the bells, whistles, tin-cans, combs and hooters breaking forth into a symphony which continued with varying degrees of intensity, but without a break, throughout the entire performance. Personal remarks, giggling cat-calls and a running stream of comment were added to the reception, these also being given forth indiscriminately before, during and after each item, and nothing could subdue Greene, who imitated a gurgling parrot during each song. Seated at the piano, I was helpless with laughter the greater part of the time, but the joke of it was that the performers (except Von Berg, who entered into the fun) carried on valiantly, raising their voices and doing their utmost to give effect to the programme as under normal conditions.

The " flapper," who was received with squeaky imitations of her voice, the ringing of bells and rattling of tins, was presented after her item with a huge bouquet of onions, carrots and straw. The Adjutant, who tried to sing a sentimental song, was received with moans and groans and as soon as he started " When I was a Boy at School," there were loud cries of " That wasn't so long ago ! " Another officer sang " I'm Captain Reginald d'Arcy of the Guards," to which the audience added " Gaw blimy," or " I don't think," after each line, but in spite of this he accepted the applause as genuine and came forward to give an encore. " What, *again* ! " shouted the transport, followed by cries of " Make it a short one ! " Which he did.

The funniest item was the doctor's songs. The M.O. possessed a sweet little voice, suitable for a parlour, but too soft for a concert hall, and when he started off pianissimo with " There's a Cottage in God's Garden," it was the signal for general snivelling and blubbing, with handkerchiefs well to the fore, this continuing throughout the item. Nevertheless he gave an encore which touched the heart of the audience so much that showers of pennies fell upon the stage. He was so wild about this that the O.C. Concert Party had great difficulty in persuading him to appear in the second half of the programme, but he was eventually induced to sing something more cheerful—at which the rows of transport men sat and giggled from first to last, finally flinging more showers of pennies at his feet. That time he did *not* give an encore.

There is no space in which to record the reception given to the officer who sang ditties at the piano, or to the song which I had to give myself in response to an insistent dirge from the back rows. Sufficient to say that the evening's events left half the performers choleric with rage and, I'm afraid, brought to a sad end that concert party's brief but breezy existence.

It will always live in the memories of certain of us as a red-letter day, when we gave sudden rein to a mixture of feelings which others more fortunate had vented on Armistice Day. Some of those who would have enjoyed it most were not present, for Macloughlin, Figg, Trendell and others had gone home on leave, where they had succeeded somehow in getting " demobbed." Figg, a civilian once more ! What must his feelings be ?

" Buck up and get leave," wrote he. " Every man who gets home on leave and obtains a letter from his employer can now get demobbed, even if he isn't a miner or a conscientious objector."

The old members of the section, of course, dwindled in numbers with every man that went on leave, for it was almost certain that none would return, but very few had as yet departed, while not one had so far received a demobilisation call from the L.R.B. orderly room. Then, five days after the memorable concert, a runner brought me a chit which set my heart a fluttering with hope, and on reporting to the Adjutant I found that demobilisation papers indeed awaited me, and

I was to start next day. The Board of Trade Overseas Trade Department had applied for me—that was all I knew or cared. If they thought I ranked as a " demobiliser " it was not for me to disillusion the authorities !

The farewell to all my old pals was mitigated by the knowledge that most of them would get leave shortly, and by the resolve to fix up a great reunion at the earliest possible date. It was therefore with a feeling as of walking on air—in spite of the weight of my equipment—that I stepped out towards the orderly room next morning in order to receive my papers. Full equipment had been handed out to me, any article of which I was short having been furnished by Q.M.S. Hamilton without demur—truly a strange state of affairs. The only thing that worried him was the disappearance of all the transport's men's bayonets which had, of course, been " lost " in a very early stage of the War, but he indented for some more and for the first time on record everything required turned up almost before one had asked for it.

The section lent me the mess-cart in order to ride into Mons, and at six o'clock on the 12th of January I joined a party of some hundreds of men of all units, bound for Blighty like myself, some of them only half tight, others well on the way to oblivion. However, we all managed to get into the train somehow and though we were disappointed to find ourselves turned out and marched into a billet in Valenciennes, it was some consolation to know that one stage of our homeward journey was accomplished. They spent a day here sorting us out into different demobilisation centres and in the evening undid all the good work by letting the men scramble into the train in any order, so that the whole process had to be repeated at Dieppe.

We arrived here also at the dead of night and spent hours being shown into tents, but the amount of grousing was negligible : we could surely suffer a few more annoyances in silence, when the end of being " bloomin' onions every time " was fast approaching. At this camp they took special precautions to ensure that no man should take home any little strangers with him. They also made a minute examination of our equipment, announcing not once but many times that we must give in our full complement on the other side and that if we needed anything, from a helmet to a housewife, we were to ask for it now.

We finally boarded the homeward-bound boat on the evening of the 15th and as we were not due to arrive at Southampton till 8 a.m. we all settled down to enjoy the eight hours' voyage as best we might. Nearly every man's " best " consisted of being violently sick over his next-door neighbour, and it was with a very turbulent tummy that I lay for hour after hour in one of the holds, listening to the sounds of revelry around me and not daring to move lest I too be tempted to take part in the celebrations.

It was a relief when we sailed calmly up Southampton Water after daybreak, crowding round the upper deck to feast our eyes upon the Homeland to which we had returned safe and sound. The last time I had stood watching those same docks and wharves was on the transport ship leaving for France on January 24th, 1915, when a thousand pairs of eyes were gazing wistfully at the South Western trains and the boat-loads of workmen and the cranes—homely sights that might never be seen again. It was a curious coincidence that the next time I should see Southampton would be on my return for demobilisation, after a period of four years almost to the very day. All the way up the Water my thoughts were back in 1915, contrasting the forebodings of that departure with our present feelings. If we had realised then that four years of Hell lay ahead of us with the alternative of death, wounds or incapacitation, our wits would probably have left us while contemplating such a prospect. What had happened to that little draft from Q Company of the 2nd Battalion with whom I had crossed the water on that occasion ? Brought vividly back to memory by these old associations came faces and names of fellows who had been comrades in those days, but had gradually drifted away, so that the intervening years had obliterated all recollection of them. Marshall, Scholefield, Box, Thomas, Stiff—what had happened to them all ? Most of the little draft had been wounded in 1915 and had never been seen in the 1st Battalion again. Poor Kimbo Vallentine, Pace, West, Tucket, Sweeting and others were buried in France. In 1917 Gernat, one of three who remained, had been gassed and sent home, leaving only two—Sergt. Munday and myself—to carry through with the 1st Battalion until the Armistice.

We moored alongside the very pier where we had previously embarked, and drew refreshments from the self-same stall. I did not recognise any of the ladies serving there, but four years undoubtedly works a great change in faces : besides, the belles of 1915 had probably long since married !

Immediately after breakfast we entrained for the Crystal Palace, and after a rapid journey through the dear old English countryside we were deposited at the famous demobilisation depot where thousands upon thousands of men were arriving from home camps all over the south-east of England, in a proportion of about ten to every single man who had arrived from France.

After waiting over an hour we were marched into a long hall where first one article of equipment and then another was handed over to a busy staff of men in khaki who had the impertinence to send a man round with a tray collecting tips from us. He had been extraordinarily successful with our predecessors, but not much change was forthcoming from the overseas men, even though many of them were little more than recruits.

" You're being demobilised and we ain't," was the cry of the cadgers.

" And you kin think yerselves blinkin' lucky you've clicked a cushy job," was the retort.

" It ain't a cushy job. We're workin' 'ere from eight in the morning——"

"—— that ! You ought to —— well pay us for fightin' for yer."

" Garn ! I was in the trenches afore you blinkin' well joined up."

" Pass along there," came the voice of a sergeant in charge, and we moved onwards again to the next collecting section.

" Bayonets, please ! "

Rather ! With the greatest of pleasure ! Rifle ! Yes, here you are ! Who wants my box respirator ? Mess tins over there ! Hullo ! I've lost the lid of my mess-tin : what's to be done ? Yesterday I could have got anything I wanted, but to arrive at the Crystal Palace minus a mess-tin lid was a heinous crime, one that necessitated my reporting at an office and thereby wasting many precious minutes. They wanted to know how, when, where and why it was lost, and after filling in several forms and making entries in my pay-book announced that the sum of 4d. would be deducted from the amount of pay due to me.

After consuming a bun and a stick of chocolate each, we waited in a so-called queue for another two hours before passing into the hands of several other officials, including the army tailors who stood with tape measures " at the alert," ready to order our civilian clothes.

" Will you have a suit or two-pounds-ten ? " asked a corporal.

" Two pounds ten," said a man three ahead of me.

" Will you have a suit or two-pounds-ten ? "

" Two-pun-ten," said the next.

" Suit or two-pounds-ten ? "

" Two pound-ten, not 'arf ! " answered the man in front of me. And my answer was substantially the same.

Then followed a terrible wait of four hours in an enormous queue which required an army of orderlies to keep it in order. We were so afraid that at the eleventh hour the Army would announce that demobilisation was suspended, that men jostled one another and became wedged tightly together. One or two were carried away in a fainting condition. Patience was finally rewarded when the foremost persons were admitted in batches of about a dozen into the final demobilisation room, which I succeeded in entering about 7.30 that evening. A man at one table collected sundry titbits of information, another gave out railway tickets and directed you to a third table where further questions were asked.

" Any special qualifications ? "

No ! Most emphatically No ! The best way to get on in the army, as Figg had once said, was to appear a fool. Surely that was the wisest course to adopt when trying to escape from its meshes.

" Are you signing on for the Reserve ? "

No ! Most decidedly not ! I would have nothing more to do with militarism for the rest of my days. Only the fact of having been through the War in a regiment like the L.R.B., imbued with a proper *esprit de corps* and a discipline enforced by sensible means, accounted for the fact that I was bound now for a decent home instead of being conveyed in a padded lorry to the nearest lunatic asylum.

At last a man handed me the precious discharge papers and five pound Bradbury notes on account. I packed the papers away securely in my pocket, and in the twinkling of an eyelash darted for the portals of Freedom. Without daring to glance over my shoulder at the authority which I half feared might even then be bestirring itself to countermand my release, I burst through the folding doors and down the magic steps.

THE END.